JEWISH WOMEN'S HISTORY FROM ANTIQUITY TO THE PRESENT

EDITED BY
FEDERICA FRANCESCONI
AND REBECCA LYNN WINER

WAYNE STATE UNIVERSITY PRESS
DETROIT

© 2021 by Wayne State University Press, Detroit, Michigan 48201. All rights reserved. No part of this book may be reproduced without formal permission.

ISBN 978-0-8143-4631-0 (paperback)
ISBN 978-0-8143-4630-3 (hardcover)
ISBN 978-0-8143-4632-7 (e-book)

Library of Congress Control Number: 2021932819

On cover: *Ruth & Naomi from The Five Scrolls*, 1984, Drawing by Leonard Baskin 13 3/8 × 7 3/4 inches. Cover design by Will Brown.

Wayne State University Press rests on Waawiyaataanong, also referred to as Detroit, the ancestral and contemporary homeland of the Three Fires Confederacy. These sovereign lands were granted by the Ojibwe, Odawa, Potawatomi, and Wyandot Nations, in 1807, through the Treaty of Detroit. Wayne State University Press affirms Indigenous sovereignty and honors all tribes with a connection to Detroit. With our Native neighbors, the press works to advance educational equity and promote a better future for the earth and all people.

Wayne State University Press
Leonard N. Simons Building
4809 Woodward Avenue
Detroit, Michigan 48201-1309

Visit us online at wsupress.wayne.edu

JEWISH WOMEN'S HISTORY FROM ANTIQUITY TO THE PRESENT

This collection is dedicated to Judith R. Baskin,
our mentor, friend, and constant support.
The breadth and depth of her scholarship continues to inspire.

CONTENTS

PREFACE

JEWISH WOMEN'S HISTORY FROM Antiquity to the Present was born out of our desire to pay homage to the scholarship of Judith R. Baskin. But Judith Baskin is not just an outstanding scholar. Professor Baskin's community-building activism transformed Jewish studies into a field that welcomes women scholars and feminist and gender studies. Over the past four decades Baskin supported countless junior scholars (like ourselves), by attending their presentations at conferences, offering invaluable feedback, and supporting and advising on the job market and concerning publication.[1] She served as a role model for so many when in 2004, Judith R. Baskin became the first female president of the Association for Jewish Studies.

Baskin's scholarship has proven equally transformative through her monographs and coedited volumes (her selected bibliography appears at the end of this book). Her original collections, the two editions of *Jewish Women in Historical Perspective* (1991 and 1998), were foundational for both of us in our scholarly formation as historians specializing in Jewish history, social history, family history, cultural history, and the history of women and gender. We like many others in the field have used them in our research and to teach. The 1998 volume of *Jewish Women in Historical Perspective* is so popular that it is still in print more than twenty years after its original publication. The histories of Jewish women that the contributors to that collection recovered have resonated with so many readers over the years, within the academy and beyond in the wider Jewish community.

This volume, although it stands on its own merits, as its breadth of chronological and geographic coverage implies, is the latest chapter in an important story in Jewish women's history. Judith R. Baskin began it, and it is truly fitting that this edition is dedicated to her. Baskin had a vision for a collection that would make two major interventions, one scholarly and one activist; that vision was realized with the first edition of *Jewish Women in Historical Perspective* in 1991. Baskin described the historical context of and the activist need for the first edition by underlining how at the turn of the twentieth century many Jewish women involved in feminist movements were altering women's status within Judaism. At the time,

Jewish movements (Reform, Reconstructionist, and Conservative) had authorized new female and egalitarian roles (including rabbinic ordination), rituals, liturgies, and publications specifically for Jewish women. However, according to Baskin, they did so without "perspectives from the past. [Furthermore,] while the growth of women's studies as a field of scholarly endeavor has led to increased academic study of women in Judaism and individual Jewish women, few recent works have attempted to illuminate contemporary dilemmas and concerns by scholarly investigations of the lives and experiences of Jewish women of previous eras."[2]

Baskin set a series of goals in the field of history, including that the grand narratives of Jewish history not continue to be written "from the point of view of the male Jew" with an (overheavy) focus on "intellectual concerns and achievements"; that the lives of ordinary women be researched (daughters, wives, divorcées, and widows, rich and poor), along with those of the famous; and that women's culture be rediscovered. She held up the autobiography of Glikl (or Glückel) Hameln (1646–1724) as the kind of primary source by a woman that she hoped to encourage future scholars to fully mine, stating boldly, "It is one of the aims of this volume to rediscover other similarly evocative expressions of Jewish women's lives and experiences."[3]

By 1998 many in the younger generation, like ourselves, were responding to Baskin and scholars like her, writing histories of ordinary Jewish women that paid attention to their age, marital status, and social rank or class. The comparisons that the 1991 volume afforded between different regions, such as Baskin's own chapter on medieval Jewish women in Ashkenaz and Egypt, influenced others to compare the Jewish women they were studying with those of different regions and with women of the Christian or Muslim majorities under whose rule they dwelt. There were calls for an updated edition of *Jewish Women in Historical Perspective*, and in her new 1998 introduction, true to form, Baskin again had her finger on the pulse of the field. She suggested more attention to the role of Rabbinic Judaism and the binary gendered separation that it imposed on society in most Jewish communities from the sixth to the eighteenth centuries, and, by contrast, she again emphasized the search for women's culture, even though the constraints imposed on women greatly limited their ability to preserve their voices postmortem.[4]

In addition to her deep understanding of the issues in Jewish history, another of Baskin's impressive strengths is her breadth of knowledge. Her familiarity with work in the field, focusing on so many different eras and geographies, made it possible for her to conceive of the *Jewish Women in Historical Perspective* project and bring it to fruition by determining just whom to ask to write each chapter. Baskin's own research boasts a breadth shared by few (as her selected bibliography clearly reveals); she has written classic articles and monographs on topics that range from biblical figures to Bella Chagall. Professor Baskin has also constantly been looking forward. She finished her introduction to the 1991 volume with selective bibliographies for two important topics not covered, using them as calls for further research: "Jewish Women's Lives in Eastern Europe" and "Jewish Women's Involvement in Zionism and the State of Israel," both topics that appear in the 1998 edition. And the 1998 edition includes the bibliographies "Women and the Holocaust" and "Women in Israel since 1948."

We have developed the current collection to answer Baskin's calls by addressing these topics and by expanding Jewish women's history into fields that have flourished in the last twenty years: women's diverse experiences in the early modern period; embodiment and gender in Jewish mysticism; women and colonialism in modern countries under Islam; lesbian activism and its challenges; and contemporary women's life in North America, Europe, and Israel.[5] We intend for the essays in this volume to honor Judith Baskin, a great interdisciplinary scholar herself, by contributing to the deepening of women and gender studies in Jewish history and by furthering her efforts to build interdisciplinary bridges with a variety of scholars throughout the disciplines.

Editors' Note: Hebrew words in common usage appear as in standard English dictionaries. Transliteration of Hebrew, Arabic, Judeo-Arabic, Ladino, Yiddish, Polish, Russian, and other languages varies from chapter to chapter according to the authors' preferences.

Notes

1 On December 14, 2020, the Women's Caucus of the Association for Jewish Studies recognized Professor Baskin's extraordinary achievements with its award for mentorship.
2 Judith R. Baskin, "Introduction," in *Jewish Women in Historical Perspective*, ed. Judith R. Baskin (Detroit: Wayne State University Press, 1991), 17.
3 Baskin, *Jewish Women in Historical Perspective* (1991), 15–16. The reassessment of this important source in Jewish women's history has only relatively recently been aided by the critical edition and introduction to Glikl Hameln's autobiography published in Hebrew by Chava Turniansky in 2006 and in translation by Sara Friedman as *Glikl: Memoirs, 1691–1719* (Waltham, MA: Brandeis University Press, 2019).
4 Baskin, *Jewish Women in Historical Perspective* (1998), 15–16, 19.
5 Contemporary developments relating to women in the United States, Europe, and Israel are addressed in the chapters by Baader, Ashton, Fishman, and Brettschneider as opposed to being given a stand-alone chapter.

INTRODUCTION

FEDERICA FRANCESCONI AND REBECCA LYNN WINER

JEWISH WOMEN'S HISTORY FROM Antiquity to the Present makes one thing emphatically clear. In 2020 Jewish women's history is a vibrant field built on the 1990s pioneering scholarship of Judith R. Baskin, Judith Hauptman, Paula Hyman, Tal Ilan, Marion Kaplan, Ross S. Kraemer, Renée Levine Melammed, Carol Meyers, Pamela Nadell, and Judith Romney Wegner, to name only a few.[1] Over the last thirty years, historians of Jewish women have reconceptualized critiques of patriarchy, moving to a more nuanced analysis of the multiple vectors of women's oppression and their negotiations of that oppression. Scholars have made strides forward in reconstructing women's experiences by analyzing every area of their lives and life course; they have shown the effects of ideologies of gender on larger processes in Jewish history, such as the ongoing question of integration.[2] In her *Gender and Assimilation in Modern Jewish History* (1995), Paula Hyman delineated the emergence of a bourgeois transnational Jewish culture with shared characteristics in America and Western and Eastern Europe through which Jewish women acculturated in different ways in different regions and at their own rates distinct from men. Scholars have developed this insight through in-depth focus on locales and have included new topics, such as how women's fashions in local or Western dresses, headdresses, or hats functioned as part of the integration process among urban Jews in the Ottoman Empire and North Africa (see Malino and Danon's essays in this volume). So, too, historians of Jewish women have reconceptualized watershed events in Jewish history. In the 1990s scholars of the Holocaust sought to recover women's history and women's writings and to explain the centrality of gender in the Nazi implementation of genocide.[3] In 2020 scholars are establishing that gender influenced every aspect of the genocide along with class, family relations, and age. Previously neglected or taboo aspects of women and girls' intimate perspectives, their affect and emotions, sexuality, and experiences of sexual violence are now being analyzed to understand their resistance, survival strategies, and responses to the genocide.[4]

Beginning in the 1990s, study of Jewish women and gender moved forward with the founding of academic research centers and new journals in the field as well as increased publication of scholarly books on Jewish women and gender studies. The Hadassah-Brandeis Institute (HBI), which opened its doors in 1997, is devoted to research on Jews and gender and publishes a wide-ranging book series on these issues.[5] In partnership with the Schechter Institute of Jewish Studies in Jerusalem, the HBI founded *Nashim: A Journal of Jewish Women's Studies and Gender Issues* in 1998.[6] The first issue of *Women in Judaism: A Multidisciplinary Journal*, an academic open-access e-journal hosted by the University of Toronto, appeared in 1997.[7] The Jewish Women's Archive, founded in 1995, now presents an easily accessible platform, the *Shalvi/Hyman Encyclopedia of Jewish Women*, with articles by major scholars in their fields.[8]

In the third decade of the twenty-first century, flagship quarterly journals in the broader field of Jewish history and Jewish studies also regularly publish articles, roundtables, and special issues on Jewish women's history.[9] A notable example is the recent roundtable "Feminist Approaches to Jewish Studies," published in *Jewish Social Studies: History, Culture, Society* (2019) for which Sarah Abrevaya Stein, Tony Michels, and Kenneth Moss assembled a group of leading feminist scholars from various disciplines who have done work in Jewish studies. The editors asked the group, which included Shir Alon, Mara Benjamin, Natalie Zemon Davis, Susan A. Glenn, Sara Imhoff, Marion Kaplan, and Alice Kessler-Harris, to reflect on the impact of feminism on their subfields from the 1970s through the present and to evaluate their dialogue with cognate fields (such as women's history, gender studies, and queer theory).[10] The roundtable recognized the pathbreaking and continuing roles of feminist historians in establishing the importance of the history of women and gender for Jewish studies as a whole. Histories of women, particularly those focusing on their everyday lives and written from a creative variety of sources (e.g., lullabies alongside newspapers), constitute some of the first major feminist inroads in the general field. These histories have inspired and informed the work of feminists in theology and Jewish thought and have been accompanied by similar advances in the fields of Jewish literature. The roundtable includes an intellectual autobiography of Davis and an interview with Kessler-Harris as historians for whom the study of Jewish history and Jewish women fostered compelling work on society, sex, labor, and class in European and American history more broadly.[11] Glenn and Kaplan situate their pioneering work on the history of American feminism and Holocaust studies, respectively, and trace the evolution of these fields over the last fifty years, taking stock of where they are now.[12] Alon and Benjamin, reflect on the need today for more work on gender themes and the increased presence of female scholars in Mizrahi and Sephardic studies and Jewish thought.[13] Finally, Imhoff calls for a transformation of the field of Jewish studies embedded in feminist inquiry and gender studies as a necessary step to become "a better, more interesting version of itself."[14] The editors recognize, and the roundtable clearly establishes, the central role of the study of gender and women's history in Jewish history. And the efforts of scholars such as Benjamin and Alon are moving their subfields forward despite continued reluctance to adopt methodological and theoretical frameworks that inform the fields of gender and sexuality studies.

Innovations of *Jewish Women's History from Antiquity to the Present*

JEWISH WOMEN'S HISTORY FROM *Antiquity to the Present* builds on this stable foundation. The collection spans biblical times to the early twenty-first century in nineteen core chapters. The view of the volume is broad also in geographic scope; essays address Jewish women's lives on three continents, focusing on Eastern and Western Europe, Britain, ancient and modern Israel, Babylonia (Iraq), Egypt, Turkey, North Africa, and North America. This global range affords readers the opportunity to appreciate how local historical context shaped the specifics of Jewish women's lives. The second edition of Baskin's pathbreaking collection *Jewish Women in Historical Perspective* appeared in 1998. Since then no study has sought to take so comprehensive a look at the field of Jewish women's history.[15]

As editors, we have endeavored to balance the need for a global reach with chapters that cover chronological ground. Each chapter focuses on a set time and place. That said, the contributors pay attention to the fact that in some areas of Jewish history the usual periodization does not always address the trends in women's history. For example, the timeline for immigration is being reassessed in Jewish American history. The old periodization delineates a "Sephardic" colonial and early national period, a "German" nineteenth-century period, and an "Eastern European" late-nineteenth-century period. As Melissa R. Klapper explains in her chapter, a newer model for Ashkenazic Jews posits a relatively continuous migration from the 1820s to the 1920s. This allows Ashkenazic Jewish women's shared concerns about and negotiations around work, family, and the freedoms of American life to come into relief.[16]

Pioneering Jewish studies scholars have identified new evidence and used new interpretative tools to analyze known sources, thus rendering any claim of not talking about women because there were not sufficient sources untenable. And as the contributions in this collection reflect, the number of additional new sources relating to Jewish women both in manuscript and print that scholars have discovered in the last decade alone is astounding. Interest in both the social history of Jews and the recovery of women's voices through research on gender has contributed to the discovery of new sources, as has the reassessment of specific processes and events. These include the rediscovery and study of the Genizah documents and the opening of access to archives in Eastern Europe since the collapse of the Soviet Union in 1993. The contributors bring an enhanced linguistic skill set to their expanded archives, having taken advantage of the opportunity for training in multiple languages now offered by departments of Jewish studies, religious studies, languages, and history in academic institutions in Europe, Israel, and the United States. They also apply new methodologies in approaching rabbinic sources, prescriptive literature, and *musar* (ethics), interrogating them about gender structures and female roles both in the rabbinic imagination and in relation to women's restrictions, agency, and quotidian actions on the ground.

In her 1998 introduction to *Jewish Women in Historical Perspective*, Judith Baskin called for a more diverse exploration of Jewish women's experiences in order to redefine our understanding of both the significance and the essence of Jews and Judaism throughout history.[17] And in a recent special issue of the journal *Clio: Women, Gender, History*, Leora Auslander and Sylvie Steinberg brought together scholars who use methodologies of the history of religion and of women's history to investigate the essential roles of Jews, Jewishness, and Judaism in both nationalistic and diasporic contexts from ancient Judea to contemporary Ethiopia, Berlin, and New York.[18] For Auslander and Steinberg, gender is central to Judaism. They call for an exploration of symbolic schemas in light of gender and an analysis of that symbolic universe in Judaism, which they define as a crossroads of diverse beliefs, rituals, and theological movements.[19] The chapters in this volume incorporate this reconceptualization of the nature of Jews and Judaism. The study of Judaism, the nature of Jewishness, and gender roles through history in this collection relies on sources that were written or dictated by women alongside biblical, rabbinic, and kabbalistic foundational texts created by male elites. For example, the Genizah letters that Jewish women dictated to professional scribes in medieval Fustat (Cairo) reveal how gender expectations shaped women's strategies when they formulated claims, addressed requests to male relatives, and took their cases to Muslim courts to redress perceived wrongs in matters of inheritance in the Jewish system (see Baskin's chapter in this volume). The letters written by the North African– and Ottoman-born female teachers of the Alliance israélite universelle at the turn of the twentieth century also show the importance of women's voices in understanding their projects and concerns. In their letters these teachers navigated Jewish French familial feminism in which gender relations and women's distinctive roles were conceived as catalysts for progressing Jewish society's civilization. They sought to reassess that system, resisting its ideological preoccupations with the so-called backwardness of the *orientales* and liberating themselves while transplanting this feminism to North Africa and the Middle East (see Malino's chapter). As other examples in the chapters demonstrate as well, our contributors, with their diverse sources, explore Jewish women's history through gender analysis of a diversified (and ultimately democratized) source base.[20]

In analyzing the histories of Jewish women, the contributors all build on the category of gender as framed for historians by Joan Wallach Scott in her classic 1986 article, which has shaped the discourse ever since. Scott defines gender as "a constitutive element of social relationships based on perceived differences between the sexes" and "a primary way of signifying relationships of power."[21] Our collection also incorporates an interdisciplinary methodology. The volume brings together social and cultural historians, literary scholars, sociologists, and political philosophers who apply their own emphases, expertise, and differing understandings of how Jewish women of the past can be studied and understood. In addition to the approaches of biblical, rabbinic, and document-based historical studies, they use the methods of anthropology, postcolonial studies, material culture studies, visual culture studies, and disability studies. The contributors shape their analyses through the prisms of class, ethnicity, sexual identity and orientation, and the fluid and historically contingent identity of Jewishness.[22] Finally, all the contributors present their understanding of the state of the conversation about the history of Jewish women in their subfields, incorporate their own and others' recent scholarship, and delineate areas for further research.

Women's historians of the 1970s often focused on famous or infamous women, whereas those of the 1980s and 1990s started to reconstruct the experiences of ordinary women. The contributors to this volume are all committed to exploring the experiences of ordinary women and to delineating the gender systems that shaped their everyday realities within families, households, communities, and societies. Extraordinary women such as Dona Gracia Nasi, Sara Copio Sullam, Glikl Hameln, Rachel Rebecca Leah Horowitz, and Henrietta Szold are incorporated into and analyzed within their own historic-societal contexts and in relation to their contemporary female peers rather than framed as sole exceptional figures.

In 2005, in their introduction to the co-edited volume *Polin: Jewish Women in Eastern Europe*, Paula Hyman and ChaeRan Freeze set a historiographical agenda whose goals have been (and are) crucial for scholarship of Jewish women: to integrate the history of Jewish women into the broader narratives, to deconstruct old interpretative lenses, and to rethink Jewish history (for them, in the area of Eastern Europe) using the new decisive understandings of research on gender.[23] In their introduction to a 2020 special issue of the journal *Jewish History*, Elissa Bemporad and Glenn Dynner remarked that scholars of modern Jewish history of Eastern and East-Central Europe are responding positively to Freeze and Hyman's call. They are integrating the history of Jewish women into the master narratives of the past, including "changes occurring in Jewish education, conversion waves, postwar relief efforts, anti-Jewish violence, Soviet productivization projects, and, more broadly, the acculturation process that animated Jewish modernization."[24] And, indeed, the contributors to this volume show that all areas in Jewish history are characterized by a similar engagement with women's history and gender that has transformed the field over the last thirty years.

In sum, *Jewish Women's History from Antiquity to the Present* is designed to make the cutting-edge work of historians of Jewish women visible to all historians and history students. The chapters lend themselves to use by historians of women outside Jewish studies who are seeking comparison with their own scholarship.[25] The contributors, although working under the constraints of tight word limits, define specialist terms and provide accessible introductions to their times, places, and the broader subfields they address. They also make comparisons between the experiences of Jewish and non-Jewish women. Jewish studies has sometimes been seen as a closed field with terms and interests divorced from the majority cultures in which Jews lived. This volume shows that such a view is inaccurate and that broader histories are greatly enriched by incorporating the experiences of Jewish women.

Intersectionality and Jewish Women

AT PRESENT, INTERSECTIONALITY OFFERS one of the most relevant and powerful theoretical tools to frame Jewish women's history. Scholars from many different disciplines use the concept to study power relations in women's lives through the concurrence of race, ethnicity, nationality, socioeconomic status, sexuality, educational opportunities, disability, age, and gender, among other factors. Researchers applying intersectionality theory analyze multifaceted identities to discern which features are salient for individuals in different circumstances, times, and places. Intersectionality theory offers a nuanced understanding of power dynamics, such as domination, subordination, and privilege.

Critical legal studies scholar Kimberlé Crenshaw introduced the term *intersectionality* in 1989 to describe the compound and overlapping discrimination that minority women face in negotiating racism and sexism.[26] Joyce Antler argues that Jewish feminists played a crucial role in conceptualizing intersectionality from its inception through their dialogues with African American feminists and members of other marginalized communities.[27] However, Jewish feminists' contributions to the development of intersectionality theory have not been widely acknowledged in critical race studies; and, as Marla Brettschneider's 2016 monograph seeks to redress, Jewish topics and perspectives are not currently much in evidence in intersectionality work.[28] In a recent article, Judith Gerson explores how scholars might use this methodology in Jewish studies, because "Jewishness and Jewish identity remain ever-changing expressions of difference and coherence, inequality and power, and are best understood in concert with other configurations of inequality and difference."[29]

The contributors to this collection apply the theory of intersectionality to explore the simultaneous phenomena that affected and changed Jewish women's lives both as Jews and as women. Although often conceived of as neat categories, gender, sexuality, and race are more complicated and fluid than presumed.[30] Rachel Adelman draws on intersectionality in her study of the Hebrew Bible and describes the multitiered systems of power that underlined biblical texts. Patriarchal structures are underpinned in the law even as divine intervention challenges the narration and saves women, as in the case of the realization of maternity for the matriarchs who suffer long periods of infertility. God assures "His" continuous protection of the patriarchal covenant, and yet, in prophetic and wisdom literature, feminine gender tropes are used to describe the divine. There is an implicit criticism of male protagonists, and perhaps the whole paternalistic system, in the ways that inheritance devolves and in the fates of female victims of sexual violence. The subsequent chapters in this collection explore the reception of gender tropes and social constructs of the masculine and feminine in the Hebrew Bible in different Jewish communities and by Jewish women throughout the centuries and in diverse locales.

ChaeRan Freeze also draws explicitly on intersectionality to investigate Jewish women's experiences in the Russian Empire, a political entity that was multinational and multiconfessional, and situates them in the matrix of imperial law, institutions, and culture as minority subjects. Freeze focuses on Jewish women's experiences in religious life, education, culture, family, economics, politics, and health, especially chronic illness. Freeze also highlights the creative strategies that Jewish women employed to take advantage of contradictions and find loopholes to ameliorate their subordinate positions, for example, by petitioning the Imperial Chancery to issue them separate passports from their husbands so that they could travel to seek cures for diabetes or tuberculosis.

Indeed, the contributors to this volume write a history of Jewish women that has evolved from a perspective of one-dimensional analytic and cultural categories of patriarchy, oppression, and subordination into one that explores the diversity of gender and Jewish women's experiences within its different sociocultural and economic contexts.

Chapter Overview: Some Important Themes

THIS VOLUME OPENS WITH two chapters on foundational Jewish texts: the Hebrew Bible (Adelman) and the classical rabbinic corpus (Tal Ilan). The texts of the Hebrew Bible were composed over hundreds of years, possibly from before 1000 BCE to the final centuries BCE.[31] Canonical rabbinic texts, the Mishnah and the Tosefta, the Palestinian and Babylonian Talmuds, and the Tannaitic and Amoraic midrashim, were redacted from the second through the seventh centuries. The connection between the two corpora of texts—the Written and the Oral Torah—is the foundational tenet of Rabbinic Judaism as it was elaborated in the aftermath of the destruction of the Temple in 70 CE and has remained crucial in Judaism and Jewish life to the present day. Rabbinic conceptions of women's position in society, emanating from interpretations of the Hebrew Bible, are not only important as a product of textual creativities in their own context of Roman Palestine and the Sassanian Persian Empire but are also key to understanding later Jewish societies because, toward the early fourth century, the Rabbis started exerting a growing influence.

Adelman and Ilan's in-depth and multilayered analyses of the biblical and rabbinic corpora allow them to delve into texts produced in fundamentally patriarchal worlds, revealing their similarities, contradictions, and dissonances and causing them to speak to one another. Adelman analyzes the status of women under biblical law and female figures through paradigmatic roles (from the matriarch to the woman warrior). Biblical law privileges men, and at its core is the need for husbands to control their progeny; yet in some texts women act successfully against these norms and defeat male privileges, such as primogeniture. Ilan reveals the layers of the rabbinic gendered system that originated in the Hebrew Bible by exploring conceptions of femininity; women's legal status and expectations of women in the domestic, religious, economic, and professional domains; and glimpses of their everyday lives across the social spectrum from matrons to enslaved women. The Rabbis interpreted women's subordination as a punishment for the consequences of Eve's transgression in the Creation narrative in the book of Genesis and, according to Ilan's analysis, they sought to build a system that excluded women from participation in Jewish cultic life with a new rule that exempted them from all time-bound commandments. By delving into contradictions in the texts, such as the prohibition against women residing in the sukkah versus the obligation to light candles on Hanukkah, Ilan proves that this new rule was an ideological move by the Rabbis aimed at excluding women's participation in the public religious sphere.

The next two contributions, by Judith R. Baskin and Renée Levine Melammed and Rebecca Lynn Winer, concentrate on Jewish women's lives in the medieval period from the seventh century (a time of expansion of the Islamic caliphates as well as the final systematization of Rabbinic Judaism) to 1492 (the expulsion of Jews from Spain) and its aftermath. The focus is on the women (and men) who lived in semi-autonomous Jewish communities in the Muslim worlds of Egypt, North Africa, the Middle East, al-Andalus (Muslim-ruled Spain) and the Latin Christian territories in Iberia (Sepharad), and England, northern France and the German-speaking regions (Ashkenaz). The contributors recover the experiences of individual women in the religious, cultural, economic, and social domains. They explore how these were influenced by notions about the nature of the Jewish woman and the politics of gender elaborated in Jewish milieus and the dominant governing societies. The abundant sources pertinent to women analyzed in both chapters show the fundamental differences between medieval Jewish women's lives under Islam and under Christianity in Ashkenaz. Medieval Jewish society under Islam (and in Christian Spain) was characterized by a greater overall population, larger communities, and the participation by its middle- and lower-class members in many economic activities, whereas in Ashkenaz smaller communities in urban enclaves with a higher average wealth and social status and a concentration on finance and merchant commerce predominated. Jewish women's economic activities were thus more diversified under Islam and in Christian Spain and were more profitable and conveyed more communal status in Ashkenaz. Read together, these two chapters also show how the study of Jewish women's experiences challenges our understanding of the crucial watersheds in both medieval general and Jewish history: the massacres and devastation of European Jewish communities during the first four Crusades (1096 to 1204) and the massacres and forced conversions of Jews in Iberia in 1391 and their expulsion in 1492. Drawing on elegies and other sources that celebrate the martyrdom of Jewish women who refused conversion in 1391, Melammed and Winer correct the misconception that, when faced with conversion or death, Sephardim always chose baptism.[32] The Iberian elegies use narrative and rhetoric similar to those of the more well-known Hebrew chronicles, analyzed by Baskin, that memorialize the exemplary resistance and heroic death of Jewish women in Ashkenaz in 1096.

Considering Jewish women and forced conversions in medieval Europe, Baskin and Melammed and Winer analyze strategies of adaptation, resistance, and agency. Jewish women in Ashkenaz were less likely than men to convert to Christianity; there were probably fewer benefits for them; and rabbinic authorities facilitated divorce for Jewish wives whose husbands were apostates and guaranteed the return of their dowries. Indeed, the authors of the Hebrew Chronicles praised women so highly to shame men who might opt for conversion. In Christian Iberia, Jewish women who had forcibly converted in 1391 were more prone to maintain Jewish practices than men through the secret observance of mitzvot (precepts), such as lighting Sabbath candles, fasting on Yom Kippur, and customary celebrations of birth called *hadas*. They created new ceremonies, such as debaptizing, which de facto became non-halakhic (not conforming to Jewish law) rituals of a new underground Jewish movement (crypto-Judaism). Even after the establishment of the Spanish Inquisition in 1481 that put their and their relatives' lives in even greater danger, crypto-Jews continued to perpetuate Judaism in the domestic domain. At the turn of the sixteenth century young female prophets led an intense messianic movement of conversos that was silenced by Spanish inquisitors. Their relevance is also related to the prophetic nature of their message.

As Sharon Koren reveals, in the third contribution centered on medieval Judaism (broadly conceived), female mysticism was a nonexistent reality in medieval Judaism, although mystical texts are permeated by female and gendered symbolisms. Koren explores the cosmic feminine, feminine imagery, gendered godhead, and cosmic gynecology in the Zohar (Book of Splendor), the most important kabbalistic text that emerged in 1280 CE as a collective effort of several authors in Castile. Indeed, the concept of the *Shekhinah*, the feminine aspect of the divine, permeates Zoharic literature, where divine attributes are described as having sex, menstruating, being pregnant, giving birth, and breastfeeding. Nonetheless, according to some Zoharic teachings, only Jewish married men can see the face of the *Shekhinah*. Despite the importance of female symbolism, the kabbalistic gender binary perpetuated women's inferiority and exalted heteronormative monogamy. Ultimately, divine feminine symbolisms (not all positive) did not imply gender parity or a call for any challenge in women's position in medieval Jewish societies. Yet, given the influence of the Zohar after the Iberian expulsions in the spiritual and cultural recovery of Sephardic Jews and the flourishing of early modern Kabbalah, Sabbateanism, and Hasidism, the prominence of female symbolism in the text is significant in and of itself, as Koren explains in her postscript. Indeed, as some contributions in this volume elaborate, these Jewish mystical movements, even if with different developments, often maintained the same dichotomy between a positive attitude toward sexuality and kabbalistic female symbolisms and the permanence of women's exclusion. Hasidism in particular persisted in excluding women and casting them as material and carnal, as demonstrated by the pioneering work of Ada Rapoport-Albert to which other contributions in this volume refer (e.g., Freeze and Ashton's chapters).[33]

Even if its chronological boundaries in early modern Jewish history are not firm, historians generally agree that 1492 was a watershed year in Jewish history and was distinctive in the trauma Sephardic Jews experienced. Furthermore, recently, European historians, in discussions of events that reshaped the early modern world, have attributed more significance to the 1492 Jewish expulsion, as the first attempt to purify an entire country of unbelievers and purge it from heresy, than to the publication of Martin Luther's Ninety-Five Theses in 1517. After 1492 Jews and, within decades, other religious communities (Dutch Anabaptists, Italian Calvinists, English Catholics, and Bohemian Hussites) became refugees on the move, all forcibly removed or deciding to leave because of religious persecution. These groups often then constituted new enclaves with the same principles of exclusiveness, purification, and purgation that had characterized the communities they left.[34] The Jewish refugee, immigrant, and servant women from Safed, Venice, Livorno, Amsterdam, Metz, and Altona whose lives are analyzed in this volume bring new foci to the study of this world; they passed through various stages of persecution, displacement, precariousness, and adjustment. For example, as explained by Melammed and Winer, former conversas in seventeenth-century Amsterdam composed the majority of the Portuguese community and effectively contributed to building their new Jewish community with donations, charitable activities, and active participation in the dowering society for orphans and girls.

The contributions by Federica Francesconi, Debra Kaplan and Elisheva Carlebach, and Moshe Rosman focus specifically on the early modern period and analyze Jewish women's history in the Italian Peninsula, Central and Western Europe, and Poland-Lithuania. Even with different emphases and outcomes, they all analyze Jewish women in the economic, legal, and religious domains from the sixteenth through the eighteenth century, addressing the dichotomy of public and private and the gender binary opposition of masculine and feminine. They use a plethora of archival and printed sources as well as material culture and the built environment, much of which has been unknown until now. The sixteenth century was certainly characterized by events that greatly influenced the lives of Jewish women (and men) in those geographic contexts.

For example, 1516 marked the establishment of the Venetian ghetto (and others starting in 1555), 1517 the start of the Protestant Reformation in German cities, and 1579 the constitution of the Polish-Lithuanian Commonwealth. Yet these contributors also analyze elements of continuity and transformation that bridge the medieval and early modern periods rather than designate a rupture; as aptly described by Kaplan and Carlebach, the medieval "culture of writing," which was more common after the mid-fifteenth century and to which Jewish women participated as copyists, continued and was impacted by the technology of printing in the early modern period and then it became a major agent of transformation and democratization of Jewish women's literacy.

Francesconi concentrates on the gradual withdrawal of Jewish women in the Italian peninsula from public life that paralleled the formation of mercantile Jewish elites and the restrictions imposed on Jewish life and ghettoization in the sixteenth and early seventeenth century. She then shows how simultaneously a slow process of feminization around the home accelerated from the seventeenth century. Female identities were shaped by new forms of cultural agency, learning and apprenticeship, fraternalism, and devotion in both the domestic and public domains. Kaplan and Carlebach analyze Jewish women's lives in Western and Central Europe through three main phenomena that occurred synchronously: a new proliferation (and enforcement) of Jewish communal and halakhic regulations, particularly evident in urban settings; a consequent vast production of records that document women's activities, families, and interactions; and the gendered aspects of the print revolution. In his exploration of Jewish women's lives in Poland-Lithuania, Rosman analyzes tension and negotiation between two social, cultural, and religious phenomena that intersected, evolved, and transformed the Polish Jewish communities: the conceptualized gendered system that saw the feminine role as a facilitation of male religious and economic objectives and Jewish women's actual roles and efforts to attain more active religious and economic participation in society.

The contributors populate Jewish history in the early modern period with women whose "informal" daily work in their family business (e.g., pawnshops, taverns, and textile workshops) does not appear in the records of guilds, charters, and other official correspondence in which only husbands are typically listed.[35] As Francesconi reveals, starting in the sixteenth century, Jewish women in Venice organized themselves in female communities of artisans challenging the anonymity that characterized their underpaid work in the sector of silk production. Through the manufacture of rich, luxurious ornaments in silk and brocade with visible dedications and signatures and at times complex iconographies, they also challenged their limited agency in the visible public space of the synagogue, the ghetto, and the city. As Kaplan and Carlebach point out, many Jewish women, such as the well-known Glikl Hameln, started out in commerce as adjuncts to the businesses their husbands ran and then continued their activities as widows. Sometimes they used the dowry they had brought into the marriage as capital for investment. Notably in early modern Jewish communities, the profession of midwifery challenged women's anonymity. For example, midwives were trained by other women in gynecology, were appointed as officials in their communities, and served as advisers to rabbinic courts in cases of illicit pregnancies, at times keeping records of births.

A typical case of formal work in the early modern period was domestic service. Many girls were expected to be trained in domestic and professional skills by Jewish matrons and, after a variable period of years, to leave their householders with savings sufficient for a dowry. Contracts of apprenticeship were often stipulated between the young women's families and their future employers; often, Jewish maidservants were sent to work far away from their own families. The lack of parental control and the cohabitation of house-holders and servants or co-workers could lead to illicit sexual relationships, which were made public when pregnancies occurred. In early modern European history this social issue was a global phenomenon that often had tragic consequences: In eighteenth-century England and France 70% of women accused of infanticide were single maidservants.[36] Francesconi and Kaplan and Carlebach showcase two different attitudes in the rabbinic and lay male establishments (both aimed at keeping social control of the community): In northern Italian cities Jewish courts tended to oblige the seducers to marry the pregnant maidservants, or, if already married, to support them as well as their illegitimate children; whereas in German states, Jewish communities often rejected women in similar conditions and abandoned them, along with their illegitimate offspring. These attitudes also mirror different conceptualizations of the Jewish household.

In assessing female agency and participation in the religious and cultural sphere, the contributors pay attention to socioeconomic status and family background. Women from rabbinic or affluent households exceeded their peers in access to education, reading, and writing. At the same time, gendered aspects of print culture produced new female readership and texts authored by women that transcended the social divide locally and globally. Kaplan and Carlebach, Francesconi, and Rosman delve into the expanded literacy of Jewish women in the early modern world with their increased access to devotional and secular literature and new genres of texts written for women or authored by women (such as the *tkhines*) in the vernacular languages and Hebrew. Prescriptive texts written for women to be educated in the mitzvot such as the *Seder Mitzvot*

Nashim (1600), because of their numerous translations and different versions in multiple languages, functioned as global educational-religious instruments. At the same time, differences in educational systems and societal dynamics emerge if we compare female-authored texts by the Venetian Sara Copio Sullam (1592–1641) and Sara Rebecca Leah Horowitz (born in the 1710s in contemporary Poland), analyzed by Francesconi and Rosman. Both authors can be considered voices of the Jewish strains of early modern proto-feminism. Sara Copio Sullam, educated in Hebrew and Italian literature, classics, philosophy, and music and yet limited during adulthood in her access to canonical and kabbalistic Jewish culture, reconfigured her intellectual world to center on poetry and literature, with Jewish and secular subjects and a strong focus on female themes, and wrote mostly in Italian. Emerging as a female Jewish published author, her public persona was permanently destroyed because of anti-Semitic and misogynistic reactions by Christian contemporary intellectuals. Sara Rebecca Leah Horowitz was immersed in Jewish religious culture and authored the *Tkhine Imohos*, or supplicatory prayer of the matriarchs, a booklet that included her own compositions of *tkhines* prayers in Yiddish and Aramaic and a commentary in Hebrew. Although accepting conventional female roles and moving within Jewish society, Horowitz demanded recognition of women's religious role through the fulfillment of commandments, participation in public synagogue prayer, and instruction in Torah study.

One of the main contributions that emerges from the chronological ordering of the chapters from antiquity to the early modern age is the diversity of Jewish women's religious experiences. Women's education and literacy are bound up with their piety and devotion in synagogal and domestic rituals. By investigating the Jewish female religious experience, the contributors analyze the changes in male-centered establishments (both rabbinic and secular) over time and in different locales, in rabbinic and prescriptive literature, and in the proliferation of communal laws, halakhic regulations, and social customs. As Ilan demonstrates, since late antiquity rabbinic authorities have sought to ratify and extend the exclusion of women from the study hall and to limit their religious practice in the synagogue. Following on the paths of recent scholarship, however, the contributors to this book dismantle what was until recently assumed to be a rigid dichotomy between public and private and propose other ways of understanding Jewish women's religion. Considering the medieval Jewish world, women's education was mostly (but not exclusively) centered in the domestic sphere and was aimed at preserving the Jewish household and supporting male performance in the synagogue. Yet the contributors here emphasize how in reality the boundaries between the two spheres, public and private, were permeable and constantly negotiated.

For example, as Baskin explains, from the eleventh through the end of the thirteenth century in Ashkenaz, Jewish women expanded their sphere of religious practice into the male-centered communal and synagogal space, performing rituals that they were not obligated to, such as acting as godmothers during circumcisions, reciting blessings for the *lulav* and sukkah in courtyards, and wearing tefillin (phylacteries) in the streets.[37] As Kaplan and Carlebach and Rosman reveal, in early modern Ashkenaz, because of the limitation on women's roles in the synagogue, a new female spirituality arose in a private devotional dimension through *tkhines* that was instrumental in women regaining their place in public worship. Beginning in the seventeenth century, *tkhine* collections with large diffusion included texts composed for every stage of the female biological cycle and the performance of sacral acts; in addition, many were intended to be recited by women together during the public prayer liturgy. These changes were reflected in the built environment; communities remodeled existing synagogues or built new ones to include women's sections (*ezrat nashim*) as an integral part of the structure instead of relegating women to temporary or outside arrangements.

Even with different emphases and assessments, the diversity of the female religious experience and the interplay between public and private and between sacred and profane are significant also in the chapters that are centered on the nineteenth century. These chapters continue the exploration of Jewish women's diverse religious, educational, and economic experiences in the home, community, and wider world in Europe, Britain, the Ottoman Empire, North Africa, and the United States (these are the chapters by Freeze, Baader, Valman, Danon, Malino, and Klapper). Although traditional histories of Jewish integration often concentrate solely on economic or intellectual elites (often male), our volume expands the sphere of inquiry to incorporate lower- and middle-class Jewish women who were affected by modern integration and emancipation, different paths of Jewish enlightenment, immigration, surrounding cultures, anti-Semitism, and the new Jewish religious denominations, cultural and philanthropic associations, and political movements. Gender, class, and ethnicity emerge as categories that simultaneously played an equal role in shaping Jewish women's lives and their societies. Together the chapters constitute a nuanced study of the plurality of women's experiences in a period of rapid and widespread change through a transnational sphere of inquiry.

Our contributors confront, complement, and challenge the theoretical model of "domestic Judaism," as theorized by Paula Hyman in the framework of the nineteenth-century bourgeois culture: "When life in the modern Western world led most assimilating Jewish men to abandon traditional Jewish culture and limit their religious expression to periodic appearances at synagogue and the performance of some communal service, their wives absorbed the dominant societal expectations of women as the guardians of religion . . . retaining some domestic aspects of Jewish tradition, including customary foods, and transforming others into ostensibly secular family celebrations, such as the Friday evening, rather than Sunday, dinner."[38] Building on Hyman's pioneering model has allowed scholars in the field to produce nuanced studies that underscore the plurality of female experiences and highlight the existence of complementary gendered systems in the modern Jewish experience.

Benjamin M. Baader tells the story of middle- and upper-class Jewish women in Germany during the nineteenth century and beyond through feminist and gender-sensitive analysis. He explains that because many Jewish men neglected Jewish religion and synagogue attendance, domestic Judaism, in which women transmitted Jewish religion and Jewish identity, took hold.[39] The little-known memoirs of Clara Geissmar (née Clara Regensburger, b. 1844) disclose this transformation of domestic Judaism in Germany through the absorption of the bourgeois culture of *Bildung*: the harmonious education of the heart, intellect, and character through engagement with literature, poetry, and art. Baader argues that a feminization of Judaism uniquely characterized nineteenth-century Germany by encompassing the formation of Reform, positive-historical (later Conservative), and Orthodox Judaisms, which affected men and masculinity as well. Women at times openly supported the adaptation of Judaism to modern sensibilities; for example, in 1855 a group of women in Mannheim petitioned the Jewish community, on behalf of their rabbi, to support the introduction of a new prayer book in which German prayers replaced some Hebrew ones. In doing so, they expressed gratitude for the opportunity to recite prayers with dignity without being excluded and silenced.

In her analysis of British and Eastern European Jewish women in Victorian England, Nadia Valman offers both a variant of and a challenge to domestic Judaism. Women became the guardians of the spiritual purity of the home that, according to the Victorian bourgeois ideology of domesticity, was to provide a shelter from the outside masculinized world of work. Yet looking at the Jewish social divide, a more complex scenario emerges in which an interplay between inclusion and exclusion shaped gender roles and female experiences. From the Victorian period to the start of World War I, English Jewish women negotiated a changing community riven by class, economics, and cultural differences; Ashkenazic Jewish immigration, especially after 1881, more than tripled the size of this tiny minority community, which expanded to 200,000 by 1914. The ways that class and culture intersected in shaping Jewish women's identities feature prominently in Valman's analysis, as do the bonds that Jewish women formed with non-Jewish women. Early in the Victorian period, as male community leaders sought emancipation, elite Jewish women were energized by the dominant Protestant culture's promotion of women's religious domestic roles and created innovative Jewish practices for their families. This was a favorable climate for the fiction of Grace Aguilar (1816–1847), who promoted Jewish women's spirituality and equality for Jews. Later, upper- and middle-class Jewish women drew on expectations for women's behavior when they founded, supported, and headed welfare organizations to support the Jewish poor. And in 1902 Lily Montagu partnered with theologian Claude Montefiore to establish the Jewish Religious Union, paving the way for gender-equal Liberal Judaism. Yet looking at the Jewish social divide through popular culture, literature, letters, and memoirs, a complex scenario emerges. Jewish female collaboration across class in the areas of health and welfare successfully accelerated social mobility. Some Jewish immigrant women still felt alienated not only from other Jewish women but also from institutional Jewish organizations and Judaism. So too did secular Jewish "new woman" intellectuals such as Amy Levy (1861–89). Some Jewish women, such as Lily Montagu, felt better able to connect with gentile women from the same social and economic backgrounds. Montagu and her sister established a household with her dear friend Constance P. Lewis.

Freeze introduces her analysis of Jewish women's changing experiences in the modern Russian Empire by building on Chava Weissler's pioneering analysis of the transformation of *tkhines* from avenues of women's agency to instruments of male control.[40] In the early modern period female-authored *tkhines* enabled the valorization of women's concerns, rituals, and domesticity, but by the nineteenth century male-authored *tkhines* (under female pseudonyms) stressed bourgeois gender roles and proper domestic hygiene according to the reformist projects of their *maskilim* (Enlightened) authors. In their vision, men were to become remasculinized through achievement in the world of work, whereas the bourgeois cult of domesticity refeminized women in the private sphere. Indeed, as Freeze explains, the *maskilim*'s vision poorly reflected the realities of Jewish women in the Russian economy and daily life, even for those from upper or middle socioeconomic classes. For example, the women of the Poliakov family, which came to dominate finance in Moscow and St. Petersburg, helped build the family fortune in the mid-1800s (although two generations later female relatives were completely sidelined from the family business). Jewish women, both ordinary and renowned, navigated modernization, industrialization, and religious and secular ideologies, from the circles of Hasidim and *mitnagdim* (their opponents) to those of political movements

(Zionism, Bund, socialism, and more), with some success. At times, exclusion from the religious sphere removed barriers to female secular education and provided cultural integration and professional opportunities; bars to Jewish women's learning in Hebrew and traditional Jewish texts had the corollary of opening opportunities for female secular education. Jewish girls matriculated at state educational institutions and universities, and by the 1870s a significant number entered medical professions, especially pharmacy, midwifery, and dentistry, and moved into Russian cities that had previously been off limits to Jews.

Through the wide production of the Ladino press, Dina Danon explores the introduction of bourgeois womanhood as a Westernizing ideology affecting women and the domestic sphere in the Sephardic Ottoman cities of Izmir, Salonica, and Istanbul. Danon places Jewish women's experiences at the matrix of political, cultural, social, and economic changes, technological advances, and Westernizing reforms. For these Sephardic Jewish women, the connection between femininity and domesticity was not new. At the end of the century, Francophone Westernization led to cultural tensions between East and West that pervaded the quotidian. Women were pulled in two different directions: They were preservers of Jewish heritage in their homes and innovators of the modern, which meant deracination from local culture. Although, according to Baader, German Jewish women adapted to the sociocultural bourgeois environment with minimal friction as their community achieved economic uplift, Ottoman Sephardic women struggled. They were encouraged to prioritize their role in the home as mother-educators and pushed to develop charity, cleanliness, and fashion, labeled as their "natural skills." Yet many were poor, and the bourgeois culture advanced by the press was out of reach. Articles in newspapers from the 1890s, such as Istanbul's *El Tiempo* and Izmir's *El Novelista*, blamed the "twentieth-century" Sephardic women for their "modern" behaviors because of a perceived opposition between life *a la turka* and life *a la franka*. On the other hand, the secularization of Jewish women in Western Europe did not have a Sephardic equivalent. In this respect, Sephardic women had more in common with their Ottoman counterparts.

One agent of modernization in the Sephardic world was the Alliance israélite universelle through its philanthropic, educational, and cultural activities. Frances Malino analyzes gender, assimilation and integration, colonialism, and Jewish women's agency through her study of the French-speaking North African–and Ottoman-born primary school teachers educated in Paris and sent by the Alliance to Jewish communities in the Islamic world from 1892 to 1934. She contextualizes her analysis within the entanglement of global colonialism, francophone Westernization, and Jewish embourgeoisement. Malino likens these Jewish women teachers to the "new women" of belle époque France, by which she means "journalists, activists, and writers." The Alliance teachers ascribed to French familial feminism and strove for the embourgeoisement of their fellow Jews.[41] Europeanized in language and dress as well as in education and yet perceived as outsiders and *orientales*, these women functioned as agents of French colonialism. Many advanced their own liberation and transformed their young female students into literate "exemplars of the new Jewish woman." Women such as Messody Pariente made independent decisions to import knitting or sewing machines and set up dress ateliers to teach their pupils to sew the latest French fashions to earn a living or to keep a "modern" home. When they attempted to transplant this feminism to North Africa and the Middle East by intervening in social and cultural issues, such as banning child marriage, and tangled with French colonial officials, these *institutrices* experienced successes. But they also expressed frustration and had a tendency to look down on the "bad habits" of their "Oriental" pupils, especially those who spoke Arabic instead of Sephardic Ladino.

Perhaps the most successful adaptation of domestic ideals to Jewish women's changing lives occurred in the United States, where Melissa Klapper traces the rise of activism at the communal, national, and international levels from the mid-nineteenth to the early twentieth century. American Jewish women were a diverse group: urbanites, small-town dwellers, and pioneers. Many were immigrants. Still, Jews experienced less class tension than in Britain. Klapper analyzes domestic Judaism as the ideal model for American Jewish women: achieved by the middle and upper classes and significantly aspirational for women from lower classes and, as such, influential on domestic and family relations. Klapper reveals how adaptation and opportunities for immigrant Jewish women depended not only on gender but also on class, social and economic conditions, family stability, and anti-Semitism. Yet, considering the diversity of Jewish women's professions and political participation at the turn of the twentieth century, Klapper suggests that Jewish women transformed and even challenged gendered domestic ideals. Jewish women worked for themselves, their families, community organizations, and large and small companies and shops; in addition, working-class married women earned at home, doing all kinds of piecework and taking in boarders. Despite the hardships of immigration (poverty, abandonment of wives, orphaned children, oppressive and sexist working conditions, and so on), Klapper demonstrates that overall Ashkenazic Jewish women seized new opportunities for socioeconomic advancement in America. Jewish teenage girls attended high school at a higher rate than those of other ethnic groups. This opened up expanded opportunities for professional growth and political participation, which prompted some to challenge gendered domestic ideals. Jewish communal institutions (such as the Jewish Theological Seminary, established in 1886) also offered opportunities to advance women's secular and religious educations. The fact that Halakhah permits a variety of contraception provided support for a movement that allowed poor Jewish women, Jewish women from Eastern Europe, and middle-class Jewish women, independently or with their partners, the means to plan their families. Political activism (including Zionism, despite the initial resistance) became one the most successful components of Jewish women's lives in the United States; these women often had previously embraced political participation in Eastern Europe. For example, American Jewish women participated avidly in Hadassah activities from their inception in the 1910s.

Indeed, as our volume shows, since the turn of the twentieth century, political activism has posed complex challenges to Jewish female associationism because Jewish women had to confront opposition that was both internal and external to Jewish society. For example, at the end of the nineteenth century in Britain, Jewish women workers at times succeeded in unionizing, despite the Jewish leadership and rabbinate's fierce resistance and the backlash of their Jewish male co-workers (see Valman's chapter). In those years, despite the strenuous opposition of both employers and their male co-workers, American Jewish women workers became the pillars of both the International Ladies Garment Workers Union and the Amalgamated Clothing Workers of America. Yet even if both Jewish lay and religious authorities supported female suffrage, in the 1920s American Jewish women rarely held leading roles in the national suffrage movement because of the persistence of anti-Semitism, and they often expressed their support as individuals rather than as members of Jewish associations (see Klapper's chapter). Also in the 1910s and 1920s, Jewish women's associations in Eastern Europe and the Yishuv (the Jewish communities of pre-state Palestine) had to face paternalistic traditional attitudes toward women and overcome the consequent opposition to female suffrage, inclusion, and self-determination in the Zionist movements (see the chapters by Freeze and Rosenberg-Friedman).

Lilach Rosenberg-Friedman's chapter expands the focus on women and political participation to Jewish women's changing lives in Mandatory Palestine in the decades leading up to the independent State of Israel. The ideology of the man as the "new Jew," a strong defender of the nation and provider for women and children, was integral to the Zionist project of establishing a Jewish state and society. In the nationalist historical narrative women were remembered as having been treated with remarkable equality in the building of the state. Although women's efforts were indeed crucial,

Rosenberg-Friedman explains that feminist and gender historians challenged this rosy picture of equality in the 1980s, when they recovered women's voices, including those that went against the grand national narrative. They argued instead that women's roles were defined as auxiliary to the new male Jew and that women's concerns were often sidelined. For example, although it was notable that women in the elite Palmach division of the army trained for combat, most of them were quickly pulled from the front lines for fear that their capture would reflect badly on the national honor. Female Zionists were encouraged above all to become mothers, and motherhood was considered their central role.

Within this context, Rosenberg-Friedman analyzes Ashkenazic and Mizrahi women's experiences and shows how at times women used the positive conceptualization of motherhood and gender discourse, both central to the Zionist enterprise, to challenge their marginality. Since the 1920s Ashkenazic women have led national initiatives in the welfare, health care, educational, and child care sectors, and in doing so, they have challenged the patriarchal control over a number of institutions without clashing with male antagonism. Volunteer work was essential in establishing institutions in the Yishuv; and women such as Henrietta Szold, founder of Hadassah, who was elected to the National Council, came to lead administrative divisions of the emerging government, in Szold's case the Department of Education and Health. Immigration on the ground happened in stages, shaping a multiethnic society of European and Arab Jews (at first mostly local), who lived in close contact with the Arab Muslim and Christian populations. The experiences of Mizrahi women, marginalized as women and as ethnic minorities, have begun to be analyzed thoroughly by scholars in the last two decades. These women often faced constraints imposed by their families and community backgrounds— for example, no access to formal education, economic impoverishment, and contempt and condescension from the larger and more influential Jewish Ashkenazic population. But they too negotiated Zionist ideals and reconfigured their own place in this society, often being the first in their families to integrate in the Yishuv.

The 1998 edition of *Jewish Women in Historical Perspective* includes a bibliography on women and the Holocaust as a call to develop what was then an emerging field. Three years later, Ruth Klüger (1931–2020), Holocaust survivor and scholar of German literature, published the English translation of her memoir in which she recounts her experiences of the genocide during her girlhood and adolescence in Vienna, Theresienstadt, Auschwitz-Birkenau, and the labor camp Christianstad (published in German in 1992 and in English in 2001). For Klüger men tried to claim possession of "wars, and hence the memories of wars, are owned by the male of the species. And fascism is a decidedly male property, whether you were for or against it."[42] This poignant observation underlines some reasons for the lack of focus on women (both as victims and as perpetrators) in the history of the Holocaust.[43] Over the last twenty years, however, as Natalia Aleksiun shows in her chapter, scholarly literature on the Holocaust and genocide studies has been transformed by the study of women and gender. As Marion Kaplan recently summarized, "Without women's memories we missed not only familial and domestic aspects of the Holocaust but also gendered public behaviors and humiliations and gendered persecutions in ghettos and camps."[44]

Aleksiun focuses on what it was like to be young and female in the ghettos and labor, concentration, and extermination camps and in hiding in Eastern Europe. The chapter is grounded in testimonies, diaries, memoirs, and oral interviews, many of which are published or analyzed here for the first time. Aleksiun mines these young women's personal accounts with careful attention to discern how the loss of family members, social taboos, and self-censorship affected these authors. She succeeds in recovering young Jewish women's insights about their roles in their families and communities, their desires and ambitions, and their exploration and understanding of womanhood. Most of the diaries and memoirs Aleksiun analyzes were written by young women who belonged to the middle class before the war, and their social status informed how they responded to the genocide, striving to retain a certain style of life at the beginning of the occupation, in ghettos, and through hiding and internment in concentration and extermination camps. Education was of particular importance for teenage girls; Janina Bauman remembers her efforts alongside her friends to locate teachers, who were paid by their parents, for an underground school in the Warsaw ghetto. Aleksiun investigates the ways in which gender shaped coming-of-age for teenage girls and their survival strategies. She argues that the major factors that influenced the experiences of young Jewish women were economic status, family relations (in particular, between teenage daughters and their parents, including how long parents survived and families remained together), age at puberty, Nazi policies (such as the age for forced labor), and individual trajectories during the Holocaust.

In the final chapters Dianne Ashton, Marla Brettschneider, and Sylvia Barack-Fishman bring the history of Jewish women up to the present day. They focus on Jewish women's religious expression, roles in their families and communities, and activism internationally, with emphasis on the United States. The North American Jewish population is currently the largest and most diverse in the Jewish world (with the full range of denominations from Reform to ultra-Orthodox represented). Thus the United States presents a compelling case study for the evolution of Jewish women's experience across the spectrum of theology and spirituality, religious practice, family life, feminism, and LGBTQ activism in the aftermath of the Holocaust, the foundation of the State of Israel, the rise of the civil rights and women's movements, and the contemporary resurgence of anti-Semitism.

Dianne Ashton explores women's spiritual expression in the Reform, Reconstructionist, Renewal, Conservative, and Orthodox Jewish worlds over the last hundred years, considering religious activities that have engaged significant numbers of women or through which women have demonstrated their religious creativity. She argues that Jewish women's spirituality has expanded in congregational services, in the home, and through singing in innovative ways anchored on Jewish women's traditional rituals. In her analysis creation and performance are intrinsically linked, and the focus is on religious activities created and promoted by women's groups, rituals performed by Jewish women at home, and musical expressions created, performed, and taught by women in Jewish institutions (congregations and cantorial schools). Ashton reveals a double process of female redefinition of the religious sphere in modern and contemporary Judaism: women as groups enabling women as individuals to reappropriate public Jewish space (synagogues and congregations in general) as well as creating new values and new rituals in the domestic sphere (e.g., the emergence of women's Passover seders with the recognition of Miriam as a central figure in the narration of Exodus). Jewish women's efforts have substantially altered contemporary Jewish practice. A prominent example of change that Jewish women's groups effected since the first decades of the twentieth century is the transformation of the Hanukkah festival from a neglected celebration into an American tradition for Reform and Conservative congregations. The simplicity of the rituals connected to the holiday, the domestic setting, the absence of rabbis (and their potential interference) during celebrations, and Hanukkah's timing near Christmas offered new pedagogical opportunities for the chapters in the National Federation of Temple Sisterhoods (now the Women of Reform Judaism) and later the Women's League for Conservative Judaism. They expanded religious experience for American Jews around the holiday in religious schools and enhanced women's participation in special activities in synagogues, social congregational centers, and homes.

Marla Brettschneider provides an overview of the beginnings and development of Jewish lesbian and queer feminism in the twentieth and twenty-first centuries, with a particular focus on the past four decades in the United States. This period has seen the development of a self-identified lesbian community as well as gender-based homophobia directed at people who were, or were imagined to be, lesbians. Jewish lesbians have been integral to the activist efforts of lesbian movements but have seen these strong alliances erode after 1980 with the increasing rise of anti-Semitism on the left. Brettschneider analyzes a rich corpus of Jewish lesbian work in the areas of literature, religion and spirituality, the arts, politics and history, scholarly endeavors, and organizational and activist life. The impressive story of Ruth Berman and Connie Kurtz that opens the chapter sheds light on this eclectic and multicultural world: Both were white Ashkenazic women from the 1930s Jewish immigrant society of Brooklyn who fell in love with each other in 1974, divorced their husbands, and lived together ever after. Their life together was characterized by lesbian activism in the Jewish world and beyond; for example, they helped found Congregation Beit Simchat Torah in New York (the world's largest gay and lesbian synagogue), fought for gay marriage, opened branches of Parents, Friends, and Family of Lesbians and Gays (PFLAG) in New York and Florida, and worked with Black Lives Matter activists on anti-racism initiatives. Brettschneider shows how many lesbian women shared the same path as Berman and Kurtz and, as individuals and in associations, influenced Jewish and non-Jewish American society.

The role of Jewish female associationism is explored in many chapters; considerable attention is devoted to the traditional participation of women in charity, philanthropy, and Jewish welfare, and female associationism came to shape Jewish women's active participation in religious change, political activism, and secular cultural production. Starting in the early modern period, we see Jewish women operating *hevrot* (confraternities) aimed at burial, charity, and religious endeavors independently of men; these Jewish sisterhoods offered women a degree of agency with the opportunity to expand their social, spiritual, and professional domains. For nineteenth-century American Jewish women, including those who no longer kept kosher or observed the Sabbath after immigration, activities in Jewish ladies auxiliaries and sisterhoods became one of the most important components of Jewish life and offered expanding access to public life that characterized the turn of the twentieth century (see Klapper's chapter). Ample changes occurred since the first decades of the twentieth century in the religious sphere because of the role played by Jewish women's groups (see Ashton's chapter). Moreover, since the nineteenth century female associationism has often expanded into political activism. Brettschneider offers perhaps the most nuanced and multilayered case of Jewish female political and cultural associationism and activism. Jewish lesbians have gathered in formal and informal social and cultural networks and formed LGBTQ synagogues across the United States since the 1970s. Often beyond the Jewish milieu, Jewish lesbians have been vital to cultural and spiritual innovation and active in social justice causes.

At the same time, their identity between different worlds has forced them to face different kinds of exclusion determined by anti-Semitism, patriarchy, heteronormativity, and cis-gender privilege.

Sylvia Barack-Fishman offers a sociological overview of the changing expectations, roles, contexts, and conditions of Jewish women's lives today, including conceptions of gender and gender roles, described and analyzed with attention to the larger contexts of Jewish movements and to ethnic and religious identification in contemporary American Jewish life. She explores demographic changes in education and occupation, marital status, and fertility; sexuality, gender, and personal and social choices; and ethnic and religious behaviors. Twenty-first-century Jewish women now regularly aspire to meaningful careers and high levels of professional achievement. The context for Jewish women's professional rise has been far-reaching social change, which has ushered in a more fluid and egalitarian sense of what constitutes a family in the Jewish community. Fishman demonstrates that American Jewish women continued the trends that Klapper located as originating in the last decades of the nineteenth century and that have come to play a proactive role in every dimension of American and Jewish societies. Fishman argues that Jewish education for girls and women has transformed contemporary Jewish life across the denominations. She also documents a measurable feminization of every aspect of non-Orthodox American Jewish life; instead of men, in the last decades women have become the signifying Jews. Women's leadership and grassroots involvement in American Jewish religious, scholarly, and communal life has increased, whereas men's commitment has waned. Fishman attributes this phenomenon to assimilation into American norms and argues that the contemporary American Jewish gender imbalance has a problematic effect on the lives of individual women and on the American Jewish community.

Finally, Fishman opens the gates to the Jewish Orthodox world and its diversity and transformations of the first two decades of the twenty-first century. The stories of Jewish Orthodox women and their achievements were largely absent from the editions of *Jewish Women in Historical Perspective*, but they are important in Fishman, Ashton, and Brettschneider's contributions here. Modern Jewish Orthodox women have taken advantage of numerous educational innovations to acquire intellectual tools to engage rabbinic texts and embrace diverse new roles in Jewish religious settings. An American Orthodox rabbinic seminary for women, Yeshivat Maharat, graduated its first rabbi, Rabba Sara Hurwitz in 2009. Transformations have gone beyond the domain of modern Jewish Orthodoxy; for example, Chabad leaders have expanded the significance of the wife-husband partnership of *sheluhim* (missionaries) and created opportunities for women as co-leaders in educational centers. Despite the intrinsic bias and frequent condemnation of gender fluidity, Orthodox rabbis engage with homosexuality in their communities. Some, even though they formally do not accept homosexuality as a reality, still welcome LGBTQ couples. Clearly the social and theoretical gender turn has affected every branch of the Jewish world. In this case, we see that contemporary Jewish transformations and scholarship nurture each other.[45]

Conclusions

AS MANY OF OUR contributors have remarked in their chapters, more research is needed in their subfields. We hope that scholars in the field will conduct further research on Jewish women in the Atlantic world, Sephardic women in the United States, Mizrahi women's pasts, and Jews of color. Furthermore, some broader topics, such as issues of demography, gender, and disability and aging call out for deeper exploration across the various contexts and time frames. Nonetheless, the diverse historical experiences of Jewish women and the approaches and sources used by the scholars in this volume to analyze them constitute global and transnational histories that contribute to fruitful comparisons in Jewish studies. This collection should also interest those outside Jewish studies. In early modern history missionary nuns and Jesuits are considered key focuses of study in shedding light on the emergence of the global,[46] but, arguably, Jews—and especially Jewish women as a minority within a minority—have played a more decisive role as agents of modernization, resistance, and change from antiquity to the present.

The study of Jewish women in historical perspective can successfully challenge Eurocentric and teleological narratives. It brings a unique and worldwide perspective; shows a vibrant variety of social strategies, political negotiations, and cultural productions in different geographic contexts; and methodologically is built on the rigorous study of sources requiring knowledge of numerous languages. Thus *Jewish Women's History from Antiquity to the Present* provides historians with the opportunity to challenge the criticism that is often leveled at global history as a discipline—that is, the lack of knowledge of languages and thus deep analytical engagement with historical sources.[47]

Moreover, the current Jewish history of gender and women contributes to the project of making feminist scholarship global and interdisciplinary. Yet often the variety and diversity of the Jewish historical experience is ignored by general historians, or, if it is taken into account, despite interdisciplinary theoretical claims, it is refashioned through vague characterizations, stereotypes, and generalizations that are unfortunately indebted to the same

Eurocentric and teleological narratives that the authors are attempting to challenge. This collection enriches the history of Jewish women and sheds additional light on their intersectional position in the past, and we intend for it to strengthen ties between Jewish studies scholars and scholars from related fields and disciplines.

Notes

We thank Judith R. Baskin, Francesca Bregoli, and Seth Koven for their insightful suggestions.

1 Some important works by these authors include Judith R. Baskin, ed., *Women of the Word: Jewish Women and Jewish Writing* (Detroit: Wayne State University Press, 1994); Judith R. Baskin, ed., *Jewish Women in Historical Perspective* (Detroit: Wayne State University Press, 1991; 2nd ed., 1998); Judith Hauptman, *Rereading the Rabbis: A Woman's Voice* (Boulder, CO: Westview Press, 1997); Paula Hyman, *Gender and Assimilation in Modern Jewish History: The Roles and Representation of Women* (Seattle: University of Washington Press, 1995); Tal Ilan, *Mine and Yours Are Hers: Retrieving Women's History from Rabbinic Literature* (Leiden: Brill, 1997); Marion Kaplan, *The Making of the Jewish Middle Class: Women, Family, and Identity in Imperial Germany* (New York: Oxford University Press, 1991); Ross S. Kraemer, *Her Share of the Blessings: Women's Religions Among Pagans, Jews, and Christians in the Greco-Roman World* (New York: Oxford University Press, 1992); Renée Levine Melammed, *Heretics or Daughters of Israel: The Crypto Jewish Women of Castile* (New York: Oxford University Press, 1999); Carol Meyers, *Discovering Eve: Ancient Israelite Women in Context* (New York: Oxford University Press, 1988); Pamela Nadell, *Women Who Would Be Rabbis: A History of Women's Ordination, 1889–1985* (Boston: Beacon Press, 1998); and Judith Romney Wegner, *Chattel or Person? The Status of Women in the Mishnah* (New York: Oxford University Press, 1992). Also see the end of this volume for Baskin's selected bibliography.

2 For the historiographical trends concerning Jewish women and gender from antiquity through 1800, including a discussion of post-1970 Jewish communities, see Judith R. Baskin, "Women's and Gender Studies: Historiographical Trends," in *The Routledge Companion to Jewish History and Historiography*, ed. Dean Bell (London: Routledge, 2019), 486–500.

3 For a review of the last four decades of scholarship, see Marion Kaplan, "Did Gender Matter During the Holocaust?" *Jewish Social Studies* 24, no. 2 (2019): 37–56. For a state of the field written in the 1990s, see the review essay by Myrna Goldenberg, "'From a World Beyond': Women in the Holocaust," *Feminist Studies* 22, no. 3 (1996): 667–87.

4 See Natalia Aleksiun's chapter in this volume; and Kaplan, "Did Gender Matter."

5 The HBI Series on Jewish Women has been published under that name since 2007; the original series title was the Brandeis Series on Jewish Women. The first volume appeared in 1999. Also notable is the small feminist Bio Press, which published

books about Jewish women, including Sondra Henry and Emily Taitz, *Written Out of History: Our Jewish Foremothers* (New York: Biblio, 1983). For a finding aid to Biblio's 1978–2000 collection, see http://collections.americanjewisharchives.org/ms/ms0669/ms0669.html (accessed December 20, 2020).

6 https://www.brandeis.edu/hbi/publications/nashim.html.

7 https://wjudaism.library.utoronto.ca/index.php/wjudaism.

8 https://jwa.org/encyclopedia.

9 And as we were going to press, a special issue on women and gender in American Jewish history in the journal *American Jewish History* was published (vol. 104, no. 2/3 [2020]).

10 Sarah Abrevaya Stein, Tony Michels, and Kenneth B. Moss, "Introduction," *Jewish Social Studies* 24, no. 2 (2019), https://muse-jhu-edu.ezp1.villanova.edu/article/717266/pdf (accessed December 21, 2020).

11 Natalie Zemon Davis, "Women, Jewish History, European History," *Jewish Social Studies* 24, no. 2 (2019): 33–36; and Tony Michaels, Lara Vapnek, Annie Polland, "An Interview with Alice Kessler-Harris," *Jewish Social Studies* 24, no. 2 (2019): 82–105.

12 Marion Kaplan, "Did Gender Matter"; and Susan A. Glenn, "Writing the Feminist Past," *Jewish Social Studies* 24, no. 2 (2019): 17–32.

13 Shir Alon, "Gendering the Arab-Jew: Feminism and Jewish Studies After Ella Shohat," *Jewish Social Studies* 24, no. 2 (2019): 57–73; and Mara Benjamin, "Agency as Quest and Question: Feminism, Religious Studies, and Modern Jewish Thought," *Jewish Social Studies* 24, no. 2 (2019): 7–16.

14 Sarah Imhoff, "Women and Gender, Past and Present: A Jewish Studies Story," *Jewish Social Studies* 24, no. 2 (2019): 74–81.

15 For the modern period, see Marion Kaplan and Deborah Dash Moore, eds., *Gender and Jewish History* (Bloomington: Indiana University Press, 2011). This collection established gender as essential to understanding modern Jewish history.

16 Klapper also makes reference to Hasia R. Diner, *The Jews of the United States, 1654 to 2000* (Berkeley: University of California Press, 2004). Part II of Diner's book is called "The Pivotal Century," which Diner defines as 1820–1924.

17 Baskin, *Jewish Women in Historical Perspective*, 21.

18 Leora Auslander and Sylvie Steinberg, "Introduction" [to the special issue Judaism: Gender and Religion], *Clio: Women, Gender, History* 44 (2016): 7–20. https://www.cairn-int.info/article-E_CLIO1_044_0007--introduction.htm (accessed December 29, 2020).

19 Auslander and Steinberg, "Introduction."

20 Charlotte Fonrobert noted progress in the field of Jewish studies through the transformation of the source base in her influential "On 'Carnal Israel' and the Consequences: Talmudic Studies Since Foucault," *Jewish Quarterly Review* 95, no. 3 (2005): 462–69.

21 Joan W. Scott, "Gender: A Useful Category of Historical Analysis," *American Historical Review* 91 no. 5 (1986): 1067.

22 The *Journal of Jewish Identities* was founded in 2008 to explore this issue and publishes empirical, theoretical, and review articles and occasional debates.

Benjamin M. Baader, Chaya Halberstam, and Beth Berkowitz co-edited the special issue "Gender Theory and Theorizing Jewishness," using methodologies of gender theory to investigate the category "Jewish" (*Journal of Jewish Identities* 11, no. 1 [2018]).

23 ChaeRan Y. Freeze and Paula Hyman, "Introduction: Historiographical Survey," in *Polin: Jewish Women in Eastern Europe*, ed. Paula Hyman and Antony Polonsky (London: Littman Library of Jewish Civilization, 2005), 3–24.

24 Elissa Bemporad and Glenn Dynner, "Jewish Women in Modern Eastern and East Central Europe," *Jewish History* 33 (2020): 1.

25 Jewish women's history is increasingly being brought into comparisons in the larger field of women's history. See the issue on the comparative history of marriage in *Gender and History*, which includes Rena N. Lauer, "In Defense of Bigamy: Colonial Policy, Jewish Law, and Gender in Venetian Crete," *Gender and History* 29, no. 3 (2017): 570–88.

26 See Kimberlé Crenshaw, "Demarginalizing the Intersection of Race and Sex: A Black Feminist Critique of Antidiscrimination Doctrine, Feminist Theory, and Antiracist Politics," *University of Chicago Legal Forum* 1989, no. 1 (1989): 139–67.

27 In the 1970s and 1980s some Jewish feminists expressed frustration that their identities were not recognized by their fellow feminists and that anti-Semitism was not a cause that feminists organized to combat, even as they were struggling against a lack of support in the Jewish community. See Joyce Antler, *Jewish Radical Feminism* (New York: New York University Press, 2018), 1–28, esp. 18–20. Antler also cites Evelyn Torton Beck, "The Politics of Jewish Invisibility," *National Women's Studies Association Journal* 1 (1988): 93–102.

28 Marla Brettschneider, *Jewish Feminism and Intersectionality* (Albany: SUNY Press, 2016).

29 Judith M. Gerson, "Gender Theory, Intersectionality, and New Understandings of Jewishness," *Journal of Jewish Identities* 11 (2018): 14, doi: 10.1353/jji.2018.0002.

30 On this in the context of Jewish history, see Federica Francesconi, "The Venetian Jewish Household as a Multireligious Community in Early Modern Italy," in *Global Reformations: Transforming Early Modern Religions, Societies, and Cultures*, ed. Nicholas Terpstra (London: Routledge, 2019), 231–48.

31 See John Barton, "The Hebrew Bible and the Old Testament," in *The Hebrew Bible: A Critical Companion*, ed. John Barton (Princeton, Princeton University Press: 2016), 3.

32 See also Miriam Bodian, *Dying in the Laws of Moses: Crypto-Jewish Martyrdom in the Iberian World* (Bloomington: Indiana University Press, 2007).

33 Ada Rapoport-Albert, "On Women in Hasidism, S. A. Horodecky, and the Maid of Ludmir Tradition," in *Jewish History: Essays in Honor of Chimen Abramsky*, ed. Ada Rapoport-Albert and Steven J. Zipperstein (London: Peter Halban, 1988), 498–525; and Ada Rapoport-Albert, *Hasidic Studies: Essays in History and Gender* (London: Littman Library of Jewish Civilization, 2018).

34 Nicholas Terpstra, *Religious Refugees in the Early Modern World: An Alternative History of the Reformation* (Cambridge, UK: Cambridge University Press, 2015).

35 For a definition of women's "informal" and "formal" work, see Michael Toch, "Jewish Women Entrepreneurs in the 16th and 17th Century: Economics and Family Structure," *Jahrbuch für Fränkische Landesforschung* 60 (2000): 256.

36 See Sara Maza, *Servants and Masters in Eighteenth-Century France: The Uses of Loyalty* (Princeton, NJ: Princeton University Press, 1983); and Cissie Fairchilds, *Domestic Enemies: Servants and Masters in Old Regime France* (Baltimore: Johns Hopkins University Press, 1984). In France, babies born to unwed Jewish mothers were taken and raised as Catholics.

37 On these aspects, see Avraham Grossman, *Pious and Rebellious: Jewish Women in Medieval Europe* (Waltham, MA: Brandeis University Press, 2004), 174–97; and Elisheva Baumgarten, *Practicing Piety in Medieval Ashkenaz: Men, Women, and Everyday Religious Observance* (Philadelphia: University of Pennsylvania Press, 2014), 138–69.

38 Hyman, *Gender and Assimilation*, 26.

39 Kaplan, *Making of the Jewish Middle Class*, esp. 54–63.

40 Chava Weissler, *Voices of the Matriarchs: Listening to the Prayers of Early Modern Jewish Women* (Boston: Beacon Press, 1998).

41 For French familial feminism Malino refers to Karen Offen, "Depopulation, Nationalism, and Feminism in Fin-de-Siècle France," *American Historical Review* 89, no. 3 (1984): 648–76.

42 Ruth Klüger, *Still Alive: A Holocaust Girlhood Remembered* (New York: Feminist Press at The City University Press, 2001), 18.

43 Quoted and discussed in Elissa Bemporad, "Memory, Body, and the Holocaust: Women and the Study of Genocide," in *Women and Genocide: Survivors, Victims, and Perpetrators*, ed. Elissa Bemporad and Joyce W. Warren (Bloomington: Indiana University Press, 2018), 4–6. Among some exceptions from the 1990s, see, for example, Dalia Ofer and Lenore Weitzman, eds., *Women in the Holocaust* (New Haven, CT: Yale University Press, 1998); and Judith Tydor Baumel, *Double Jeopardy: Gender and the Holocaust* (London: Vallentine Mitchell, 1998).

44 Kaplan, "Did Gender Matter," 39.

45 For another recent example, see the special issue on the feminism and art of Jewish Orthodox and Haredi women in *Shofar* (vol. 38, no. 2, 2020), especially the introduction: Rachel S. Harris and Karen E. H. Skinazi, "Was I afraid to Get Up and Speak My Mind? No, I Wasn't: The Feminism and Art of Jewish Orthodox and Haredi Women," *Shofar* 38, no. 2 (2020): 1–20.

46 See, for example, Luke Clossey, *Salvation and Globalization in the Early Jesuit Missions* (Cambridge, UK: Cambridge University Press, 2008), 1: "Every respectable account of early-modern history spotlights the global range of the missionary orders, especially of the Jesuits."

47 For example, Francesca Trivellato, "Is There a Future for Italian Microhistory in the Age of Global History?" *California Italian Studies* 2, no. 1 (2011), http:// escholarship.org/uc/item/0z94n9hq (accessed December 20, 2020).

NEW DIRECTIONS IN READING GENDER AND WOMEN IN THE HEBREW BIBLE

RACHEL ADELMAN

THE HEBREW BIBLE IS a complex anthology of twenty-four books that draws on various sources which were authored and redacted (presumably by men) over the course of hundreds of years, from before the period of the monarchy to the Persian exile.[1] The historical setting of the biblical account itself spans two millennia, divided roughly into four distinct periods in ancient history: (1) the legends in Genesis of the patriarchs and matriarchs (1600–1300 BCE); (2) the period of the Exodus from Egypt through the conquest of Canaan (1300–1000 BCE); (3) the period of the monarchy (1000–586 BCE); and (4) the post-exilic period of the neo-Babylonian (586–539 BCE) and Persian Empires (539–322 BCE). Given the composite nature of the text and the paucity of original sources that date to this period, confounded by the absence of "herstory" in the androcentric tradition, the attempt to uncover or recover the stories of women by scholars is fraught. Can we say *anything* for certain about the historical experience of women in the biblical world on the basis of such a multivocal collection?[2] As a literary scholar and a close reader, all I can confidently attempt to understand is how women have been depicted through voices both complicit in and resistant to that patriarchal world. Further, biblical scholarship has expanded to include the concept of gender, enhancing our understanding of the portrayal of both male and female figures, as well as of God, in the biblical narrative. As Simone de Beauvoir once famously asserted, "One is not born a woman, but, rather, becomes one."[3] Contemporary feminist scholars, informed by historical-contextual and literary reading strategies, can reveal how gender tropes are performed—by man, woman, or deity—as "masculine" and "feminine" social constructs in the Hebrew Bible.[4]

In the first part of this chapter I survey the status of women under biblical law and investigate how various narratives either reinforced or subverted that law. In the second part I analyze the primary female figures in the Hebrew Bible under the aegis of four paradigmatic roles that women fulfill: (1) the matriarch, whose primary role is to bear and advance the legendary hero and heir to the patriarchal covenant (1800–1300 BCE); (2) the woman warrior, who battles with unconventional weaponry for the nation's survival from the Exodus through to the end of Judges (1300–1000 BCE); (3) the wives and wise women in the king's court, who present a critique of regnal power during the period of the monarchy (1000–586 BCE); and (4) the female victims of sexual violence across the biblical record (often referred to in the text as daughters), who never emerge into a maternal role. In the final part I turn to theology, exploring figurative gender tropes in prophetic and wisdom literature. Classically, God is portrayed in masculine terms as a father or husband figure, whereas Israel is represented as the bride and wayward wife. Less well known are those passages in which God is depicted in maternal terms as a woman in travail (childbirth), a nursemaid (breastfeeding), or a mother grieving for her lost children, particularly in the composition known as "Second Isaiah" (Isa. 40–66) (postdating 586 BCE, after the Babylonian exile). Through attention to context and setting and interpretations that reclaim women's agency, in this chapter I explore the diverse and often conflicting biblical representations of women and gender in the Hebrew Bible.

Status of Women in Biblical Law and Narrative

BIBLICAL LAW REFLECTS A patriarchal, patrilocal, and patrilineal society in which women's agency seems highly circumscribed; the stories in the Bible suggest otherwise. The term *patriarchy* refers to "a hierarchical society in which power resides in the male property-owning father-figure both at the familial level and, by extension or parallel, at the state level. . . . [It also refers more widely] to a system in which males in general are privileged over women in general."[5] In the biblical context the term *patrilineal* refers to the inheritance of property and to the covenantal promise and blessings that pass from father to son, and *patrilocal* refers to the presumed abode of the family unit.[6] With the development of postcolonial studies and intersectionality theory, power relations have come to be understood as multitiered; Elisabeth Schüssler Fiorenza thus suggests the term *kyriarchy* (literally "rule of the master") as a more expansive term than *patriarchy*. The broad feminist agenda then entails a critique of the system of oppression, because gender intersects with socioeconomic status, religion, race, sexual orientation, and (dis)ability.[7]

According to biblical norms,[8] a woman was under the aegis of her father until she married, whereupon she moved to her husband's family home. Marriage was unidirectional, and the woman had little say. The man would "take" a wife in matrimony (Deut. 22:13), and she might, likewise, be divorced by him at his will (Deut. 24:1–4). The woman was expected to be a virgin, and the bride price was set accordingly (Deut. 22:13–21).[9] Rape was not determined on the basis of the woman's lack of consent but rather was contingent on whether it could be presumed or proved that she had resisted in crying out (Deut. 22:23–27). In the case of adultery, it was incumbent upon the woman, not the man, to be strictly monogamous, as the last of the proverbial Ten Commandments intones, "You shall not covet your neighbor's *wife*" (Exod. 20:14; Deut. 5:18); the "married woman" was bound by monogamy, but her husband was not, for he could take another woman as a wife or concubine.[10] Adultery (by definition with a married *woman*), was punishable by stoning both for the woman and the man who had relations with her (Deut. 22:22; Lev. 20:10). Furthermore, a child conceived of this illicit union was deemed a *mamzer*, "misbegotten," and could not marry into the community (Deut. 23:3). If a jealous husband suspected his wife of adultery, he could subject her to the trial by ordeal of the *sotah* ritual (Num. 5:11–31), in which the wife was compelled by the High Priest to drink "the bitter-cursing waters," and if guilty, she would miraculously suffer the terrible consequences—a prolapsed uterus or perhaps death.[11] All these laws point to a double standard, whereby the man could control his wife and guarantee that the progeny she bore would be unambiguously his own. At the heart of patriarchy's legal strictures lies the question of paternity and the need to rule over female sexuality and procreation. Many stories in the Hebrew Bible underscore the practice of these laws, whereas others chafe against their norms.

The paradigm of the wife-sister tales, for example, demonstrates the tension between social norms in a foreign land and the precarious status of the matriarchs and patriarchs as "strangers in a land not their own" (Gen. 15:13). Fearing the power of the local king, Abraham twice passes his wife, Sarah, off as his sister, and she is taken by the local monarch—in Egypt (Gen. 12:10–20) and in Gerar (Gen. 20:1–18); Isaac follows in his father's footsteps with his wife, Rebekah (Gen. 26:6–11).[12] In the first two stories, God intervenes, striking the pharaoh and his household with plagues and warning the king of the Philistines, Abimelech, in a dream to save Sarah from being violated. Critique of the patriarchs is muted in the biblical text, as though to say that they had been right to fear for their lives in a land where a man might be killed and his beautiful wife abducted, where adultery is deemed more heinous than murder.[13] No such salvation comes to Esther, taken into the palace of Ahasuerus, the Persian king, during a period in biblical history when God has seemingly disappeared; there are no overt miracles or prophetic messages from on high.[14] An intersectional analysis highlights the women's status as doubly "other"— both foreigner (Israelite or Jew) and female—as they are passed, like chattel, from one male figure to another. Sympathetic to their plight, these stories point to an ethic that transcends the patriarchal historical context. They also highlight the difference between the overt presence of God in the patriarchal narratives and the seeming absence of God during the historical context of Esther, in the Achaemenid Empire (ca. fifth century BCE). Although biblical law mandates that a woman's sexuality belongs solely to her husband, the patriarchs sometimes undermined their wives' fidelity when in fear of their lives. Divine intervention to save the women poses a critique of the heroes' actions and, perhaps, the paternalistic system that undergirds them.

This contrast between legal norms and divine fiat also applies to inheritance, where the law favors the eldest son. Repeatedly in narratives about divinely ordained leadership, the younger son becomes the chosen one. In a seminal essay, Robert Cover contextualizes the normative world of law in relation to the foundational narratives that give it meaning.[15] To illustrate the dynamic between law and narrative, Cover draws on the precept of succession (primogeniture) in scripture, where the first born inherits a double portion from his father's estate, even if he is the son of the less beloved wife (Deut. 21:15–17)—yet Isaac displaces Ishmael, Jacob displaces Esau, Ephraim displaces Menashe, Joseph comes to rule over his brothers, and even David, the eighth of Jesse's sons, is chosen over his older brothers for the Judean kingship. In all these cases, the younger son is favored by God over the firstborn. The recurrent theme illustrates a broader theological principle, in which divine election is at odds with legal or social norms. Narrative challenges *nomos* (law) to show how the process of God's choice of heir for the patriarchal covenant or monarchy does not follow any natural law or norm. As Cover avers, these foundational biblical narratives "always retained their subversive force—the memory that divine destiny is not lawful."[16] As I discuss later, women often played an active role as agents of the divine hand in history, advancing their son as the chosen heir.

A tension between *nomos* and narrative also inheres in relation to the "Holiness Code" in Leviticus (chaps. 17–26), which includes a list of forbidden sexual relations. For example, the code specifies that a man must not marry his brother's wife—"It is the nakedness of your brother" (Lev. 18:16)—even if the brother dies or divorces his wife (perhaps based on the belief that a man and wife become one flesh; [cf. Gen. 2:24]). The laws of levirate marriage, however, qualify these strictures. Should a woman become widowed without progeny, then the man's brother is obligated to cohabit with her to conceive a child, who would then become heir to the deceased (Deut. 25:5–10). The stories of Judah and Tamar (Gen. 38) and Ruth, Naomi, and Boaz (Ruth 1:11–13, 15 and 4:5–6, 10), directly allude to levirate marriage with interesting permutations.[17] Although the widow was an object of pity, subject to community charity along with the orphan and the stranger,[18] these formidable widows (Tamar, Ruth, and Naomi) overcome their childlessness and poverty by taking matters into their own hands to ensure an inheritance and continuity for themselves.

These two quasi-levirate marriage cases are part of the triptych leading up to the birth of David and the founding of the Judean dynasty (later identified with the messianic line). Three narratives intersect; all entail a seduction or near seduction: The daughters of Lot make their father drunk and seduce him, conceiving the eponymous ancestors of Moab (literally "of the father") and Ammon ("of kin") (Gen. 19:30–38); Tamar dresses up as a harlot by the roadside and seduces her father-in-law, Judah (Gen. 38); and Ruth nearly seduces Boaz in the granary (Ruth 3). What ultimately sanctions these women's initiative is the imperative of life and continuity. Ruth "the Moabite" becomes part of the Israelite people (despite the injunctions against the Moabites in Deut. 23:4 and Neh. 13:1–3), precisely *because* she redeems the illicit acts of her predecessors, Tamar and the daughters of Lot.[19] She is then identified as the great-grandmother of King David in the conclusion to the book of Ruth.

The issue of exogamy (marriage outside the tribe or nation) also points to a range of attitudes toward the other, especially "the foreign woman," across the biblical historical terrain. The so-called rape of Dinah by Shechem (Gen. 34) may be more concerned with the taboo not to intermarry with the indigenous people of Canaan, the Hivites in this case, than with the issue of forced sexual relations with a daughter of Jacob and the dishonor brought on the patriarch.[20] According to the law, the rapist was required to marry the virgin and pay the bride price (Exod. 22:15–16 and Deut. 22:28–29); her consent was not taken into consideration. The story of Dinah, however, did not end in marriage but in the slaughter of all the male residents of Shechem; the Hivites were one of the Canaanite peoples with whom Israel was not to intermingle (Deut. 7). Passages in Exodus and Deuteronomy reinforce this taboo about exogamy (Exod. 34:11–16; Deut. 7:1–6 and 23:4–9), justified in part because the local Canaanite woman would lead the Israelite men astray to worship other gods, as the Moabite and Midianite women did in the case of Ba'al-Peor (Num. 25). In the historical account, this same critique of intermarriage undergirds the downfall of Solomon, with his 700 wives and 300 concubines who turned his heart astray to worship other gods (1 Kgs. 11:1–5). Yet Moses married a

Midianite, who bore him two sons with no hint of reprobation in the biblical text (Exod. 2:21, 4:25, and 18:2–4). Although Miriam seemingly casts aspersions on Moses' having taken a Cushite wife (Num. 12:1), she is sorely rebuked by God for doing so (Num. 12:3–15). The biblical account reflects multivocal attitudes to the "foreign woman" across the sources, some critical and others laudatory.

Consider, for example, the Canaanite harlot Rahab of Jericho, who heroically hid the spies that Joshua had sent and allied herself with the Israelites; she was saved, along with her family, and integrated into the community (Josh. 2, 6:17, 22–23). Whether a figure like Rahab historically existed is impossible to determine. What is significant here is the use of the cross-cultural motif of "the harlot with a big heart" to demonstrate the appeal of the Israelite God and the Exodus story for this Canaanite woman. In yet another passage in Deuteronomy, echoed in the post-exilic writings of Ezra and Nehemiah (ca. sixth to fifth century BCE), the Ammonite and the Moabite people are maligned; they can never be admitted into the congregation of the Lord (Deut. 23:4, Neh. 13:1–3). It is at this point, when "Jews" (historically descended from Judean returnees to the land) and their religion emerge as distinct from the earlier ancient Israelite people.[21] Invoking the threat of the other in the form of foreign women, Ezra and Nehemiah force the Judeans to separate from their foreign wives and banish them along with the progeny of these "illicit" unions (Ezra 9–10; Neh. 10:31, 13:23–27). Yet, according to the biblical chronology, roughly 500 years earlier, Ruth "the Moabite" married Boaz and became the great-grandmother of King David. The book of Ruth, though set in the premonarchic period of the Judges (c. 900 BCE), might have been written much later as a critique of Ezra and Nehemiah's attitude toward marriage with "foreign women" and/or as a justification of David's ancestry.[22] Most scholars point to the polyphonic nature of the biblical corpus—one set of legal codes is xenophobic, whereas alternative passages openly embrace the other. In the discrepancy between law and narrative, we must read between the lines and along the grain of historical context to understand the shifts in attitude—the opening and closing of the apertures where foreign women, as doubly other to the Israelite, become the focal point of change.

Biblical Matriarchs and Mothers

THE FIRST WOMAN TO become a mother is Eve as "the mother of all living" (Gen. 3:20). But that biological imperative is weighed down with the consequence of sin. Because Eve succumbed to the wily words of the serpent, she (and all women) are "cursed" (Gen. 3:16). Feminist scholars have uncovered the way that the myth of the so-called Fall from Eden and later interpretive tradition have served to inscribe men's power over women.[23] Gender and maternity emerge, uniquely and ironically, as the woman is born of man (Gen. 2:21–23). Whereas traditional commentary blames the first woman for the frailty of human existence—illness, travail in childbirth, mortality, hardship in working the earth, and even patriarchy itself, all consequences of the banishment from Eden—feminist interpretation suggests otherwise. In a historical contextual reading, women are not condemned to be ruled by men because of Eve's error but because the myth has been understood to be a *prescriptive* curse (the fate of all women) rather than a *descriptive* look at the conditions of the agrarian setting in which the stories in Genesis were composed. The story of disobedience in the Garden of Eden is an etiological tale, a "just so story" that accounts for women's fecundity but also for their hardship in birth and child rearing, subject to male control of female sexuality.[24]

From Eve onward, however, maternity becomes a uniquely female arena of control. Never again would man give birth to woman as he did in the primordial Garden. One might read the stories of mothers in the Hebrew Bible as a kind of corrective to the Eden story, where God lets the woman in on the divine plan and they become the directors in determining the heir to the covenantal promise.[25] Further, in contrast to Adam's role in naming, *women* take on the task of naming their progeny for the most part.[26] Yet three of the four matriarchs could not initially bear children. Their stories are part of a larger paradigm where barrenness and conception become the fertile ground for the working of divine providence.

The Hebrew Bible recounts six stories of barren women who become mothers of legendary heroes: Sarah, Abraham's wife and mother of Isaac (Gen. 18:9–15, 21:1); Rebekah, Isaac's wife and mother of Jacob (Gen. 25:19–26); Rachel, Jacob's wife and mother of Joseph (Gen. 30:1–8, 22–24); the unnamed wife of Manoah and mother of Samson (Judg. 13:1–24); Hannah, wife of Elkanah and mother of Samuel the prophet (1 Sam. 1:1–28); and the Shunnamite woman, an acolyte of the prophet Elisha (2 Kings 4:8–17). Metaphorically, "Fair Zion" (who represents the people and land) marks the seventh barren woman, who will eventually rejoice in her many children (Isa. 54:1).[27] All these women suffer a prolonged period of infertility, sometimes exacerbated by the presence of a less beloved though more fertile co-wife. These episodes all include variations on an annunciation scene in which a prophet, divine messenger, or even God appears to the woman with the promise of conception. The son born of this divine intercession is then heroically given over to the service of God: Isaac is bound and nearly sacrificed by his father (Gen. 22); Jacob sires the twelve tribes of Israel but first must flee for his life from his murderous brother, Esau

(Gen. 27); Joseph becomes "the great Provider" in Egypt but only after an act of near fratricide and being sold into slavery (Gen. 37); and both Samson and Samuel are consecrated as Nazirites even before conception (Judg. 13 and 1 Sam. 1–2), but, though Samson dies a martyr's death (Judg. 16:30), Samuel dedicates his life as a prophet to the service of God, anointing the first two kings of Israel (1 Sam. 8–16). As Susan Ackerman avers, "God who opens the womb has the right to demand, in some fashion, the life that comes from it."[28]

Once the "hero" is born, the matriarch plays a critical role in advancing her son as heir to the promise. Although Sarah was the one to bring in the "rival wife" (Gen. 16)—Hagar, her Egyptian maidservant, who bore Abraham Ishmael, his firstborn son—she later insists that the "slave woman and her son" be banished, for they present a threat to Isaac; God endorses her initiative, to the patriarch's dismay (Gen. 21:10–12).[29] In utero, Rebekah alone is privy to the divine oracle that two nations are in her womb and the older (son) will serve the younger (Gen. 25:25–26), but she never tells Isaac, who favors Esau. Instead, she resorts to deceit, disguising Jacob as his older hairy brother to steal the blessing from his blind father (Gen. 27:41–28:10). This trope is part of an overarching trend, discussed earlier, in which the younger son overturns the right of the firstborn. Here the women seem to be in cahoots with God's plan.[30] The only narrative in which the rival wife is *not* displaced and *all* the sons inherit the patriarchal covenant is in the story of Jacob's wives, Rachel and Leah—sisters and first cousins to Jacob of the Terahide clan.[31] Although sororal rivalry for Jacob's love and fertility percolates throughout their story (Gen. 29–31), their sons all stay within the covenantal promise as the founding fathers of the twelve tribes of Israel. As discussed earlier, the daughters of Lot, Tamar, and Ruth transgress legal and social norms to ensure that "life finds a way." Likewise, the midwives Shifra and Puah defy the king of Egypt in their "conscientious objection" against the decree to slay all the Hebrew male infants (Exod. 1:15–21);[32] and three women collaborate to sustain the life of the Redeemer, Moses, as an infant: his mother, his sister, and the daughter of the pharaoh (2:1–10). All these women are held up as heroic for their dedication to the continuity of life through motherhood.

Female Warriors and the Unconventional Weaponry of Women

FEMALE FIGURES ALSO PLAY a crucial role in the death of the enemy, deploying unconventional weaponry of women. They step in during a crisis in leadership when there is no man (or an emasculated man) at the helm—characteristic of the chaos that reigned during the time of the Judges.[33] To be slain by a woman, in patriarchal terms, implied that something was not right in the state of Israel or Judea.[34] When Abimelech, the self-appointed king of the Shechemites, begged his servant to finish off the job of killing him, he explained, "Let it not be said 'a woman slew him'" (Judg. 9:54), because he had been mortally wounded when a woman dropped a millstone from a tower that crushed his skull. Deemed shameful to be killed by a woman, the story became proverbial (cf. 2 Sam. 11:21).

Both Deborah and Jael set the precedent for this paradigm (Judg. 4–5). When asked by Barak to join him in battle, the prophetess and judge Deborah warned, "Know that Sisera [the enemy general of the Canaanites] will be delivered into the hands of a woman" (Judg. 4:9). The statement was meant to shame Barak for his less than manly appeal to her. Deborah may have been ironically thinking she would vanquish Sisera; but Jael, wife of Heber the Kenite, slays him when he flees to her tent for shelter. Under her offer of protection (and perhaps more), he falls asleep, whereupon she kills him by piercing his temple with a tent peg (Judg. 4:19–22; cf. 5:25–27).[35] Reading gender as a social construct and feminine or masculine behavior as performative, Deryn Guest points out that Jael performs both in the feminine mode of seduction and the masculine mode of penetration as she fells the enemy, thereby disrupting the gender binary.[36] Likewise, during the Maccabean period (second century BCE), Judith (of the Apocrypha), slays Holofernes, the Assyrian general, by a carefully orchestrated seduction, which ends with his decapitation and the salvation of her Judean town from the siege.[37] One might attribute the fall of Haman, the archenemy of the Jews in the book of Esther, to the queen's subtle plot to host two exclusive wine feasts with Ahasuerus and Haman, thereby arousing the king's jealousy (Esther 5 and 7). In all these stories, the enemy is defeated ignominiously by feminine wiles and a literal or figurative blow to the head.

When the narrative deploys a woman warrior, it implies a critique of the sociopolitical hierarchy in its historical setting; inadvertently, however, it also undermines the masculine-feminine binary. According to social convention and biblical law, woman may not put on man's apparel (Deut. 22:5). By extension, a female does not bear arms. Yet women such as Deborah, Jael, Judith, and even Esther emerge as powerful figures, wielding their unconventional weapons during periods of "serious social dysfunction"[38] and decentralization, at liminal junctures in the history of the Israelite and, later, the Jewish people.

The Role of Women in the King's Court

WOMEN PLAY A FORMATIVE role in the narratives of the monarchies in Israel and Judah. The First Commonwealth can be divided into two periods: the United Kingdom (1050–930 BCE), under Saul, David, and David's son, Solomon (1 Sam. 10–1 Kgs. 11); and the Divided Kingdoms of the Northern and Southern Tribes, Israel and Judah, respectively (1 Kgs. 12–2 Kgs. 25). The Northern Kingdom collapsed with the Assyrian conquest (722 BCE), when the proverbial ten lost tribes were dispersed; the Southern Kingdom, Judah (along with the remnant of Israel), persisted until the Babylonian conquest (586 BCE). Whereas the queen mothers of Judah are named consistently throughout 1 and 2 Kings, the biblical narrative recounts only the names of the most notorious queen mothers of the Northern Kingdom. Jezebel, the infamous wife of Ahab (1 Kgs. 16:30–2 Kgs. 9:36), daughter of a Phoenician king, established idolatry as the central form of worship in the Northern Kingdom and set up her own prophets of Baal and Asherah (1 Kgs. 18:19), waging an ideological battle with Elijah and the prophets of YHWH (the God of Israel) (1 Kgs. 17–19).[39] In addition, she seized the vineyard of Naboth for her husband after plotting his death in Jezreel (1 Kgs. 21) and was finally killed by the successor to the throne, Jehu (2 Kgs. 9:30–37), thrown ignominiously to the dogs, measure for measure, in Jezreel according to Elijah's curse (1 Kgs. 21:23; 2 Kgs. 9:10, 36–37). The notorious Queen Athaliah, daughter of Ahab (or Omri), who married Jehoram of Judah, followed in Jezebel's footsteps. After Ahaziah, their son, was killed in a dynastic struggle (2 Kgs. 11:1), she slew all but one of the rival descendants and usurped the throne, reigning for six years (842–836 BCE) as the only woman reported to have ruled as queen in Israel/Judah (2 Kgs. 11; 2 Chron. 22:10–23:21).[40] In seizing power, causing the death of innocent people and introducing Baal and Ashera worship as the official religion, the characterization of these "bad" queens supports the theodicy underlying the historical account: Israel was condemned to exile because of the corruption of the monarchy.[41]

During the period of the United Kingdom (1050–930 BCE), before the division of the monarchy under Rehoboam, Solomon's son, women also played a critical role both in Saul's court and in the court of his rival, David. Three of David's wives—Michal, Abigail, and Bathsheba—were pivotal in determining the successor to the throne, passively (by virtue of their lineage or status) as well as actively (through their behavior and speech).[42] Despite the epigram that history is written by the victors, the women's split loyalties expose the machinations of the king as Machiavellian. Michal, Abigail, and Bathsheba are torn between powerful men (either father and husband or husband and king).

David is not just a rival pole; he ultimately determines the outcome of their alliance. For Michal, her dual loyalty is poignantly expressed in the epithets attached to her name: "Saul's daughter" or "David's wife."[43] As the only woman said to love a man (1 Sam. 18:20, 28), Saul uses his daughter, Michal, as a trap to fell the young warrior in battle, and David's boundless success only fans the flames of jealousy and paranoia for the incumbent king. So when Michal betrays her father to protect her husband (19:10–17), King Saul hands her over to another man in marriage (1 Sam. 25:44). Later, she is reclaimed by David as he moves the capital to Jerusalem in a bid to unite the monarchy (2 Sam. 3:14–16). She is the tragic pawn in the game of chess between kings. As a conduit of the Saulide line, which is destined to be cut off (cf. 2 Sam. 21:8), Michal's role in securing continuity through an heir to the throne is essentially sealed by their last bitter repartee (2 Sam. 6:20–23). Her fate? A barren scepter in her grip, no son of hers succeeding.[44]

Like Michal who initially allies with David against her father, Abigail aligns herself with David and his band of outlaws *against* her husband, Nabal, a wealthy landowner in Carmel (1 Sam. 25).[45] Of all the women in the Bible, she is uniquely introduced as both beautiful and intelligent, in contrast to Nabal, her foolish husband (1 Sam. 25:3). When the man refuses to feed David and his henchmen as compensation for "protecting" the landowner's shepherds and flocks, David swears to slay Nabal and all the males of the household. Abigail, upon hearing his bloody intentions, secretly intercepts David on the path. Replete with gifts of drink, food, and eloquent speech, she intervenes to prevent a bloodbath. In doing so, she breaks faith with her husband, and, after his death, marries the future king of Israel. However, her message prophetically extends beyond the context of her own household. She auspiciously warns him, "Let this not be a trembling or stumbling block of the heart to my lord, to have shed blood for no cause" (1 Sam. 25:31).[46] Not only does it resonate with how David must restrain himself from slaying Saul in the episodes that frame this chapter (chaps. 24 and 26), but it also foreshadows how the king will later slip in succumbing to lust and bloodshed in the incident with Bathsheba and Uriah (2 Sam. 11). In that episode, David *does* shed blood for no cause, trying to cover up his adultery. Abigail's wise words of caution, like the speech of other wise-woman figures, serve as a critique of unbridled power.[47]

Most infamously, Bathsheba, "the wife of Uriah," is forced to betray her husband in submitting to David's illicit desire.[48] The consequences? Adultery. Uriah's murder. The death of the infant born of their adulterous union. And the unraveling of David's authority and kingdom. Yet it is Bathsheba who bears Solomon their second son and the successor to the throne. Bathsheba sews a life-giving thread after broken faith and heinous crimes in the dénouement to the David story. It is she who guarantees Solomon's succession. Prompted by the prophet Nathan, the queen invokes an oath at the king's sickbed, which David had supposedly made to her (though no such words are recorded in the biblical narrative): "My lord, you swore to your servant by YHWH your God, saying: 'Your son Solomon shall succeed me as king, and he shall sit on my throne'" (1 Kgs. 1:17). Invoking God's name in the oath (her own innovation on the prophet's script in v. 13), she shrewdly forwards her son Solomon as successor. As a result, her name, Bathsheba, takes on a new vocalization: "woman of oath" (*bat shevu'ah*).[49] Although passive initially, her ultimate role as aligned with that of the prophet Nathan and ultimately God underscores divine forgiveness and the transformation of heinous transgression under divine grace in the overarching redemptive narrative.

Daughters, Victims of Violence

FEMALE FIGURES KNOWN PRIMARILY by the epithet "daughter of" (*bat*) all meet a tragic fate: Dinah, the daughter of Jacob, is raped (Gen. 34); Jephthah's daughter submits to her father's vow and is sacrificed (Judg. 11:34–40); King Saul plays his daughter Michal as a pawn to fell his rival (1 Sam. 18–19 and 25:44); the Levite takes his concubine back from her father's home in Bethlehem, and she is gang-raped in Gibeah (Judg. 19); and Tamar, David's daughter, is raped by her half-brother, Amnon (2 Sam. 13). As a consequence of rape, rejection, or sacrifice, these women (who should be under the protective aegis of their father) never accede to the primary role of wife or mother in the Hebrew Bible.[50] The five daughters of Zelophehad, whose father died leaving no male heir, provide the one exception that proves the rule; they inherit their father's landholding (Num. 27:1–11, 36:1–10; Josh. 17:1–6).[51] In all the other instances, the father is implicated in his daughter's debasement, as David is when he sends his daughter to attend to Amnon's sickbed, though he ostensibly does not know his son's intentions in feigning illness (2 Sam. 13:6–7). The king/father not only fails to protect Tamar but also does nothing when he hears of her violation (like Jacob in response to Dinah's debasement) (2 Sam. 13:21; Gen. 34:5, 30). David is further held culpable when her brother, Absalom, takes matters into his own hands (2 Sam. 13:20–39; like Dinah's brothers, Simeon and Levi Gen. 34:24–31). Despite the vengeance enacted, there is no redemption for the daughter: Dinah disappears from the Genesis narrative, and Tamar remains effectively silenced and "desolate" (*shomemah*) in her brother's house (2 Sam. 13:20). In every other instance but here, *shomemah* is used with regard to the devastation of a city or land.[52]

The desolation of Tamar, King David's daughter, can be read as a fore-shadowing of the fate of Daughter Zion (*Bat Tzion*), the personification of Jerusalem across Psalms, Lamentations, and prophetic passages. The metaphor hinges on the presumed status of the beautiful daughter as the most vulnerable figure, the most sheltered and precious treasure of her father's regard in patriarchal society. Jerusalem is first introduced as *Bat Tzion* (Fair or Daughter Zion) in Isaiah's prophecy against Sennacherib (2 Kgs. 19:21; Isa. 36–37), highlighting the sense of her protected status and invincibility (e.g., see Ps. 46 and 48). But the metaphor is expanded in the poetry and prophecy of lament, when she (Jerusalem) is devastated, even ravaged (Isa. 1:8; Lam. 1:6, 2:1, 4, 8, 10, 13, and 4:22).[53] In the latter prophecy of consolation and return, *Bat Tzion* is restored (as in Isa. 52:2, 62:11; Mic. 4:8, 19, 13; Zeph. 3:14; and Zech. 14, 9:9). After the conquest of the neo-Babylonian Empire, a period of "return to Zion" (*shivat Tzion*) is initiated by the Persian king Cyrus (539 BCE). The prophet promises that Jerusalem will one day rejoice and metaphorically conceive and bear children: "For the children of the desolate woman [*shomemah*] will be more than the children of her that is married" (Isa. 54:1).[54] With regard to Tamar or Dinah, however, we never hear of them again.[55] They are merely removed from view as "abject" (Julia Kristeva's term), neither subject nor object in the social and symbolic order.[56]

Why include the stories of women's debasement and consequent abjection in the Bible—the story of Dinah and Shechem (Gen. 34), the gang rape of the concubine of Gibeah (Judg. 19), and the story of Amnon and Tamar (2 Sam. 13)? How do we teach these "texts of terror" (feminist scholar Phyllis Trible's term), in their historical context, and expose their patriarchal values? These narratives were not intended to applaud women's oppression and silence the victims but rather to convey the full horror of the women's violation. Biblical scholar Tikva Frymer-Kensky maintains that "these stories are frequently told as critiques of the social situations that they portray."[57] She urges the contemporary reader to "read with a 'hermeneutics of grace,' a method of interpretation that recognizes the basic decency and well-meaning character of the biblical authors," but she warns that "if we tell the biblical stories about women without taking note of the social system that gives them symbolic value, and naming its inequities, then we unwittingly help to perpetuate the skewed system that the Bible assumes."[58] The protected status of the daughter and her vulnerability undergird the rape stories; she is deprived of sexual agency in betrothal and marriage. By exposing the assumptions embedded in the text and inviting the women's voice to speak between the lines of the narrative, we can transform Dinah, Tamar, and even the concubine of Gibeah from an object of male abuse into a subject of feminist critique. I now turn to the prophetic narratives, where

God answers and figuratively redeems those daughters in their desolation by taking on the feminine mantle of mother.

Gendered Tropes in Prophecy

As THEOLOGIAN MARY DALY once remarked, "When God is male, then male is God."[59] What, then, do we do with the anthropomorphic metaphors of God as a "man of war" (Exod. 15:3; Isa. 42:13), a protective and punitive father (as in Jer. 1:8 and Mal. 1:6), or a possessive husband? In this third paradigm, perhaps the most egregious, God is represented as a man who marries a woman—Israel, symbolic both of land and nation—and then rejects her when she goes astray in worshipping foreign gods (Hosea 1–3; Jer. 2–3; Ezek. 16 and 23).[60] The relationship mirrors the unilateral and exclusive nature of marriage in the Bible, where the man "takes" a woman, just as God "took" Israel out of Egypt, betrothed to him through the covenant at Sinai. When Israel (the northern tribes) and later Judah (the southern tribes) breach the covenant by worshipping idols, the prophet asks: Can a husband take back his promiscuous wife if the Law forbids it?[61] Yet God overrides the Law, that is, if Israel endures a period of penance, while the land is laid waste, and she repents. The problem with this allegory for the relationship between Israel and God is that abuse follows the breach; the Almighty banishes the people to the desert and subjects them to thirst and hunger, affliction, and enforced servitude in exile, just as Hosea does with his promiscuous wife, Gomer (Hosea 2–3). Does the metaphor not covertly sanction wife abuse? There are two approaches one could take: transform the paradigm or search for alternative metaphors.

The feminist scholar Rachel Adler radically rereads the allegory in Hosea. In the biblical text God vows to take back the woman that he has cast off after she has had many lovers.

> And in that day—declares YHWH—You will call Me *Ishi* [literally "my man"], And no more will you call Me *Ba'ali* [literally "my master"/the Canaanite god]. . . . And I will espouse you forever: I will espouse you with righteousness and justice, And with goodness and mercy, And I will espouse you with faithfulness; Then you shall know YHWH. (Hosea 2:18–22)

Consonant with Robert Cover's understanding of the redemptive arc of history, the prophetic narrative depicts God constructively violating the Law to preserve the covenant. God willingly takes back his wayward wife but on new terms: No longer will they call God "Ba'al" (the Canaanite god and also "master"), but "my man," which suggests an egalitarian relationship based on mutual recognition, as in the act of naming the first man and woman (Gen. 2:23). Furthermore, it is the supposed male God who vows fidelity to Israel, the woman, on new terms (righteousness, justice, goodness, mercy, and faithfulness), while *she* will "know" God. In the conventional biblical idiom, men are the subjects of the verb "to know" (*y-d-ʿ*) as a euphemism for intimate, sexual relations, as in "And the man knew his wife" (Gen. 4:1).[62] Adler argues, "Because the constructive violation of law is depicted metaphorically, it affects not only the law but also the metaphor that is its carrier. . . . The introduction of reconciliation into the breached covenant marriage accomplishes a constructive violation of metaphor . . . [redefining] marriage . . . based not upon ownership but upon mutual responsiveness."[63] This reading not only transforms the misogynist trope of God as the possessive husband and Israel as the wayward wife but also provides us with a new model for marriage itself as a relationship forged in reciprocal terms that are both binding and eternal, grounded in a covenant of love.

We might also address the underlying conventional misogynist metaphors by turning to alternatives, where God plays female roles: a woman in mourning (Jer. 8:21), a woman in labor (Isa. 42:14, 51:1–2, 12), a mother lamenting her lost children (Jer. 31:15–20) and rejoicing in their return (Isa. 49:13–15, 66:7–14),[64] or a midwife (Ps. 22:10–11, 71:6).[65] Phyllis Trible suggests that the maternal metaphors for God may stem from the Hebrew term for compassion, *rahamim*, an abstract noun derived from the word *rehem*, meaning "womb." The root, *r-ḥ-m*, is both the locus and the metaphorical locution for divine love.[66] God remembers Ephraim, her darling child, and "therefore My womb trembles for him, I will truly show motherly-compassion upon him [*rahem 'araham-menu*], declares YHWH" (Jer. 31:20). The personification of God as mother ripples out from the womb into other images for the Exodus from Egypt and the sojourn through the wilderness: an eagle hovering over her nestlings, bearing them aloft on pinions (Deut. 32:11; cf. Exod. 19:4); a nursing mother who suckled them on "honey from the crag, oil from the flinty rock" (Deut. 32:13), though the children neglected "the Rock who begot" them and the God "who labored to bring them forth" (Deut. 32:18, echoed in Isa. 42:14 and 51:2). These images in the later post-exilic prophecies broaden the "Personhood of God"[67] through metaphor or simile expanded into allegory and surpass the biological boundaries—a mother might abandon her children, but God would never forget Zion (Isa. 49:15, 66:13). Yet a cautionary note must be sounded even among these moving poetic female images. Underlying the metaphor of Fair Zion as a desolate daughter or barren wife lie patriarchal values. These tropes associate the land with women and women's bodies as an image for the collective social body. We must be wary of reifying the paternalism embedded in these metaphors that cover over the woman's violation, where the male acts upon the passive female body.

Conclusion

IN THIS ESSAY I have surveyed some of the central female roles and gender tropes in the Hebrew Bible—mother, daughter, warrior, and wise woman—within the patriarchal world that undergirds their lives. As the handmaidens of history, women figures may be agents in fulfilling the divine plan. The matriarchs in Genesis—Sarah, Rebekah, Rachel, and Leah—all play a central role in selecting the heir to the patriarchal covenant, whereas the initiative of Lot's daughters, Tamar (Judah's daughter-in-law), and Ruth account for the foundation of the Judean (and messianic) dynasty. Although I am cognizant of the different sources and voices throughout this complex anthology of works, in the end the texts speak to one another in the final form. In recent years, scholars, poets, and writers of modern midrashim have begun to articulate creative rereadings of the stories that give voice to women figures who have been marginalized or silenced in the biblical text. The primary agenda in this reading strategy, in Trible's words, is to "depatriarchalize" biblical interpretation and recover themes that "disavow sexism."[68] Under this category, I include modern midrashim, which reclaim the silenced voices of women (Alicia Ostriker's poetry, the songs of Alicia Jo Rabins of "Girls in Trouble," Tamar Biala's collection of Israeli women's midrashim, *Dirshuni*, and Wilda Gafney's *Womanist Midrash*). Other scholars highlight the subversive role of biblical women (Ilana Pardes, Tikva Frymer-Kensky, Tamara Cohn Eskenazi, Amy Kalmanofsky, Rachel Adelman, and Judy Klitsner), showing how narratives that feature female agency chafe against and even transform legal and gender norms. For those interested in feminism and the history of women's roles and status in the Hebrew Bible, new scholars have broken open the field of biblical studies. Not only do they deconstruct the Bible's patriarchal values, but they also enable us to hear the muted voices of women percolating up from the fissures of the text.

Notes

1   Authorship of the sources of the Pentateuch is ascribed to J, E, P, and D according to the documentary hypothesis. The priestly source (P) was most likely of male authorship, because the priesthood and the scribal tradition were restricted

to men. Yet given the lively female characters Eve, Sarah, Rebekah, and Tamar, Harold Bloom suggests that the J source may have been authored by a woman, perhaps a princess of the Davidic royal house; see Harold Bloom, *The Book of J* (New York: Grove Weidenfeld, 1990), 24–36. See also Richard Elliot Friedman, *Who Wrote the Bible* (San Francisco: Harper & Row, 1987), 86. Other scholars conjecture that the Song of Songs may have been written by a woman, given the centrality of the female lover's voice; see Cheryl Exum, *Song of Songs: A Commentary* (Louisville, KY: Westminster John Knox Press, 2005), 64–66; Athalya Brenner, "Women Poets and Authors," in *A Feminist Companion to the Song of Songs*, ed. Athalya Brenner (Sheffield, UK: Sheffield Academic Press, 1993), 86–97; and S. D. Goitein, "Women as Creators of Biblical Genres," *Prooftexts* 8 (1988): 1–33 (translation of the 1957 Hebrew version).

2   On questions of method and methodology, see Susanne Scholz, "Methods and Feminist Interpretation of the Hebrew Bible," in *Feminist Interpretation of the Hebrew Bible in Retrospect*, vol. 3, *Methods*, ed. Susanne Scholz (Sheffield, UK: Sheffield Phoenix Press, 2016), 19–34; and Susan Niditch, "Portrayals of Women in the Hebrew Bible," in *Jewish Women in Historical Perspective*, ed. Judith Baskin, 2nd ed. (Detroit: Wayne State University Press, 1998), 25–45.

3   Simone de Beauvoir, *The Second Sex* (New York: Vintage Books, 1973), 301. For a critique of de Beauvoir's characterization of "feminine" and "woman," see Judith Butler, *Gender Trouble* (New York: Routledge, Chapman & Hall, 1990), esp. 8–34.

4   See the comprehensive study by Amy Kalmanofsky, *Gender Play in the Hebrew Bible* (New York: Routledge 2017).

5   Deborah W. Rooke, "Patriarchy/Kyriarchy," in *The Oxford Encyclopedia of the Bible and Gender Studies*, ed. Julia M. O'Brien (New York: Oxford University Press, 2014), 2: 1.

6   Biblical law specified only sons as heirs, with a double portion awarded the first-born (Deut. 21:15–17).

7   Kimberlé Crenshaw introduced the term *intersectionality*; see Kimberlé Crenshaw, "Mapping the Margins: Intersectionality, Identity Politics, and Violence Against Women of Color," *Stanford Law Review* 43 (1991): 1241–99. Elisabeth Schüssler Fiorenza applies the concept to biblical studies; see Elisabeth Schüssler Fiorenza, *But She Said: Feminist Practices of Biblical Interpretation* (Boston: Beacon Press, 1992), 115–17, 122–25. See also Kwok Pui Lan, "Elisabeth Schüssler Fiorenza and Post-Colonial Studies," *Journal of Feminist Studies in Religion* 25, no. 1 (2009): 191–207.

8   For an overview, see Victor H. Matthews, Bernard M. Levinson, and Tikva Frymer-Kensky, eds., *Gender and Law in the Hebrew Bible and the Ancient Near East* (Sheffield, UK: Sheffield Academic Press, 1988).

9   See Tikva Frymer-Kensky's foundational article, "Virginity in the Bible," in *Gender and Law in the Hebrew Bible and the Ancient Near East*, ed. Victor H. Matthews, Bernard M. Levinson, and Tikva Frymer-Kensky (Sheffield, UK: Sheffield Academic Press, 1998), 79–96.

10   Although a man was bound to honor the "conjugal rights" of his first wife (Exod. 21:10).

11 For a historical-contextual analysis of this strange ritual, see Tikva Frymer-Kensky, "The Strange Case of the Suspected Sotah (Numbers V 11–31)," in *Women in the Hebrew Bible: A Reader*, ed. Alice Bach (New York: Routledge, 1999), 463–74; Jacob Milgrom, "The Case of the Suspected Adulteress, Numbers 5:11–31: Redaction and Meaning," in *Women in the Hebrew Bible: A Reader*, ed. Alice Bach (New York: Routledge, 1999), 475–82; and Michael Fishbane, "Accusations of Adultery: A Study of Law and Scribal Practice in Numbers 5:11–31," in *Women in the Hebrew Bible*, ed. Alice Bach (New York: Routledge, 1999), 487–502.

12 See Susan Niditch, "The Three Wife-Sister Tales of Genesis," in *A Prelude to Biblical Folklore: Underdogs and Tricksters*, by Susan Niditch (San Francisco: Harper & Row, 1987), 23–69.

13 As Abraham averred, in ascribing "no fear of God in this place" (Gen. 20:11).

14 Some interpretive traditions identify Esther as Mordecai's wife. See Adele Berlin, *The JPS Bible Commentary: Esther* (Philadelphia: Jewish Publication Society, 2001), 26; and Rachel Adelman, *The Female Ruse: Women's Deception and Divine Sanction in the Hebrew Bible* (Sheffield, UK: Sheffield Phoenix Press, 2015), 204, 222–24.

15 Robert Cover, "The Supreme Court, 1982 Term—Foreword: Nomos and Narrative," *Harvard Law Review* 97, no. 4 (1983): 4–68. For an exploration of how female figures in subsequent Jewish culture made an impact on the Jewish interpretation of law, see Jane L. Kanarek, *Biblical Narrative and the Formation of Rabbinic Law* (New York: Cambridge University Press, 2014).

16 Cover, "Supreme Court, 1982 Term," 24.

17 For the tension between *nomos* and narrative in these stories, see Adelman, *Female Ruse*, 96–103. For levirate marriage in the Hebrew Bible and rabbinic corpus, see Dvora Weisberg, *Levirate Marriage and the Family in Ancient Judaism* (Hanover, NH: University Press of New England, 2009).

18 See, for example, Deut. 10:18; 14:29; 16:11, 14; 24:19–21; 26:12–13; and 27:19.

19 See Harold Fisch, "Ruth and the Structure of Covenant History," *Vetus Testamentum* 32, no. 4 (1982): 425–37; and Adelman, *Female Ruse*, 90–125. Ruth Kara-Ivanov Kaniel has identified a literary paradigm called "the mother of the Messiah," where the illicit behavior of these outsider women leads to the conception of the progenitor of the messianic line; see Ruth Kara-Ivanov Kaniel, *Holiness and Transgression: Mothers of the Messiah in the Jewish Myth* (Boston: Academic Studies Press, 2017).

20 See Alison Joseph, "Who Is the Victim in the Dinah Story?" TheTorah.com, 2017, http://thetorah.com/who-is-the-victim-in-the-dinah-story/ (accessed December 20, 2020).

21 Shaye J. D. Cohen, "From Ethnos to Ethno-Religion," in *The Beginnings of Jewishness: Boundaries, Varieties, Uncertainties*, by Shaye J. D. Cohen (Berkeley: University of California Press, 1999), 109–39.

22 See Yair Zakovitch, *Ruth: Introduction and Commentary* (Tel Aviv: Am Oved; and Jerusalem: Magnes, 1990), 19–20, 24 (Hebrew). Others argue that the issue during the period of Ezra and Nehemiah was not necessarily ethnic rejection of the outsider but rather assimilating the children into Judean practice, belief, culture, and even language. See Jacob Wright and Tamara Cohn Eskenazi,

"Contrasting Pictures of Intermarriage in Ruth and Nehemiah," TheTorah.com (2015), http://thetorah.com/contrasting-pictures-of-intermarriage-in-ruth-and-nehemiah/ (accessed December 20, 2020).

23 See Phyllis Trible, "A Love Story Gone Awry," in *God and the Rhetoric of Sexuality*, by Phyllis Trible (Philadelphia: Fortress Press, 1978), 72–142; and Mieke Bal, *Lethal Love: Feminist Literary Readings of Biblical Love Stories* (Bloomington: Indiana University Press, 1987), 104–30.

24 See Carol Meyers, *Rediscovering Eve: Ancient Israelite Women in Context*, 2nd ed. (New York: Oxford University Press 2013), 81–102.

25 See Judy Klitsner, *Subversive Sequels in the Bible* (Philadelphia: Jewish Publication Society, 2009), 131–58.

26 See Ilana Pardes, *Countertraditions in the Bible: A Feminist Approach* (Cambridge, MA: Harvard University Press, 1992), 39–59; and Karla G. Bohmbach, "Names and Naming in the Biblical World," in *Women in Scripture*, ed. Carol Meyers, Toni Craven, and Ross S. Kraemer (Boston: Houghton Mifflin, 2000), 33–99.

27 This metaphor is based on the typology of the barren wife and her rival (cf. 1 Sam. 2:5 and Ps. 113:9). See Mary Callaway, *Sing, O Barren One: A Study in Comparative Midrash* (Atlanta: Scholars Press, 1986), 59–90.

28 Susan Ackerman, "Child Sacrifice: Returning God's Gift," *Bible Review* 9, no. 3 (1993): 56. See also Jon D. Levenson, *The Death and Resurrection of the Beloved Son* (New Haven, CT: Yale University Press, 1993).

29 Sympathy in the text toward Hagar and Ishmael is clear, despite their exclusion from the patriarchal covenant. Hagar is the first woman to whom an angel of God speaks, and Ishmael is granted a unique divine destiny. See Phyllis Trible, *Texts of Terror* (Philadelphia: Fortress Press, 1984), 9–35; and Tikva Frymer-Kensky, *Reading the Women of the Bible* (New York: Schocken, 2002), 224–337. Contemporary "womanist" Bible scholars, who embrace their identity as African American women of color, have reclaimed the voice of Hagar; see Renita Weems, *Just a Sister Away* (San Diego: Lura Media, 1988), 1–21; and Wilda C. Gafney, *Womanist Midrash: A Reintroduction to the Women of the Torah and the Throne* (Louisville, KY: Westminster John Knox Press, 2017), 38–44.

30 See Adelman, *Female Ruse*, 12–37.

31 See Amy Kalmanofsky, *Dangerous Sisters in the Hebrew Bible* (Minneapolis: Fortress Press, 2014), 19–36; and Adelman, *Female Ruse*, 38–67.

32 See Judy Klitsner, "The Rebirth of the Individual: The Tower of Babel and the Midwives of Israel," in *Subversive Sequels in the Bible*, by Judy Klitsner (Philadelphia: Jewish Publication Society, 2009), 31–62.

33 See Jo Ann Hackett, "In the Days of Jael: Reclaiming the History of Women in Ancient Israel," in *Immaculate and Powerful: The Female in Sacred Image and Social Reality*, ed. Clarissa Atkinson, Constance Buchanan, and Margaret Miles (Boston: Beacon Press, 1985), 15–38.

34 See Gale A. Yee, "By the Hand of a Woman: The Metaphor of the Woman Warrior in Judges 4," in *Women, War, and Metaphor: Language and Society in the Study of the Hebrew Bible*, ed. Claudia V. Camp and Carole R. Fontaine (Atlanta: Scholars Press, 1993), 99–132.

35 See Susan Ackerman, *Warrior, Dancer, Seductress, Queen: Women in Judges and Biblical Israel* (New York: Doubleday, 1998), 89–127; and Susan Niditch, "Eroticism and Death in the Tale of Jael," in *Gender and Difference in Ancient Israel*, ed. Peggy L. Day (Minneapolis: Fortress Press, 1989), 43–57.

36 Deryn Guest, "From Gender Reversal to Genderfuck: Reading Jael Through a Lesbian Lens," in *Bible Trouble: Queer Reading at the Boundaries of Biblical Scholarship*, ed. Teresa J. Hornsby and Ken Stone (Atlanta: Society of Biblical Literature, 2011), 9–43.

37 See the comparison by Sidnie White, "In the Steps of Jael and Deborah: Judith as Heroine," in *No One Spoke Ill of Her: Essays on Judith*, ed. James VanderKam (Atlanta: Scholars Press, 1992), 5–16.

38 Hackett, "In the Days of Jael," 25.

39 See Phyllis Trible, "The Odd Couple: Elijah and Jezebel," in *Out of the Garden: Women Writers on the Bible*, ed. Christina Büchmann and Celina Spiegel (New York: Fawcett Columbine, 1994), 166–79, 340–41; Tina Pippin, "Jezebel Re-Vamped," in *A Feminist Companion to Samuel and Kings*, ed. Athalya Brenner (Sheffield, UK: Sheffield Academic Press, 1994), 196–206; and Amy Kalmanofsky, "Jezebel and Ahab," in *Gender-Play in the Hebrew Bible: The Ways the Bible Challenges Its Gender Norms*, by Amy Kalmanofsky (New York: Routledge, 2016), 95–113.

40 See Reuven Chaim Klein, "Queen Athaliah: The Daughter of Ahab or Omri?" *Jewish Bible Quarterly* 42, no. 1 (2014): 11–20; and Stuart Macwilliam, "Athaliah: A Case of Illicit Masculinity," in *Biblical Masculinities Foregrounded*, ed. Ovidiu Creangă and Peter-Ben Smit (Sheffield, UK: Sheffield Phoenix Press, 2014), 69–85.

41 See Ginny Brewer-Boydston, *Good Queen Mothers, Bad Queen Mothers: The Theological Presentation of the Queen Mother in 1 and 2 Kings* (Washington, DC: Catholic Biblical Association of America, 2016).

42 For the roles of David's wives as critique of the monarchy, see Adelman, *Female Ruse*, 126–97.

43 See David Clines, "The Story of Michal, Wife of David, in Its Sequential Unfolding," in *Telling Queen Michal's Story: An Experiment in Comparative Interpretation*, ed. David J. A. Clines and Tamar C. Eskenazi (Sheffield, UK: Sheffield Academic Press, 1991), 129–40; and Lillian R. Klein, "Michal, the Barren Wife," in *A Feminist Companion to Samuel and Kings*, ed. Athalya Brenner (Sheffield, UK: Sheffield Academic Press, 2000), 37–46.

44 Paraphrasing Shakespeare, *Macbeth*, III; i.

45 See Jon D. Levenson and Baruch Halpern, "The Political Import of David's Marriages," *Journal of Biblical Literature* 99, no. 4 (1980): 507–18; and Jon D. Levenson, "1 Samuel 15 as Literature and as History," *Catholic Bible Quarterly* 40 (1978): 11–28.

46 According to rabbinic tradition, the word *this* alludes to the incident of Bathsheba (*b. Megillah* 14b). Uriel Simon also notes the dramatic irony; see Uriel Simon, "The Poor Man's Ewe-Lamb: An Example of a Juridical Parable," *Biblica* 48 (1967): 236.

47 Such as the wise woman of Tekoa (2 Sam. 14) and her counterpart in the town of Abel (2 Sam. 20:14–22). Claudia V. Camp argues that the personification of "Lady Wisdom" in Proverbs (1:5–6 and *passim*) derives not from the Near Eastern goddess or from the Greek *Sophia* but from this female role in Israelite history, comparable to the (male) town elder; see Claudia V. Camp, "The Wise Women of 2 Samuel: A Role Model for Women in Early Israel," *Catholic Biblical Quarterly* 43 (1981): 14–29; and Claudia V. Camp, *Wisdom and the Feminine in the Book of Proverbs* (Sheffield, UK: Almond Press, 1985). See also Carol Newsom, "Woman and the Discourse of Patriarchal Wisdom: A Study of Proverbs 1–9," in *Gender and Difference Gender and Difference in Ancient Israel*, ed. Peggy Day (Minneapolis: Augsburg/Fortress Press, 1989), 142–60.

48 Some scholars have argued that Bathsheba is ostensibly raped because, given the king's power, she does not have the right to refuse. But rape language is not deployed in this passage, and the only significant factor here is that she is married and, by virtue of her status, passively serves in the downfall of the king. See Alexander Izuchukwu Abasili, "Was It Rape? The David and Bathsheba Pericope Re-examined," *Vetus Testamentum* 61 (2011): 1–15; Frymer-Kensky, *Reading the Women of the Bible*, 156; Adelman, *Female Ruse*, 166–84; and Sara M. Koenig, *Isn't This Bathsheba?* (Eugene, OR: Pickwick, 2011).

49 See Moshe Garsiel, *Biblical Names: A Literary Study of Midrashic Derivations and Puns* (Ramat Gan: Bar-Ilan University Press, 1991), 129–30; and Koenig, *Isn't This Bathsheba*, 43–44, 94.

50 See Kimberly D. Russaw, *Daughters in the Hebrew Bible* (London: Rowman & Littlefield, 2018).

51 See Tal Ilan, "The Daughters of Zelophehad and Women's Inheritance: The Biblical Injunction and Its Outcome," in *Exodus to Deuteronomy: A Feminist Companion to the Bible*, ed. Athalya Brenner (Sheffield, UK: Sheffield Academic Press, 2000), 176–86; Yael Shemesh, "A Gender Perspective on the Daughters of Zelophehad: Bible, Talmudic Midrash, and Modern Feminist Midrash," *Biblical Interpretation* 15, no. 1 (2007): 80–109; and Zafrira Ben-Barak, *Inheritance by Daughters in Israel and the Ancient Near East: A Social, Legal, and Ideological Revolution* (Jaffa: Archaeological Center Publications, 2006).

52 *Shomemah* comes from the verb *sh-m-m*, "laid waste," "desolated," "appalled," as in Exod. 23:29; Isa. 49:19; Jer. 51:26; Ezek. 6:14, 33:28, 29, 35:3, 7, 15; and Lam. 1:13, 16 and 3:11. See Francis Brown, S. R. Driver, and Charles A. Briggs, *A Hebrew and English Lexicon of the Old Testament* (Oxford, UK: Clarendon Press, 1966), entry 10073, 1031.

53 Barbara Bakke Kaiser, "Poet as 'Female Impersonator': The Image of Daughter Zion in Biblical Poems of Suffering," *Journal of Religion* 67, no. 2 (1987): 164–82; Mary L. Conway, "Daughter Zion: Metaphor and Dialogue in the Book of Lamentations," in *Daughter Zion: Her Portrait, Her Response*, ed. Mark. J. Boda, Carol J. Dempsey, and LeeAnn S. Flesher (Atlanta: Society of Biblical Literature), 101–27.

54 See Mark J. Boda, "The Daughter's Joy," in *Daughter Zion: Her Portrait, Her Response*, ed. Mark. J. Boda, Carol J. Dempsey, and LeeAnn S. Flesher (Atlanta: Society of Biblical Literature, 2012), 321–42.

55 Although Absalom poignantly names his daughter Tamar (2 Sam. 14:27).

56 Julia Kristeva, *Powers of Horror: An Essay on Abjection*, trans. Leon Roudiez (New York: Columbia University Press, 1982).

57 Frymer-Kensky, *Reading the Women of the Bible*, 353.

58 Frymer-Kensky, *Reading the Women of the Bible*, 353.

59 Mary Daly, *Beyond God the Father* (Boston: Beacon Press, 1973), 9.

60 For a discussion of the problematic nature of these metaphors, see Renita J. Weems, *Battered Love: Marriage Sex, and Violence in the Hebrew Prophets* (Minneapolis: Fortress Press, 1997); Gerlinde Baumann, *Love and Violence: Marriage as Metaphor for the Relationship Between YHWH and Israel in the Prophetic Books* (Collegeville, MN: Liturgical Press, 2003); and Kalmanofsky, *Dangerous Sisters*, 53–68.

61 See Jer. 3:1, based on Deut. 24:1–4.

62 The same inversion is conveyed by Jer. 31:22b: "For YHWH has created a new thing on earth: female encompasses/courts [*tesovav*] man."

63 Rachel Adler, *Engendering Judaism* (Boston: Beacon Press, 1998), 164.

64 Mayer I. Gruber, *The Motherhood of God and Other Studies* (Atlanta: Scholars Press, 1992), 3–15; Sarah J. Dille, *Mixing Metaphors: God as Mother and Father in Deutero-Isaiah* (London: T & T Clark International, 2004); Irmtraud Fischer, "Isaiah: The Book of Female Metaphors," in *Feminist Biblical Interpretation*, ed. Luise Schottroff and Marie-Theres Wacker (Grand Rapids, MI: Eerdmans, 2012), 303–18; and Riannon Graybill, "Yahweh as Maternal Vampire in Second Isaiah," *Journal of Feminist Studies in Religion* 33, no. 1 (2017): 9–25.

65 Juliana M. Claassens, *Mourner, Mother, Midwife: Reimagining God's Delivering Presence in the Old Testament* (Louisville, KY: Westminster John Knox Press, 2012).

66 See Phyllis Trible, "Journey of a Metaphor," in *God and the Rhetoric of Sexuality*, by Phyllis Trible (Minneapolis: Fortress Press, 1978), 31–59.

67 Yochanan Muffs's term; see Yochanan Muffs, *The Personhood of God: Biblical Theology, Human Faith, and the Divine Image* (Woodstock, VT: Jewish Lights, 2005).

68 Phyllis Trible, "Depatriarchalizing in Feminist Interpretation," *Journal of the American Academy of Religion* 41, no. 1 (1973): 31.

GENDER AND WOMEN'S HISTORY IN RABBINIC LITERATURE

TAL ILAN

HOW DOES ONE WRITE women's history using sources that were not written as history and are not interested in women and their experiences? Rabbinic literature is composed, first and foremost, of a legal codex—the Mishnah, ca. 200 CE—with a complex and at times highly imaginative commentary attached to it: the Talmudim (Palestinian, or *Yerushalmi*, third–fourth century CE; and Babylonian, or *Bavli*, fourth–sixth century CE) and the Midrashim (the ones relevant for us dating from the third to seventh century). Legal codices such as the Mishnah are by definition prescriptive rather than descriptive. In other words, they posit an ideal society, and many of their rulings hint more at behavior they wish to combat than at standards currently in practice. The commentaries (i.e., the Talmudim) are thematically linked with the Mishnah's legal matter. The Midrashim are imaginative interpretations of the Bible for both legal and other information. Although the Mishnah (and the Bible) lead the commentators into many exciting avenues of discussion, history and historical inquiry are usually not part of them.

From a feminist perspective, Rabbinic literature is a typical cultural product of late antiquity: It was written by men and for men and presents a patriarchal and androcentric outlook, which is sometimes misogynistic. The study of women's history from Rabbinic literature is hampered by the Rabbis' disinterest in the lives of women as human subjects rather than as appendices to their husbands' households and property. The Rabbis were a small group of scholars who began their exegetical and legal activity in the wake of the destruction of the Temple in 70 CE and who, over several centuries, sought to become and eventually succeeded in becoming the leaders of the Judaism that survived from antiquity into the Middle Ages. Aside from their legal program, which aimed at bringing Jewish women under men's direct judicial control,[1] the Rabbis were primarily interested in themselves—an intellectual male elite who made the study house and Torah study the center of the world, and everything else, including women, subsidiary. Only a select group of men occupied the benches of the study houses that produced Rabbinic literature; no women were among them. Yet, in their everyday lives, each of the Rabbis was surrounded by women—mothers, wives, daughters, and others. In this chapter I describe the way the Rabbis imagined women and expected women to behave; I contrast this with information the Rabbis disclose about real women and what they actually did. At times, of course, the two aspects coincided, but sometimes they were distinctly different.

The Rabbis did not view postbiblical Jewish women as equal to men, just as women were not viewed as equal in the Greco-Roman, Semitic Mediterranean, or Babylonian societies in which Jews lived. Rabbinic literature viewed women's position as emanating from the injunctions of the Hebrew Bible. Their subordination was understood as resulting from the consequences of Eve's role in the creation narrative, both as being created secondarily and as being guilty of the first transgression, namely, eating from the forbidden Tree of Knowledge in the Garden of Eden. In midrashic literature women are punished for Eve's involvement in this transgression and therefore suffer while giving birth, are subjected to their husbands (as already suggested in the Bible), and are also locked up at home as in a prison and must go out with their heads covered (*Avot de Rabbi Nathan* B, 42). Their functions at funerals (preparing the body, mourning the dead) are understood as consequences of their involvement in bringing death to the world. Even the special commandments reserved for women—lighting the Sabbath candles (*hadlaqat ha-ner*), setting aside the *challah* portion when baking, and avoiding contact with their husbands during menstruation (*niddah*)—were viewed as punishments for that sin (see *Genesis Rabbah* 17:8).[2]

The Rabbis' innovation was systemization of dispersed biblical texts. In some cases they formulated in law what must have been common practice for generations. Thus it is doubtful whether women ever participated in communal prayer. Yet the Rabbis also formulated a law that women were exempt from all time-bound commandments (*m. Qiddushim* 1:7), and before that law came into being, they certainly could. For example, the exemption of women from participation in Sukkot festivities, particularly the prohibition to reside in the sukkah (*t. Qiddushim* 1:10), was the result of this new law; it was completely new and probably entailed some opposition.[3]

The law of women's exemption from time-bound commandments is understood as a generalization (*kelal*) and the rabbis themselves insist that one does not learn about specific rulings from generalizations (*b. Eruvin* 27a). Indeed, a survey of specific time-bound commandments shows clearly that they do include women. Women are expected to participate in prayer and the blessing on food (*m. Berakhot* 3:3). They are expected to drink four glasses of wine on Passover (*b. Pesahim* 108a–b). They are commanded to light candles on Hanukkah (*b. Shabbat* 23a), and so on. Thus the fact that the exempting law contradicts specific rulings that compel women to follow some time-bound commandments indicates that it was an ideological move on the Rabbis' part rather than a practical one.

Time-bound commandments, as the Rabbis themselves make clear at the same place where they formulate the law about women's exemption, are, as a rule, cultic commandments. The list, which follows the ruling in its parallel Tosefta, includes "building the sukkah, taking the *lulav*, and donning phylacteries" (*t. Qiddushin* 1:10). The list also registers examples of commandments that are not time bound and therefore from which women are not exempt: "[the return of] lost property and the sending away of the [mother bird from the] nest [when taking the young for consumption] and [building] a railing [around one's roof]" (*t. Qiddushin* 1:10). These commandments are clearly noncultic.

Many scholars have speculated on the reason for the exemption of women from time-bound commandments. A charitable interpretation claims that exemption is not exclusion and that by allowing woman to abstain from time-bound commandments, the lawgivers understood their special circumstances of childbearing and child rearing, which left them little time for participation in the cult. I suggest a less charitable interpretation here: Women's exclusion from these commandments meant their expulsion from Jewish cultic life. The lists themselves clearly indicate that the issue at hand was women's cultic participation and that the Rabbis were more interested in removing women from Jewish cultic life than they were about their time and commitments.

Contemporary concerns and Hellenistic influence tampered further with biblical justification for women's subordination. In one midrash the Rabbis compare the biblical story of the creation of woman with the Greek Pandora myth, in which women are seen as created secondarily and as the source of all the evils in the world. In the Rabbis' parable Eve is compared to a woman whose husband gave her all his property to use, save one barrel, which she had to keep shut. The property is of course the Garden of Eden and the "one barrel" is the Tree of Knowledge. The wife cannot contain her curiosity, opens the barrel, and finds it full of scorpions and snakes (*Genesis Rabbah* 19:10). This is compared to Eve eating fruit from the Tree of Knowledge and giving some to Adam. Consequently, Eve and Adam both suffered and still suffer today. The Pandora myth, in which the first Greek woman is given a box, which she is told not to open but does, thereby releasing all evils, including death, into the world, is used by the Rabbis as a parable with which to clarify the Garden of Eden story, reducing Eve to the root cause of human misery and death.

The Crystallization of the Role of Women in Rabbinic Literature

LIKE JEWISH WOMEN'S IMAGE, Jewish women's legal position was also based on the Hebrew Bible, particularly on injunctions mentioned in the legal sections of the Pentateuch. Biblical law was of Semitic origin and supported a society that upheld polygyny and bride-price marriages. Internal developments, as well as the influence of the Western civilizations under whose aegis the Jews had come, beginning in the third century BCE (the Greeks and then the Romans), tended toward monogyny and dowry marriages. Thus the Rabbis reevaluated and reformed some key biblical injunctions associated with women (such as the *yibbum*, i.e., levirate marriage, which they basically rejected).[4] Other issues associated with women's position had not been tackled by the biblical legislators at all, first and foremost, the marriage settlement.

According to Rabbinic sources, the sage Shimeon ben Shatah instituted the Jewish marriage contract, the *ketubbah*, during the Second Temple period (*t. Ketubbot* 12:1; *y. Ketubbot* 8:11, 32b–c; *b. Ketubbot* 82b). The meaning of this innovation was that several of the woman's rights in marriage were made legally binding by a written document. It made support for a widowed or divorced wife part of the legal system of marriage and not an act of charity. Marriage contracts were produced by some of the societies with which the Jews came into contact, such as the Egyptians and the Greeks. Evidence from the fifth-century BCE Jewish community in Elephantine Egypt reveals that marriage documents were produced by Jews that far back.[5] Furthermore, we know that this institution continued to be viable in Jewish society, because Jewish marriage documents from slightly earlier than the Mishnah (ca. 100–150 CE) were discovered in the Judean Desert. Although they are all written for Jews, they are diverse in nature, written in Aramaic or in Greek, and display a plethora of traits that are occasionally compatible with the Rabbinic *ketubbah*, but not always.

Scholars have attempted to harmonize the legal injunctions of these Dead Sea documents with Rabbinic rulings of the Mishnah. Documents have been reread and amended so as to comply with Rabbinic requirements.[6] However, because these documents predate the Mishnah by several decades, they should instead serve as witnesses to Jewish women's legal position before Rabbinic intervention. Although documents from the Judean Desert are occasionally quite close to Rabbinic formulations and demands, this is more an indication that Rabbinic tradition did not begin its foray into women's legal status from scratch but rather based it on an early Aramaic tradition. Indeed, many of the *ketubbah* clauses are formulated in Aramaic in the Mishnah, although the codex is composed in general in Hebrew, indicating that these clauses are citations of earlier formulas.

The Judean Desert documents indicate that, as time went by, more and more Jews chose to write marriage contracts in Greek, promising that, when necessity arose, the document would be quickly executed by a functioning court of law. As the scholar Hannah Cotton has emphasized, these Greek documents were not Greek translations of Aramaic documents but were composed in the Hellenistic legal tradition.[7] Women who owned a Greek marriage contract could effectively bring their legal suits to a functioning Roman court in Palestine (and not to the voluntary Rabbinic legal system).

The conflict between the self-proclaimed Rabbinic legal system, which served as a voluntary arbitration institution, and the legal systems run by the state was a reality with which the Rabbis needed to contend. By their own admission, women were important clients of the Rabbinic courts. Many Rabbinic stories repeatedly present women appearing before the Rabbis demanding justice and arguing their cases.[8] Yet the Jerusalem Talmud informs us that one woman by the name of Tamar, who disliked the ruling given to her by the Rabbis, took her case before the Roman court at Caesarea (*y. Megillah* 3:2, 74a).

Unlike in the case of the *ketubbah*, in the case of a *get* (divorce), the Mishnah did not choose to follow in the footsteps of the Aramaic tradition of the documents found in the Dead Sea region. The right to divorce in the Bible is described incidentally, as part of the law that forbids a man to remarry his wife after she was married to another (Deut. 24:1–4). Thus divorce is not formulated as an exclusive prerogative of the husband. However, Rabbinic literature leaves no doubt that divorce was a unilateral action, reserved for the husband alone (*m. Yevamot* 14:1). Nevertheless, one document discovered in the Judean Desert indicates that outside Rabbinic circles women could and did initiate divorce proceedings. In this document a woman by the name of Shelamzion daughter of Joseph of Ein Gedi, sends her husband, Eleazar son of Hananiah a document terminating their marriage, describing the transaction as "a bill of divorce and release," just as in the Mishnaic text (*m. Gittin* 9:3). This is one example of how taking Rabbinic literature alone as a reflection of social reality distorts our historical view.[9] The Rabbis made a decision on divorce detrimental to women that still strongly influences women's position in Judaism today.

An important institution that connected marriage and divorce was the *yibbum* (levirate marriage). As discussed in Deuteronomy 25:5–9, this is a legal procedure that obligates a widow to marry her dead husband's brother, if the husband died without heirs. The Bible also includes, albeit grudgingly, a move to release the levirate bride from her levir (Deut. 25:7–9). This action is called *halitzah* and requires a ritual in which the reluctant levir is denigrated—his rejected-intended spits in his face and removes his shoe. The Rabbis of the Mishnah paid lip service to levirate marriage. An entire tractate in the Mishnah (*Yevamot*) is devoted to its intricacies. Praise for its merits is voiced in the Talmudim; Rabbi Yosi (mid-second century CE), who took his sister-in-law in levirate marriage, is greatly praised for this action (e.g., *y. Yevamot* 1:1, 2b). Yet despite this praise, levirate marriage itself was almost completely abandoned by the end of the second century CE, because it often clashed with the move toward monogyny. One Talmudic text suspects all levirate matches as emanating from lust of the partners and likens the offspring of such unions to bastards (*mamzerim*; *b. Yevamot* 39b). The Rabbis also ceased to view *halitzah* as negative, maintaining that in their day it was the norm (*m. Bekhorot* 1:7). Thus we see again how in some cases postbiblical Judaism maintained biblical law without maintaining its spirit.

Crucial to women's legal status was inheritance, the form of which also originated in biblical law. The crucial biblical passage discussing the daughter's rights in her father's inheritance is that of the daughters of Zelophehad (Num. 27:1–11). The daughters of Zelophehad had no brothers and demanded from Moses the right to inherit in the absence of male heirs. Moses recognized the justice of their claim, ruling in their favor, but his decision clearly stated that Jewish daughters could inherit from their fathers only when there were no sons. Although this ruling is often upheld as an example for an emendation made in the biblical law in favor of women, it was not broadly egalitarian (because it denied other daughters the right to inherit). It also prevented further egalitarian legislation in this field in late antiquity, because the Bible made a clear distinction between sons and daughters. Thus Second Temple Pharisees, in their legal dispute with a Sadducee opponent (*y. Bava Batra* 8:1, 16a), zealously upheld Moses's ruling as the final word. Their opponents, on the other hand, were probably influenced by the Greco-Roman world, in which women were equal heirs to the paternal estate. They claimed that this law was unfair and therefore could not reflect the divine intention; and their reliance on the sages of the gentiles (*hakhmei goyim*) is stated explicitly. Another discussion on the matter in the Babylonian Talmud associates the egalitarian ruling on the daughters' inheritance with Christian communities (*b. Shabbat* 116a–b). In Rabbinic literature the Pharisee position, of course, won the day; the Pharisees—a Second

Temple sect mentioned by several sources (foremost Josephus and the New Testament)—were the predecessors of the Rabbis.

Yet despite their seemingly wholehearted acceptance of biblical precedent in the case of inheritance, Rabbinic reaction to this issue was ambivalent, changing over time. The inheritance rights of daughters were also close to most Rabbis' hearts; many had daughters themselves and worried about their futures and welfare. It is thus not surprising that the Rabbis of the later Talmudim invented all kinds of legal instruments with which to circumvent their own predecessors' draconian endorsement of the biblical injunction.[10] The most common was the deed of gift.[11] Because the biblical law of inheritance is clearly spelled out and because the deed of gift as a Jewish legal tool was an inno-vation, in their legal discussions the Rabbis made sure that their formulation of the deed of gift did not appear to be a violation of the law of inheritance. The Rabbinic conversation about the deed of gift is constructed so that no one would suspect its gendered character. After all, deeds of gifts could be written on behalf of friends, distant relatives, and other beneficiaries. Yet every single Jewish deed of gift found in the Judean Desert and in the earlier Jewish archives of Elephantine, dating from the Persian period (fifth–fourth centuries BCE), was written for women—wives and daughters.[12] Although deeds of gift did much to ensure a daughter's welfare, whatever property she might come to own in her own right depended entirely on the goodwill of her father, who could, if he wished, write her a deed of gift and make her economically independent. If no such goodwill existed, a daughter would probably remain dependent on others throughout her life.[13] The Rabbis chiefly aimed to allow fathers the legal leeway to support their daughters should they so wish.

Canonization of the Role of Women in the Mishnah and the Babylonian Talmud

As CORRECTLY FORMULATED BY pioneering scholar Jacob Neusner, the Rabbis were the first Jews to produce a complete legal system that dealt with women's place in society.[14] Yet the Mishnaic Order of Women (*Nashim*) is not interested in women per se. Thus Tractate *Niddah*, which is devoted to menstruation reg-ulations, is found in the Order of Purities (*Tohorot*) rather than in *Nashim*. The order of *Nashim* is devoted to the wife's legal relationship to her husband. It defines the husband's acquisition, ownership, and dissolution of ownership of his wife. For Neusner, the Mishnah is a document that allows Jewish men to con-trol potential chaos in their lives by sanctifying times, objects, and dependents. He identified "women" as one of the areas in a Jewish man's life that has to be controlled and sanctified, because by their very nature women were potentially unruly and therefore dangerous.

Feminist Talmudic scholar Judith Wegner has shown that the Mishnah is a neatly edited document, with a full agenda about women. Men, according to this system, own women's reproductive capacities. The transactions they conduct concern the acquisition of these capacities by the husband from the father. According to Wegner, in these transactions women are treated as chattel. A woman could gain control of her own reproductive capacities and thus become an independent legal agent through divorce or widowhood. Wegner concluded that independent women (i.e., widows and divorcees) were treated as their own legal agents by the Rabbis where private transactions were concerned. Yet even independent women were seen as a threat to the public order, and thus the Mishnah attempted to confine all women to the private spaces of the home and to bar them from participating in public activities of cult and Torah study.[15] Rabbinic literature excludes women altogether from serving as witnesses in a court of law (*m. Rosh Hashanah* 1:8; *Sifre Deuteronomy* 190). During the Second Temple period, however, women apparently did serve in such a capacity. One text from the Dead Sea sect, a Second Temple Jewish sect (third century BCE–first century CE) whose literature was discovered in caves on the northwestern coast of the Dead Sea, suggests that wives were encouraged to give evidence against their husbands in the sect's tribunal (1QSa 1:10–11). Also, Josephus reports that in Herod's court women gave evidence in important trials (e.g., Josephus, *Antiquities of the Jews*, 17:65).[16] Obviously, in earlier times Jewish women could serve as witnesses, and the fact that the Rabbis chose to bar them from this activity indicates that they chose to be more restrictive toward women.

Neusner's and Wegner's theories are useful tools for viewing the Mishnah as a unified whole, and *Nashim* as an integral part of it. Yet Rabbinic literature is seldom a site of unity and agreement. The principle of the dispute is at the heart of even the carefully edited Mishnah. At least one Rabbinic tradition identifies the disputes of Beit Shammai and Beit Hillel (legal schools founded by these two Rabbis), as the foundation of Rabbinic learning (*t. Eduyot* 1:1). Despite this assertion, it is well known that the entire corpus of rulings suggested by Beit Shammai was rejected by the descendants of Beit Hillel who edited the Mishnah (*t. Eduyot* 2:3). What is less known is that, although this Shammaitic corpus may have in general displayed a more somber view of life, it likewise presented a more benign view of the position of women. The members of Beit Shammai supported a woman's right to run her business transactions independently of her husband (*m. Ketubbot* 8:1). They argued for the reliability of a widow's testimony regarding the death of her husband and demanded a full payment of her wedding settlement (*m. Eduyot* 1:12). And because they accepted the unilateral nature of Rabbinic divorce, they limited the grounds on which a husband could sue for divorce (*m. Gittin* 9:10).[17] The rejection of the entire Beit Shammai corpus was not beneficial to women's legal position in the canons of Judaism.

We find these relatively benign disputes inside the Mishnah itself. When we come to compare Rabbinic opinions preserved in competing Rabbinic corpora, they become a battlefield. The system of the Mishnah was edited over and against strong opposition, traces of which are still preserved in other documents. Judith Hauptman has shown that many of the rulings on the issue of women in the Mishnah are more restrictive than those in the loose compilation of traditions in its contemporary Tosefta (another early compilation of Rabbinic legal thought, a twin of the Mishnah).[18] She stressed, for example, that women in the Mishnah are absent in association with many aspects of the Passover celebration (*m. Pesahim* 2:6, 10:1; 4), where the Tosefta shows their participation (*t. Pesahim* 2:22; 10:4; 11 [Erfurt Ms]); the Mishnah does not see them as equal heirs of their mothers (*m. Bava Batra* 8:4), but the Tosefta allows daughters to inherit their mother's property equally with sons (*t. Bava Batra* 7:10); further, Hauptman shows that, though the Mishnah reserves procreation as a commandment to men alone (*m. Yevamot* 6:6), the Tosefta envisions a situation where women are equally so commanded (*t. Yevamot* 8:4). The rulings of the more benign Tosefta never became law.

Other examples of the editorial dictatorship of the Mishnah in relation to women's rights are evident in halakhic midrashim, Rabbinic commentaries on the legal sections of the Pentateuch. One halakhic midrash, usually assigned to the influential school of Rabbi Aqiva (ca. 250 CE), *Sifre* on Deuteronomy, using the masculine language of the biblical text, exempted women from many roles and activities. Thus it interpreted the phrase "and you shall teach them [i.e., the laws and statutes of the Torah] to your sons" (Deut. 11:19) to mean that the Bible viewed only sons but not daughters as entitled to learn Torah (*Sifre Deuteronomy* 46). It is now clear that the competing Rabbinic school, that of Rabbi Yishmael, which produced the halakhic midrash *Sifre* on Numbers (also ca. 250 CE), used a completely different midrashic principle—that of inclusion—regarding women. It ruled, for example, that a woman could participate in the ritual of burning the red heifer to produce ashes from which water of purification was produced (*Sifre Numbers* 124). And that women, just like men, are obligated to wear fringes (*tzitzit*) on their garments (*Sifre Numbers* 115); the school of Rabbi Aqiva rejected this opinion (*Sifre Zuta* 15:38).[19]

In light of the existence of opposing opinions, which were systematically ignored by the Mishnah or declared void, it becomes clear that, in formulating their first legal codex and in their bid for sovereignty over the Jewish people, the Rabbis sought to control women. They regulated every aspect of their legal existence and compartmentalized their movement to make control easier. Rabbinic literature made women silent partners in their marriages and systematically barred them from all public functions, such as cult and Torah study. In what follows, my focus is on how the Rabbis imagined women's lives in the legal, domestic, professional, religious, and intellectual spheres.

Women in the Domestic Sphere

ALTHOUGH THE PUBLIC-PRIVATE DIVIDE for men and women did not always hold true, the idea that a woman's place was in the home was clearly and strongly espoused in Rabbinic literature (e.g., *Genesis Rabbah* 8:12; *t. Sotah* 5:9; *m. Ketubbot* 7:6; *t. Ketubbot* 7:6). A whole range of halakhically incumbent women's activities were performed in the home: cooking, baking, laundering, sweeping, bed making (*m. Ketubbot* 5:5). Rabbinic literature is also full of incidents portraying women as engaging in homebound activities. The Mishnah, when discussing the impurity of the *am ha-aretz* (an ignorant, non-Rabbinic Jew), incidentally describes two women grinding wheat within the confines of the house (*m. Tohorot* 7:4). When debating how close to the beginning of Shabbat one may begin a new labor, the Tosefta describes a woman placing a bowl of lupine on the fire (*t. Shabbat* 3:1). In a discussion of consecrated fruits, the Jerusalem Talmud tells us of a woman who laid vegetables on her roof to dry (*y. Ma'asrot* 5:7, 52a); another passage, concerning smoke pollution and fire hazards, mentions a woman lighting a fire in her backyard (*y. Bava Batra* 2.2, 13b).

A major duty envisioned by the Rabbis for the woman at home was raising children, particularly babies, dependent on her for sustenance. The Mishnah, which makes household chores halakhically binding for women, includes the woman's obligation to breastfeed her children (*m. Ketubbot* 5:5). Raising children is also mentioned incidentally; when the Mishnah rules how people may conduct themselves on Shabbat without violating it, it allows a woman to assist her toddler when walking (*m. Shabbat* 18:2). In an episode illustrating the law of Temple donations, a mother is described as vowing to donate her sick daughter's weight in gold if she lives and then fulfilling her vow (*m. Arakhin* 5:1). The law of individuals who took a Nazirite (consecrating) vow and then became polluted is illustrated with the story of Miriam of Palmyra, who polluted herself to be by her dying daughter's side (*m. Nazir* 6:11). *Lamentations Rabbah*, one of the oldest works of midrashic literature (fourth century CE?), tells of a woman mourning her dead son to excess (*Lamentations Rabbah* 1:24b). In a later story (sixth century CE?), a woman scolds her Rabbi husband for not mourning their daughter as she does (*b. Shabbat* 151b). These stories illustrate a certain conviction on the part of the storytellers about the special mystical relationship between mother and child. I refer here to these sources, rather than to Rabbinic injunctions to women to stay home and keep house, because they tell us incidentally of the kinds of nuanced activities in the home that women were engaged in.

Not all women were housewives. The rich were exempt from engaging in household chores, even by the same Halakhah that confined women to them. A woman who owned domestic slave women could, halakhically, exempt herself (*m. Ketubbot* 5:5). Thus we are entitled to inquire whether rich women were nevertheless confined to their homes. At the other end of the social ladder were women who needed to leave their houses to work for a living because their husbands alone could not support the household. And enslaved women, even halakhically, were not expected to live in the same way that free Jewish women were. All these women were as much a part of Jewish society as the "normative" women of Rabbinic Halakhah, but they are practically ignored when the Rabbis speak of "women."

Women in the Professional Sphere

NOT SURPRISINGLY, JEWISH WOMEN's labor was worth money. This is acknowledged by the Rabbis when they describe the business relationship between husband and wife: He is required to feed and cloth her, and in return the work of her hands belongs to him (*m. Ketubbot* 4:4).[20] One source states that if a husband does not maintain his wife, she may retain the fruit of her handwork (*m. Ketubbot* 5:9). That a husband could demand of his wife a certain quota of work is suggested by a complementary ruling stating that a nursing mother's work quota should be reduced and her food supply increased (*m. Ketubbot* 5:9). Breastfeeding was considered labor that could be compensated. The Rabbis discuss situations in which a divorced woman refused to nurse "her husband's" (!) child and he was compelled to hire a wet nurse in her stead (*t. Ketubbot* 5:5; *y. Ketubbot* 5:6, 30a). Other sources discuss the prospect of a Jewish woman serving as wet nurse for the child of a pagan, and vice versa (*m. Avodah Zarah* 2:1).[21]

Rabbinic imagination envisioned the working woman primarily at her spindle or loom.[22] In the Mishnaic tradition that enumerates the chores a wife does for her husband, spinning takes pride of place. Rabbi Eliezer (first–second centuries) is reputed to have remarked that even a rich woman with a hundred slaves is expected to work in wool, because idleness brings about fornication (*m. Ketubbot* 5:5). Elsewhere, he is quoted as saying a woman's only wisdom is in the distaff (*y. Sotah* 3:4, 19a). This evidence presents an attitude viewing textile work as a woman's domain. Women's surplus textile work may have been an important source of income in the economy of the Jewish household. The Rabbis mention that there were women who sold their linens in Galilee and woolens in Judea (*m. Bava Qama* 10:9).

The Rabbis envisioned the woman wool worker laboring piously over her loom in her house. In a ruling describing rites of mourning, work in general is precluded. Yet one source specifically exempts from this rule labors carried out within the confines of the house. A woman, this source continues, is allowed to spin and weave indoors during the period of mourning (*b. Mo'ed Qatan* 21b). Textiles could be manufactured in a cottage industry, where the wife produced and her husband sold her work. This gendered vision of a correctly governed household made wool work suitable in the eyes of the Rabbis for Jewish women. Yet they themselves were aware that this vision was far from reality. Owning a loom was expensive, and a household with one was relatively well-off. One can imagine that textiles were also produced on an industrial scale and that women went out to work in various sweatshops. This may be the reality hinted at in the Halakhah that requires a husband to divorce his wife if she is seen spinning in the marketplace (*m. Ketubbot* 7:6). The Rabbis often stressed that a woman should not be found in the market (most emphatically, *Genesis Rabbah* 8:12).[23]

Yet the sources draw a varied picture of women engaging in a plethora of occupations in the marketplace on top of spinning. Women produced leaven (yeast or bread starter), which they sold to bakers (*m. Hallah* 2:7; *t. Hallah* 1:8), and pickled vegetables to sell at their doorstep (*t. Bava Qama* 11:7). Sources even add that they did this because it was demeaning for husbands to engage in such lowly trade. Women also served as shopkeepers (*m. Ketubbot* 9:4; *t. Ketubbot* 9:3); and contrary to Rabbinic expectations of Jewish women to stay confined away from the gaze of strange men, the Jewish female innkeeper was a common phenomenon (e.g., *m. Demai* 3:5; *t. Demai* 4:32; *m. Yevamot* 16:7). These trades are just a few examples that managed to fall through the Rabbis' tight net of prescriptive texts intended to shape reality according to their vision. There is little doubt that women engaged in many more occupations.

Rabbinic literature also supplies meager evidence about women engaging in nonskilled labor outside the home. In a society that was mostly agricultural, the harvesting season was a time when many laborers were in demand and extra income could be earned. The Rabbinic Halakhah regulates economic relationships between landowner and seasonal laborer. One Rabbinic source tells us that, if a man were hired as an agricultural laborer, his wife could assist him in harvesting (*b. Bava Metzia* 12a). I suggest that the situation described is of a laborer paid on condition that he harvests a certain quota of produce. Obviously, in such a situation, a family team could more easily meet the landowner's quota. From another source we hear of a woman coming back to town during the harvest on her own and testifying to her husband's death working in the field; the Rabbis suggest that she may have come from an olive grove, where olive picking was taking place (*m. Yevamot* 15:2; cf. *m. Eduyot* 1:12). Poorer women certainly worked together with men in agriculture.

In addition, some professions were reserved exclusively for women. The wet nurse has already been mentioned. Professional keeners or mourners are always described as female (*m. Mo'ed Qatan* 3:9; *m. Ketubbot* 4:4).[24] Midwifery was also only practiced by women because the intimate female experience of childbirth was considered unfit for a male gaze. Thus the various words used to describe the midwife are all feminine (*hakhamah, m. Shabbat* 18:3; *hayah, t. Bava Batra* 7:2). All the episodes involving midwives are told of females (e.g., *y. Shabbat* 18:3, 16c), and all Halakhah associated with midwifery is transmitted in female language (e.g., *m. Avodah Zarah* 2:1).

Because women were midwives and domestic cooks, they often understood physical processes and chemical dietary combinations that placed them ideally as potential healers. Thus, for example, the Jerusalem Talmud mentions a certain Timtinis, who was Rabbi Yohanan's doctor (*y. Avodah Zarah* 2:2, 40d). Em, a woman associated with Abbayye in the Babylonian Talmud, is reputed to have possessed a great repository of practical knowledge of medicinal and therapeutic charms and recipes.[25] In a source absent from the printed editions of the Talmud but present in the manuscripts of Tractate *Berakhot*, the fourth-century Babylonian sage Rami bar Hamma's mother teaches him a protective ritual that will allow him to remain untouched during his visit to a demon-ridden privy (*b. Berakhot* 62a).[26]

Jewish women are often portrayed in Rabbinic and other sources as primary agents of magic. Exploring these accounts opens another window onto women's activities within and outside the house. Women were certainly purchasers of amulets. Of the forty-two Jewish amulets I have reviewed, twenty-six were written for women.[27] It is also likely that women were involved in producing them. In one tradition in the Babylonian Talmud a description is given of an amulet written on the skin of a hyena to avert rabies. This is followed by a story about a certain sage, Abba bar Manyumi, also called Abba bar Martha, whose mother made him a certain golden tube, probably an amulet to protect him from rabies (*b. Yoma* 84a). The story also reflects the truism that all amulets name the customer after his or her mother. Before mentioning Abba bar Martha, Abbayye explains that such an amulet should be addressed to so and so, son of a certain woman (*planaya bar planayta*). This practice suggests a reverse gender hierarchy, making the mother more important than the father. Amulets represent an alternative religious tradition, from which women seem not to have been excluded.

However, when women's healing efforts did not succeed, failures were often perceived as malicious malpractice, sorcery, and poisoning. At one point in Second Temple history this disparaging attitude toward women's activity seems to have erupted into a full-scale witch hunt. This probably took place during the reign of Queen Shelamzion Alexandra (76–67 BCE, whom I discuss more in the "Political History" section). The Mishnah states simply that Shimeon ben Shatah (apparently Shelamzion's Pharisee adviser) hung eighty women in Ashkelon (*m. Sanhedrin* 6:4). The Jerusalem Talmud specifically identifies the women as witches (*y. Sanhedrin* 6:9, 23c). I argue elsewhere for a historical kernel to this story.[28]

Women's Religion

MAGIC WAS THUS A unique female religious expression. But was the use of amulets, medical formulas, and adjurations always defined by the Rabbis as magic? They devote a long chapter in the Tosefta to condemnation of the "ways of the Ammorites" (*t. Shabbat* 6), which to the lay reader may appear to be magical practice. Several of these "ways" are formulated in feminine verbs (*t. Shabbat* 6:14–15; 17–19), indicating that women were their prime practitioners. The descriptions of these ways, which are completely forbidden, suggests an intimate knowledge of alternative religious practices. Yet the Rabbis do not designate them as magic (*kishuf*). They do define women's activities among themselves, over and over again, as magic: They accused most women of practicing sorcery (*perutzot bi-kheshafim*) (*b. Eruvin* 64b; and see also *y. Sanhedrin* 7:19, 25d; and *b. Sanhedrin* 67a). Most stories of witchcraft in Rabbinic literature involve women. The Israelite witches of Babylonia had an official leader, with whom the Rabbis negotiated (*rishtinhi de-nashim kashfaniyot*, "chief of sorcerous women") (*b. Pesahim* 110a). All women, when they grew old, were suspected of practicing magic (*keshafim*) (*b. Sanhedrin* 100b). Two women sitting on two sides of the road were assumed to be practicing magic (*vadai be-keshafim asqinan*, "certainly they practice magic") (*b. Pesahim* 111a). The daughters of Rav Nahman were said to mix a boiling cauldron with their bare hands by practicing magic (*b. Gittin* 45a). These are but a few of the examples in the literature. Rather than accepting these descriptions as true or discarding them as disparaging and false, however, they should be understood as the

Rabbis' unsympathetic (male) interpretation and misunderstanding of women's religious expression and even skilled labor, of which we know very little.[29]

We know much more about women's participation (or lack thereof) in the official religious institutions in the time of the Rabbis and before. I turn now to these issues.

Women in the Temple

ALTHOUGH MOST RABBINIC LITERATURE postdates the destruction of the Temple, the Rabbis do have some things to say about what women may have done in it. This includes their contribution to the production of the temple veil (*parokhet*). Because weaving was a traditional feminine occupation, as we have seen, women weavers producing sacred garments were present in many Greek temples at the time, as well as in the Jerusalem Temple. Nevertheless, even this minor appearance of women on the scene of the Temple was downplayed by the Rabbis. Thus, though the Tosefta clearly mentions the women weavers (*t. Sheqalim* 2:6), its more authoritative counterpart, the Mishnah, in a parallel passage, mentions only the male supervisor of these activities (*m. Sheqalim* 5:1).

The Rabbis also retroactively exempted women from going on pilgrimages to the Temple. Yet all our sources from Second Temple times and from Rabbinic literature itself show that women were indeed pilgrims. Thus a Talmudic story innocently relates how in the distant past sons and daughters, competing for their father's good opinion, rushed on a pilgrimage to Jerusalem and the daughters outran the sons (*b. Nedarim* 36a). For obvious chronological reasons, the Rabbis had no control over the way pilgrimages had been conducted. Yet in their reconstruction of the past, when one Rabbi, in order to dispute this new ruling, mentions the wife of Jonah, who used to go to Jerusalem on pilgrimages, he is countered with a retort that the Rabbis forced Jonah's wife back from her intended journey (*y. Berakhot* 2:3, 4c).

The Rabbis also exempted women from residing in the sukkah (ritual booth), but in the Tosefta, the sage Rabbi Judah (mid-second century CE) mentions the ancient precedent of the proselyte Queen Helene (mid-first century CE) residing in an enormous sukkah in Jerusalem (*t. Sukkah* 1:1). This source indicates that when the wife of Jonah went on a pilgrimage to Jerusalem, women also built and resided in sukkot. Another minor episode may hint at a similar conclusion. On the Mishnah that states, "Women, slaves, and minors are exempt from [residing in the] sukkah. A minor who does not need his mother is obligated [to reside in the] sukkah," we are informed that "once Shammai the Elder's daughter-in-law gave birth, he removed the ceiling [over her] and covered it with branches." The Mishnaic text today states that he did this "for the sake of the minor" (*m. Sukkah* 2:8), because Shammai, unlike other Rabbis, thought that this commandment was incumbent on all male children. However, scholars have shown that these words are clearly a gloss.[30] The Mishnah had just exempted both women (i.e., Shammai's daughter-in-law) and children who are dependent on their mothers (i.e., her son) from this commandment. Shammai's actions are a violation of any one of these two commandments, or of both. This is one indication that when the Rabbis exempted women, they were innovating, over and against previous practice and even against another Rabbi, in this case, Shammai.

Women in the Synagogue

THE FOREMOST RELIGIOUS INSTITUTION that substituted for the Temple, after its destruction by the Romans in 70 CE, was the synagogue. Rabbinic literature mentions women regularly attending synagogues without comment (*b. Avodah Zarah* 38a–b; *b. Sotah* 22a; *y. Sotah* 1:4, 16d). One tradition suggests that in a town where all the residents are priests, when they bless the congregation in the house of prayer, it is the women and children who answer "Amen" (*y. Berakhot* 5:4, 9d). A heated debate is still under way over whether or not when attending synagogue women were segregated from men, but either way they attended prayer sessions.[31]

The synagogue was not included in the biblical cultic system; it probably developed in the Diaspora well before the Temple fell. For this reason, the gender division and segregation of the Temple functions were initially not imitated there. Bernadette Brooten has shown that, just like men, women carried such titles as *Archisynagogos* (head of synagogue), *Presbyter* (elder), or *Mater Synagogos* (mother of the synagogue) on inscriptions from varied locations, such as Smyrna, Crete, Caria, Thrace, Venosa (Italy), Rome, and Tripolitana (Libya).[32] Significantly missing from among these officials are women from Palestine and Babylonia. There seems to be a correlation between this absence and the regions over which the Rabbis purported to wield power. The Rabbis would have barred women from holding positions of influence in the synagogues.

Women in the Study House

FOR THE RABBIS, AFTER the destruction of the Temple, the public (secular) domain became the space of the study house, and the most significant noncultic public activity was Torah study. Learning became an important status symbol and a means of achieving social mobility. Because it endowed its initiates with social privileges that the Rabbis appropriated to themselves, men were encouraged to learn Torah and become literate.

The Rabbis' attitude toward women's literacy and the learning of Torah is thus of special importance. They declared that women were exempt from them (e.g., *b. Eruvin* 27a). Yet exemption is not always associated with exclusion. Whether a man is permitted to teach his daughter Torah is discussed often in the sources (*Sifre Deuteronomy* 46; *m. Sotah* 3:4), and although the ultimate answer is usually no, one source inquires whether a man could teach his daughter Greek wisdom (*y. Sotah* 9:16, 24c). This sort of wisdom may have been complex and interesting, but it lay outside the sphere of Torah study, which was the only form of study really valued by the Rabbis. Also, the private instruction of Torah within the confines of the home was not compatible with the presence of Torah-learned women exerting themselves in the study house.

The sort of evidence adduced in the process of ascertaining that women were not altogether absent from the study house is even more circumstantial than that adduced for topics discussed thus far. The enigmatic mention of a woman by the name of Beruriah making a halakhic decision in the Tosefta (*t. Kelim Bava Metzia* 1:6) is a good start. Who this woman was and how she came to be present in the study house is not clear. Her mention engenders no comment other than Rabbi Yehoshua (first–second century CE) commending her halakhic knowledge. Later Rabbis found this allusion and this woman disconcerting. The Mishnah engaged the technique of editing her out. Beruriah's ruling is mentioned in the Mishnah, but it is assigned to the sage who commended her, Rabbi Yehoshua (*m. Kelim* 11:4). The Babylonian Talmud chose a different technique to deal with this gender interference. It inflated Beruriah's Torah competence but at the same time made her unique and inimitable (*b. Pesahim* 62b).[33] Both these reactions show that even if Beruriah and women of her sort were possibly found in the early tannaitic study houses (Rabbi Yehoshua, Beruriah's contemporary benefactor in the Tosefta, was already a grown man when the Temple was destroyed), by the time the Mishnah was edited, they had become a complete anomaly. The study house developed into an all-male segregated environment.

Political History

AFTER THE DESTRUCTION OF the Temple, the Jews did not write a political history in which kings and wars feature. Up to the destruction of the Temple, we rely on the works of a historian, Josephus. After the destruction, we need to resort to Rabbinic literature, a source that shows no interest in history per se and has no pretensions to historical accuracy. Yet ironically, because Rabbinic literature is a source that is wholly independent of Josephus, in some cases it preserves important and different traditions about issues that Josephus relates. In two cases, Rabbinic literature is also an important source for politics and women in the Second Temple period. In both cases, this derives from the fact that the Pharisees were the forerunners of the Rabbis. Their point of view on the events reflects the point of view of the Pharisees, whose own sources have not come down to us in any other way.

In the most Jewish dynasty of Second Temple times, the Hasmoneans, a woman served as queen (Queen Shelamzion Alexandra, 76–67 BCE; Josephus, *Antiquities of the Jews*, 13: 407–32). According to Josephus, the most significant action taken by this woman once she became queen was to reverse her husband's policies and remove the Sadducees from office, replacing them with the Pharisees (Josephus, *War of the Jews Against the Romans* 1: 110–11; Josephus, *Antiquities of the Jews*, 13: 409). This action suggests that she had been a Pharisee supporter.

Josephus's overall judgment of the queen's "illegal" reign was scathingly negative. Yet he ends his long diatribe with the observation that hers was a reign of peace and prosperity (Josephus, *Antiquities of the Jews*, 13: 432). The Rabbis were also no fans of women's rule. In the halakhic midrash on Deuteronomy, where the "law of the king" is expounded, they interpret the biblical words "You shall set up a king over you" (Deut. 17:14) to absolutely exclude queens (*Sifre Deuteronomy* 157). Yet the same composition mentions with great admiration the queenship of Shelamzion (*Sifre Deuteronomy* 42). In her days, so this midrash says, the biblical blessing of rain in its season, promised to Israel only if they do God's will, was realized. Obviously, this extremely positive judgment of the queen's reign is the residue of a Pharisee legacy, whereas the categorical rejection of queenship represents their new position as nonsectarian, consensus-seeking Rabbis. The textual history further supports this. In the slightly later halakhic midrash on Leviticus, the description of rain in its season as a sign of divine blessing is assigned not just to the queen but also to her contemporary, sage Shimeon ben Shatah (*Sifra, be-Huqqotai* pereq. 1:1), but in the Babylonian Talmud the queen disappears altogether, leaving the sage as responsible for this positive outcome (*b. Taanit* 22b–23a).

Aside from his story about Queen Shelamzion, Josephus tells us that the Pharisees easily won the support of women and ruled them (Josephus, *Antiquities of the Jews*, 17: 41). Rabbinic literature provides circumstantial evidence for Josephus's claim. In one source the Rabbis relate how Sadducee women consulted them concerning their menstrual purity (*m. Niddah* 4:1–2). This probably implies a female following of the Pharisees.

The most important source for women's active participation in the Pharisee movement is found in the Rabbinic description of the Second Temple *havurah* (i.e., fellowship). The *havurah* is the internal name that the Pharisees chose for themselves. Tosefta *Demai*, chapter 2, is an ancient catalog of the sect's ordinances, when still only a table fellowship. In the Mishnah these ordinances are condensed in two verses and severely edited (*m. Demai* 2:2–3); they mention no women. However, *t. Demai* 2:16–17 does mention women and makes demands on these women equal to those on the men of the *havurah*. In light of this observation, I also consider the "Pharisee woman" mentioned in *m. Sotah* 3:4 as referring to a woman member of the sect.[34] Her denigration in the Mishnah (she is said to be one of those who wear out the world) results from an androcentric authorship and a deliberate attempt of the later Rabbis to erase all sectarian characteristics tying them with the earlier Pharisees. This includes turning their backs on the women who had supported them in the earlier, sectarian phase of their existence.

Conclusion

RABBINIC LITERATURE IS FAR from being a trustworthy historical source for any field and most certainly not for women. However, in the absence of other sources, the historian has to make do with it—and make the most of it. Although Rabbinic texts are prescriptive in nature, we have seen that by reading between the lines concerning references to events and phenomena that contradict their prescriptions, we discover some faithful portrayals of the sort of "ills of society" they attempted to combat, reflecting historical events. The gender historian must be resourceful and look for evidence outside Rabbinic texts: in the Greco-Roman world at large, at other sources reflecting Jewish society (such as inscriptions or papyri), and at the observations of gender scholars the world over. With these it becomes possible to gain a glimpse at what women did and what they were not permitted to do in the fundamentally patriarchal Rabbinic world.

Notes

1   Jacob Neusner, ed., *A History of the Mishnaic Law of Women, Part 5: The Mishnaic System of Women* (Leiden: Brill, 1980).

2　And see the thoughtful discussion in Judith R. Baskin, *Midrashic Women: Formations of the Feminine in Rabbinic Literature* (Hanover, NH: University Press of New England, 2002), 44–87.

3　See also Shulamit Valler, *Massekhet Sukkah* (Tübingen: Mohr Siebeck, 2009), 10.

4　Michael Satlow, "Reconsidering the Rabbinic *Ketubbah* Payment," in *The Jewish Family*, ed. Shaye J. D. Cohen (Atlanta: Scholars Press, 1993), 133–51.

5　Bezalel Porten and Ada Yardeni, *Textbook of Aramaic Documents from Ancient Egypt*, vol. 2, *Contracts* (Winona Lake, IN: Eisenbrauns, 1989).

6　See, for example, Ranon Katzoff, "Papyrus Yadin 18: Legal Commentary," *Israel Exploration Journal* 37 (1987): 239–42; and Adiel Schremer, "Divorce in Papyrus Se'elim 13 Once Again: A Reply to Tal Ilan," *Harvard Theological Review* 91 (1998): 193–202.

7　Hannah M. Cotton, "The Rabbis and the Documents," in *Jews in a Graeco-Roman World*, ed. Martin Goodman (Oxford, UK: Oxford University Press, 1998), 177.

8　For a good source collection, see S. Valler, *Women in Jewish Society in the Talmudic Period* (Tel Aviv: Hakibbutz Hameuchad, 2000), 103–49 (Hebrew).

9　See Tal Ilan, "Notes and Observation on a Newly Published Divorce Bill from the Judaean Desert," *Harvard Theological Review* 89 (1996): 195–202. This article triggered the following responses: Schremer, "Divorce in Papyrus Se'elim"; Robert Brody, "Evidence for Divorce by Jewish Women?" *Journal of Jewish Studies* 50 (1999): 230–34; Joseph A. Fitzmyer, "The So-Called Divorce Text from Wadi Seiyal," *Eretz Israel* 26 (1999): 16*–22*; Hannah M. Cotton and Elisha Qimron, "XHev/Se ar 13 of 134 or 135 CE: A Wife's Renunciation of Claims," *Journal of Jewish Studies* 49 (1998): 108–18; and David Instone Brewer, "Jewish Women Divorcing Their Husbands in Early Judaism: The Background to Papyrus Seelim 13," *Harvard Theological Review* 92 (1999): 349–57.

10　See Judith Hauptman, *Rereading the Rabbis: A Woman's Voice* (Boulder, CO: Westview Press, 1998), 177–95.

11　Still relevant is Reuven Yaron, *Gifts in Contemplation of Death in Jewish and Roman Law* (Oxford, UK: Oxford University Press, 1960).

12　See Hannah M. Cotton, "Deeds of Gift and the Law of Succession in the Papyri from the Judaean Desert," *Eretz Israel* 25 (1996): 410–15 (Hebrew); and Tal Ilan, "Women's Archives in the Judaean Desert," in *The Dead Sea Scrolls: Fifty Years After Their Discovery*, ed. Lawrence H. Schiffman, Emanuel Tov, and James VanderKam (Jerusalem: Israel Exploration Society, 2000), 755–60.

13　I discuss this in greater detail in Tal Ilan, "The Daughters of Zelophehad and Women's Inheritance: The Biblical Injunction and Its Outcome," in *A Feminist Companion to The Bible: Exodus to Deuteronomy*, ed. A. Brenner, 2nd ser. (Sheffield, UK: Sheffield Academic Press, 2000), 176–86.

14　Neusner, *History of the Mishnaic Law*, 13–42, 239–72.

15　Judith R. Wegner, *Chattel or Person: The Status of Women in the Mishnah* (Oxford, UK: Oxford University Press, 1988). The terms *public* and *private* are used by Wegner. For a critique of these concepts, with a fresh approach, see Cynthia M. Baker, *Rebuilding the House of Israel: Architectures of Gender in Jewish Antiquity* (Stanford, CA: Stanford University Press, 2002).

16 Editions and translations of the works of Josephus are available in the Loeb Classical Library.

17 See T. Ilan, *Integrating Women into Second Temple History* (Tübingen: Mohr Siebeck, 1999), 43–81.

18 Judith Hauptman, "Mishnah *Gittin* as a Pietist Document," in *Proceedings of the Tenth World Congress of Jewish Studies*, ed. David Assaf and World Union of Jewish Studies (Jerusalem: World Union of Jewish Studies, 1990), Div. C, 1: 23–30 (Hebrew); Judith Hauptman, "Maternal Dissent: Women and Procreation in the Mishnah," *Tikkun* 6, no. 6 (1991): 80–81, 94–95; Judith Hauptman, "Women's Voluntary Performance of Commandments from Which They Are Exempt," *Proceedings of the Eleventh World Congress of Jewish Studies*, ed. World Congress of Jewish Studies (Jerusalem: World Union of Jewish Studies, 1994), Div. C, 1: 161–68 (Hebrew); Judith Hauptman, "Women and Inheritance in Rabbinic Texts: Identifying Elements of a Critical Feminist Impulse," in *Introducing Tosefta: Textual, Intratextual, and Intertextual Studies*, ed. Harry Fox and Tirzah Meacham (Hoboken NJ: KTAV, 1999), 221–40; Judith Hauptman, "Women in Tractate Pesahim," in *Atara L'Haim: Studies in the Talmud and Medieval Rabbinic Literature in Honor of Professor Haim Zalman Dimitrovsky*, ed. Daniel Boyarin, Shama Friedman, Marc Hirshman, Menahem Schmelzer, and Israel M. Tashma (Jerusalem: Magnes Press, 2000), 63–78 (Hebrew); and Judith Hauptman, "Women in Tractate *Eruvin*: From Social Dependence to Legal Independence," *Jewish Studies* 40 (2000): 145–58 (Hebrew). See also Gail Labovitz, "'These Are the Labors': Constructions of the Woman Nursing Her Child in the Mishnah and Tosefta," *Nashim: Journal of Jewish Women's Studies and Gender Issues* 3 (2000): 15–42; and Tal Ilan, *Silencing the Queen* (Tübingen: Mohr Siebeck, 2006), 111–23.

19 And see Ilan, *Silencing the Queen*, 215–41.

20 Further, a baraita in the Babylonian Talmud delineates the reciprocal relationship between maintenance and handwork; see *b. Ketubbot* 47b.

21 On wet nursing, see also Labovitz, "These Are the Labors."

22 On this construction of gender, see Miriam Peskowitz, *Spinning Fantasies: Rabbis, Gender, and History* (Berkeley: University of California Press, 1997).

23 See Baker, *Rebuilding the House of Israel*, 77–112. Baker suggests a nuanced view of these texts.

24 On a Rabbinic connection between women and death, see *Genesis Rabbah* 17:8.

25 See the discussion in Charlotte E. Fonrobert, *Menstrual Purity* (Berkley: University of California Press, 2000), 151–59; and Valler, *Women in Jewish Society*, 161–72.

26 See The Friedberg Project for Talmud Bavli Variants (https://bavli.genizah.org), which shows that this addition is found both in the Munich 95 and Paris 671 manuscripts and in a genizah fragment, T-S F 1(2).109.

27 See Jean-Baptist Frey, *Corpus Inscriptionum Iudaicarum* (Rome: Pontificial Institute, 1936), vol. 1, nos. 518 and 674; vol. 2 (1952), nos. 802, 819, 874, and 1167; David Noy, *Jewish Inscriptions of Western Europe* (Cambridge, UK: Cambridge University Press, 1993), vol. 1, no. 156; Joseph Naveh and Shaul Shaked, *Amulets and Magic Bowls* (Jerusalem: Magnes, 1985), 44, no. 2; 68, no. 7; 78, no. 8;

82, no. 9; 90, no. 11; 94, no. 12; 98, no. 13; 106, no. 15; Joseph Naveh and Šhāûl Šhāked, *Magic Spells and Formulae: Aramaic Incantations of Late Antiquity* (Jerusalem: Magnes, 1993), 50–52, no. 17; 57, no. 18; 77, no. 23; 85, no. 25; 91, no. 27; 95, no. 28; 101, no. 30; Moshe Schwabe and A. Reiffenberg, "A Judaeo-Greek Amulet," *Bulletin of the Israel Exploration Society* 12 (1945–1946): 68–69 (Hebrew); and Roy Kotansky, "Two Inscribed Jewish Aramaic Amulets from Syria," *Israel Exploration Journal* 41 (1991): 270, 275.

28 See Ilan, *Silencing the Queen*, 215–23.

29 For the argument that women wrote (some of) the Babylonian magic incantation bowls, see Dorit Kedar, *She Wrote Incantation Bowls* (Tel Aviv: Idra, 2019).

30 Isaiah Sonne, "The Schools of Shammai and Hillel Seen from Within," in *Louis Ginzberg Jubilee Volume*, ed. Saul Lieberman, Solomon Zeitlin, Shalom Spiegel, and Alexander Marx (New York: American Academy for Jewish Research, 1945), 280–81, no. 13.

31 See Immanuel Löw, *Gesammelte Schriften* (Szegedin, Hungary: A. Bába, 1898), 4: 55–71; Shmuel Safrai, "Was There a Women's Gallery in the Ancient Synagogue?" *Tarbiz* 32 (1963): 329–30 (Hebrew); Bernadette Brooten, *Women Leaders in the Ancient Synagogue: Inscriptional Evidence and Background Issues* (Chico, CA: Scholars Press, 1982), 103–38; and William Horbury, "Women in the Synagogue," in *Cambridge History of Judaism*, ed. William Horbury, William D. Davies, and John Sturdy (Cambridge, UK: Cambridge University Press, 1999), 3: 358–401.

32 Brooten, *Women Leaders*. See also Ross S. Kraemer, "A New Inscription from Malta and the Question of Women Elders in Diaspora Jewish Communities," *Harvard Theological Review* 78 (1985): 431–38; Marisa Conticello De'Spagnolis, "Una testimonianza ebraica a Nuceira Alfaterna," in *Ercolano 1738–1988: 250 anni di ricerca archeological*, ed. Luisa Franchi dell'Orto (Rome: L'Erma di Bretschneider, 1988), 242–52; Bernadette Brooten, "Iael Prostates in the Jewish Donative Inscription from Aphrodisias," in *The Future of Early Christianity: Essays in Honor of Helmut Koester*, ed. A. Thomas Kraabel, George W. E. Nickelsburg, Birger R. Peterson (Minneapolis: Fortress Press 1991), 149–62; and Daniel Stökl Ben Ezra, "A Jewish 'Archontesse': Remarks on an Epitaph from Byblos," *Zeitschrift für Papyrologie und Epigraphik* 169 (2009): 287–93.

33 See Ilan, *Integrating Women*, 175–94, for a detailed discussion of Beruriah. See also David Goodblatt, "The Beruriah Traditions," *Journal of Jewish Studies* 26 (1975): 68–85; Rachel Adler, "The Virgin in the Brothel and Other Anomalies: Character and Context in the Legend of Beruriah," *Tikkun* 3, no. 6 (1988): 28–32, 102–5; and Daniel Boyarin, *Carnal Israel: Reading Sex in Rabbinic Culture* (Berkeley: University of California Press, 1993), 167–96.

34 For both see Ilan, *Silencing the Queen*, 71–110.

MEDIEVAL JEWISH WOMEN IN MUSLIM AND CHRISTIAN MILIEUS

JUDITH R. BASKIN

THE MAIN EXPECTATIONS FOR Jewish women in medieval times were domestic. "May she sew, spin, weave, and be brought up to a life of good deeds" is the prayer with which one set of parents in Northern Europe recorded their daughter's birth.[1] An additional desire, expressed in another milieu of the Jewish Middle Ages, Muslim Egypt, was that a newborn daughter "might come into a blessed and auspicious home," that is, marry well and have children.[2] Many medieval Jewish women fulfilled these aspirations, and some were also active in economic endeavors and in religious and communal roles; others endured lives of struggle and poverty or died as martyrs sanctifying the divine name.

During the Middle Ages, between 650 and 1500 CE, most Jews lived outside the Land of Israel, with significant populations in the Muslim worlds of Egypt, North Africa, the Middle East, and Spain and in the Orthodox Christian Byzantine Empire; smaller numbers of Jews lived in Ashkenaz, as Jews referred to their communities in northern France, England, and German-speaking regions of Europe. Places in northern Italy where Jews from Germany and France settled are also part of this medieval milieu.[3] Jewish communities enjoyed a great degree of autonomy over their lives and internal affairs in all these locales, so long as they paid substantial taxes. Jewish self-government, across geographic and political boundaries, was based on the mandates of the Babylonian Talmud (Halakhah), which provided a uniform pattern for Jewish family, communal, religious, and economic life. Even though Talmudic legislation affirms women's human status and furthers fulfillment of her physical and emotional needs, in general its mandates relegate females to secondary enabling positions, whereas men are privileged as the central participants in Jewish worship, study, and communal authority.[4]

The norms and customs of local environments also influenced how Jewish social and family life developed and diverged from place to place. Jews assumed the language, dress, and many of the practices of their gentile neighbors, as well as prevailing cultural attitudes about appropriate female behaviors. Jewish women, named and unnamed, appear in literary and historical works by Jewish and non-Jewish authors and are mentioned in legal and economic documents. However, medieval Jewish women left few words of their own, so discovering their spiritual lives and personal aspirations is difficult. Recent scholarship focusing on images of Jewish women in Jewish and Christian illuminated manuscripts offers rich insights into Jewish women's lives, as do material objects recovered by archaeologists.[5]

In the Muslim World

THE CAIRO GENIZAH DOCUMENTS have expanded knowledge of medieval Jewish society and institutions under Islam. Discovered shortly before 1890 in the attic genizah, a storage area for sacred writings, of the Ben Ezra synagogue in Old Cairo, these religious texts and business records, correspondence, court proceedings, and other legal records illuminate virtually every aspect of Jewish life, particularly between the tenth and thirteenth centuries.[6] During this mainly peaceful and prosperous era, Jews did not have the full rights of Muslims, but they were tolerated, as long as required taxes were paid. Many of these urban Mediterranean Jews were involved in trade, often over long distances. Some Jews were wealthy, but Jewish communities were largely middle class, although there were also Jews on the lower rungs of the social ladder. Jews spoke Arabic, the language of their larger milieu, and usually wrote in Judeo-Arabic, a form of Arabic written in Hebrew characters.

Jewish communal norms generally dictated that women's place was in the home. This is reflected in the observation of the preeminent legal scholar, philosopher, and physician Moses ben Maimon (Maimonides, also known as the Rambam; 1135–1204), who lived much of his life in Cairo, that "there is nothing more beautiful for a wife than sitting in the corner of her house" (Maimonides, *Mishneh Torah*, "Code of Women, Marriage," 13:11).[7] Maimonides went on to say that a woman is not a prisoner, but he suggested that visits to family and friends should not exceed one or two a month. In fact, Jewish women usually insisted on freedom of movement, and many records of marital squabbles in the Cairo Genizah make this an explicit right if reconciliation is to be achieved.[8] According to Shlomo Dov Goitein, women created their own world within a world dominated by men: "They customarily flocked together, whether in the women's gallery in the house of worship, the bathhouse, the bazaar, the gatherings on happy or mournful occasions, or through the visits of friends and relations."[9] Nevertheless, Jewish women were prepared to venture beyond their usual comfort zones to fight for their legal rights, particularly in matters of inheritance. Oded Zinger has documented how Jewish women sometimes resorted to Muslim courts in such cases, even though they faced significant communal and familial resistance and were criticized more severely than men who made similar choices.[10] As Renée Levine Melammed points out, "The fact that women were utilizing or threatening to utilize Muslim law and courts means that they were aware of the options available to them" and that they were knowledgeable about the differences in Jewish and Islamic law that affected their lives.[11]

The Jewish community saw marriage as the natural state for both men and women[12] and a woman's life was determined by the marriage arranged for her. According to documents in the Cairo Genizah, Jews did not follow rabbinic norms that favored betrothing a daughter while she was still a minor (before the age of 12½); rather, girls remained under the close care of parents or guardians until they married in their late teens or early 20s.[13] Marriages were sometimes orchestrated within the extended family, a strategy intended to conserve wealth and offer security and familiarity to a young bride.[14] However, marrying outside the family and across distance was an opportunity for merchant families to establish valuable connections; the Cairo Genizah has records of marriages between, for example, young men in Persia and young girls from Syria or Egypt.[15] Sometimes businessmen from abroad would endeavor to marry into a successful local family as a way of establishing a foothold and eventually attaining a higher position in a society where mobility depended on patronage relationships. Similarly, a young man might seek to marry into a family that was known for its scholarly attainments.[16]

The marriage contract (*ketubbah*) stated the economic terms of the union. The husband agreed to provide his wife's food and clothing and to maintain her in general. Jewish grooms also contributed a marriage gift (*mohar*); part was paid to the bride's father at marriage, and a portion was reserved for the bride in case of a divorce or her husband's death. Similarly, the bride brought a dowry, which was to be returned to her should the marriage end. The dowry was generally far more valuable than the husband's marriage gift and gave a prosperous family leverage in finding a suitable match for their daughter and ensuring her proper treatment.[17] The dowry was a form of protection for the bride, because the expense of repaying it could discourage a husband from an impulsive divorce. Its contents, which might include gold and silver jewelry, real estate holdings, household objects, one or more enslaved maidservants,[18] and occasionally books, were evaluated by assessors, and an itemized list was attached to the marriage contract. Often a mother would pass on items from her dowry to her daughters when they married.[19]

A marriage contract could mandate protections for the wife, a way of altering Jewish laws and practices that were unfavorable to women. These might include guarantees that if the union dissolved, the husband would immediately produce a divorce document (*get*); that the husband would not marry another wife;[20] that he would not beat his wife; that he would not separate her against her will from her parents; or that he would not travel anywhere without her consent. Often the contract stipulated that the husband would write a conditional bill of divorce before setting out on a journey to protect his wife from becoming an *agunah*, a deserted wife, who could never marry again if her husband disappeared and there were no witnesses to his death. He might also be required to deposit the delayed installment of her marriage gift as well as the sums needed for her maintenance during his absence.[21]

In addition to the unilateral *ketubbah*, a contract issued in the husband's name, which has generally been the norm in rabbinic practice, examples of another *ketubbah* form have been found in the Cairo Genizah, written according to the custom of the Land of Israel. These documents define marriage as a partnership (*shutafut*) and state that the wife may initiate divorce proceedings against her husband if she is unable to live with him.[22] In fact, divorce was frequent in the Cairo Jewish community, where arranged marriages, geographic mobility, and the "greater attentiveness to a wife's sufferings to be expected in a cosmopolitan bourgeois society" all contributed to marital strife.[23] Moreover, the larger Muslim society also permitted divorce, so no particular stigma was attached to the practice in the Jewish community. Divorce in this milieu was facilitated by a *takkanah* (an alteration in Jewish law) from mid-seventh century Baghdad. It stated that if a woman claimed that she could not bear to live with her husband, a Jewish court would force him to grant her an immediate divorce on the condition that she relinquish all or most of her financial entitlements. This *takkanah* of the rebellious wife (*moredet*) was intended to prevent women from seeking divorces in Muslim courts, thereby circumventing the halakhic process.[24] Divorced women who had support from wealthy and well-connected family members were able to remarry without difficulty. Less fortunate divorcées were left in want and joined the considerable number of other indigents, including impoverished widows and deserted wives, who wandered from place to place dependent on public charity.[25]

Two legal queries (responsa) to Maimonides tell of a deserted wife who made herself independent by running a school, assisted by her eldest son. Years later her husband reappeared and demanded that she give up the school because it injured his dignity for his wife to be a teacher; otherwise, he requested permission to take a second wife. The wife, in turn, argued that her husband had been repeatedly undependable and that she could not easily resume her school should her husband again disappear. Maimonides advised the wife to take advantage of the *takkanah* of the *moredet* by refusing all relations with her husband and forfeiting her marriage portion (likely gone, in any case). After that, Maimonides wrote, "She will have disposition over herself, she may teach what she likes, and do what she likes," but "if she remained with her husband, he could forbid her to teach."[26]

Although the *ketubbah* obligated husbands to support their wives, many women of all social classes earned money, mostly through needlework, although some wealthy women owned property. A wife usually kept her earnings for private use, but they sometimes caused marital friction. In a petition to a twelfth-century rabbinic court a wife requested that her husband not require her to do embroidery in other people's houses for his benefit; should she work, she wished to retain her wages.[27] Women served as brokers who collected the spun threads, textiles, and embroidery work of other women and sold them to merchants; other occupations included "bride-combers" (wedding coordinators), midwives, and "washers," who prepared the dead for burial. Some women taught needlework to young girls, were astrologers, or were caretakers of synagogues and schools. Genizah documents mention female physicians and oculists, although Shlomo Dov Goitein notes that these women "had not gone through the expensive apprenticeship of scientific medicine but were practitioners whose knowledge and skill had come to them by tradition."[28]

Genizah documents refer to the twelfth-century businesswoman Karima ("dear one") more than any other woman. Also known as al-Wuhsha ("object of yearning") al-Dallala ("the broker"), her marriage ended in divorce after the birth of a daughter; she later bore a son in a nonmarital relationship, a scandal that led to her expulsion from Cairo's Iraqi synagogue on the Day of Atonement. Al-Wuhsha's extensive will detailed her assets and their disposition, comprising bequests to communal, religious, and charitable institutions (including the Iraqi synagogue), and to family members, and gave directions for an elaborate funeral. Al-Wuhsha clearly made a strong impression on her community; later writings refer to her survivors as the daughter, son, and granddaughter of Al-Wuhsha.[29] Although al-Wuhsha was exceptional, Goitein observes that she had business dealings with other women, "and by no means only in small matters," an indication that other Jewish women may have approached her degree of success and autonomy.[30] However, most women's money-making endeavors were small and marginal to the larger economy. Married women, who rarely possessed resources outside the nuclear family, relied on their husbands; in his absence, they turned to male relatives or a husband's business partners, a dependence that could be humiliating and precarious.[31]

Women's economic activities raise questions about their education and their involvement in Jewish communal and religious life. The schoolmistress discussed earlier had received an elementary education from someone, whether her unworthy husband, as he claims in his letter, or another family member.[32] But significant learning among Jewish women was rare. The only documents in the Cairo Genizah that can be attributed to women are letters, and most of these were dictated to professional scribes.[33] Goitein sees the absence of any spiritual matter created by or for women in the Cairo Genizah as evidence that "the inner worlds of men and women certainly were separated from each other"; women could never compete intellectually with men who had been exposed to Hebrew language and sacred texts from early childhood, both in study and in synagogue worship.[34]

Despite their lack of learning, women's pious observance of the home-based laws incumbent on them and their synagogue attendance, where they prayed in a women's gallery, are documented in Genizah writings. Prosperous women donated Torah scrolls and oil and books for study, and they left legacies for the upkeep of the synagogue,[35] ways of imprinting their presence on a realm in which they were otherwise secondary. The Cairo Genizah does preserve an account of a young woman who wished to spend her life serving God through fasting, prayers, and almsgiving. Although she was compelled to marry, matrimony did not diminish her spiritual life, and her visions ultimately led to messianic upheavals in Baghdad in 1120.[36] But this was an extraordinary case. Most Jewish women lived within their extended kinship circles, contributing to their family's finances as they could, practicing piety as appropriate, and devoted to their children's well-being.

Jewish Women's Lives in Ashkenaz

BEFORE 1000 CE ONLY A few Jews lived in Germany and northern France; their numbers increased as Jews moved to Ashkenaz in response to new economic opportunities.[37] This transition was not without challenges; Jews, essentially the only minority religious community in northern Christian Europe, presented ideological and practical problems to religious and secular rulers, even as they were perceived as bringing economic benefits to a developing urban mercantile culture. As the Middle Ages progressed and ongoing hostilities with the Muslim world led to increasing xenophobia, Jews became subject to outbreaks of popular violence. At the same time, the growth of the European economy and increasing exclusion of Jews from international trade in the aftermath of the first four Crusades (1096 to 1204), led many to concentrate their economic energies on moneylending, a denigrated and dangerous but essential occupation. Moreover, Jews were subject to ever-increasing taxation and legal disabilities, including wearing distinctive clothing and badges. By the end of the fifteenth century, Jews had been expelled altogether from areas where they had long lived, including England (1290), France (fourteenth century), and Spain (1492), although communities remained in German-speaking Europe.

The Jews of Ashkenaz lived in small urban enclaves under the protection of local rulers; many community members were involved in commerce, and the general standard of living was high. As Jews prospered, Jewish women played increasingly vital and often autonomous roles in their families' economic lives, both as merchants and as financial brokers, allowing them to achieve almost unprecedented position and power in Jewish communal life.[38] Women's public visibility and impact is in sharp contrast to that of Jewish women in Muslim lands but comparable to that of Christian women of bourgeois and noble status, including women who assumed leadership roles in religious communities. Jews spoke the local language in daily activities, but religious scholarship flourished in Hebrew, a pattern analogous to the separation between vernacular expression in ordinary life and the use of Latin for religious ritual and written expression by the learned Christian elite. One significant sign of Jewish acculturation to Christian society and language is women's names, which frequently originated in the majority culture. Before the mid-twelfth century, many Jewish men traveled extensively. Jewish women, like Christian women in the urban bourgeoisie, ran their households and economic affairs effectively during their husbands' absences; both groups of women achieved a degree of literacy and acquired requisite financial skills. As Martha Keil writes of the later Middle Ages, "Jewish upper-class women used their own seals, were able to ride, and followed patrician ways with regard to clothing, eating habits, music, and book illumination."[39]

Jewish family norms were considerably influenced by the practices of the majority culture. One example is the eleventh-century *takkanah* forbidding polygyny for Jews in Christian countries.[40] This legal alteration is attributed to Rabbi Gershom ben Judah (ca. 960–1028), the first rabbinic authority of Ashkenazic Jewry, who is also credited with the pronouncement that no woman could be divorced against her will. These rulings, along with the large dowries they brought into marriage, indicate the high social standing of Jewish women in this milieu, as opposed to the Muslim world. Because the capital with which a young couple started life mainly originated in the bride's portion, parents demanded guarantees in the *ketubbah* that the bride would be treated with respect, that her marriage would have some permanence, and that she would have financial security. It was also the custom in Ashkenaz, as in the Cairo Genizah world, for a husband to leave his wife a conditional divorce document when he set out on a journey so that the wife would be free to remarry should the husband fail to return after a specified time.[41] According to Halakhah, the dowry of a deceased childless wife belonged to her husband. However, a twelfth-century enactment, attributed to Rabbi Jacob ben Meir Tam (Rabbenu Tam; 1100–1171), made it returnable to the father should his daughter die without offspring in the first year of marriage; if a woman died childless in the second year, one-half was returned. These legal alterations, which bear inadvertent witness to the dangers of childbirth for young wives, were likely intended to encourage fathers to endow their daughters generously.[42]

Jewish girls, despite rabbinic prohibitions, were often betrothed at the age of 8 or 9. A young woman might be married at 11 or 12 to a husband of almost the same age. The responsa of Rabbi Meir of Rothenburg (the Maharam; d. 1293) records the case of a young girl, married before the age of 12, who went to court against her mother who had interfered in a marital dispute. Rabbi Meir ruled that the young wife, whom he describes as in control of the couple's possessions, was not bound by agreements her mother made without her knowledge.[43] A thirteenth-century Talmudic commentary justified child marriages on grounds of difficult social realities: "If a person is now in a financial position to give his daughter an adequate dowry, he fears that in the future he will be unable to do so and his daughter will remain unwed forever."[44] Moreover, settling a daughter early proved her desirability and increased her family's prestige; conversely, a broken engagement might generate rumors concerning the rejected bride and her relatives. Such anxieties contributed to an eleventh-century *takkanah* imposing excommunication against those who violated a betrothal agreement; in most cases the culprits were bridegrooms and their families.[45]

The sages of France and Germany spoke out against spousal abuse, another indication of women's powerful place in the Jewish family. Wife beating was grounds for divorce, and enforcing a divorce in such cases was taken more seriously in Ashkenaz than elsewhere in the Jewish world. Certainly, spousal harmony was valued, and most Jewish writers viewed marital sexuality positively, an attitude that was at odds with the Christian requirement of celibacy for those who took religious vows and with church teachings that sexual activity within marriage should be limited to procreation. The church also forbade divorce, frowned on remarriage after the death of a spouse, and had strict rules on consanguinity, according to which many Jewish marriages among relatives (such as first cousins) were deemed incestuous. It is not surprising that Christian writers criticized Jewish marital patterns and sexual behavior, real and imagined, or that Jews were often perplexed by Christian teachings.[46] Influence from the larger environment may account for the anxiety about sexuality characteristic of the Ḥasidei Ashkenaz, the German Jewish pietists of the twelfth and thirteenth centuries whose writings, such as *Sefer Ḥasidim* (The Book of the Pious), express a deep consciousness of sexual temptations and a profound ambivalence about the joys of licensed sexual activities. Their works had a profound impact on subsequent Jewish pietistic writings.[47]

Despite the importance placed on marital happiness, Jewish marriages in Ashkenaz often ended in divorce. Women's strong economic status and the support of their birth families allowed for plentiful opportunities for remarriage.[48] In the Muslim world, as discussed earlier, the *takkanah* of the *moredet* enabled a woman to initiate divorce if she stated to a rabbinic court that her husband was repugnant to her and that she was prepared to relinquish all or most of her marriage portion. Most medieval sages in Ashkenaz did not accept this exit strategy. Instead, women used another Talmudic option to leave unhappy marriages: rebellion by refusing sexual relations (*b. Ketubbot* 63b). This was accomplished by a woman's refusal to immerse in the ritual bath (*mikveh*) following her state of *niddah*.[49] In becoming a rebel (*moredet*), the woman would lose her *ketubbah* over time, based on daily fines, and then the court would compel her husband to divorce her.[50] Rabbinic leaders, following the lead of Rabbenu Tam, vehemently attacked the frequency of such divorces, and Rabbi Meir of Rothenburg attempted to combat the practice by ruling that a *moredet* had to give up not only her *ketubbah* but also all her personal property and the wealth she had inherited or acquired through her business undertakings. As Avraham Grossman points out, these efforts indicate that a major social crisis was under way and that the rabbinic leadership was all but helpless to stop it.[51] However, in the fourteenth and fifteenth centuries, as hostile political pressures increased and prosperity declined, women began to lose their social and economic standing and rabbinic authority was gradually reasserted. At the same time, rabbinic leaders increasingly limited women's ability to coerce divorce by any means, not only in Ashkenaz but in Spain, North Africa, and ultimately the rest of the Jewish world.[52] By the mid-sixteenth century mechanisms for a woman to initiate divorce had disappeared entirely from normative Jewish practice.[53]

Jewish women's high standing in Ashkenaz derived from their economic success; in some cases, a wife's business acumen allowed her husband to devote himself to study and teaching. Halakhah permitted women to manage the capital and property they acquired through dowry, inheritance, and, in the case of divorce or widowhood, their marriage contract payment; and it allowed them to earn funds through various entrepreneurial undertakings. Medieval responsa literature refers to women's frequent meetings with Jewish and gentile men for business purposes as a matter of course, even though such activities were viewed negatively by religious leaders. The German sage Rabbi Eliezer ben Joel Halevi (1140–1225) wrote, "Day after day women go forth with two or three men and seeing that the sages of Torah offer no protest, are unaware that it is forbidden."[54] Jews, both female and male, accepted the risk of violent attacks while traveling as a part of their economic lives. *Sefer Ḥasidim* states that a Jewish woman journeying in dangerous circumstances could dress in nun's clothing to avoid rape.[55]

Among women's commercial occupations, moneylending was preferred.[56] These complex operations required a degree of literacy in the vernacular (rendered in Hebrew characters) and training in mathematics and bookkeeping skills. Extant records in various European archives indicate that Jewish women acting alone or as the head of a business consortium were responsible for half of all loans in northern France in the thirteenth and fourteenth centuries and for a third of all loans in German and Austrian communities between 1350 and 1500; these figures do not take into account women partnered with their husbands or a male relative.[57] Although most women dealt in small loans to other women, small groups, usually widows, were active in major business transactions with nobility and rulers. Resentment over the power of Pulcellina, a moneylender in the court of Blois in France, led to the ritual murder slander of 1171 that resulted in her martyrdom, along with at least thirty other Jews of the city.[58] Licoricia of Winchester had direct dealings with the king of England; her five sons, who described themselves as "sons of Licoricia," were also moneylenders, continuing their mother's business after her murder in 1277.[59] Some women learned artisan trades from fathers or husbands, and there are references in Jewish and Christian sources to Jewish women who were midwives and oculists. Several medieval obstetric treatises in Hebrew, apparently intended for midwives, indicate that at least some women were literate in that language.[60]

Women's elevated status in Ashkenaz is also reflected in their religious practices. From the eleventh century to the end of the thirteenth century, some women performed rituals for which they were not obligated by Halakhah, including reciting blessings for the *lulav* and sukkah, participating in the benediction after meals, and taking a more significant role in synagogue worship. In twelfth-century Germany and northern France some women wore tefillin (phylacteries) and fringed garments. There are strong indications that prominent women, whose financial support was necessary to their communities' survival, insisted on these practices, and it is evident that rabbinic authorities felt powerless to prevent them. To establish a halakhic justification for the prevalence of women reclining during the Passover seder, the twelfth-century Tosaphists designated all Jewish women in Ashkenaz as "important."[61] When Rabbi Jacob ben Moses Moelin (the Maharil; ca. 1365–1427) was asked why he did not reproach Rabbanit Bruna, who lived in his city and always wore a *tallit qatan* (fringed garment), he replied that he feared she might not listen to him.[62] Grossman suggests that women such as Bruna may have been inspired by a contemporaneous Christian religious revival in which women were influential in shaping communal worship.[63]

Some prominent women served as godmother (*sandeka'it*), which entailed holding a male infant during his circumcision in the synagogue. Rabbi Meir of Rothenburg vehemently but unsuccessfully attempted to abolish this practice, because he believed that the presence of perfumed and well-dressed women in the synagogue was immodest. He wrote, "It is not a seemly custom for a woman to enter all bedecked among the men and before the Divine Presence."[64] His students were also unable to prevent this "phenomenon of 'godmothers,'" because "there is no one who takes heed," and the custom continued until the beginning of the fifteenth century.[65] By that time, rabbinic leaders had apparently succeeded in excluding women from the main synagogue sanctuary. Henceforth the godmother's role was limited to carrying the infant from his mother to the synagogue entrance where he was handed over to the *sandak*, the honored godfather who held him during the circumcision ritual.[66] The Maharil wrote of this exclusion that "all that increases the separation of [men and women] is praiseworthy."[67]

Martha Keil has suggested that the construction of women's areas in synagogues in the thirteenth and fourteenth centuries was another demonstration of the rabbinic desire to distance women from the sanctuary containing the Torah scrolls. These women's sections, which were built in Worms (1212) and Speyer (1230) among other cities, were separated from the main sanctuary by a wall with narrow windows.[68] Women could barely see or hear male worship, nor could they be heard. As Keil writes, "Because they had their own room now, the women were absolutely prohibited from entering the place of public honor, something which had not been the case in the eleventh and twelfth centuries."[69] Jewish women conducted their own services in these rooms, led by a learned woman; such prayer leaders included the thirteenth-century Urania of Worms, whose headstone epitaph commemorates her as "the daughter of the chief of the synagogue singers. . . . She, too, with sweet tunefulness officiated before the women to whom she sang the hymnal portions."[70] Jewish customary law concerning the menstruating woman (*niddah*) also became more exclusionary in medieval Ashkenaz in the late Middle Ages. Based on the highly influential *Baraita de Niddah*, a book apparently from the geonic period, the *niddah* was forbidden to enter a synagogue, to come into contact with sacred books, to pray, or to recite God's name. These customs were followed in many locales during the medieval and early modern eras, although they have no basis in Halakhah, and they were generally endorsed by rabbinic authorities who praised compliant women for their piety.[71]

Women were excluded from the male realms of the synagogue in the later medieval centuries, but they could not be excluded from economic life. As women thrived in business, some submitted their financial disputes to non-Jewish courts and took oaths, despite rabbinic objections. Swearing oaths was essential in business agreements, and usually men validated the oath by touching the Torah scroll. Keil points out that because women were no longer allowed to enter the sanctuary, fifteenth-century rabbis compromised by placing the Torah "in the arms of the woman taking the oath at the entrance to the synagogue."[72] In a few cases wealthy Jewish women also became leaders in the communal realm. At least one, Selda, acquired administrative authority as a tax collector in Austria in 1338.[73] In 1354 Kändlein of Regensburg was the chief of her community's five leaders (*parnassim*), apparently because of her economic standing and significant tax payments; twenty years later a woman named Josephine was elected to Regensburg's eleven-member community administrative council (*kehillah*). The lives of such powerful Jewish businesswomen were not without risk; Kändlein, like Licoricia of Winchester and Dolce of Worms, was murdered in her home during a robbery.[74]

Women's maternal roles were central to their families and communities. Elisheva Baumgarten has shown that medieval Jewish writers assumed that mothers bore the primary responsibility for child care, because the requisite love and compassion were natural and particular to them. In cases of divorce, boys remained with their mothers until the age of 6, when their formal education began, whereas girls stayed with their mothers until marriage.[75] Mothers educated their daughters in household and business skills and in halakhic regulations applicable to home and marriage; these included dietary laws, domestic observance of the Sabbath and festivals, and the commandments relevant to marital relations. Particular anxiety is expressed in several sources that women should be instructed to be assiduous and expeditious in observing the laws of *niddah*.[76] Most Jewish boys were literate in Hebrew and some became learned, but higher educational standards rarely applied to girls, and then only to a few from scholarly families. Although some women were able to lead prayers for the other women of their communities, lack of Hebrew was not seen as an impediment to piety for either women or men. *Sefer Ḥasidim* advises, "One should learn the prayers in a language one understands, for prayer is first and foremost an entreaty of the heart, and if the heart does not understand what issues from the mouth, how can the one who prays benefit?"[77]

Jewish women were less likely than men to convert to Christianity, probably because the benefits were fewer. Rabbinic authorities did everything possible to facilitate a divorce for a Jewish wife whose husband had converted and to guarantee the return of her property so that she could remarry.[78] When crusading frenzy first swept France and Germany in 1096, many Jewish communities were threatened with death if they refused to convert. According to Hebrew chronicles of the events, few Jews accepted the choice of baptism and some women are described as killing their children and themselves rather than submit. The chroniclers extol such women as active exemplars of piety under stress and describe them as "beautiful and comely" and "saintly and pious" as they urged their husbands on and actively chose to sanctify God's name by their martyrdom.[79] Grossman writes, "There is no other genre in the medieval Jewish world in which women occupy such a central and important place, and are portrayed in such a sympathetic and admiring manner as in these stories."[80] Although it is difficult to determine the historicity of these depictions, Grossman emphasizes that the aura of sanctity that characterizes the chroniclers' accounts demonstrates women's exalted status.[81] Some scholars have suggested that these representations are as much literary as historical and were intended to provide didactic models of martyrdom for future generations. Susan Einbinder, for example, has suggested that women are praised so highly in order to shame men who might opt for conversion in similar circumstances.[82]

Esteem for a beloved wife and a description of her activities appear in the prose and poetic laments of Rabbi Eleazar ben Judah of Worms (the Rokeah; d. 1238), a pietist leader, in memory of his exemplary wife, Dolce,[83] and their two daughters, killed by intruders in 1196. He relates that Dolce supported her family and her husband's students through business ventures; she knew "what was forbidden and what was permitted," attended synagogue regularly, sewed together forty Torah scrolls, made wicks for synagogue candles, and instructed women and led their prayers. Their daughters too, the Rokeah wrote, learned Hebrew prayers and songs from their "saintly" mother. Eleazar's elegies for his murdered wife and children echo the martyrdom language of the Hebrew Crusade chronicles; at the lament's conclusion, he imagines his beloved martyred spouse wrapped in the eternal life of Paradise.[84]

Similar values are expressed in the fourteenth-century ethical will of Eleazar ben Samuel of Mainz. In this Hebrew testament, which expressed his convictions and his hopes for his children, he urged his sons and daughters to attend syna-gogue daily and to devote time to "Torah, the Psalms, or works of charity." His daughters must obey the laws applying to women, because "modesty, sanctity, and reverence should mark their married lives"; they should, moreover, "respect their husbands and be invariably amiable to them." The young, both female and male, must be instructed "in the Torah." Marriages should be celebrated as early as possible and prospective spouses are to come from respectable families. Elea-zar's daughters should prepare candles for the Sabbath and refrain from risking money in games of chance, although they may amuse themselves for trifling stakes on New Moon (Rosh Chodesh) days, customarily celebrated as holidays by Jewish women. He also advised against "mixed bathing, mixed dancing, and all frivolous conversation" and stated that his daughters should "be always at home and not gadding about . . . since idleness leads first to boredom, then to sin. Rather, let them spin, cook, or sew."[85] It is difficult to know where the personal overtakes the formulaic in such writings, but Eleazar's obvious concern for his daughters' education, their mode of life, and the pitfalls they might encounter reveal a Jewish society in which women played many active roles.

Conclusion

JEWISH WOMEN'S LIVES IN the Muslim world changed little in the early mod-ern era. In the course of the fifteenth and sixteenth centuries, however, sig-nificant changes occurred in Jewish life in Northern Europe. These included exiles and migrations from traditional areas of settlement; the impact on Jew-ish communities of the Protestant Reformation and the Catholic response; and the ramifications of the invention of printing. Printed books, including legal codes, facilitated an increasing uniformity of halakhic practice across the Ash-kenazic world. Printers also published inexpensive works in the vernacular for those who were not learned in Hebrew; such books and pamphlets furthered women's literacy and provided new patterns of female piety.[86] These and other developments are discussed in the chapters that follow.

Notes

1 Isidore Epstein, "The Jewish Woman in the Responsa (900 CE–1500 CE)," in *The Jewish Library*, vol. 3, *Woman*, ed. Leo Jung (New York: Soncino Press, 1934), 123.
2 Shlomo Dov Goitein, *A Mediterranean Society: The Jewish Communities of the Arab World as Portrayed in the Documents of the Cairo Geniza*, vol. 3, *The Family* (Berkeley: University of California Press, 1978), 49.

3　Jews first applied the biblical place name Ashkenaz (Jer. 51:27) to these areas of Europe in the eleventh century. On medieval Jewish communities, see Goitein, *Mediterranean Society*; Norman A. Stillman, "The Jewish Experience in the Muslim World," in *The Cambridge Guide to Jewish History, Religion, and Culture*, ed. Judith R. Baskin and Kenneth Seeskin (Cambridge, UK: Cambridge University Press, 2010), 85–112; and the articles in Robert Chazan, ed., *The Cambridge History of Judaism*, vol. 6, *The Middle Ages: The Christian World* (Cambridge, UK: Cambridge University Press, 2018).

4　Judith R. Baskin, "Jewish Traditions About Women and Gender Roles: From Rabbinic Teachings to Medieval Practice," in *The Oxford Handbook of Women and Gender in Medieval Europe*, ed. Judith Bennett and Ruth Mazo Karras (Oxford, UK: Oxford University Press, 2013), 35–51.

5　Katrin Kogman-Appel, "Material Culture and Art," in *The Cambridge History of Judaism*, vol. 6, *The Middle Ages: The Christian World, ed. Robert Chazan* (Cambridge, UK: Cambridge University Press, 2018), 860–81; Thérèse Metzger and Mendel Metzger, *Jewish Life in the Middle Ages: Illuminated Hebrew Manuscripts of the Thirteenth to the Sixteenth Centuries* (New York: Alpine Fine Arts Collection, 1982); and Sara Lipton, *Dark Mirror: The Medieval Origins of Anti-Jewish Iconography* (New York: Metropolitan Books, 2014).

6　The Cairo Genizah contained 200,000 documents written mostly in Hebrew characters in languages including Hebrew, Arabic, and Aramaic. See Goitein, *Mediterranean Society*; Eve Krakowski, *Coming of Age in Medieval Egypt: Female Adolescence, Jewish Law, and Ordinary Culture* (Princeton, NJ: Princeton University Press, 2018); and Renée Levine Melammed, "A Look at Women's Lives in Cairo Genizah Society," in *The Festschrift Darkhei Noam: The Jews of Arab Lands*, ed. C. Schapkow, S. Shepkaru, and A. T. Levenson (Leiden: Brill, 2015), 64–85.

7　For an English translation, see Isaac Klein, *Mishneh Torah of Moses Maimonides*, Book 4, *The Book of Women*. Yale Judaica Series, vol. 19 (New Haven, CT: Yale University Press, 1972).

8　Goitein, *Mediterranean Society*, 3: 153–55; and see Mordechai A. Friedman, "The Ethics of Medieval Jewish Marriage," in *Religion in a Religious Age*, ed. S. D. Goitein (Cambridge, MA: Harvard University Press, 1974), 83–102, esp. 87–95.

9　Goitein, *Mediterranean Society*, 3: 359. See also Eve Krakowski, "The Genizah and Family History," *Jewish History* 32, nos. 2–4 (2019): 175–97.

10　Oded Zinger, "'She Aims to Harass Him': Jewish Women in Muslim Legal Venues in Medieval Egypt," *Association for Jewish Studies Review* 42, no. 1 (2018): 159–92; and Oded Zinger, "Jewish Women in Muslim Legal Venues: Seven Legal Documents from the Cairo Genizah," in *Language, Gender, and Law in the Judaeo-Islamic Milieu*, ed. Zvi Stampfer and Amir Ashur (Leiden: Brill, 2020), 37–87.

11　Renée Levine Melammed, "A Look at Medieval Egyptian Jewry: Challenges and Coping Mechanisms Discerned in the Cairo Genizah Documents," in *From Catalonia to the Caribbean: The Sephardic Orbit from Medieval to Modern Times— Essays in Honor of Jane S. Gerber*, ed. F. Francesconi, S. Mirvis, and B. M. Smollett (Leiden: Brill, 2018), 100–116, 107.

12 Goitein, *Mediterranean Society*, 3: 53.

13 Krakowski, *Coming of Age*, 113–41, 240.

14 On endogamous marriages, see Goitein, *Mediterranean Society*, 3: 55–56; and Krakowski, *Coming of Age*, 213–24.

15 Goitein, *Mediterranean Society*, 3: 56–58; Judith R. Baskin, "Mobility and Marriage in Two Medieval Jewish Societies," *Jewish History* 22, nos. 1–2 (2008): 223–43.

16 On patronage culture, see Krakowski, *Coming of Age*, 294–97, 226–28. On marital connections between scholarly families, see Goitein, *Mediterranean Society*, 3: 58–60; and Krakowski, *Coming of Age*, 228–29.

17 Mordechai A. Friedman, "Marriage as an Institution: Jewry Under Islam," in *The Jewish Family: Metaphor and Memory*, ed. David Kraemer (New York: Oxford University Press, 1989), 31–45, 33.

18 On enslaved non-Jewish women in Jewish homes, see Craig Perry, "An Aramaic Bill of Sale for the Enslaved Nubian Woman Na'im," *Jewish History* 32, nos. 2–4 (2019): 451–61. On Jewish men's sexual involvement with enslaved women, see Craig Perry, "'No One Sees and Every Man Does as He Sees Fit': Slavery and Masculinity in the Jewish Community of Medieval Egypt," http://medievalslavery.org/middle-east-and-north-africa/source-no-one-sees-and-every-man-does-as-he-sees-fit-slavery-and-masculinity-in-the-jewish-community-of-medieval-egypt/ (accessed November 24, 2020); and Moshe Yagur, "Captives, Converts, and Concubines: Gendered Aspects of Conversion to Judaism in the Medieval Near East," in *Language, Gender and Law in the Judaeo-Islamic Milieu*, ed. Zvi Stampfer and Amir Ashur (Leiden: Brill, 2020), 88–109.

19 Goitein, *Mediterranean Society*, 3: 125.

20 Jewish polygyny was more common in wealthy families, given the expense of maintaining several spouses and their children. Polygyny also occurred when a first wife appeared to be infertile after a decade of marriage and in cases of levirate marriage. On this topic, see Friedman, "Marriage as an Institution," 38–40.

21 Goitein, *Mediterranean Society*, 3: 142–47; see also Amir Ashur, "Legal Documents: How to Identify Prenuptial Agreements," *Jewish History* 32, nos. 2–4 (2019): 441–49.

22 Friedman, "Marriage as an Institution," 34–35; Mordecai A. Friedman, *Jewish Marriage in Palestine: A Cairo Genizah Study*, 2 vols. (Tel Aviv: Jewish Theological Seminary of America, 1980–1981).

23 Goitein, *Mediterranean Society*, 3: 263.

24 Gideon Libson, "The Age of the Geonim," in *An Introduction to the History and Sources of Jewish Law*, ed. N. S. Hecht, B. S. Jackson, S. M. Passamaneck, D. Piattelli, and A. M. Rabello (Oxford, UK: Oxford University Press, 1996), 234–38; Goitein, *Mediterranean Society*, 3: 267; Robert Brody, *The Geonim of Babylonia and the Shaping of Medieval Jewish Culture* (New Haven, CT: Yale University Press, 1998), 62–63; and Judith R. Baskin, "The *Taqqanah* of the *Moredet* in the Middle Ages," in *Accounting for the Commandments in Medieval Judaism: New Studies in Law, Philosophy, Pietism, and Kabbalah*, ed. Jeremy P. Brown and Marc Herman, 45–57 (Leiden: Brill, 2021).

25 Goitein, *Mediterranean Society*, 3: 324; Mark Cohen, *Poverty and Charity in the Jewish Community of Medieval Cairo* (Princeton, NJ: Princeton University Press, 2005); and Mark Cohen, *The Voice of the Poor in the Middle Ages: An Anthology of Documents from the Cairo Genizah* (Princeton, NJ: Princeton University Press, 2005).

26 Moses Maimonides, *Responsa of R. Moses b. Maimon*, vol. 1, ed. Yehoshua Blau (Jerusalem: Mekitze Nirdamim, 1958), no. 34, no. 45 [Hebrew]. For a translation and analysis of these documents, see Renée Levine Melammed, "He Said, She Said: The Case of a Woman Teacher in Maimonides' Twelfth Century Cairo," *Association for Jewish Studies Review* 22, no. 1 (1997): 19–36.

27 Goitein, *Mediterranean Society*, 3: 133.

28 Shlomo Dov Goitein, *Mediterranean Society*, 1: 128; on female economic options, see 3: 324–42. On the far larger male-dominated ambit, see Jessica L. Goldberg, *Trade and Institutions in the Medieval Mediterranean: The Geniza Merchants and Their Business World* (Cambridge, UK: Cambridge University Press, 2012).

29 Goitein, *Mediterranean Society*, 3: 346–52; and Oded Zinger, "Goitein and Strong Women," *Jewish History* 32, nos. 2–4 (2019): 541–45.

30 Goitein, *Mediterranean Society*, 3: 350.

31 Goitein, *Mediterranean Society*, 3: 332; and Judith R. Baskin, "Independent Jewish Women in Medieval Egypt: Enterprise and Ambiguity," in *From Catalonia to the Caribbean: The Sephardic Orbit from Medieval to Modern Times—Essays in Honor of Jane S. Gerber*, ed. F. Francesconi, S. Mirvis, and B. M. Smollett (Leiden: Brill, 2018), 83–99.

32 See Judith R. Baskin, "Some Parallels in the Education of Medieval Jewish and Christian Women," *Jewish History* 5, no. 1 (1991): 41–51, 46. On female teachers in Cairo, see Levine Melammed, "He Said, She Said," 28–29.

33 Some Cairo Genizah letters written by women appear in Franz Kobler, ed., *Letters of Jews Through the Ages*, vol. 1, *From Biblical Times to the Renaissance* (Philadelphia: Jewish Publication Society, 1952), 145–50, 233–34; see also Joel Kraemer, "Women Speak for Themselves," in *The Cambridge Genizah Collections: Their Contents and Significance*, ed. Stefan C. Reif (Cambridge, UK: Cambridge University Press, 2002), 178–216; and Renée Levine Melammed and Uri Melammed, "Epistolary Exchanges with Women," *Jewish History* 32, nos. 2–4 (2019): 411–18.

34 Goitein, *Mediterranean Society*, 1: 93, 3: 34.

35 Goitein, *Mediterranean Society*, 3: 359; Sara Reguer, "Women and the Synagogue in Medieval Cairo," in *Daughters of the King: Women and the Synagogue*, ed. Susan Grossman and Rivka Haut (Philadelphia: Jewish Publication Society, 1992), 51–57, 54.

36 Goitein, *Mediterranean Society*, 3: 47–48.

37 On the growth of this community in the second half of the Middle Ages, see Robert Chazan, "Jewish Life in Western Christendom," in *The Cambridge Guide to Jewish History, Religion, and Culture*, ed. Judith R. Baskin and Kenneth Seeskin (Cambridge, UK: Cambridge University Press, 2010), 113–39.

38 For discussions of Jewish women's lives in this milieu, see Elisheva Baumgarten, "Gender and Daily Life in Jewish Communities," in *The Oxford Handbook of*

Women and Gender in Medieval Europe, ed. Judith Bennett and Ruth Mazo Karras (Oxford, UK: Oxford University Press, 2013), 213–28; and Elisheva Baumgarten, "The Family," in *The Cambridge History of Judaism*, vol. 6, *The Middle Ages: The Christian World*, ed. Robert Chazan (Cambridge, UK: Cambridge University Press, 2018), 440–62.

39 Martha Keil, "'She Supplied Provisions for Her Household': Jewish Business Women in Late Medieval Ashkenaz," in *The Jews of Europe in the Middle Ages*, ed. Historisches Museum der Pfalz Speyer (Speyer, Germany: Hatje Cantz, 2004), 84. See also Avraham Grossman, *Pious and Rebellious: Jewish Women in Medieval Europe* (Waltham, MA: Brandeis University Press, 2004), 114–17.

40 Avraham Grossman stresses women's high status as motivating this ruling (*Pious and Rebellious*, 76–77) and also suggests that the ordinance was intended to prevent Ashkenazic merchants from taking second wives while in Muslim lands (74–77); the problem of deserted wives and their children is an ongoing theme in the Cairo Genizah documents.

41 Kenneth R. Stow, *Alienated Minority: The Jews of Medieval Latin Europe* (Cambridge, MA: Harvard University Press, 1992), ch. 9; Grossman, *Pious and Rebellious*, 68–101; Simcha Goldin, *Jewish Women in Europe in the Middle Ages: A Quiet Revolution* (Manchester, 2016).

42 Grossman, *Pious and Rebellious*, 150; Avraham (Rami) Reiner, "Rabbenu Tam's Ordinance for the Return of the Dowry: Between Talmudic Exegesis and an Ordinance That Contradicts the Talmud," *Diné Israel: An Annual of Jewish Law and Israeli Family Law* 33 (2019): 71–98.

43 Irving Agus, *Rabbi Meir of Rothenburg: His Life and His Works*, 2nd ed. (New York: KTAV, 1970), nos. 284, 320.

44 Irving Agus, *The Heroic Age of Franco-German Jewry* (New York: Yeshiva University Press, 1969), 281, citing *tosafot* (twelfth- to fourteenth-century Talmudic commentary) to *b. Kiddushin* 41a; Grossman, *Pious and Rebellious*, 33–55.

45 Grossman, *Pious and Rebellious*, 51–55; see also Ephraim Kanarfogel, "Rabbinic Conceptions of Marriage and Matchmaking in Christian Europe," in *Entangled Histories: Knowledge, Authority, and Jewish Culture in the Thirteenth Century*, ed. Elisheva Baumgarten, Ruth Mazo Karras, and Katelyn Mesler (Philadelphia: University of Pennsylvania Press, 2017), 23–37.

46 Stow, *Alienated Minority*, 207–9.

47 Judith R. Baskin, "From Separation to Displacement: The Problem of Women in *Sefer Hasidim*," *Association for Jewish Studies Review* 19, no. 1 (1994): 1–18.

48 Grossman, *Pious and Rebellious*, 251–52.

49 Rabbinic legislation (Halakhah) regarding the *niddah*, the menstruating woman, ordains that intimacy is forbidden from the time the woman expects her menses until seven "clean" or "white" days on which no blood is seen have elapsed. On the evening of the seventh day without sign of blood, marital relations may resume following the wife's immersion in a ritual bath (*mikveh*). Several medieval ritual baths in Germany have been excavated and restored as museum exhibits; these include *mikvaot* in Speyer (1120), Worms (1185–1186), Cologne (twelfth century), and Erfurt (mid-thirteenth century).

50 Grossman, *Pious and Rebellious*, 240. Women's timely immersions played a central role in both medieval Jewish piety and marital politics; see Judith R. Baskin, "Women and Ritual Immersion in Medieval Ashkenaz: The Sexual Politics of Piety," in *Judaism in Practice: From the Middle Ages Through the Early Modern Period*, ed. Lawrence Fine (Princeton, NJ: Princeton University Press, 2001), 131–42; and Judith R. Baskin, "Male Piety, Female Bodies: Men, Women, and Ritual Immersion in Medieval Ashkenaz," *Journal of Jewish Law: Studies in Medieval Halakhah* 17 (2007): 11–30.

51 Grossman, *Pious and Rebellious*, 244–46, 249.

52 Elimelech Westreich, "The Rise and Decline of the Law of the Rebellious Wife in Medieval Jewish Law," *Jewish Law Association Studies* 12 (2002): 207–18.

53 The *takkanah* of the *moredet* does not appear in the *Shulhan Arukh* (Set Table), completed in 1563 by the Sephardic scholar Joseph Karo (1488–1575); this work, with the *Mappah* (Tablecloth), a supercommentary by the Ashkenazic authority Moses Isserles (1530–1572), became the standard code of Jewish law and practice.

54 Grossman, *Pious and Rebellious*, 117–21; the responsum is cited in Grossman, *Pious and Rebellious*, 30.

55 *Sefer Ḥasidim* [Bologna version], ed. Reuven Margoliot (Jerusalem: Mosad Ha-Rav Kook, 1964), par. 702.

56 Grossman, *Pious and Rebellious*, 117–21; William C. Jordan, "Jews on Top: Women and the Availability of Consumption Loans in Northern France in the Mid-Thirteenth Century," *Journal of Jewish Studies* 29 (1978): 39–56; Cheryl Tallan, "Medieval Jewish Widows: Their Control of Resources," *Jewish History* 5, no. 1 (1991): 63–74; Cheryl Tallan, "Opportunities for Medieval Northern-European Jewish Widows in the Public and Domestic Spheres," in *Upon My Husband's Death: Widows in the Literature and Histories of Medieval Europe*, ed. Louise Mirrer (Ann Arbor: University of Michigan Press, 1992), 115–27.

57 Keil, "She Supplied Provisions," 84.

58 Susan Einbinder, "Pucellina of Blois: Romantic Myths and Narrative Conventions," *Jewish History* 12, no. 1 (1998): 29–46; and Judith R. Baskin, "Pulcellina of Blois," in *Shalvi/Hyman Encyclopedia of Jewish Women*, www.jwa.org/encyclopedia (forthcoming in 2021).

59 Suzanne Bartlett, *Licoricia of Winchester: Marriage, Motherhood, and Murder in the Medieval Anglo-Jewish Community* (Edgware, UK: Vallentine Mitchell, 2009).

60 On education and vocational training, see Baskin, "Some Parallels"; and Judith R. Baskin, "Educating Jewish Girls in Medieval Muslim and Christian Settings," in *Making a Difference: Essays in Honor of Tamara Cohn Eskenazi*, ed. David Clines, Kent Richards, and Jacob L. Wright (Sheffield, UK: Sheffield Phoenix Press, 2012), 19–37. On female Jewish physicians and midwives, see Joseph Shatzmiller, "Femmes médecins au Moyen Ages: Témoignages sur leurs pratiques (1250–1350)," in *Histoire et société: Mélanges offerts à Georges Duby I* (Aix-en-Provence: Université de Provence, 1992), 167–75; Ron Barkai, *A History of Jewish Gynaecological Texts in the Middle Ages* (Leiden: Brill, 1998); and Elisheva Baumgarten, "Ask the Midwives: A Hebrew Manual of Midwifery from Medieval Germany," *Social History of Medicine* 32, no. 4 (2019): 712–33.

61 According to *b. Pesahim* 108a, "A woman who is by the side of her husband need not recline; but if she is an important woman, she must recline." On women's assumption of ritual practices, see Grossman, *Pious and Rebellious*, 174–97; and Elisheva Baumgarten, *Practicing Piety in Medieval Ashkenaz: Men, Women, and Everyday Religious Observance* (Philadelphia: University of Pennsylvania Press, 2014), 138–69.

62 Grossman, *Pious and Rebellious*, 194, 281.

63 Grossman, *Pious and Rebellious*, 178–79.

64 Cited in Grossman, *Pious and Rebellious*, 185–86.

65 Grossman, *Pious and Rebellious*, 185. Grossman suggests a connection between this custom and the participation of Christian women in the baptism ceremony, a topic also discussed by Elisheva Baumgarten, *Mothers and Children: Jewish Family Life in Medieval Europe* (Princeton, NJ: Princeton University Press, 2004), 55–89.

66 Martha Keil, "Public Roles of Jewish Women in Fourteenth and Fifteenth-Centuries Ashkenaz: Business, Community, and Ritual," in *The Jews of Europe in the Middle Ages (Tenth to Fifteenth Centuries)*, ed. Christoph Cluse (Turnhout, Belgium: Brepols, 2004), 317–30. See also *Sefer Maharil: Minhagim*, ed. Shlomo J. Spitzer (Jerusalem: Machon Yerushalayim, 1989), *Hilkhot Milah*, no. 22, 487.

67 *Sefer Maharil, B'rit Milah*, no. 22, 487.

68 Keil, "Public Roles of Jewish Women," 325.

69 Keil, "Public Roles of Jewish Women," 328. See also Grossman, *Pious and Rebellious*, 180–82; and Elisheva Baumgarten, "Praying Separately? Gender in Medieval Ashkenazi Synagogues (Thirteenth–Fourteenth Centuries)," *Clio: Women, Gender, History* 44, no. 2 (2016): 43–62. https://www.cairn-int.info/article-E_CLIO1_044_0043--praying-separately-gender-in-medieval.htm# (accessed December 29, 2020).

70 For female prayer leaders, see Emily Taitz, "Women's Voices, Women's Prayers: Women in the European Synagogue of the Middle Ages," in *Daughters of the King: Women and the Synagogue*, ed. Susan Grossman and Rivka Haut (Philadelphia: Jewish Publication Society, 1992), 59–71. On cemetery epitaphs, see Ephraim Shoham-Steiner, "The Sources," in *The Cambridge History of Judaism*, vol. 6, *The Middle Ages: The Christian World*, ed. Robert Chazan (Cambridge, UK: Cambridge University Press, 2018), 330–34; and Elisheva Baumgarten, "Reflections of Everyday Jewish Life: Evidence from Medieval Cemeteries," in *Les vivants et les morts dans les sociétés médiévales: XLVIIIe Congrès de la SHMESP (Jérusalem, 4-7 mai 2017)* (Paris: Éditions de la Sorbonne, 2018), 95–104.

71 See Baskin, "Women and Ritual Immersion"; Baskin, "Male Piety, Female Bodies"; and Baumgarten, *Practicing Piety*, 24–50.

72 Martha Keil, "Rituals of Repentance and Testimonies at Rabbinical Courts in the 15th Century," in *Oral History of the Middle Ages: The Spoken Word in Context*, ed. Gerhard Jaritz and Michael Richter (Budapest: Central European University Press, 2001), 164–76.

73 Keil, "She Supplied Provisions," 85–86.

74 Keil, "She Supplied Provisions," 86–87; and Keil, "Public Roles of Jewish Women," 323–24, 327. On Licoricia, see Bartlett, *Licoricia of Winchester*; for Dolce, see Judith R. Baskin, "Dolce of Worms: The Lives and Deaths of an Exemplary Medieval

Jewish Woman and her Daughters," in *Judaism in Practice: From the Middle Ages Through the Early Modern Period*, ed. Lawrence Fine (Princeton, NJ: Princeton University Press, 2001), 429–37.

75 Baumgarten, *Mothers and Children*, 22–24, 158–59.

76 Israel Abrahams, *Hebrew Ethical Wills* (Philadelphia: Jewish Publication Society, 1926; rep. 2006), 209–10; *Sefer Ḥasidim* [Bologna ed.], par. 506; par. 873.

77 *Sefer Ḥasidim* [Bologna ed.], par. 588.

78 On conversion, see Paola Tartakoff, *Conversion, Circumcision, and Ritual Murder in Medieval Europe* (Philadelphia: University of Pennsylvania Press, 2020); Rachel Furst, "A Return to Credibility? The Rehabilitation of Repentant Apostates in Medieval Ashkenaz," in *On the Word of a Jew: Religion, Reliability, and the Dynamics of Trust*, ed. Nina Caputo and Mitchell B. Hart (Bloomington: University of Indiana Press, 2018), 201–21; and Shalem Yahalom, "Apostasy, Conversion, and Marriage: Rabbeinu Tam's Ruling Permitting the Marriage of a Female Apostate," *Jewish History* 33 (2020): 299–324.

79 Robert Chazan, *European Jewry and the First Crusade* (Berkeley: University of California Press, 1987). The Hebrew term for martyrdom is *kiddush ha-shem*, "sanctification of the Divine Name."

80 Grossman, *Pious and Rebellious*, 198–99. Robert Chazan describes these mid-twelfth century texts as interpretive and tendentious narratives that focus on the valor of Jewish martyrs to console later generations and prompt supplications to God (Chazan, *European Jewry*, 45–47). However, he goes on to rate their reliability as "fairly high," noting that the Jewish chronicles are corroborated by "Christian sources" (49).

81 Grossman, *Pious and Rebellious*, 201.

82 Susan Einbinder, "Jewish Women Martyrs: Changing Representations," *Exemplaria* 12, no. 1 (2000): 105–28. Also see Jeremy Cohen, *Sanctifying the Name of God: Jewish Martyrs and Jewish Memories of the First Crusade* (Philadelphia: University of Pennsylvania Press, 2006), esp. 106–29, on the diverse themes, Jewish and Christian, that inform the various literary portrayals of the 1096 martyrdoms of Rachel of Mainz and her children; and Judith R. Baskin, "Female Martyrdom," in *Shalvi/Hyman Encyclopedia of Jewish Women*, www.jwa.org/encyclopedia (forthcoming in 2021).

83 This Italian name, from the Latin *dulcis* ("sweet" or "pleasant"), is sometimes rendered Dulcie or Dulcea by contemporary authors; Dolce, the most accurate rendering of the Hebrew, also reflects the Italian origins of the leadership elite of this Rhineland community.

84 The elegy is based on Proverbs 31:10–31, the description of the "woman of valor." For a translation and commentary, see Baskin, "Dolce of Worms"; for the Hebrew text, see A. M. Haberman, *Sefer Gezerot Ashkenaz ve-Zarfat* (Jerusalem: Tarshish Books, 1945), 164–67.

85 Abrahams, *Hebrew Ethical Wills*, 207–18.

86 Judith R. Baskin, "Jewish Women's Piety and the Impact of Printing in Early Modern Europe," in *Culture and Change: Attending to Early Modern Women*, ed. Margaret Mikesell and Adele Seeff (Newark: University of Delaware Press, 2003), 221–40.

JEWISH WOMEN AND GENDER IN IBERIA (SEPHARAD) AND BEYOND

From Medieval to Early Modern

Renée Levine Melammed and Rebecca Lynn Winer

During the Middle Ages, Iberia (the Iberian Peninsula) was home to one of the largest Jewish communities in the world. Gender hierarchies and political power went hand in hand in Iberia, where Jews, Christians, and Muslims all lived and negotiated a modus vivendi as frontiers shifted.[1] Honor and status in society for individuals and groups were tied to sexual access to or protection of women. In this chapter we sketch out the history of Jewish women between the Muslim conquest (of most of the peninsula) in 711–ca. 720 CE to the Spanish monarchs' expulsion of the Jews in 1492 and beyond. Studying Jewish women and gender in Iberia is vital to understanding how this society functioned over time and in different spaces and regions. The experiences of Iberian Jewish women, real and imagined, serve as an important counterpoint to the experiences of their coreligionists in Ashkenaz and the wider Islamic world, enriching our understanding of gender roles and medieval Jewish life. Finally, this history serves as an indispensable background to the Sephardic Diaspora, because the crucible of Sephardic culture originated in the Iberian Peninsula (Sepharad in Hebrew).

Mapping continuity and change over such a long period can be challenging with sometimes limited sources and unavoidable gaps. Nevertheless, treasure troves do survive in the form of rabbinic sources, fatwas by Muslim authorities, royal charters, chronicles, notarial and ecclesiastical records, literature, and art. More material, especially documents concerning the wealthy and widows, is encountered after 1200 CE. The position of a widow, without the control of a husband, granted her a higher degree of legal autonomy and simultaneously forced many widows to engage in more economic activities, increasing their visibility in the records. Moving from Muslim conquest through Christian expansion, massacres and forced conversions of Jews in and around 1391, the expulsion of the Jews of Spain in 1492, and the early generations in exile, we narrate the roles that real Jewish women played and explore how concepts of Jewish women as sexual partners, wives, mothers, and potential converts shaped Iberian consciousness.

Persecution Under the Visigoths: Targeting Jewish Family and Community

JEWS IN IBERIA WERE subject to three roughly consecutive rules during the medieval and early modern periods: Visigoth, Muslim, and Christian. From late Roman times on, Jewish freedoms in Spain were curtailed; for example, it was illegal for Jewish men to marry or have sex with Christian women. After the Visigothic kings converted from Arian Christianity to Catholicism in 587 CE, they instituted harsh policies against Jews seeking to impose uniformity on their previously diverse people. Church council records and royal legislation reveal a coordinated, if uneven, effort to stamp out Judaism, leaving written precedent that fifteenth-century authorities would draw on in the decades leading up to the 1492 expulsion. Forced conversion was mandated around 613 CE, expulsion in 681 CE, and mass enslavement in 694. Converts from Judaism were still referred to as Jews, contributing to the view that baptism was insufficient to change them. Jews and converts were kept under the watchful eyes of local priests instructed to surveil women and children (some of whom were probably taken away from their parents); circumcisions, marriage partners, and nuptial rites were all areas of concern.[2]

We are not sure how well the Jews of Visigothic Spain survived persecution. Their population may never have been large; the ideological work that theoretical Jews did for Visigothic leaders intent on holding their kingdom together was perhaps more important than their numbers.

Jewish Culture and Life in al-Andalus: Women's Opportunities and Limitations

JEWISH LIFE CAME TO flourish in the wake of the rapid Muslim conquest of most of the Iberian Peninsula, from 711 to ca. 720. Although stories would circulate in the later Middle Ages that a Jewish fifth column betrayed the Visigoths to the invading Muslims, many in the new Jewish community hailed from North Africa,[3] from where the majority of the rank-and-file members of the invading army originated (their leaders were Arabs).[4] The subsequent cultural developments that transpired in al-Andalus (Muslim-ruled Spain) during the Umayyad emirate and the caliphate of Córdoba (756–ca. 1031) refashioned Jewish life. Arabic was readily spoken by Jews, and serious interest in poetry, grammar, astronomy, philosophy, philology, and medicine was inspired by contact with Islamic culture. The Jewish elite created its own Andalusian cultural milieu while never abandoning its Jewish roots. More educated and wealthy Jewish men were active as poets and writers, merchants, physicians, philosophers and scientists, courtiers, and tax farmers.

We know far less about women and nonelites. One mark of Muslim hegemony in the Iberian Peninsula was the ability of an elite Muslim man to have sexual access to women of all three faiths. Intermarriage and interfaith sexual relationships between Muslim men and Christian or Jewish women were allowed by jurists, who then guided interfaith families with an eye to ensuring that all progeny grew up to be good Muslims. Christians made up a majority of the population in al-Andalus for the first century or more of Muslim rule, and Andalusi Islamic jurists spent more of their time ruling on issues relating to Muslims marrying Christian women than on their unions with Jewish women.[5] However, some Muslim elites, such as Sa'id ibn Djudi, poet warrior from Granada, are known to have had Jewish concubines.[6]

In al-Andalus Jewish women may have acted as patrons of the arts, as did their Muslim counterparts who sponsored art and architecture and supported the construction of schools, mosques, tombs, and hospitals.[7] Evidence from the eleventh century and later in Muslim and then Christian Spain indicates that Jewish women funded the supply of oil for lamps in synagogues, the writing of Torah scrolls, and the casting of Torah crowns and covers and patronized goldsmiths, embroiderers, writers, and builders.[8] In 1286 Sara, the widow of David de Cabestany, established a trust fund for educating poor boys and a dowry fund for needy girls.[9] Dowry funds and dowering societies would play a major role in facilitating the marriages of orphaned and less fortunate Sephardic girls for centuries.

In al-Andalus Muslim women wrote poetry, enslaved women (who were trained as potential concubines for the elite) composed erotic love songs (*ghazal*), and elite freeborn women wrote elegies (*ritha*).[10] Some elite Jewish women participated in this cultural flowering. One talented tenth-century Jewish author was the wife of the trailblazing Hebrew poet Dunash ibn Labrat (920–990 CE), who unabashedly described her as erudite. Ezra Fleischer's work on fragments from the Cairo Genizah, the storehouse of assorted international papers written in Hebrew letters, mainly dating from 950–1250, led him to conclude that Ibn Labrat's wife was the "first Hebrew woman poet."[11]

Her "Will Her Love Remember?", written in the new Andalusian Hebrew style, was originally thought to have been penned by Ibn Labrat.[12] These poignant and sophisticated verses were written when Ibn Labrat was forced to leave her and their infant behind.

> Will her love remember his graceful doe,
>   her only son in her arms as he parted?
> On her left hand he placed a ring from his right,
>   on his wrist she placed her bracelet.
> As a keepsake she took his mantle from him,
>   and he in turn took hers from her.
> Would he settle, now, in the land of Spain,
>   if its prince gave him half his kingdom?[13]

The wives and daughters of other celebrated poets and scholars make brief appearances in the works of their husbands and fathers. The Jewish elite sought marriages that linked lineages known for achievement in traditional Jewish scholarship, wealth, and power. Shmuel Ha-Nagid (993–1056) relates that his wife's family did not consider him as her first choice of a potential spouse, but eventually this daughter of the judge of the Jewish court in Granada married the poet-warrior, bearing him four children.[14] Their son Joseph married the learned daughter of a scholar from Kairouan (now in Tunisia); following Joseph's demise during the pogrom of 1066 in Granada, his wife fled with their son to Lucena (near Córdoba), where they received community support as honored refugees.[15] When Shmuel Ha-Nagid's unnamed young daughter died in 1044, he sent his son a poem of lamentation.[16]

Scholars have wondered whether Ha-Nagid might have been the father of the talented Arabic woman poet Qasmuna. Qasmuna bint Isma'il al-Yehudi ("the Jew") was supposedly trained by her father, Isma'il ibn Bagdalah; Shmuel Ha-Nagid's Arabic name, Isma'il ibn Nagre'la, sounds similar.[17] Fragments of Qasmuna's poetry were recorded in Arabic anthologies, a testament to her talent; such anthologies usually include biographical information, but no details have been found for her.[18] Qasmuna's poems belong to a genre known as muwaššaḥ, which entails frequent changes of rhyme, meter, and strophe; extant verses are original and polished, revealing a witty and highly educated young woman. Eliyahu Ashtor, the eminent historian of Jewish life in al-Andalus, maintains that Qasmuna was not the only Jewish woman who acquired a reputation for her Arabic verses.[19]

Jewish women were not just involved in the literary sphere. As Avraham Grossman argues, although Jewish and Muslim men might have been uncomfortable seeing "women active in public as merchants and property owners"[20] and although men undertook these activities (especially those that involved travel) more often than women, some women undoubtedly functioned in precisely these roles. Material concerning women's work and public presence during Islamic rule is sparse, but documents in the Cairo Genizah reveal many active women—wealthy and poor, married, divorced, and widowed—who were not restricted to their homes. Widows and wealthy women actively managed personal assets, and wives whose husbands were away on business naturally took over for them.

Jewish Women's Everyday Lives in Christian Spain

From the late eleventh century, Christian rulers from the north of the peninsula expanded their realms. In the wake of Muslim Almoravid (1086) and Almohad (1146) invasions from North Africa, many Jews fled north from their homes in al-Andalus or were captured in the upheaval. In 1138 Christian Toledo, traces of communal activities to ransom Jewish women captives come to light; the famous poet, physician, and philosopher Yehuda Ha-Levi collected funds for one young woman's release.[21]

Another problem that arose with increased migration was the abandonment of married or betrothed women as Jewish men traveled or changed their places of residence, even opting to marry other women. Some *ketubbot* included clauses limiting absences to four months; the aim of these provisions was to discourage the traveler from being tempted to take a second wife while abroad. In the eleventh and twelfth centuries, respectively, Isaac Alfasi (a North African halakhist whose work had enduring influence in Spain and beyond) and Moses Maimonides (whose family fled al-Andalus under Almohad persecution) attempted to deal with this phenomenon. Alfasi recommended that the husband work where he resided; he also ruled that a man needed to obtain his wife's consent before traveling and should not wed another while absent.[22] Both authorities restricted absences to a year. In addition, before setting forth, married men were to leave behind a divorce writ to enable their wives to terminate the marriage if the husband did not return within the agreed amount of time.[23] The goal was to avoid the abandonment of wives, for whom there was little legal remedy. Spanish communities also confronted men who were not honoring their commitments to abandoned wives or fiancées by imposing fines on them.[24]

By the late twelfth century municipal charters were promulgated in Léon, Castile, Aragon, and Catalonia, and by the mid-thirteenth century there was a veritable revolution in the generation of notarial registers and royal chancery documents, particularly in the Crown of Aragon (the main territories of which were Aragon, Catalonia, Roussillon, Valencia, and the Balearics). This Latin documentation, surviving Hebrew deeds (*shetarot*) drafted by Jewish scribes, and rabbinic literature (especially responsa, i.e., questions concerning Jewish law answered by prominent scholars) reveal much about Jewish women. They attended synagogue, where some vied for control of seats in their section and where women who felt unjustly treated by the courts could interrupt services publicly to obtain justice.[25] Women also frequented bathhouses, municipal or private, not only when required to undergo ritual immersion in the *mikveh* (ritual bath), signifying their clean days after monthly menstruation, but also on a weekly basis. This was a social event, and prosperous Jewish ladies were often accompanied on these outings by their daughters, maidservants, and neighbors.[26]

When men were away or held public or military roles, Christian women managed businesses, properties, and estates. Women in Castilian towns owned shops and market stalls and peddled goods in the marketplace.[27] Jewish women likewise were involved in moneylending, trade, handicrafts (including making veils and coral beads), weaving, work in furs, shoe selling, and manufacturing. The less well-to-do went into domestic service, some as orphans hoping to earn dowries or wives seeking extra money and connections for their families as wet nurses.[28] Contracts for young Jewish women servants are more common from the late fourteenth century on. In 1390 Hasdai Crescas, crown rabbi of Aragon and philosopher, hired a 13-year-old Jewish girl named Dolça, daughter of Astruch de Bonastre, as a domestic servant for a four-year period.[29] Jewish women were also found in more traditional roles, such as embroiderers, seamstresses, midwives, keeners, and bathers of the deceased.[30] Jewish wives worked as members of family businesses and on their own, sometimes because of financial stress, bankruptcy, or an absentee husband.[31] The Latin record for the town of Perpignan (in Roussillon) shows both that Jewish women made transactions much less frequently than Jewish men and that Jewish women displayed financial knowledge and a sophisticated sense of the realities of doing business through the loans and investments that they did make.[32] And if women's loans were generally more modest than those of the men, substantial sums were still recorded in the transactions of wealthier women.

Husbands (in deathbed declarations in Hebrew or in Latin wills) and Christian courts or notary's offices often named Jewish widows as guardians to enable them to administer their children's finances, given that they would be most apt to try to disperse these funds wisely. Many Jewish widows administered their deceased husbands' properties and cared for their offspring. These women gained both legal and economic power. The prospect of remarriage was not always appealing to them, because they risked losing custody of their children (particularly older boys; girls might be raised with their mothers until they were eligible to marry). At the same time, local Jewish law did not exactly encourage widows with progeny to remarry; widows who did not choose to remarry and/or claim the sums owed to them in their marriage contracts (*ketubbah*) were entitled to support. No one could compel them to act otherwise. In the communities of the Crown of Aragon, it could even be to a widow's advantage not to remarry if it were economically feasible.[33]

The presence of widows in the public sphere was not only tolerated but also sometimes promoted; placing limitations on the earning potential of widows would result in creating a burden for their families and the community. The activities of an eleventh-century Toledan are revealed in a letter she received from her brother. Balluta, most likely a widow, because no male relatives are mentioned, was in charge of her household and had provided her daughter's dowry.[34] In 1284 in Perpignan, Reina (Regina in Latin), widow of Bonsenyor Jacob of Montpellier, served as the head of a panel of guardians for her children; as such, she arranged the marriage of her teenage daughter Mayrona and promised to continue to assist the young couple by contributing to their share of a communal debt owed the king.[35] In 1392 an eminent widow from Girona secured her property by turning to King John I of Aragon, who supported her case.[36] A financier's widow from Medina del Campo turned to both the rabbinic and royal courts in the 1480s to save her dowry from being appropriated to cover her husband's debts.[37]

Jewish families often supported the financial interests of their womenfolk. Jewish women who were property owners conducted business by themselves or with agents, sometimes choosing their sons or brothers as partners. When problems arose, they could petition the courts or initiate a lawsuit as they sought to protect their interests. In thirteenth-century Catalonia, Christian widows could function as heirs to their husbands or exercise usufruct (lifelong power) over the estate. These customs enabled Jewish women to feel more secure about their own management of marital property and inheritances.[38] Jewish women often maintained strong ties to the families they were born into, even after they married, and the rights of a woman's natal kin to her property were sometimes supported by law. In thirteenth-century Toledo, a Jewish widower could not receive all of his wife's estate but was able to share it equally with their children and, if childless, with heirs from her father's family; in particular, if the bride's surviving mother had helped provide her dowry, she received half.[39] Instructions were often left in wills, including bequests to guarantee support for widows or to provide daughters with dowries.[40] Jewish women named other women as recipients of money or property. Evidence from Latinate wills dictated by fourteenth-century Catalonian Jewish women might have had Hebrew counterparts with the intention of doubly ensuring validity. In 1338 one female testator instructed her sister to commission a Torah scroll and provide needy brides with dowries. Some left valuables to the synagogue; one willed all her possessions to her husband, but with the condition, commonly placed on women but rarely on men, that he remain chaste and not remarry.[41] One gets the sense that women chose causes that were personally dear to them and that reflected the ideals of their community.[42]

Sex and the "Jewess": Gender and Hierarchy in Christian Spain

As WOMEN'S HISTORIANS, WE seek to recover the experiences of individual women, such as those whose values and priorities are preserved in their wills; as historians of gender, we also find it important to underline that notions about the nature of the Jewish woman did ideological work in this society. David Nirenberg has stressed the role of Christian prostitutes in policing communal boundaries and blocking interfaith sex in Christian-ruled Iberia; according to most law codes, Jewish (and Muslim) men were not to sleep with them on pain of death to both parties. The gendered hierarchy meant that there was a double standard. Despite some variations in the laws (some openly permitting Christian men having Jewish and Muslim concubines, and others condemning sex across religious boundaries), Christian men who had sex with Jewish or Muslim women were not usually punished. Their intercourse was believed to reinforce the right ordering of society through Christian conquest and colonial control of Jews and Muslims.[43] Jewish women were portrayed as eroticized objects of desire in Christian literature and art, as Sara Lipton and David Nirenberg, among others, have noted.[44]

Prostitution among Christians was widely accepted in Christian Spain as a conduit for the sexual impulses of (unmarried) men who otherwise might engage in sexual crimes, such as rape and adultery. Fears of sexual mixing and notions of elite Jewish male privilege may have contributed to the establishment of Jewish bordellos and the arrangement that *aljama* (community) officials should provide the workers with stipends.[45] Not all the rabbis approved of these conditions or even maintained that it was appropriate for Jewish men to frequent brothels. Some were certain that because purity laws were not being observed by Jewish prostitutes, who were not frequenting the ritual bath, sexual contact with them was a transgression.[46] Others echoed Christian leaders, claiming that opting to meet sexual needs by means of a prostitute was preferable to having adulterous relations.[47]

Polygamy was more prevalent when Jews lived under Muslim rule, as the dominant majority permitted it. A common Jewish response, however, was to include a clause in marriage contracts preventing the groom from taking a second wife or bringing an enslaved woman into the home without his wife's approval.[48] Once Christian rule was established, bigamy was not eradicated, but in effect monogamy became the only legal option with two exceptions:[49] A wealthy Jew averse to divorcing his first wife, possibly when she had not been able to conceive, could petition the crown, which set a fee for confirmation of the legitimacy of any children born to a co-wife.[50] (This was not completely unlike a childless Christian notable seeking the legitimation of his children born out of wedlock). Hasdai Crescas, whose only son was murdered in Barcelona in the 1391 massacres, petitioned to take a second wife. Because Crescas's first wife was beyond childbearing age, he married an additional spouse in hopes of producing an heir. This wife, Jamila, bore him three daughters and a son.[51] Polygamy could also result from levirate marriage. A childless widow was at the mercy of her brothers-in-law, who determined whether she would be forced to marry one of them or be released from this fate. The preference in Spain was for levirate marriage when a surviving brother was not married, yet the prospect of a polygamous marriage for a brother-in-law was not always ruled out. Spanish rabbis were not overly considerate toward widows. Maimonides gave widows little leeway, stating that they could demur only if the prospective groom was deformed; otherwise, if they refused, such a widow was equivalent to a rebellious woman. In the thirteenth century, however, Rabbi Solomon ibn Adret (Rashba) of Barcelona mentioned a fictitious marriage (and divorce) by a widow to avoid the levirate union. Dealings with widows and their brothers-in-law often involved tensions around inheritance as well as potential complications concerning polygamy.[52]

Elite Jewish men, like their Christian counterparts, took Muslim and Jewish concubines, despite the fulminations of rabbinic authorities.[53] Yom Tov Assis attributes this to "the general sexual permissiveness of medieval Spain," which perturbed the rabbis.[54] Nirenberg perceived instead an expression of the privileges of wealth and status.[55] Jewish men might not have sex with Christian women, but they would exercise their privilege to do so with their enslaved Muslim women and with Jewish women (of lower status). If feasible, rabbinic authorities urged Jewish men to convert their enslaved concubines, free them, and then marry them so that their children would be Jewish. This practice became more rare after 1300 as Christian fears concerning Jewish men sexually corrupting not only Christian women but also slaves who otherwise might become Christian converts increased.[56] In Saragossa, even though the monogamy clause prevalent among Jews in the Islamic world appeared in the standard *ketubbah*, the Jewish husband Açach Abenaçora cohabited openly with a lover (*amiga*). His wife, Durona, persuaded the authorities to imprison him, but he was released on appeal to a Christian judge in 1383. Durona then had recourse to the king, who supported her case.[57]

Interfaith sexual relations were feared by Christian and Jewish authorities as a possible step on the way to apostasy. A late-eleventh-century upper-class Christian woman from Provence fell in love with a member of an elite Jewish family, converted to Judaism, married him, and fled south to Castile. Her brothers objected vehemently to their sister's betrayal of church and family. The couple fell victim to a violent attack on the Jews of Muño (near Burgos), and the widowed convert received letters of support from the Jewish community for funds to redeem her children, who were taken captive. She later remarried and moved to Nájera, yet her brothers tracked her down and she was sentenced to death. In a scene worthy of cinematic reproduction, some Jews bribed the jailer and smuggled her out of prison in the still of the night.[58] Conversion to Christianity was more common, however, and Jewish women sometimes made the choice to apostatize to escape domestic abuse, leave unhappy unions for new partners, or marry those forbidden to them by Jewish law.[59]

Hence Jewish leaders defended communal honor by strongly discouraging relationships between Jewish women and non-Jewish men. In fourteenth-century Saragossa, Jewish officials sought to punish Oro de Par because she had a non-Jewish lover; her face was disfigured and she was exiled.[60] In 1311 a woman who married a Christian man was murdered by her brothers when she became pregnant.[61] A wealthy widow from Trujillo was arrested for "scandalous behavior," namely, affairs with three different Christian men between 1481 and 1490.[62]

The events that transpired in Spain at the end of the fourteenth century would forever alter the history of Spanish Jewry, including Sephardic women. Attacks on Jews and Jewish communities began in July 1391 in Seville at the instigation of a charismatic anti-Semitic archdeacon and demagogue who had devoted years to roaming the countryside delivering vitriolic sermons and had not been deprived of his position in the Church. This impetus, and various other factors, came into play as community after community faced plunder, destruction, conversion, and death. Individual Jews sought protection from the crown or municipal leaders. Families and congregations were given cover in castles and fortresses, but all this did not necessarily save them.[63]

Resistance and Adaptation in the Wake of
1391 and 1492: Jewish Women and *Conversas*

THERE HAS BEEN A preconception that, when faced with conversion versus death, Ashkenazim chose martyrdom and Sephardim chose baptism. Many indeed converted, but thousands of Spanish Jews died during the riots and attacks in 1391, which lasted nearly a year. A Hebrew elegy from Toledo mourns the loss of nine synagogues, five study houses, and numerous rabbinic figures. Verse 13 reports the demise of pious and merciful women who were murdered, and verse 15 refers to Rabbi Yehuda, who first sacrificed his own wife and children before being murdered by the attackers.[64] Guillem Macaró, a jurist who chronicled the events in Barcelona in August, explained that many Jews converted because they were dying of hunger and thirst (after being protected in castles and elsewhere); he added that women, in particular, were killed because they were "more resistant to receive the sacrament of baptism than the men."[65]

After the dust settled, Christian authorities hoped converts would bring their Jewish spouses with them into their new faith, yet they sought to limit neophytes' interactions with Jews. Tolrana of Girona was asked in September 1391 if she was willing to cohabit with her husband, a baptized Christian, "without blaspheming Christ or attempting to attract him to her faithless Judaism." Her response was a clear refusal to live with him, convert, or renounce her religion.[66] During the attacks, one apostate husband pressured his wife to follow suit. According to an inquiry by royal judges in Tortosa on August 13, 1391:

> One of the converts, Pere March, knocked on the door of his wife, who was "then being a Jewess," and directed her to get out of bed because today was going to be a bad day. Against the background of looming violence, the visitors attempted to persuade family members to become Christian. . . . The conversos descended from the fortress, they escorted a number of people, including the wife of En Pere March, Na Caixixa, and the mother, wife, and young children of the converso Gonçalbo Tranxer. All of whom, of their own will, according to the judge, went to the house of Bernat Tranxer to be baptized.[67]

Caxixa's Jewish parents were anxious to alter the situation, paying the jailer to prevent her conversion and to return her to the castle, but they apparently arrived too late. When only one spouse converted, life became complicated. Some Jewish wives found their economic circumstances markedly reduced after their apostate husbands abandoned them.[68] If a couple had wed as Jews and the husband converted, the Jewish wife could not always obtain a divorce writ, whether in Spain or from afar if she had fled. One conversa left and remarried without divorcing her Jewish husband; she and her new husband returned to Judaism, moving to Málaga, where they were wed, only to discover that her first husband, who had been assumed to be dead, was still alive. The rabbis wanted to determine whether she had converted voluntarily or under duress; if the former, she was an adulterer and her children would be bastards. In the meantime, both marriages were dissolved.[69]

During the final century in Iberia many Jewish women tried to carry on their lives in the same manner as in the past, despite the major changes and traumas that occurred. For example, Tolosana, the erudite wife of Don Benveniste de la Cavalleria of Saragossa, wrote a dirge with her husband when their son died.[70] In 1443, when she was already widowed, she bequeathed a free-loan fund with a condition: In case the governmental administration of the *aljama* of Saragossa was no longer functioning, the funds should be transferred to the largest extant Aragonese Jewish community. In her will she also left monies for a burial society, a Talmud Torah (school), a *bikur holim* (society to care for the sick), and modest sums for her two Christian sons, three Christian daughters, and two Jewish daughters. *Aljama* officials in Morvedre (an urban center that rose in prominence in the fifteenth century as Jewish refugees settled there) legislated against women "flaunting their wealth" of jewelry and fine clothing.[71]

By the mid-fifteenth century, Visigothic legal precedent that dictated that converted Jews were never quite Christian enough was resurrected, and conversos, or New Christians, were discriminated against through purity of blood statutes (instituted first in Toledo in 1449), preventing them from assuming public offices. Intermarriages between New Christians and Old Christians were not common but did occur more frequently by the 1500s, making rabbinic decisions concerning their offspring challenging. Simha Asaf has claimed that older conversa women knew family genealogies and could help keep family names straight, especially regarding claims of belonging to a priestly or Levite family.[72] Around 1498 the conversa Juana Rodríguez of Toledo explained to the Tribunal of the Inquisition that she had observed Judaism while married to her first husband but that because her second husband was an Old Christian, it was too risky for her to continue.[73]

The effects of the mass conversions of tens of thousands of Jews between the massacres of 1391 and the 1414 conclusion of the Disputation of Tortosa, with its accompanying proselytizing campaigns, rocked Spanish society. For Jews and conversos living in their wake, their place in society was constantly and dangerously being negotiated in the century leading up to the expulsion. Women who opted to observe Judaism secretly did so with increased fear of endangering their lives or the lives of their coreligionists after 1481, when the Spanish Inquisition began to function. Afterward, many examples of the secret observance of female *judaizantes* (Judaizers) appear in the Inquisition's records. They range from minimal, such as lighting Sabbath candles or fasting on Yom Kippur, to almost complete descriptions of rituals enacted for the most part in their homes. Thus some women obtained new dishes for Passover or insisted on using separate dishcloths (for dishes and utensils that came into contact with pork versus those that did not).[74] The Inquisition was concerned with deeds as well as the intentions behind them; thus nonhalakhic activities, such as debaptizing, and Jewish cultural celebrations of birth called *hadas* were equally incriminating.[75] Many conversos belonged to the middle and upper-middle classes and employed household servants. These individuals were built-in witnesses for the prosecution, appearing time and again in the Inquisition files, despite the objection of the pope against using their unreliable testimonies. Because the home was the natural locale for observance of numerous Jewish practices, crypto-Jewish women more or less took on the responsibility of perpetuating Judaism to the best of their ability.[76] Moriscas (forced converts from Islam to Christianity) would be plagued by the Inquisition for playing similar roles in their communities until they were expelled in the early 1600s.[77]

Young women played a central role in a brief but intense messianic movement that took off at the beginning of the sixteenth century. It originated in 1499: An 11-year-old named Inés of Herrera began to prophesy to the conversos who flocked to her hometown, a center for leather goods. Numerous young women and girls, after exposure to her visions and descriptions of the Promised Land, began to fast on Mondays and Thursdays (the two weekdays when the Torah is read in synagogue) and to observe the Sabbath. Their families had chosen conversion rather than exile in 1492. The prospect of salvation in a Jewish mode, a mere seven years after their apostasy, was extremely appealing.[78] The Inquisition reacted vehemently to the news of this maiden's and two other prophets' activities. Inés was burned at the stake, and many of her followers were arrested, imprisoned, and convicted of heresy. By 1503 this movement was effectively wiped out, but that this artisan circle of conversos was energized by the visions of a young girl is significant.[79]

New Communities in Traditional Modes: Women Negotiate the Sephardic Diaspora

THE SPANISH EXPULSION OF 1492 and the forced conversion of all Portuguese Jews in 1497 deeply affected the lives of Jewish and conversa women.[80] Several wealthy and powerful conversas were able to regain their Jewish heritage and have come down in history as benefactors of their fellow crypto-Jews. Benvenida Abravanel left Spain for Italy, where her husband headed the Jewish community of Naples. After Don Samuel's death in 1547, she continued to conduct his business affairs, was actively charitable, made her home a center for study, and was extremely strict about the distribution of inheritances to her children and her husband's illegitimate son.[81] Another eminent Iberian widow was Dona Gracia Nasi, born in 1510 in Portugal to a family of prominent Spanish exiles. She was wed at age 18 to Francisco Mendes, a wealthy banker from the Benvenist family, and widowed by 1535. Realizing in 1536 that the newly established Portuguese Inquisition was about to investigate the lives of the New Christians, Gracia departed with her daughter, sister, and two nephews. In Antwerp she joined her husband's brother and talented business partner, Diogo, who inherited half the family fortune; most of the remainder was left to Gracia's young daughter under the management of her mother as guardian. Although Gracia planned to head eastward, her awareness that other conversos were anxious to flee Iberia led her to establish an underground escape route for them. Many of those she saved became her loyal agents, enabling her to spread her wealth and extend her activities across Europe and the Ottoman Empire. Gracia's trials and tribulations were many, especially in Italy, where her sister may even have betrayed her to the authorities.[82] She eventually headed to Constantinople by way of Ragusa (Dubrovnik), where she could finally live openly as a Jew. In Turkey Gracia attempted to organize an international economic boycott of the port of Ancona to avenge the arrest and burning of conversos in 1556. She planned the creation of an economically self-sufficient Jewish settlement in Tiberias, having received a permit from the sultan. In addition, Gracia funded and supported numerous publications, synagogues, study houses, and charities throughout the Balkans.[83] Gracia was devoted to her fellow Sephardim; her status as a wealthy widow enabled her to execute most of her plans, attesting to the brilliance of this businesswoman and philanthropist who was always looking to the future.

Sephardim settled in such numbers in the Ottoman Empire that they virtually displaced the native "Romaniot" Jews (of the former Byzantine Empire). Some Sephardic women fulfilled important roles as members of a religious minority. An active widow in the Ottoman Empire was Esther Handali, of Istanbul, *kiera* (lady), intermediary for the women in the harem and the outside world in the late sixteenth century. She and others, such as Esperanza Malakhi, served in the palace, but mirroring the faction-ridden climate there—each of the women of the Ottoman harem sought to raise a son who would reign after his father and eliminate his half-brothers—Jewish women intermediaries often became involved in intrigues and complications.[84]

Spanish exiles settled in Italy, North Africa, and the Ottoman Empire, which included Salonika, Istanbul, Syria, Palestine, and Egypt. In Middle Eastern communities, women's names appear as owners of property, moneylenders, in markets, and as artisans; widows took on the most active roles.[85] Ruth Lamdan has found earlier attempts by rabbinic authorities in these regions to separate men and women in the workforce, at synagogue services, and at holy sites, but the arrival of immigrants from Spain and North Africa led to changes. Separation was no longer as stringently adhered to, partly as a result of the hardships that these individuals had endured, which created a high degree of social and geographic mobility.[86] In the end rabbinic leaders were not very successful in curbing the activities and public appearances of women.

Partly in reaction to the trauma of the expulsion from Spain and the flourishing of new kabbalistic devotions, mysticism developed in numerous communities in the Middle East through the early modern age. J. H. Chajes argues that there was "significant involvement of women in the phenomena of spirit possession, divination, and dream interpretation," especially in the late sixteenth century in Jerusalem, Safed, and Damascus.[87] The noted mystic Hayyim Vital (1542–1620) referred to a number of women who had divination skills, were practitioners of magic, and were able to mediate with the dead. Perhaps the most impressive phenomenon that Vital, and other Jewish sages who were his contemporaries, respected was that of women beneficiaries of the positive possession (dybbuk) of a good soul (*maggid*). Indeed, Francesca Sarah of Safed and the young daughter of Raphael Anav in Jerusalem, both active in the 1570s, were considered especially pious. They appeared in the synagogue and study hall, had spiritual experiences, decreed fasts, and practiced divining in this community.[88] The fact that rabbinic leaders believed in these possessed Jewish women is remarkable. In contemporary European contexts women with similar manifestations were often condemned as witches, the only exception being Quaker communities in which such women were considered emissaries of God. The new kabbalistic devotions with Iberian roots that developed in the sixteenth-century Middle East later took an unexpected turn with the rise of the Sabbetai Tzevi movement in the late seventeenth century.[89] There women emerged as religious performers in the synagogue, although with ambiguous behaviors; in some contexts they were seen as holy virgins, and in others as incestuous whores.[90]

The conversas who settled in the Portuguese community of Amsterdam brought a strong Iberian heritage with them. Their identification with the "Portuguese Nation"[91] and commitment to Judaism were openly declared in their wills and other donations. In the seventeenth century, women made up the majority of the Portuguese community. Rabbinic leaders were concerned with their moral conduct because so many had arrived on their own or routinely had husbands who were away on business. Most had been born as Catholics with an extremely limited knowledge of Judaism.[92] Nevertheless, as Levie Bernfeld has shown, they were, on the whole, devoted to their faith, attended synagogue, and were active philanthropists, donating to the local yeshiva, the boys' orphanage, and funds for ransoming captives and for supporting the Holy Land.[93] Women helped other women through donations to the Santa Companhia de dotar orfans e donzeles pobras (commonly known as the Dotar), the Portuguese dowering society established in Amsterdam in 1615 and modeled on the Venetian precedent, founded in 1613.[94] The Dotar was dedicated to providing dowries and respectable marriages for less fortunate girls of Portuguese lineage; this implied the exclusion of other Jewish girls. In Amsterdam, in the first decades of the seventeenth century during which these men and women were redefining their Jewishness, the distinctiveness, unity, and solidarity of the Portuguese Nation were the most important components of their identities.[95] The candidates for the Dotar's lottery had to "believe in oneness of God" and identify "spiritually with Judaism."[96] Recipients could claim dowries only after proving they had married (circumcised) Jewish partners in ceremonies performed by rabbis. In 1641 the administrators of the Dotar started admitting women as members.[97]

Conclusion

RECENT STUDIES HAVE REVEALED the powerful gender hierarchy that all Jews lived under in medieval Iberia, stressing the intersectionality of Jewish women's experience. Still, Sephardic women were not hidden under veils or cloistered in their homes; a great many found the means to express themselves, whether in the business world, by defying the Inquisition, as poets, or as benefactors of the poor. Reconstructing the activities of women in Iberia and beyond allows one to see the influence of the surrounding culture, whether Muslim or Christian. Although Jewish law and values played a central role in the medieval and early modern periods, exigencies allowed for degrees of fluidity that led to women's participation, most notably in the economic sphere. One can also see the tremendous strength required in overcoming traumatic historical developments, such as forced conversions and expulsions. When life in Iberia came to an end, these Jewish women maintained their ties to Judaism as they relocated and reestablished themselves in new communities. They did not forsake their Sephardic roots.

Notes

1 Before the thirteenth century those who spoke Arabic, Spanish/proto-Castilian, Galician-Portuguese, and Catalan, among other languages, could be enemies or allies depending on current realpolitik.

2 For a historical overview, see Roger Collins, *Early Medieval Spain: Unity in Diversity 400–1000*, 2nd ed. (New York: St. Martin's Press, 1995), 128–43 and the classic study of Jews under Christian rule in Iberia Yitzhak Baer, *A History of the Jews in Christian Spain*, 2 vols. (Philadelphia: Jewish Publication Society, 1992 [orig. English translation 1961]), 1:15–22. For Visigothic sources on Jews in translation, see Olivia Remie Constable, ed., *Medieval Iberia: Readings from Christian, Muslim, and Jewish Sources*, 2nd ed. (Philadelphia: University of Pennsylvania Press, 2012), 17, 21–26. Constable's volume includes excerpts from over twenty sources on Jews in medieval Iberia.

3 See Michael M. Toch, "The Jews in Europe, 500–1050," in *The New Cambridge Medieval History c. 500–c. 700*, ed. P. Fouracre (Cambridge, UK: Cambridge University Press, 2005), 1: 551.

4 Collins, *Early Medieval Spain*, 150.

5 See Janina M. Safran, *Defining Boundaries in al-Andalus: Muslims, Christians, and Jews in Islamic Iberia* (Ithaca, NY: Cornell University Press, 2013).

6 See Eliyahu Ashtor, *The Jews of Moslem Spain*, 3 vols. (Philadelphia: Jewish Publication Society, 1973–1984), 1: 316.

7 See Gavin R. G. Hambly, "Becoming Visible: Medieval Islamic Women in Historiography and History," in *Women in the Medieval Islamic World*, ed. Gavin R. G. Hambly (New York: St. Martin's Press, 1998), 3–27; and D. Fairfield Ruggles, "Women Patrons," in *Medieval Islamic Civilization: An Encyclopedia*, ed. Josef W. Meri (New York: Routledge, 2006), 2: 864.

8 See Eleazar Gutwirth, "*Qilusin*: el mecenazgo femenino medieval," in *La mujer judía*, ed. Yolanda Morena Koch (Córdoba, Spain: Ediciones El Almendro, 2007), 115–19, 120–27.

9 See Rebecca Winer, *Women, Wealth, and Community in Perpignan, c. 1250–1300: Christians, Jews, and Enslaved Muslims in a Medieval Mediterranean Town* (Aldershot, UK: Ashgate, 2006), 78–79. For the territory in which Sarah lived, the Crown of Aragon, see Yom Tov Assis, *The Golden Age of Aragonese Jewry: Community and Society in the Crown of Aragon, 1213–1327* (London: Littman Library of Jewish Civilization, 1997). In the 1330s an elegy alluded to the donation of a house to the synagogue by the deceased, Dona Mira; see Gutwirth, "*Qilusin*," 128.

10 See Magda Al-Nowaihi, "Elegy and the Confrontation of Death in Arabic Poetry," in *Transforming Loss into Beauty: Essays on Arabic Literature and Culture in Honor of Magda Al-Nowaihi*, ed. Marlé Hammond and Dana Sajdi (Cairo: American University in Cairo Press, 2008), 3–20; and Tahera Qutbuddin, "Women

Poets," in *Medieval Islamic Civilization: An Encyclopedia*, ed. Josef W. Meri (New York: Routledge, 2006), 2: 866.

11 See Ezra Fleischer, "Al Dunash ben Labrat ve-'ishto uvno" [About Dunash ben Labrat and His Wife and Son], *Jerusalem Studies in Hebrew Literature* 5 (1984): 201–2.

12 See S. J. Pearce, "Bracelets Are for Hard Times: Economic Hardship, Sentimentality, and the Andalusi Hebrew Poetess," *Cultural History* 3, no. 2 (2014): 148–69. Pearce has questioned the attribution of the poem to Dunash ibn Labrat's wife but stresses that "the work of the supposed Andalusi Hebrew poetess reflects economic and social realities faced by women in Muslim Spain" (148).

13 Peter Cole, ed. and trans., *The Dream of the Poem: Hebrew Poetry from Muslim and Christian Spain, 950–1492* (Princeton, NJ: Princeton University Press, 2007), 27.

14 See Renée Levine Melammed, "*The Jews of Moslem Spain*: A Gendered Analysis," *Journal of Sefardic Studies* 2 (2014): 79.

15 Levine Melammed, "*Jews of Moslem Spain*," 81–83. See also Ashtor, *Jews of Moslem Spain*, 2: 164–65.

16 Ashtor, *Jews of Moslem Spain*, 2: 98.

17 See María Ángeles Gallego, "Approaches to the Study of Muslim and Jewish Women in Medieval Iberian Peninsula: The Poetess Qasmuna bat Isma'il," *Miscelánea de Estudios Árabes y Hebraicos* 48 (1999): 70–72.

18 See Gallego, "Approaches," 63–75.

19 Ashtor, *Jews of Moslem Spain*, 3: 8.

20 See Avraham Grossman, *Pious and Rebellious: Jewish Women in Medieval Europe* (Lebanon, NH: University Press of New England, 2004), 114.

21 See Renée Levine Melammed, "Spanish Women's Lives as Reflected in the Cairo Genizah," *Hispania Judaica* 11, no. 2 (2015): 97–98.

22 See the *Responsa of R. Isaac ben Jacob Alfasi*, ed. Wolf Leiter (Pittsburgh: Mekhon ha-Rambam, 1954), no. 120, 83–84, quoted in Yom Tov Assis, "Sexual Behaviour in Mediaeval Hispano-Jewish Society," in *Jewish History: Essays in Honor of Chimen Abramsky*, ed. Ada Rapoport-Albert and Steven J. Zipperstein (London: P. Halban, 1988), 55n61.

23 See *Teshuvot haRambam* [R. Moses b. Maimon's responsa], ed. Jehoshua Blau (Jerusalem: Rubin Mass, 1986), 2, no. 347, 624; and the Hebrew edition of Grossman, *Pious and Rebellious* (Jerusalem: Zalman Shazar Center for Jewish History, 2003), 130n47 and 141n80.

24 See Avraham Grossman, "Metsuqoteha shel ha-'isha ha-netusha bi-Sfarad ba-me'ot ha-'ahat 'esre-shlosh 'esre" [The Struggle Against Abandonment of Wives in Muslim Spain in the Eleventh–Thirteenth Centuries], *Hispania Judaica* 10 (2014): 5–19.

25 See Elka Klein, "Public Activities of Catalan Jewish Women," *Medieval Encounters* 12, no. 1 (2006): 48–61. Klein includes the use of *ikuv tefillah* (disturbing the prayers) by a widow in 1261.

26 Women of all three religions might have used the municipal bathhouse simultaneously; see Heath Dillard, *Daughters of the Reconquest: Women in Castilian Town Society, 1100–1300* (New York: Cambridge University Press, 1984), 152.

27 See Dillard, *Daughters*, 158–63; Grossman, *Pious and Rebellious*, 111–12; and Teófilo Ruiz, "Women, Work, and Daily Life in Late Medieval Castile," in *Women*

at Work in Spain from the Middle Ages to Early Modern Times, ed. Marilyn Stone and Carmen Benito-Vessels (New York: Peter Lang, 1998), 112.

28 See Anna Rich Abad, "Able and Available: Jewish Women in Medieval Barcelona and Their Economic Activities," *Journal of Medieval Iberian Studies* 6, no. 1 (2014): 71–86; Anna Rich Abad, "Coral, Silk, and Bones: Jewish Artisans and Merchants in Barcelona Between 1348 and 1391," *Nottingham Medieval Studies* 53 (2009): 53–72; and Sarah Ifft Decker, "Jewish Women, Christian Women, and Credit in Thirteenth-Century Catalonia," *Haskins Society Journal* 27 (2016): 161–78.

29 See Anna Rich Abad, *La comunitat Jueva de Barcelona entre 1348 i 1391 a través de la documentació notarial* (Barcelona: Fundació Noguera, 1999), 183.

30 In Amsterdam women worked in the *mikveh* and served as *mortalhadeyras*, washing the dead and preparing shrouds. See Tirtsah Levie Bernfeld, "Sephardi Women in Holland's Golden Age," in *Sephardi Family Life in the Early Modern Diaspora*, ed. Julia R. Lieberman (Waltham, MA: Brandeis University Press, 2010), 187–88.

31 Winer, *Women, Wealth*, 87–89.

32 Winer, *Women, Wealth*, 89.

33 See Elka Klein, "The Widow's Portion: Law, Custom, and Marital Property Among Medieval Catalan Jews," *Viator* 31 (2000): 154; and Richard Emery, "Les veuves juives de Perpignan (1371–1416)," *Provence Historique* 37, fasc. 150 (1987): 559–69.

34 The document is T-S 13J 9.4 in the Cairo Genizah collection. See Levine Melammed, "Spanish Women's Lives," 94–95.

35 Winer, *Women, Wealth*, 123–24.

36 See Sílvia Planas Marcé, *Na Blanca, jueva de Girona (s. XIV)* (Bellcaire d'Empordà, Spain: Edicions Vitel·la, 2010).

37 From an unpublished study by Marina Girona Berenguer, from the Royal Chancellor's Archive in Valladolid.

38 Klein, "Widow's Portion," 163; and Elka Klein, "Splitting Heirs: Patterns of Inheritance Among Barcelona's Jews," *Jewish History* 16 (2002): 49–71.

39 Grossman, *Pious and Rebellious*, 151.

40 Klein, "Splitting Heirs," 56, 63.

41 See Robert I. Burns, *Jews in the Notarial Culture: Latinate Wills in Mediterranean Spain, 1250–1350* (Berkeley: University of California Press, 1996), 114–16.

42 For a fascinating will in Catalan by an erudite Gironan, see Sílvia Planas Marcé, "Na Goig fa testament: les darreres voluntats d'úna dama jueva de la Girona medieval," *Afers* 73 (2012): 513–34.

43 See David Nirenberg, *Communities of Violence: Persecution of Minorities in the Middle Ages* (Princeton, NJ: Princeton University Press, 1996), 145–48, 152–59.

44 Sara Lipton, "Where Are the Gothic Jewish Women? On the Non-Iconography of the Jewess in the *Cantigas de Santa Maria*," *Jewish History* 22, nos. 1–2 (2008): 139–77; and David Nirenberg, "Deviant Politics and Jewish Love: Alfonso VIII and the Jewess of Toledo," in *Neighboring Faiths: Christianity, Islam, and Judaism in the Middle Ages and Today*, by David Nirenberg (Chicago: University of Chicago Press, 2014), 55–74.

45 See Simha Asaf, "'Anuse' Sfarad u-Portugal be-sifrut ha-Teshuvot" [The "Anusim" of Spain and Portugal in the Responsa Literature], *Me'assef Zion* 5 (1933): 35–36, esp. n. 1.

46 About the ruling of Rabbi Judah of Toledo to expel Jewish prostitutes, see Grossman, *Pious and Rebellious*, 139.

47 Assis, "Sexual Behaviour," 52–53.

48 See Mordechai Akiva Friedman, *Ribbui Nashim biyme ha-benayim: Te'udot Hadashot me-ha-Gniza ha-Qahirit* [Jewish Polygyny in the Middle Ages: New Documents from the Cairo Geniza] (Jerusalem: Bialik Institute, 1986), 28–46.

49 Assis, "Sexual Behaviour," 30.

50 See Yom Tov Assis, "Herem de-Rabbenu Gershom ve-nissu'e kefel bi-Sfarad" [The Ordinance of Rabbenu Gershom and Polygamous Marriages in Spain], *Zion* 46 (1981): 257.

51 This permission was granted on May 18, 1393. See Fritz Baer, *Die Juden im christlichen Spanien: Urkunden und Regesten I. Aragonien und Navarra* (Berlin: Akademie Verlag, 1929), 711, no. 452.

52 Grossman, *Pious and Rebellious*, 98.

53 See David Nirenberg, "Love Between Muslim and Jew in Medieval Spain: A Triangular Affair," in *Jews, Muslims, and Christians in and Around the Crown of Aragon*, ed. Harvey J. Hames (Leiden: Brill, 2004), 127–55; and Jonathan Ray, *The Sephardic Frontier: The "Reconquista" and the Jewish Community in Medieval Iberia* (Ithaca, NY: Cornell University Press, 2006), 170.

54 Assis, "Sexual Behaviour," 36–37, 40, 51.

55 Nirenberg, *Communities of Violence*, 141, 184–85; and Assis, "Sexual Behaviour," 36–37, 40, 51.

56 See Rebecca Lynn Winer, "Jews, Slave-Holding, and Gender in the Crown of Aragon Circa 1250–1492," in *Cautivas y esclavas: el tráfico humano en el Mediterráneo*, ed. Aurelia Martín Casares and María Cristina Delaigue Séris (Granada, Spain: University of Granada, 2016), 43–60.

57 See Asunción Blasco Martínez, "Mujeres Judías Aragoneses entre el amor, el desamor, la rebeldía y la frustracíon (siglos XIV–XV)," *El Prezente: Studies in Sephardic Culture* 3 (2010): 34.

58 See Edna Engel, "Gilguleha shel giyyoret mi-Provens: Tatsref shel shlosha qta'im mi-gnizat Qahir" [The Wandering of a Provençal Proselyte: A Puzzle of Three Genizah Fragments], *Sefunot* 7 (1999): 13–21; and Yosef Yahalom, "Igrot Maño: Ma'ase yadav shel sofer kafri mi-tsfon Sfarad" [The Maño Letters: The Work of a Village Scribe from Northern Spain], *Sefunot* 7 (1999): 23–33.

59 Paola Tartakoff, "Jewish Women and Apostasy in the Medieval Crown of Aragon, c. 1300–1391," *Jewish History* 24 (2010): 7–32.

60 David Nirenberg concluded that Oro de Par took lovers of both faiths but that the Jewish officials feared retaliation by the Christians; see Nirenberg, *Communities of Violence*, 136. Asunción Blasco Martínez concluded that she had married a Muslim; see Blasco Martínez, "Mujeres Judías," 31.

61 Baer, *Die Juden*, 203, no. 164, item 6.

62 See Haim Beinart, *Trujillo: A Jewish Community in Extremadura on the Eve of the Expulsion from Spain* (Jerusalem: Magnes Press, 1980), 20–24.

63 See Benjamin R. Gampel, *Anti-Jewish Riots in the Crown of Aragon and the Royal Response, 1391–1392* (New York: Cambridge University Press, 2016).

64 See Cecil Roth, "A Hebrew Elegy on Martyrs of Toledo, 1391," *Jewish Quarterly Review* 39 (1948–1949): 137.

65 Gampel, *Anti-Jewish Riots*, 103.

66 Gampel, *Anti-Jewish Riots*, 132.

67 Gampel, *Anti-Jewish Riots*, 150–51.

68 Rebecca Lynn Winer, "Un conte de deux femmes juives: la vie dans le *call* de Perpignan entre 1250 et 1415," trans. Aymat Catafau, in *Histoire de Perpignan*, ed. Patrice Poujade (Perpignan, France: Éditorial Trabucaire, in press).

69 Numerous cases of marital complications appear in Dora Zsom, *Conversos in the Responsa of Sephardic Halakhic Authorities in the 15th Century* (Piscataway, NJ: Gorgias Press, 2014), 70–71.

70 See J. Targarona Borrás, "The Dirges of Don Benvenist and Doña Tolosana de la Cavalleria for the Death of Their Son Solomon," in *Studies in Arabic and Hebrew Letters in Honor of Raymond P. Scheindlin*, ed. J. P. Decter and M. Rand (Piscataway, NJ: Gorgias Press, 2007), 211–23.

71 See Mark D. Meyerson, *A Jewish Renaissance in Fifteenth-Century Spain* (Princeton, NJ: Princeton University Press, 2004), 89.

72 See Asaf, "'Anuse' Sfarad," 23.

73 Archivo Histórico Nacional, Madrid, leg. 180, no. 10.

74 See Renée Levine Melammed, *Heretics or Daughters of Israel: The Crypto-Jewish Women of Castile* (New York: Oxford University Press, 1999).

75 See Renée Levine Melammed, "Noticias sobre los ritos de los nacimientos y de la pureza de las Judeo-conversas del siglo XVI," *El Olivo* 13, nos. 29–30 (1989): 235–43.

76 Renée Levine Melammed, "Crypto-Jewish Women Facing the Spanish Inquisition: Transmitting Religious Practices, Beliefs, and Attitudes," in *Christians, Muslims, and Jews in Medieval and Early Modern Spain*, ed. Mark D. Meyerson and Edward D. English (Notre Dame, IN: University of Notre Dame Press, 2000), 197–219.

77 See Mary Elizabeth Perry, *The Handless Maiden: Moriscos and the Politics of Religion in Early Modern Spain* (Princeton, NJ: Princeton University Press, 2005); and Renée Levine Melammed, "Judeo-Conversas and Moriscas in Sixteenth-Century Spain: A Study of Parallels," *Jewish History* 24 (2010): 155–68.

78 There was also a Christian worldview informing their acceptance of a woman mystic; see Sharon Koren's chapter in this volume.

79 See Haim Beinart, "Tenuat ha-nevi'a Ines be-Pueblo de Alcocer uve-Talarrubias va-'anusehen shel ayarot eleh" [The Prophetess Inés and Her Movement in Pueblo de Alcocer and Talarrubios], *Tarbiz* 51 (1982): 633–58; Haim Beinart, "Anuse Chillón ve-Siruela ve-ha-nevi'ot Mari Gomes ve-Ines bat Juan Estevan" [Conversos of Chillón and Siruela and the Prophecies of Mari Gómez and Inés, the

Daughter of Juan Esteban], *Zion* 48 (1983): 241–72; Haim Beinart, "Ha-nevi'a Ines u-tenuatah be-Herrera moledetah" [The Prophetess Inés and Her Movement in Her Hometown, Herrera], in *Studies in Jewish Mysticism, Philosophy, and Ethical Literature*, ed. Y. Dan and Y. Hacker (Jerusalem: Magnes Press, 1986), 459–506; and Haim Beinart, "The Prophetess of Extremadura: Inés of Herrera del Duque," in *Women in the Inquisition: Spain and the New World*, ed. Mary Giles (Baltimore: Johns Hopkins University Press, 1999), 42–52. See also Levine Melammed, *Heretics or Daughters*, 45–72, 216–19.

80 See Renée Levine Melammed, "The Jewish Woman in Medieval Iberia," in *The Jew in Medieval Iberia, 1100–1500*, ed. Jonathan Ray (Boston: Academic Studies Press, 2012), 273–80.

81 See Renata Segre, "Sephardic Refugees in Ferrara: Two Notable Families," in *Crisis and Creativity in the Sephardic World, 1391–1648*, ed. Benjamin R. Gampel (New York: Columbia University Press, 1997), 164–85, 327–36.

82 See Howard Adelman, "The Venetian Identities of Beatrice and Brianda de Luna," *Nashim* 25 (2013): 10–29.

83 Many books and novels have been written about Dona Gracia Nasi. One of the first was Cecil Roth, *Doña Gracia of the House of Nasi* (Philadelphia: Jewish Publication Society, 1977).

84 See Paméla Dorn Sezgin, "Jewish Women in the Ottoman Empire," in *Sephardic and Mizrahi Judaism: From the Golden Age of Spain to Modern Times*, ed. Zion Zohar (New York: New York University Press, 2005), 220.

85 See Ruth Lamdan, *A Separate People: Jewish Women in Palestine, Syria, and Egypt in the Sixteenth Century* (Leiden: Brill, 2000), esp. 110–26.

86 Lamdan, *A Separate People*, 127–38.

87 See J. H. Chajes, "Women Leading Women (and Attentive Men): Early Modern Jewish Models of Pietistic Female Authority," in *Jewish Religious Leadership: Image and Reality*, ed. J. Wertheimer (New York: Jewish Theological Seminary, 2004), 237–62; and J. H. Chajes, "He Said, She Said: Hearing the Voices of Pneumatic Early Modern Jewish Women," *Nashim* 10 (2005): 99–125.

88 Chajes, "Women Leading," 247–57.

89 See J. H. Chajes, *Between Worlds: Dybbuks, Exorcists, and Early Modern Judaism* (Philadelphia: University of Pennsylvania Press, 2003), 101–18.

90 See Ada Rapoport-Albert, *Women and the Messianic Heresy of Sabbatai Zevi, 1666–1816*, trans. Deborah Greniman (Oxford, UK: Littman Library of Jewish Civilization, 2011).

91 See Renée Levine Melammed, *A Question of Identity: Iberian Conversos in Historical Perspective* (New York: Oxford University Press, 2004), 61–66, 70–77.

92 See Tirtsah Levie Bernfeld, "Religious Life Among Portuguese Women in Amsterdam's Golden Age," in *The Religious Cultures of Dutch Jewry*, ed. Yosef Kaplan and Dan Michman (Leiden: Brill, 2017), 79–97.

93 See Bernfeld, "Religious Life"; and Tirtsah Levie Bernfeld, *Poverty and Welfare Among the Portuguese Jews in Early Modern Amsterdam* (Oxford, UK: Littman Library, 2012).

94 On Venetian dowering societies, see Francesconi's chapter in this volume.

95 See Miriam Bodian, "The 'Portuguese' Dowry Societies in Venice and Amsterdam: A Case Study in Communal Differentiation Within the Marrano Diaspora," *Italia* 6 (1987): 30–61.

96 Bernfeld, "Religious Life," 63.

97 See Jessica V. Roitman, "Marriage, Migration, and Money: The Santa Companhia de dotar orphãs e donzelas pobres in the Portuguese Sephardic Diaspora," *Portuguese Studies Review* 13, no. 1 (2005): 348.

GENDER AND
WOMEN IN THE ZOHAR

Sharon Faye Koren

FEMININE SYMBOLS AND EROTIC imagery undergird theosophical Kab-balah,[1] with symbolic Kabbalists describing God as a multifaceted divine force of masculine and feminine attributes, which they often depict in ma-ternal or sensual terms.[2] Feminine aspects engage in sexual intercourse, become pregnant, give birth, nurse, and menstruate. References to *Shek-hinah*, one of God's feminine forms, appear on almost every page of the standard printed edition of the Zohar (Book of Splendor), the most famous work of medieval Kabbalah.[3] Building on that imagery, medieval mystics infused deeper meaning into their own observance, believing that every ritual action empowers the divine feminine and creates harmony between the masculine and feminine potencies within the godhead. Despite the cen-trality of feminine symbols in the literature, human women are notably ab-sent. Although wives may have served as amanuenses to their husbands' spiritual pursuits, medieval Zoharic texts do not directly address real his-torical women. Therefore, in contrast to the other essays in this volume that discuss the lives of actual Jewish women, I focus on the lives of the cosmic feminine, describing the gendered godhead, feminine imagery, and cosmic gynecology in Zoharic literature to suggest that kabbalistic in-terest in the divine feminine does not translate into advocacy for gender parity. These explorations prompt consideration of why feminine imagery is so pronounced in a literature written by and for men.

What Is Kabbalah?

THEOSOPHICAL KABBALAH EMERGED IN southern France in the late twelfth and early thirteenth centuries in response to the challenges of Aristotelianism and Maimonidean philosophy, newly introduced to the Latin West. Following Aristotle, Maimonides (d. 1204) posits that God is an infallible, unchanging, self-sufficient power that set the entire universe into motion. Human beings cannot describe God because they are, by their nature, incapable of understanding all that God is. All the anthropomorphisms and the anthropopathisms in the Bible must be interpreted allegorically because an infinite God cannot have a body or display emotion. Our only recourse is to describe what God is not.[4] The Unmoved Mover does not need humans' prayers or their good deeds. Indeed, according to some interpretations of Maimonides, God does not even hear human prayers; the proper way to engage with Maimonides's immovable God is through awed silence.[5] Commandments serve as a useful spiritual purpose in keeping individuals mindful of God and in creating and preserving community, but God has no book of reward and punishment.[6]

The concept of such a remote God felt new and appealing to many of the Provençal intelligentsia, but it also differed significantly from the midrashic mentality of traditional rabbinic Judaism. Moreover, such an abstract idea of God could be spiritually unsatisfying to those yearning for a deeper and more personal connection with their creator. In response, some traditionalists enlarged on earlier mystical and midrashic traditions, combining them with the Neoplatonic philosophy popular in southern France to create a form of Jewish philosophy deeply rooted in tradition: Kabbalah (literally "tradition").[7]

Like many of their Neoplatonic contemporaries, these theosophical Kabbalists believed that one aspect of God lies beyond the realm of human comprehension and as such can be described only in negative terms. They refer to this unknowable power as the 'Ayn Sof, the Without End. Ten divine attributes, known as sefirot (singular sefirah), emanate from this ineffable source to inhere into the realm of being. This divine structure provided mystics with both the remote and unknowable God of the philosophers and a revealed accessible God with whom they could engage. Medieval Kabbalists often divided the sefirot into two groups: an upper group of three and a lower group of seven (see Figure 1). The upper three sefirot, the focus of early Kabbalah, were often associated with cerebral qualities. The lower seven were analogized to the days of the week, colors, biblical figures, and more. The creative possibilities were infinite because, as Arthur Green explains, the sefirot must be understood not as "'hypostatic entities' but as symbolic clusters, linked by association, the mention or textual occurrence of any of which automatically brings to mind all others as well."[8] Shekhinah, for example, is described in images that range from human mother to mother earth, from the Land of Israel to the moon.

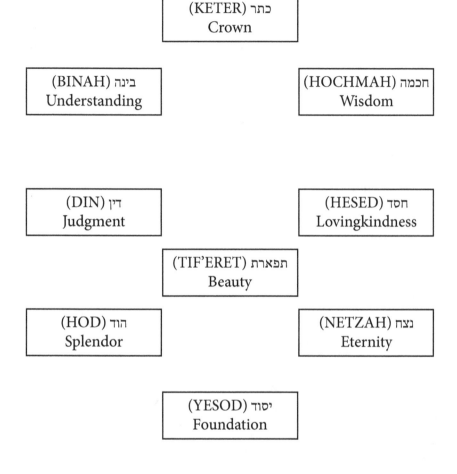

	(KETER) כתר Crown	
(BINAH) בינה Understanding		(HOCHMAH) חכמה Wisdom
(DIN) דין Judgment		(HESED) חסד Lovingkindness
	(TIF'ERET) תפארת Beauty	
(HOD) הוד Splendor		(NETZAH) נצח Eternity
	(YESOD) יסוד Foundation	
	(SHEKHINAH) שכינה Presence-Indwelling	

The *sefirot*.

Medieval Jewish mystics sought to uncover the mysteries of the revealed divine realm; however, in contrast to other medieval philosophers, their goal was not just divine knowledge. Theosophical/theurgic Kabbalists believed in an essential reciprocity between God and human beings. They thought, of course, that human beings needed God. At the same time, they held that

God needed human beings. Knowledge of the inner workings of the divine realm and Jewish ritual enabled Kabbalists to ensure intradivine harmony. Just as a physician must know the anatomy and physiology of the human body to treat patients and ensure homeostasis, theosophical Kabbalists used their knowledge of divine mysteries to maintain cosmic harmony through Jewish ritual. In so doing, mystics ensured that divine light would flow unimpeded from the first *sefirah*, *Hokhmah*, through the sefirotic realm and ultimately overflow into our own world, guaranteeing balance and peace. Prayer and keeping the commandments were, according to these mystics, essential ways to effect change and restore the divine realm.[9]

The twelfth-century midrashic compilation *Sefer ha-Bahir* (Book of Brightness) is traditionally believed to contain the earliest expressions of symbolic Kabbalah. Many also credit Kabbalah's origins to the Provençal scholar Isaac the Blind (1160–1238) and his circle. Isaac's teachings spread into Catalonia, where his students Ezra and 'Azriel of Gerona experimented with the Neoplatonic potential of Kabbalah. Their contemporary Nahmanides (Moshe ben Nahman; 1194–1270), also of Gerona, the leading figure of the Jewish community in Catalonia, more conservatively focused on the midrashic and earlier mystical aspects of Kabbalah and only hinted at kabbalistic secrets in his Torah commentary.[10] Medieval symbolic Kabbalah achieved its most innovative flowering in central Spain, where King Alfonso "the Wise" facilitated a cultural Renaissance, creating ripe conditions for Castile to become the center of kabbalistic activity.[11] Mystics flocked to Castile, free to express their religious devotion in new and inventive ways. These scholars wrote hundreds of kabbalistic works, including commentaries on the ten *sefirot*, rationales for the commandments, short works on mystical secrets, and interpretations of the Torah. The main body of the Zohar contains teachings that date to this creative period. Much of this kabbalistic literature describes the teachings and peregrinations of Rabbi Shimon bar Yochai (Rashbi, 2nd century CE) and his circle. Although the corpus is traditionally attributed to Rashbi, academics have proven it to be the product of a circle of medieval mystics likely helmed by Moses de Leon (d. 1305) in the thirteenth century, with later accretions from the fourteenth century through its printing in the sixteenth century.[12]

Male and Female

UNLIKE MAIMONIDES, WHO REJECTED anthropomorphisms and desexualized God, theosophical Kabbalists embraced a lexicon of embodiment, gender, and sexuality to describe the inner working of the divine realm. Medieval Kabbalists posit that everything in our terrestrial world, including human bodies, reflects a higher cosmic reality. Through somewhat circular logic, they assume that, because human beings are made in God's image and our form is a human body, the divine form must also be an *anthropos*. They compare the first three *sefirot*, *Keter* (crown), *Hokhmah* (wisdom), and *Binah* (understanding), to a human head; the seven lower *sefirot* include arms (*Hesed* [for the right arm] and *Din* [for the left]); a torso (*Tif'eret*); legs, kidneys, or testicles (*Netzah* [for the right side] and *Hod* [for the left]);[13] a phallus (*Yesod*); and the *Shekhinah*, sometimes representing a general feminine symbol, or in some passages, a womb, vagina, clitoris, or the corona ('*atarah*) of the phallus.[14]

Zoharic literature endeavors to uncover the mysteries of this divine body through a close reading of the Bible. For the Zoharic circle, the description in Genesis of the creation of terrestrial 'adam (the human being) also describes the mythic origins of primordial Adam ('adam qadmon)—the sefirotic realm.[15] In Genesis 1:27 we read

Elohim created the adam, in the image of *'Elohim*,
He [*'Elohim*] created the earthling [*'adam*], male and female,
He [*'Elohim*] created them.[16]

In this first creation account, the first human being is created sexless. As noted by Rachel Adler,[17] 'adam is a Hebrew term, not yet a proper name. The 'adam is quite literally an earthling, a being derived from the red ('adom) earth ('adamah). The Hebrew original uses masculine pronouns because Hebrew has no neuter form. A Zoharic interpretation of this verse and its parallel in Genesis 5:1–2 seems to apply a similarly egalitarian understanding to the sefirotic realm (I have bold-faced and italicized terms to help clarify the Zohar's hermeneutical method).

Rabbi Shimon said, "Supernal secrets are revealed in these two verses, Male and Female He created them—revealing supernal glory, mystery of faith, for out of this mystery Adam was created."

"Come and see: With the secret by which heaven and earth were **created**, *Adam* was **created**. Of them is written: 'These are the ***generations*** of heaven and earth' (2:4). Of Adam it is written: 'This is the book of the ***generations*** of Adam' (5:1). Of them is written: 'when they were **created**' (2:4). Of Adam is written: 'on the day they were **created**' (5:2).

'Male and female He created them.' From here we learn: Any image not embracing male and female is not fittingly supernal (cf. BB74b). . . .

Anywhere male and female are not found as one, the Blessed One does not place His abode. Blessings are found solely where male and female are found, as it is written: He blessed them and named them Adam. It is not written: He blessed him and named him Adam. One is not even called 'adam, human, unless male and female are as one."[18]

God created the first human being in the image and likeness of the male and female sefirotic realm. The Zohar "proves" this mystery of faith by noting that the terms *generations* and *created* appear in the verses describing the creation of the heavens and the earth as well as those describing the creation of the 'adam (human being). The use of identical terms points to a corresponding meaning. The divine realm is sefirotic *Adam* ('adam qadmon), who, like the human 'adam, was created male and female.[19] This balance between male and female is the "mystery of faith" that undergirds Zoharic theology and is, through the Zoharic lens, the goal of all Jewish ritual.

The male *sefirah*, *Hokhmah*, is balanced by the female *Binah*.[20] *Din/Gevurah* (Judgment) is associated with the feminine and must therefore remain in balance with the masculine *Hesed* (lovingkindness).[21] And the central *sefirah*, *Tif'eret*, is the bridegroom who must unite with his bride, the *Shekhinah*, through the agency of *Yesod* (the divine phallus). Much of Zoharic literature describes intradivine dynamics in terms of the erotic relationship between these couples. The gendered framework is essential to the inner workings of the *sefirot* and offers a mystical rationale for heterosexual marriage.[22] According to several teachings in the Zohar, "One who is not male and female is called half a body."[23]

The Feminine *Sefirot*

THE FEMININE SEFIROT BINAH and *Shekhinah* are identified with a wide array of associated symbols. *Binah*, "mother," is the cosmic womb who gives birth to the seven lower *sefirot*. The biblical matriarch Leah, who also gives birth to six sons and one daughter, personifies her sefirotic drama.[24] *Binah* is the sea from which all rivers of illumination flow. She is the palace "home" of her partner, *Hokhmah*, and her seven "children."[25] As the upper mother, she is the point of ultimate repentance and return (both *teshuvah* in Hebrew).[26] She represents the supernal jubilee, the end of the seventh seven-year cycle of *shemittah*, when all property returns to its original owners, all debts are forgiven, and all slaves are freed.[27] *Binah* is a stork (*hasidah* in Hebrew) because she gives birth to the *sefirah* of *Hesed*.[28] The appearance of any of these images in biblical verses cues Kabbalists to her activity within the sefirotic realm.

Despite *Binah*'s symbolic import, *Shekhinah* is the *sefirah* most discussed in kabbalistic and academic literature.[29] The term's origins may be traced to rabbinic texts, where she represents God's indwelling in our world (from the Hebrew root *sh-kh-n*, to reside). In later midrashim the symbol evolves from a representation of God's presence in the world into a separate independent force existing alongside God—God and his *Shekhinah*. However, it was not until the mid-thirteenth century that the *Shekhinah* became fully realized as a divine feminine cosmic force associated with myriad symbols. In the main body of the Zohar, almost every biblical verse becomes an invitation to uncover the inner workings of *Shekhinah* with the other *sefirot*. *Shekhinah* is *Binah*'s daughter, *Tif'eret*'s bride, and the mother of human souls. She is the Earth, the moon, a field, the Land of Israel, Zion, and Jerusalem. Incorporating imagery from the Song of Songs, she is a beautiful rose, the community of Israel (*knesset yisra'el*), and a merciful deer that feeds her fawns. She is the Temple cult's Throne of Glory and the Ark of the Covenant. As the seventh *sefirah*, she is the seventh day of the week, the Sabbath, and the seventh-year, *shemittah*, the agricultural Sabbath during which the land lies fallow (Lev. 25:2).

Sefirotic Physiology and Gynecology

BECAUSE ZOHARIC LITERATURE POSITS that human physiology, like everything in the human dimension, reflects a higher divine reality, its authors map their understandings of the human body's function onto the sefirotic realm. For example, many Zoharic passages explain Genesis 2:10, "A river issues from Eden, to water the garden," as describing the emanative flow of the sefirotic realm from its source in *Hokhmah*, Eden, through to the *Shekhinah*, the garden. Some interpretations describe this intradivine process in overtly sexual terms. For them, *Hokhmah* is Eden, the divine father who implants his seed in *Binah*, the divine mother, in a matter so satisfying that the two live in constant harmony. Through this union, *Binah* crowns their holy son, *Tif'eret*, with divine energy. Thus aroused, *Tif'eret* desires his lady, the *Shekhinah*. At that moment, *Yesod*, the divine phallus, ejaculates, thereby literally "watering the garden" so that the *Tif'eret* and *Shekhinah* can unite. The Zohar describes the cosmic, emanative flow of the *sefirot* in human physiological terms that mirror medieval medical theories on the origin of semen: that it originates in the brain's white matter and then flows to the penis.[30]

Theosophical Kabbalists not only focus on the cosmic parallel to their own male physiology but also imagine that the feminine *sefirot Binah* and *Shekhinah* mirror female life-cycle functions as well. As noted, each can engage in intercourse with her partner: *Binah* with *Hokhmah* and *Shekhinah* with *Tif'eret* through the agency of *Yesod*. *Binah*, the upper mother, becomes pregnant and gives birth to the seven lower *sefirot* (see Figure 1); *Shekhinah*, the lower mother, gives birth to human souls. *Binah* suckles the seven lower *sefirot*, providing spiritual nourishment to the sefirotic realm; *Shekhinah* suckles the lower worlds, offering divine illumination and succor to the human realm.[31] According to Ellen Haskell, maternal symbols, which developed from earlier rabbinic associations between nursing and spiritual transmission, enabled the mystic to cultivate a tender relationship with God that "was not reliant on associations with sexuality or rulership."[32]

Some texts describe the *Shekhinah* as a menstruant (*niddah*). Just as menstruation suspends sexual relations on earth, *Shekhinah*'s menstruation interrupts divine union.[33] Zoharic teachings adjust the length of the *Shekhinah*'s flow to correspond with their exegetical needs. Some teachings describe *Shekhinah* as a *niddah* on weekdays. On Friday morning, *Binah*, her mother, purifies and adorns her so that she can reunite with her husband *Tif'eret* on *Shabbat* evening (Friday night). Another teaching suggests that the *Shekhinah* came under the sway of the demonic "other side" (*sitra 'ahra*) and became a *niddah* while the Israelites were slaves in Egypt. After they were freed, she had to wait seven weeks of the *'omer* (a 49-day period of partial mourning between the second day of Passover and Shavuot [the Feast of Weeks]) before she could reunite with her husband, *Tif'eret*, on the eve of Shavuot.[34]

Gender Fluidity in Theosophical Kabbalah

KABBALISTS' CHRISTIAN NEIGHBORS SIMILARLY sought a tender maternal relationship with divinity, the most obvious manifestation being the burgeoning cult of the Virgin Mary, discussed later. Thirteenth-century Christian texts also describe Jesus as a mother, providing his followers with food, sheltering small children, and ministering to the weak and the sick—all traditional female roles. Christian mystics describe his blood on the cross as nourishing, and he is even said to lactate.[35] Yet, although Christian mystics used maternal images to describe their relationship with Christ, Jesus remained male. By contrast, some thirteenth-century theosophical Kabbalists conceived of the divine gender in more fluid terms.[36] For them, *Binah* is the feminine upper mother and is perceived as a womb when she receives the effluxes (seed) of *Hokhmah*; however, she is part of the "world of the male" (*'olam ha-zakhar*) when she exerts power over the lower *sefirot*.[37] *Shekhinah*, too, can be described in both male and female terms. Many Zoharic texts similarly describe *Shekhinah* in masculine terms, such as David and kingdom (*malkhut*) when she is active, and in feminine terms when she displays qualities of containment, passivity, or even evil.[38]

Zoharic literature often describes evil as a necessary aspect of the godhead. On the sefirotic tree, *Binah* and *Din/Gevurah* both appear on the left, "sinister" in Latin. Several early Kabbalists located the origin of evil in *Binah* or in excess *Din* (judgment). Later, some Castilian Kabbalists entertained a more dualistic conception of evil as the demonic *sitra 'ahra*, literally the "other side" of the sefirotic realm jutting out of *Din*. *Shekhinah*, who is often described as an empty vessel having nothing of her own, is especially vulnerable to the sway of excess judgment or the *sitra 'ahra*. The myth of the menstruating *Shekhinah* points to Kabbalah's close association of the feminine with evil. Some teachings in the Zohar suggest that the *sitra 'ahra* occasions *Shekhinah*'s flow; menstrual blood is red like its fiery source. She is therefore *niddah*, literally "banned" from the holy *sefirot*.[39] This association between menstruation and evil on the cosmic level may have influenced restrictions on real women's access to the sancta.[40]

Feminine Symbols as Exegetical Tools

ZOHARIC LITERATURE ALSO IDENTIFIES *Binah* and *Shekhinah* with the biblical matriarchs. According to Joseph Gikatilla, "*Shekhinah* in Abraham's time was called Sarah, in Isaac's time Rebecca, and in Jacob's time Rachel."[41] Jacob meets Rachel—young, beautiful, and loved—at a well; he appreciates her beauty at first sight and immediately falls in love. Her sister Leah, by contrast, remains unseen at home and is depicted as older, nearsighted, and hated (Gen. 29–30). The Zohar understands this narrative as a historical event and a key to a cosmic reality. Leah is *Binah*, "older" than her sister because she is an earlier emanation. Leah as *Binah* gives birth to six sons and one daughter. Her weak eyes and hated status are marks of her inscrutability to the uninitiated.[42] In contrast, younger Rachel is the *Shekhinah*, a portal to the divine, easily accessible and perceived. Her cosmic function is embedded in the narrative. Rachel/*Shekhinah* first meets Jacob in public because she is the beautiful public face of the sefirotic realm. Jacob, who has not yet achieved his full mystical potential, immediately appreciates Rachel. He works for her for seven years because she is the seventh and lowest *sefirah*.[43] His unwitting (blind) marriage with Leah enacted a divine plan that he could not yet understand. Jacob simply could not yet perceive Leah as *Binah*. He thinks her eyes are weak, but it is truly Jacob who does not see. Leah is not hated; rather, she is undervalued, invisible, or misunderstood.[44] The literal sense of the biblical narrative thus provides a key to the inner workings of the divine realm.

As the lowest *sefirah*, Rachel/*Shekhinah* is the entry point to divine secrets. Like the female figure of wisdom in Proverbs 9:6 who invites the "simple into her home so that they give up simpleness and walk in the way of understanding [*binah* in Hebrew]," *Shekhinah* invites initiates to learn the mysteries of Torah. One of the Zohar's most famous parables describes *Shekhinah* as a beautiful maiden, hidden deep in her palace, whose lover, the mystic, hovers around her gates hoping to catch a glimpse of her. She encourages him, coquettishly revealing and concealing herself to arouse his desire. The Zohar describes their romance.

> So it is with words of Torah: she reveals herself only to her lover. Torah knows that one who is wise of heart circles her gate every day. What does she do? She reveals her face to him from the palace and beckons him with a hint, then swiftly withdraws to her place, hiding away. None of those there knows or notices—he alone does, and his inner being and heart and soul follow her. Thus the Torah reveals and conceals herself, approaching her lover lovingly to arouse love in him. . . . Once he has grown accustomed to her she reveals her face to him—face to face, and tells him all the hidden secrets and all the hidden ways, concealed in her heart since primordial days. Then he is a complete man, husband of Torah, master of the house, for all her secrets she has revealed to him, concealing nothing. . . . Human beings must be alert, pursuing Torah to become her lovers.[45]

Here the eros that we have come to expect in the sefirotic realm is mirrored in the romance between the mystic and *Shekhinah*. She is the oral Torah, portrayed as a princess, who, like Rapunzel, is hidden away in a tower. She calls out to her lover to arouse love in him, and when he loves her with all his heart, soul, and might (evoking the words of the daily Shema prayer from Deut. 6:5), she reveals herself to him "face to face," echoing God's revelation to Moses on Sinai (Exod. 33:11). This illumination changes his very essence, and he becomes "complete." The parable imagines engagement with the biblical text as the means to achieve a mystical experience.[46] The *Shekhinah* as oral Torah thus becomes the portal to mystical illumination.[47]

Other Zoharic texts describe mystics as the "initiates of the Matronita's (*Shekhinah's*) palace."[48] For the initiate, there are preconditions to entry: A mystic must be male, circumcised, ritually pure, married to a woman, and righteous.[49] Having entered, however, the mystic is no longer the *Shekhinah's* inferior. On the contrary, once the adept becomes husband of Torah, he becomes "master of the house."[50] Beyond this privileging of the masculine, many Zoharic texts portray *Shekhinah* as a damsel in distress. As noted by Art Green, Kabbalists, like knights in a medieval romance, endeavored to save their lady, the Matronita, from demonic forces and exile, ensuring her safety and returning her to her husband, *Tif'eret*.[51] Punctilious observance of Jewish ritual provided an opportunity to unite *Tif'eret* and *Shekhinah* through the agency of *Yesod*. This participatory salvation is apparent in the preponderance of thirteenth- and fourteenth-century mystical rationales for the commandments that encourage adherents to observe the commandments to activate these cosmic occurrences.

Human Sex Echoing the Divine

FOR THE MYSTIC THE commandments to procreate provided the most direct theurgic parallel to celestial union. Engaging in licit sexual union on Friday night was the most obvious way for the mystic to restore *Shekhinah*, the Sabbath Queen, to her rightful partner, *Tif'eret*. The Talmud required Torah scholars to pay their marriage debt on Friday evenings,[52] and the Zohar's teachings imbued this established custom with cosmic import. The male mystic represents *Tif'eret*; his wife, the *Shekhinah*; their licit heterosexual intercourse invigorates divine union. At the same time, marital intercourse also serves as a means for the adept to have a mystical experience and unite with *Shekhinah*.[53] Although Zoharic texts enjoin mystics to pleasure their wives on Friday nights, these sexual encounters were ultimately meant for the sake of heaven.[54] Indeed, many texts describe what Elliot Wolfson has coined "an ascetic eroticism," in which mystics sublimated their desire for terrestrial partners for their love for God.[55] Kabbalists' wives were vessels for *Shekhinah*, amanuenses for a male mystical encounter.[56]

The role of women as spiritual facilitator is mirrored in the narrative portions of the Zohar. The main body of the Zohar frames homilies with stories that enrich Zoharic teachings.[57] The authors of these narratives seldom cast women, but the handful that do mention mothers, wives, and daughters offer a lens into their understanding of women's roles. For example, after a precocious adept interprets the mystical meaning of the verse "out of the eater came something to eat" (Judg. 14:14), the boy and his companions "reached the outskirts of his mother's village. As soon as she saw them, she prepared the house and they stayed there for three more days." Her son teaches the kabbalistic mysteries of eating; his mother prepares food for his friends.[58] This gender divide reflects conventional earthly roles that are much more prosaic than the elevated and fluid notions of gender to which the mystics adhere in their Zoharic interpretations.

In another frame narrative, two rabbis stay at an inn. When they rise at midnight to study Torah, the innkeeper's daughter lights a lamp for them and silently stands behind them unnoticed, listening.

> Rabbi Abba opened, saying, "For the mitzvah is a lamp and Torah is light, and reproofs of discipline are the way to life" (Proverbs 6:23).
>
> "For a mitzvah is a lamp"—whoever engages in this world in those commandments of Torah has a lamp arranged before him by every single commandment, to illumine him in that world. "And the Torah is light"—one who is occupied with Torah attains the light by which the lamp is lit. For a lamp without a light is nothing; light without a lamp similarly, cannot shine; so each needs the other completely. Action is needed to prepare the lamp, and studying Torah is needed to light the lamp. Happy is he who engages in them—in light and in lamp.[59]

As Eitan Fishbane teaches, Rabbi Abba suggests every mitzvah "must be actualized from its potential. Just as the candle may be prepared but is inert until it is lit, so too the study of Torah ignites the candle of the commandment."[60] Rabbi Abba continues and applies this dynamic to the relationship between *Tif'eret* and *Shekhinah*: "*Shekhinah* is the candle; *Tif'eret* is the flame that ignites and causes the light to shine."[61]

Rabbi Abba turns around and finally notices the innkeeper's daughter—the young woman who had lit the lamp enabling his teaching. Seeing her, he offers yet another interpretation.

> He said, "for a lamp is a mitzvah." What is "a lamp?" A lamp is a mitzvah attained by women, namely the Sabbath lamp. For although women do not attain Torah, men attain Torah and illumine this lamp that women prepare by this mitzvah. Women by preparing this lamp; men by Torah, illuminating this lamp—adorning the mitzvah that is incumbent upon women.[62]

All the gendered actions and relationships of this frame coalesce in this final interpretation. Lighting Sabbath candles is one of three mitzvot traditionally assigned to women.[63] Human women may light the material Sabbath lamp. However, women cannot attain and illumine Torah; that is the *Shekhinah*.

Women may only prepare the lamp; male mystics can ignite the lamp and make it shine. Women are matter; men are the cause.[64]

As this frame demonstrates, women were the material means through which men achieved their spiritual ends. They were not partners in their husband's mystical experiences, nor do we have any evidence that medieval Jewish women were aware of their theurgic contributions or able to understand theosophical mysteries. On the contrary, Spanish Kabbalah was the carefully guarded esoteric property of a few elite Jewish men. Indeed, as Judith Baskin argues, it is unlikely that women, or most men for that matter, would have had the educational background necessary to understand kabbalistic mysteries.[65] Medieval kabbalistic rituals were written by men and addressed to men. Isolated examples of men's nods to women's involvement, like those just cited, serve only to highlight the glaring absence of women's meaningful involvement in this exclusively male realm.[66]

Behind the Feminine Focus

ALTHOUGH THE KABBALISTS' PSYCHOLOGICAL motivations remain obscured, I suggest several possible historical reasons that feminine imagery may feature so prominently in a literature written by and for men.

Some scholars suggest that some Zoharic teachings use sexuality as a polemic against monasticism and Christian celibacy.[67] Jewish men were commanded to procreate; they could not abandon their communities and focus all their energies on God. In response to the twelfth-century emphasis on clerical celibacy, Kabbalists may have elevated sexuality and developed the notion of the *Shekhinah* as the divine's feminine element through which they could engage with God and, in so doing, distance themselves from the monasticism often associated with spiritual enlightenment.

Other passages in Zoharic literature that expatiate on the importance of procreation, endogamous unions, and sexual purity are internal Jewish polemics against the perceived sexual impropriety of many contemporary upper-class Jews who engaged in extramarital affairs (often with their Christian and Muslim household help).[68] Because premodern Jews believed in matrilineal descent, any progeny born from such a union would not be Jewish unless the mother converted before giving birth. This kabbalistic concern for endogamy and sexual purity is conveyed by the symbols associated with the *sefirah Yesod*, "foundation." *Yesod*, the divine phallus, is the site of the cosmic covenant (*brit*) reinscribed on every Jewish man.[69] Any man who engages in illicit sexual relations would be literally inserting the holy into the profane.[70] Joseph, the biblical hero who resisted the advances of Potiphar's (his Egyptian employer) wife, was therefore the perfect symbol of the celestial *Tsaddiq* (righteous man). According to several Zoharic teachings, only a man who is married and circumcised can see the face of the *Shekhinah*, reinforcing the mystics' exaltation of heteronormative monogamy.

Although an effort to stave off intrareligious relationships may have guided the Kabbalists' thinking, they may also have been responding to the popularity of the Marian cult in the surrounding culture. The parallel feminine symbols of the Virgin Mary and the *Shekhinah* each functioned as mediators between heaven and earth for their supplicants. Both were identified with the wisdom in Proverbs and with the exegesis of the Song of Songs. Christians prayed through Mary; adepts attained a mystical experience through the *Shekhinah*. Arthur Green and Peter Schafer independently assert that the symbol of the feminine *Shekhinah* must be understood within the context of the Marian cult.[71] Indeed, it would have been impossible for Kabbalists in Castile to be unaware of the burgeoning cult of the Virgin Mary. She was lauded in song, her image appeared on the exterior monumental sculpture of Castilian churches and cathedrals, and her likeness was paraded through the streets on holy days. However, several scholars have questioned the scope of influence. Feminine images and sexual symbolism in Jewish sources predate the rise of Kabbalah in the late twelfth century. Moreover, numerous aspects of the feminine symbols of the Zohar cannot be explained by Marian parallels, such as the role of *Binah* or that of the divine family and, perhaps most notably, the Kabbalists' unabashed sexuality. The *Shekhinah* was not the Jewish Virgin Mary, but, as many scholars have shown, medieval Jewry acculturated particular aspects of the dominant culture and made them their own. And certain descriptions of the *Shekhinah*—such as the reinvigoration of the symbol of the *Shekhinah* suffering in exile with her children, which may be a reaction to Mary suffering at the foot of her son's cross—reflect potential parallels to Marianism.[72] Because there is no single or canonical book of the Zohar until its publication in the sixteenth century, we cannot definitively ascribe influence of the Virgin Mary on all Zoharic texts, nor can we definitively deny that Kabbalists knew about the Virgin Mary.

The Eve/*Shekhinah* Dichotomy

THE ZOHARIC AUTHORS PROJECT their own erotic yearnings and their physiological needs onto the divine to convey their desire for God. Their emphasis on procreation allows them to participate in the act of creation.[73] And their theology responds to the needs of the Jewish communities in which they live. However, their use of feminine symbols is in no way a cry for gender parity. For medieval theosophical Kabbalists, the sefirotic realm provides an etiology for the status quo.

Gender and feminine imagery in medieval Kabbalah is a product of its time. Moshe Idel explains, "The theosophical theurgic Kabbalists create a metaphysical construct to validate given order."[74] Kabbalah is the creation of a male world in which women's inferiority is assumed and implicit. The kabbalistic gender binary is read in Aristotelian terms: men active, women passive; men form, women matter; and men right, women left. Just as courtly love literature has been described as a source of medieval misogyny and just as the rise of the Virgin Mary amplified the Eve and Mary dichotomy, feminine symbols in Zoharic literature validated and perpetuated the inferior status of Jewish women in medieval Iberia.

Postscript

WOMEN'S SPIRITUAL OPPORTUNITIES IMPROVED somewhat in early modern Kabbalah. After the expulsion of the Jews from Spain in 1492, the epicenter of kabbalistic activity moved to Safed. Whereas Spanish Kabbalah was the carefully guarded esoteric property of a few elite Jewish men, Safedian Kabbalists, though by no means populists, democratized certain theurgic elements of Kabbalah in an effort to hasten redemption and *tiqqun* (restoration). Pious acts by all Jews, including women, were believed to be instrumental in effecting changes in the cosmos, and, consequently, women may have achieved a new spiritual status. Some Kabbalists believed that both partners, not just the husband, needed to have the correct intention when engaging in physical union in order to empower *Shekhinah*.[75]

In the seventeenth and eighteenth centuries the Zohar was adapted and translated into Yiddish, giving women access to mystical literature and opening up new possibilities for their spiritual expressions. Chava Weissler describes how male and female writers used vernacular Kabbalah in *tkhines* (Yiddish supplications) to enrich women's observance.[76] Women participated actively in the heretical Sabbatian and Frankist movements, and many functioned as prophets.[77] In Hasidism, some women—most famously the Maid of Ludmir (Hannah Rochel Verbermacher)—functioned as spiritual leaders.

Jewish mysticism, however, was not immediately transformed into an egalitarian spiritual system. The accounts of these premodern women maintained the cultural norms of their period and reinforced the notion of mysticism as a social construct. The opportunities for women in Safed, Sabbatianism, and early Hasidism perpetuated rather than abolished the patriarchal status quo.[78] Ada Rapoport-Albert persuasively argues that the Maid of Ludmir tradition perpetuates rather than changes the status of women in the Jewish mystical tradition. Hannah Rochel Verbermacher denied her sexuality and led an ascetic, celibate life to pursue her spiritual and scholarly path. Once she was persuaded to marry and assumed her "rightful" position as wife in the Jewish world, she lost her following and she died in obscurity.[79]

We have begun to see a change in the modern period as feminist theologians and all spiritual seekers reclaim the feminine symbols in Kabbalah as their own.[80] In *Standing Again at Sinai*, Judith Plaskow advises:

> There are obvious advantages to having a feminine element in God that is a firmly established aspect of the tradition. Yet when the tradition is a male one—both with regard to Judaism in general and Kabbalism in particular—female images are apt to come with certain limitations. Two of the virtues on the image of the Shekhinah from a feminist perspective are that it is an image of divine immanence and an image of God in nonhierarchical relation. It deliberately offsets the picture of God as a dominating Other and at the same time fits well with the emphasis on mutual relationship in feminist spirituality. The Shekhinah, as opposed to the totally unknowable *kadosh barukh hu* (Holy One blessed be He), is precisely the aspect of God with which we can be in relation, and it is experienced in joint study, community gatherings, lovemaking, and other moments of common and intimate human connection. These positive aspects of the image are tied to its shortcomings, however, for this immanent, relational element in God has never been on equal footing with the ineffable masculine Godhead. . . . The Shekhinah is a usable image for feminists only if it is partly wrenched free from its original context, so that the tradition becomes a starting point for an imaginative process that moves beyond and transforms it.[81]

Pursuers of truth need to be honest about their sources. Zoharic literature provides spiritual seekers with the hermeneutical tools to find God in every verse of the Torah and a theological framework that gives meaning and agency to human existence. Jewish mystics throughout the ages have contextualized their understanding of the divine through their daily experiences and through Jewish texts. The Zoharic teachings can and should be unburdened by their patriarchal framework, but that framework should not be forgotten.

Notes

1 Feminine symbols and erotic imagery are essential to medieval Jewish mysticism and have been a central aspect of scholarship. It would be impossible to provide a complete picture of the multifaceted nature of the feminine in Kabbalah in a chapter-length work. This chapter is meant as an introduction to the major gender themes in Zoharic literature.

2 There are two types of Kabbalah: theosophical/theurgic and prophetic/ecstatic. Theosophical/theurgic Kabbalah, the focus of this paper, uses symbols to explore the inner workings of the sefirotic realm; ecstatic Kabbalah uses divine names and letters to achieve *unio mystica*. Although the emphases are different, there can be overlap between the two. Moshe Idel, "Defining Kabbalah: The Kabbalah of the Divine Names," in *Mystics of the Book*, ed. R. A. Herrera (New York: P. D. Lang, 1993), 97–122.

3 *Sefer ha-Zohar*, 3 vols., ed. Reuven Margaliot (Jerusalem: Mossad ha-Rav Kook, 1964). All references are to the Margaliot edition of the Zohar; all translations, unless noted, are taken from *The Zohar: Pritzker Edition*, ed. and trans. Daniel Matt (vols. 1–9), Nathan Wolski (vols. 10, 13), and Joel Hecker (vol. 12) (Stanford, CA: Stanford University Press, 2004–2018).

4 Moses Maimonides, *The Guide of the Perplexed*, 2 vols., ed. Shlomo Pines (Chicago: Chicago University Press, 1963), 1:1–36 (pp. 1: 21–85).

5 Maimonides, *Guide of the Perplexed*, 1:59 (p. 1: 139).

6 Maimonides, *Guide of the Perplexed*, 3:26–34 (pp. 2: 506–38).

7 Mark Brian Sendor, "The Emergence of Provençal Kabbalah: Rabbi Isaac the Blind's Commentary on Sefer Yetsirah." PhD diss., Harvard University, 1994.

8 Arthur Green, *A Guide to the Zohar* (Stanford, CA: Stanford University Press, 2004), 36.

9 Moshe Idel, *Kabbalah: New Perspectives* (New Haven, CT: Yale University Press, 1988), 173–99; Daniel Matt, "The Mystic and the Mizwot," in *Jewish Spirituality 1: From the Bible through the Middle Ages*, ed. Arthur Green (New York: Crossroads, 1986), 367–404.

10 Moshe Idel, "Nahmanides: Kabbalah, Halakhah, and Spiritual Leadership," in *Jewish Mystical Leaders and Leadership*, ed. M. Idel and M. Ostow (Northvale, NJ: Jason Aronson, 1998), 15–96; Elliot Wolfson, "By Way of Truth," *AJS Review* 14 (1989): 103–78.

11 Moshe Idel, "The Kabbalah's 'Window of Opportunities,' 1270–1290," in *Meʾah Sheʾarim: Studies in Medieval Jewish Spiritual Life in Memory of Isadore Twersky*, ed. Ezra Fleischer (Jerusalem: Hebrew University Magnes Press, 2001), 171–208.

12 Yehudah Liebes, "How the Zohar Was Written," in *Studies in the Zohar*, trans. Stephanie Nakache (Albany, NY: SUNY Press, 1993), 85–138; Ronit Meroz, "Zoharic Narratives and Their Adaptations," *Hispania Judaica Bulletin* 3 (2000): 3–63 (Hebrew); Daniel Abrams, "The Invention of the Zohar as a Book," *Kabbalah* 19 (2009): 7–142; Daniel Abrams, *Kabbalistic Manuscripts and Textual Theory* (Los Angeles: Cherub Press, 2010); Boaz Huss, *Like the Radiance of the Sky* (Jerusalem: Ben Zvi Institute and Bialik Institute, 2008) (Hebrew).

13 *Sefer ha-Zohar*, 3: 296a.

14 Daniel Abrams, *The Female Body of God in Kabbalistic Literature* (Jerusalem: Magnes Press, 2004) (Hebrew). On the *Shekhinah* as *'Atara*, see the many works of Elliot Wolfson, including, Elliot Wolfson, *Circle in the Square: Studies in the Use of Gender in Kabbalistic Symbolism (Albany: SUNY Press, 1995)*.

15 *Sefer ha-Zohar*, 1: 15b.

16 Translation my own.

17 Rachel Adler, *Engendering Judaism* (Jerusalem: JPS Press, 1998), 123.

18 *Sefer ha-Zohar*, 1: 55b, *Zohar: Pritzker Edition*, 1: 314.

19 Using a *gezerah shavah*, a rabbinic exegetical tool.

20 *Sefer ha-Zohar*, 3: 290a (*Idra Zuta*).

21 This understanding is most pronounced in the writings of Isaac the Blind's father, Abraham ben David (Rabad) Moshe Idel, *Kabbalah and Eros* (New Haven, CT: Yale University Press, 2005), 66.

22 It is important to note here that, though a fluid binary is the most common, it is certainly not the only representation of male and female dynamics in Kabbalah. Moshe Idel categorizes several different models of male and female in Kabbalah, including (1) the dyadic (the model I describe), (2) a triadic model in which a male power exists in-between two female powers (either wife or concubine), and (3) Elliot Wolfson's integrative model in which the feminine power is subsumed into the masculine, creating an androgynous male divinity. Idel, *Kabbalah and Eros*, 131–33. On the *sefirot* as male androgyne and traces of homoeroticism in kabbalistic literature, see the many articles and books by Elliot Wolfson, including Elliot Wolfson, *Language, Eros, Being: Kabbalistic Hermeneutics and Poetic Imagination* (New York: Fordham University Press, 2005), 142–89. On the *sefirot* as a female androgyne, see Abrams, *Female Body of God*, 68–91.

23 This interpretation of male and female in Kabbalah assumes and reinforces a heteronormative status quo. See *b. Yerushalmi* 63b–64a; *b. Genesis Rabbah* 17:2; and *b. Midrash Tehillim* 59:2. See also *Sefer ha-Zohar* 1: 34b, 47a, 55b, 150a–b, 165a, 182a, 233a–b, 239a, 248a; 2: 144b; 3: 5a–b, 7a, 7b, 17a, 33b–34a, 46b, 57b, 74b, 81b, 141b (IR), 145b, 148a. See also Idel, *Kabbalah and Eros*, 32–33; and Yehuda Liebes, "Messiah of the Zohar: On R. Simeon bar Yohai as a Messianic Figure," in *Studies in the Zohar*, ed. Yehuda Liebes; trans. Arnold Schwartz, Stephanie Nakache, and Penina Peli (Albany: SUNY Press, 1993), 68.

24 I am currently completing a book on the matriarchs in the Zohar. I devote a chapter to Leah.

25 Rabbinic literature often describes women in architectural terms—his home connotes his wife. Charlotte Fonrobert, *Menstrual Purity: Rabbinic and Christian Representations of Biblical Gender* (Stanford, CA: Stanford University Press, 2000), 40–68.

26 On *Binah* and redemption, see Moshe Idel, "The Jubilee in Jewish Mysticism," in *Millenarismi nelle cultura contemporanea: Con un'appendice su yovelabraico e giubileo cristiono*, ed. E. I. Rambaldi (Milan: Franco Angeli, 2000), 209–32.

27 *Sefer ha-Zohar*, 1: 261b; Lev. 25:8–13.

28 On the image of the stork, see Elisheva Baumgarten, *Practicing Piety in Medieval Ashkenaz: Men, Women, and Everyday Religious Observance* (Philadelphia: University of Pennsylvania Press, 2014), 1.

29 Academic literature on the *Shekhinah* is enormous. See, for example, Abrams, *Female Body of God*; Idel, *Kabbalah and Eros*; Arthur Green, "The Shekhinah, the Virgin Mary, and the Song of Songs," *AJS Review* 26 (2002): 1–52; Biti Roi, *Love of the Shekhina: Mysticism and Poetics in Tiqqunei Zohar* (Tel Aviv: Bar Ilan University Press, 2017) (Hebrew); Peter Schäfer, *Mirror of His Beauty* (Princeton, NJ: Princeton University Press, 2002); Gershom Scholem, "The Feminine Element of Divinity," in *On the Mystical Shape of the Godhead*, ed. Jonathan Chipman (New York: Schocken, 1991), 140–96; and Wolfson, *Language, Eros, Being*.

30 Danielle Jacquart and Claude Thomasset, *Sexuality and Medicine in the Middle Ages* (Princeton, NJ: Princeton University Press, 1988), 52–56.

31 *Sefer ha-Zohar*, 3: 296a. Ellen Haskell, *Suckling at My Mother's Breasts: The Image of a Nursing God in Jewish Mysticism* (Albany: SUNY Press, 2013), 65–89; Abrams, *Female Body of God*, 123–40.

32 Haskell, *Suckling at My Mother's Breasts*, 3–5; Abrams, *Female Body of God*, 125.

33 Lev. 15:19–24; Fonrobert, *Menstrual Purity*.

34 *Sefer ha-Zohar*, 3: 97a–b, 3: 255b; Elliot R. Wolfson, *The Book of the Pomegranate: Moses de Leon's Sefer ha-Rimmon* (Providence, RI: Brown Judaic Studies, 2020), 136. Note that, although *Binah* is described as having female physiological functions, I have not found a reference to her as a *niddah*. She is third in the flow of emanations and cannot come under the sway of the *sitra 'ahra*.

35 Caroline Walker Bynum, *Jesus as Mother: Studies in the Spirituality of the High Middle Ages* (Berkeley: University of California Press, 1982), 115–18.

36 Elliot Wolfson has devoted many books and articles to this theme. See, for example, Elliot Wolfson, "Crossing Gender Boundaries in Kabbalistic Ritual and Myth," in Elliot Wolfson, *Circle in the Square*, 99–104, 108–10.

37 Idel, "Jubilee in Jewish Mysticism," 226; Melila Hellner-Eshed, *A River Runs Through Eden: The Language of Mystical Experience in the Zohar* (Stanford, CA: Stanford University Press, 2011), 73; Wolfson, *Language, Eros, Being*, 70–77, 81–86.

38 Pregnancy is clearly the example of containment, and it is interesting to note that in some texts (e.g., *Sefer ha-Zohar*, 1: 232a) her pregnant state is viewed negatively.

39 The roots of the Hebrew term for menstruant (either *n-d-h* or *n-d-d*) suggest expelling. Moshe Greenberg, "The Etymology of Niddah (Menstrual Impurity)," in *Solving Riddles and Untying Knots*, ed. Ziony Zevit, Seymour Gitin, and Michael Sokoloff (Winona Lakes, IN: Eisenbrauns, 1995), 69–70.

40 Sharon Faye Koren, *Forsaken: The Menstruant in Medieval Jewish Mysticism* (Waltham, MA: Brandeis University Press, 2011), 75–83, 97.

41 Joseph Gikatilla, *Gates of Light / Sha'arei 'Orah*, trans. Avi Weinstein (New York: Harper Collins, 1994), 230, f. 59b.

42 *Sefer ha-Zohar*, 1: 153b, 1: 223a.

43 *Sefer ha-Zohar*, 1: 153b, 2: 354.

44 Sharon Faye Koren, "'Two Voices Heard in Castile': Rachel and Mary Weep for Their Children in the Age of the Zohar," in *Mothers in the Jewish Cultural Imagination*, ed. Jane Kanarek, Marjorie Lehman, and Simon Bronner (Liverpool, UK: Littman Library of Jewish Civilization, 2017), 225–53.

45 *Sefer ha-Zohar*, 2: 99a; *Zohar: Pritzker Edition*, 5: 33–34. This Zoharic passage is part of the "Old Man of *Mishpatim*" (*Sefer ha-Zohar*, 2: 94a–114a), an independent teaching on Exodus 21–24.

46 Elliot R. Wolfson, "The Hermeneutics of Visionary Experience: Revelation and Interpretation in the *Zohar*," *Religion* 18 (1988): 311–45.

47 Rabbinic literature often describes women in architectural terms. In *Mishnah Niddah* 2:5, rabbis compare female reproductive anatomy to a room (*ḥeder*), a hallway (*prozdor*), and an upper chamber (*aliyah*). The term *door* most often refers to the vagina. The *Shekhinah* as divine door is an unsubtle allusion to the intensely erotic relationship between her and the adept.

48 *Matronita* is an Aramaication of the Latin *matrona* (married woman). Hellner-Eshed, *A River Flows from Eden*, 73.

49 Elliot Wolfson, "Circumcision and the Divine Name: A Study in the Transmission of Esoteric Doctrine," *Jewish Quarterly Review* 78 (1987): 77–112; Elliot Wolfson, "Circumcision, Vision of God, and Textual Interpretation: From Midrashic Trope to Mystical Symbol," *History of Religions* 27 (1987): 189–215.

50 His house connotes his wife.

51 Green, *Guide to the Zohar*, 52.

52 The rabbis specify the requirements for marital debt according to profession. A man of leisure every day, a laborer twice a week, and so on, but according to *b. Ketubot* 62b, a Torah scholar is required to engage in sexual relations with his wife only on Friday night. On rabbinic ambivalence regarding sexuality, see Daniel Boyarin, *Carnal Israel: Reading Sex in Talmudic Culture* (Berkeley: University of California Press, 1993), 134–66.

53 Moshe Idel, "Sexual Metaphors and Praxis in the Kabbalah," in *The Jewish Family: Metaphor and Memory*, ed. David Kraemer (Oxford, UK: Oxford University Press, 1989), 191–224.

54 See, for example, *Sefer ha-Zohar*, 1: 50a.

55 Wolfson, *Language, Eros, Being*, 296–332, esp. 297–99.

56 Assi Farber imagines the life of Rashbi's wife in her heart-wrenching poem "The Kabbalist's Wife, Castile, End of the Thirteenth Century," *Te'uda* 21–22 (2007): 21 (Hebrew).

57 There are many new and exciting studies on Zoharic narratives. One of the earliest and most influential is Liebes, "Messiah of the Zohar," 1–84.

58 *Sefer ha-Zohar*, 1: 240b; *Zohar: Pritzker Edition*, 3: 467. See also *Sefer ha-Zohar*, 1: 93a, about a wife mentioned in the context of a *brit* invitation.

59 *Sefer ha-Zohar*, 2: 166a; *Zohar: Pritzker Edition* 5: 460–61.

60 Eitan Fishbane, *The Art of Mystical Narrative* (New York: Oxford University Press, 2018), 146.

61 Fishbane, *Art of Mystical Narrative*, 146.

62 *Sefer ha-Zohar*, 2: 166a; *Zohar: Pritzker Edition*, 5: 460–61.

63 According to *Mishnah Shabbat* 2:6, women's observance of *niddah, challah*, and lighting Sabbath candles forestalls death in childbirth. See also Fishbane, *Art of Mystical Narrative*, 146. In a shorter parallel teaching in *Midrash ha-Neelam Ruth*, the Rabbi Bun notices the innkeeper's daughter and teaches, "Through three things does a woman acquire merit: laws of menstrual impurity, separating a portion of dough, and kindling lamps." *Zohar Hadash Rut*, 86c; *Zohar: Pritzker Edition* 11: 216. *Midrash Tanhuma Buber, Metsora* 17, associates each with Eve's sins.

64 On the influence of Aristotelian thought on thirteenth-century Kabbalah, see Sharon Koren, "Kabbalistic Physiology," *AJS Review* 28 (2002): 317–39.

65 Judith Baskin, "Dolce of Worms: Women Saints in Judaism," in *Women Saints in World Religions*, ed. Arvind Sharma (Albany: SUNY University Press, 2000), 42.

66 Jewish women's absence from Spanish Kabbalah is a jarring contrast to spiritual trends in medieval European Christianity and Islam. Indeed, Caroline Bynum explains that by the thirteenth century—contemporaneous with the male circle of the Zohar in Castile—"Christian women were more likely than men to be mystics, to gain reputation based on their mystical abilities and . . . were primarily responsible for encouraging and propagating some of the most distinctive aspects of late medieval piety" (Bynum, *Jesus as Mother*, 172). Muslim women engaged in Sufi practices as early as the eighth century. The most celebrated Islamic female, mystic Rábi'a al-'Adawiyya of Basra, transformed the harsh asceticism of early Sufism into love mysticism in eighth-century Iraq. In thirteenth-century Iberia, Muhammed ibn 'Ali ibn al-'Arabī (1165–1240), one of the most well-known Andalusian mystics, studied with female Sufi guides; he, in turn, championed women's spiritual opportunities and developed a mystical theology that embraced and elevated women. See Annemarie Schimmel, *Mystical Dimensions of Islam* (Chapel Hill: University of North Carolina Press, 1975), 426–36; and Sa'diyya Shaikh, *Sufi Narratives of Intimacy: Ibn Arabi, Gender, and Sexuality* (Chapel Hill: University of North Carolina Press, 2012).

67 Wolfson, *Language, Eros, Being*, 312.

68 See Yom Tov Assis, "Sexual Behaviour in Medieval Hispano-Jewish Society," in *Jewish History: Essays in Honour of Chimen Abramsky*, ed. Ada Rapoport Albert and Steven J. Zipperstein (London: Peter Halban, 1988), 25–59; Yitzhak Baer, "The Historical Background of the *Raya Mehemmna*," *Tsion* 5 (1940): 1–44 (Hebrew); Yitzhak Baer, "Todros Abulafia and His Time," *Tsion* 2 (1936): 19–55 (Hebrew); Sharon Koren, "The Symbol of Rebekah in the Zohar," *Journal of Medieval Iberian Studies* 6, no. 1 (2014): 87–102; and Michal Kushnir-Oron, "A Sermon of Rabbi Todros Abulafia," *Da'at* 11 (1983): 47–51 (Hebrew).

69 Wolfson, "Circumcision and the Divine Name," 77–112; Wolfson, "Circumcision, Vision of God," 189–215.

70 *Sefer ha-Zohar*, 1: 131b.

71 Schäfer, *Mirror of His Beauty*; Green, "The Shekhinah."

72 Koren, "Two Voices Heard in Castile."

73 Idel, *Kabbalah and Eros*, 244–45.

74 Idel, *Kabbalah and Eros*, 70.

75 Idel, *Kabbalah and Eros*, 147–49.

76 Chava Weissler, "Vernacular Kabbalah," in *Gender and Jewish History*, ed. Marion Kaplan and Deborah Dash Moore (Bloomington: Indiana University Press, 2011), 215–32; Chava Weissler, *Voices of the Matriarchs: Listening to the Prayers of Early Modern Jewish Women* (Boston: Beacon Press, 1998).

77 Ada Rapoport-Albert, *Women and the Messianic Heresy of Sabbatai Zevi: 1666–1816* (Oxford, UK: Oxford University Press, 2011).

78 Rapoport-Albert, *Women and the Messianic Heresy*.

79 Ada Rapoport-Albert, "On Women in Hasidism, S. A. Horodecky, and the Maid of Ludmir Tradition," in *Jewish History: Essays in Honour of Chimen Abramsky*, ed. Ada Rapoport-Albert and Steven Zipperstein (London: Peter Alban, 1988), 508. For a different perspective, see Nehemiah Polen, "Miriam's Dance: Radical Egalitarianism in Hasidic Thought," *Modern Judaism* 12, no. 1 (1990): 17–18, 26; and Naftali Loewenthal, "'Daughter/Wife of Hasid' or 'Hasidic Woman'?" *Jewish Studies* 40 (2000): 21–28. Koren, *Forsaken*, 3–4.

80 Chava Weissler, "The Meaning of the Shekhinah in the Jewish Renewal Movement," in *Women Remaking American Judaism*, ed. Riv Ellen Prell (Detroit: Wayne State University Press, 2007), 51–81; Chava Weissler, "Women of Vision in the Jewish Renewal Movement," in *New Age Judaism*, ed. Celia Rothenberg and Anne Vallely (London: Vallentine Mitchell, 2008), 52–72.

81 Judith Plaskow, *Standing Again at Sinai: Judaism from a Feminist Perspective* (New York: Harper Collins, 1991), 139–40.

JEWISH WOMEN IN
EARLY MODERN ITALY

FEDERICA FRANCESCONI

THE OPENING PAGE OF *Orah Hayyim* (Way of Life), in a 1435 manuscript from Mantua of Jacob ben Asher's legal code *Arba'ah Turim* (Four Rows), is representative of Italian Jewish life and perhaps also women's place in it. It is illuminated in the international Gothic style dominant in the area, features full borders with exuberant acanthus florals inhabited by putti and miniature figures typical of Italian illumination, and showcases an illustration depicting a scene related to the text. Men and women seem to pray together in a small synagogue, all wearing *tallitot* (prayer shawls, at the time usually associated only with men), around the *aron ha-kodesh* (Torah ark) without separation of the sexes (*mechitzah*).[1] Such a synagogue was likely arranged in a room in a well-off Jewish house in Mantua; the room was probably used for storage during the week and was transformed into a prayer space during the Jewish holidays. The synagogue would have been attended by a relatively small community, whose settlement started as a result of the municipality inviting a Jewish moneylender to move to the city. The domestic overlapped with the communal, and during the special time of Shabbat and other Jewish holidays a domestic place was turned into a community space, made sacred every time the Torah scroll was taken out of the *aron ha-kodesh*. The combination of artistic Italian elements in the masterful layout of the page and the halakhic contents of the book mirror the cultural hybridization that characterized Italian Jewry.[2] Read through the lens of gender, despite the norms this text espoused, but, as perhaps the absence of the *mechitzah* makes clear, we can even hypothesize that Jewish women appeared as prayer performers, cross-dressers, and ultimately actors standing as equals to men in front of God. These female roles were lost, negotiated, and even regained in evolving Italian Jewish communities through the late medieval and early modern ages.

The opening page of *Oraḥ Ḥayyim* in the *Arba'ah Turim* by Jacob ben Asher, preserved in Cod. Ross. 555, fol. 12v. (1435) from Mantua. Biblioteca Apostolica Vaticana, Vatican City. Photograph © Ursula and Kurt Schubert Archive, Center for Jewish Art, Jerusalem.

By the late fifteenth century, after the medieval expulsions from England, France, Germany, Spain, and Portugal, Italian Jewish communities in Northern and Central Italy became safe ports for Ashkenazic and Sephardic Jewish refugees. Even after the expulsions from the Kingdoms of Sicily (1492–93) and Naples (1510), Italy remained the only Western European region in which Jews could live in relative stability. New challenges affected not only Italian Jewish women and their families during the sixteenth century but also Jews from the Ottoman Empire, Eastern Europe, and conversos from the Iberian Peninsula who settled in Italy. In 1516 the government of the Serenissima in Venice established the first Italian ghetto, a restricted quarter where Jews were forced to reside, in an attempt to establish a compromise between the religious teachings of the Catholic state and its socioeconomic needs. Jewish lives were also dramatically affected in the second half of the sixteenth century by conversionary efforts initiated by Paul IV (r. 1555–1559) and Counter-Reformation policies that targeted various forms of European heresy, including baptized Jews seeking to return to Judaism. The Talmud was publicly burned in 1553; and the bull *Cum Nimis Absurdum* (1555), which created the Roman ghetto, restricted Jewish economic activity and property ownership in the Papal States,[3] and ultimately led to the establishment of ghettos throughout the Italian peninsula and local expulsions.[4]

In Venice, Rome, Florence, Ferrara, Mantua, Modena, and elsewhere, ghettoized Jews were intentionally secluded as polluters of the civic Christian body. They were oppressed by state fiscal pressures and violent intrusions from the Inquisition and the Case dei Catecumeni (Neophyte Houses) and, in the Papal States, were purposefully impoverished in an attempt to push them toward conversion. Still, they pursued a complex, ongoing process of cultural, social, and legal negotiation. The walls of the Italian ghettos enclosed Jewish life in a permanent state of separation from the Christian world but did not bar continuous exchange with the outside society and culture.[5]

The restrictions imposed on Jewish life and ghettoization coincided with the recession of Jewish women from public life. This process was paralleled by women's retreat from the religious sphere, the masculinization of Jewish spaces, and the reconfiguration of the female domain. These changes were related to the consolidation of many local Jewish mercantile and male-centered elites, the emergence of new forms of Jewish kabbalistic piety, and Counter-Reformation influences. Rabbinic authorities reimagined the reality of Jewish women's lives in the domestic domain and did so with unprecedented sophistication, including new rituals and prayers specifically for women. Through a slow process of feminization invested in the house, female identities were shaped by new forms of cultural agency, learning and apprenticeship, frater-nalism, and devotion, domestic and public.[6]

In this chapter I explore early modern Jewish women's lived experience by taking into consideration options available to women of various regions, social classes, and life statuses. The early modern period in Jewish history has no firmly established chronological boundaries. I single out the period between the early sixteenth century and the end of the eighteenth century. I address rabbis' and elite men's prescriptive pronouncements about the female nature and ways in which women's choices were conditioned and limited alongside the new options men were imagining—a complexity often neglected or underestimated by Jewish and general historians. I concentrate on four main areas: rabbinic and secular attitudes toward gender and women; women's agency in Jewish society, confraternity, and family; religious devotion, book culture, and literary expression; and ritual life and material culture in the domestic, religious, and public domains. In so doing, I mine rabbinic literature; notarial wills; confraternity *pinkasim* (record books); correspondence from Jewish, municipal, and ecclesiastical institutions; records of rabbinic tribunals; and records of trials and testimonies released in Jewish civil courts, civic magistracies, and local Inquisitions—all read in light of scholarship produced in the last thirty years. In addition to these written archives, I also address material culture and the built environment.

Ambivalent Jewish Male Writers:
Reflections of Real Women and Female Agency?

NOT UNLIKE THEIR CHRISTIAN counterparts, Jewish male writers in the six-teenth and seventeenth centuries expressed convictions that women were men-tally weak and more prone to frivolity and vice in the contemporaneous debate known as *querelle de femmes*. Some expressed obsessions regarding women's supposed uncontrolled sexual desire and cowardice in a variety of media—ethical works, poetry, and sermons. They often pitted the good woman and the evil woman against each other. In his poem "Against Women Who Pursue Religious Studies," Immanuel Frances (1618–1710) states that, whereas the good woman concentrates her efforts on fostering the piety of her children, the evil one reinforces her debauchery through religious studies and knowl-edge of the Torah.[7] Frances's attitude reflects a long rabbinic tradition against women's literacy and the learning of the Torah, but his view was not unequiv-ocally shared. In fact, in Italy prescriptive literature, rabbinic imagination, and actual practice developed ambiguous and intriguing realities.

In the fifteenth century, Jewish women were not encouraged to devote themselves to the study of the Torah and the Talmud. Nonetheless, quite a few worked successfully as copyists of Hebrew books. They encountered no opposition in doing so, because of their expertise in Hebrew and halakhic literature, and were proud of their work, as evidenced in the prayers and dedications that they composed and attached. The note that Paula added to a copy of a biblical commentary made for herself and the members of her household reads, "Thus is concluded this work, the Commentary on the Prophets, copied by Paula, daughter of R. Abraham the Scribe . . . in the city of Rome. . . . May the Omnipresent allow us to read it, me and my seed and my seed's seed to the end of all generations."[8]

In his commentary to *Eshet Ḥayil* (1606) Abraham ben Hananiah Yagel de Gallichi (1553–ca. 1623), a celebrated scholar, physician, and kabbalist who lived between Mantua and Modena, describes this ambivalent atmosphere. He addresses men and married women as equals in relation to their reciprocal obligations and respective duties but elaborates on the potentially ambivalent duality of women. He expresses strong concern regarding the negative consequences of women, under the category of the "other woman," contrasted with the woman of valor: becoming too zealous with fasts, prayers, and wearing sackcloth and neglecting their husbands. Yagel's concerns also extend to the entire household that would be neglected. By contrast, referring to the archetype in Proverbs 31, at the center of a long tradition of commentaries by Italian Jewish scholars starting with Emanuel of Rome (1261–1328) and Messer Leon (ca. 1427–ca. 1497), Yagel includes instructing her children and household members to follow God's commandments and providing food for the poor among the woman of valor's duties.[9] She was also to wear modest clothes and jewelry, because her heart should be only for her husband, her household, and her father in heaven. As Roni Weinstein demonstrates, Yagel's woman of valor, through her conduct, shapes the masculine roles in the household and affects moral and worldly inclinations, sexual passions, and the relationship between God and all household members. Finally, her embrace of virtue and moral balance cultivates her family's worth of divine remuneration for their good deeds.[10]

Some Jewish women became partners to their husbands in the professional arena, even though their presence is concealed in the official records of guilds, charters, and official correspondence, where only husbands are typically listed. Autobiographies, notarial acts, and inquisitorial records reveal a more variegated reality. Yagel himself mentions that in the early 1570s he had an official partnership with Rina, the wife of Jacob de Lacairo, for a bank in the town of Luzzara that ended in bankruptcy and consequently Yagel's imprisonment.[11] Only because of the inquisitorial trial against the Jewish banker and philanthropist Moisè Modena (1539–1630) from Modena (the surnames of Italian Jews often came from where they resided) do we know that his wife, Marianna, was an active partner in the family bank and that her daughters-in-law were probably involved as well.[12]

The "other woman" that Yagel describes—the one who is too devout—had her Catholic counterpart in the living saints (*sante vive*), tertiaries, and independent religious women who were active from the mid-fifteenth through the early sixteenth century in Italy.[13] In the mid-sixteenth century the confinement of these women, who had previously found satisfying roles outside convents, became one of the primary goals of the new social discipline imposed by Catholic reformers. Whereas Christian religious women were cloistered, Jewish women were ghettoized. Christian religious women's bodies were made recognizable and, at the same time, anonymous through specific dress according to different orders. Jewish women's bodies had been publicly stigmatized through the imposition of the badge, enforced in Christian Europe since 1215. Later in Italy, Jews were marked through gendered objects; women were obliged to wear earrings, and men had to wear a badge.[14]

Using texts from Proverbs and the Song of Songs in his 1556 bilingual (Hebrew and Italian) poem "Magen Nashim" (In Defense of Women), Leone de Sommi Portaleone (1527–1592), the celebrated playwright from Mantua, defended women by focusing on men's wrongdoings to women and the virtues of women by chronicling Greek, Roman, and Jewish women of valor.[15] In so doing, he paralleled the Christian-Western tradition that extends from Christine de Pizan (1364–1430) to Cornelius Agrippa (1486–1535), questioning consolidated beliefs in innate gender traits and naturally dictated gender roles by holding up illustrious, knowledgeable women of the past to refute the charges that male scholars had made against woman's nature.[16] De Sommi also expanded the Western canon, praising not only the Jewish heroines Jael, Hadassah (Esther), and Judith, appreciated at the time in the humanistic tradition as strong women (*femmes fortes*) and as the center of new debates on the *querelle de femmes*, but also Rachel, Leah, Abigail, and Hannah. By so doing, he emphasizes the importance of the biblical matriarchs and heroines in their own Jewish tradition in relation to Christian writers and painters.

To de Sommi, the principle of love and the role of women in its domain were a larger social issue that went beyond the personal sphere or literary convention. In his *Tsaoth b'Dihutha d'Kiddushin* (Comedy of Betrothal), written in Hebrew, the author describes the trials of Jewish youth in matters of love, emphasizing young Jewish women's struggle for free consent in marriage and the pressure exercised by both parents and Jewish society at large to make matches based on wealth, advantage, and dowry.[17] The vicissitudes of love for the two protagonists, Beruriah and Yedidiah, whose engagement is broken by Beruriah's parents because of the apparent disinheritance of Yedidiah at the death of his father, reflect emerging social issues. In the sixteenth century dowry inflation was challenging Jewish communities and *patria potestas* (parental, especially paternal, rights) at times clashed with the next generation's inclinations. Similar trends have been traced among contemporary Italian Christians. They are at the center of *Le tre sorelle* (The Three Sisters), another comedy by de Sommi, written in Italian in 1588, which focuses on the world of Italian Christian youth in the sixteenth century.[18]

A Jewish synod held in Ferrara in 1555 reiterated that no man could betroth a woman except with her consent and also stipulated that a daughter could not be married (*nissuin*) "without the assent of two of her closest relatives, should her father be dead.[19]" Kenneth Stow examines how in the same period Italian rabbis were more ready than others to take into consideration the principle of *ḥibbah* (the affection or even sexual desire) of both boys and girls. Italian rabbis extended the halakhic category of the refusal (*me'un*), traditionally applied to betrothals, when orphaned adolescent girls under the age of 12 claimed the right to terminate these matches. In Italy the *me'un* began to be applied to engagements (*shiddukhin*) and betrothals (*kiddushin*) that were both legally binding and used by adolescent girls older than 12, orphaned or not, who were obtaining the right to terminate engagements; Menachem Azariah da Fano wrote that "even a grown daughter [*bogeret*] [can] refuse [*me'un*] her father's initiative."[20] In sixteenth-century Rome young Jewish women succeeded on the grounds that both the prospective groom and the bride "must suit each other, he and she, she and he" or because "they don't love each other." In 1537 Lariccia, a poor girl, declared herself to be "the unhappiest of all women" because of an unwanted match. She had been crying for days, saying that her brothers had tricked her into an engagement and then her father had tricked her into a betrothal. According to a washerwoman who testified on her behalf, Lariccia had clearly said to her father, "I do not like this man, nor do I want him." Lariccia was neither an orphan nor had she been betrothed under the age of 12. Nevertheless, assisted by the lawyer and rabbi Pompeo del Borgo, she advocated the *me'un* and was freed from any engagement. In the halakhic system and rabbinic court young women's affection, desire, and attraction mattered.[21] Yet, to have access to social stability and fulfill Jewish values through good marriages, girls such as Lariccia needed a decent dowry. To achieve this, Jewish maidens often left their homes to work as domestic servants for Jewish families in their own or other Italian cities, hoping to save enough money. In the seventeenth century this phenomenon became quite common in all Jewish communities in Northern Italy and Central and Eastern Europe.

Gender, Community, and
Domestic Service in the Jewish Household

LACK OF PRIVACY AND physical proximity, conditions apparent in the ghettos, where space was constrained, could foster the development of intense sentiments. In the Venetian ghetto Italian and Sephardic mercantile households hosted Jewish, Muslim, and Christian female co-workers, servants, and slaves—some Spanish, Black African, and mixed race—and thus became an unusual crossroads for multiethnic and multireligious communities.[22] Reciprocal declarations of affection, loyalty, and gratitude are often expressed in testaments and other notarial acts dictated by mistresses and servants. Despite their disadvantaged social class and limited choices, Jewish servants in Venice exercised a certain agency in the disposal of their modest wealth through donations and bequests to individuals, surrogate families, and institutions. Pacientia Mora was a Levantine Black servant in the house of the Sephardic matron Rachel Aboaf; she dictated her last will in September 1664. She left her small estate to her mistress and friends in the ghetto.[23] This process was not unidirectional; some mistresses left their assets to their servants.[24] Rabbinic literature seems to have moved toward appreciation of affection in the household beyond close family relatives. Some Italian responsa and Hebrew contracts from the second half of the sixteenth century include reciprocal expressions of affection between male and female householders and their female servants, as do rabbinic discourses and prescriptive literature.[25] Moreover, as happened in contemporary European Christian households, many girls were expected to be trained in domestic and professional skills. Contracts of apprenticeship were stipulated between the young woman's family and her future employers in front of notaries. For example, in Rome in 1541 the Jewish matron Fioruccia accepted the daughter of a certain Annella (also Jewish) as an apprentice for one year to teach her various *lavori femminili* (fine embroidery and so forth) that Fioruccia's own daughter knew.[26]

The cohabitation of householders and servants or co-workers could lead to the development of illicit sexual relationships. Although women's involvement in these relationships was not always due to physical coercion, often coercive tactics were at play.[27] Apparently Jewish courts intervened only when pregnancy made an illegitimate relationship public. Only then did the systemic problems that poorer young Jewish women faced become visible to the Jewish elites, who wanted to control events that could have destabilizing repercussions on order and hierarchy in the community. If servants were minors, their employers were considered responsible for their safety—in this context, their virginity—and in cases of pregnancy employers were obliged to pay the expenses of childbirth, nursing, and support for the child until adulthood. If the woman and her seducer were both single, the court tended to pressure him into marrying her; if that was not possible, the father rather than the mother was responsible for the care of the child resulting from illicit sex. In 1749 the physician Moisè Vaigler of Mantua was forced to marry his servant, Rachel Arezzi from Modena, whom he had impregnated. He had to add to the *ketubbah* that he would never divorce the woman and that he would take care of their child, recognizing him as his own son. In fact, when he tried to divorce Rachel two years later, the Jewish courts of both Modena and Mantua denied his petition.[28] According to a 1778 *psak halakhah* (legal decision) written in Modena, unprecedented in the European context, the first responsibility for pregnant maidservants fell to the *ba'al habait* (the owner of the house); the *kahal kadosh* (Jewish community) was absolved from obligation and discouraged householders from corrupting Jewish young women under their roofs. Tolerating this behavior risked both public shame and economic burden.[29] In Venice, rabbis found halakhic solutions for transitioning Euro-African children of Italian and Sephardic Jewish men, trapped in a liminal ambiguous ethnic, religious, and social status, into Judaism; in their responsa, bias against blackness is absent.[30]

Jewish courts and civil magistracies handled cases where things went wrong, and notarial acts, such as marriage contracts, often depict everyday reality. Smeralda Foa, who "had with her toil earned [a dowry] as a servant over the course of about eighteen years in the house of the merchant Moyse Pescarollo," was married in Turin in 1721.[31] Sara Tedeschi from Turin worked as a servant girl in Venice, and "with her works, industries, and salaries" provided herself with a dowry and married in 1773.[32] Although they may have married later, after long terms of service, the dowries of these maidservants were no smaller than those of more fortunate girls both Jewish and non-Jewish in eighteenth-century Turin.[33] Recent studies have stressed the importance of the dowry in sixteenth-century Rome, seventeenth-century Livorno, and eighteenth-century Turin as a tool to preserve family estates and to ensure the growing autonomy of Italian Jewish women from the early modern through the modern era.[34]

A Multilingual World: Religious Devotion, Book Culture, and Literary Expression

STARTING IN THE FOURTEENTH century or earlier, dedicating a literary work (such as de Sommi's) to a woman was not a rarity in the Italian Jewish and

Christian milieus. Jewish women could be both dedicatees and recipients of precious illuminated manuscripts, such as the fourteenth-century master-piece *Golden Haggadah*, given in 1602 to Rosa, the daughter of Rabbi Yoav Gallico, and her groom, the teacher Elia, son of Rabbi Menahem Rava, in Carpi.[35]

In Old Yiddish literature the production of books dedicated to individual women or the female public appears most prominently in Italy. Genres of Yid-dish books, such as Bible translations, that would as a rule be addressed to male readers only or, less often, to readers of both genders were addressing women. The translation of the Pentateuch published by Leo Bresh in Cremona in 1560 adds a distinct mention of a female addressee and promises "every woman or girl will know about God's Torah and what piousness means when she reads this book every Saturday and holiday and does not waste her time reading other kinds of Yiddish books which are nonsense."[36] Here the translator is probably referring to secular literature such as *Paris un' Viene* (Verona, 1594), an adaptation of the fourteenth-century chivalric poem composed originally in Provençal and then translated into French, which contains the first roman-tic declaration in a Yiddish book. Moreover, the author criticizes men's neglect of the study of the Bible and its negative repercussions for women: "When the married women and single women and the young girls see that the men do not study, they don't either."[37]

In both Catholic and Jewish literary production, whether in Hebrew, Yiddish, or Italian translation, the general process of the masculinization of society also involved attempts to limit women's access to secular culture by pushing them into a cloistered sort of *bibliotheca selecta*. In 1614 Yaakov ben Elhanan Heilprun, translator of Rabbi Binyamin Aharon Slonik's *Seder mitzvot nashim* (Book of the Commandments for Women), printed in Padua in 1625, wrote in his introduction, "And so your daughters, even if they are not betrothed and are not yet brides, should read it. . . . It is less harmful to read this book than Ariosto, the Hundred Novellas [*Decameron*], Amadís de Gaula and other such profane literature that are forbidden to [be] read on the Shabbat as Moses our teacher stated, since one can only learn obscenity and vanity from them."[38] Only a few years earlier Antonio Possevino, the noted Jesuit scholar and author of *Bibliotheca Selecta*, one of the masterpieces of the Counter-Reformation, charged that the *Amadís de Gaula* and Ariosto's works diminished piety and opened the door to magic, libidinous desire, and satanic thoughts.[39] However, despite fears about corrupting Italian texts, female read-ership increased tremendously among Jewish women in Italy, as elsewhere in Europe, as Jews embraced the invention of print. Venice became one of the main centers for Jewish books in Hebrew and Yiddish through the eighteenth century, and the publication of multilingual books of customs, precepts, and prayers written for women proliferated.[40]

In the seventeenth century Italian rabbis attempted to confine Jewish women to the domestic sphere, and likely some women supported these efforts. Aaron Berekhiah Modena (1578–1639) from Modena, one of the most influential Kabbalists in seventeenth-century Italy, imagined women's lives in the domestic domain and articulated the sacred aspects of female Jewish space with sophistication. According to Modena, a woman in difficult labor must be given a candle from the synagogue to light herself to draw merit from the blessings she usually pronounced on Shabbat and holidays, including the Day of Atonement, to speed the safe delivery of her baby. Modena thus introduced a new feminine ritual. The moment of birth was considered crucial because the *sefirot* (spheres) are attracted here from below, and the life of the mother and her baby are thus in danger. The connection between the woman in danger and the candle mirrors the link between purity and light: If the woman does not respect the prescriptions of the laws of purity, she puts herself as well as her unborn child in danger.[41] In Modena's conception, however, women were not to be unsupervised; kabbalistic rituals, such as the husband's recitation of Psalm 20, rather than the rituals of a midwife or female relative or friend would ensure a more proper and holy childbirth. The presence of the husbands in the room would also ensure that Jewish parturients held a candle instead of a Torah scroll to their breasts to relieve them from the distress of a closed womb, a custom widespread in Italian Jewish communities (and elsewhere) and widely denounced by local rabbis.[42] Modena's *Maavar Yabbok* (1626) includes two other Hebrew prayers, known in Yiddish versions in early modern Europe, to be recited at the moment of childbirth. The first invokes the merit of Sarah, Rachel, Hannah, and other barren women, and the second requests that God, who heard the prayers of the matriarchs, hear this prayer as well.[43]

Lived experience did not conform, at least not completely, to prescriptions of the public arena as the domain of men, and the domestic space as the natural environment for women. Italian literature that was not supposed to be in the hands of Jewish men and that certainly was not to fall into those of Jewish women seemingly did. In 1636 Modena inquisitor Giacomo da Lodi discovered that 35-year-old Allegra Carmi Poggetti, wife of Rabbi Leone and mother of three toddlers, was in possession of a number of non-Hebrew books kept in the closet of her bedroom: Boccaccio's *Genealogia degli Dei*, Isabella Andreini's "La chanzione" (probably *Mirtilla: Pastorale*, published for the first time in 1588), Ovid's *Metamorphoses*, and Dante's *Divina Commedia*.[44] The discovery of Allegra Poggetti's books allows for a broader understanding of dual gender

Jewish readership and culture. Widowhood could at times provide important learning opportunities. After raising her grandchild Aaron Berekhiah, the widow Fioretta Modena chose to move to Safed at the end of the sixteenth century because of her desire to pursue kabbalistic studies. She died shortly after her arrival.[45] A similar choice would have been inconceivable during the years of marriage, but getting back their dowries allowed women to make choices, such as entering a second marriage, supporting their children financially, and even embarking on new cultural, religious, and devotional paths. In a *siddur* (prayer book) that a certain Giuseppe Coen commissioned for his wife, Yehudit Kutscher, in 1786, Psalm 20 is included with instructions that the husband recite it for his wife, although interestingly this text of the psalm, unlike the original, addresses a woman and not a man.[46] Finally, despite Modena's wishes, Italian Jewish women continued to hold a Torah scroll while lying in bed during childbirth.[47]

Perhaps the most intriguing—and exceptional—case of female cultural accomplishment and its challenges during the ghetto age was that of the Venetian Sara Copio Sullam (1592–1641), a poet, playwright, and patron of the literati. Sara Copio was born to a mercantile Jewish family and married Jacob Sullam, an illustrious banker. In her father's house she was well educated in both Hebrew and Italian literature, classics, philosophy, and music. Contemporary Italian Jewish authors' cultural formation was based in disciplines such as Kabbalah, rhetoric, and historiography, scholastic and Neoplatonic philosophy, magic, medicine and the sciences, and music.[48] We can assume that the education Copio Sullam received was similar to that described in 1523 by a Jewish observer from Salonica. He stated that daughters of wealthy Italian Jewish families in Parma were trained in rhetoric and "Boethius, Terentius, Ovid, Tullius [Cicero], Petrarch, Dante and many other similar books together with works on history from the time of Carthage and Troy [*Aeneid* and *Iliad*], and some that can be read in the idiomatic language and Studia Humanitatis."[49] The emphasis was more on Renaissance culture than Jewish subjects. At times this uneven education could become an important resource for cultural survival and even literary production. Limited in her access to Kabbalah, the Hebrew Bible and biblical commentaries, and Talmudic treatises, Copio Sullam reconfigured her intellectual world to center on poetry and literature with Jewish and secular subjects.

Once married, Copio Sullam opened a literary salon—attended mostly by Christian men of letters along with the celebrated rabbi Leone Modena—in her new home in the Venetian *ghetto vecchio*. Christian intellectuals gave her lessons, sonnets, and letters, and in exchange she provided financial backing and intellectual conversation. In 1618 Copio Sullam initiated an intellectual correspondence with noted Genoese poet Ansaldo Cebà (1565–1623), and, ultimately, he pressured her to apostatize. Her refusal led to her ruin and accusations of blasphemy, plagiarism, and dishonesty from Cebà and other Christian intellectuals.[50] In the summer of 1621 she published a manifesto in Italian rebutting accusations from Baldassarre Bonifacio (1585–1659), a cleric, jurist, and intellectual who belonged to her literary circle. Bonifacio accused her publicly of blasphemy and the denial of the immortality of the soul, a common belief in Judaism and Christianity. In her manifesto Copio Sullam articulated her defense using the Torah and its humanistic goals, explaining the history of the immortality of the soul drawing on Jewish historian Josephus (first century CE) and the historical Jesus from Matthew's gospel, and defending her Jewish identity, principles, and beliefs. In doing so, she used the Hebrew Bible and the New Testament, Aristotle, Virgil, and Dante.[51] She also characterized Bonifacio's attacks against her as a pretext to attack all women; in so doing, she used a gendered perspective and even the "woman question" as rhetorical strategies. Copio Sullam's was not only a story of attacks against a Jew who became too visible and then refused conversion, but also an episode in the long history of defamation of intellectual women in seventeenth-century Venice whose social profiles did not correspond to what Virginia Cox defines as "the 'honest' [Christian] woman of good family, socially integrated and conventional in her mores."[52] Only the fact of being Jewish excluded Copio Sullam from this idealistic social profile. Arcangela Tarabotti (1604–1652), a self-proclaimed dissident nun, shared a similar destiny. Copio Sullam survived this plot, as well as accusations of plagiarism and attempts to extort money from her, but her public persona as a Venetian of letters was permanently destroyed.[53]

Jewish Women, Fraternalism, and Professional Activities

IN EARLY MODERN ITALIAN Jewish communities, the presence of women in the public sphere was at times challenged by cultural transformations and negotiated with the lay and rabbinic male establishments, as emerges in the history of Jewish confraternities. According to Elliott Horowitz, new forms of Jewish piety, such as the adoption of Lurianic Kabbalah, and Counter-Reformation influences, such as restriction of popular expressions that were considered dangerous and subversive, led to a change in Italian Jewish society. Jewish women were accepted into the new Italian Jewish confraternities during the sixteenth century.[54] The confraternity Hevrat Nizharim (heedful, observant) was established in Bologna, the second city in the Papal States after Rome, in

1546. It had religious and philanthropic purposes that included the observation of three major precepts: learning Torah, praying together, and participating in charity work. Its statutes show that, at the time of its foundation, women were admitted as members.[55] A civil trial in Bologna reveals that an affluent and illustrious woman, Fiammetta da Pisa, the wife of one of the most important Jewish bankers in the city, was leading the female chapter in 1556, the year the ghetto was established in Bologna. Local Christian judges identified her as "the *priorissa* [prioress] of the Jewish women in the city."[56] Her story, as well as those of the other members of the Ḥevrat Nizharim, were not recovered beyond this trial, probably because of the expulsion of the Jews from Bologna in 1569.

In the following century ghettoized Italian Jewish societies were in transformation. Fearing women's potentially transgressive behaviors, seventeenth-century Jewish confraternities in Italy appear as almost exclusively male spaces. The only exceptions were dowering sisterhoods, often known as Compagnia delle Donne, for which we have scattered documentation in Rome, Venice, and Florence.[57] However, across Europe and the Atlantic world, the most successful dowering societies were established, organized, and led by male Jewish merchants, because, according to the Talmud, marrying off a son is one of the six obligations that a father has in raising him (the others are circumcision, redemption of a firstborn son through a donation to a priest, and teaching him Torah, a profession, and to swim) (*b. Kiddushin* 29a). In seventeenth-century Venice, the Italo-Ashkenazic Ḥassi Betulot, the Ponentine Hebrà para Casar Orphaos, primarily composed of ex-conversos and their descendants, and the Levantine Ḥassi Betulot were active. Women donated funds, but the members were all men.[58] In seventeenth-century Italy the only Jewish dowering confraternity that allowed the participation of both men and women was the Hebrà para Cazar Orfas e Donzelas, established in Livorno in 1644.[59]

By the eighteenth century, women had regained a voice and role in communal charity. When on November 22 of 1735 twenty-two well-to-do Jewish women in Modena established the sisterhood Soʿed Ḥolim (to benefit the sick) they took a firm stand on mutual aid for women.[60] Inspired by the famous verse "You shall love your neighbor as yourself [Lev. 19:18]," the stated aim of the sisterhood was to "help and assist all sick women, rich and poor, in the ghetto." The *ḥevrah* was established in the house of the founder, Miriam Rovigo. Its activities were remarkably wide ranging. The confraternity employed women and girls over 10 years old as assistants, servants, administrators, and representatives, and it involved them in their weekly and monthly meetings; both confraternity members and day laborers in charge of medical assistance to the sick practiced various forms of midwifery as well as gynecology.

Fifteen years after its founding, the members of So'ed Ḥolim were making "public" donations of community charity: dowries to poor Jewish girls and wood for the fireplaces of all poor families in the ghetto.[61] The confraternity honored the minor holiday of the new moon (Rosh Chodesh of the month of Tevet), of special significance to women; on that day they avoided heavy work and demonstrated the sanctity of their confraternity through an explicit reference to the month in which its activities began.[62] Over the years the women of So'ed Ḥolim issued loans and invested in bonds and property, using collective profits for their activities. So'ed Ḥolim worked to ease living conditions through systematic charity provided to the most vulnerable groups in Modena's ghetto. The confraternity offered "invisible" Jewish women a degree of agency without subverting the existing social and halakhic structures.[63]

Ritual Life, Material Culture, and Gendered Apprenticeship

IF PERHAPS IN MANTUA in 1435 women would pray publicly together with men wearing *tallitot* in a synagogue, according to a 1478 manuscript copied by the illustrious rabbi Abraham Farissol, in the morning in the intimacy of her own bedroom at least one Jewish matron proudly recited, "Praised are You, Lord our God, King of the Universe, Who has made me a woman and not a man."[64] The normative male version of the prayer, established by the Rabbis in the Talmud, is "Blessed are You . . . who has not made me a woman," with women reciting, "who has made me according to Your will."[65] The rituals of these fifteenth-century Jewish women are intriguing not only for the obvious devotional challenges to men's primacy but also because those challenges were associated with objects—*tallitot* and *siddurim* (Hebrew plural for *siddur*). At times, objects created for, donated to, and owned by Jewish women brought together linguistic, domestic, and devotional elements. A well-known and precious fifteenth-century *niello* small casket that was used to contain keys and that was presumably donated to a young bride has representations and inscriptions attached to the front, illustrating the three commandments for women: *challah* (a woman dressed in Renaissance style kneads bread dough), *niddah* (a naked woman standing in a knee-high tub, holding a scroll), and *hadlakat ha'ner* (a woman in Renaissance dress lights the candles on a candelabrum). Above each scene the appropriate Hebrew benedictions are inscribed. On the lid are two rows of dials, four in each row; each dial has a single hand and has Hebrew letters as numerals to presumably list the quantity of linens or trousseau for each room. Above each dial is an Italian inscription (dialect from Veneto) in Hebrew characters, a frequent linguistic strategy in the late medieval and early modern age when the knowledge of Hebrew was declining. Those inscriptions document an inventory of linens (sheets, towels, shirts, etc.). Another inscription is in Yiddish: *schurztuch*, aprons of a particular kind.[66] The small casket was probably made for a matron who wanted to police servants who were illiterate in the Hebrew alphabet.[67] It encapsulates Jewish women's cultural hybridization, bridging Jewish traditions and Renaissance culture. It resembles similar small caskets for keys, as protection from potential thieves in the house, documented in rabbinic sources from thirteenth- and fourteenth-century Rhineland.[68] It also shows similarities with the *cofanetto* or *forzierino* filled with jewels and other presents, a typical wedding gift from groom to bride in contemporary Italian gentile upper-middle-class families, often decorated with representations of well-known classical or biblical scenes.[69]

In the early modern ghettos (and, in the case of Livorno, mostly but not exclusively a specific neighborhood after 1604),[70] Jewish women reconfigured their ritual lives; material culture and the built environment played important roles. We also see the emergence of communities of Jewish women gathering

Small casket (*cofanetto*) made by a Jewish artist from northern Italy (probably from the area of Veneto). Second half of the fifteenth century. Israel Museum, Jerusalem. Photo © Israel Museum, Jerusalem, by Yoram Lehmann. Image in the public domain.

in private homes, implying that forms of fraternalism shaped female agency beyond confraternities. Sixteenth- and seventeenth-century community records, manuscripts, printed *Haggadot*, and books of customs show that Venetian Jewish women and their servants and former slaves shared praying, reading, and the fulfillment of mitzvot, such as preparation for Passover, lighting Shabbat candles, and immersion in the ritual bath (*mikveh*) after menstruation (*niddah*).[71] We know that Jewish women from the upper and middle classes at times used private *mikva'ot*, even tubs built in their houses, for monthly purity rituals despite rabbinic authorities' concerns.[72] The celebration of this female ritual within the domestic domain was part of the process of feminization invested in the house that allowed women's gatherings to occur without community control. At times, female rituals moved beyond the domestic walls; for example, in seventeenth-century Venice, multiples of ten women in the Jewish Italian Society for Aiding the Poor (Ozer Dalim) used to accompany each new bride with candles in the courtyard of the ghetto.[73]

Bronze Hanukkah lamps bearing a representation of the heroine Judith were prominently displayed in affluent Jewish homes in Northern Italian cities beginning in the early seventeenth century, a feature unique to Italian Jewish society. Hanukkah lamps were hung on the walls. Lamps were adorned with motifs adapted from classical art, such as putti, wreaths, and mythical beings (centaurs and sirens), and revealed a deliberate preference for and borrowing from Renaissance art.[74] Judith was at the center of Renaissance iconography, completely decontextualized from her original Jewish setting and transformed into a symbol of the victorious Christian Church or the Commune's humanistic *res publica*.[75] However, since the medieval period, in the eyes of Jews Judith was a Jewish heroine associated with the holiday of Hanukkah; she served as a symbol of the Jewish people, their victory over their enemies, and their deliverance by a woman with the help of Israel's God.[76] These lamps thus embodied a new female agency, shaped within the domestic sphere. Finally, female affections and intimacy in the household could also produce unorthodox rituals that challenged masculinity. In her 1673 will, the Livornese Sephardic Ricca Mochora Santigliana asked an aunt to recite the mourner's Kaddish prayer for her soul, usually said by men.[77]

Early modern Italian synagogues often included women's galleries located on upper floors. Although female sections excluded Jewish women from participation in the religious services as actors with men, the "windows" of their galleries or rooms provided the opportunity to conduct parallel services. In 1600 in Rome, a certain Anna d'Arpino was appointed and paid to recite the daily *tefillah* (prayer) to the women in the synagogue called Quattro Capi.[78] In addition, these galleries allowed women an exclusive gaze on men. Jewish women could look out onto the male section below without being observed. There they gathered, prayed, conversed, and even gossiped undisturbed.

During the sixteenth and seventeenth centuries in Venetian synagogues, well-to-do Jewish women had their own voices during the religious services. Their names and expressions of both devotion to God and dedication to dear ones were displayed in front of the *aron ha-kodesh* in *meilim* (Torah mantles), *parokhot* (Torah curtains), and *mappot* (Torah binders). These were rich, luxurious ornaments in silk and brocade with visible dedications and signatures and, at times, complex iconographies. Made by the women in their homes, these fabrics served to beautify the synagogue and were displayed to the whole community during services on Shabbat and other Jewish holidays.[79] The Babylonian Talmud includes a specific mention of women's contribution to the production of the temple veil (*parokhet*), yet the role of Italian Jewish women as donors of textiles for Torah scrolls, curtains, and binders was so prominent that it was even incorporated into the liturgy of Roman Jews with a specific blessing: "He who blessed Sarah, Rebecca, Rachel, and Leah, may He bless every daughter of Israel who fashions a coat or covering with which to adorn the Torah. May the Holy One, blessed be He, pay her reward and grant her the good that she deserves, and let us say: Amen."[80]

In sixteenth- and seventeenth-century Venice middle- and upper-middle class women, both Jewish and non-Jewish, often owned looms that at the time served as tools for exercising a remunerative profession as well as acquiring a prestigious educational skill. At least since the 1520s, Venetian Jewish women and girls were quite active in reeling, throwing, spinning, and embroidering in their own homes.[81] Indeed, they emerged as female artisans, challenging the anonymity that characterized their underpaid work in the sector of silk production, and challenged women's limited agency in the visible "public" space of the synagogue, the ghetto, and the city. For example, in 1680–1681 Simḥah Levi Meshullam manufactured in silk and metallic thread an impressive *parokhet* with a complex iconography; it is preserved in the Jewish Museum of New York.[82] At the center of the piece the tablets of the Covenant are surrounded by a glory of clouds above Mount Moriah, and below is a Venetian version of messianic Jerusalem, with a temple whose hexagonal domed structure was modeled on the Dome of the Rock by Renaissance artists. Yet in the *parokhet* the temple represents the unknown Temple that will come at the end of days (Hag. 2:9), which in the Venetian ghetto was the object of new religious fervor, messianic expectations, and kabbalistic *tikkunim* (midnight rites).[83] Simḥah embellishes this impressive scene with her embroidery: "'He shall carry away a blessing from the Lord' [Psalms 24:5]; 1680–1681, the work of Simḥah, wife of Menachem Levi Meshullami."[84] Jewish women not only developed languages of memory and identity but also challenged gendering apprenticeship and gendered literacy.

Since childhood Jewish men's literacy was almost exclusively centered on the medium of the book in all its variants, but for Jewish girls from different social strata (as evidence from Rome also confirms, as examined in a section above) apprenticeship in literacy happened through reading from the printed book, stitching on linen, and embroidering silk fabrics. Indeed, Jewish women's writing appears much more secure on textiles than on paper. During the early seventeenth century, in their embroidery they also shifted from Ashkenazic to Sephardic letters (which are square) exactly when Venetian printers adopted the Sephardic letters for the production of Hebrew books. Considering the use of biblical quotations and theological turns illustrated, fabric textiles also became vehicles for learning, studying, and participating in the transnational world of Hebrew literature, Kabbalah and instances of messianism, and visual and material culture, techniques, and know-how, at times shared with gentiles.[85]

Conclusion

I HAVE ILLUSTRATED SOME features of the history of Jewish women in Italy from the fifteenth through the eighteenth century and how their lives were affected, shaped, and imagined by male Jewish intellectuals, lay leaders, and rabbis. The tension between women's lived experiences and prescriptive literature was based on a complex give-and-take between Jewish women and male-centered establishments. As elsewhere, in Italy we find a paucity of Jewish women's voices compared to the rich variety of women's voices that survive from the contemporary Christian world.

Moreover, American and Israeli scholars often privilege Hebrew sources and concentrate on cultural and intellectual histories, whereas Italian scholars focus on Italian and Latin community records and notarial and inquisitorial acts. I have brought together Italian, Latin, Yiddish, and Hebrew sources analyzed through my own and other scholars' contributions from the last thirty years. I hope to stimulate future research into both Jewish women in Italy and broader Italian Jewish society through the prism of gender, taking into account the development of Jewish history, culture, and society in Europe and the Mediterranean on the one hand and the specific context of Italy and its multifaceted cultural and social realities on the other.

Notes

I thank Cornelia Aust, Alexander Dawson, Natalie Dohrmann, Anne Oravetz Albert, Angelo Piattelli, and Tzipora Weinberg for their feedback.

1 Biblioteca Apostolica Vaticana, Vatican City, Cod. Ross. 555, fol. 12v. Another possible interpretation of the iconography is that instead of women, male youths are portrayed. For a cogent and sophisticated reflection on Jewish women in Italy performing functions that were male rites exclusively with examples from early sixteenth-century Mantua, see Robert Bonfil, "The Historian's Perception of the Jews in the Italian Renaissance: Toward a Reappraisal," *Revue des Études juives* 143 (1983): 59–82, esp. 71–75.

2 My definition of cultural hybridization responds to Peter Burke, *Hybrid Renaissance: Culture, Language, Architecture* (Budapest: Central European University Press, 2016). Jews in Italy did not submit to cultural colonization: Italian and Hebrew cultures were equal in their eyes, and agency and intention were often included in the process.

3 For an overview, see Kenneth Stow, *Catholic Thought and Papal Jewry Policy, 1555–1593* (New York: Jewish Theological Seminary Press, 1977).

4 The bibliography on the Jewish communities in the Italian peninsula is vast. For a synthesis, see Attilio Milano, *Storia degli ebrei in Italia* (Turin: Giulio Einaudi, 1963).

5 For an assessment, see Kenneth Stow, *The Roman Ghetto in the Sixteenth Century* (Seattle: University of Washington Press, 2000), 3–4.

6 I have elaborated on this thesis in Federica Francesconi, *Invisible Enlighteners: The Jewish Merchants of Modena, from the Renaissance to the Emancipation* (Philadelphia: University of Pennsylvania Press, 2021).

7 The poem can be found in T. Carmi, ed. and trans., *The Penguin Book of Hebrew Verse* (New York: Viking, 1981), 60–62.

8 Abraham Grossman, *Pious and Rebellious: Jewish Women in Medieval Europe* (Waltham, MA: Brandeis University Press, 2004), 164, 172.

9 Abraham b. Hanania Yagel-Gallico, *Eshet Ḥayil* (Venice: Daniel Zanetti, 1606); see the analysis in Roni Weinstein, "Abraham Yagel Galico's Commentary on *Woman of Valor*: Commenting on Women, Family, and Civility," in *Tov Elem: Memory, Community, and Gender in Medieval and Early Modern Jewish Societies—Essays in Honor of Robert Bonfil*, ed. Elisheva Baumgarten, Amnon Raz-Krakotzkin, and Roni Weinstein (Jerusalem: Bialik Institute, 2011), 118–35.

10 Weinstein, "Abraham Yagel Galico's Commentary."

11 Shlomo Simonsohn, *History of the Jews in the Duchy of Mantua* (New York: KTAV, 1977), 252–53.

12 Archivio di Stato di Modena, Archivio per Materie, Inquisizione, Processi, busta 69, fasc. 12, February 12, 1624.

13 Gabriella Zarri, "Living Saints: A Typology of Female Sanctity in the Early Sixteenth Century," in *Women and Religion and Medieval and Renaissance Italy*, ed. Daniel Bornstein and Roberto Rusconi (Chicago: University of Chicago Press, 1996), 219–303.

14 See Diane Owen Hughes, "Distinguishing Signs: Ear-Rings, Jews, and Franciscan Rhetoric in the Italian Renaissance City," *Past and Present* 112 (August 1986): 3–59; and Flora Cassen, *Marking the Jews in Renaissance Italy: Politics, Religion, and the Power of Symbols* (Cambridge, UK: Cambridge University Press, 2017).

15 De Sommi's poem is edited and translated in Erith Jeff-Berg, "Magen Nashim: An Early-Modern Defense of Women," *Metamorphoses* 16, no. 2 (fall 2008): 105–28.

16 See Merry Wiesner, *Women and Gender in Early Modern Europe*, 3rd ed. (Cambridge, UK: Cambridge University Press, 2008), 22–60.

17 Leone de' Sommi, *Tsaoth b'Dihutha d'Kiddushin* [Comedy of Betrothal], trans. Alfred S. Golding (Toronto: Dovehouse, 1988).

18 Leone de' Sommi, *The Three Sisters*, trans. Donald Beecher and Massimo Ciavolella (Toronto: Dovehouse, 1993).

19 Kenneth Stow, "Marriages Are Made in Heaven: Marriage and the Individual in the Roman Jewish Ghetto," *Renaissance Quarterly* 48 (1995): 445–91.

20 Stow, "Marriages Are Made in Heaven," 471.

21 Kenneth Stow, *The Jews in Rome*, 2 vols. (Leiden: Brill, 1995–1997), 1: 131–32.

22 Federica Francesconi, "The Venetian Jewish Household as a Multireligious Community in Early Modern Italy," in *Global Reformations: Transforming Early Modern Religions, Societies, and Cultures*, ed. Nicholas Terpstra (Abingdon, UK: Routledge, 2019), 231–48.

23 Archivio di Stato di Venezia, Fondo Notarile, Testamenti, Andrea Calzavara, busta 260, pratica 739, September 9, 1664.

24 For example, Archivio di Stato di Venezia, Fondo Notarile, Testamenti, busta 258, Andrea Calzavara, pratica 344, September 25, 1641.

25 Howard Adelman, "Servants and Sexuality: Seduction, Surrogacy, and Rape— Some Observations Concerning Class, Gender, and Race in Early Modern Italian Jewish Families," in *Gender and Judaism: The Transformation of Tradition*, ed. Tamar Rudavsky (New York: New York University Press, 1995), 81–82; Francesconi, "Venetian Jewish Household," 234–35.

26 Stow, *Jews in Rome*, 1: 206; document 516, February 1541, Archivio Storico Capitolino di Roma, sezione 3 (Notai ebrei), 11m l.4, f.37r.

27 For example, Cristina Galasso, "'Solo il loro servigio si brama, sia fedel, accurato e sincer': Il servizio domestico nella comunità ebraica di Livorno (secc. XVII–XVIII)," *Società e Storia* 97 (2002): 457–74; and Francesconi, *Invisible Enlighteners*, 300–303.

28 Archivio della Comunità ebraica di Modena, busta 71, "Accademia di Mantova dichiara indissolubile il stato matrimoniale contratto dal Dottore Moisè Vaigler colla Rachelle Arezzi di Modena," December 14, 1755, and "Causa vertente fra la Signora Rachel Arezzi di Modena da una parte e il Signor Dottor Moise Vailer dall'altra," December 17, 1755.

29 Archivio della Comunità ebraica di Modena, busta 71, "Lodo assunto da Israel Ghedalia Cases, Salomon Lampronti, Jacob Vita Jacchia, 1778."

30 Francesconi, "Venetian Jewish Household," 235–37.

31 Archivio di Stato di Torino, SR 1721, l. 4, vol. v. II, cc. 969v–970v, analyzed in Luciano Allegra, "A Model of Jewish Devolution: Torino in the Eighteenth Century," *Jewish History* 7, no. 2 (1993): 29–58, 41.

32 Archivio di Stato di Torino, SR 1773, l. 10, vol. v. II, cc. 1229v–1230v; Allegra, "Model of Jewish Devolution," 41.

33 Allegra, "Model of Jewish Devolution," 41.

34 See Stow, *Jews in Rome*; Galasso, "Solo il loro servigio"; and Allegra, "Model of Jewish Devolution."

35 British Library, *Golden Haggadah* (1602), title page, fol. 2.

36 Chava Turniansky and Erika Timm, *Yiddish in Italia: Yiddish Manuscripts and Printed Books from the 15th to the 17th Century* (Milan: Associazione Amici dell'Università di Gerusalemme, 2003), 130.

37 Turniansky and Timm, *Yiddish in Italia*, 130.

38 Turniansky and Timm, *Yiddish in Italia*, 132. The book has recently been beautifully translated and published as Edward Fram, *My Dear Daughter: Rabbi Benjamin Slonik and the Education of Jewish Women in Sixteenth-Century Poland* (Cincinnati: Hebrew Union College, 2007), but it does not report the mentioned introduction to the Paduan edition I have used.

39 Antonio Possevino, *Bibliotheca Selecta* (Venice: Ciotti, 1597), 113.

40 For example, the early-seventeenth-century *Seder Mizvot Nashim*, published by Maria Modena Mayer, "Il Sefer Miswot di Casale Monferrato," *Italia* 4.1 (1985), i–xix, 1–108.

41 Sylvie Anne Goldberg, *Crossing the Jabbok: Illness and Death in Ashkenazi Judaism in Sixteenth Through Nineteenth-Century Prague* (Berkeley: University of California Press, 1996), 108–9.

42 See Shalom Sabar, "Torah and Magic: The Torah Scroll and Its Appurtenances as Magical Objects in Traditional Jewish Culture," *European Journal of Jewish Studies* 3, no. 1 (2009): 143–52.

43 Michelle Klein, *A Time to Be Born: Customs and Folklore of Jewish Birth* (Philadelphia: Jewish Publication Society, 2000), 298n27.

44 Archivio di Stato di Modena, Inquisizione, Causae Hebreorum, busta 247, fasc. 25, December 9, 1636.

45 See Leone Modena, *The Autobiography of a Seventeenth-Century Venetian Rabbi: Leon Modena's Life of Judah*, ed. Mark R. Cohen (Princeton, NJ: Princeton University Press, 1988), 79; Aaron Berekhiah Modena, *Sefer Maʾavar*, fol. 7a. See also S. Assaf, *Mekorot le-toledot ha-Hinnukh be-Yisrael* (Tel Aviv: Hotsaʾat Devir, 1954), 2: 54.

46 Nina Beth Cardin, ed. and trans., *Out of the Depths I Call You: A Book of Prayers for the Married Jewish Woman* (Northvale, NJ: Jason Aronson, 1995), 90–91.

47 Isaac Lampronti, *Pahad Yitzhak* (Venice, 1750), vol. 3, pt. 4, 11a, *Yoledet*.

48 Don Herran, ed. and trans., "Volume Editor's Introduction," in *Jewish Poet and Intellectual in Seventeenth-Century Venice: The Works of Sarra Copia Sulam in Verse and Prose Along with Writings of Her Contemporaries in Her Praise, Condemnation, or Defense* (Chicago: University of Chicago Press, 2009), 1–38. On Copio Sullam, see also Lynn Lara Westwater, *Sarra Copia Sulam: A Jewish Salonnière and the Press in Counter-Reformation Venice* (Toronto: University of Toronto Press, 2020), and the bibliography therein. On Italian Jewish scholars' cultural formation, see David Ruderman, "Introduction," in *Cultural Intermediaries: Jewish Intellectuals in Early Modern Italy*, ed. David Ruderman and Giuseppe Veltri (Philadelphia: University of Pennsylvania Press, 2004), 1–23.

49 Benjamin Richler, "On the Education of Daughters of Wealthy Jews in Renaissance Italy," *Kiryat Sefer* 68, suppl. (1998): 276 (Hebrew).

50 Herran, "Volume Editor's Introduction."

51 *Manifesto di Sarra Copia Sulam Hebrea nel quale è da lei riprovata, e detestata l'opinione negante l'immortalità dell'Anima, falsamente attribuitale dal Sig. Baldassare Bonifaccio* (Venice: Antonio Pinelli, 1621).

52 Virginia Cox, *Women's Writing in Italy, 1400–1650* (Baltimore: Johns Hopkins University Press, 2008), 205.

53 Herran, "Volume Editor's Introduction," 38.

54 Elliott Horowitz, "The Eve of the Circumcision: A Chapter in the History of Jewish Nightlife," *Journal of Social History* 23, no. 1 (1989): 45–69.

55 Mauro Perani and Bracha Rivlin, eds., *Vita religiosa ebraica a Bologna nel Cinquecento: Gli Statuti della Confraternita dei solerti* (Florence: Giuntina, 2000), esp. 121–24.

56 Archivio di Stato di Bologna, Torrone, 1567, 456, cc. 288v–289r, 290r, cited in Roseella Rinaldi, "Donne in Fuga: Casi giudiziari di avanzato Cinquecento," in *Donne nella storia degli ebrei d'Italia: Atti del IX Convegno internazionale "Italia Judaica," Lucca, 6–9 Giugno 2005*, ed. Michele Luzzati and Cristina Galasso (Florence: Giuntina, 2007), 109–24, quotation on p. 120.

57 Federica Francesconi, "The Generative Space of Jewish Confraternities in Medieval and Early Modern Europe," in *A Companion to Medieval and Early Modern Confraternities*, ed. Konrad Eisenbichler (Leiden: Brill, 2019), 307–25, esp. 317–19 and the bibliography therein.

58 Miriam Bodian, "The 'Portuguese' Dowry Societies in Venice and Amsterdam: A Case Study in Communal Differentiation Within the Marrano Diaspora," *Italia* 6 (1987): 30–61; Elliott Horowitz, "The Dowering of Brides in the Ghetto of Venice: Between Tradition and Change, Ideas and Reality," *Tarbiz* 56 (1987): 347–70 (Hebrew).

59 Renzo Toaff, *La nazione ebrea a Livorno e a Pisa (1591–1700)* (Florence: Leo Olschki, 1990), 263–68; Moisés Orfali, "The Portuguese Dowry Society in Livorno and the Marrano Diaspora," *Studia Rosenthaliana* 35, no. 2 (2001): 143–56.

60 Archivio della Comunità ebraica di Modena, Archivio aggregato della So'ed Holim (SH-Register), November 22, 1735.

61 Archivio della Comunità ebraica di Modena, SH-Register, November 8, 1750, and August 23, 1751.

62 For a specific reference to the Italian Jewish context, see Leone Modena, *Historia de gli riti hebraici: vita e osservanze degl'Hebrei di questi tempi* (Venice: Calleoni, 1638), 63.

63 Francesconi, *Invisible Enlighteners*, 284–316.

64 See Evelyn M. Cohen, "Women's Illuminated Hebrew Prayer Books in Renaissance Italy," in *Donne nella storia degli ebrei: Atti del IX Convegno internazionale "Italia Judaica," Lucca, 6–9 Giugno 2005*, ed. Michele Luzzati and Cristina Galasso (Florence: Giuntina, 2007), 305–12 and the bibliography therein.

65 Farissol also copied a more famous manuscript for another Jewish matron in Ferrara in 1480 with the same benediction; Jewish Theological Seminary, Ms. 8255.

66 I thank Daniele Nissim for sending me his forthcoming publication on this.

67 The small casket has been widely discussed, but the classic is still Mordechai Narkiss, "An Italian Niello Casket of the Fifteenth Century," *Journal of the Warburg and Courtauld Institutes* 21, nos. 3/4 (1958): 288–95. Yet, as the forthcoming article by Daniele Nissim demonstrates, Narkiss's analysis shows some minor lacunas (e.g., instead of the Yiddish inscription, the name of an artisan, Jeshurun Tovar, is given in Hebrew).

68 Narkiss, "Italian Niello Casket," 289–90.

69 Marta Ajmar and Flora Dennis, eds., *At Home in Renaissance Italy* (London: Victoria & Albert Museum, 2006), 108.

70 Lucia Frattarelli Fischer, "Proprietà e insediamenti ebraici nella Livorno dalla fine del Cinquecento alla seconda metà del Settecento," *Quaderni storici* 18, no. 54/3, *Ebrei in Italia* (1983): 879–96.

71 Numerous examples are published in Turniansky and Timm, *Yiddish in Italia*.

72 For example, Paris BN [Bibliothèque nationale] Ms. Héb. 586 from 1500, thoroughly analyzed by Diane Wolfthal, *Picturing Yiddish: Gender, Identity, and Memory in Yiddish Books of Renaissance Italy* (Leiden: Brill, 2004); and the small casket from Veneto analyzed in this essay. On pertinent legal literature, see Abraham Ya'ari, "An Unknown Document Concerning the Controversy in Rovigo," in *Mehkerei Sefer*, by Abraham Ya'ari (Jerusalem: Hebrew University, 1958), 420–29 (Hebrew); and Daniel Carpi, *Pinkas va'ad kehillah kedoshah Padua* (Jerusalem: Israel National Academy of Sciences and Humanities, 1973), vol. 1, no. 118.

73 Jewish Theological Seminary, *Pinkas Hevrat Ozer dalim ve-avelim*, Ms. 8468, fols. 9a, 12a.

74 For examples of Hanukkah lamps, see *Arte e cultura ebraiche in Emilia Romagna: Catalogo della mostra, Ferrara, 20 sett. 1988–15 gen. 1989* (Milan: De Luca, 1988); and the website of the Jewish Museum of New York, https://thejewishmuseum.org/collection/9099-hanukkah-lamp.

75 For Judith in the arts, see Roger J. Crum, "Judith Between the Private and Public Realms in Renaissance Florence," in *The Sword of Judith: Judith Studies Across the Disciplines*, ed. Kevin R. Brine, Elena Ciletti, and Henrike Lähnemann (Cambridge, UK: Open Book, 2010), 291–306; and Sarah Blake McHam, "Donatello's Judith as the Emblem of God's Chosen People," in *The Sword of Judith: Judith Studies Across the Disciplines*, ed. Kevin R. Brine, Elena Ciletti, and Henrike Lähnemann (Cambridge, UK: Open Book, 2010), 307–24.

76 Debora Levine Gera, "Shorter Medieval Hebrew Tales of Judith," in *The Sword of Judith: Judith Studies Across the Disciplines*, ed. Kevin R. Brine, Elena Ciletti, and Henrike Lähnemann (Cambridge, UK: Open Book, 2010), 81–96.

77 Cristina Galasso, *Alle origini di una comunità: Ebree ed ebrei a Livorno nel XVII secolo* (Florence: Leo Olschki, 2002), 82.

78 Stow, *Jews in Rome*, 1: xxxv, 2: no. 5, 116r.

79 For the most detailed collection of examples, see Vivian B. Mann, ed., *Gardens and Ghettos: The Art of Jewish Life in Italy* (Berkeley: University of California Press, 1989).

80 Aliza Lavie, *Jewish Woman's Prayer Book* (New York: Spiegel & Grau, 2008), 224.

81 Luca Molà, "Le donne nell'industria serica veneziana del rinascimento," in *La seta in Italia dal Medieovo al Seicento: Dal banco al drappo*, ed. Luca Molà, Reinhold Mueller, and Carlo Zanier (Venice: Marsilio, 2000), 423–59, 439–40.

82 https://thejewishmuseum.org/collection/8162-torah-ark-curtain.

83 Shalom Sabar, "Messianic Aspirations and Renaissance Urban Ideals: The Image of Jerusalem in the Venice Haggadah, 1609," *Jewish Art* 23–24 (1998): 294–312.

84 Mann, ed., *Gardens and Ghettos*, catalogue no. 144, 276–77.

85 These ideas are developed in my forthcoming book, tentatively titled *The Jewish Home in Early Modern Venice: Cosmopolitan Intimacy, Global Networks, and Diasporic Material Culture*.

JEWISH WOMEN IN EARLY MODERN CENTRAL EUROPE, 1500–1800

Debra Kaplan and Elisheva Carlebach

When early modern Jewish women bought meat, cheese, or fish to feed their families, used a particular bathhouse for ritual immersion, or invited other women to celebrate the birth of a new child, they acted within (or against) a web of regulations whose goal was control over many activities that had not been closely regulated by communal ordinances before the sixteenth century. One of our central arguments in this essay is that women became more visible in Jewish written records in the early modern period than they had been in the medieval period. The culture of writing had become more common since the late medieval period (beginning ca. 1450), particularly in times of greater mobility and rupture.[1] The early modern period witnessed the proliferation of a wealth of different kinds of documents, both in manuscript and in print. In this chapter we survey four intersections between Jewish written records and Jewish women's lives: regulations, literary expression, ritual, and economic activity. Our focus is on Ashkenazic women living in Central and Western Europe from the sixteenth through the eighteenth century. At the outset we should note that this survey is not meant to be an exhaustive treatment of women's lives or a comprehensive picture of all sources that might be mined to study them. Rather, these four areas exemplify the rich source material that scholars who are interested in the lives of early modern women have at their disposal. Written documents permit us to discern women's experiences; they also shaped women's lives during this period.

Records and Regulations

The wealth of records and documents in the early modern period show a general increase in detailed regulations of areas of life that had not been subject to such rules earlier or had not been subject in this detailed way. By regulating areas of life previously left to custom, the informal became formal, and private acts became matters of public concern. This was a sea change for all affected but for women in particular, because their presumed sphere was the domestic and private and therefore their daily activities had often slipped under the radar of public law. The early modern period in Europe was one of aggressive creation of new and detailed regulations over many previously untouched areas of daily life, and this is the case for Jewish communal and halakhic regulations as well. As Elchanan Reiner has argued, the growth of Jewish population in some urban concentrations necessitated control and supervision over aspects of social and religious life that had not been necessary in small communities.[2] This can be seen in regulations concerning many types of foods. Everything to do with the slaughter, preparation, and sale of meat came under both the religious and civil regulation of the Jewish community. The Worms regulations of 1684 warned that the sale of meat, milk, cheese, wine, and liquor would be strictly regulated and overseen by the community.[3] Other communities' statutes regulated baked goods, types of fish and poultry that may be eaten, the consumption of coffee, and the like. In many communities food that had not been granted the communal seal of approval "was to be considered nonkosher."[4] Although the import, production, or sales of these items may have been primarily in the hands of men, the retail purchase, preparation, and consumption in the home was mainly the responsibility of Jewish women. Women who failed to follow the regulations could be harshly punished. In one instance in the protocols of the Ashkenazic community of Amsterdam from 1758, Hendele bat Abraham was accused of obtaining meat from a non-Jewish butcher and feeding it to her family and of selling the meat to others. Wishing to make an example of her, the parnassim sentenced her (with the complicity of the non-Jewish government) to six months of imprisonment in the Spinhuis (where criminally charged women were subjected to forced labor and horrible conditions) followed by eternal banishment from the city.[5] As regulation of daily life increased, aspects of Jewish women's lives that had not been subject to formal regulation before came under its scope. Regulation of the food supply did not generally single out women, but it exemplifies the way that regulations can be read (or read against their grain) to illuminate women's lives.

An important dimension in the rise of regulation of the formerly private sphere is the extent to which this affected the lives of women disproportionately. Much ink has been spilled on the question of how closely the public-private distinction maps onto a gendered binary. Strict lines of difference are unsustainable, as European women were never locked behind closed doors (with the exception of convents) and rigid lines of domestic versus public did not run along gendered lines in many respects. Yet there were some significant areas of congruence, and it is these areas of previously unregulated space coming under the gaze of the law that interest us.

The expansion of small states policing ever more aspects of their subjects' lives began in German lands in the sixteenth century and intensified greatly after the Thirty Years' War in the mid-seventeenth century.[6] In Protestant states the elimination of the Catholic Church allowed the secular princes to extend their regulation of the moral lives of their subjects into areas that had not been the domain of the state earlier.[7] The reliance on the existing infrastructure of corporate entities to carry out new goals of administration from above, a characteristic of this period, can be applied as well to much of the regulation instituted and enforced in Jewish communities, which internalized these developments.

With regulation came the intensification of the culture of record keeping. The enforcement of regulations reflected in myriad records written to keep track of hundreds of individuals' religious, economic, and social lives provide us with a base of sources that exceed in quantity and in quality those available concerning Jewish women in earlier times. Cultures of Jewish record keeping arose and intensified in the sixteenth century, in the milieu of Italian cities and their notarial culture and in areas of the Holy Roman Empire and Habsburg lands with their renewed focus on administrative, scribal, and archival practices.[8] The record-keeping culture in German lands, which arose in tandem with and as a reflection of the remarkable efflorescence of a legal culture of regulation, is crucial to understanding the rise of its Jewish parallels.

For much of the twentieth century legal historians have analyzed the rise of regulations and, more recently, historians have focused their attention on the culture of record keeping, but the impact on Jewish communal law and life has been less noted. Jewish communal records are commonly referred to as *pinkassim*, a term that refers to a logbook or record.[9] Some *pinkassim* served purely to record regulations, termed variously *takkanot* or *haskamot* or, in Sephardic communities, *escamot*. These regulations cover the founding agreements made by original community members, including matters of governance (such as representation, membership, elections, and taxes) and the regulation of communal spaces.[10] Larger communities kept multiple types of records in addition, sometimes folded into the *pinkas takkanot*, in many cases as stand-alone volumes. These included minute books of meetings of the lay leaders and appointments of communal personnel,[11] of the regulations and ongoing administration of the tax assessors and collectors (*shama'im*; *govim*), of fines and penalties assessed for various infractions,[12] of announcements made by the community council to the public,[13] and of the charity custodians (*gaba'im*)[14] (sometimes including separate lists of wood distribution in winter and distribution of matzo and wine for Passover) and record books of the overseers of education for the poor, both of the students and parents' obligation, the cost of books for the students, and the contracts and salaries of the teachers (*melammdim*).

The education records provide a wonderful example of how regulations not ostensibly about women can nevertheless uncover ways in which the communities circumscribed women's lives. Regulations from Altona (a Danish port city whose Jewish community was closely linked to that of Hamburg) contain two paragraphs dealing with the families of schoolteachers. "*Melammdim* . . . who are already here have no membership rights in the community and the community has the right to retain them or not. But from this day forward, *melammdim* who come with their wives may not be hired. Anyone who deceives and brings his wife after [he is hired], the *parnas* of the month must expel him to leave within eight days."[15] This ordinance banning schoolteachers from residing with their wives in the community is immediately followed by another that banned foreign *melammdim* from residing in town for more than three years.[16] By refusing to allow foreign married *melammdim* to reside in Altona together with their wives for periods up to three years, Altona (along with similar communities) created myriad social problems. Women who lost track of where their husbands were or whether they ever intended to return could turn into *agunot*.[17] Children were deprived of the presence of their fathers. The ordinances were responsible for the formation of a cadre of adult men who lived without the companionship of their wives or the comforts of home. Such restrictions may have inadvertently moved them to seek such comforts elsewhere, contributing to the breakdown in family and sexual morality.

Rabbinic courts sometimes kept records,[18] as did small claims civil courts composed of judges who were members of the lay and or scholarly elite.[19] Some communities made copies of marriage agreements (or at least the amounts each party was liable for), last wills and testaments, and inventories of the deceased's property. Many burial, charitable, and learned societies (*hevrot*) kept their own records of ordinances, members, contributions, and expenditures.[20] In some cases, such as in Mainz and Halberstadt, women operated *hevrot* (both burial societies and charity circles) independently of men, some even maintaining their own takkanot, and the community strove to keep these *hevrot* under its control. Executive secretaries (*shamashim*) of the community council or the rabbinic courts sometimes kept their own semiprivate records of matters they reckoned important to the community.[21] Both midwives and *mohalim* (circumcisers) kept records of the births or circumcisions over which they presided, the only type of Jewish birth records before states took over the function from the church.[22] Finally, many Jews kept records of their personal financial lives, their merchant and household accounts. In one example, a widow of a communal leader was asked "to search the *pinkas* of her deceased husband to ascertain whether her husband made a yearly payment of four Reichsthaler" to another party.[23] Routine requests that wives or widows relay such information, repeated in court records, testify to the partner status of women in access to and understanding of the family business records. Such records often served as valid evidence in court cases of loans and debts, owed and repaid.[24]

Pinkassim reflected communal borders and self-definitions. The border-lines can often be detected in the wording of entries. Women were sometimes called by their husband's or father's name (wife of or daughter of), but even when their own names are mentioned, they are prefaced by "the woman" (*ha-isha*) (or if the woman were single or widowed, that might be her sole designation). Men's appellations refer to their status, but women's refer to their gender alone, indicating that they were beyond a certain universe of discourse controlled by men. It is precisely this distancing we seek to subvert. By showing that women availed themselves of many possibilities, we try to show them as they saw and acted themselves rather than as they were reflected in the writings of others in their own time and in later scholarship.

Jewish Women as Readers and Writers

THE PROLIFERATION OF WRITING and literacy that marked the late medieval period created new communities of readers and writers across Europe. This is one of the reasons print technology was adopted so quickly: It amplified the ever-widening circulation of texts, which created new communities of readers, who became ever more alert to the possibilities of becoming writers themselves.

The invention of movable type by Johannes Gutenberg in the late fifteenth century and the subsequent proliferation of printed materials directly affected the lives of Jewish women.[25] Not long after the advent of the printing press, books designed for common men and specifically for female Jewish readers were printed. Sixteenth-century homiletical books in Yiddish, such as the *Brantspiegel* and the *Tsene u'rene*, summarized portions of the Bible and provided readers with moral content. Although both men and women throughout the Yiddish-speaking world could read these books, these texts were gendered as female. The publisher of the *Brantspiegel*, Moses ben Hanoch Yerushalmi

Altschuler, explained that the choice to publish in Yiddish reflected his desire to provide "women and men who are like women" with access to the book's contents.[26] Altschuler thus defined male readers who preferred the vernacular Yiddish over the scholarly Hebrew as being "like women," gendering Yiddish a women's language. This is the first time in history that an entire literature was directed at Jewish women readers. This gendered turn had monumental consequences, as it advanced Ashkenazic women into the circle of near universal literacy.

Average and even poor women and girls had familiarity with Yiddish printed works and with the Hebrew alphabet, and thus these texts had a broad readership and impact. The increasing number of available printed materials in the vernacular allowed greater numbers of women to become literate. Reading literacy was not limited to the daughters and wives of rabbis, who had often been educated at home. Although some elite women were able to read Hebrew, the Yiddish printed books allowed women from different classes to access a wealth of texts and ideas. The audience for these texts even extended to women who could not read but who might listen to the texts as they were being read aloud, a common pastime in early modern Europe.[27] It was not long before some early modern authors assumed that Ashkenazic women would own copies of these texts. Moses Porges, a seventeenth-century charity collector from Jerusalem, instructed European Jews wishing to move to the Land of Israel as to what books were worth bringing along on their journey. He listed several Hebrew books, including the Bible and liturgical and legal texts, that men were to bring on their journey, and he simultaneously advised women to bring a different list of Yiddish books. These included a Bible (likely the *Tsene u'rene*), a prayer book, *tkhines* (or "supplications" discussed later in this section), and other vernacular literature. The list suggests that these texts, unavailable in the Holy Land, were essential to a woman's library.[28]

As Porges's gendered lists indicate, women formed a discrete market for books.[29] Handbooks such as *Seder mitzvot nashim*, as the title indicates, were published to instruct women on proper observance of the three "women's commandments," namely, separating dough from the challah bread, lighting Sabbath candles, and the laws of menstrual purity. The proliferation of such handbooks exemplifies how print quickly provided women with wide access to these laws in written form. In the fifteenth century, Rabbi Jacob Molin (d. 1427) strongly warned Rabbi Hayyim of Augsburg against composing a handbook to teach men and women the laws of menstrual purity. These traditions were to be passed on mimetically, and questions were to be posed to rabbinic authorities.[30] In sharp contrast to Rabbi Molin, Rabbi Benjamin Slonik (d. ca. 1619) indicated that his edition of *Seder mitzvot nashim* could be useful for women who were embarrassed to share the specifics of their questions about menstrual purity with rabbis.[31] Five editions of Rabbi Slonik's text were published between 1577 and 1627, with an additional volume comprising excerpts from his text appearing in Prague in 1629. Four Italian adaptations were published between 1616 and 1711.[32] The volume's success attests to the new ways in which knowledge was transferred through print and to the acceptance of print as a suitable medium for such transfer by contemporary elites.[33]

Beyond consuming texts written and printed for them by men, the availability of more works in many genres stimulated women to find their own voices. Some of their writing made its way into print. Other texts were intended for family readerships or for particular women and had a limited but notable impact. Thus Rivka Tiktiner of Prague (d. 1605) wrote her own Yiddish handbook, *Meneket Rivka*.[34] Tiktiner stressed the importance of child rearing and household duties and their religious significance for women. Claiming, for example, that a woman could earn heavenly merit by cooking meals for a scholar, she highlighted the proper roles delineated for women and the value of such domestic devotion. These handbooks, like some of the moral teachings contained in the *Brantspiegel* and *Tsene u'rene*, prescribed behavior for women and sought to direct their religious observance.[35] Similar handbooks were composed by Catholics and Protestants to teach the running of a pious and holy household.[36]

Print also served to establish and disseminate uniform prayers particular to women's life-cycle events and rituals. Women had always maintained oral traditions of prayers, often in the vernacular, to be uttered at life-cycle and other events not covered in the formal synagogue services. (The biblical Hannah served as model and seal of approval for this tradition.) The rise of printed collections of *tkhines*, Yiddish prayers for women to be recited on occasions such as immersion in a ritual bath and childbirth, mark another example of texts designed for female consumption.[37] The publication of *tkhines* facilitated their circulation among a wide group of women and fostered piety through the reading of texts. Like the handbooks, these prayers were written by both men and women. Perhaps most famous among the female authors was Sarah Rebecca Rachel Leah Horowitz, whose volume of *tkhines* was accompanied by her own introductions in Hebrew and Aramaic.[38]

Even though reading and writing remained separate subjects in this period, the availability of more materials to read fueled a cycle of literacy whose results were evident in the written output of more women. It is during the early modern period that we have a sudden explosion of texts authored by women in a variety of genres. Toybe Pan, a seventeenth-century author, penned a Yiddish *lid*, a song in which a historical event is commemorated, in the wake of a plague in Prague.[39] Bella Perlhefter (d. 1709), a native of Prague who later lived in the village of Schnaittach, composed with her husband, Ber, a Yiddish encyclopedia of Jewish history and destiny, with healthy doses of midrash, mysticism, and moralism. She titled the work *Be'er Sheva* (Seven Wells); each of the seven chapters was devoted to one of her children who did not live to adulthood. This remarkable work never reached print, despite its authors' intentions. Nevertheless, despite its great length (its closely printed modern edition is almost 600 pages long), eight manuscript copies were produced in the decades after it was written, and there is evidence of more lost copies.[40] Bella Perlhefter's writerly talents were manifested in other ways as well. A few pieces of her correspondence with Ber and with Christian Hebraist Johann Christoph Wagenseil were preserved by Wagenseil. Wagenseil was interested in Jewish epistolarity, and he collected but never printed a rich sample of Jewish letters, including those of the Perlhefters and letters of other Jewish women.[41] Aside from her own letters, Bella also noted that she wrote letters on behalf of other Jewish women. Personal letters, which reflect a particular moment in time, provide glimpses into the daily lives of women that are unmatched in any other source.[42] Yiddish collections of letters have attracted the attention of scholars primarily interested in their linguistic aspects. They have yet to be mined fully to enlarge our knowledge of Jewish women's lives.[43]

The vast number of sources written for and by women creates a treasure trove of material about their lives and accomplishments yet to be mined by scholars of early modern Jewish history. This is all the more relevant when it comes to diarists, such as Glikl Hameln. Glikl's text recounts details of her first and second marriages, her business endeavors as wife and widow, her exchanges with her children, and daily life as lived by women of her class in Hamburg and Metz.[44] Many scholars have sought to extrapolate specifics about women's lives from her diary.[45] The fact that family events—the loss of Bella's children and Glikl's melancholy—compelled these two women to write emphasizes the solemnity and gravity with which recording, writing, and creating texts were viewed in this period. It also marks female writers as familiar with the conventions of their age, as Christian women also created consolations for the departure of loved ones and shaped a picture of their lives for posterity with their own words.[46]

Women took other active roles in creating books. Several colophons record the labor of women in Jewish print houses. Thus Estellina Conat, the wife of Abraham Conat, a printer in Mantua and Ferrara in the late fifteenth century, recorded that it was she who arranged the letters to be printed based on the exemplar.[47] Such labor did not necessitate understanding the text, as being able to recognize the Hebrew letters was sufficient for copying their arrangement on the page.⁴⁸ Indeed, in one Yiddish book the colophon includes a Yiddish statement by Ella, daughter of a printer in Dessau, excusing any mistakes one might find by explaining that she was merely 9 years old.⁴⁹ Similarly, Rivka and Reichel, the daughters of a printer in Wilmersdorf, worked in their father's print shop. Having acquired these skills, Reichel went on to work in print shops in Sulzbach and Fürth.⁵⁰ The colophon in a *mahzor* [High Holiday prayer book] printed in Lublin in 1567 similarly records that the printers' families participated in the production of the text. The wives arranged the letters, and the sons dealt with the ink.⁵¹ This division of labor reflects the structure of premodern economies, in which families worked together at a particular craft, often with gendered division of labor. The print shop created a new space in which men and women worked side by side and brought women into more immediate contact with letters and literacy.

Women also served as patrons of texts, providing the necessary funding to authors or publishers so that a particular text could be printed. Some women specifically sought to support the publication of volumes for other women. These women were then acknowledged and commemorated as patrons in the printed texts.⁵² This is yet another example of the intense significance with which commemorating a person or an event in writing was perceived in this period. By supporting the publication of a book, individual men and women ensured that they would be remembered in its pages. Women were also commemorated through dedications. Rabbi Yair Hayyim Bacharach (d. 1702) named his books of responsa *Havot Yair* in memory of his grandmother Hava, herself the granddaughter of the Maharal of Prague. In his introduction, Bacharach extolled his grandmother's wisdom and knowledge, specifically referring to her as a learned reader and writer: "She had a *Midrash rabbah* without translation and she studied it according to her capacity and intelligence. . . . She . . . commented on *mahzorim* [Hebrew plural for *mahzor*] and *selihot* [penitential prayers], as well as on Rashi's commentary to the Bible and the twenty four [biblical books] as well as the *targumim* [Aramaic biblical homiletic paraphrases] and external books. Several times when the titans of the generation struggled [with the meaning] she came and extended her quill and excelled in writing in the clearest language."⁵³ Although it is not unusual for women raised in rabbinic households to have access to a greater range of books and an education that exceeded that of their peers, the range of works mentioned by Bacharach indicates that his grandmother had access to and familiarity with a rich library of printed books.

Jewish Women and Ritual Life

EARLY MODERN PRACTICES OF writing, recording, and regulating created a rich body of sources documenting women's participation in local rituals. Custom books, printed handbooks and liturgical texts, and communal decrees all make reference to communal and life-cycle rituals performed by women. Memorial books, texts commemorating the pious acts of community members, highlighted women's synagogue attendance, noting when women came to pray early in the morning and late at night.[54] The women's sections in synagogues also serve as architectural evidence that women attended communal prayers.[55] Special charity collections were taken up by women, many of which were collected in the synagogue, as collections among men were. A Yiddish letter from poor women in Jerusalem to potential female donors in Ashkenaz and Poland requested that the donors appoint *gabbaʾot*, official female charity collectors, to collect funds for poor women, particularly widows and orphans, on Mondays and Thursdays, the days on which the Torah was read, and on the first day of the new month, a minor holiday that was traditionally associated with women.[56] Moreover, a *pinkas* from Prague records the appointment of official female charity collectors in its list of yearly communal appointees.[57]

In Worms, on holidays such as Simchat Torah, women held their own dances and ceremonies in the synagogue, parallel to male celebrations. These took place in the women's section and the adjacent courtyard.[58] On Shabbat ha-Bahurim, the Sabbath after Purim, marked with carnivalesque rituals to celebrate male youth, the young men of the community transgressed norms by entering the women's section in a festive procession. They were then blessed by the *rabbanit*, the rabbi's wife.[59]

The *rabbanit* also took a leading role in communal celebrations of marriage. Weddings were typically conducted on Wednesdays, although pre- and postnuptial ceremonies lasted well over a week.[60] On the afternoon before the formal marriage ceremony took place, all the women of the community came to the bride's house to braid her hair.[61] The *rabbanit* was the first among the women to do so.[62] The women would also give the bride gifts, placing these into a large bowl that was in her lap while singing special Yiddish marriage songs.[63]

Rituals of marriage frequently comprised same-sex gatherings, where women celebrated with one another.[64] Some of these rituals were limited to the bride and her unmarried friends, whereas others included all the women of the community, regardless of marital status. One such ritual was a procession in which married women, single women, and jesters accompanied the bride to the bathhouse on the day before the wedding.[65] This was a procession of women celebrating the bride through communal space. Dances, both single-sex and mixed, also took place in the community's *Brauthaus*, the location in which wedding festivities were celebrated.

Women also marked additional life-cycle events through rituals conducted both in communal spaces and in the home. Labor and delivery normally took place at home, except in cases in which an extremely poor (and often foreign) mother gave birth in the communal hospice, the *hekdesh*. Amulets and even Torah scrolls were used to ward off the dangers of childbirth. After the birth, the parturient remained at home for a period of about 6 weeks, and other women helped her with her domestic duties. In the case of a newborn boy, a special ritual took place in the home on the eve before the circumcision. The mother used a sword to protect her baby at this liminal time.[66] When the mother resumed her duties, a special ceremony called *Shabbat yetziat ha-yoledet* (the coming out of the parturient) was performed, marking the mother's reintegration as she returned to synagogue. The baby's *wimpel*, or swaddling cloth, was presented to the community at a later date, to be used as a binding for the Torah scroll.[67] As Elisheva Baumgarten has demonstrated, the Shabbat ritual closely paralleled the Christian practice of churching, highlighting both the relationships that developed among female neighbors of different communities of faith and their shared concerns around the perils of premodern childbirth.[68]

Descriptions of these rituals can be found in Jewish custom books, in the writings of converts from Judaism to Christianity, and in the works of Christian Hebraists.[69] In some texts, both manuscript and print, images accompany the descriptions. Jewish women are depicted performing rituals of birth, marriage, divorce, and ritual immersion as well as domestic rituals, such as kindling Sabbath candles, cleaning for Passover, and baking matzo.[70] A similar gendered division of labor can be seen in rituals of death, where men built coffins and carried them to the cemetery and women sewed shrouds and warmed the water used to wash the body of the deceased.[71] Sewing and preparing water were daily tasks that women generally performed, and rituals reflected that reality.

The *tekufah* ritual is another example in which women were tasked with a practice on behalf of the community because of its connection with their daily housework and responsibilities. There were four times during the year when it was considered dangerous to consume water that had been left in a vessel, unless metal or iron was placed in the vessel. Women were either to pour out the water or ensure its safety by immersing iron into the vessel, because they were responsible for drawing water for their families. Various Jewish calendar books, *sifrei evronot*, describe and illustrate women and the *tekufah* ceremony.[72]

Early modern images also depict women performing rituals relating to neither domestic work nor life-cycle events. One Yiddish custom book depicts a woman counting the *omer*, the period of forty-nine days between Passover and Shavuot that were counted on a daily basis.[73] Another image portrays a woman erasing the memory of the biblical Amalek by stepping on a soldier's head.[74] Other custom books contain images in which women are present during the Havdalah ceremony that marks the transition from Sabbath to the ensuing weekdays.[75]

Whereas the aforementioned images and texts describe women's involvement in rituals, by contrast, communal decrees and *pinkassim* highlight the increasing regulation of women's ritual activities. Thus, for example, with the establishment of communal ritual baths in early modern Altona, women were charged a fee for immersing in the *mikveh*, and official communal attendants were to monitor these payments.[76] The community also sought to dictate which ritual baths women would use.[77] With the coming of the eighteenth century, which, as noted, was a period of intense regulation of private and public behavior, various communal *takkanot*, particularly in Metz and Fürth, sought to further control and limit women's presence at rituals performed in the public sphere. Women were no longer permitted to join the communal ritual procession to pray at the graves of the righteous on the eves of Rosh Hashanah and Yom Kippur; instead, they were to do so at a different time and day than the men of the community.[78] Women were also barred from attending funerals. Only mourners and women from the *hevrah kaddisha* were permitted to attend, and in Fürth they were to remain in a designated room rather than appear by the graveside.[79] Indeed, in Fürth women were barred from using the communal *etrog* (the citron fruit blessed during Sukkot) in the synagogue or the adjacent courtyard. Rather, they were instructed to recite the blessing in their homes, as had been the custom among Ashkenazic Jewish women since medieval times.[80]

Jewish Women: Economic Life and Status

THE ROLE OF JEWISH women in business can be measured on two levels, as Michael Toch has argued: the "formal" one that appears in records and can be easily measured; and the far larger "informal" one that does not appear in the written records but in which Jewish women participated as part of their family businesses on an everyday basis.[81] Unlike other written sources from the early modern period that make women more visible, economic records in premodern times tended to treat "married couples as an economic unit."[82]

Commercial documents generally privileged husbands as the legal heads of the family unit, even though their lone signatures on contracts might totally obscure the participation of their wives.[83] Evidence of women's skills as entrepreneurs and partners surfaced when husbands died and their widows took over, sometimes seamlessly. Brendele, resident of "zum Hirsch," in Frankfurt am Main, can serve as a typical case. To collect the funds owed to her deceased husband, Anselm (d. 1541), she played court systems against one another, pursuing her cases for over twenty years until her debtors paid. She then appeared in the records as an independent businesswoman.[84] Because many Jews were involved at some point in lending money at large to small levels, the pursuit of the capital tied up in debt was an important aspect of solvency, and considerable diplomacy was involved in compelling debtors to repay loans, often in far-flung jurisdictions. Jewish widows across this period appear repeatedly in the records acting to protect themselves in this way.

Widows form one of the most prominent categories of female entrepreneurs in businesses large and small and of taxpayers in community records. This is true in both the late medieval and the early modern periods.[85] Surviving court and communal records are skewed toward illuminating the activity of widowed women, obscuring the large number of married women whose role in their family economies was sizable. Traces of married women's activities were documented in cases before both Jewish and Christian courts, in which they appeared as parties.[86] In addition, certain contractual forms indicated married women's involvement in familial business endeavors, or at least the expectation that they would be responsible for repaying related debts. Certain transactions were recorded with the word be'ohev, a Hebrew acronym indicating that a husband and wife had joint accountability for all associated debts. This form was used widely in Metz and at times in Frankfurt.[87]

This accounts for another facet of Jewish family life that appears markedly in the early modern period: Women who became single as a result of death or abandonment are a familiar "type" in this period.[88] Death was far from the only thing that took husbands away. Commerce, begging, and employment opportunities in distant places kept many Jewish men far from their homes and their wives. Abandoned women often ended up at the bottom of the economic ladder, desperate to keep their homes warm and their children fed. Widows, by contrast, often came to control considerable assets independently for the first time in their lives. A famous example is Glikl of Hameln, who came into control of her first husband Hayyim's assets after his death.

Many Jewish women started out in commerce as adjuncts to businesses that their husbands ran, sometimes with money they had brought into the marriage as dowry. Every Jewish woman was entitled by her ketubbah (marriage contract) to a certain sum upon the husband's death or dissolution of the marriage, if she was not at fault. Thus women had an interest in the family's economic health from the start of their marriages. Commerce often entailed considerable travel, skills at negotiation, and deep knowledge of the prices and quality of commodities. Regardless of class, women often acted as partners in the family business. They traveled to local markets and international fairs, where they were immersed in buying and selling, settling of debts, and tending to networks of social and economic credit.[89] Widowed women served as guarantors of loans taken by family members.[90] In the seventeenth century, as the figure of the court Jew became prominent, husbands supplied provisions for courts or nobles while their wives often did the same with women of the court. Women were not accepted in these roles without restraint. The large number of responsa and regulations regarding the propriety of women appearing in public spaces and on the road shows that conflicts of values arose between notions of female modesty and the need for Jewish women's mobility.[91] Still late-eighteenth-century court records contain evidence of many routine partnerships between Jewish women and Jewish men who were not their husbands.[92] They formed joint ventures in Altona in a staggering array of commodities that came through the port, investing, buying, selling, borrowing, and lending with Jewish and Christian partners alike.

Beyond women pursuing commercial ventures, the records show that there were skilled professions for which women were compensated, some supporting their families with the money they earned. Perhaps most notable among female professions is midwifery. From the first regulations of Jewish communities of the early modern period, midwives were hired as community professionals and granted community membership, a prized privilege, for themselves and their families. Like some merchant women, midwives were trained record keepers whose writings are only now being evaluated as a resource for women's and communal history.[93] Women also served as matchmakers, agents in arranging meetings of prospective brides' and grooms' families, with fees regulated by the community and their skills in high demand.[94] In eighteenth-century Altona, women ran the equivalent of agencies for placing Jewish domestic servants in homes; Klerche the butcher sold meat; Bella Perlhefter of Prague and Schnaittach wrote letters for women less literate than she, presumably for payment. Many women worked on the side producing fine fabrics such as lace and luxury garments such as silk stockings (Glikl and her mother), and ordinary women were involved in the creation, upkeep, and reuse of garments until they fell apart.[95] In an age when fabric was not yet mass produced, bolts of cloth represented capital, and clothes were among the most valuable items people possessed. Coats and overclothes often appear in litigation as security for loans and as items for auction or sale and are itemized in contracts from midwives to maidservants.

Poorer women created opportunities for income wherever they could find them. They rented out quarters in their homes, took in laundry from better-off households, repaired or dyed clothing, and in rural areas sold produce, eggs, and milk to their neighbors.[96] In the late eighteenth century the poor widow Spiegelin in Frankfurt supported herself and her young children by preparing 30 to 50 pounds of coffee each Thursday evening, which she would distribute to customers over the Sabbath.[97] Women were employed as nurses to the sick and to parturient mothers. Some married (and more unmarried) Jewish women served as wet nurses for pay, one of the lowest rungs on the economic scale that could still provide sustenance for a poor woman's family.[98]

One ubiquitous mode of employment for young adolescent girls in this period was domestic service. This was a fixed feature of life for girls across Europe and not unique to Jews. Nevertheless, the reasons for its strength and persistence in the early modern period relate to the economic requirements for marriage. In rabbinic law the dowry served two primary functions: It allowed fathers to give their daughters sizable portions of family assets in place of inheritance, which favored sons, and it served to attract suitable husbands. The latter motivation predominated in various Jewish societies; it became virtually impossible for young women to get married without a substantial minimum dowry.[99] The need to support a family homestead and acquire the furnishings and sustenance of life often meant that women, regardless of ownership of assets, often played a role in the family economy, even before a family was formed. This need to accumulate significant funds even before a groom was identified played a central role in young women's lives between girlhood and marriage. In the early modern period, Jewish communities became involved in recording the amounts and enforcing the promises of dowry so that young couples would not fall into poverty and onto the charity rolls. Ashkenazic *pinkassim* contain frequent regulations and entries for *hatarat kiddushin*, the permission for marriage agreements in advance of the marriage. In Metz fathers of young women were required to put the dowry amount they had promised on deposit 30 days before the wedding. Failure to do so could constitute grounds for deferral or cancellation of the wedding.[100] Those whose parents could not endow an appropriate dowry were forced to become either recipients of communal or private charity designated for dowering poor or orphaned brides, or economic actors on their own behalf, usually by entering service as domestics for a set period of years. In the ideal scenario, after a period of service in which a young woman worked and was trained in household management, she would leave with her accumulated salary, and in certain places, an additional stipend from the Jewish community, and start her own home. The reality was more grim and complicated; many young women were abused economically and sexually and left without recompense for their service. This is one of many instances in which the price for community ideals of morality fell disproportionately on vulnerable women.

Dowry at marriage was but one point in the conventional life cycle of Jewish women and girls that involved the transfer of significant family assets; as daughters, they were affected by laws and customs of inheritance. Parents who strictly followed Torah and rabbinic law would end up functionally disinheriting daughters (sometimes in favor of granddaughters by sons, for example). To circumvent this, many parents wrote wills with specific terms that did not accord with Talmudic law. Jay Berkovitz notes that *shtar hatzi helek zakhar*, a work-around to inheritance laws that favored sons over daughters, while existing much earlier, came into broad use in the seventeenth century and was routinely used in settling estates among seventeenth- and eighteenth-century Ashkenazic Jews.[101] Hirsch Oppenheim of Hamburg stated explicitly in his will (1777) that the dowry granted to his married daughter be considered a portion of her inheritance equal to that of her unmarried siblings.[102] Regarding the question of whether rabbinic courts honored such written wills, Berkovitz notes that by the late eighteenth century the Metz rabbinic court tended to respect written wills even if not in conformity with halakhic guidelines. Both the communities of Metz and Altona left *pinkassim* containing copies of wills that included many written by women.[103]

Any inheritance they may have received, gifts upon betrothal, and dowry settled upon their marriage became the cornerstones of women's assets. Martha Howell has analyzed two types of communal approaches to marital assets: a "communal property regime" in which all the properties of a husband and wife were merged and treated as one unit and in which the survivor generally inherited the joint estate; and a "separate property regime," in which each party guarded the assets they brought into the marriage separately, the disposition of which was far more complicated when one partner died.[104] Jews of early modern Europe inherited a combination of approaches. Multiple sequential marriages were not uncommon, and neither were divorces. Each of these added a layer of complication to the disposition of a family's wealth. They also provide something of a gift to historians, for it is at these complex junctures—when *ketubbah* or other support payments were at stake, when written testaments and wills were contested, when inventories were taken of property and litigation over them ensued—that written documents illuminate economic aspects of women's lives. One eighteenth-century Jewish man, after disposing of various obligations in his will, wrote that he left the remainder of all he had to his wife as a gift in his lifetime, "so that my wife would not have to make a list, an accounting, or an inventory" for any debtor or heir.[105] Women's wills not only listed the contents of their homes and personal effects but also revealed their involvement in the community, from synagogue seats to cemetery plots and their wishes to endow religious benefactions to benefit their souls.

Although gender formed the most significant dividing line between early modern people, class came as a close second. Women shared aspects of their living conditions depending on their class status and in many ways regardless of religion. The greater access they had to wealth, the greater access women had to education, to networks of kinship and commerce, and to material comforts, living space, and decent nutrition for themselves and their families. However, their role in producing a share of that wealth did differ across religious lines in the early modern period to some extent. Historians of women in Western European economies, such as Natalie Zemon Davis and Merry Wiesner, working from court documents and archival materials, note a general decline in the participation of Christian women in their family and community economy during the sixteenth and seventeenth centuries, compared with the earlier period of the late fourteenth through fifteenth centuries described by Martha Howell. Early assessments of the role of Jewish women show that they continued to play crucial roles in their families and the larger communal economies during the same period.[106] About 40% of parties appearing before the rabbinic courts in late-eighteenth-century Metz were women, and they initiated a quarter of the suits. Certainly, as Berkovitz has argued, despite the harsh language in prescriptive community regulations, the courts recognized that women acted on their own, appeared often before the Jewish courts, and in many cases represented themselves.[107]

Conclusion

THE VARIOUS GENRES AND texts that were recorded and printed in early modern Central Europe and the visibility of women in these sources attest to the fact that the sweeping changes of the early modern period affected women as well as men. The age of print rendered a far more literate Jewish population, and the texts that proliferated in this period, some of which were written by women, tell us much about women's quotidian lives. Similarly, the vast number of records that documented and regulated individual and communal life are replete with information about women's activities, families, and interactions. Although we have highlighted the rich source material available for the study of early modern women, we have not touched on many important aspects of women's lives, which remain to be probed further. Demographic themes, including life span, age at marriage, the number of times an individual might marry over the course of her life, and divorce and fertility rates are among the many subjects that deeply affected the quality of women's lives, the status they held, and the Jewish community more broadly. These topics, along with other more specialized local studies, hold out the prospect of expanding our knowledge of how Jewish women were affected by the transitions that characterized early modern times.

Notes

Both authors contributed equally to this article.

1 Rachel Zohn Mincer, "The Increasing Reliance on Ritual Handbooks in Pre-Print Era Ashkenaz," *Jewish History* 31 (2017): 103–28.

2 Elchanan Reiner, "Aliyat 'ha-kehillah ha-gedolah': al shorshe ha-kehillah ha-yehudit ha-ironit be-Folin ba-et ha-hadashah ha-mukdemet" [The Rise of the Large Kehillah: On the Roots of the Urban Kehilla in Early Modern Poland], *Gal-Ed* 20 (2006): 13–37.

3 Stefan Litt, *Jüdische Gemeindestatuten aus dem aschkenasischen Kulturraum 1650–1850* (Göttingen: Vandenhoeck & Ruprecht, 2014), 98, par. 82.

4 See, for example, Elhanan Tal, *Ha-kehillah ha-Ashkenazit be-Amsterdam ba-me'ah ha-18* [The Ashkenazic Kehillah of Amsterdam in the 18th Century] (Jerusalem: Merkaz Shazar, 2010), 125.

5 Tal, *Ha-kehillah ha-Ashkenazit*, 209.

6 Marc Raeff, "The Well-Ordered Police State and the Development of Modernity in Seventeenth and Eighteenth Century Europe: An Attempt at a Comparative Approach," *American Historical Review* 80, no. 5 (1975): 1221–43.

7 Raeff, "Well-Ordered Police State," 1226.

8 Emperor Maximilian's reign (d. 1519) is marked by numerous attempts to rationalize governance and power in the Holy Roman Empire, culminating in the adoption of the legal code Carolina in 1532.

9 For an overview of this literature, see Stefan Litt, *Pinkas, Kahal, and the Mediene: The Records of Dutch Ashkenazi Communities in the Eighteenth Century as Historical Sources* (Leiden: Brill, 2008), 7–19, 92–113.

10 The Pinkassim Project, accessed through the NLI/Ktiv, site is digitizing a growing number of *pinkassim*. See http://web.nli.org.il/sites/NLI/English/collections/jewish-collection/pinkassim (accessed May 2, 2018).

11 Compare Robert Bonfil and Isaac Yudlov, eds., *Minute Book of the Jewish Community of Casale Monferrato, 1589–1657* (Jerusalem: Magnes, 2012) (Hebrew), with *Pinkas terumot le-bet ha-keneset be-Casale Monferrato*, Columbia University, Rare Books and Manuscripts Library, ms X893 P653. These are quite different

types of records; the former is a community minute book, whereas the latter is a *pinkas* containing records of donations to the synagogue on the Sabbath.

12 For example, Central Archives for the History of the Jewish People, Jerusalem (CAHJP), AHW 15 consists primarily of fines paid for violations of communal order.

13 For example, CAHJP, AHW 85a consists of announcements proclaimed in the synagogue in eighteenth-century Altona.

14 For example, CAHJP, AHW 31b, AHW 36 a–b and AHW 37 are *pinkassim* detailing poor relief in Hamburg and Altona in the seventeenth and eighteenth centuries.

15 CAHJP, AHW 10, par. 150, published in Heinz Mosche Graupe, *Die Statuten der Drei Gemeinden Altona, Hamburg und Wandsbeck*, 2 vols. (Hamburg: Hans Christians Verlag, 1973), 2: 90.

16 CAHJP, AHW 10, par. 151, in Graupe, *Statuten*, 2: 90.

17 For an analysis of communal bans against young men bringing their families and their impact on women, see Noa Shashar, *Gevarim neʾelamim- Agunot ba-merhav ha-Ashkenazi, 1650* [Vanished Men] (Jerusalem: Carmel, 2020).

18 See Edward Fram, *A Window on Their World: The Court Diaries of Rabbi Hayyim Gundersheim Frankfurt Am Main, 1773–1794* (Cincinnati: Hebrew Union College Press, 2012); and Jay Berkovitz, *Protocols of Justice: The Pinkas of the Metz Rabbinic Court, 1771–1789* (Leiden: Brill, 2014).

19 CAHJP, AHW 121/1 is apparently a record of civil cases before the Jewish court in Altona from the end of the eighteenth century.

20 For example, CAHJP, HM2/5182, which is composed of records of the burial society in Worms from 1716 to 1828.

21 For *pinkassim* kept by the *shamash*, see, for example, CAHJP, AHW 20; and Jewish Theological Seminary, ms 10772.

22 On midwives' records, see Jordan R. Katz, "Jewish Midwives, Medicine, and the Boundaries of Knowledge in Early Modern Europe, 1650–1800," PhD diss., Columbia University, 2020; and Elisheva Carlebach, "Community, Authority, and Jewish Midwives in Early Modern Europe," *Jewish Social Studies*, n.s., 20, no. 2 (2014): 5–33. Record books of circumcisers from the early modern period survive in relative abundance.

23 Jewish Theological Seminary, ms 10772, fol. 73r, entry for Thursday, 25 Kislev [5]327 [1767]. The woman is identified as the "wife of [Altona community leader] R. David L"D [Leidsdorf]."

24 CAHJP, D/Fr3/32 is an example of a similar record of individual financial transactions conducted in Frankfurt am Main in the seventeenth century, maintained by the community.

25 On the impact of print in early modern Europe, see Elizabeth L. Eisenstein, *The Printing Press as an Agent of Change: Communications and Cultural Transformations in Early-Modern Europe* (Cambridge, UK: Cambridge University Press, 1980); and Adrian Johns, *The Nature of the Book: Print and Knowledge in the Making*, 1st ed. (Chicago: University of Chicago Press, 2000).

26 Chava Weissler, *Voices of the Matriarchs: Listening to the Prayers of Early Modern Jewish Women* (Boston: Beacon Press, 1998), 52.

27 Edward Fram, *My Dear Daughter: Rabbi Benjamin Slonik and the Education of Jewish Women in Sixteenth-Century Poland* (Cincinnati: Hebrew Union College Press, 2007). On reading aloud among lower classes and women, see Roger Chartier, "Leisure and Sociability: Reading Aloud in Early Modern Europe," trans. Carol Mossman, in *Urban Life in the Renaissance*, ed. Susan Zimmerman and Ronald F. E. Weissman (Newark: University of Delaware Press, 1989), 103–20; and Tessa Watt, *Cheap Print and Popular Piety, 1550–1640* (Cambridge, UK: Cambridge University Press, 1993).

28 Moses Porges, "Darkhei Zion," in *Masaòt Eretz Israel shel olim yehudim me-yeme ha-benayim ve-ad le-reshit shivat Zion* [Travels to the Land of Israel of Jewish Immigrants from the Middle Ages Until the Beginning of the Return to Zion], by Avraham Yaari (Tel Aviv: Moden, 1996), 277. On Porges, see Yifat Mor-Rozenson, "Ba-derekh me-Yerushalayim le-Ashkenaz: Darkhei Zion le-Rav Moshe Porges u-kehal korim be-Ashkenaz ba-et ha-hadashah ha-mukdemet" [On the Path from Jerusalem to Ashkenaz: *Darkhei Zion* by Rabbi Moshe Porges and the Reading Public in Early Modern Ashkenaz], MA thesis equivalent, Bar Ilan University, 2018.

29 Natalie Zemon Davis, "Printing and the People," in *Society and Culture in Early Modern France*, by Natalie Zemon Davis (Stanford, CA: Stanford University Press, 1975), 189–226.

30 Fram, *My Dear Daughter*, 12–15.

31 For an English translation of Rabbi Slonik on this point, see Fram, *My Dear Daughter*, 156.

32 Fram, *My Dear Daughter*, xviii.

33 For resistance to print by some rabbis, see Elchanan Reiner, "The Ashkenazi Elite at the Beginning of the Modern Era: Manuscript Versus Printed Book," *Polin* 10 (1997): 85–98.

34 Rivka Bat Meir, *Meneket Rivkah: A Manual of Wisdom and Piety*, ed. Frauke Von Rohden (Philadelphia: Jewish Publication Society, 2009).

35 Yemima Chovav, *Alamot ahevukha: Hayye ha-dat veha-ruah shel nashim ba-hevrah ha-ashkenazit be-reshit ha-et ha-hadashah* [Maidens Love Thee: The Religious and Spiritual Life of Jewish Ashkenazic Women in the Early Modern Period] (Jerusalem: Merkaz Dinur and Carmel, 2009).

36 Rudolph Bell, *How To Do It* (Chicago: University of Chicago Press, 1999); Lyndal Roper, *The Holy Household: Women and Morals in Reformation Augsburg*, Oxford Studies in Social History (Oxford, UK: Clarendon Press, 1989).

37 Weissler, *Voices of the Matriarchs*, 66–148.

38 Moshe Rosman, "Lehiyot isha be-Folin-Lita be-reshit ha-et ha-hadasha" [To Be a Woman in Poland-Lithuania in the Early Modern Period], in *Kiyyum ve-shever: Yehudei Polin le-dorotehem* [The Broken Chain: Polish Jewry Through the Ages], 2 vols., ed. Israel Bartal and Israel Gutman (Jerusalem: Merkaz Shazar, 1987), 2: 415–31; and see Rosman's chapter in this volume.

39 See Chava Turniansky, "Yiddish Song as Historical Source Material: Plague in the Judenstadt of Prague in 1713," in *Jewish History: Essays in Honour of Chimen Abramsky*, ed. Ada Rapoport-Albert and Steven J. Zipperstein (London: Peter

Halban, 1988), 189–98; and Kathryn Hellerstein, *A Question of Tradition: Women Poets in Yiddish, 1586–1987* (Stanford, CA: Stanford University Press, 2014).

40 Nathanael Riemer and Sigrid Senkbeil, eds., *Be'er Sheva by Beer and Bella Perlhefter: An Edition of a Seventeenth Century Yiddish Encyclopedia* (Wiesbaden: Harrasowitz Verlag, 2011).

41 Wagenseil Collection, University Library, Leipzig, B.H. 18.

42 Elisheva Carlebach, "Letter into Text: Epistolarity, History, and Literature," in *Jewish Literature and History: An Interdisciplinary Conversation*, ed. Eliyana R. Adler and Sheila E. Jelen (Bethesda: University Press of Maryland, 2008), 113–33; Elisheva Carlebach, "The Letters of Bella Perlhefter," https://fordham.bepress .com/emw/emw2004/emw2004/11/ (accessed November 29, 2017).

43 See, most recently, Arthur Arnheim and Chava Turniansky, *Yiddish Letters from the World of Glikl Hamel* (Jerusalem: Magnes Press, 2020).

44 Chava Turniansky, ed. *Glikl: Zikhroynes, 1691–1719* (Jerusalem: Merkaz Zalman Shazar, 2006), in translation by Sara Friedman as *Glikl: Memoirs, 1691–1719* (Waltham, MA: Brandeis University Press, 2019).

45 See, for example, Monika Richarz, *Die Hamburger Kauffrau Glikl: Jüdische Existenz in der Frühen Neuzeit* (Hamburg: Christians, 2001).

46 Cornelia Niekus Moore, "The Quest for Consolation and Amusement: Reading Habits of German Women in the Seventeenth Century," in *The Graph of Sex and the German Text: Gendered Culture in Early Modern Germany 1500–1700*, ed. Lynne Tatlock (Leiden: Brill Rodopi, 1994), 247–68; Natalie Zemon Davis, *Women on the Margins: Three Seventeenth Century Lives* (Cambridge, MA: Harvard University Press, 1997).

47 Abraham Meir Haberman, *Nashim ivriot be-tor madpisot, mesadrot, motziot le-or ve-tomkhot be-mehabrim* [Jewish Women as Printers, Typesetters, Publishers, and Patrons of Authors] (Berlin: Reuven Maas, 1933), 7.

48 Fram, *My Dear Daughter*, 54n88.

49 Haberman, *Nashim ivriot*, 13.

50 Haberman, *Nashim ivriot*, 12–13.

51 Fram, *My Dear Daughter*, 54.

52 Haberman, *Nashim ivriot*.

53 Yair Hayyim Bacharach, *Havat Yair* (Frankfurt am Main, 1699), introduction.

54 On gender and the Memorbuch of Frankfurt, see Tzvia Koren-Loeb, "Das Memorbuch zu Frankfurt am Main: Erschließung und Kommentierung Ausgewählter Themenkreise," PhD diss., Universität Duisberg Essen, 2008.

55 Barry L. Stiefel, *Jews and the Renaissance of Synagogue Architecture, 1450–1730* (London: Routledge, 2016); Helen Hills, *Architecture and the Politics of Gender in Early Modern Europe* (Aldershot, UK: Ashgate, 2003).

56 Avraham Yaari, "Shnei kuntresim me-Erets Yisrael" [Two Letters from the Land of Israel], *Kiryat Sefer* 23, no. 2 (1947): 140–59. On women and the new month, see *y. Pesachim* 4:1.

57 This can be found in the logbook from the Pinkas Synagogue in Prague; CAHJP, HM2/4024.

58 Juspe Schammes, *Minhagim de K"K Warmaisa*, 2 vols., ed. B. S. Hamburger and E. Zimmer (Jerusalem: Mif'al Torat Hakhmei Ashkenaz, 1988), no. 186.

59 Juspe Schammes, *Minhagim*, no. 224. On youth, see Elliott S. Horowitz, "A Jewish Youth Confraternity in 17th-Century Italy," *Italia* 5 (1985): 36–97.

60 Daniel Sperber, *The Jewish Life Cycle: Custom, Lore, and Iconography: Jewish Customs from the Cradle to the Grave* (Oxford, UK: Oxford University Press, 2008), 173–74.

61 On the medieval practice, see Avital Davidovitch-Eshed, "Bein keliah le-keliah: Al se'ar u-betulim ba-tarbut ha-Ashkenazit be-yeme ha-benayim" [Between Plaits: On Hair and Virginity in Medieval Ashkenazic Culture], *Zmanim* 118 (2012): 50–61.

62 Juspe Schammes, *Minhagim*, no. 231.

63 Diana Matut, "Singing for the Bride and Groom in Early Modern Ashkenaz," paper presented at the YIVO Institute for Jewish Research, New York, September 19, 2017.

64 Lyndal Roper, "'Going to Church and Street': Weddings in Reformation Augsburg," *Past and Present* 106 (1985): 62–101; Debra Kaplan, "Rituals of Marriage and Communal Prestige: The Breileft in Medieval and Early Modern Germany," *Jewish History* 29, nos. 3–4 (2015): 273–300.

65 Juspe Schammes, *Minhagim*, no. 230.

66 Elisheva Baumgarten, *Mothers and Children: Jewish Family Life in Medieval Europe* (Princeton, NJ: Princeton University Press, 2004), 100–105.

67 Robert Weyl and Freddy Raphael, *Juifs en Alsace: Culture, société, histoire* (Toulouse: Privat, 1977), 184–94.

68 Baumgarten, *Mothers and Children*, 105–18.

69 See, for example, Elisheva Carlebach, *Divided Souls: Converts from Judaism in Germany, 1500–1750* (New Haven, CT: Yale University Press, 2001); and Yaacov Deutsch, *Judaism in Christian Eyes: Ethnographic Descriptions of Jews and Judaism in Early Modern Europe* (New York: Oxford University Press, 2012).

70 *Sefer Minhagim* (Venice, 1593), Bodleian Libraries, University of Oxford, Opp. 4° 1006, fol. 19r; and the images in Diane Wolfthal, *Picturing Yiddish: Gender, Identity, and Memory in the Illustrated Yiddish Books of Renaissance Italy* (Leiden: Brill, 2004).

71 Juspe Schammes, *Minhagim*, no. 248.

72 Elisheva Baumgarten, "'Remember That Glorious Girl': Jephthah's Daughter in Medieval Jewish Culture," *Jewish Quarterly Review* 97 (2007): 180–209; Elisheva Carlebach, *Palaces of Time: Jewish Calendar and Culture in Early Modern Europe* (Cambridge, MA: Harvard University Press, 2011), 160–88.

73 Wolfthal, *Picturing Yiddish*, fig. 12.

74 Wolfthal, *Picturing Yiddish*, fig. 53.

75 *Sefer Minhagim* (Venice, 1600), Bodleian Libraries, University of Oxford, Opp. 4° 1004, fol. 63v.

76 For mikveh fees in the Netherlands, see Litt, *Pinkas, Kahal, and the Mediene*, 79–80.

77 Debra Kaplan, "'To Immerse Their Wives': Communal Identity and the 'Kahalishe' Mikveh of Altona," *AJS Review* 36, no. 2 (2012): 257–79. Similar regulation can be found in the printed *pinkassim* of Amsterdam and Padua.

78 Litt, *Jüdsche Gemeindestatuten*, 262, par. 456; 375, par. 62.

79 Litt, *Jüdische Gemeindestatuten*, 262, par. 460; 375, par. 62.

80 Litt, *Jüdische Gemeindestatuten*, 262, par. 458.

81 Michael Toch, "Jewish Women Entrepreneurs in the 16th and 17th Century: Economics and Family Structure," *Jahrbuch für Fränkische Landesforschung* 60 (2000): 256. For a more extended discussion of this subject, see Debra Kaplan, "Women and Worth: Female Access to Property in Early Modern Urban Jewish Communities," *Leo Baeck Institute Year Book* 55, no. 1 (2010): 93–113.

82 Berkovitz, *Protocols*, 136.

83 Berkovitz, *Protocols*, 169; Fram, *Window on Their World*, 35.

84 Toch, "Jewish Women Entrepreneurs," 258.

85 Michael Toch notes that the rate for late medieval female entrepreneurship for rural women in fifteenth-century southern Germany was twice as high as the rates for the sixteenth and seventeenth centuries. See Toch, "Jewish Women Entrepreneurs," 256.

86 Debra Kaplan, *Beyond Expulsion: Jews, Christians, and Reformation Strasbourg* (Stanford, CA: Stanford University Press, 2011), 79; Berkovitz, *Protocols of Justice*.

87 Berkovitz, *Protocols*; CAHJP, D/Fr3/32. For additional *takkanot* that dealt with this issue in Frankfurt, see Kaplan, "Women and Worth."

88 Shashar, *Gevarim ne'elamim*.

89 For the Leipzig fair, see Max Freudenthal, *Leipziger Messgäste: Die jüdischen Besucher der Leipziger Messen in den Jahren 1675 bis 1764* (Frankfurt am Main: J. Kauffmann, 1928); Richard Markgraf, *Zur Geschichte der Juden auf den Messen in Leipzig von 1664–1839* (Bischofswerda, Germany: Friedrich May, 1894).

90 Fram, *Window on Their World*, 117, no. 48.

91 Debra Kaplan, "'Because Our Wives Trade and Do Business with Our Goods': Gender, Work, and Jewish-Christian Relations," in *New Perspectives on Jewish-Christian Relations: In Honor of David Berger*, ed. Elisheva Carlebach and Jacob J. Schacter (Leiden: Brill, 2012), 241–61.

92 See, for example, CAHJP, AHW 121/1; and Berkovitz, *Protocols*, 171.

93 See Carlebach, "Community"; and Katz, "Jewish Midwives."

94 See, for example, Fram, *Window on Their World*, 97, no. 39, in which one woman and two men served as matchmakers for one couple; and 105, no. 42, in which three men and one woman served as matchmakers for another match.

95 Daniel Lord Smail, *Legal Plunder: Households and Debt Collection in Late Medieval Europe* (Cambridge, MA: Harvard University, 2016), index *s.v.* clothing.

96 For repairing clothing, see Toch, "Jewish Women Entrepreneurs," 259, regarding Sara, wife of Isaac of Alsfeld (1529), who "used to sew shirts and collars for her customers." On rural women, see Kaplan, "Women and Worth."

97 Robert Liberles, *Jews Welcome Coffee: Tradition and Innovation in Early Modern Germany* (Waltham, MA: Brandeis University Press, 2012), 71.

98 Mary Lindemann, *Patriots and Paupers: Hamburg, 1712–1830* (Oxford, UK: Oxford University Press, 1990), 48.

99 Eve Krakowski provides an illuminating discussion of the relationship between dowry, female adolescence, and labor. See Eve Krakowski, *Coming of Age in*

Medieval Egypt: Female Adolescence, Jewish Law, and Ordinary Culture (Princeton, NJ: Princeton University Press, 2017), 143–65.

100 Berkovitz, *Protocols*, 141–42.

101 Berkovitz, *Protocols*, 153.

102 Heinz Moshe Graupe, "Jewish Testaments from Altona and Hamburg (18th Century)," *Michael: On the History of the Jews in the Diaspora* 2 (1973): 29.

103 For Metz, see Berkovitz, *Protocols*, 152n43, referring to Jewish Theological Seminary of America, Archives, ms. 9835; for Altona and Hamburg, see the will of Pesche, wife of Moses Hamm (1763), in Graupe, "Jewish Testaments," 24–26.

104 Martha C. Howell, *Women, Production, and Patriarchy in Late Medieval Cities* (Chicago: University of Chicago Press, 1986), 9–20.

105 Graupe, "Jewish Testaments," 13.

106 Merry Wiesner, *Working Women in Renaissance Germany* (New Brunswick, NJ: Rutgers University Press, 1986), 7; Howell, *Women, Production, and Patriarchy*; Kaplan, "Women and Worth."

107 Berkovitz, *Protocols*, 172.

JEWISH WOMEN IN THE POLISH-LITHUANIAN COMMONWEALTH

From Facilitation to Participation

MOSHE ROSMAN

THE POLISH-LITHUANIAN COMMONWEALTH WAS officially created by the 1569 Union of Lublin in which Crown Poland (roughly, today's Poland plus Ukraine west of the Dnieper River) was confederated with the Grand Duchy of Lithuania (encompassing today's Belarus, Lithuania, much of Latvia, and at times parts of Estonia). It was this commonwealth that was partitioned three times (1772, 1793, 1795) and erased from the map by its neighbors, Prussia, Russia, and Austria.

The Commonwealth was a large country stretching from the Baltic Sea in the north to just shy of the Black Sea in the south and from somewhat east of the Dnieper River in the east to the Oder River in the west. It was multi-ethnic (including, in addition to the main groups of its constituent countries, Germans, Armenians, Scots, Italians, and Jews) and multireligious (Roman Catholic, Greek Catholic, Orthodox, Protestant, Jewish, etc.). The economy was based on agriculture, organized in a feudal manner with the land owned by the king, the churches and, especially, the nobility, although it was worked by medieval-style serfs who owed fealty and labor to their lords. The country was a commonwealth with a legislative parliament (Sejm) composed of representatives of the nobles (about 10% of the population), and all nobles had the right to participate in elections for the king.

Ashkenazic Jews from German lands began establishing permanent communities in Poland in the twelfth century. Along with economic opportunity, the Commonwealth's relative religious toleration attracted Jewish settlement. By the mid-eighteenth century Jews were some 7% of the population and approximately half of the urban population; numbering 750,000, they constituted the largest Jewish community in the early modern world.

They enjoyed a significant measure of communal autonomy, with their own legislative and judicial institutions. They were prosperous enough to support a vibrant religious and educational culture with many synagogues, schools, and yeshivas.

Like the larger Polish society and European society in general, Polish Jewish society was patriarchal.[1] In this context *patriarchal* denotes the fact that men dominated public political and religious life and overwhelmingly held the most powerful economic positions. They also benefited from more legal rights than women. Women, however, were not without agency. As we will see, they were active in the marketplace, had property rights, managed matters of health (especially gynecology), were often heads of households, and conducted an articulated religious life. Moreover, marriage was indeed a partnership with the division of domestic power decided on a case-by-case basis.

That said, most sources for the history of the Jews in the Polish-Lithuanian Commonwealth were written by men for men. It is therefore no surprise that historiography has turned its attention to Polish Jewish women's lives only relatively recently. Yet, once one asks what life was like for Jewish women in the early modern Polish-Lithuanian Commonwealth, it turns out that there are sources that relate to women's experiences and that it is possible to combine "her-story" with "his-story," transforming the historical narrative.

Gender Stereotypes

WE CAN BEGIN BY attempting to delineate the attributes of "women" in this society. What characteristics were denoted by the gender "female" as opposed to "male"? A manuscript from the Jewish Division of the Vernadsky Library in Kiev, titled *Sefer Haḥeshek*, offers us a convenient typology.[2] *Sefer Haḥeshek* was written in northern Ukraine (Volhynia) around 1740 by a man named Hillel Ba'al Shem. Hillel was an itinerant *ba'al shem*[3] who made his living by ministering to the medical, spiritual, and material problems of people he encountered in the communities he visited. His stock-in-trade consisted of natural folk remedies and the magical methods of practical Kabbalah. Hillel dreamed of settling down as the resident *ba'al shem* in some Jewish community. This would offer a steady livelihood, status, and the comfort of a permanent home. To further his objective, Hillel wrote *Sefer Haḥeshek*, a work that can be classified as a *segulah* book, that is, a book of prayers, incantations, amulet drawings and inscriptions, medicament recipes, and instructions for rituals—all of which were involved in the prevention or treatment of a litany of diseases, spirit possession, bad luck, and financial, social, and other problems.[4] As a man of his time Hillel did not differentiate between medical and other realms. He treated constipation, infertility, and epilepsy as well as unrequited love and annoying neighbors. The book was intended to prove Hillel's bona fides as a professional, experienced *ba'al shem*. He hoped his book, as evidence of his expertise, would help persuade the leaders of some Jewish community to permit him to settle among them and offer his *ba'al shem* services.

Sefer Haheshek is a significant cultural document that reflects the mental infrastructure of the lives of the people the author wished to convince of his knowledge and talents. Focusing on the problems of everyday life, the book lends insight into the beliefs, values, assumptions, conventions, fears, and hopes—all self-evident to the people of the time—that guided the behavior of the people of this society. One of the main foundations of social life was the construction of gender, and *Sefer Haheshek* reveals how masculinity and femininity were understood.

Hillel gave a straightforward typology of gender in his time and place by listing the attributes and fates that supposedly typified those born on the various days of the months. For example, "The sixth day: he born on it will be cunning and will live long, a female as well."[5] In all, Hillel listed thirty-four character traits or fates. Fourteen of them might be found with the members of either gender. These were long life, honor, wisdom, cleverness, bad luck, difficult death, hard work, finding favor in the eyes of God and man, beauty, agility, rhetorical ability, mercantile skill, loyalty, and success. With respect to women, three of the attributes are not typically associated with female stereotypes: rhetorical ability, mercantile skill, and success (undefined). As we will see, women in this society were economically active. As to rhetorical ability, it may be that this is a hint to one type of behavior that marked a woman as exceptional ("important") in a positive way, whether in the family setting or in the larger society. Hillel's strictly male characteristics do fit the usual stereotype. A man might be erudite, strong, courageous, blessed, or weak. Some men are afraid of danger and liable to commit (bad) involuntary actions. The attributes specified for women include modesty, ugliness, bashfulness, and charm. These were all typical for European women of the time.[6] A woman might also be "important" (*hashuvah*), making her mark on society through her qualities, wealth, or personal stature.

Most of the medical problems raised in *Sefer Haheshek* relate to women, especially fertility, pregnancy, and birth. Hillel kept returning to the problems engendered by these biological processes, continually prescribing different treatments. Some examples:

To keep Lilith, the female demon, away from the marital bed: beat two copulating dogs with a stick and put the stick in the bed.

To diagnose which member of the couple is infertile: take urine samples from each one and place bran in each container. The sample that produces worms first, belongs to the person responsible for the infertility.

To ease a difficult birth: without her realizing it, give the parturient woman to drink dried and powdered horse or mouse turd boiled and mixed in wine or water.[7]

These are just a few examples of dozens of remedies proffered by Hillel for a variety of concerns. Such remedies were in addition to a range of incantations and amulets. With respect to gynecological problems, Hillel was confident which remedy should be prescribed. However, his book does not exhibit any knowledge (even mistaken) of female anatomy or physiology. This ignorance was another aspect of the gendered organization of life. Jewish men, even *ba'alei shem*, were not to cross the gender boundary into women's realm, especially not into the labor and delivery room. Women's health problems were to stay almost exclusively in women's sphere. Hillel assumed that there would always be midwives supervising births, and he trusted in their expertise. His role was to advise them when an unusual problem arose, based on their oral description, not his clinical examination. The initiative remained with these women.[8] Even after turning to this man for consultation, it was the midwife, not he, who actually administered the remedy.

This is illustrated by Hillel's contemporary, Pinhas Katzenellenbogen's description of the use of a birth amulet. Katzenellenbogen requested an amulet from the *ba'al shem* Benjamin Beinish of Krotoszyn to ensure an easy, successful birth. The *ba'al shem* gave the rabbi a bundle of mystical inscriptions[9] to be fastened to the navel of the birthing woman. He stressed that the timing was essential. The amulet must not be placed on her too early or left in place once the baby came out. Those responsible for the all-important timing of the placement were women.

> You must take great care not to place the bundle too soon, but only when it is the proper time for the newborn to come out. *The midwife* will know instantly how to determine the right time. Also, be very careful that *the woman herself or the women attending* her remove it as soon as the infant emerges.[10] (emphasis added)

A man might be an expert in women's matters in theory, but in practice the gender boundary remained and at the end of the day women bore responsibility for their own health.[11]

Hillel repeatedly advised or demanded that a woman suffering from an ailment recite the incantations or the prayers herself rather than listen and say amen to the words of some man.[12] In general *Sefer Haheshek* creates the impression that women spent much of their lives diagnosing health problems for themselves and the members of their families, preparing and administering medicaments, and reciting incantations and prayers. These activities were a significant part of the ritual behavior of Jewish women, paralleling to some extent the ritual life of men.[13] Men were supposed to attend the synagogue daily and set aside time for Torah study. Women, following the instructions of the local *ba'al shem*, were charged with medical or magical protection of the family's health. This entailed a psychological burden. If the remedy failed (the woman did not conceive, the infant died in utero, etc.), the easiest expedient was to blame the woman's faulty application of the instructions or her character flaws or misbehavior.

The Feminine Ideal

THE GENDER SYSTEM THAT characterized Polish Jewish society, which Hillel Ba'al Shem reflected, also gained expression through other representatives of Polish Jewry. For example, the Vilna Gaon, Elijah ben Solomon Zalman, wrote a letter to his wife, Hannah, during his unsuccessful attempt to travel to the Holy Land (ca. 1770). In the letter, the Gaon noted various attributes that he expected would characterize his children. With regard to sons he was most concerned that they study intensively. With respect to his daughters he urged his wife:

> I also make an especial and emphatic request that you train your daughters to the avoidance of abjurations, oaths, lies or contention. Let their whole conversation be conducted in peace, love, affability and gentleness. I possess many moral conduct books with German [i.e., Yiddish translations];[14] let them read these regularly; above all on the Sabbath—the holy of holies—they should occupy themselves with these ethical books exclusively. For a curse, an oath or a lie, strike them; show no softness in the matter. For (God forbid!) the mother and father are punished for the corruption of the children. . . .

Therefore be most rigorous in their moral training, and may Heaven help you to success! So with other matters, such as the avoidance of slander and gossip; the regular recital of grace before and after meals, the reading of the Shema, all with true devotion. The fundamental rule, however, is that they not gad about in the streets, but incline their ear to your words and honor you and my mother and all their elders. Urge them to obey all that is written in the moral conduct books. . . .

Sin crouches at the door and people are ruled by their impulses. For men, the remedy is Torah study; and for women, modesty.[15]

The supreme objective for boys was erudition; girls, above all, were supposed to behave modestly, politely, and piously. Girls' textbooks were moral conduct (*musar*) books. Rather than presenting Torah interpretations, these books urged their readers to be God-fearing, mitzvah observant, modest, and humble. A boy excelled by *knowing*; a girl, by being pious, modest, quiet, and obedient.[16]

It was axiomatic that the members of both sexes were to refrain from sexual contact until marriage. Guarding girls' virginity was paramount, as implied by the following enactment in the record book (*pinkas*) of the Talmud confraternity (*hevrat shas*) of the Zhitomir *kloyz* (place of advanced study) from 1775:

Be it a testimony in Israel and a memorial for the future that the scholar Samuel ben Elijah came before us, the leaders [*gabbaim*] of the Ner Tamid confraternity asserting that his daughter, Rachel Leah, aged two years, fell off a chair today onto the ground and broke her hymen. Thus we the undersigned investigated and found and realized that this was indeed true. Therefore, so that in the future this will not be a handicap, slander or evil defamation for the girl Rachel Leah, we have recorded this for safe-keeping in the book as a protection for her open to all.[17]

A girl who was not a virgin would have low value on the marriage market. Therefore it was imperative that the public record show that the toddler Rachel Leah lost her hymen as the result of an accident and not a premarital sexual contact.

In his letter the Vilna Gaon epitomized the essence of his society's conventional view of gender: "Sin crouches at the door and people are ruled by their impulses. For men, the remedy is Torah study; and for women, modesty."[18]

His ideal was for a boy to grow into a scholar and a girl to be his supportive, modest wife facilitating his life of Torah. Hannah, his own wife, described him as "not caring about worldly matters, his household, the health of his children or his livelihood." These were her proper concern.[19] This approach was enunciated as early as the Talmud.[20] In Poland it was given expression by Rabbi Moses Isserles (known as Rama or Remu): "If a woman helps her son or husband study Torah, she shares their reward."[21]

Sara Rebecca Rachel Leah Horowitz

IT IS INSTRUCTIVE TO compare the ideal of the facilitating wife with the ideas of Sarah Rebecca Rachel Leah Horowitz. Probably born in the second decade of the eighteenth century, Leah (the name she was commonly known by) lived in different places in southeast Poland-Lithuania and was an unusually learned Jewish woman. This is obvious from a booklet that she wrote titled *Tkhine Imohos*, or supplicatory prayer of the Matriarchs. The booklet contained three sections: (1) an introduction in Hebrew in which Leah, a woman, justifies her daring to write a prayer and also gives her opinion about women's place in Jewish religion; (2) a version of the *tkhine* in Aramaic; and (3) the Yiddish *tkhine*. It is clear from the many citations in her texts as well as her ability to write in Aramaic that Leah was a scholar who was conversant with the Bible, Talmud, midrashim, and even the Zohar.[22]

Leah accepted much of the conventional wisdom of her time with respect to women.[23] For example, some of her ideas match those of the Vilna Gaon as to the desirable attributes of Jewish women. Both of them quote the rabbinic maxim "A proper woman obeys her husband."[24] Like the Gaon, Leah recognized the negative effects that female synagogue attendance might bring. The Gaon asserted, "It would also be better for your daughter not to go to the synagogue because there she will see embroidered clothing and the like and become jealous and say something at home. This leads to slander and other things."[25] Leah also pointed out the female jealousy that could result from synagogue attendance: "Women talking [rather than praying] in the synagogue arouse jealousy, even in such a holy place. When she gets home a woman argues with her husband over finery. She says, 'In the synagogue I should be outfitted as beautifully as so-and-so.'"[26] Leah also shared the opinion that a common sin of Jewish women was talking during the prayer service: "Women are talkative, gabbing in the synagogue on the Sabbath."[27]

Leah's overall conclusions, however, differed from those of the male authorities. Because of the potential for negative effects, the Gaon preferred to keep his daughters away from the synagogue (although he was not enthusiastic about men's behavior there either).[28] By contrast, Leah asserted that it was important for women to attend synagogue daily. If women were given prayers to say, such as the *tkhine* that she wrote, or even if they just cried in spontaneous, improvised prayer, and if female prayer were given the respect it warranted, then women's participation in the synagogue service might serve a noble purpose.

> "A person's prayer is only heard in the synagogue" [*Yalkut Shimoni*, I Kings, 190; *b. Berakhot* 6a]. Therefore, because "the day of the Lord is near" [Isa. 13:6], it is proper that our women come to the synagogue morning and evening to pray "with copious tears" [Isa. 59:20]. . . . Perhaps in the women's merit "the redeemer will come to Zion" [Ps. 80:6].[29]

Moreover, Leah challenged the declaration of the Talmud: "How do women gain merit? By bringing their sons to the synagogue [to study] and waiting for their husbands until they return from the bet midrash."[30] Leah did not understand how the Talmud could pronounce that women's role was limited to religious facilitation. She noted that women were responsible for observing all 365 negative commandments in the Torah in addition to 46 of the 60 positive commandments still relevant to individual practice (since the Temple was destroyed). In that case, why were no other merits for women mentioned?[31]

For Leah it was imperative for every Jew to study Torah and discover for her- or himself what God asks of each person. Yiddish books were the vehicle by which women—and uneducated men—could connect to the Torah. Describing appropriate behavior for the Sabbath, she wrote, "They should only speak words of Torah and study, each according to his ability. Moreover, those [men] incapable of study and also the women should read in Yiddish so they also will understand how to serve God. They must know how to keep the mitzvot that apply to them that God has set forth."[32] Leah did not explicitly challenge the conventional expectation that women should facilitate the religious fulfillment of their menfolk. She demanded recognition that women's religious role properly included observing a plethora of commandments, public synagogue prayer, and Torah study.

A Literature Accessible to Women

THE YIDDISH LITERATURE THAT the Gaon and Leah commended was a development of early modern Ashkenazic European Jewry in both the West and the

East. Beginning in the sixteenth century, as print became widespread, a new Yiddish library grew for women and uneducated men (*nashim ve'amai ha'aretz*). This library included several genres of religious literature: literal translations of the Bible (Konstanz, 1544; Cremona, 1560) and works such as the *Melokhim Buch* (Augsburg, 1543) and the *Shmuel Bukh* (Augsburg, 1544), which retold the biblical stories from the books of Samuel and Kings as epic poems. The most popular book, *Tsene u'rene* (Go Forth and See; Lublin? ca. 1600), was a retelling of the Torah portions weaving the main rabbinic midrashim into the translated Torah text. Books such as *Azhoras Noshim* (Kraków, 1534), *Seder Noshim* (Kraków, 1541), and *Seder Mitzvos Hanoshim* (Kraków, 1577) belong to the genre of literature (referred to as *seder mitzvot nashim*, "the order of women's precepts") that explained the commandments considered to apply especially to women. Moral conduct books, such as *Brantspiegel* (Burning Mirror; Kraków, 1596) and *Menekes Rivke* (Rebecca's Nurse; Prague, 1609),[33] instructed their readers how to behave as pious, modest women, warned them against sinning, and illustrated their strictures with legends and anecdotes. Anthologies of stories with a moral, such as the *Ma'aseh Bukh* (Basel, 1602), provided entertainment with a religious message. Beginning in the seventeenth century, *tkhine* collections gave women especially a means of religious expression attuned to the rhythms of their life. Some of these *tkhines* were intended for recitation in the synagogue as a component of public prayer liturgy. Others were said by women in private according to their personal spiritual needs. There were *tkhines* geared to every stage of the female biological cycle: menstruation, immersion, coitus, pregnancy, birth; *tkhines* accompanying the performance of sacral acts such as lighting Sabbath candles or visiting the cemetery; and *tkhines* for sickness, death, and other misfortunes.[34]

The development of the Yiddish library during the sixteenth–eighteenth centuries was tacit recognition on the part of the male rabbinic elite, whose members composed most of this literature, that, religiously speaking, women counted. As early as 1589 the Kraków printer Isaac ben Aaron of Prossnitz insisted, "Women are also obligated to learn; that is, Pentateuch, Bible, all of the laws of purity and impurity and of what is permitted and what is prohibited, just as well as the men."[35]

It was necessary to prepare women for their cultural roles in an efficacious manner. In the maelstrom of religious trends of Reformation and Counter-Reformation Europe, Jewish women needed new means of education that could immunize them against alien influences and ensconce them securely within the circle of Jewish culture. With the newly accessible library women could acquire knowledge parallel to what was contained in the books belonging to the erudite men. They were introduced to Judaism's fundamental beliefs and lore. A woman who read or listened to *Tsene u'rene* could learn the rabbinic interpretation of the Torah, loosely parallel to what a scholarly man would glean from Rashi's commentary. The *Ma'aseh Bukh* presented many of the legendary stories from rabbinic literature, echoing the classic *Ein Ya'akov*, often studied by men. The *Brantspiegel*, an encyclopedic guide to proper daily thought and behavior throughout the seasons of the year, was full of halakhic material. There were *tkhines* that cited the Zohar and other kabbalistic works, along with explanations of various halakhic rules and customs.[36] As a result, women could potentially understand basic Jewish theology and Halakhah.

Women in the Synagogue

IT IS EVIDENT THAT in this period women's participation in public prayer in the synagogue was on the rise. In his *Mappah* glosses on the *Shulḥan Arukh*, the leading Polish rabbi Moses Isserles (1520–1572) declared:

> Some wrote that a menstruant woman may not enter the synagogue, worship, speak God's name or touch a book during the days she sees blood. Others say she is permitted to do all of these things; and *this is the primary opinion*. However, the custom of these lands is to follow the first opinion. But during the white days[37] it was customary to be lenient. Even where they were stricter, on the High Holidays and such occasions when many gather to attend the synagogue it is permitted to [menstruants], like other women, to attend the synagogue because their standing outside when everyone is gathered together [inside] causes them great pain.[38] (emphasis added)

Isserles's sixteenth-century ruling apparently reflects a conflict between a veteran practice, distancing menstruants, and a more recent trend to encourage women to attend synagogue. In the passage Isserles challenges the legal basis of the prohibitory custom and cites two further leniencies that would facilitate more female participation in public ritual.

The tendency to favor women's participation in public worship found expression in Ashkenazic synagogue architecture of this period. From the late sixteenth century, beginning in Ashkenaz and moving into Poland, communities remodeled existing synagogues and built new ones to include dedicated women's sections (*ezrat nashim*) under the main roof of the building as an integral part of the structure. This architectural element brought women physically into the synagogue and announced that they had a permanent place there. This contrasted with earlier arrangements where women remained outside or were relegated to an adjacent *weibershul* (women's synagogue), to a basement below the prayer hall, or to a temporarily partitioned-off space in the main prayer hall on special occasions, such as the priestly blessing on holidays or the shofar blowing on Rosh Hashanah.[39]

In a similar spirit, many of the *tkhines* composed in Poland in the eighteenth century, like Horowitz's *Tkhine Imohos*, were written for recitation in the synagogue during services there, rather than in private.[40] This was a further sign of the expansion of women's role in public prayer.

The bylaws of the community of Nieśwież (ca. 1740) confirm the presence of women in the synagogue, at least on the Sabbath. They also allude to problems with women's ostentatious dress that the Vilna Gaon referred to. One rule forbade Jewish women to walk in the street dressed in a garment embroidered with gold and silver thread, called a *zaleska*. The reason was so as not to arouse gentile jealousies. On the Sabbath, however, there was some leniency: "When a woman goes to synagogue wearing a *zaleska* inlaid with gold or silver embroidery, she must wear it inside out until she arrives at the synagogue. There she may turn the *zaleska* to the gold and silver side. But when she leaves the synagogue to go home, she must again turn it inside out."[41] The 1759 bylaws of a different community, Iwieniec (near Minsk), imply that women also attended synagogue services on weekdays. One of a series of prohibitions intended to prevent informal, unsupervised social contact between women and men ordered that "the women must leave the synagogue during the *daily morning service* before the Torah ark is opened and *in the evening* before the aleinu prayer" (emphasis added).[42]

Women's Economic Status

IF IN THE REALM of religion and culture paying more attention to women's needs was a new trend,[43] in the economic sphere Jewish women's active role had long been a given. In Poland, with regard to real estate, from a legal perspective all married women—Christian and Jewish—were partners with their husbands. Municipal court records document many real estate transactions. Consistently, the names of both members of the couple were recorded as owners of the sold property. There was evidently fear that failure to list the woman might serve as future grounds to annul the sale, claiming that she objected to it as a rightful owner.[44] On the other hand, these same real estate transaction records point to a weakness in at least some women's economic status. From the recovery after the Chmielnicki massacres of the mid-seventeenth century through the 1780s, in real estate deals involving both Jews and Christians, east of the Vistula, the tendency was for the Christian to be the seller and the Jew the buyer. This fits the general pattern of a rise in the Jewish population, the geographic spread of Jewish settlement to towns in the east of the country, and the creation of the Jewish shtetls, market towns with a Jewish majority. However, there was an exception to this pattern. When the Jewish party to the real estate deal was an unmarried female rather than a male, it was almost always she who was the seller.[45] This is because these sellers were typically widows, forced to sell their homes to have enough money for the ongoing support of their families. These widows could not continue in the trades or businesses of their late husbands and suffered a decline, frequently precipitous, in their economic capabilities. Such real estate sales testify to the dependence of these women and their families on the economic activities of their husbands.

Such dependence and economic descent are illustrated by the case of Dobraszka.[46] Dobraszka was married to Jospa. When Jospa died, sometime before 1715, Dobraszka was left with a total debt of 4110 zlotys owed to creditors. The property that Jospa left did not equal the debt. Dobraszka signed a prenuptial agreement with her second husband, Moszko Berkowicz. There she promised to transfer all of her property to Moszko. In exchange, Moszko committed to pay off Dobraszka's debts, buy her three sets of clothing, and set up an 800-zloty fund that her fatherless son could draw on in the future. When her first husband died, Dobraszka was, practically speaking, bankrupt. Instead of selling her house and attempting to scrape by, Dobraszka utilized her property as a dowry and attained economic security through remarriage.

Other cases reinforce the impression of the general economic dependence of Jewish women on their husbands. In 1710 the arrendator (revenue lessee) Abramko, husband to Szejna, was arrested, beaten, and died of his wounds.[47] Szejna could not continue managing her *arenda* (leasehold) on her own. She even paid a Jewish agent to find someone who would take it off her hands. The agent disappointed. Szejna became ill and did not even have enough money to pay for a doctor.[48]

Sometime in the mid-1780s Oron Kusznierz died, leaving his wife, Ruchl, with a 50-zloty debt to the *kahal* of Winnica (Vinnytsia, Ukraine). Communal elders demanded her property in payment of the debt. She refused and appealed to the Winnica municipal court. The Polish court decided that Ruchl was indeed liable for the debt but did not require her to hand over her home. Instead, it ruled that she should sell the house, using part of the proceeds to pay off the debt but keeping the balance. Without her husband, Ruchl's only option was to sell her biggest asset and slide down the economic ladder.[49] This was typical for widows.[50]

These types of cases would appear to indicate that the circumstances of a woman lacking an economic connection to a man were, generally, unenviable. The example of Drezl Roth is instructive. During wartime in the 1630s she fled with her husband, Tevele, from Glogau (Głogów, Poland) to Poznań. The couple lived there for six years as refugees, without receiving a residence license (*hezkat yishuv*) from the Jewish community. By the time Tevele was able to pay the license fee and gain permanent residence status, the couple had divorced. This development meant that the husband's payment did not count for his ex-wife and Drezl was required to leave Poznań. With insufficient money of her own, Drezl lost her chance at residence rights.[51]

Women with Economic Agency

IN THIS PERIOD THE economic dependence of Jewish women on their husbands was not unambiguous. Women generally mixed domestic duties with income-producing economic activity. The family was an economic unit with the husband usually in the role of senior partner, but the wife was still a partner, albeit typically a junior one. For example, in a 1721 Kraków Jewish court case concerning a domestic dispute over marital property, the husband charged that his (second) wife, Temerl, did not "go to Kraków to do business and make a livelihood for the couple and their children, as is the way of *men and women*" (emphasis added).[52] That is, both men and women were expected to contribute to the family livelihood.

A central female occupation in this gender-organized economy was moneylending. Jewish women appear in lists as creditors of nobles and townsfolk in Poland from at least the fourteenth century. By the seventeenth and eighteenth centuries, Jews were, as a group, more borrowers than lenders. Still, petty moneylending remained a sideline for some Jews, and it was women who filled a central role in this economic niche. This is implied by the requests filed in municipal courts to sell unclaimed pawns, which came more and more from women. Likewise the number of cases concerning debt collection in which Jewish women were involved was on the increase.[53]

A different common Jewish women's occupation in Poland was also connected to traditional gender-assigned duties. In municipal court testimonies in various civil cases, Jewish women stand out as tavern keepers, either independently or in partnership with their husbands.[54] This was the *Żydówka* (Jewess) running the *karczma* (tavern, inn): greeting and making small talk with the patrons, serving food, preparing the sleeping quarters, safekeeping valuables and merchandise, solving various problems. In short, mothering the customers as well as seeing to the needs of her own family, whose home was usually the inn.

There were strong, independent women such as the widow *Żydówka* Fejga Lokacka of Dubno in the 1740s. She held her own in an ongoing, almost violent dispute with her Jewish neighbors and managed her own affairs with the municipality. However, the dictates of gender conventions influenced the behavior of most married women innkeepers. For example, in 1710 the anonymous wife of Abramko, innkeeper in Satanów (Sataniv, Ukraine), who was in charge of the tavern alone while her husband was away on a three-week trip to a commercial fair, set gender-determined limits for herself. When "gypsies" showed up to purchase beer for a wedding, she did not want to deal with them. She asked a man who was on hand, Moszko Szajowicz, to wait on them, saying, "You, as a man, know well how to haggle with them over this."[55] Sima was another Satanów tavern keeper who limited her contact with some male customers. Early one Friday evening in 1720, when her husband, Jos, had already gone off to the synagogue for Sabbath evening prayers, two Christian travelers arrived at the inn seeking lodging. They asked Sima to keep their money for them while they were at the inn. Sima "did not want to take the money from them for safekeeping because of the Sabbath and the absence of her husband."[56]

Hebrew sources indicate an additional typical women's occupation. In 1628 the Jewish Council of Lithuania forbade Jewish women peddlers to frequent gentile homes unless they were accompanied by their husbands or another Jewish man, in addition to a Jewish boy.[57] This prohibition confirms that women were active as itinerant peddlers in towns and villages. Moreover, economic circumstances being what they were, the prohibition was not effective. Indeed, the requirement that a peddling woman have chaperones would make peddling impractical and unprofitable. For a long time the Jewish authorities chose to overlook what they could not hope to control, and women's peddling just increased. In 1751, however, the Council tried again to stop this occupation, by outlawing it completely.

> Earlier sages and authorities diligently decreed, set restrictions and established safeguards to prevent women from going to Gentile homes with various merchandise, as recorded at several past Council sessions. . . . Many violators proliferated in all of the communities who carelessly let their wives loose,[58] making a living from this practice to support their families. Their children are borderline bastards.[59]

Acknowledging the failure of its previous restrictions, this time the Council attempted to combat this women's economic activity by forbidding all female peddling, whether chaperoned or not. The new prohibition included a ban (*herem*) declared against women peddlers (*tendlerin*), their husbands, and any merchant who consigned merchandise to them for sale. However, this time too the attempt to prevent female peddling failed. In 1761 the Council, again attempting to control what it could not outlaw, announced that Jewish women should take care not to visit gentile homes without a chaperone.[60] A comparison of the 1761 decree mandating a single undefined chaperone with the 1751 one that forbade female peddling completely and with the 1628 one that required two chaperones (one a married man) implies that, even though it was perceived as reflecting negatively on female modesty and male honor, female peddling was so important economically that its opponents were forced to compromise with reality. It is doubtful that even the 1761 directive was observed. Women peddlers continued to ply their trade.[61]

If women were circulating among villages as sellers and buyers, it stands to reason that they also appeared in the marketplace. In the Kraków Jewish court case mentioned earlier, the wife Temerl allegedly did not follow conventional practice and engage in some moneymaking enterprise. Furthermore, Joel Sirkes (1561–1640), in connection with the question of biblically prohibited cross-dressing, offered his opinion that "the male garment, called *żupica*, and other similar men's outfits that women are accustomed to put on and wear in the marketplace and sit in them in the store, are not forbidden."[62] Thus it appears that women would normally run stalls and stores in the market. This is confirmed by lists of taxpayers. For example, in Międzybóż in 1742, out of 66 stores on the marketplace, 11 (16.6%) were owned by women (7 Jews and 4 Christians). All but one of the Jewish women seem to have been widows. Some women, like the fishmongers of Bar in 1766, sold from nothing more than a stand or a table.[63]

This means that, alongside the widows who were forced by economic necessity to sell their homes, there were women who could support themselves through mercantile activity after the death of their husbands. To be sure, once the husband died, the standard of living often declined for these women as well. Ber of Bolechów (1723–1805) mentioned "the late Ms. Raizl, mother of the aforementioned Reb Ber, who ran a store with all manner of goods, even after the death of her husband."[64] Another example is Pearl, widow of Jacob Reis Katz, who, in 1638, upon arriving in Poznań after her husband's death, established a store on the market there. The Poznań *kahal* permitted Pearl to sell textiles in her store on a wholesale basis only. Presumably this was to prevent her from competing with the Jewish merchants already operating in Poznań.[65]

Powerful Women

Widows such as Pearl, supporting themselves and often their families as household heads, appear in virtually all lists of Jewish taxpayers in Polish towns. Frequently, there is a notation that the household includes a married son or son-in-law. That is, despite the presence of a young family man, the woman was the owner of the house and the head of the family.[66] In Poland, then, there were women similar to Glikl bas Yehuda (1645–1724; also known as Glikl of Hameln, but actually more of Hamburg) in Germany. Such women were involved in their husband's business while he was alive, and after his death they successfully managed the enterprise, property, and family, overseeing the marriage matches and business careers of their children.[67]

An extreme example of such a woman is Gitl, widow of Todros Kożuchowski, one of the richest Kraków Jewish merchants in the mid-seventeenth century. In his will Todros commanded that after his death, his wife, Gitl, should manage his diverse mercantile and financial affairs. He specified that Gitl would inherit all his movable property and would be the executor of all of his estate, deciding what to keep and what to sell. She also decided what each child would inherit. Some of them were already married, and Gitl had to determine which house each would receive, which permanent place in the synagogue, how much financial support she could offer, and which of the children to take into the business. She arranged betrothals and set the sums of dowries. With respect to business, her job was "to deal in every type of commerce according to her desires, *as she has always done*, for her benefit and the benefit of all the heirs. . . . For she is the principal of the house, the power, the ruler over the entire estate and the business for her whole life" (emphasis added).[68] "As she has always done" implies that, like Glikl of Hamburg, Gitl of Kraków was her husband's business partner. When Todros was alive, Gitl was active in business affairs and prepared to become the chief once he died.

Women who were not active in the day-to-day running of a business might still be involved in basic family economic decisions. Ber of Bolechów's second wife, Leah, exemplified this model. According to his memoirs, it was Leah, together with some other family members, who convinced Ber to open a store rather than become a moneylender. Moreover, it was only after Leah consented that the couple moved to Bolechów and started trading in wines. The decision to invest the nuclear family's nest egg in a partnership with Ber's father was also a joint one.[69]

It was also possible to find strong women in the *arenda* leasing business, which was a main pillar of the Polish Jewish economy. In the 1640s in the Pinsk region the most powerful arrendators were the Szymszyc family.

When the husband, Eliezer, died in 1645, his wife, Deborah, took over the management of three large estates, including agricultural lands and forests, rivers, and lakes, with their timber, honey, fish, game, and other products. She essentially oversaw the work of more than a thousand townspeople and peasant serfs who lived on these lands. Deborah collected the various taxes and fees they were required to pay and supervised the labor they were obligated to provide. Her staff included her two sons, her brother, and a complement of Jewish clerks, supervisors, and subarrendators. Deborah Szymszyc was determined and assertive. When the peasants of Lulin refused to pay the road toll, Deborah showed up in the village one market day with a posse of people who worked for her. They confiscated merchandise as payment for the unpaid tolls and injured twelve villagers. When the nobleman owner of one of the villages decided he wanted to abrogate the *arenda* contract, he began stirring up the peasants to attack Deborah's staff people and hurt her business. She responded by organizing her employees as a fighting force and successfully restored order.[70]

Conclusions

JEWISH WOMEN IN THE early modern Polish-Lithuanian Commonwealth played a complex role in their society and culture. Like European, including Polish, women in general, Jewish women were supposed to be modest, quiet, obedient, and pious. Their main mission was to facilitate the achievements of their husbands and sons. In the religious and economic spheres their activities were supposed to support the efforts of their menfolk, which were considered primary. However, to facilitate others' (men's) roles, the women also had to be successful, both practically and spiritually. Without women the Jewish economy would not have functioned smoothly. Typically, women were largely financially dependent on their husbands. However, women were usually partners, not bystanders, in the family economic endeavor. Women's moneylending, innkeeping, peddling, trade, *arenda* leasing, and crafts (not treated here) were an inseparable part of the family enterprise.[71] For widows they were its essence. With respect to religion, it became taken for granted that, for women to do their part in strengthening religious life, they had to attain a certain level of knowledge as well as a means of religious expression and ritual participation. Developing a many-faceted Yiddish literature offered one avenue for women to gain the knowledge they needed and to use it in the service of their faith. There were various religious activities that women carried out in private and semiprivate. At the same time, between 1500 and 1800, the synagogue gradually opened up to them. Conventional gender hierarchy did not change, but the gender boundary began to move.

Notes

Earlier versions of some of the material presented here appeared in Hebrew in Israel Bartal and Israel Gutman, eds., *The Broken Chain: Polish Jewry Through the Ages* (Jerusalem: Zalman Shazar Center, 2001), 2: 415–34; and in English in Moshe Rosman, *Categorically Jewish, Distinctly Polish: Polish Jewish History Reflected and Refracted* (Liverpool, UK: Liverpool University, Littman Library of Jewish Civilization, 2021), chaps. 14 and 15.

1 See Maria Bogucka, *Women in Early Modern Polish Society: Against the European Background* (Oxon, UK: Ashgate, 2004), 9–15 and *passim*; Shaul Stampfer, "Was the Traditional East European Jewish Family in the Recent Past Patriarchal?" in *Families, Rabbis, and Education: Traditional Jewish Society in Nineteenth-Century Eastern Europe*, by Shaul Stampfer (Oxford, UK: Littman Library of Jewish Civilization, 2010), 121–41.

2 *Sefer Haheshek* means "book of desire or devotion," referring to one's relationship with God; cf. Psalms 91:14. *Sefer Haheshek*, Jewish Division, Vernadsky Library, Kiev, Or 178. The work was first identified by Yohanan Petrovsky-Shtern; see Yohanan Petrovsky-Shtern, "The Master of an Evil Name: Hillel Ba'al Shem and His *Sefer Ha-Heshek*," *AJS Review* 28 (2004): 217–48. Compare my construction here of Eastern European Jewish gender with that of Chava Weissler, *Voices of the Matriarchs* (Boston: Beacon Press, 1998), 51–65.

3 *Ba'al shem* literally means "master of [God's] name" and is the title given to Jewish miracle workers or shamans. See Immanuel Etkes, *The Besht: Magician, Mystic, and Leader* (Waltham, MA: Brandeis University Press, 2005), 7–45; and Moshe Rosman, *Founder of Hasidism: A Quest for the Historical Ba'al Shem Tov* (Oxford, UK: Littman Library of Jewish Civilization, 2013), 11–26.

4 On *segulah* books, see Hagit Matras, "From Creation of Man to Healing Him: Studies in Segulah and Medical Books," in *Creation and Re-Creation in Jewish Thought: Festschrift in Honor of Joseph Dan on the Occasion of His Seventieth Birthday*, ed. Rachel Elior and Peter Schäfer (Tübingen: Mohr Siebeck, 2005), 147*–164*, esp. 159*–162* (Hebrew).

5 *Sefer Haheshek*, 249–50.

6 For non-Jewish women, see Bogucka, *Women*, 113–24; Merry Wiesner, *Women and Gender in Early Modern Europe* (Cambridge, UK: Cambridge University Press, 2000), 13–35.

7 These remedies appear in *Sefer Haheshek*, 37, 59, 10.

8 Cf. Elisheva Baumgarten, "'Thus Say the Wise Midwives': Midwives and Midwifery in Thirteenth-Century Ashkenaz," *Zion* 65 (2000): 45–74 (Hebrew); and Edward Fram, *My Dear Daughter: Rabbi Benjamin Slonik and the Education of Jewish Women in Sixteenth-Century Poland* (Cincinnati: Hebrew Union College Press, 2007), 80.

9 Literally, "a bundle of names" (*kerekh shel shemot*).

10 Pinḥas Katzenellenbogen, *Yesh Manḥilin*, ed. Yitzḥak Feld (Jerusalem: Makhon Ḥatam Sofer, 1986), 99.

11 On vicarious gynecology, cf. Fram, *My Dear Daughter*, 80; and Wiesner, *Women and Gender*, 30–37, 78–81.

12 For example, *Sefer Haḥeshek*, 23, 45.

13 Cf. Weissler, *Voices of the Matriarchs*, 76–85, 96–103, 177–88.

14 For a discussion of such *musar* (moral conduct) literature in Hebrew and Yiddish, see Zev Gries, *Conduct Literature: Its History and Place in the Life of Beshtian Hasidism* (Jerusalem: Bialik Institute, 1989) (Hebrew).

15 Israel Abrahams, *Hebrew Ethical Wills* (Philadelphia: Jewish Publication Society of America, 1926 [1976]), 316–17; cf. Fram, *My Dear Daughter*, 48–60 and the notes to the full text on 153–307.

16 The ideal stereotype of the facilitating, pious, chaste, silent, modest, and obedient woman was common in Poland and Europe in general; see Bogucka, *Women*, xxii, 6, 111–19.

17 Jewish Division, Vernadsky Library, Kiev, Or 56, no. 28; cf. Mordecai Nadav, ed., *The Minutes Book of the Jewish Community Council of Tykocin*, 2 vols. (Jerusalem: Israel Academy of Sciences, 1996), 1: 425, par. 600 (Hebrew). The possibility that the children in these cases were victims of sexual abuse cannot be excluded.

18 Abrahams, *Hebrew Ethical Wills*, 319.

19 Eliyahu Stern, *The Genius: Elijah of Vilna and the Making of Modern Judaism* (New Haven, CT: Yale University Press, 2014), 19.

20 *b. Brakhot* 17a.

21 *Shulḥan Arukh, Yoreh Deiʾah* 246:6. Cf. Mordecai Yoffe, *Levush Ateret Zahav Gedolah* (Prague, 1609), 246:6; Yaakov Emden, *Megillat Sefer*, ed. Y. Bick (Jerusalem: Jerusalem Jewish Classics, 1979), 93; Bogucka, *Women*, 25, 119. It is instructive to compare the ideal of the facilitating wife with the ideas of Leah Horowitz, expressed in her booklet *Tkhine Imohos* (Lviv, ca. 1790). See below, and Moshe Rosman, "Leah Horowitz's *Tkhine Imohos*: A Proto-Feminist Demand to Increase Jewish Women's Religious Capital," *Polin* 33 (2021): 17–50.

22 *Tkhine Imohos*, National Library of Israel, R8° = 41A460, *Tkhines*, vol. 6, no. 2. On Leah Horowitz and her composition, see Haim Liberman, *Ohel Raḥel* (New York: Haim Liberman, 1980), 432–38; Weissler, *Voices of the Matriarchs*, 104–25, 183–85; and Rosman, "Leah Horowitz's *Tkhine Imohos*."

23 For further discussion of beliefs about women and attitudes toward them, see Fram, *My Dear Daughter*, 37–43 (Jewish women); and Bogucka, *Women*, 77–109 (Polish women).

24 Meir Ish-Shalom, ed., *Seder Eliyahu Rabbah ve-Seder Eliyahu Zuta* (Jerusalem: Wahrman, 1969), 51; *Yalkut Shimoni, Shoftim*, 42. Wives' subordination to husbands' authority was universal in Europe in this period; cf. Abrahams, *Hebrew Ethical Wills*, 318; Rosman, "Leah Horowitz's *Tkhine Imohos*," n. 59; and Wiesner, *Women and Gender*, 13–35.

25 Abrahams, *Hebrew Ethical Wills*, 321. There was a preference for women and girls to stay at home; see Fram, *My Dear Daughter*, 50–52. In Poland, particularly in

various Protestant denominations, some women played more active roles; see Bogucka, *Women*, 57–73.

26 Rosman, "Leah Horowitz's *Tkhine Imohos*," 26.

27 Rosman, "Leah Horowitz's *Tkhine Imohos*," 23. Pointedly, Leah also criticized men who talked in the synagogue (25–26). Another female *tkhine* author, Sara bas Tovim, cited talking during prayer services as a women's sin; see T. G. Klirs, comp., *The Merit of Our Mothers: A Bilingual Anthology of Jewish Women's Prayers* (Cincinnati: Hebrew Union College Press, 1992), 28–31.

28 Abrahams, *Hebrew Ethical Wills*, 321.

29 Rosman, "Leah Horowitz's *Tkhine Imohos*," 24–25.

30 *b. Berakhot* 17a.

31 What Leah was claiming here is that it cannot be that women gain religious merit solely by facilitating the religious activities of men. Women have almost as many religious obligations as men do. Like men, their path to religious fulfillment is through performance of the mitzvot in their own right, not by facilitating the performance of others. Cf. Rabbi Ephraim Solomon Lunshits's observation that women "were exempted from most of the commandments." *Ir Gibborim*, cited by Edward Fram, *My Dear Daughter*, 37, 57–62. On Polish women's religious status and activities, see Bogucka, *Women*, 53–75.

32 The citation is from the Yiddish section of Leah's *Tkhine Imohos*; cf. Rashi (on *b. Megillah* 21b) and other medieval authorities who emphasized that "women and unlearned men" should be provided with translations in their own vernacular so that they understand the commandments.

33 For analysis of two such books, see Jacob Elbaum and Chava Turniansky, "Householders' Morality: The Book *Sam Ḥayyim* by R. Avraham Ashkenazi Apitiker of Ludmir," in *Creation and Re-Creation in Jewish Thought: Festschrift in Honor of Joseph Dan on the Occasion of His Seventieth Birthday*, ed. Rachel Elior and Peter Schäfer (Tubingen: Mohr Siebeck, 2005), 109*–144* (Hebrew); and Noga Rubin, *Conqueror of Hearts: Sefer Lev Tov by Isaac ben Eliakum of Posen, Prague 1620* (Tel Aviv: Hakibbutz Hameuchad, 2013) (Hebrew). There were analogous books in Polish reinforcing similar messages; see Tamar Salmon-Mack, *On Marriage and Its Crises in Early Modern Polish and Lithuanian Jewry* (Tel Aviv: Hakibbutz Hameuchad, 2012), 38–39 (Hebrew).

34 Israel Zinberg, *A History of Jewish Literature*, vol. 7, *Old Yiddish Literature*, trans. Bernard Martin (Cincinnati: Ktav, 1975); Khone Shmeruk, *Yiddish Literature in Poland: Historical Studies* (Jerusalem: Magnes Press, 1981), 11–74 (Hebrew); Weissler, *Voices of the Matriarchs*, 3–35.

35 Cited in Shmeruk, *Yiddish Literature in Poland*, 89.

36 Weissler, *Voices of the Matriarchs*, 92–103; Klirs, *Merit of Our Mothers*, 14–28.

37 These are the seven days after the menses have ceased to flow when sexual contact is still prohibited.

38 *Shulḥan Arukh, Oraḥ Ḥayyim* 88:1. Cf. Elisheva Baumgarten, "'They Are Doing the Right Thing': A New View of Women's Custom in Medieval Ashkenaz Not to Enter the Synagogue During Menstruation," in *Ta-Shma: Studies in Judaica in Memory of Israel M. Ta-Shma*, 2 vols., ed. Rami Reiner (Alon Shvut: Tevunot Press, 2012),

1: 85–104 (Hebrew); Elisheva Baumgarten, "Gender in der Aschkenasischen Synagoge im Hochmittelalter," in *Die SchUM Gemeinden Speyer–Worms–Mainz: Auf dem Weg zum Welterbe*, ed. Pia Heberer and Ursula Reuter (Regensburg: Schnell & Steiner, 2013), 73–85; and Avraham Grossman, *Pious and Rebellious: Jewish Women in Medieval Europe* (Waltham, MA: Brandeis University Press, 2004), 25.

39 Baumgarten, "Gender in der Aschkenasischen Synagoge"; Grossman, *Pious and Rebellious*, 181; Fram, *My Dear Daughter*, 63–64. For analysis of women's place in the early modern Ashkenazic Polish synagogue, see Yemima Chovav, *Maidens Love Thee: The Religious and Spiritual Life of Jewish Ashkenazic Women in the Early Modern Period* (Jerusalem: Dinur Center, Hebrew University, 2009), 357–67 (Hebrew); and Vladimir Levin, "The Architecture of Gender: Women in the Eastern European Synagogue," https://www.bac.org.il/sdrvt/sdarot/beyond-religion -synagogues-in-eastern-europe-dr-vladimir-levin/video/the-architecture-of -gender-with-dr-vladimir-levin/ (accessed December 7, 2020).

40 Weissler, *Voices of the Matriarchs*, 25; cf. Fram, *My Dear Daughter*, 65–70.

41 Jewish Division, Vernadsky Library, Kiev, Or 104, no. 65, Nieśwież community pinkas, 58b.

42 Jewish Division, Vernadsky Library, Kiev, Or 59, no. 31, Iwieniec community pinkas, par. 21. See also Ukrainian Central State Historical Archive, Kiev (UCSHA), Satanów 50 I 1, p. 312b, 1725. For other examples of women in synagogue daily, see Simon Dubnow, ed., *Pinkas Hamedinah: Pinkas va'ad hakehillot haroshiyot bemedinat Lita* [Minute Book of the Council of the Chief Jewish Communities of Lithuania] (Berlin: Ajanoth, 1925), 272, par. 1023; Fram, *My Dear Daughter*, 53, 53n81.

43 Cf. Moshe Rosman, "The History of Jewish Women in Early Modern Poland: An Assessment," *Polin* 18 (2005): 26–56.

44 For examples, see UCSHA, Satanów 50 I 1, Bar 1387 I 2, and Dubno 33 I 7, 16, 17, 21; and Bogucka, *Women*, 13–15, 104.

45 For examples, see UCSHA, Satanów 50 I 1, pp. 302, 474b; Bar 1387 I 2, pp. 2, 26, 79, 89; and Potocki 49 II 2944, no. 2. There were exceptions to this; for example, Yenta of Satanów purchased a house and store from the Christian Jan Szafranko around 1709; see UCSHA, Satanów 50 I 1, p. 5.

46 UCSHA, Potocki 49 III 56, p. 5; and Tarlo 256 I 1269, p. 17. The location was apparently the town of Waręż. Cf. Nadav, *Minutes Book*, 1: 121, par. 186; and 1: 146, par. 229.

47 We do not know what his alleged crime was.

48 Biblioteka Czartoryskich, Kraków, Ew 86, undated petition of Szejna.

49 UCSHA, Winnica 45 I 1, no. 207, p. 53a. For other examples, see UCSHA, Potocki 49 III 439, pp. 13–14; Lubomirski 236 II 188, pp. 50–51, 66–69; and Ossolineum (Wrocław), Oss 2560 III, pp. 106, 117–18.

50 Cf. Sandra Cavallo and Lyndan Warner, eds., *Widowhood in Medieval and Early Modern Europe* (London: Taylor & Francis, 1999).

51 Bernard D. Weinryb, *Texts and Studies in the Communal History of Polish Jewry* (New York: American Academy for Jewish Research, 1950), Hebrew section, 4, par. 4. We do not know whether Drezl was actually forced to leave the town.

52 Weinryb, *Texts and Studies*, Hebrew section, 216, par. 30.

53 Shmuel Artur Cygielman, *The Jews of Poland and Lithuania Until 1648* (Jerusalem: Zalman Shazar Center, 1991), 255–71 (Hebrew); UCSHA, Potocki 49 II 2944, no. 14; and Dubno 33 I 7, 17 passim; Jewish Division, Vernadsky Library, Kiev, Or 104, no. 65, Nieśwież community pinkas, 59b. Cf. Bogucka, *Women*, 50: "Small-scale money lending was almost entirely monopolized by women."

54 For examples of these women innkeepers, see UCSHA, Winnica 45 I 1, no. 203, pp. 51b–52b: Esterka and Rywka; Satanów 50 I 1, p. 20b: Kreyna Markowa; Lubomirski 236 II 10, pp. 13–14: anonymous; and Beresteczko 1400 I 1, pp. 102a–b: Gierszanka.

55 UCSHA, Dubno 33 I 17, pp. 1–2; Satanów 50 I 1, p. 14.

56 UCSHA, Satanów 50 I 1, p. 200. On the Sabbath Jews are forbidden to touch money.

57 Dubnow, *Pinkas Hamedinah*, p. 34, par. 133; cf. Fram, *My Dear Daughter*, 39. On Polish women peddlers, see Andrzej Karpiński, "Przekupki, kramarki, straganiarki: Zakres feminzacja drobnego handlu w miastach polskich w drugiej połowie XVI–XVII wieku" [Women Hawkers, Hucksters, and Stall Keepers: Feminization of Petty Trade in Polish Towns in the Second Half of the Sixteenth and the Seventeenth Centuries], *Kwartalnik Historii Kultury Materialnej* 38 (1990): 81–91.

58 At least in some cases the husband was back in town managing the family store.

59 Dubnow, *Pinkas Hamedinah*, 257–58, par. 547.

60 Dubnow, *Pinkas Hamedinah*, 270, par. 1005; cf. Iwieniec community pinkas on p. 2. For an example of a Jewish woman peddler, see UCSHA, Dubno 33 I 21, no. 71, p. 34.

61 Attempts to restrict women peddlers were also motivated by an economic consideration that was at least as strong as the manifest fear for the virtue of Jewish women. Women peddlers, by going to the customers' homes, posed a threat to the merchants in the marketplace, who had to wait for customers to come to them. See Jacob Katz, *Tradition and Crisis* (New York: Schocken, 1993), 21, 262n17; and Yitshak Rivkind, "The Jewish Woman in Past Jewish Economic Life," *Di Zukunft* 38 (1933): 110–15 (Yiddish). In Polish society there also was negative evaluation of competition from women laborers and peddlers, who typically were willing to accept lower compensation; see Bogucka, *Women*, 50; and Karpiński, "Feminization," 87; cf. Salmon-Mack, *On Marriage*, 148–49.

62 Yoel Sirkes, *Bayit Ḥadash*, gloss on *Tur Yoreh Dei'ah*, par. 182.

63 Biblioteka Czartoryskich, Kraków, 4085; UCSHA, Bar 1387 I 2, p. 60; cf. Karpiński, "Feminization."

64 Ber of Bolechow, *The Memoirs of Ber of Bolechow*, trans. and ed. Mark Vishnitzer [Wischnitzer] (New York: Arno Press, 1973), 97.

65 Weinryb, *Texts and Studies*, Hebrew section, 25, par. 65. On women's economic activities, cf. Fram, *My Dear Daughter*, 57. Expedients, such as the one cited here, to prevent commercial competition were standard in both Polish and Jewish communities and between Polish municipalities and Jewish *kahals*; see Moshe Rosman, *Categorically Jewish, Distinctly Polish: Polish Jewish History Reflected*

and Refracted (Liverpool, UK: Liverpool University, Littman Library of Jewish Civilization, 2021), Introduction.

66 For example: Biblioteka Czartoryskich, Kraków, 4085; Ossolineum, Wrocław, Oss 9640/III Przemyśł 1661; Jewish Division, Vernadsky Library, Kiev, Or 59, no. 31, Iwieniec community pinkas, pp. 20–21; and Or 127, no. 82, Smolein community pinkas, pp. 14–69; UCSHA, Potocki 49 II 147, p. 1079.

67 Chava Turniansky, ed., *Glikl: Memoirs, 1691–1719*, trans. Sara Friedman (Waltham, MA: Brandeis University Press, 2019). See also Natalie Zemon Davis, *Women on the Margins: Three Seventeenth Century Lives* (Cambridge, MA: Harvard University Press, 1997), 12–15, 203–5, 226–27.

68 Feival H. Wetstein, *Kadmoniyot Mipinkasaot Yeshanim* [Historical Events from Old Record Books] (Kraków, 1892), 31–37, document 12. For an English translation of the will, see Moshe Rosman, "How Family Wealth and Power Are Organized," in *Early Modern Workshop: Resources in Jewish History*, vol. 3, *Gender, Family, and Social Structures* (Middletown, CT: Wesleyan University, 2006), https://fordham.bepress.com/cgi/viewcontent.cgi?article=1036&context=emw (accessed December 7, 2020). On Polish widows' commercial activities, see Bogucka, *Women*, 33–51 and *passim*.

69 Ber of Bolechow, *Memoirs*, 84, 86, 90.

70 Mordechai Nadav, *The Jews of Pinsk: 1506–1880*, ed. Moshe Rosman, trans. Moshe Rosman and Faigie Tropper (Stanford, CA: Stanford University Press, 2007), 91–92. Cf. M. J. Rosman, *The Lords' Jews: Magnate-Jewish Relations in the Polish-Lithuanian Commonwealth During the Eighteenth Century* (Cambridge, MA: Harvard University Press, 1990), 138–39; Janusz Nowak, "Feyga Lejbowiczowa arendarka w Końskowoli Sieniawskich" [The Woman Lessee, Feyga Lejbowicz, in the Sieniawski Family's Town Końskowola], *Rocznik Biblioteki Naukowej PAU i PAN w Krakowie* 48 (2003): 212–36; and Ossolineum, Wrocław, Oss 2560 III, p. 143. On Polish women estate managers, see Andrzej Wyczański, "Kobiety kierowniczki folwarków w starostwie sieradzkim w XVI w" [Women Managers of the Sieradz District Demesne], *Zapiski Historyczne* 41 (1976): 41–49.

71 On Jewish participation in crafts, see Mark Wischnitzer, *A History of Jewish Crafts and Guilds* (New York: J. David, 1965); and Maurycy Horn, "The Chronology and Distribution of Jewish Craft Guilds in Old Poland, 1613–1795," in *The Jews in Old Poland, 1000–1795*, ed. Antony Polonsky, Jakub Basista, and Andrzej Link-Lenczowski (London: I. B. Tauris, 1993), 249–65.

THE INTERSECTIONAL EXPERIENCE OF JEWISH WOMEN IN THE RUSSIAN EMPIRE

CHAERAN Y. FREEZE

IN 1899 KHAIA BERKOVA Burshtein filed a petition in the Kiev Orphan's Court requesting full custody over her granddaughter Liubov (Liuba) Betgilel following her daughter Deberta's death. Deberta had been legally separated from her husband, Samuil Betgilel, because of their "very stormy relationship" and his need to live in "the remotest parts of Russia" to work as a civil engineer of transportation. Burshtein claimed that this proved to be a hardship for her daughter, who needed treatment for her tuberculosis. In his testimony, Samuil conceded that he "was forced to go to the Saratov steppes for the construction of the Tambov-Lamyshin railroad line," but he blamed his wife's illness for the breakdown of his marriage. Not only did Deberta spend "a part of the year and our marriage" receiving treatment at various spas in Europe, but also "she was strictly forbidden to have a true married life [sexual relations] to avoid having consumptive offspring. I was to stay away from her." He demanded that the court uphold his rights as a father "by virtue of the laws of guardianship established in family procedure." Despite Burshtein's protests that her grandchild barely knew her father, the court awarded full custody of Liubov to her father, who was by then living in St. Petersburg.[1]

The court case reveals that before her death Deberta Betgilel (née Burshtein) had lived a complex life, simultaneously experiencing privilege and oppression based on her multiple subject positions. As the daughter of a first-guild merchant, she had enjoyed residency rights in Kiev, a city outside the Pale of Settlement where only "useful" categories of Jews were permitted to settle starting in 1859; later, as the wife of a university-educated civil engineer, she retained her residency privileges. As a chronically ill patient, Deberta suffered numerous disabilities and long periods of convalescence; however, her wealth allowed her to travel abroad for treatments at the best European spas.

As a woman, Deberta was legally dependent on her husband; imperial family law prohibited her from living apart from Samuil unless he granted her a separate passport. His failure to furnish her with proper documentation forced Deberta to procure a false passport, leading to her arrest before her death. The husband also refused to grant her a travel passport for her treatments abroad unless she left their daughter with him. Because Jewish law governed family law in the absence of civil marriage in Russia, Deberta could not obtain a divorce, which was her husband's sole prerogative.

This case vividly illustrates how intersectionality—a theory developed by Black feminist theorists—might help to illuminate the lives of Jewish women in the Russian Empire. Using the analogy of a traffic accident, Kimberlé Crenshaw argues that the victim suffers injuries (such as discrimination) from simultaneous collisions, "frustrating efforts to determine which driver caused the harm."[2] According to this analogy, Deberta experienced multiple harms simultaneously as a result of the confluence of gender, religion, marital and estate status, and disability—all facets of her intersectional identity. Intersectionality can expose not only the "interlocking systems of oppression" or "matrix of domination" (to use Patricia Hill Collin's concept)[3] that marginalized Jewish women but also the creative strategies they used to take advantage of contradictions in these systems to ameliorate their disadvantages and subordination.

In this chapter I provide a broad survey of the state of the field, which has remained relatively fallow since Paula Hyman and ChaeRan Freeze published their historiographical survey in *Polin: Jewish Women in Eastern Europe* over a decade ago.[4] In her recent assessment, Eliyana Adler similarly concludes that the integration of women into master narratives and reconceptualization of existing paradigms such as periodization "remain elusive."[5] The "add women and stir" approach and the assumption that the male experience is the universal one still dominate the general scholarship; yet a few promising developments merit attention. An important caveat: rather than use the traditional term *Eastern Europe* (a vague historical construction), I investigate life in the Russian Empire, a coherent political entity that was multinational and multiconfessional. According to the All-Russian Census of 1897, there were 2,653,217 Jewish women in the empire (compared with 2,536,184 men),[6] and their narratives must be brought from the "margins to the center."[7] Placing Jewish women in the context of the empire situates them in the matrix of imperial law, institutions, and culture in which they were intimately embedded as minority subjects. I explore Jewish women's experiences in religious life, education and culture, family, economics, and politics and evaluate new directions in scholarship.

Religious Life

FOLLOWING THE FIRST PARTITION of Poland in 1772, Catherine II of Russia promised her new Jewish subjects "all the freedoms which they now enjoy [in Poland] with regard to their religion."[8] Jewish women's religious lives were shaped by gender-based segregation, which led to separate expressions of piety, reading practices, and even subversive behavior that challenged the norms of Jewish religious culture.

Chava Weissler argues that *tkhines* (supplicatory prayers in Yiddish) in the early modern period represented an important form of "women's participation in [the mystical] pietistic revival and its popular literature" in Poland.[9] Reciting *tkhines* provided a uniquely female experience; in contrast to the obligatory Hebrew liturgy that men chanted in a public congregation, *tkhines* were personal, voluntary, and recited at home in the vernacular Yiddish. The prayers addressed specific female concerns and rituals, such as pregnancy, childbirth, and the women's three commandments (taking challah when baking, lighting Shabbat candles, and attending the *mikveh*). Women invoked the biblical matriarchs as models of piety and advocates in times of trouble. Weissler suggests that *tkhines* (especially by female authors) provided a means for women to transcend gender roles, if only momentarily, and valorized female rituals and domestic culture. For instance, in the "*Tkhine* of Shifrah's Words," the author (Shifrah bas Joseph of Brody from a rabbinic family) endowed the lighting of the Sabbath candles with mystical meaning, countering rabbinic views that this action served to compensate for Eve's sin of extinguishing the light of the world. Shifrah connected candle lighting with the unity of the *sefirot* (emanations of revealed divinity in Kabbalah) and cast women in the symbolic role of the high priest who facilitated the union of the male and female aspects of God—an unthinkable role for women in traditional Judaism. By the nineteenth century, Weissler observes that male-authored *tkhines* (under female pseudonyms) reflected the reformist agendas of the Haskalah (Jewish Enlightenment) movement, which stressed bourgeois gender roles and proper domestic hygiene.[10]

Women also read separate Yiddish religious and ethical books, such as the popular "women's Bible," the *Tsene u'rene*. A Yiddish adaptation of the weekly Torah readings accompanied by midrashim, aggadot, commentaries, and more, this text became "a Yiddish language laboratory" and shaped reading practices.[11] By reading the stories in their entirety, girls acquired broader comprehension of the text. Yehuda Leib Katzenelson (1846–1917) admitted that the *Tsene u'rene* opened his eyes because he had studied only "discontinuous sections of the Five Books, with no relation or connection between them."[12]

Women read the *Tsene u'rene* not only in private but also communally. Zvi Scharfstein recalled that after the men went to the *beit midrash* to pray, sometimes neighbors would drop by and "sit by my mother to hear the contents of the weekly portion."[13] The collective experience of reading the *Tsene u'rene* or ethical books such as the *Brantspiegel* fostered intimate and active engagements with the texts—opportunities for women to add their own personal interpretations and responses.[14]

Jewish women's religious lives were also influenced by the milieu in which they lived. In many Ukrainian, Polish, and Belorussian towns, the distinctive customs of Hasidism dominated. Ada Rapoport-Albert rejects the claims made by scholars in the last century that women were especially receptive to Hasidism because of its emotional character and that they gained "complete equality" because of its egalitarian spirit. In fact, she argues that Hasidism persisted in casting women as "irredeemably material," their carnality precluding the attainment of spiritual transcendence.[15] Women, who were excluded from the intimate courts of the rebbes (Hasidic leaders), could never assume leadership positions or practice male forms of piety because of the deliberate construction of strict gender boundaries. The life of Hannah Rachel Verbermakher (b. ca. 1815), known as the Maid of Ludmir, is a case in point. Born in Volhynia, the Maid began to observe all the male rituals and gained a widespread reputation as a teacher and miracle worker. However, her desire to embrace an ascetic lifestyle (sanctioned exclusively for men for Torah study) met with strong opposition and pressure to marry. "Had this tradition bestowed any legitimacy on the ascetic piety of women," Rapoport-Albert contends, "the Maid might have found an outlet for it even within marriage as did men who managed to achieve it without altogether renouncing their . . . obligation toward worldly existence."[16] Marcin Wodziński concurs that Hasidism was a "distinctly masculine enterprise" that strictly excluded women from male spaces and rituals, even in the writing of intimate *kvitlekh* (petitionary notes to the rebbe), which women submitted in the name of a male representative. As a result, he interrogates the category of "hasidic women," because women rarely defined themselves in such terms (even though they lived in Hasidic households and communities) until after World War I, not to mention declarations like those of Rabbi Meir of Apt, who proclaimed in 1824, "Women generally are not Hasidim."[17]

The exclusion of women from Hasidic institutions and spaces provided opportunities for subversion of the norms, especially in the realm of dress. In her memoirs, Ita Kalish recalled that her grandfather Rabbi Simhah Bunem hired a special tailor to sew the women's clothing: "grotesque" feminine garments of black or red satin adorned with gaudy headpieces. Female subversion was creative. Aunt Revele, for instance, wore the "Vurke garment" only with her husband's family but exchanged "her veil for a modern bonnet and housecoat for a beautiful, modern dress" when visiting her father's house in Lodz. The women also took advantage of festive occasions such as weddings to order dresses from Madame Keller of Warsaw. However, there were limits to female agency over dress. When Aunt Tsivyele entered the wedding hall in her "lemon-yellow satin dress, embroidered with blue velvet flowers with a long train . . . a malicious murmuring arose: such a dress was better suited for an actress than a Vurke rebbe's daughter."[18] Ironically, the Russian state claimed to protect women from the oppression of modest dress norms. For instance, in 1862 the general governor of Kiev received a report that the followers of tzaddik Twersky "attacked women who wore crinolines on the street, inflicting insults and blows," so that "one girl barely escaped with her life from the fury of the mob." She managed with difficulty to get home "under the escort of the police attendants and a soldier."[19] When the state instituted strict bans against distinctive Jewish dress in public spaces in 1851, it had expected stiff resistance but was surprised that the laws emboldened some women to shed their traditional clothing.[20]

Mitnagdism, a religious subculture in the northern provinces of Lithuania and Belorussia that vehemently opposed Hasidism and valorized Torah study, also used sex segregation to consolidate the power of the scholarly male elite, their ideology, and institutions.[21] Immanuel Etkes observes that the *mitnagdim* co-opted the tacit acceptance of women to assume the burden of breadwinning so that men could travel to remote yeshivas (rabbinic academies) and study Torah.[22] They cast female work to support scholars as a privilege and means to gain spiritual merit, thereby shifting cultural prestige from matters of the economy and income to the spiritual undertakings of men.[23] Even in this well-established structure, some women, such as Rayna Batya Berlin, the wife of Rabbi Naftali Tzvi Berlin (head of the Volozhin yeshiva), challenged their marginality. According to her nephew Barukh Epstein, Rayna neglected her domestic duties and devoted herself exclusively to the study of Jewish texts. He recounted her complaints about the devaluation of women inherent in their prohibition to study Torah, which clearly left an imprint on him because he devoted an entire chapter to her titled "The Wisdom of Women."[24] Epstein's decision to include his aunt's voice allows "her powerful presence" to "destabilize the very worldview [of the scholarly elites] he is ostensibly defending." Although Rayna Batya retreats into silence, she never "makes peace with her condition" of being relegated to the margins of the male study house.[25]

Jewish Education and Culture

BECAUSE JEWISH LAW DID not mandate instruction for females, Jewish girls remained outside the formal religious educational system. Some towns established a special heder for girls, but in most instances female education was private, informal, and practical, with an emphasis on both reading and writing (a skill that boys did not necessary acquire in the heder).[26] Iris Parush argues that because women remained outside the disciplinary system, they were free to learn foreign languages, study secular subjects, and read whatever books they desired, unencumbered by rabbinic surveillance—what she calls the "benefit of marginality."[27] The *maskilim* also took advantage of female marginality to open up the first private schools for girls; they recognized that the modern curricula would arouse less hostility in Jewish society because they were designed for female students, who mattered little to the religious authorities. In his petition for state funds to open the first private school for girls in Vil'na in 1831, Shevel' Perel' justified the request in terms of the value for Jewish boys: "It is common knowledge that the education of the female sex represents one of the most important means to the spread of enlightenment among men."[28] The marginality of girls' schools afforded the teachers greater freedom to experiment with the language and literature curriculum. In his report to the Society for the Dissemination of Enlightenment Among the Jews of Russia, Rabbi Zelig Minor observed that only a few Jewish boys had mastered Russian in their private school because their curriculum focused primarily on traditional Jewish texts; in contrast, "[the girls] study the reigning language five times a week in each grade and consequently, the girls' comprehension of the Russian language is quite good." He complained, however, that "as to the Law of Faith [the religion class], they know nothing" because of the lack of emphasis and the poor qualifications of the teachers.[29] Concerns about religious education for Jewish girls became more urgent in the interwar period, when traditional Jewish society struggled against the tide of assimilation.

In the absence of barriers to female secular education, Jewish girls flocked to state educational institutions, where they encountered Russian students and radical political ideas. Mariia Rashkovich, who later became a doctor, recalled "with warm feelings" her experiences at the Mariinskaia gymnasium in Odessa, where the students enjoyed lessons from first-rate teachers, including senior lecturers from the Novorossiisk University. Through her intimate reading circle (*kruzhok*), she became acquainted with the radical writings of Vissarion Belinskii, Nikolai Dobroliubov, and Dmitrii Pisarev.[30] The writer Shmuel Leib Tsitron identified these "bosom books" in his memoirs as the cause of the "radical spirit that rose among the young Jewish women of Minsk in the 1870s."[31] Female students were especially drawn to Nikolai Chernyshevskii's novel *What Is to Be Done* (1863), which espoused a doctrine of personal emancipation and sexual freedom and stressed individual effort, above all through "books, tutoring by friends, and circles."[32]

The *zhenskii vopros* (women's question) raised questions about the desirability of women in higher education, which critics argued represented the first step toward female emancipation from hearth and home. Starting in 1859, professors opened their university lectures to women as auditors (*slushatel'nitsy*), but the Statute of 1863 soon banned female students from all Russian universities after student riots raised the specter of women as a threat to public morality and stability. Jewish women who could afford to study abroad left for Switzerland and France, but many returned in the 1870s with the establishment of the "Higher Women's Courses" in Moscow, St. Petersburg, Kiev, and Kazan.[33] Anna Pavlovna Vygodskaia (1868–1943), who discovered Professor Petr Lesgaft's lectures on anatomy in St. Petersburg, described her new identity as a *kursistka* (a student at a highly respected women's college): "A special type of *kursistka* was formed under the influence of this remarkable scholar—a 'Lesgaftian' was known for her energy, persistence, hard work, and passion for social causes."[34] Medicine (especially midwifery and dentistry) was an attractive field of study for Jewish women. As the matriculation records show, the number of Jewish female students in women's medical courses in St. Petersburg increased exponentially—from 4.3% of the total student body in 1872 to 33.8% in 1879. By the end of the nineteenth century, Jewish women made up 19% of all midwives in the empire.[35]

By the early twentieth century, the rabbinic elite became aware that the gendered system of education had created a significant gap between the sexes. Rabbi Isaac Reines, who was invested in the marital alliances between daughters of *balebatim* (wealthy householders) and yeshiva students, recognized that the marital partners were worlds apart. His solution, however, was not to reform female education to include more religious subjects but to establish a modern yeshiva in Lida (Grodno Province) that included general subjects to acquaint Torah scholars with "the ways of the world."[36] Knowledge of Hebrew remained fairly rare among women until the 1880s, because men policed the holy tongue, describing it as "a man's apparel [which] a woman must not don" (to quote the writer David Frishman).[37] Women such as Miriam Markel Mosessohn (1839–1920), who dared to write in Hebrew, internalized the notion of language cross-dressing: "I have violated the law by dressing like a man [Deut. 22:5]. Who knows whether a crowd of people will gather and strip this garment from me?"[38] Breaking down the barriers to Hebrew for women was challenging, even in Zionist circles. Puah Rakovsky (1865–1955), who sought to expand

Hebrew education for girls in Poland in the late nineteenth century, observed that "Jewish parents, even intelligent ones, felt that girls should not have the same education as boys—never mind the idea of a girl wanting to learn the Holy Tongue!"[39] It was only in the interwar period that Hebrew became integrated into formal religious education for girls, especially after Sarah Schenirer established the Bais Yaakov schools. Naomi Seidman explores this innovative movement that came to encompass elementary schools, high schools, teacher's seminaries, vocational schools, summer programs, and youth movements as a "revolution in the name of tradition."[40]

The Family

ALTHOUGH JUDAISM AS A religion remained fairly autonomous, the institution of the family was governed by two separate, sometimes contradictory, systems of law: imperial family law and Halakhah (Jewish law). Secular family law emphasized "authority, obedience, filial duty, and paternalistic obligations," which reflected the "autocratic socio-political order."[41] A wife was "obliged to obey her husband as the head of the family, to live with in love, respect, and unlimited obedience, and to render him all pleasure and affection as mistress of the household." The law conceded that daughters who married were primarily obligated to their husbands rather than to their parents, for "one person cannot satisfy completely two such unlimited powers as that of the parents and the husband"; however, in reality, there were "overlapping structures of authority."[42] A husband exercised tremendous power over his wife by controlling her access to a passport (as seen earlier in the Betgilel case) and employment. As wife beating and drunkenness emerged as urgent social issues in the 1870s, the Imperial Chancellery for the Receipt of Petitions began to issue separate passports for women who suffered from exceptional abuse or neglect. Jewish women such as Dora Faivilevich turned to the Chancellery to obtain a passport to travel abroad for treatment of her diabetes. She explained that her husband was a "person with the highest measure of pettiness, maliciousness, rudeness, and a deficiency in his moral and spiritual development" who "ignored my human and feminine attributes."[43] The investigator confirmed her accusations, and she received a separate passport to travel to Carlsbad. However, she was unable to receive a divorce because the jurisdiction over such matters lay with the rabbinate.

Whereas most European states had established a system of civil marriage, the Russian state gave each religious confession the authority to deal independently with questions of marriage and divorce. Hence rabbis and the traditional *batei-din* (rabbinic courts) retained complete and final authority. Increasingly, however, the state began to question and, in practice, to violate that autonomy. Starting in 1853, the state recognized only those marriages performed by "state rabbis" (elected by their communities) and registered in communal metrical books. I argue that Jewish women became increasingly vulnerable in matters of divorce under the confusing dual system of law. Husbands whose marriages had been conducted by a "spiritual rabbi" (often an expert in Jewish law but without official standing in the eyes of the state) could simply declare their marriages invalid, abandoning their wives, who could never remarry because Jewish law still recognized their unions as valid. Equally important was the breakdown of rabbinic control that previously checked the broad rights of the husband. Because the tsarist state refused to concede any coercive power to the rabbis, they lacked any enforcement power to assist in woman-initiated divorces for wife beating, poverty, impotence, and more. I argue elsewhere that women began to use new strategies, resorting to the state courts to secure rightful monetary settlements (the dowry, alimony, and child support). Ironically, the very patriarchal state that enforced women's subordination to their husbands intervened to save Jewish women in the name of protecting them from depraved Jewish men and "backward" Jewish customs. The state, however, was not the only institution that castigated Jewish family practices.[44]

The traditional family was also the target of the Haskalah movement, which sought to articulate its own vision for reordering power in Jewish society. David Biale argues that the *maskilim* critiqued early and arranged marriage as crass financial transactions, devoid of love and consent. In its place, the *maskilim* proposed a new romantic model of marriage.[45] Novels such as Avraham Mapu's popular *The Love of Zion*—the first Hebrew novel—"made Jews fall in love with love and with literature." As Naomi Seidman puts it, "The novel exerted erotic and romantic power, drove a nail in the old system of arranging marriage, and provided a template for modern courtship, marriage, and family practices." She argues that as an "alternative to traditional rabbinic texts," the modern Jewish novel provided a "sentimental education" to its readers, who learned the scripts of romantic love from books rather than from life.[46] Olga Litvak reads Mapu's *Love of Zion* as a product of male anxiety about unruly female desire. She interrogates the text: "Why does female desire have to be so carefully stage-managed by the author? Why does an exciting romance end up as the most conventional social contract of marriage?" Litvak explains, "That is the way it has to be, because once the fly of desire has been released into the ointment of history there is nothing to ensure that [the protagonist] Tamar will, in fact, stay tamed." In fact, Litvak contends that "Mapu must contain the subversive Tamar through the institutions of family, community, and state—the very same sites of authority that he was initially prepared to let her flout in the name of love."[47]

The *maskilim* also criticized traditional gender roles for being "unproductive," because parasitic men lived off their in-laws or wives, who supported them through their labor in the marketplace. In lieu of these roles, they propagated the bourgeois cult of domesticity that would, as Biale puts it, "shelter Jewish women from the allegedly corrupting influences of commerce and refeminize them as mothers, wives, and homemakers in the private sphere." Biale also suggests that behind "this revolt against a perceived matriarchal family" lay a desire on the part of the *maskilim* to usurp power from the very women who had dominated them in their adolescent marriages.[48] Yet the vision of the *maskilim* had little in common with the realities of Jewish women in the Russian economy.

The Economy

THROUGHOUT THE IMPERIAL PERIOD, Jewish women played a significant role in the family economy either as independent breadwinners or as partners in traditional Jewish occupations. However, this was not simply due to the Jewish religious ideals (as described and stressed in the scholarship) but to the general Russian legal framework that protected women's property and inheritance rights and recognized their independent status as merchants and artisans. Women's subordinate status in Russian law coexisted with extraordinary rights—unique in Europe—to acquire, own, and manage immovable and movable property "without the consent of husbands" and "to buy, sell, and enter contracts" independently.[49] In Russia, women from most social groups, even noblewomen, engaged in economic activities, so this was not unique to Jews.[50]

Examining gender roles in the Poliakov family—which dominated Russian big business and finance with banking houses in Moscow and St. Petersburg and which built a quarter of the railroads in the empire—illustrates significant changes over three generations. The family hailed from the small town of Dubrovno (Mogilev Province), where Solomon Poliakov (1812–1897) ran a small retail shop with his wife, Zlata (née Rabinovich; 1812–1851), of Minsk until hard times forced him to travel to Moscow in 1842. Zlata, like other female merchants of her generation, singlehandedly ran the family business, but stiff competition eventually forced her to sell her goods in the larger district town of Orsha. Having earned the trust of her customers, Zlata independently secured loans and "opened her own store with beautiful merchandise" that was tailored to the "tastes and demands of her clients." Her ability to obtain her wares directly from Moscow (instead of a warehouse in Shklov, which supplied most of the province) made her business extremely successful.[51]

Zlata's sons also married women who were active in trade. When her son Iakov Poliakov moved to Voronezh to manage a cloth mill factory and alcohol distillery for Count Ivan M. Tolstoi, his wife, Amalia (née Lifshchitz), managed their family business in Orsha. In a paternalistic tone, Iakov remarked: "[My] wife absolutely demonstrated that a woman is no worse than a man. . . . They [wives] understand perfectly and can conduct any business. They can even adapt well in financial difficulties."[52] His younger brother Lazar's wife, Rozaliia (née Vydrin), was also famed for her business acumen, as Iakov observed: "The Vydrins ran an iron goods business in Mogilev. The bride Rozaliia managed a store and was considered knowledgeable in her business."[53] She remained active in the family's enterprises and banks in Moscow as a major stockowner and decision maker. Much to Iakov's chagrin, she refused to bank risky loans to rescue his failing banks and often chided him about loans he had failed to repay.[54]

The women in the Poliakov family were not unique. According to the *Guide to Factories and Plants* for 1879, which included information about female entrepreneurs, 3.9% of all proprietresses of industrial enterprises in the empire were Jewish (compared with 75.7% Russian, 9.6% Polish, 5.3% German, 1.4% Ukrainian, and 2.6% other women)—a fairly large percentage, because Jews made up only 4.1% of the total population in 1897. For instance, Sophia Brodskaia owned a tobacco factory in Voronezh (which was situated outside the Pale of Settlement) with twenty workers and "produced goods to the value of 20,000 rubles."[55] Other female enterprises specialized in the production of textiles, vodka, lard candles, matches, leather, and porcelain. By 1884 the percentage of Jewish female entrepreneurs had risen to 4.9%, reflecting a general trend in the empire of increased female participation in Russian industries.[56] These figures did not include Jewish involvement in small trade and business, which was more characteristic of the economy in the Pale of Settlement—a topic addressed at length by Ol'ga Sobolevskaia in her study on everyday Jewish life in Belorussia.[57] Women such as Zlata Poliakova ran small shops in the market, selling fruit, bread, textiles, and other domestic items in the towns, whereas other women in rural areas engaged in the liquor trade and innkeeping, which led to daily interactions with non-Jewish customers. Daily conflicts in the marketplace, inns, and taverns between small business owners and clients over the poor quality of goods, accusations of inaccurate scales and theft, and so forth escalated into catastrophic violence during waves of pogroms in the late nineteenth and early twentieth centuries.[58]

By the third generation of the Poliakov family, Rozaliia's three daughters— Ziniada, Khaia, and Raia—knew practically nothing about their family business, whereas their brothers served as board members of their banks and railroad enterprises. As the Poliakov records reveal, banking, commerce, communication, and transportation were fields largely dominated by men by the late imperial period.[59] The memoirist Pauline Wengeroff, whose brother-in-law Avram Isaakovich Zak was well acquainted with the Poliakovs because of his work at the Gintsburg bank, experienced similar shifts in her own family.[60] When her husband insisted on excluding her from business decisions, she was outraged: "I had no voice with him in financial matters. He called my advice meddling and would hear nothing of it. It was his opinion that a wife, especially his, had no aptitude in this sort of thing and that my 'meddling was a disparagement of his ability.'" Despite his string of financial failures (even with an influential relative like Zak in St. Petersburg), her husband claimed that the "man, the breadwinner, has the duty to support his family, and therefore he is master." Wengeroff rejected his claims, citing Chonen's own grandfather, who "bent his will" to his wife "because he knew that she was more than a match for him in every respect" and deferred to her decisions in their innkeeping business.[61] Wengeroff's memoirs are ultimately about her "disempowerment by her liberated husband and children, all of them complicit in the 'silencing' of the mother who refuses to sit quietly by, knitting and watching her spoiled and selfish offspring 'speak about their [own] lives and ideals.'"[62]

In Russia, Jewish women could enroll with their husbands in their respective social estates and enjoy the privileges and restrictions of their status or register independently if they were unmarried. When the state began to permit "useful" categories of Jews (first-guild merchants, retired soldiers, skilled artisans, and university students) to leave the Pale of Settlement starting in 1859, Jewish women took advantage of these new opportunities to settle in the Russian interior. In 1879 all students with degrees in dentistry, midwifery, and pharmacy—categories to which more educated Jewish women belonged— were included in this selective emancipation. For instance, Tauba Korenblat, who earned her degree from the Imperial Khar'kov University in 1883, opened a private practice in Chuguev (Khar'kov Province) to provide "greater accessibility for the poor class of people and for male and female students." In 1908 she decided to move her practice outside the Pale of Settlement to Koroch (Kursk Province), but the governor rejected her petition on the grounds that "any newcomers to the town of Koroch, especially Jews, are extremely undesirable" given the revolutionary mood of the times. The governor's argument failed to convince an official in the Ministry of the Interior, who scribbled on Korenblat's file, "Under the statutes pertaining to the practice of a specialty [i.e., dentistry], she has the right to live in Koroch and open an office for that. . . . This order is incorrect."[63]

The alleged revolutionary mood was prevalent not only in Kursk but also in the Pale of Settlement, where the empire experienced a belated and accelerated industrialization in the mid-1880s. According to the 1897 census, 48.7% of Jews resided within the prescribed urban centers, where they dominated crafts such as tailoring, weaving, shoemaking, and the production of food and beverages. Long hours (sixteen to eighteen hours a day in the northwest cities), meager wages, and seasonal employment left many workers in dire poverty.[64] Female workers, especially young girls, were vulnerable to unfair treatment. For instance, in 1901 protests broke out at the Gal'pern matchbox factory in Pinsk after the foreman ordered the female workers to pack thinner matches in bigger boxes. "Those changes significantly reduced our wages," complained 20-year-old Sora Breitbord, who was paid per unit of packed boxes. "For example, before I received up to thirty-five kopecks, but now no more than twenty kopecks."[65] Archival sources reveal that work in factories, printing presses, and artisan shops also made women vulnerable to sexual harassment, assault, and unwanted pregnancies.[66] Female workers found themselves oppressed not only by the factory regime but also by the state police, who kept them under surveillance for revolutionary activities, arresting them for strikes even when they sought to address specific grievances and were not organized by a revolutionary party.

Women on the Margins

UNTIL RECENTLY, MARGINALIZED GROUPS such as unwed mothers, domestic servants, the mentally ill, the disabled,[67] and Jewish converts to Christianity have been ignored in the historiography. In part, this is because they did not leave a written record of diaries, letters, or memoirs; however, some voices found their way into the court and administrative records because of unexpected encounters with the tsarist state.

The most regulated group of women was registered prostitutes. Upon registration, they received a yellow ticket (*zheltyi bilet*) from the state, which "protected them from police harassment" but also subjected them to intense medical-police surveillance and regulation.[68] In Vil'na, for example, Jewish prostitutes in brothels had to submit to a twice-weekly medical examination for venereal diseases. Incentives for complying with these invasive examinations included free medical care at the city hospital and documentation in case of lawsuits. Hence, when a client accused Brokha Kagan (a Jewish prostitute at Natina's brothel) of infecting him with syphilis in 1893, the city doctor testified that "she has never been ill, has never had any symptoms of syphilis, and was not considered syphilitic on the [weekly] list."[69] Public debates in state and society about the high visibility of Jews in the sex trade led to the creation of a Jewish branch of the Russian Society for the Protection of Women in St. Petersburg through the patronage of Baroness Roza Gintsburg and her husband, Baron Goratsii Gintsburg, in 1901. The goal was to protect young Jewish women from prostitution by providing them with financial assistance, creating spaces such as libraries, dormitories, and summer colonies where they could spend their "free time" and organizing such wholesome activities for them like walks in nature.[70]

The world of Jewish brothels, illegal abortion clinics, and other marginal spaces came into sharp focus during a major court case in Vil'na in 1890. The previous year, a group of Jewish children who had gone mushroom picking in the forest on the outskirts of Vil'na found an abandoned baby wrapped in rags. The state investigation uncovered a network of Jewish women who ran a baby-farming business in Vil'na that hired out unwed mothers (mainly domestic servants) as wet nurses and extorted their salaries in exchange for the care of their illegitimate offspring, most of whom died from neglect and abuse. Testimonies of the unwed mothers revealed the vulnerability of domestic servants and factory workers who experienced sexual assault, harassment, and "seduction" based on promises of marriage (which the men rarely fulfilled).[71]

Although the Vil'na court case dealt with the murder of newborn infants, it referred to the mentally ill in the Jewish hospital. The care of the mentally ill fell mainly on the shoulders of the family or sometimes on the communal *hekdesh* (which served a dual role as a poorhouse and a hospital). By the late nineteenth century, more families began to turn to the Jewish hospitals in Vil'na, Kiev, and Warsaw for assistance. In the case of Rivka Arliuk, the community of Oshmiany complained to the police in 1902 that "[she] beats passers-by and neighbors, throws stones at people, and tries to set fire to the house where she lives. She has bitten several people." They cast her as a "threat to the public safety" and requested her institutionalization in the Jewish hospital.[72] Petitions to the state, which highlighted the suffering of the family and a short history of the mentally ill individual, provide faces and narratives to the nameless "mad" women wandering the street and reveal how society and the medical regime sought to erase their visibility by removing them from public spaces.

Converts to Christianity also lived on the fringes of both Jewish and Christian society. As recent studies have shown, baptism did not dissolve the old ties that bound them to the Jewish family. Women who converted for marriage and sought reconciliation with their Jewish families experienced severe conflicts with Christian husbands who felt threatened by their crossing of religious boundaries.[73] Christian missionaries active among Jews also expressed alarm at the fate of converts who, "after accepting holy baptism . . . are deprived of their sources of livelihood in a Jewish environment" and "must either die from starvation [or] live with the Jews, pandering to them, painstakingly fulfilling their loathsome rituals."[74] When the impoverished Rybakov family came to the attention of the Mariinsko Sergievskii Shelter in St. Petersburg, the staff observed that the family lived on the margins because the converted father was constantly drunk, leaving the "ailing mother, burdened with five minor children."[75] The shelter, which sought to remake Jewish converts into "honest" and "useful" Russian citizens, stressed their need to abandon old "Jewish" vices (such as greediness) and occupations (trade). The discourse reflected a trend toward racialization that emphasized their otherness—that is, treating converts not on the basis of religious confession but as a separate racial group with deeply ingrained traits regardless of sincere or nominal conversions.[76]

Politics

SCHOLARS HAVE NOTED THE increased political participation of Jewish women in imperial Russia, but no comprehensive study yet exists. Little archival work has been conducted, and the existing historiography consists largely of biography-based studies that rely on women's memoirs and literary represen-tations.[77] By the late 1870s, Jews began to join the populist (*narodnik*) move-ment, making up a staggering 20% of the Chaikovskii circle, the best organized group of revolutionaries. Populists turned to political terrorism to rouse the peasantry and overturn the political order. On March 1, 1881, Gesia Gel'fman (d. 1882), a member of the self-declared terrorist organization Naraodnaia volia (The People's Will), was arrested for her participation in the assassina-tion of Tsar Alexander II in 1881. During her trial, she refused to answer any questions but admitted to her role in the movement. Because of her pregnancy and calls for clemency from socialists in the West, the state commuted her death sentence to lifelong penal servitude.[78] She became a symbol of Jewish "treachery" among the *pogromshchiki* (perpetrators of violent pogroms), who claimed to punish the Jews for attacking the autocracy.

By the time of the Revolution of 1905–1907, several revolutionary parties, which included Jewish women in their ranks, competed for dominance. Jewish working women in northwestern cities, for example, Vil'na and Minsk, opted to join the Bund, which embraced the vision of a proletarian revolution. They participated in the strike movements to protest the terrible working conditions in the factories and artisan shops.[79] Zionism, the Bund's main rival, did not attract a mass following before World War I. However, female activists such as Puah Rakovsky were drawn early to Hibbat Zion (Lovers of Zion); much to her dismay, she discovered that the "first bearers of idea of Hibbat Zion . . .

did not admit women into their circles."[80] To address the exclusion of women, Rakovsky attempted to raise awareness about the issue among the male leadership and organize women in independent associations, such as Bnos Tsyion (Daughters of Zion), a Polish Zionist woman's organization founded in 1917, to fight for female suffrage, inclusion, and self-determination.[81]

Jewish women who rejected the industrialist vision of Marxism or Zionism and embraced terrorism as a strategy for overthrowing autocracy joined the Socialist Revolutionary Party, making up about 30% of its membership.[82] The desire for vengeance for the oppression of the Jews motivated women such as Mariia (Mania) Shkol'nik to join the Combat Organization, which carried out the group's acts of terror. Shkol'nik attributed her decision to assassinate Nikolai Kleigels, the general governor of Kiev, to his cruelty: "[He] had organized the Jewish pogroms, and . . . become universally hated."[83] In stark contrast, some Jewish women (usually the wives of liberal Jewish politicians) completely rejected the idea of overthrowing the tsarist state and were repulsed by the violence and disorder of the revolutionary parties. Instead, they pressed for legal reforms through the Kadet Party. Roza Vinaver, whose husband, Maksim Vinaver, was elected as a Jewish representative to the first Russian Duma, affirmed her liberal Kadet values and ethos, which espoused the rule of law, basic civil liberties, constitutional democracy, and above all, *vsenarodnost'*—a broad, supra-ethnic nationality that upheld patriotism without chauvinism and narrow sectarianism.[84] This kind of vision imagined that Jews would be liberated from the matrix of oppression through liberal politics.

New Directions

ONE WAY TO UNDERSTAND Jewish women in the tsarist empire, as demonstrated in this chapter, is through the feminist lens of intersectionality—that is, to explore the matrix of domination that shaped their lives in an imperial setting. Jewish women simultaneously had to contend with their gender, social estate status, marital status, ethnicity, religious laws and customs, cultural norms, class, able-bodiedness or disability, and so forth in their daily lives. As illustrated, Jewish women sometimes found creative ways to subvert the norms or to use contradictory systems (i.e., state law versus religious law) against each other to secure their rights. They could appeal to the patriarchal character of the state to protect them as women from the discrimination of Jewish law; conversely, some women relied on rabbis to protect them from the power of the state that viewed their marriages as invalid because they were not conducted by a state rabbi.

This survey of Jewish women's history and culture in the tsarist empire reveals that the new scholarship, though meager in quantity, is rich in quality. For instance, new interpretations of maskilic literature through a sharp gendered lens or female reading practices can provide new perspectives on hackneyed representations of the Haskalah and sex segregation in Jewish life. The study of women and gender, however, is still in a nascent stage; much research remains to be done on such topics as female disabilities (e.g., mental illness, deafness, muteness), sexuality, dress and fashion, emotions, and cultural production. Finally, the task ahead is to the rewrite the master narratives, not simply to "add and stir" but to offer new paradigms on Jewish history in the Russian Empire based on new research.

Notes

1 Derzhavnyi arkhiv mista Kyieva, f. 164, op. 1, d. 1197, ll. 1–4, 7–7 ob., 14–16.
2 Kimberlé Crenshaw, "Mapping the Margins: Intersectionality, Identity Politics, and Violence Against Women of Color," *Stanford Law Review* 43, no. 6 (1991): 1241–99.
3 Patricia Hill Collins, *Black Feminist Thought: Knowledge, Consciousness, and the Politics of Empowerment* (Boston: Unwin Hyman, 1990), 221–38.
4 ChaeRan Y. Freeze and Paula Hyman, "Introduction: Historiographical Survey," in *Polin: Jewish Women in Eastern Europe*, ed. ChaeRan Y. Freeze and Paula Hyman (London: Littman Library of Jewish Civilization, 2005), 3–24.
5 Eliyana Adler, "Out of the Ghetto: Historiography on Jewish Women in Eastern Europe," *Polin: Writing Jewish History in Eastern Europe* 29 (2017): 301–17.
6 "Naselenie," *Evreiskaia Entsiklopediia* (St. Petersburg: Obshchestvo dlia nauchnykh evreiskikh izdanii), 11: 538. These figures included the Kingdom of Poland. The total Jewish population was 5,189,401, or 4.13% of the total population.
7 bell hooks, *Feminist Theory: From Margin to Center* (Cambridge, MA: South End Press, 2000).
8 Andreas Kappeler, *The Russian Empire: A Multi-Ethnic History*, trans. Alfred Clayton (New York: Routledge, 2001), 58.
9 Chava Weissler, "Tkhines," in *The YIVO Encyclopedia of Jews in Eastern Europe*, ed. Gershon David Hundert (New Haven, CT: Yale University Press, 2008), 2: 1885.
10 Chava Weissler, *Voices of the Matriarchs: Listening to the Prayers of Early Modern Jewish Women* (Boston: Beacon Press, 1998).
11 Jacob Elbaum and Chava Turniansky, "Tsene-rene," in *The YIVO Encyclopedia of Jews in Eastern Europe*, ed. Gershon David Hundert (New Haven, CT: Yale University Press, 2008), 2: 1912–13.
12 Iris Parush, *Reading Jewish Women: Marginality and Modernization in Nineteenth-Century Eastern European Society* (Waltham, MA: Brandeis University Press, 2004), 66.

13 Parush, *Reading Jewish Women*, 137.

14 Jean Baumgarten, "Listening, Reading, and Understanding: How Jewish Women Read Ethical Yiddish Literature (Seventeenth to Eighteenth Centuries)," *Journal of Jewish Studies* 16, no. 2 (2017): 262.

15 Ada Rapoport-Albert, *Hasidic Studies: Essays in History and Gender* (London: Littman Library of Jewish Civilization, 2018).

16 Ada Rapoport-Albert, "On Women in Hasidism, S. A. Horodecky, and the Maid of Ludmir Tradition," in *Jewish History: Essays in Honor of Chimen Abramsky*, ed. Ada Rapoport-Albert and Steven J. Zipperstein (London: Peter Halban, 1988), 508; see also Nathaniel Deutsch, *The Maid of Ludmir: A Holy Jewish Woman and Her World* (Berkeley: University of California Press, 2003).

17 Marcin Wodziński, *Hasidism: Key Questions* (Oxford, UK: Oxford University Press, 2018), 48.

18 ChaeRan Y. Freeze and Jay Harris, *Everyday Jewish Life in Imperial Russia* (Waltham, MA: Brandeis University Press, 2013), 24.

19 TsDIAK-Ukraïny, f. 1423, op. 1, d. 6, ll. 56–58 (September 12, 1862).

20 See Eugene Avrutin, *Jews and the Imperial State: Identification Politics in Tsarist Russia* (Ithaca, NY: Cornell University Press, 2010), 42–44.

21 Naomi Seidman, *The Marriage Plot, Or, How Jews Fell in Love with Love and with Literature* (Stanford, CA: Stanford University Press, 2016), 254.

22 Immanuel Etkes, "Marriage and Torah Study Among the *Lomdim* in Lithuania in the Nineteenth Century," in *Jewish Family: Metaphor and Memory*, ed. David Kraemer (Oxford, UK: Oxford University Press, 1989), 153–78.

23 Paula Hyman, *Gender and Assimilation in Modern Jewish History* (Seattle: University of Washington Press, 1995); Parush, *Reading Jewish Women*, 58.

24 Eliyana Adler, "Reading Rayna Batya: The Rebellious Rebbetzin as Self Reflection," *Nashim: A Journal of Jewish Women's Studies and Gender Issues* 16 (fall 2008): 130–52.

25 Dan Seeman and Rebecca Kobrin, "'Like One of the Whole Men': Learning Gender and Autobiography in R. Barukh Epstein's *Mekor Barukh*," *Nashim* 2 (1999): 84–85.

26 Shaul Stampfer, "Gender Differentiation and the Education of the Jewish Woman in Nineteenth Century Eastern Europe," *Polin* 7 (1992): 63–85; Eliyana Adler, *In Her Hands: The Education of Jewish Girls in Tsarist Russia* (Detroit: Wayne State University Press, 2010).

27 Parush, *Reading Jewish Women*, 57.

28 Adler, *In Her Hands*, 29.

29 Parush, *Reading Jewish Women*, 90.

30 Mariia Rashkovich, *Vospominaniia vrachei Iulii Al. Kviatkovskoi i Mariia Rashkovich* (Paris: [s.n.], 1937), 151–56.

31 Parush, *Reading Jewish Women*, 180.

32 Richard Stites, *The Women's Liberation Movement in Russia: Feminism, Nihilism, and Bolshevism, 1860–1930* (Princeton, NJ: Princeton University Press, 1978), 93.

33 Carole B. Balin, "The Call to Serve: Jewish Women Medical Students in Russia, 1872–1887," in *Polin: Jewish Women in Eastern Europe*, ed. ChaeRan Y. Freeze and Paula Hyman (London: Littman Library of Jewish Civilization, 2005), 133–40.

34 Anna Pavlovna Vygodskaia, *The Story of a Life: Memoirs of a Young Jewish Woman in the Russian Empire*, trans. Eugene M. Avrutin and Robert H. Greene (Dekalb: Northern Illinois University Press, 2012), 116.

35 Balin, "Call to Serve," 141.

36 ChaeRan Y. Freeze, *Jewish Marriage and Divorce of Jews in Imperial Russia* (Waltham, MA: Brandeis University Press, 2001), 34.

37 Parush, *Reading Jewish Women*, 228. On the gendered division of Hebrew as the masculine holy tongue for prayer and literature and Yiddish the feminine vernacular for the mundane and everyday life, see Naomi Seidman, *A Marriage Made in Heaven: The Sexual Politics of Yiddish and Hebrew* (Berkeley: University of California Press, 1997).

38 Carole B. Balin, *To Reveal Our Hearts: Jewish Women Writers in Tsarist Russia* (Cincinnati: Hebrew Union College Press, 2000), 36.

39 Puah Rakovsky, *My Life as a Radical Jewish Woman: Memoirs of a Zionist Feminist in Poland*, ed. Paula Hyman (Bloomington: Indiana University Press, 2002), 25.

40 Naomi Seidman, *Sarah Schenirer and the Bais Yaakov Movement: A Revolution in the Name of Tradition* (London: Littman Library of Jewish Civilization, 2019).

41 William Wagner, *Marriage, Property, and Law in Late Imperial Russia* (Oxford, UK: Clarendon Press, 1994), 62.

42 Wagner, *Marriage, Property, and Law*, 63–64.

43 Freeze, *Jewish Marriage and Divorce*, 174–75.

44 Freeze, *Jewish Marriage and Divorce*, 201–42.

45 David Biale, *Eros and the Jews: From Biblical Israel to Contemporary America* (Berkeley: University of California Press, 1997), 150; David Biale, "Eros and Enlightenment: Love Against Marriage in East European Jewish Enlightenment," *Polin* 1 (1986): 63.

46 Seidman, *Marriage Plot*, 21, 26, 35, 46.

47 Olga Litvak, *Haskalah: The Romantic Movement in Judaism* (New Brunswick, NJ: Rutgers University Press, 2012), 145. For more on Yiddish literature and love, also Olga Litvak, "Khave and Her Sisters: Sholem-Aleichem and the Lost Girls of 1905," *Jewish Social Studies* 15, no. 3 (2009): 1–38.

48 Biale, *Eros and the Jews*, 161.

49 Galina Nikolaevna Ul'ianova, *Female Entrepreneurs in Nineteenth-Century Russia* (London: Pickering & Chatto, 2009), 2–4.

50 Ul'ianova, *Female Entrepreneurs*, 1–5. For noblewomen's work, see Michelle Marrese, *A Woman's Kingdom: Noblewomen and the Control of Property in Russia, 1700–1862* (Ithaca, NY: Cornell University Press, 2002).

51 See Iakov Poliakov, "Istoriia semeinye nachinaniia [s] 1748 goda," Central Archives of the History of the Jewish People, Israel; ChaeRan Y. Freeze, *A Woman of Distinction: Zinaida Poliakova's Life and Diaries in Imperial Russia* (Waltham, MA: Brandeis University Press, 2019). First names will be used here to identify family members because of the multiple Poliakovs.

52 Poliakov, "Istoriia semeinye nachinaniia," l. 22.

53 Poliakov, "Istoriia semeinye nachinaniia," l. 16.

54 Poliakov, "Istoriia semeinye nachinaniia," ll. 1–17.

55 Ul'ianova, *Female Entrepreneurs*, 122.

56 Ul'ianova, *Female Entrepreneurs*, 122.

57 Ol'ga A. Sobolevskaia, *Povsednevnaia zhizn' evreev Belarusi v kontse XVIII–pervoi polovine XIX veka* (Grodno, Belarus: GrGU im. Ia. Kupaly, 2012).

58 For examples, see Freeze and Harris, *Everyday Jewish Life*, 448–56.

59 Freeze, *Woman of Distinction*.

60 Pauline Wengeroff, *Memoirs of a Grandmother: Scenes from the Cultural History of the Jews of Russia in the Nineteenth Century*, trans. Shulamit Magnus (Stanford, CA: Stanford University Press, 2014); Shulamit Magnus, *A Woman's Life: Pauline Wengeroff and Memoirs of a Grandmother* (London: Littman Library of Jewish Civilization, 2016). See also Judith R. Baskin, "Piety and Female Aspirations in the Memoirs of Pauline Epstein Wengeroff and Bella Rosenfeld Chagall," *Nashim* 7 (spring 2004): 65–96.

61 Wengeroff, *Memoirs of a Grandmother*, 86–94.

62 Olga Litvak, "Jocasta Speaks," *Jewish Review of Books* (winter 2011), https://jewishreviewofbooks.com/articles/136/jocasta-speaks/ (accessed December 19, 2020).

63 Rossiiskii gosudarstvennyi istoricheskii arkhiv, St. Petersburg, f. 1284, op. 224, d. 260, ll. 25–30.

64 Ezra Mendelsohn, *Class Struggle in the Pale: The Formative Years of the Jewish Worker's Movement in Tsarist Russia* (Cambridge, MA: Cambridge University Press, 1970), 20–22.

65 Lietuvos Valstybes Istorijos Archyvas, Vilnius, f. 446, op. 3, d. 234, ll. 10–12 ob., 85–87, 95–97, 125–28.

66 For examples, see ChaeRan Y. Freeze, "Lilith's Midwives: Jewish Newborn Child Murder in Nineteenth-Century Vil'na," *Jewish Social Studies* 16, no. 2 (2010): 1–27.

67 Hanna Wegrzynsk explores the fascinating custom of "black weddings" of orphans and Jews with "physical deformities" at the cemetery to ward off the plague—a practice that the rabbinic council in Warsaw sought to abolish during the cholera plague of 1892. Hanna Wegrzynsk, "Shvartze Khasene: Black Weddings Among Polish Jews," in *Holy Dissent: Jewish and Christian Mystics in Eastern Europe*, ed. Glenn Dynner (Detroit: Wayne State University Press, 2011), 55–68.

68 For a comprehensive study of prostitution in Russia, see Laurie Bernstein, *Sonia's Daughters: Prostitutes and Their Regulation in Imperial Russia* (Berkeley: University of California Press, 1995), 22.

69 Lietuvos Valstybes Istorijos Archyvas, Vilnius, f. 383, op. 1, d. 205, l. 203 (1893).

70 Rossiiskii gosudarstvennyi istoricheskii arkhiv, St. Petersburg, f. 1335, op. 1, d. 2, l. 37. For the Jewish branch of the association in Kiev, see Natan Meir, "Jews, Ukrainians, and Russians in Kiev: Intergroup Relations in Late Imperial Associational Life," *Slavic Review* 65, no. 3 (2006): 489–92. For statistics on the number of prostitutes and brothel keepers in the Pale of Settlement and public debates about Jews and the sex trade, see Bernstein, *Sonia's Daughters*, 161–66.

71 Freeze, "Lilith's Midwives," 1–27.

72 Lietuvos Valstybes Istorijos Archyvas, Vilnius, f. 383, op. 3, d. 268, ll. 5–10.

73 See also ChaeRan Y. Freeze, "When Chava Left Home: Gender, Conversion, and the Jewish Faith in Tsarist Russia," in *Polin: Jewish Women in Eastern Europe*, ed. ChaeRan Y. Freeze and Paula Hyman (London: Littman Library of Jewish Civilization, 2005), 153–88; Rachel Manekin, "The Lost Generation: Education and Female Conversion in Fin-de-Siècle Krakow," in *Polin: Jewish Women in Eastern Europe*, ed. ChaeRan Y. Freeze and Paula Hyman (London: Littman Library of Jewish Civilization, 2005), 189–229; and Ellie R. Shainker, *Confessions of the Shtetl: Converts from Judaism in Imperial Russia, 1817–1906* (Stanford, CA: Stanford University Press, 2016).

74 ChaeRan Y. Freeze, "Fallen from the Faith: Jewish Converts in Imperial Russia," in *Church and Society in Modern Russia: Essays in Honor of Gregory L. Freeze*, ed. Manfred Hildermeier and Elise Kimerling Wirtschafter (Wiesbaden: Harrasowitz, 2015), 166.

75 ChaeRan Y. Freeze, "The Mariinsko Sergievskii Shelter for Converted Jewish Children in St. Petersburg," in *Jews in the East European Borderlands: Essays in Honor of John D. Klier*, ed. Eugene M. Avrutin and Harriet Murav (Boston: Academic Studies Press, 2012), 27–49.

76 Freeze, "Mariinsko Sergievskii Shelter," 48–59.

77 For instance, see Naomi Shepherd, *A Price Below Rubies: Jewish Women as Rebels and Radicals* (Cambridge, MA: Harvard University Press, 1993); and Deborah Hertz, "Dangerous Politics, Dangerous Liaisons: Love and Terror Among Jewish Women Radicals in Czarist Russia," *Histoire, Économie et Société* 4 (2014): 94–109.

78 Barbara Alpern Engel, "Gesia Gelfman: A Jewish Woman on the Left in Imperial Russia," in *Jewish and Leftist Politics: Judaism, Israel, Antisemitism, and Gender*, ed. Jack Jacobs (Cambridge, UK: Cambridge University Press, 2017), 183–99.

79 Harriet Davis-Kram, "The Story of the Sisters of the Bund," *Contemporary Jewry* 5, no. 2 (1980): 27–43.

80 Paula Hyman, "Discovering Puah Rakovsky," *Nashim* 7 (2004): 105.

81 Rakovsky, *My Life*, 70–88.

82 Amy Knight, "Female Terrorists in the Russian Socialist Revolutionary Party," *Russian Review* 33, no. 2 (1979): 145.

83 Freeze and Harris, *Everyday Jewish Life*, 584.

84 Victor Kelner and Oleg A. Korostelev, "Vospominaniia Rozy Vinavera," *Arkhiv evreiskoi istorii* 7 (2012): 11–134; ChaeRan Y. Freeze, "The Evolution of Roza Georgievna Vinaver: The Making of a Jewish Liberal Politician's Wife in Imperial Russia," in *The Individual in History*, ed. ChaeRan Y. Freeze, Sylvia Fuks Fried, and Eugene R. Sheppard (Waltham, MA: Brandeis University Press, 2015), 317–32.

WOMEN, GENDER, AND MODERNITY IN NINETEENTH-CENTURY GERMAN JEWISH HISTORY

BENJAMIN M. BAADER

NINETEENTH-CENTURY GERMANY WAS THE cradle of modern Jewish historiography, meaning the writing of Jewish history as a secular and critical enterprise; and more than 100 years later, German Jewish women's and gender history was the site of pioneering feminist historiography. Over the course of the nineteenth century, German Jewish men self-consciously and courageously began to create the academic field that they called *Wissenschaft des Judentums* (scholarly study, or science, of Judaism) and that is known today as Jewish studies. Thus male Jewish writers and historians began to study Jewish literature and Jewish culture in the detached and purportedly objective manner in which university scholars had started studying the texts of all civilizations, rather than engaging with Jewish texts from a religious perspective, in which all study of Hebrew literature was essentially an act of worship, designed to explore God's will and to absorb God's teachings. Modern Jewish historiography was an integral part of *Wissenschaft*, a project by which Jews sought to establish themselves in modern German culture and society.[1]

The context for this rise of modern Jewish scholarship and modern Jewish historiography was German Jews' efforts to adapt to the radically changing circumstances of their lives in the first half of the nineteenth century. In fact, between the onset of the Enlightenment in the middle of the eighteenth century and the founding of the German Empire in 1871, German lands underwent dramatic changes, as industrialization transformed the economic and social structure of society and the German nation-state took shape. Jews were a small population—in 1871, just over 1% of Germans—and in the eighteenth century, many of them were desperately poor, and all suffered under debilitating legal and economic restrictions.[2] With the modernization of German society, these restrictions began to decrease and the economic position of German Jews started to improve. Step by step, Jews integrated into the emerging German middle classes and into the culture of bourgeois respectability and aimed at gaining full citizenship while holding onto their Jewishness and working to adapt Jewish culture and religion to new and radically transformed circumstances.

The *Wissenschaft* project and the creation of modern historical narratives about the Jewish people were designed to support these endeavors. In the new political and cultural universe of modern culture, nation-states drew legitimacy from the history they began telling about themselves, and for the small Jewish population in German lands, the historical works of Jewish scholars such as Isaac Marcus Jost (1793–1860) and Heinrich Graetz (1817–1891) were paramount in the quest for a modern Jewish identity and for acceptance as both equal (as German citizens) and different (as Jews). For instance, history could demonstrate that Jews had always been useful members of the societies in which they had lived and that they possessed a rich legacy of intellectual, cultural, and economic achievements. Jewish history provided the grounds for a renewed and reconceptualized self-esteem and for a platform for political agency. As German Jewish men pioneered writing modern Jewish history, the narrative of how German Jews entered modernity became the model of Jewish modernization. Until a generation ago, our understanding of what it means to be modern and Jewish was shaped primarily by the German story.[3]

This modern German Jewish historiography was a masculinist enterprise. The *Wissenschaft* scholars were exclusively men; they wrote primarily for other men about texts that men before them had written and about a history in which almost exclusively men figured as actors. In their hands, Jewish history was intellectual history, the history of texts and ideas that women had for centuries been able to access in only very restricted ways. Jewish history was a political and economic history in which Christian kings gave charters to male Jewish community leaders, and Jewish men traded goods (and books) from Tangier to Vilna and made fortunes. Women barely figured in these accounts.[4] Only in the 1970s, the era of second-wave feminism and decades after World War II and the Nazi persecution and attempted extermination of European Jewry, did Jewish women scholars in the United States, some of them descendants of emigrants from Germany, systematically challenge the exclusivist male character of nineteenth-century *Wissenschaft* on its most cherished grounds: German Jewish history. At the time, such an endeavor constituted a provocation and lacked precedents in the academic world, but these historians pioneered in developing a true modern Jewish women's history and feminist historiography and changed Jewish history for good. The account of German Jewish women's history and of gender in German Jewish history that I present in this chapter is known and accessible to us because of the achievements of these feminist historians.

Drawing and building on decades of such feminist scholarship, I first relate the fascinating story of a group of prominent and highly unusual women who led salons in Berlin in the era of the Enlightenment around 1800. These women achieved an outstanding degree of integration into German society, but to the horror of Jewish observers, most of them converted to Christianity. Next, I use the memoir of a not particularly well-known Jewish woman who lived in the nineteenth century, Clara Geissmar, to discuss a much more representative trajectory of successful upward mobility and slow disengagement from Jewish practice, although short of apostasy. However, by no means did all German Jews abandon Jewish practice, and in the third section of this chapter, I elaborate on the transformation of Jewish religious culture in this period that comes sharply into focus when a gender analysis is applied to the history of modernization of Judaism. By studying nineteenth-century Judaism through a feminist and gender-sensitive lens, we can see that Germany was not only the site of the formation of the Jewish denominations of Reform, positive-historical (later Conservative), and Orthodox Judaism but also the cradle of a culture of bourgeois religiosity in which women were much more prominent than they had been previously. Finally, I end with some comments on German Jewish women's and gender history from the late nineteenth century to the present, a period that saw the climax of Jewish integration and Jewish cultural creativity in Germany, persecution and genocidal destruction, and the emergence of a new German and European Jewish feminist culture today.

Salon Women and Apostasy

ARGUABLY, THE HISTORY OF German Jewish women in modern times begins with the Jewish women who hosted and socialized in the salons of Berlin and Vienna's Enlightened society in the last two decades of the eighteenth century and the first years of the nineteenth century.[5] A salon was literally a living room in a private house, and in the context discussed here the term refers to regular gatherings that took place most commonly in private houses. In salons, intellectuals, writers, clergy, nobles, diplomats, government officials, artists, and other guests read aloud and discussed literature, some of which they had written themselves, listened to music, recited poetry, discussed philosophical and religious issues, and exchanged news on the social, cultural, political, and economic life in their city and country and in Europe. The salons were a part of a new type of sociability, and in fact they belonged to a completely novel social formation and new political space that had emerged in the era of the European Enlightenment in the second half of the eighteenth century and that we call the public. In this novel Enlightened public sphere, people gathered as equals to exchange ideas, to educate and improve themselves and each other, and to work toward the betterment of society at large. For centuries in medieval and early modern Christian Europe, humans had been defined by their social and legal status as, for instance, nobles, clergy, Christian burghers, peasants, or Jews, and the concept that people could meet and communicate with each other as rational and moral individuals, irrespective of their standing in the hierarchical order of the corporate society, was revolutionary.[6] This radically novel concept allowed Jews, who were a separate group and lived under a particular set of legal and social restrictions, to participate in the new Enlightened sociability.

The emerging public realm encompassed discourse in newspapers, journals, and various other publications, often referred to as the Republic of Letters; voluntary associations, such as reading clubs and civic societies; coffeehouses, where patrons could read newspapers and discuss news and ideas; and salons. What distinguished the salons from other institutions of Enlightened sociability was that coffeehouses and most voluntary associations were strictly male spaces, whereas in salons men and women mixed.[7] Moreover, most typically, salons were hosted by women. And in Berlin, nine of the fifteen or so salons that operated in the city between 1780 and 1806 were led by Jewish women, and eleven more Jewish women were members of salons, meaning they frequented at least one on a regular basis. This means that twenty Jewish women were actively involved in the salon culture, which is an extraordinarily high number considering that Jews constituted less than 2% of the Berlin population. On the other hand, in relation to the perhaps 640 adult Jewish women who lived in Berlin at the time, 20 Jewish salon women were not more than 3.1% of the Jewish population. These numbers show that, although Jewish women were dramatically overrepresented in the salon culture of the city, most Jewish women did not frequent salons.[8]

The same was the case for Christian women too, of course. Some Christian women led salons and were involved in salon culture, but most had no ties to the world of salons. And as a population, Jewish women were not more likely to host or frequent salons than Christian women. Yet the statistic creates this impression, because a small group of highly educated young women from wealthy Jewish families came to play a leading role in Berlin salons. These women were not representative of German Jewry. Their story is the account of a particular cluster of women in a unique setting and a distinct historical moment.

Also, only a few Jewish men seem to have been regulars in salons. The Jewish salon women of Berlin belonged to an elite of Jewish merchant families, and the brothers and husbands of the women who hosted and attended salons were businessmen. If the men engaged in intellectual and cultural matters, at least some of them were more likely to pursue the traditional study of religious texts rather than experiment with the novel intellectual activities that took place in the salons. And even those men who pursued new modes of secular learning and engaged in Enlightened sociability could cultivate their interests and cultural ambitions in a variety of venues, not just in salons. Thus the male relatives of the salon women tended not to embrace salon culture as enthusiastically as their sisters and wives.[9]

The young, wealthy, and, by all reports, beautiful salon women had received a new style of secular Enlightenment education,[10] and they created salons and joined salon culture to cultivate their love for literature and music in a well-tempered social setting. They were eager to discuss the new ideas about culture, religion, and society that they had been exposed to, with like-minded and cultured peers beyond their own familial circles. In fact, the egalitarian ethos of salon culture allowed them to mingle with Christian noblemen, who disregarded deeply ingrained social conventions, attended gatherings in Jewish homes, and interacted with their hostesses freely and warmly. This in itself was unheard of and indeed close to scandalous, and it must have been exhilarating for the Jewish women.[11] In the uninhibited setting and open atmosphere of the salons, where all participants relished genuine intellectual and personal exchange, the Jewish women and Christian noblemen developed intense friendships and even romantic involvements. In fact, ten of the twenty Jewish salon women eventually married Christian men whom they had met in the salons, most of them nobles, and nine of the women first divorced Jewish husbands. And to marry their Christian suitors, the Jewish women had to convert to Christianity, because a marriage between a Jewish and a Christian partner was impossible at the time. Yet perhaps even more shocking, seven salon women embraced Christianity without marrying a Gentile. Indeed the majority of the Jewish salon women, seventeen of the twenty, left Judaism for Christianity.[12]

The most prominent among them was Rahel Levin (1771–1833), who underwent baptism before she married the young noble poet Karl August Varnhagen (1785–1858) in a match that has received extensive attention.[13] And perhaps the most famous image of a Berlin Jewish *salonière* who was to leave the fold is the captivating portrait of Henriette Herz (1764–1847) by Anna Dorothea Therbusch (1721–1782), a painter who worked for the Prussian court and also the Berlin bourgeoisie.[14]

Also alarmingly, this group of women who, from the Jewish perspective, went so disgracefully astray included Brendel Veit, née Mendelssohn, later Dorothea Schlegel (1764–1839), one of the daughters of Moses Mendelssohn.[15]

Henriette Herz, oil on canvas, by Anna Dorothea Lisiewska Therbusch (1778). Berlin State Museum. Image in the public domain.

Moses Mendelssohn (1729–1786) had been the towering figure of the Jewish Enlightenment, the Haskalah, and his life's work had consisted in propagating the compatibility of European modernity and Judaism. In defiance of Christians who expected Jews to convert to attain citizenship in a modern nation-state, Mendelssohn had modeled that a Jew could be a citizen of the emerging civil society and still remain religiously fully committed and observant.[16] When Brendel Mendelssohn divorced her first husband, Simon Veit (1754–1819), converted to Christianity, and married the noble Friedrich Schlegel (1772–1829), after her father had died, she seemed to undo her father's legacy.

The dramatic story of the Berlin Jewish salon women, relayed here in broad strokes, shocked contemporaries and has for 200 years attracted much attention. For generations of German Jews, scholars of German Jewish history, and various other observers, the drama of the salon women has provided the opportunity to reflect on the complexities of the Jewish entry into modernity and on the modern Jewish condition.[17] Thus when feminist scholars set out to challenge the male-centered narrative of Jewish history, the Berlin salon women unsurprisingly were on their agenda. Among these scholars, Deborah Hertz devoted herself to the study of the Jewish *salonières*, applying rigorous and novel social-history and quantitative history methodologies.[18] Hertz interpreted the salon women's course of action as a female mode of pursuing emancipation. These well-educated and economically privileged Jewish women had great success as *salonières*, and they became deeply involved with the non-Jewish members of the salons. But the salons were a utopian microcosm, and all other realms of society were closed to Jewish women as women and as Jews. Yet the Jewish salon women wanted to be part of the world beyond the boundaries of the Jewish community. Like many of their male Jewish counterparts, they longed for true access to non-Jewish society, full integration, and legal emancipation. Converting and marrying a Christian noble seemed to be a gender-specific path for achieving these goals.[19] Moreover, historian Natalie Naimark-Goldberg has recently suggested that at least some of these women were ambivalent about the institution of marriage. For instance, Brendel Mendelssohn Veit pursued the divorce from her husband long before she met Schlegel; her sister, Henriette Mendelssohn (1775–1831), never married; and another woman of their circle, Fradchen Liebmann, née Marcuse (1771–1844), cultivated romantic friendships with other women.[20] Hertz and Naimark-Goldberg focus on these women's agency. They tell the story of Jewish women actively shaping their destinies, trying to defy the constraints that defined their lives. Naimark-Goldberg even reads the life choices of this group of Jewish Enlightened women in Berlin as a rejection of and an assault on the existing gender order and the subordination of women in marriage.[21]

The Berlin salon women's agency could get them only so far, however, and their story did not end in triumph. These women left behind the social framework of their families and community by converting. They gave up economically secure marriages or splendid marriage prospects to enter into love matches with often not very well-off Christian nobles. They gained unprecedented access to the most distinguished circles of Prussian society. Yet when the Napoleonic occupation in 1806 changed the intellectual climate in Berlin, the 25-year period of the egalitarian and open-minded sociability of the Enlightenment salons ended. Patriotic and anti-Semitic attitudes gained ground, ex-Jewish spouses and even friends turned into liabilities for Prussian nobles, and the social and economic situation of converted Jews became precarious. The loneliness and even poverty of some former Jewish *salonières* during the final decades of their lives is striking.[22] Jewish salon women had

ventured into a utopian space, ahead of its time, that had existed at a particular historical moment under specific conditions in Berlin. Yet as an island
of the future, the salon world of this era and its culture of radical integration
collapsed. The twenty well-educated young salon women from a small group
of wealthy Jewish families had been able to gain an amount of freedom, status,
and fame—if not notoriety—unheard of for Jewish women, but their achievements could not be sustained, and their story is exceptional.

Upward Mobility, Memoirs, and
Disengagement from Judaism

As a rule and different from the small group of salon women whose unique
story I just relayed, Jews in German lands did not enter modernity by way of
illegitimate romances and scandalous acts of apostasy. Rather, German Jews
integrated into modern German society in the first half of the nineteenth century in a process of massive structural transformation, which was dramatic
in its own ways. As they did so, this impoverished and culturally marginal
population joined the emerging German middle classes. In fact, around 1800
the lifestyle of the overwhelming majority of Jews in German lands stood
in stark contrast to that of the Jewish salon women of Berlin (and Vienna),
who belonged to a small elite of wealthy families. At the time, most Jews in
Germany were economically struggling, if not in distress, and they were only
beginning to be touched by the culture of the European Enlightenment. In the
ensuing decades, however, industrialization revolutionized German society
as a whole, and in an enormous effort German Jews achieved a breathtaking
upward mobility. By 1871, when the unification of Germany and the founding of the German Empire under the leadership of the conservative military
man Chancellor Otto von Bismarck brought full legal emancipation—at least
on the national level—the Jews in German lands had become socially, economically, and culturally middle class.[23] This process can be summarized by
the term *embourgeoisement*: German Jews became bourgeois. As a group, they
did not become wealthy, and many continued to work extremely hard to maintain a lower-middle-class income level and lifestyle—and sometimes failed.
But as a community, German Jews had escaped mass poverty by 1871.[24]

Much scholarship has examined these developments in their structural
dimension, but autobiographical accounts give the most vivid insight into
how this transformation played out in people's everyday lives. A rich memoir
collection, edited by historian Monika Richarz, includes a significant number
of narratives by female authors, including Clara Geissmar, who was born in

1844 as Clara Regensburger. The story of Geissmar's life both resembles and differs from that of Brendel Mendelssohn Veit (Dorothea Schlegel), Henriette Herz, and Rahel Levin Varnhagen.[25] Geissmar's story is similar to that of the salon women, who lived three-quarters of a century before her, as all these Jewish women moved from the socially, religiously, and culturally Jewish settings of their childhoods into the new and exciting world of modern German society. However, whereas the salon women were a small and exceptional group that achieved an unusual degree of integration in the utopian social microcosm of Enlightenment salon culture, by the middle of the nineteenth century Geissmar's experience was unremarkable, even typical.

According to Geissmar's account, Jewish life in Eppingen, the small town in the southern German region of Baden where she was born, was framed by religious practice and tradition. Geissmar describes at length the festivities and customs on Jewish holidays such as Passover, Sukkot, Hanukkah, and Purim that structured the year.[26] Also with much emotion, Geissmar evokes the Friday evenings in the home of her childhood, "the freshly cleaned rooms, the cozy warmth in the winter, the seven-armed brass lamp with its seven little flames whose wicks were braided from cotton wool in the morning."[27] Geissmar goes on to describe the traditional foods and the solemn moment when her father, after returning from synagogue, quietly blessed the children.[28]

Yet at the same time, Geissmar's parents were devoted to German *Bildung*, an essential feature of nineteenth-century bourgeois culture in German lands. The term is often translated as "education," but it literally means "formation" and denotes the harmonious cultivation of one's mind, intellect, and moral capacities that was believed to result from engagement with literature, poetry, and art. As an extension of Enlightenment culture, the culture of *Bildung* became defining for the emerging middle classes in Germany, and through its politics, ethics, and aesthetics, it staked out a territory beyond the confines of religious and confessional divisions and particularisms. Since the early nineteenth century, German Jews had enthusiastically embraced this culture of *Bildung* and the promise it offered to fully belong, and by the 1840s no Jewish family in German lands was untouched by it.

In fact, Geissmar's mother loved German and English literature, and Geissmar reports that the family particularly revered Friedrich Schiller, perhaps the most iconic author and playwright of the German national awakening in the Enlightenment era. And they adored the writings of Henrich Heine, a witty, radically democratic poet of a slightly later period, who was incidentally also Jewish. According to Geissmar, she still knew many poems by Heine by heart decades after she had left her parents' home. In her childhood, even the family's cook learned Schiller's ballads. In fact, in a memorable incident, the cook served up the family's soup with a volume of Schiller, after she hid the book in the empty soup tureen when Geissmar's mother entered the kitchen.[29] This mishap is funny on its own terms, but historians like to refer to it, because by literally imbibing Schiller's poetry with their soup, the Geissmar family enacted what is considered characteristic for nineteenth-century German Jews: They devoured German literature, driven by their love for *Bildung* and German culture and their eagerness to attain middle-class status and to fully integrate into German society. Non-Jewish families that were middle class or aspired to middle-class status of course likewise embraced this German culture of *Bildung*. Yet for Jews, who still needed to convince their neighbors and the German authorities of their Germanness, these cultural practices had particular weight.

According to Geissmar's account of her childhood in Eppingen in the middle of the nineteenth century, her parents and the Jews in her community seamlessly and harmoniously integrated the new culture of German *Bildung* into a life shaped by religious practice and centuries-old Jewish custom. However, Clara Geissmar also describes how this changed when she married a young Jewish lawyer at age 18. The couple lived in Konstanz, a town about 240 kilometers south of Eppingen. There, they were the only Jewish family.[30] This was not unusual at the time, as German lands lifted residency restrictions for Jews and thus Jews moved to towns where they had not been allowed to reside for centuries.[31] Without any communal support and frame, the young couple seems to have dropped most religious practice, and Geissmar describes how secular moral and political worldviews took the place of religion for her. At the same time, she reports that she missed religion and considered converting to Protestantism, especially to give the couple's children a religious upbringing. Yet not only did her husband oppose this move, but also Geissmar herself was "not interested in Christ."[32] The Protestantism she valued was rather the religion of Lessing, Schiller, and Goethe, she explains. It was *Bildung* as religion, or a culture of bourgeois sensitivity and morality, that was close to religiosity for her and her contemporaries.

This disengagement from Judaism that Geissmar describes was a common experience in German Jewish families between the early nineteenth century and the beginning of the twentieth century. Jews moved from a life embedded in Jewish practice and observance to a middle-class existence in which religion constituted an aspect of the culture of *Bildung*. Typically, this shift was not accompanied by conversion to Christianity.[33] And differently from Geissmar, Jews tended to move to large urban centers with significant and growing Jewish communities rather than to towns without Jewish life.[34] Cities such as Berlin, Hamburg, Frankfurt, and Munich offered a degree of anonymity, but they also housed a Jewish subculture in which Jews maintained their own professional and social networks, regardless of their religious commitments. This is the setting in which Clara Geissmar composed her detailed descriptions of Jewish holiday celebrations and rural Jewish customs, when she wrote her memoir in 1913, in her late 60s. In the account, she expresses her nostalgic longing for religious forms no longer practiced in her world. Thus memoirs always both provide information on the period they discuss, and they are historical documents of the time in which they were created.[35] By 1913, religion for German Jews had become optional in a way that had not been the case a century earlier. Judaism and the performance of ritual had become a choice. The same was the case for Christians too, of course, many of whom had withdrawn from religious practice and beliefs. But they had not experienced any pressure to convert to a different religion, and their move into a more secularized form of Christian culture was much less problematic.

Gender and the Transformation of Jewish Religious Culture

YET THE STORY ABOUT Jews entering modernity is not just about disengagement from Judaism in a society in which religion was no longer pervasive. The history of the modernization of Jewish civilization is also the history of religious change. For Judaism, this story has been told since the nineteenth century as the account of the three branches of modern Judaism coming into existence: Jewish Reform, positive-historical Judaism, and modern Orthodoxy. The Reform movement emerged in the first decades of the nineteenth century, when Enlightenment ideas of rationality and morality and the culture of *Bildung* began to made inroads into Jewish religious life and when Jews set out to show that they were fit for German citizenship. Then, (male) teachers at newly founded modern Jewish schools and (male) preachers who had made themselves familiar with the canon of German literature and culture experimented with a new style of synagogue devotion. They emphasized decorum and aesthetics and introduced choirs, German-language prayers, hymns, and edifying sermons into overall shortened services. And these Jewish leaders developed a distinct Reform theology, according to which ritual law (Halakhah) was an outdated and dispensable shell of Judaism and the spirit of Judaism constituted the religion's eternal core.[36] Positive-historical Judaism and modern Orthodoxy constituted themselves in opposition to Reform, although they were also engaged in adapting Judaism to the modern world. The positive-historical movement, which later in the United States developed into Conservative Judaism, proposed a more measured change of halakhic practices than

Reform Judaism. It understood Judaism as continuously evolving through-out history and held that contemporary changes needed to be grounded in careful scholarly investigation. Thus the founder of the movement, Zacharias Frankel (1801–1875), came to head the world's first modern institution for the academic instruction and professional training of Jewish clergy, the Jewish Theological Seminary, which opened in Breslau in 1854.[37] Modern Orthodox leaders categorically disagreed with both Reform and positive-historical Judaism and developed a theology that declared Halakhah to be eternal and unchanging. Modern Orthodox Jews established their own congregations when Reform Judaism became dominant in their communities. Yet, like all other Jewish Germans, modern Orthodox Jews aspired to German citizenship and enthusiastically participated in German cultural life, which they considered compatible with full ritual observance.[38]

Since the days in nineteenth-century Germany when male Jewish leaders, rabbis, and scholars began to narrate the account of these developments and of the modernization of the Jewish religion, this was a story focusing on the thought and deeds of the men involved, the theological differences that set the emerging three movements apart from each other, and the institutions that male leaders founded. Unsurprisingly, women appear in these accounts only in occasional comments, if at all.[39] The history of religious thought, synagogue life, and Jewish communal institutions evidently and naturally seemed to be an all-male affair.

However, as I show in my own work, women were far from invisible in the Jewish texts and documents of this era. A case in point is the first significant Jewish German-language periodical, *Sulamith*. This was a seminal publication of the early Reform movement that every scholar of the Jewish religion in nineteenth-century Germany before me has consulted without exploring the fact that the journal is named after a female biblical figure, its cover features the image of a woman, and a significant number of the articles in the journal are either addressed to women or discuss questions that relate to women and religion.[40] In addition to this new interest that male Jewish leaders took in women, which I discuss in some detail later, I also found that women actively supported the modernization of religious life in the nineteenth century and at times advocated for change themselves. For instance, in 1855 a group of women in Mannheim submitted a petition on behalf of their rabbi, Moses Präger (1817–1861), who had come into conflict with his superior in the Jewish community because of the modernized prayer book that Präger had published. In the book Präger had removed Hebrew prayers and replaced some of them with German-language devotions. In their petition the women applauded the change and expressed gratitude for living in an era in which they could worship God with dignity and were no longer excluded, rejected, and silenced. A regression to previous conditions, they claimed, would deprive them of "the just gained and already so much cherished good of religious edification."[41]

In another case, the leading figure in the German kindergarten movement, Johanna Goldschmidt of Hamburg (1806–1884), and four of her female relatives honored the preacher Gotthold Salomon (1784–1862) on the occasion of his twenty-fifth anniversary at the Hamburg Temple, Germany's model Reform synagogue. During the ceremony in 1843, the women presented Salomon with a richly embroidered album in red velvet in which they had collected almost a hundred letters of congratulations to Salomon from friends and noted personalities from across the Jewish world. Salomon, who has been called "the favorite preacher of the female sex," asserts in his autobiography that this "memorial of friendship" still brought tears to his eyes twenty years later.[42] Similarly, Rabbi Leopold Stein (1810–1882) in Frankfurt highly valued his ties with Louise von Rothschild (1820–1894) and her seven daughters, for whom he served as religious instructor; and he translated and published their writings, including a learned apologetic treatise by Clementine von Rothschild (1845–1865), titled *Letters to a Christian Friend: About the Fundamental Truths of Judaism*, which appeared first in German in 1867.[43]

Thus women were by no means absent from the history of religious culture in nineteenth-century Germany. Rather, they played active roles in adapting Judaism to modern sensibilities, and if their contributions are omitted, the story of the modernization of Judaism is incomplete. Furthermore, as I show in my work, male German Jewish educators and rabbis took a novel type of interest in women's synagogue attendance and in religious instruction for girls. These leaders declared women to be the guardians of Judaism and their domestic and motherly functions to be central to the future of Judaism. In practical terms, this meant that girls were included in modernized programs of religious instruction, culminating in confirmation ceremonies. For Jewish boys the confirmation competed with the customary bar mitzvah celebration and at times replaced the established ceremony. Girls remained excluded from the bar mitzvah rite, but the confirmation ceremonies, which by the end of the nineteenth century had become the norm in all but the relatively small number of Orthodox synagogues in Germany, offered girls an unprecedented degree of inclusion in public Jewish worship.[44] Girls and women also came to sing in mixed synagogue choirs; and Jewish communities lowered the balustrades of women's balconies and removed the lattice in front of them in an uneven yet mostly uncontested process.[45]

These changes and the mitigation of women's inferior position in the synagogue were not driven by an emancipatory impulse or ideas of gender equality, and although they seem to have been welcomed by women, there is no evidence that women actively fought for them. Rather, contemporary publications by rabbis, pedagogues, and other male Jewish leaders indicate that, above all, ideas of nineteenth-century bourgeois culture, shared by Christians and Jews, motivated the changes.

According to this rising worldview, women were the noble and moral sex that had a particular propensity for religious sentiment and values, and women's benevolent influence as mothers and wives in the domestic realm was indispensable for the moral and religious character of the family and society. Thus it seemed essential to male Jewish leaders that the female sex be exposed to the beneficial influence of religious education and synagogue devotion, which developed and sustained the inner beauty and morality of Jewish daughters, wives, and mothers. In fact, the new emphasis on early childhood education and on mothers' roles in the moral, intellectual, and religious development of their children brought women into the center of concern. The future of Judaism was thought to depend on Jewish mothers' religious and moral character and on them being prepared and equipped for their exalted religious function in the home.

Thus even the founder and leader of the modern Orthodox movement, Samson Raphael Hirsch (1808–1888), considered girls' religious education so important that he condoned mixed-sex classes until a separate girls' school could be established by the Orthodox Frankfurt community.[46] Hirsch developed a true cult of the Jewish mother: "Women of the House of Jacob! Mothers of the Jewish people!" he exhorted the female members of his community in 1862, "Our continued survival and freedom depend solely on our willingness and ability to fulfill the vow . . . 'To hearken to the voice of God and to keep His covenant.' . . . Save your child for humanity and Judaism."[47]

Hand in hand with this idealization of the Jewish woman and mother went a quasi-religious elevation of domesticity and family life. In fact, nineteenth-century German Judaism was no longer primarily defined by ritual observance, rabbinic learning, and formal prayer. Rather, it became a religiosity of *Bildung*, virtue, and emotionalized spirituality, in which women were believed to excel. Accordingly, women's place in Jewish society changed. This was more pronounced in Reform-oriented settings than in modern Orthodox congregations, which remained strictly committed to the halakhic framework. Even in Orthodox synagogues, however, the style of services changed, and worshipers highly valued decorum, edifying German-language sermons, and beautiful choirs, and they sought cultural improvement, moral ennoblement, and emotionally and aesthetically satisfying religious experiences in public worship. This is the "cherished good of religious edification" that the Mannheim women referred to in their petition. And the German-language prayers that they defended are aspects of the same new culture of bourgeois religiosity, distinct from rabbinic Judaism, and focused on *Bildung*, *Sittlichkeit* (morality), and edification. The ideal of Jewish religious life was represented not by the learned Talmud scholar any longer but by the cultivated, culturally refined, and spiritually sensitive person; and religious sensitivity, inner beauty, morality, and virtue were considered feminine attributes. Christian religious culture in nineteenth-century Germany experienced the same trend toward a bourgeois religiosity in which women and femininity were highly valued. However, premodern Judaism had been considerably more gendered, with women in a distinctly marginal and inferior position. Accordingly, the implications of the embourgeoisement of religious culture were more significant in the Jewish setting than in the Christian one.

As I have shown, a gender analysis of Jewish religious culture in nineteenth-century Germany sheds light on acts and perspectives of women that had been neglected previously—the story of half the population that had hitherto been untold. In addition, a gender-sensitive reading of nineteenth-century sources also brings into focus an enormous shift in Jewish religious culture that was invisible, when scholars restricted their inquiries to male leaders, narrowly defined intellectual history, and the history of institutions. By broadening our horizons, a new account of the modernization of Judaism emerges. This modernization is not defined solely by the rise of the three different branches of Judaism, their relationship to and their definition of Halakhah, and other theological and philosophical differences between them; rather a gender analysis shows a deep structural transformation throughout. In the nineteenth century, German Judaism ceased to be most of all a culture of Talmud Torah and Hebrew prayer, in which men had a privileged position; it became a culture of bourgeois religiosity, in which beauty, edification, and morality, all strongly identified with femininity, were the highest religious ideals for men and for women.[48] Thus it is not misguided to talk about a feminization of Judaism in nineteenth-century Germany and to claim that inquiring about women leads to new insights into men and masculinities.[49]

German Jewish Women and the Jewish Family from 1871 to Today

IN THIS ACCOUNT I have focused on German Jewish women's and gender history from the late eighteenth century through the first half of the nineteenth century. As we have seen, however, Clara Geissmar, looking back as an older woman during the first decade of the twentieth century, noted how much her Jewish world had changed. In this final section, I thus wish to make a few comments on Jewish life in Imperial Germany, the period from the unification of Germany in 1871 to the end of World War I in which Geissmar wrote. And in closing I briefly survey the course of German Jewish women's and gender history beyond World War I.

In Imperial Germany Jews consolidated the middle-class status that many of them had attained in the earlier decades of the nineteenth century. This process—in particular, the rise of family businesses and Jewish men's entry into professions—had been well studied by the 1980s, but it was feminist historian Marion Kaplan in her work from 1991 who showed that women's activities in the family played a central role in Jewish upward mobility in Germany.[50] Heavily based on memoir literature, Kaplan's work details how women labored to cultivate the steady, tranquil, and orderly lifestyle of the middle classes with regular meal times, leisurely walks, and other regulated activities for children and adults in a clean, tasteful, and well-maintained domestic setting. Perhaps most important, not only did Jewish women ensure that their children were tidy and well behaved, but they also introduced them to German literature, music, and art and thus anchored the culture of *Bildung* in Jewish homes. In doing so, women laid the foundations for a middle-class existence, and their contributions were indispensable for the German Jews' entry into bourgeois society.[51]

At the same time that Jewish women created and sustained the cultured German character of their families' homes, they also safeguarded the Jewishness of their families. In a setting in which religious observance and in fact religious practice declined, women preserved the Jewishness of their homes, for instance, by adhering to Jewish foodways, even if they abandoned the formal observance of dietary laws in the kitchen. Thus feminist scholarship has redefined our understanding of what constitutes Jewish culture. Rabbinic literature, liturgy, religious poetry, and philosophical treatises shape the parameters of Judaism and Jewish life, but today it has become common to hold that Jewish culture is also constituted by what is practiced in the kitchen, in the nursery, and in the social realm.[52] Along these lines, Jewish women in Imperial Germany were responsible for cultivating their families' ties to other Jewish families—friends and relatives—and they ensured that through these social networks their sons and daughters would be introduced to other young Jewish men and women when they reached a marriageable age.[53] Jewish women maintained a web of Jewishness beyond the world of Jewish texts that shaped the present and the future of their communities.

Whereas Jewish women defined Jewish life from within the domestic realm, in the late nineteenth century they also began entering German universities and professions, and they became active in the feminist movement. Their organization, the Jüdische Frauenbund (Jewish Women's League), played a leading role in the German women's movement from its inception in 1904 to its dissolution in the Nazi era.[54] In fact, the feminist, self-determined, wage-earning Jewish woman, called the New Jewish Woman, became the symbol of Weimar (interwar) German society. And Weimar was a setting in which the ordination of the first woman rabbi, a lively Jewish youth culture, Jewish engagements in Communist and the nascent Zionist movements, and intensifying anti-Semitism all coexisted with unprecedented levels of Jewish integration and public recognition.[55]

The rise of National Socialism brought an end to this lively culture and its ambiguities. In this era of increasing restrictions, economic strangulation, social isolation, and soon outright persecution, Jewish women labored alongside their husbands, brothers, fathers, and sons to maintain dignity and as much normalcy as possible. For a variety of reasons, women often advocated for their family's emigration, whereas their husbands were more hesitant to undertake this step. However, in many cases women were the ones to stay behind, for instance, to care for elderly parents, and they perished in larger numbers than German Jewish men did.[56]

For the period after 1945, we possess little gender-sensitive scholarship on the small, beleaguered, and traumatized Jewish postwar community in Germany.[57] However, today German and European Jewish culture has begun to reemerge as a third pillar of Jewish civilization, next to North American and Israeli Jewish life worlds, and German Jewish women are contributing to the development of a distinctly European twenty-first-century Jewish feminism. Still very much entangled with the reverberations of the Shoah and deeply marked by it, they are set to recreate Jewish life after the genocide in a manner and with a type of deliberateness that differs from Jewish lifestyles and politics in other Jewish centers.[58] Aware of and loyal to their history and its burdens and promises, German Jewish women are forging their own Jewish future, in the land of *Wissenschaft* and the cradle of modern Jewish historiography.

Notes

1 For a short introduction to *Wissenschaft* historiography, see Michael A. Meyer, ed., *German-Jewish History in Modern Times*, vol. 2, *Acculturation, 1780–1871* (New York: Columbia University Press, 1997), 336–41. On premodern Jewish historical consciousness, or the lack thereof, and the rise of modern Jewish historiography, see Ismar Schorsch, *From Text to Context: The Turn to History in Modern Judaism* (Hanover, NH: University Press of New England, 1994); and

Yosef Hayim Yerushalmi, *Zakhor: Jewish History and Jewish Memory* (Seattle: University of Washington Press, 1982).

2 Michael A. Meyer, ed., *German-Jewish History in Modern Times*, vol. 1, *Tradition and Enlightenment, 1600–1780* (New York: Columbia University Press, 1996), 134–43, 244–51; Monika Richarz, ed., *Jewish Life in Germany: Memoirs from Three Centuries* (Bloomington: Indiana University Press, 1991), 6.

3 For two classical accounts, see Jacob Katz, *Out of the Ghetto: The Social Background of Jewish Emancipation, 1770–1870* (Cambridge, MA: Harvard University Press, 1973); and Robert Seltzer, *Jewish People, Jewish Thought: The Jewish Experience in History* (Upper Saddle River, NJ: Prentice Hall, 1980), 513–618. Yet as this volume demonstrates with its wide range of contributions, including innovative scholarship on Italian, Sephardic, Ottoman, and Eastern European Jewries, the era of Germanocentrism is over. Today, the German and Western European experience is no longer considered the privileged site and the measure of how Jews engineered modernity.

4 For exceptions, see Meyer Kayserling, *Die jüdischen Frauen in der Geschichte, Literatur und Kunst* (Leipzig: Brockhaus, 1879); and Nahida Ruth Lazarus (Nahida Remy), *Das jüdische Weib: Mit einer Vorrede von M. Lazarus*, 3rd ed. (Berlin: Siegfried Cronbach, 1896). In the 1930s the Weimar Jewish intellectual Hannah Arendt wrote a biography of Rahel Varnhagen. See Hannah Arendt, *Rahel Varnhagen: The Life of a Jewess* (London: East and West Library, 1957). Even though *Rahel Varnhagen* first appeared in 1957 in London, Arendt had completed the manuscript in 1933 in Germany. See Liliane Weissberg, "Introduction," in *Rahel Varnhagen: The Life of a Jewess*, by Hannah Arendt (Baltimore: Johns Hopkins University Press, 1997), 5, 42.

5 On the Vienna salons, see Hilde Spiel, *Fanny von Arnstein: A Daughter of the Enlightenment, 1758–1818* (New York: Berg, 1991). The Berlin salons are discussed later in this chapter.

6 Deborah Hertz, *Jewish High Society in Old Regime Berlin* (New Haven, CT: Yale University Press, 1988), 14–18; Dorinda Outram, *The Enlightenment* (Cambridge, UK: Cambridge University Press, 1995), 14–30, 91–93.

7 Natalie Naimark-Goldberg, *Jewish Women in Enlightenment Berlin* (London: Littman Library of Jewish Civilization, 2013), 183.

8 Hertz, *Jewish High Society*, 35–47, 97–118, 191–94. See also Naimark-Goldberg, *Jewish Women*, 183–215.

9 Hertz, *Jewish High Society*, 39–43, 147–55, 188–89; Naimark-Goldberg, *Jewish Women*, 211–15.

10 Hertz, *Jewish High Society*, 188–89.

11 Hertz, *Jewish High Society*, esp. 127. See also Naimark-Goldberg, *Jewish Women*, 278–87.

12 Naimark-Goldberg, *Jewish Women*, 200–222, 244–50.

13 See, for example, Deborah Hertz, *How Jews Became Germans: The History of Conversion and Assimilation in Berlin* (New Haven, CT: Yale University Press, 2007), 43–76, 109–11, 116–33, 165–72, 201–5, 215; and Deborah Hertz, "Leaving Judaism for a Man: Female Conversion and Intermarriage in Germany, 1812–1819,"

in *Zur Geschichte der jüdischen Frau in Deutschland*, ed. Julius Carlebach (Berlin: Metropol, 1993), 113–28. The classic study on Rahel Varnhagen née Levin is Arendt, *Rahel Varnhagen*. For a recent feminist treatment, see Barbara Hahn, *The Jewess Pallas Athene: This Too a Theory of Modernity* (Princeton, NJ: Princeton University Press, 2005), 13, 42–55.

14 Ekhart Berckenhagen, "Therbusch, Anna Dorothea," *Grove Art Online*, 2020 (accessed December 20, 2020).

15 Hertz, *Jewish High Society*, 106–7, 211–13.

16 For the most important biographical studies, see Alexander Altmann, *Moses Mendelssohn: A Biographical Study* (Tuscaloosa: University of Alabama Press, 1973); and Allan Arkush, *Moses Mendelssohn and the Enlightenment* (Albany: State University of New York Press, 1994).

17 These are major themes in both Arendt, *Rahel Varnhagen*, and Hahn, *The Jewess Pallas Athene*.

18 See Hertz, *Jewish High Society*; Deborah Hertz and Judith R. Baskin, "Emancipation Through Intermarriage? Wealthy Jewish Salon Women in Old Berlin," in *Jewish Women in Historical Perspective*, 2nd ed., ed. Judith R. Baskin (Detroit: Wayne State University Press, 1991), 193–207; Hertz, "Leaving Judaism," 113–46; and Deborah Hertz, "The Troubling Dialectic Between Reform and Conversion in Biedermeier Berlin," in *Towards Normality? Acculturation and Modern German Jewry*, ed. Rainer Liedtke and David Rechter (Tübingen: Mohr Siebeck, 2003), 103–26.

19 Hertz, *Jewish High Society*, 249–50. For a critique of conceiving of the salons as a utopian microcosm, see Naimark-Goldberg, *Jewish Women*, 188–91.

20 Naimark-Goldberg, *Jewish Women*, 224–26, 233–39, 248–56.

21 Naimark-Goldberg, *Jewish Women*, 237, 256.

22 Hertz, *Jewish High Society*, 251–81, esp. 270.

23 Michael A. Meyer, ed., *German-Jewish History in Modern Times*, vol. 3, *Integration in Dispute, 1871–1918* (New York: Columbia University Press, 1997), 1, 155.

24 For the definitive survey of German Jewish history at this time, see Meyer, *German-Jewish History*, vol. 2.

25 For the abridged English edition of the original three-volume German publication, see Richarz, *Jewish Life*.

26 Richarz, *Jewish Life*, 157–59.

27 Richarz, *Jewish Life*, 156.

28 Richarz, *Jewish Life*, 157.

29 Richarz, *Jewish Life*, 159.

30 Richarz, *Jewish Life*, 155.

31 Meyer, *German-Jewish History*, 2: 296, 298.

32 Richarz, *Jewish Life*, 161.

33 For two classical texts on this process, see Jacob Katz, "German Culture and the Jews," in *The Jewish Response to German Culture*, ed. Jehuda Reinharz and Walter Schatzberg (Hanover, NH: University Press of New England, 1985), 1–16; and George L. Mosse, *German Jews Beyond Judaism* (Bloomington: Indiana

University Press, 1985). However, these studies focus only on men and disregard the realm of the family.

34 Meyer, *German-Jewish History*, 2: 298–99.

35 See Miriam Gebhardt, *Das Familiengedächtnis: Erinnerung im deutsch-jüdischen Bürgertum, 1890–1932* (Stuttgart: Franz Steiner, 1999).

36 Michael A. Meyer, *Response to Modernity: A History of the Reform Movement in Judaism* (Oxford, UK: Oxford University Press, 1988), 28–77, 89–119, 131–42.

37 Meyer, *German-Jewish History*, 2: 140–41.

38 The most important study on the first modern Orthodox synagogue community in Germany is Robert Liberles, *Religious Conflict in Social Context: The Resurgence of Orthodox Judaism in Frankfurt Am Main, 1838–1877* (Westport, CT: Greenwood Press, 1985). On the leading rabbinic figure of the early modern Orthodox movement, Samson Raphael Hirsch, see also Meyer, *Response to Modernity*, 77–79. On the theology of all three modern Jewish movements discussed in this paragraph, see Meyer, *German-Jewish History*, 2: 138–51.

39 See, for instance, Michael Meyer's account from 1988, for his brief references to women in a narrative that otherwise engages with men only: Meyer, *Response to Modernity*, 47, 55. However, a more recent publication by Meyer shows how much the field has changed: Michael A. Meyer, "Women in the Thought and Practice of the European Jewish Reform Movement," in *Gender and Jewish History*, ed. Marion A. Kaplan and Deborah Dash Moore (Bloomington: Indiana University Press, 2010), 139–57.

40 Benjamin Maria Baader, *Gender, Judaism, and Bourgeois Culture in Germany, 1800–1870* (Bloomington: Indiana University Press, 2006), 19–41.

41 Adolf Lewin, *Geschichte der badischen Juden seit der Regierung Karl Friedrichs (1738–1909)* (Karlsruhe: G. Braunsche Hofbuchdruckerei, 1909), 323–32, quotation on 331.

42 Meyer Kayserling, *Bibliothek jüdischer Kanzelredner: Eine chronologische Sammlung der Predigten, Biographien und Charakteristiken der vorzüglichsten jüdischen Prediger* (Berlin: Springer, 1870), 1: 155; Gotthold Salomon, *Selbst-Biographie* (Leipzig: Otto Wigand, 1863), 42. For more information on the album and the women who prepared it, see Baader, *Gender, Judaism, and Bourgeois Culture*, 199–206.

43 Clementine von Rothschild, *Briefe an eine christliche Freundin: Über die Grundwahrheiten des Judenthums* (Frankfurt am Main: Reinhold Baist, 1867). For more on Stein and the von Rothschild women in Frankfurt, see Baader, *Gender, Judaism, and Bourgeois Culture*, 191–99.

44 Baader, *Gender, Judaism, and Bourgeois Culture*, 146–51.

45 Baader, *Gender, Judaism, and Bourgeois Culture*, 143–44, 152.

46 Mordechai Breuer, *Modernity Within Tradition: The Social History of Orthodox Jewry in Imperial Germany* (New York: Columbia University Press, 1992), 123–24.

47 Samson Raphael Hirsch, "Woman's Role in Jewish Education," in *The Collected Writings of Rabbi Samson Raphael Hirsch* (New York: P. Feldheim, 1992), 7:

396–97, 399. The essay was published originally in German in *Jeshurun* 8 (1862): 413–31.

48 For a fuller account of this shift and its multiple aspects and dimensions, see Baader, *Gender, Judaism, and Bourgeois Culture.*

49 See Baader, *Gender, Judaism, and Bourgeois Culture*, 116, 123, 132, 143, 178, 216–19; and also Benjamin Maria Baader, "Jewish Difference and the Feminine Spirit of Judaism in Mid-Nineteenth-Century Germany," in *Jewish Masculinities: German Jews, Gender, and History*, ed. Benjamin Maria Baader, Sharon Gillerman, and Paul Lerner (Bloomington: Indiana University Press, 2012), 50–71.

50 Marion A. Kaplan, *The Making of the Jewish Middle Class: Women, Family, and Identity in Imperial Germany* (New York: Oxford University Press, 1991).

51 Kaplan, *Making of the Jewish Middle Class*, esp. 54–63.

52 See, for instance, Ruth Abusch-Magder, "'Eating Out': Food and the Boundaries of Jewish Community and Home in Germany and the United States," *Nashim: A Journal of Jewish Women's Studies and Gender Issues* 5 (2002): 53–82; Andrew Buckser, "Keeping Kosher: Eating and Social Identity Among the Jews of Denmark," *Ethnology* 38, no. 3 (1999): 191–209; and Sarah Wobick-Segev, "'The Religion We Plant in Their Hearts': A Critical Exploration of the Religiosity of a Secular German-Jewish Family at the Beginning of the Twentieth Century," *Jewish History* 28, no. 2 (2014): 159–85.

53 Kaplan, *Making of the Jewish Middle Class*, 85–116.

54 Marion Kaplan, *The Jewish Feminist Movement in Germany: The Campaigns of the Jüdischer Frauenbund, 1904–1938* (Westport, CT: Greenwood Press, 1979).

55 See, most importantly perhaps, Sharon Gillerman, *Germans into Jews: Remaking the Jewish Social Body in the Weimar Republic* (Stanford, CA: Stanford University Press, 2009); Elisa Klapheck, *Fräulein Rabbiner Jonas: The Story of the First Woman Rabbi* (San Francisco: Jossey-Bass, 2004); Tamara Or, *Vorkämpferinnen und Mütter des Zionismus: Die Deutsch-Zionistischen Frauenorganisationen (1897–1938)* (Frankfurt: Peter Lang, 2009); Alison Rose, *Jewish Women in Fin de Siècle Vienna* (Austin: University of Texas Press, 2008); Till van Rahden, "Intermarriages, the 'New Woman,' and the Situational Ethnicity of Breslau Jews from the 1870s to the 1920s," *Leo Baeck Institute Year Book* 41 (2001): 125–50; Stefanie Schüler-Springorum, "Die 'Mädelfrage': Zu den Geschlechterbeziehungen in der deutsch-jüdischen Jugendbewegung," in *Jüdische Welten: Juden in Deutschland vom 18. Jahrhundert bis in die Gegenwart*, ed. Marion Kaplan and Beate Meyer (Göttingen: Wallstein, 2005), 136–54; and Naomi Shepherd, *A Price Below Rubies: Jewish Women as Rebels and Radicals* (Cambridge, MA: Harvard University Press, 1993).

56 Marion Kaplan, *Between Dignity and Despair: Jewish Life in Nazi Germany* (New York: Oxford University Press, 1998), 63–69, 138–44, 236–37.

57 The most significant is Atina Grossmann, *Jews, Germans, and Allies: Close Encounters in Occupied Germany* (Princeton, NJ: Princeton University Press, 2007).

58 For the most important European Jewish feminist network today, see https://www.bet-debora.net. For some background, see Debora Antmann, "Welche

Bedeutung hatte der Lesbisch Feministische Schabbeskreis als Teil einer intersektional denkenden und handelnden sozialen Bewegung der 1980er und 1990er Jahre in der BRD?" bachelor's thesis, Alice Salomon Hochschule Berlin, 2016; Lara Dämmig and Elisa Klapheck, "Debora's Disciples: A Women's Movement as an Expression of Renewing Jewish Life in Europe," in *Turning the Kaleidoscope: Perspectives on European Jewry*, ed. Sandra Lustig and Ian Leveson (New York: Berghahn Books, 2006), 147–63; and Jessica Jacoby, Claudia Schoppmann, and Wendy Zena-Henry, eds., *Nach der Shoa Geboren: Jüdische Frauen in Deutschland* (Berlin: Elefanten Press, 1994).

HOME INFLUENCE

Jewish Women in Nineteenth-Century Britain

NADIA VALMAN

NINETEENTH-CENTURY BRITISH JEWISH HISTORY is typically narrated as the story of political emancipation, religious change, and the development of community infrastructure.[1] In these decades Jews successfully campaigned for the right to participate fully in national and local government and to attend the ancient universities of Oxford and Cambridge. They formalized and diversified religious organization, bringing together established synagogues under the aegis of the United Synagogue, establishing the schismatic Reform congregation, and, later in the century, convening smaller immigrant congregations as the Federation of Synagogues. They established the Board of Deputies of British Jews to mediate the relationship between Jews and the state, and the Jewish Board of Guardians to administer aid to the Jewish poor. In Victorian Britain, Jews were bankers, journalists, lawyers, and master tailors, and several—the diplomat Sir Moses Montefiore, the prime minister Benjamin Disraeli, and the writer and political activist Israel Zangwill—were prominent in public life. Beginning the century as a tiny religious minority, the Jewish population expanded through large-scale Ashkenazic immigration to around 200,000 by the end. Like the broader Victorian population, the community was deeply divided by class, economic status, and culture and further splintered by differing relationships to Eastern European language and memory.

Throughout the Victorian period, Jewish women could not take part in political life as parliamentary candidates or electors and were excluded from religious leadership and the management boards of synagogues and welfare institutions. Their lives were therefore invisible to the major social and political historians of Anglo-Jewry. When this gap was finally addressed in the new feminist historiography of the 1990s, female social workers, writers, and trade union organizers were rediscovered and enthusiastically recovered.[2] Yet these accounts tend to elide differences and conflicts among Jewish women and to produce instead a catalog of brave heroines drawn from the powerful Jewish elite. In this essay, in contrast, I draw on personal writing, popular culture, and oral history as well as institutional records to bring into juxtaposition the achievements of upper-class Jewish women and the experiences of working-class women with whom they increasingly interacted. Indeed, it is worth considering the salience of the category "Jewish women" in a period when such sharp social and religious divisions fractured the Jewish population. I aim also to interpret the changing lives of Jewish women within the broader context of Victorian Britain, when women's exclusion from political participation alongside their central role in domestic religion meant that in many respects Jewish women had more in common with gentile women than with Jewish men.

Cultivating Jewish Domesticity

Autobiographical writing from early Victorian England demonstrates the eclecticism of religious practice among the Jewish upper class and the formative role played by women in shaping the religious ethos of their homes. In the mid-nineteenth century, for example, Louisa de Rothschild (1821–1910), who married into the wealthy banking family, usually observed the Sabbath with a short service in the family home followed by Bible lessons for her daughters. Louisa did not write letters or ride in her carriage but spent the day studying devotional literature by both Jews and Christians. She could not read Hebrew but ensured that her two daughters learned it thoroughly. Yet even as a young girl, Louisa's religiosity resembled that of earnest Victorian Protestants, emphasizing spiritual self-examination and an effort to conquer worldliness.[3] On Friday evenings in the upper-middle-class household of Agnes Henriques (1841–1919), the family would read prayers together; then each of her six children would recite the Ten Commandments and kneel before Henriques as she (not her husband) blessed them with the customary priestly benediction.[4] The Judaism of the Victorian elite, Todd Endelman argues, though earnestly felt, "was a religion without sharply defined doctrines," not overly concerned with theology but associated with "reasonable behavior, fraternal responsibility, ethnic loyalty, intellectual courtesy, and communal charity."[5] Idiosyncratic and often syncretic in form, it was a marker of decency rather than private belief. However, in emphasizing the conventional character of Victorian Judaism, Endelman underrates its novelty. Religious culture in Victorian England gave women an unprecedented role as spiritual guardians. Influenced by the theology of Evangelical Protestantism, a new emphasis on the humanity, meekness, and humility of Christ brought women into closer identification with his redemptive mission. Evangelicalism prescribed an exalted role for women through their powers of influence; the mother, God's deputy in the home, occupied a key position in the crusade for national regeneration.[6] Rothschild's and Henriques's domestic religious practice suggests the influence on Jewish life of the new spiritual authority accorded to women in Victorian middle-class Christian culture.

Moreover, it was this climate that enabled the success of British Jewry's first popular writer, Grace Aguilar (1816–1847), whose best-selling domestic novels *Home Influence* (1847) and *The Mother's Recompense* (1851), written in the 1830s and published posthumously in the 1840s and 1850s, contributed significantly to the cult of domesticity. However, the few works that Aguilar published during her lifetime display her also as a robust apologist for the Jews. In her most accomplished writing, she brought together political argument and popular fictional genres to represent Judaism in terms comprehensible to the English woman reader.[7] Jewish congregations and networks broadly fostered such efforts, sponsoring and publicly endorsing fiction by Aguilar's contemporaries Maria Polack and Celia and Marion Moss in the hope that literature might play a role in improving the Jews' public image.[8]

The urgency of this task was given impetus by the campaign for Jewish emancipation, which began to unfold in the 1830s. Elite members of the small Jewish community in England and their supporters petitioned for the removal of the requirement that those elected to Parliament or certain civic offices swear an oath of allegiance "on the true faith of a Christian." The question was seen as a symbolic struggle over whether the character of the state should remain exclusively Christian.[9] Keenly following the debate, upper-class Jewish women strongly identified with the cause of Jewish emancipation. For a decade after the election of her brother-in-law Lionel de Rothschild as an MP in 1847, Louisa de Rothschild and her sister Charlotte Montefiore regularly attended debates in Parliament over whether the Christian oath should be removed. "Ah me," wrote Montefiore in frustration, "when will religion be understood—be felt to be not a matter of mere creed and of doctrine but a spirit breathing love and peace and charity, binding us all lovingly to God."[10]

The fiction of Grace Aguilar publicly advocated for the Jews by displaying their dignity and deep patriotism. Her earliest published stories, *Records of Israel* (1844), historical romances that showcased the heroic suffering and loyalty to their country of the Iberian Jews under the Inquisition, were "offered to the public generally, in the hope that some vulgar errors concerning Jewish feelings, faith and character may, in some measure, be corrected."[11] Like her popular novel about the persecution of Spanish crypto-Jews, *The Vale of Cedars; or, The Martyr* (1850), the stories in *Records of Israel* drew on the strong anti-Catholic feeling prevalent in England in the 1840s and sought to identify the beleaguered Jewish heroine with the Protestant woman reader. Both texts successfully adapted the generic and ideological conventions of popular middle-class fiction, especially the focus on a brave, devoted, and humble female protagonist, to promote the cause of religious toleration.

To foster Jewish women's pride in their own spiritual heritage, Aguilar published *The Women of Israel* (1845), an appropriation of the popular Evangelical form of scripture biography, which was designed to counter the targeting of Jewish women by Evangelical conversionists. In Aguilar's version, which aimed to refute the contemporary charge that Judaism degraded women, Old Testament heroines appear as pious, modest role models for Victorian readers.[12] Her insistence that Jewish women should engage in scripture study is often understood as a demand for female equality, but it rather reflects Aguilar's identification with the religious ethos of early Victorian England, which put Bible reading at the center of religious practice.[13] The form of domestic spirituality expressed in and popularized by Aguilar's writing was to have a far-reaching influence on the next generation, when the gendered values generated among the early Victorian middle class were to define, enable, and limit the expectations of a new, demographically different Jewish population.

Gender and Jewish Immigration

BETWEEN 1881 AND 1914, an open immigration policy attracted between 100,000 and 150,000 Jews to Britain, the largest immigrant group in the period. They arrived from towns and villages in Russia, Romania, and Galicia (modern-day Poland and Ukraine), with the largest numbers settling in the East End of London and significant groups settling in provincial northern cities. Unlike other migrant groups, men were frequently accompanied by women and children. More than one-third of the Jews arriving in London in this period were nearly or completely penniless.[14]

New arrivals were not warmly welcomed by Anglo-Jewry's governing elite, who sought to discourage immigration, to repatriate immigrants or facilitate onward migration, and to mitigate the impact of immigration through philanthropy. They regarded the immigrants not only as an obligation but also as a threat to their own social status because, as the *Jewish Chronicle* argued, the English formed their "opinion of Jews in general as much, if not more, from them than from the Anglicised portion of the community."[15] Anxiety about public opinion was exacerbated by the rise in popular anti-alien feeling in the

1890s, when the housing shortage, depression of wages, and crime in east London were widely ascribed to the Jews. The *Jewish Chronicle* reminded readers that immigrants, "in accepting the hospitality of England . . . owe[d] a reciprocal duty of becoming Englishmen," and the wealthy directed concentrated

In Grace Aguilar's novella *The Perez Family* (1843), a young working-class Jewish woman, Sarah, is advised by the elderly Esther that Jewish girls should not be too proud to take employment as servants. Illustration by T. H. Robinson in Grace Aguilar, *The Vale of Cedars and Other Tales* (London: J. M. Dent; and Philadelphia: Jewish Publication Society of America, 1902), 273.

philanthropic efforts at Anglicizing the poor through education and social and welfare provision.

Organized ministration to the needs of poor immigrants had a precedent. A few decades earlier, attempts to mediate the integration of Irish migrants, a population of over 800,000, were undertaken by the clergy of the Roman Catholic Church. Catholics too were a precarious minority who had only recently been granted emancipation and continued to endure widespread hostility in Protestant England. Supported by middle-class Catholics, the Church sought to shape the moral and social values of nonpracticing rural migrants who had been dislocated to English cities. It provided material aid, employment training, and church-based leisure activities, encouraging intramarriage and fostering affective ties to Ireland and Rome. Through popular ritual the Church also reinforced the reverence of female chastity and motherhood. While exerting social discipline, the clergy also helped migrants adapt to metropolitan society, building a Catholic urban subculture.[16]

The established Jewish community also developed a wide-ranging material and ideological response to immigrant poverty. It should be noted, though, that their anxiety over Anglicization belied the many ways in which the state welfare and criminal justice systems were notably accommodating toward Jews. From the 1870s onward, destitute Jews who entered the workhouse were provided with kosher food, and single mothers charged with infanticide appear to have been considered with particular sympathy.[17] Nonetheless, the Jewish Board of Guardians (JBG), established in 1859 to centralize charitable relief for the Jewish poor, sought to keep Jews away from public support. Although its provision was among the most progressive in England and included soup, clothes, apprenticeships, and loans for establishing businesses or onward migration, the JBG exerted the strict discipline and emphasis on self-help characteristic of Victorian philanthropy. For example, abandoned wives were refused financial support by the JBG because the board believed that this policy would compel errant husbands to assume their family responsibilities.[18] The JBG's approach to charity brought it into conflict with the ethos of immigrant-organized practices of mutual aid: friendly societies and *chevroth* that were structured democratically and distributed assistance according to Jewish tradition, aiming to avoid stigmatizing the recipient.[19] The methods and strategies through which members of the Anglo-Jewish elite sought to mold the acculturation of Jewish immigrants are of particular interest for women's history. This agenda shaped the opportunities of both immigrant and native Jewish women in the late nineteenth century and the relationships among them.

The social and economic effects of emigration also had a significant impact on gender roles in public and domestic life. Oral history testimony from immigrants to Manchester suggests that in nineteenth-century Eastern Europe, "male status was closely bound up with religious scholarship, which represented a primary avenue to social recognition and an important source of political influence," whereas women had little religious status in their own right.[20] Women's responsibilities were in the domestic sphere, although their role could also extend to earning, usually as petty merchants and sometimes as the sole breadwinner. In this context women's work was desirable, because it enabled husbands to attain higher social and religious status through study. The primary distinction was between the spheres of the sacred and the profane, contrasting with the Victorian bourgeois ideology of gender, which distinguished instead between the spheres of public and private: men engaged in earning income and secular pursuits and women safeguarding the spiritual purity of the home.[21]

Once in England, most immigrant women continued to play only a minimal role in formal religious life. Few attended synagogue or were literate in Hebrew. Careful observance of dietary laws and extensive preparations for festivals and Sabbath continued. However, women's domestic religious practice assumed increasing significance in defining a household's Jewish identity as the status accorded to male scholarship and piety declined, Sabbath observance waned because of employment pressures, and the synagogue faded from its dominance in communal life.[22] In immigrant life the religious role of women came to resemble the English bourgeois model. Yet the environment of the modern metropolis also pulled against these ideals. As Vivi Lachs has shown, the bawdy, irreverent Yiddish music hall songs of late Victorian London reflect the new leisure, social, and sexual opportunities that were changing the horizons of immigrant women.[23] Several music hall songs portray women as their own matchmakers, earning their dowry or subverting arranged marriages with older men by taking lovers. These images suggest the disruption of traditional courtship patterns and parental control that followed emigration and the sharp awareness in immigrant popular culture of the impact of modernity.

Jewish Women and Labor

IN LATE-NINETEENTH-CENTURY ENGLAND IMMIGRANT Jewish women had fewer employment options—domestic service or employment in a factory or workshop—and lower wages than men. Nonetheless, in this period women were entering the workforce in dramatic numbers, especially in tailoring, where subdivision and deskilling had created new work opportunities with simple, low-paid tasks such as buttonholing, paid as piecework.[24] Typically, however, this work did not provide a living wage. That few Jewish women were officially recorded on the census as employed in workshops suggests that their labor in family enterprises or on a casual basis was not generally recognized as work. The vast majority worked at home, unseen by the census and unprotected by workplace regulations: Widows, young mothers, or wives of men on intermittent wages worked long hours for low pay to support the family economy.[25] These preindustrial labor conditions, their isolation from political activists, their limited understanding of capitalism, and the cost of union membership meant that London Jewish women were reluctant to organize into unions.[26] Another perspective was offered by Lily Montagu (1873–1963), who ran a working girls' club and concluded from her observations in the 1890s that persecution had made the older generation of immigrant women "individualistic"—exhausted from their own struggle for a living and "inclined to teach their children to get on with their work, mind their own business and let other people get on with theirs."[27]

Sweated Jewish women workers also encountered mixed messages about trade unions. They were repeatedly urged to organize by Jewish members of the Women's Trade Union League (WTUL).[28] But most of the Jewish leadership and rabbinate strenuously discouraged unions.[29] In addition, male Jewish trades unionists, like their non-Jewish counterparts, regarded women workers as a threat to their jobs and wages. In Leeds a strike by the (Jewish) Leeds Tailoresses' Trade Union in 1889 was the first tailors' strike to have an impact; however, although the male clothing factory operatives subsequently established their own union, they did not support the women's efforts.[30] Although it is tempting to celebrate the resourceful leadership of the WTUL or, as one historian has claimed, that the few Jewish women's trades unions that had been formed by the turn of the century demonstrated more "solidarity, discipline and persistence" than the men's unions, the bigger picture is of sporadic and largely unsuccessful union action among Jews until the early twentieth century.[31]

Family and Home in the Jewish East End

IN THE LATE NINETEENTH century the Jewish immigrant home became a topic of fierce controversy. The presence of foreign Jews in east London was causing a "sanitary problem," claimed an article in the medical journal *The Lancet*, because of "[t]heir uncleanly habits and ignorance of English ways of living."[32] In an immediate response the JBG appointed sanitary inspectors to help make complaints about inadequate conditions to landlords and the local authority and to issue advice about keeping homes clean.[33] Yet it was also widely noted that, despite extreme overcrowding and insanitary conditions, infant mortality was significantly lower among Jews. Indeed, Jewish immigrant mothers were seen by health and social work practitioners in late-nineteenth-century London as a model to their gentile neighbors.[34] Although a number of factors may have contributed to lower infant and maternal mortality, including Jewish ritual practices around food preparation, cleanliness of utensils, and handwashing before meals, and the custom among Jewish immigrant women of longer breastfeeding, most significant was the high standard of health care available to Jewish women in east London.[35]

Health care was a complex matter for immigrants. Much of it was offered by Anglican institutions, and for both Jewish and Irish Catholic women, without family and unfamiliar with English language and medical practices, childbirth could be a time of great stress.[36] Jews were also targeted by well-funded medical missionaries, who communicated in Yiddish and regarded the provision of physical and emotional care as an opportunity to demonstrate Christian kindness (though their efforts at conversion were generally unsuccessful).[37] However, excellent medical care was available to Jewish women at local teaching hospitals, which served non-Anglican patients, and through supplementary social services provided by Jewish organizations.

A key innovation responding to Jewish immigrant women's needs was the Sick Room Helps Society (SRHS), established in 1895, which offered Jewish home helpers to new mothers. As well as creating employment for destitute East End widows, this service enabled poor mothers to convalesce from childbirth in their homes. The SRHS was partly funded by weekly penny contributions from its clients, a scheme designed to foster self-sufficiency among the poor. The SRHS also promoted independence among its clients with the Provident Fund, to which women contributed a penny a week as insurance for their periods of confinement. West End Jewish ladies also established mothers' meetings and home visiting in the East End with the purpose of imparting wisdom about hygiene and household economy.[38] In the early twentieth century, when national concern about maternal and infant care increased, the services of the SRHS expanded to the provision of a maternity home and infant welfare center.

Immigrant maternity services have become the focus for differing interpretations of the Victorian Jewish welfare system. The drive for medical and sanitary improvement is frequently seen as part of the coercive machinery of Anglicization.[39] Yet oral history interviews with immigrant women indicate that the middle-class management of maternity provision was not experienced as unwelcome condescension because it provided health care in a familiar homelike environment, suggesting that the immigrant ethos was at least partly maintained.[40] Moreover, historians often neglect the fact that philanthropic aid to poor Jewish women was not exclusively a top-down operation, and several charities, including the Jewish Lying-In Charity and the Foreign Jewish Ladies Benevolent Society, were organized and funded by the Jewish working class.[41] Rickie Burman argues that women's organizations such as the Manchester Jewish Ladies' Visiting Association, established to support new mothers, like the London SRHS, helped to humanize the disciplinarian approach of the Jewish Board of Guardians.[42] Caring for new mothers, then, represented one sphere in which traditional and modern practices coexisted and sometimes merged, and the involvement of women volunteer workers changed the overall tenor of welfare provision.

The most influential interventions in the lives of immigrant women undoubtedly came from youth clubs and settlement houses established, funded, and run by members of the Anglo-Jewish elite. Clubs enabled the Jewish leadership to continue some surveillance of young people, who were increasingly entering the workforce after they left school. The first such clubs were founded in the 1880s for girls, in response to the heightened dangers that working girls were thought to be facing. Part of the broader urban youth club movement of the late Victorian period, Jewish clubs were modeled on their Christian counterparts and designed to build respectability. Their programs reinforced middle-class values and gender roles: sports for boys and needlework and music for girls. As Sharman Kadish notes, Anglo-Jews saw nothing incongruous in seeking to "graft English public school ideals onto a population which came from an entirely different tradition, with a vibrant cultural life of its own, and which lived under economic and social conditions which were not at all comparable."[43] Classes at Lady Katie Magnus' Jewish Girls' Club in London's East End, for example, included plain and fancy needlework, cooking, musical drill, gymnastics, and instruction in English and French.

The guiding ethos in girls' clubs was friendship. The dedication of the West Central facilities in Soho in 1896 declared its purpose to be to help "protect our sisters all from the temptations and pitfalls of a great city" through "rest and innocent pleasures, and loving companionship, and mutual helpfulness and improvement."[44] That these high ideals could also involve resentment and resistance is suggested in the writing of Emily Marion Harris (1844–1900), manager of the West Central club, who, in her novel *Benedictus* (1887) describes the trepidation felt by a middle-class philanthropist in the presence of noisy, assertive adolescent girls, and by Amelia B. Davidson, organizer of Free School Concerts for the Poor, who complained about the "disorderly conduct" of cigar factory women.[45] Dissent came from within Anglo-Jewry too; the philanthropist Helen Lucas (1835–1918), daughter of the Liberal MP Frederick Goldsmid, considered that girls' clubs served "to destroy home and family life, and influence, which used to be such a splendid feature among our children" by teaching girls "to seek their pleasures away from their homes."[46] This terror of letting girls out onto the streets pointed to the underlying motivation driving philanthropic work with immigrant girls: the broader moral panic in the late nineteenth century about Jewish involvement in networks of vice.

Sex Work and Rescue Work

THE EXPANSION OF COLONIES of migrant single men together with new technologies of transport and communication in the late nineteenth century offered new opportunities for the sex industry. Jews, connected both with emigrant destinations and with Eastern Europe, where prostitution had burgeoned in the mid-nineteenth century, played a role in the expansion of the international traffic in women.[47] Emigration rendered young Jewish women particularly vulnerable. Because more men than women emigrated, women left in Eastern Europe had fewer prospects of marriage. Parents, naively or in financial desperation, consented to their daughters being married to visiting foreigners, or women were persuaded to leave with the promise of well-paid work. They were then taken abroad and sold into prostitution. This practice was made easier by the fact that the *ketubbah* (Jewish marriage contract) was not recognized in nineteenth-century British civil law if the marriage had not been registered by the state, so marriages contracted only through a *ketubbah* afforded women no protection as wives once they reached Britain.[48]

Jewish involvement in the traffic in women was interpreted in the context of what Judith Walkowitz describes as a "cultural paranoia" that overtook Britain in the late nineteenth century.[49] It was a frequent reference point in anti-alien rhetoric of the 1890s and a source of acute embarrassment to the established Anglo-Jewish community. The Jewish Association for the Protection of Girls and Women (JAPGW), established in London in 1885, set up a range of preventive measures, working closely with Christian antitrafficking groups such as the National Vigilance Association. Indeed, the JAPGW's founder, Lady Constance Battersea (1843–1931), daughter of Louisa de Rothschild, described the association as extending the work of national social purity campaigners Josephine Butler and W. T. Stead.[50] The Anglo-Jewish rescue movement gradually gained influence and became a model for other such operations throughout the British empire and South America.[51] The JAPGW established a Gentlemen's Committee that sent representatives to meet unaccompanied women arriving at ports—work that was considered inappropriate for ladies.[52] Volunteers met several hundred ships a year, and an average of two unaccompanied young women were found on each.[53] In 1898 the JAPGW extended its reach by establishing Sara Pyke House, a supervised temporary hostel for vulnerable working-class girls in the East End. By the early twentieth century, the JAPGW was taking an even more holistic approach, including offering marriage counseling to help avoid the financial desperation that could follow marital breakdown.

Besides working to prevent women from entering the sex trade, the JAPGW hoped to rescue those who already had and others who were sexually active and unmarried. Like its Protestant and Catholic counterparts, also established by middle-class ladies, the JAPGW set up Jewish institutions for the purpose of reforming such "fallen" women. As unmarried mothers, both Jewish and Irish migrant women often faced isolation from conformist communities and kinship networks. The organizers of Charcroft House, the Jewish maternity home for "the girl who has fallen through her ignorance, her weakness or her folly," regarded such women as redeemable and saw Charcroft as a home that could provide the family and community support that was unavailable to Jewish unmarried mothers. The home employed Yiddish-speaking staff for the many who had been sent from Eastern Europe to conceal their pregnancy and spoke no English. Charcroft required clients to enter for a full year, learn English, and train in domestic work; laundry work helped raise funds for the home.[54] The aim was to render inmates respectable and capable of supporting their children.

The JAPGW was significant in demanding that Anglo-Jewry recognize the prevalence of the sexual exploitation of young Jewish women. Yet, although rescue workers have been characterized as the vanguard of Anglo-Jewish feminism,[55] their politics were decidedly conservative. Like non-Jewish rescue organizations of this period, the JAPGW's work was underpinned by the belief that women, by nature, were innocent and in need of protection, discipline, and correct instruction. The JAPGW's organizers attended to their clients' ethnic and religious needs, but "[a]t the same time as dispensing comfort and support," argues Lara Marks, "they also insisted on a type of behaviour which mirrored the codes of modesty and motherhood enforced in the wider society."[56] Moreover, feminist historiography has drawn our attention to the agency of some women in choosing to work in the sex trade, which their Victorian defenders found difficult to grasp. As Edward Bristow has shown, figures from the early twentieth century indicate that large numbers of Jewish prostitutes in London engaged in the trade voluntarily.[57] Women might turn to sex work to avoid destitution, to supplement poor wages, or to gain a measure of independence. The disciplinarian approach of reforming institutions was not always embraced; some residents of Charcroft House struggled against the humiliating conditions set by the home, and others later returned to life on the streets.[58] And although rescue workers believed that only a religious atmosphere would redeem them from a life of "sin," Jewish prostitutes did not necessarily feel that they had turned their back on Judaism; some, for example, asserted their religious affiliation by deliberately avoiding missionary rescue homes that offered nonkosher food.[59] Unlike middle- and upper-class women, they did not see a contradiction between their religious faith and their sexual activity.

Even if their mission was largely unsuccessful, for privileged Victorian Jewish ladies involvement in social work could be transformative. Members of the JAPGW visited Jewish women in workhouse infirmaries and prisons, and ladies' visiting associations talked to new mothers in their own homes, encountering worlds that were quite different from their own. As Lady Magnus argued, the companionship fostered in girls' clubs was intended to benefit working girls through intimacy with "women more happily circumstanced," yet wealthy women had "a hundred sympathies in common" with working girls and "with some things it may well be . . . the teachers are the learners."[60] This expression of humility suggests that it was not just class interest that motivated Jewish community workers or that, whatever their motivations, the impact of these encounters could be liberating in ways they did not anticipate. Such relationships of what Seth Koven calls "intimate inequality" were a result of the particular conjunction of friendship, passion, and service that characterized Victorian middle-class women's culture.[61]

In learning about the lives of others and reflecting on their own, Victorian Jewish female philanthropists also learned about leadership. They came from Anglo-Jewry's ruling elite—Helen Lucas and Lily Montagu were daughters of Liberal MPs, and Nettie Adler (1868–1950) was the daughter of the chief rabbi—but their knowledge of social inequality and organizational governance was gained in the many Jewish organizations they ran for years: the Jewish Board of Guardians' apprenticeship scheme, the North London Grocery Fund, the Domestic Training Home, the Sick Room Helps' Society, Jewish Children's Penny Dinners, and numerous girls' clubs. In Manchester in the 1880s, sanitary visiting was undertaken by Jewish and Christian women working together, and, as Anne Summers has argued, brought like-minded Jewish and Christian women into contact with one another and fostered their sense of belonging to the same civic community.[62]

Philanthropy also led to more formal links with women campaigners outside the British Jewish community. Rescue work in London entailed Jewish women cooperating with partner organizations both locally (with the non-Jewish social purity campaigners of the National Vigilance Association) and internationally (with the Jewish feminist Jüdischer Frauenbund in Germany). It could involve working with non-Jewish clients too; services offered by the JAPGW, including help at the point of arrival and temporary hostel accommodation, were provided to both Jewish and non-Jewish immigrant women.[63] Such work led some in the early twentieth century to larger ambitions, whether in the Jewish world, such as Lily Montagu's rethinking of Judaism in terms that could appeal to working women, or on the national stage, such as Nettie Adler's successful career as a Liberal politician or the involvement of several elite Jewish women in English suffragist organizations. The formation in 1902 of the Union of Jewish Women (UJW), belated though it was in comparison with the coordinated national women's movement, brought together these women—some from Orthodox families and others who had married non-Jews—to create what the UJW called "a bond between Jewish women of all degrees and all shades of opinion, religious, social and intellectual."[64] Its object, however, as the Irish Jewish philanthropist Lady Ellen Desart (1857–1933) declared in a speech to the UJW, was "to promote the social, moral and spiritual welfare of Jewish women" on the basis that "Woman's sphere, her real power, lies in the Home."[65] At the start of a new century, as Jewish women began to articulate new forms of self-consciousness and solidarity, they also grounded their authority by looking back to the early Victorian rhetoric of femininity.

The perspectives of immigrant and working-class women are largely absent from both elite Anglo-Jewish women's accounts of their work and subsequent analyses of it. The fervid intimacy that characterized middle-class women's religious culture was not part of theirs. Many historians argue that the myth of the "Jewish woman" served the class interests of the wealthy, expanding the authority of middle-class Jewish women through constraining the freedoms of the poor.[66] Sisterhood was more rhetoric than reality. As Tony Kushner puts it, "Immigrant women shared with their richer and anglicised sisters the exclusion from synagogue power . . . yet there was little else that united the women of Whitechapel with those of Maida Vale."[67] Sharman Kadish, however, has claimed that the Jewish club movement, unlike its gentile counterpart, promoted social mobility and closer relations between classes.[68] We can find evidence in support of this argument in welfare workers' evolving philosophies. Although she never became a socialist, Lily Montagu's firsthand acquaintance with working girls' lives through the club movement led to her support for trade unions and her campaigning work to improve conditions in workshops.[69] She believed that as long as women remained unskilled and low paid, they would fall into early marriage as an escape from the drudgery of work; her club was therefore intended to raise its members' aspirations and self-respect through education and mutual support.[70] Similarly, whereas Victorian organizations such as the JAPGW originally aimed to move their clients into domestic service, by the early twentieth century the UJW was helping women to secure positions as teachers, governesses, clerks, and nurses. Although they did not share the bourgeois ideology of female mission that fueled the activism of the Jewish elite, working-class Jewish women benefited from their practical help as supporters and mentors.

New Women

WITH THE INAUGURATION OF women's colleges at the University of Cambridge in 1869 and the opening of London University degrees to women in 1878, a new intellectual and professional class of Jewish women emerged in the late nineteenth century. Based neither in the West End nor the East End Jewish worlds, the writer Amy Levy (1861–89) and her friend the activist and translator Eleanor Marx (1855–98) joined networks of female trade union organizers, social investigators, and writers who frequented the British Museum Reading Room in Bloomsbury.[71] In her essay "Middle-Class Jewish Women of To-Day," published in the *Jewish Chronicle* in 1886, Levy lists the Nietzsche scholar Helen Zimmern, the poet and translator Mathilde Blind—both German émigrés—and the mathematician and electrical engineer Phoebe Sarah Marks (later Hertha Ayrton), the daughter of a Polish immigrant.[72] Yet as Levy notes in her essay, for women such achievement "often means the severance of the closest ties, both of family and of race"; indeed, these women saw themselves as secular intellectuals and moved primarily in non-Jewish circles.[73]

As a feisty 17-year-old, Levy had written to the *Jewish Chronicle* in 1879 to demand that Jews take seriously the "large class of intelligent, capable women who are willing and able to perform work from which they find themselves shut out by the tradition of ages."[74] In her later essay, she lamented middle-class Jewry's archaic fixation on marriage as the only destiny for women, on whom, she declared, "the shadow of the harem" has rested too long.[75] Levy developed this theme in her tragic novel *Reuben Sachs* (1889), in which the young protagonist, "despite her beauty, her intelligence, her power of feeling, saw herself merely as one of a vast crowd of girls awaiting their promotion by marriage."[76] Levy's critique was eagerly seized on by a number of Jewish contemporaries, from the conversionist Violet Guttenberg to the radical assimilationist Cecily Sidgwick, who produced imitations of *Reuben Sachs* featuring a Jewish heroine frustrated with the patriarchal and philistine character of middle-class Jewish society.[77] Picking up on the feminist mood of the 1890s, this trope harkened back, at the same time, to an older Evangelical tradition of representing Judaism as oppressive to women.[78]

Yet the failure of Victorian Judaism to fulfill the spiritual and intellectual needs of women was also expressed beyond the realm of literary discourse. As a girl growing up among the midcentury Jewish elite, Louise de Rothschild's daughter Constance longed for "true, pure, bright, simple-eyed faith." She had no desire to renounce Judaism, yet she confided in her diary her delight in the emotional uplift she felt during a service in Westminster Abbey, which, unlike the singing and sermon in synagogue, felt "truly ennobling."[79] In her memoir, Lily Montagu recalled that her Orthodox upbringing during the 1880s was "shaped by my father" and characterized by "small regulations which, in the name of Judaism, restricted my liberty." She described feeling alienated in synagogue on the Day of Atonement, where she obediently sat in the women's gallery remote from the leaders of the service and observed a congregation whose behavior, she thought, conveyed no sense of reverence or emotion.[80] In 1902 Montagu and the theologian Claude Montefiore inaugurated the Jewish Religious Union, which led to the establishment of Liberal Judaism. Montefiore described this as "a living, growing, spiritual conception, not a hard and fast collection of laws. It helped man [sic] to live and to think, to hope and to pray, not merely to obey and to sacrifice" and Montagu felt that it was a "teaching [that] seemed to set me free from my spiritual fetters."[81]

Even more boldly, in her first novel, *Naomi's Exodus* (1901), Montagu retells the story of this spiritual journey from the perspective of a young Jewish shop worker. As she had concluded through her work in girls' clubs, unreformed Judaism was especially unsatisfying for immigrant girls and women, who on the one hand "were not expected to join in public worship" but on the other bore the brunt of the economic strain of festival observance.[82] For Montagu, their common experience as Jewish women provided the grounding for the cross-class friendships that she saw as key to her work of raising girls' aspirations. Equally, in her early forays into leading synagogue services, she favored a democratic structure of worship in which "the leader must actually pray with the Congregation as one of the group. . . . She must invite her congregation to seek God with her, realizing the dignity and the difficulty of the search, never speaking for them."[83] For Montagu, religious and political innovation went hand in hand; she was later to become the first woman to preach a sermon in an English synagogue and to be active as a moderate suffragist in the Jewish League for Woman Suffrage. Her most underrecognized innovation, though, was to try to reconcile the class divisions of Anglo-Jewry, bringing Jewish women of different social status together through a return to the synagogue.

Intimate Lives

LILY MONTAGU'S MOVE FROM the Jewish philanthropic milieu of girls' clubs to the broader political world of campaigning for the rights of women workers was also facilitated by her close friend, the socialist feminist Margaret MacDonald (1870–1911).[84] As Anne Summers has shown, through personal friendships and cooperation between their organizations, Victorian middle- and upper-class women, for whom the experience and meaning of religion was more similar than different, were brought together by devout belief. The National Union of Women Workers, for example, an organization of philanthropists and reformers established in the late nineteenth century, had a strongly Christian ethos with few concessions for religious minorities, yet their language of religion and obligation was deeply familiar to Jewish women.[85]

Interest in the private experience of friendship across religious difference is a new departure for Jewish women's history. Evolving beliefs were a subject of intense discussion between Montagu and MacDonald; and MacDonald compared Montagu's conflict over rejecting her father's Orthodoxy with her own decision to switch allegiance from her father's Liberal Party to the socialist Independent Labour Party.[86] Equally passionate was the personal and working friendship between Montagu's older sister, Netta Franklin (1866–1964), and her Christian friend Charlotte Mason, founder of the child-centered home education movement, the Parents' National Education Union. Both were uncomfortable with their respective strict religious upbringing, and Mason's friendship provided Franklin with a calling that gave spiritual meaning to her private and public life. Franklin established a school based on Mason's philosophy of education, and Mason became a valued adviser when, in the early 1900s, Franklin was writing Liberal Judaism textbooks for children.[87] The particular intimacy of these friendships was generated by their common experience as women struggling with inherited forms of religious faith.

More enigmatic are the interior lives that can be glimpsed obliquely in the archive, sometimes only at moments of crisis. In her will, Lily Montagu appointed as sole executors her sister Marian and Constance P. Lewis, describing them as her "two beloved friends." Montagu declared that she had confidence that she and Marian would join each other after death, because "God could not have given us the power to love like this if it was not a love which should go on forever" and "My dear Constance has been wonderful to me always. Her love and devotion have contributed much to my happiness."[88] In the ambiguous words of Montagu's biographer, Constance "shared a home" with Lily and Marian from 1918 until she died in 1952, but the depth of their relationship was publicly articulated only after Montagu's death.

The same euphemistic phrase was used in a newspaper obituary for the pianist and composer Agnes Zimmerman, whose "public career was a good deal interrupted for eighteen years by her devoted attention to Louisa Lady Goldsmid, whose home she shared after the death of [Louisa's husband] Sir Francis Goldsmid."[89] There are no personal papers that might bring to light the nature of the relationship between Louisa Goldsmid (1819–1908) and her protégée Agnes but, as Sophie Fuller argues, whether sexual or not, their queer history is one that "inhabited emotional worlds in which they were not subservient to men and children."[90] Goldsmid's family was famously philanthropic; her husband had founded the Jews' Infant School and was a significant patron of University College London, where Louisa herself endowed three piano scholarships for women. But she was unusual among the mid-Victorian Anglo-Jewish elite for her leading role in many feminist political campaigns, including women's suffrage, higher education, and trade unions, and in publicizing the pogroms against Russian Jews in the 1890s.[91] Even more remarkably, Louisa Goldsmid came from Anglo-Jewry's elite world of banking, philanthropy, and the conservative West London Synagogue of Reform Jews, whereas Agnes Zimmerman was a devout Roman Catholic. One reason that a cross-denominational, same-sex relationship was effectively invisible was that it was understood within the language of female spiritual devotion that was normative throughout the century, a language that conceals more than it reveals.[92]

Conclusion

IN THE PRIVACY OF their homes or on the public stage, women were makers of Anglo-Jewish history, whether through Grace Aguilar's advocacy of Jewish equality through the medium of popular fiction, the creation and staffing of new welfare organizations, or the development of a spiritual, gender-equal Judaism by Lily Montagu. Overwhelmingly, as the wives and daughters of Anglo-Jewry's dominant elite and as women of the upper middle class, they were doing the work that was expected of them, yet many were also innovators.

However, popular culture and literary and private writings have complicated a simple progressive narrative of Jewish women's history in Britain. They suggest that if some felt a "bond between Jewish women of all degrees and all shades of opinion, religious, social and intellectual," as the Union of Jewish Women asserted at the turn of the century, others felt alienated—from Jewish women of different social status and from institutional forms of Judaism established during the nineteenth century. The fluidity with which some individuals moved between Jewish and non-Jewish worlds and the common experience of religious minorities in England must also make us reconsider the boundaries of the Jewish "community" and the ways in which Jewish and gentile women's histories overlapped.

Viewing Anglo-Jewry through the lens of women's history enables us to see some of its previously occluded dimensions. For example, the eclectic and improvised nature of religious practice outside the regulations established by synagogues is discernible in women's accounts of their domestic rituals. The health and welfare advantages for Jews, compared with other immigrant groups, also a subject rarely discussed, come into sharp focus when we consider the resources, services, and attention proffered by female volunteer workers, cultivating the cultural capital that was to facilitate rapid social mobility in the twentieth century. And in attending to the detail of interactions and conversations among female friends within and across denominations, we can trace women's distinctive experience of being Jewish in a Victorian religious culture of obligation and intimacy.

Notes

1 Eugene C. Black, *The Social Politics of Anglo-Jewry, 1880–1920* (Oxford, UK: Blackwell, 1988); David Cesarani, *The* Jewish Chronicle *and Anglo-Jewry, 1841–1991* (Cambridge, UK: Cambridge University Press, 2005); David Feldman, *Englishmen and Jews: Social Relations and Political Culture, 1840–1914* (New Haven, CT: Yale University Press, 1994).

2 The foundational studies are Linda Gordon Kuzmack, *Woman's Cause: The Jewish Woman's Movement in England and the United States, 1881–1933* (Columbus: Ohio State University Press, 1990); and Michael Galchinsky, *The Origin of the Modern Jewish Woman Writer: Romance and Reform in Victorian England* (Detroit: Wayne State University Press, 1996).

3 Lucy Cohen, *Lady de Rothschild and Her Daughters, 1821–1931* (London: John Murray, 1935), 8.

4 Todd M. Endelman, *Radical Assimilation in English Jewish History, 1656–1945* (Bloomington: Indiana University Press, 1990), 81–83.

5 Endelman, *Radical Assimilation*, 84.

6 Jane Rendall, *The Origins of Modern Feminism: Women in Britain, France, and the United States, 1780–1860* (Basingstoke, UK: Macmillan, 1985), 74–77; Catherine Hall, "The Early Formation of Victorian Domestic Ideology," in *White, Male, and Middle Class: Explorations in Feminism and History*, by Catherine Hall (Cambridge, UK: Polity Press, 1992), 75–93.

7 Nadia Valman, "From Domestic Paragon to Rebellious Daughter: Victorian Jewish Women Novelists," in *Jewish Women Writers in Britain*, ed. Nadia Valman (Detroit: Wayne State University Press, 2014), 10–34 (11–18); Nadia Valman,

The Jewess in Nineteenth-Century British Literary Culture (Cambridge, UK: Cambridge University Press, 2007), ch. 4.

8 Valman, *The Jewess*, 115. On Aguilar's fiction, see also Galchinsky, *Origin of the Modern Jewish Woman Writer*; Michael Ragussis, *Figures of Conversion: "The Jewish Question" and English National Identity* (Durham, NC: Duke University Press, 1995), ch. 4; and Michael Scrivener, *Jewish Representation in British Literature, 1780–1840: After Shylock* (New York: Palgrave Macmillan, 2011), ch. 6. On Aguilar's poetry, see Cynthia Scheinberg, *Women's Poetry and Religion in Victorian England: Jewish Identity and Christian Culture* (Cambridge, UK: Cambridge University Press, 2002), ch. 5.

9 On the campaign for Jewish emancipation, see Feldman, *Englishmen and Jews*; and M. C. N. Salbstein, *The Emancipation of the Jews in Britain: The Question of the Admission of the Jews to Parliament, 1828–1860* (Rutherford, NJ: Fairleigh Dickinson University Press, 1982).

10 Cohen, *Lady de Rothschild*, 42.

11 Grace Aguilar, *Records of Israel* (London: John Mortimer, 1844), x.

12 Valman, *The Jewess*, 85–115.

13 Michael Galchinsky, "Engendering Liberal Jews: Jewish Women in Victorian England," in *Jewish Women in Historical Perspective*, 2nd ed., ed. Judith R. Baskin (Detroit: Wayne State University Press, 1999), 221.

14 Figures from the Royal Commission on Alien Immigration of 1903, cited by Lara Marks, *Model Mothers: Jewish Mothers and Maternity Provision in East London, 1870–1939* (Oxford, UK: Clarendon, 1994), 11.

15 *Jewish Chronicle*, August 12, 1881, cited by Susan L. Tananbaum, *Jewish Immigrants in London, 1880–1939* (London: Pickering & Chatto, 2014), 24.

16 Lynn Hollen Lees, *Exiles of Erin: Irish Migrants in Victorian London* (Manchester, UK: Manchester University Press, 1979), 164–212.

17 Daniel J. R. Grey, "'Almost Unknown Amongst the Jews': Jewish Women and Infanticide in London, 1890–1918," *London Journal* 37, no. 2 (2012): 122–35.

18 On the practice of irregular marriage by immigrant rabbis outside the jurisdiction of the chief rabbi, which rendered wives vulnerable to desertion and weakened the authority of the Anglo-Jewish leadership, see David Englander, "*Stille Huppah* (Quiet Marriage) Among Jewish Immigrants in Britain," *Jewish Journal of Sociology* 34, no 2 (1992): 85–109.

19 Marks, *Model Mothers*, 31–37.

20 Rickie Burman, "Women in Jewish Religious Life: Manchester, 1880–1930," in *Disciplines of Faith*, ed. Jim Obelkevich, Lyndal Roper, and Raphael Samuel (London: Routledge & Kegan Paul, 1987), 38–39. See also Rickie Burman, "The Jewish Woman as Breadwinner: The Changing Value of Women's Work in a Manchester Immigrant Community," *Oral History* 10, no. 2 (1982): 27–39; Rickie Burman, "'She Looketh Well to the Ways of Her Household': The Changing Role of Jewish Women in Religious Life, c. 1800–1930," in *Religion in the Lives of English Women, 1760–1930*, ed. Gail Malmgreen (London: Croom Helm, 1986), 234–59; and Rickie Burman, "Jewish Women and the Household Economy in Manchester,

c. 1890–1920," in *The Making of Modern Anglo-Jewry*, ed. David Cesarani (Oxford, UK: Basil Blackwell, 1990), 55–75.

21 Burman, "Jewish Woman as Breadwinner," 30.

22 Burman, "Women in Jewish Religious Life," 46–51. Paula E. Hyman notes this pattern throughout Jewish communities in Western Europe; see Paula E. Hyman, *Gender and Assimilation in Modern Jewish History: The Roles and Representation of Women* (Seattle: University of Washington Press, 1995), 24–27.

23 Vivi Lachs, *Whitechapel Noise: Jewish Immigrant Life in Yiddish Song and Verse, London, 1884–1914* (Detroit: Wayne State University Press, 2018), 135–64.

24 Anne J. Kershen, *Uniting the Tailors: Trade Unionism Amongst the Tailors of London and Leeds, 1870–1939* (Portland, OR: Frank Cass, 1995), 12–14.

25 James A. Schmiechen, *Sweated Industries and Sweated Labor: The London Clothing Trades, 1860–1914* (Urbana: University of Illinois Press, 1984), 40–41, 50–79.

26 Schmiechen, *Sweated Industries*, 99–104.

27 Lily H. Montagu, *My Club and I: The Story of the West Central Jewish Club* (London: Neville Spearman & Herbert Joseph, 1944), 64.

28 Kuzmack, *Woman's Cause*, 107–16.

29 Schmiechen, *Sweated Industries*, 104–14.

30 Kershen, *Uniting the Tailors*, 72–81.

31 Black, *Social Politics of Anglo-Jewry*, 229.

32 London City Council, Public Health Department, "Report by the Medical Officer on the Sanitary Condition and Administration of Whitechapel," October 15, 1894.

33 Marks, *Model Mothers*, 65.

34 Infant mortality in the late nineteenth century was significantly lower in areas of high Jewish population in London and Manchester than in the rest of England and Wales; a similar pattern was seen in Jewish immigrants to the United States and indeed in the Pale of Settlement. See Marks, *Model Mothers*, 49–50.

35 Marks, *Model Mothers*, 68–78.

36 Marks, *Model Mothers*, 107.

37 Ellen Ross, "'Playing Deaf': Jewish Women at the Medical Missions of East London, 1880–1920s," in *19: Interdisciplinary Studies in the Long Nineteenth Century* 13 (2011), doi: http://doi.org/10.16995/ntn.622.

38 Marks, *Model Mothers*, 113–19.

39 Tananbaum, *Jewish Immigrants in London*, 53.

40 Marks, *Model Mothers*, 125.

41 Black, *Social Politics of Anglo-Jewry*, 221.

42 Rickie Burman, "Middle-Class Anglo-Jewish Lady Philanthropists and Eastern European Immigrant Women: The First National Conference of Jewish Women, 1902," in *Women, Migration, and Empire*, ed. Joan Grant (Stoke-on-Trent, UK: Trentham Books, 1996), 123–49.

43 Sharman Kadish, *"A Good Jew and a Good Englishman": The Jewish Lads' and Girls' Brigade, 1895–1995* (London: Vallentine Mitchell, 1995), 38. English public schools are elite private schools.

44 *Jewish Chronicle*, January 24, 1896.

45 Valman, "Domestic Paragon," 21–22; Black, *Social Politics of Anglo-Jewry*, 229–30.

46 Helen Lucas, "Letter to Editor," *Jewish Chronicle*, March 29, 1898, cited in Black, *Social Politics of Anglo-Jewry*, 137.

47 Edward J. Bristow, *Prostitution and Prejudice: The Jewish Fight Against White Slavery, 1870–1939* (Oxford, UK: Clarendon Press, 1982).

48 Englander, "*Stille Huppah*," 91–93.

49 Judith R. Walkowitz, *Prostitution and Victorian Society: Women, Class, and the State* (Cambridge, UK: Cambridge University Press, 1980), 247.

50 Kuzmack, *Woman's Cause*, 58.

51 Bristow, *Prostitution and Prejudice*, 237.

52 Lara Marks, "Race, Class, and Gender: The Experience of Jewish Prostitutes and Other Jewish Women in the East End of London at the Turn of the Century," in *Women, Migration, and Empire*, ed. Joan Grant (Stoke-on-Trent, UK: Trentham Books, 1996), 31–50.

53 Figures cited in Tananbaum, *Jewish Immigrants in London*, 134.

54 Lara Marks, "'The Luckless Waifs and Strays of Humanity': Irish and Jewish Immigrant Unwed Mothers in London, 1870–1939," *Twentieth Century British History* 3, no. 2 (1992): 113–37, esp. 125–28.

55 Kuzmack, *Woman's Cause*, 53.

56 Marks, "Luckless Waifs and Strays," 136.

57 Bristow, *Prostitution and Prejudice*, 241.

58 Marks, "Luckless Waifs and Strays," 128.

59 Marks, "Race, Class, and Gender," 46–48.

60 K. M. [Katie Magnus], "A Word About Girls' Clubs," *Jewish Chronicle*, April 15, 1898, cited by Black, *Social Politics of Anglo-Jewry*, 138.

61 Seth Koven, *The Matchgirl and the Heiress* (Princeton, NJ: Princeton University Press, 2014), 160.

62 Anne Summers, *Christian and Jewish Women in Britain, 1880–1940: Living with Difference* (London: Palgrave Macmillan, 2017), 55–57.

63 Summers, *Christian and Jewish Women*, 36.

64 Cited in Kuzmack, *Woman's Cause*, 49.

65 Lady Desart, speaking to the Union of Jewish Women in 1907, Union of Jewish Women, *First Annual Report 1903* and *Fifth Annual Report 1907*, cited in Tony Kushner, "Sex and Semitism: Jewish Women in Britain in War and Peace," in *Minorities in Wartime: National Racial Groupings in Europe, North America, and Australia During the Two World Wars*, ed. Panikos Panayi (Oxford, UK: Berg, 1993), 122.

66 Black, *Social Politics of Anglo-Jewry*, 230.

67 Kushner, "Sex and Semitism," 124.

68 Kadish, *A Good Jew*, 70.

69 Jean Spence, "Working for Jewish Girls: Lily Montagu, Girls' Clubs, and Industrial Reform, 1890–1914," *Women's History Review* 13, no. 3 (2004): 491–510, esp. 495.

70 Spence, "Working for Jewish Girls," 503.

71 Deborah Epstein Nord, "'Neither Pairs nor Odd': Women, Urban Community, and Writing in the 1880s," in *Walking the Victorian Streets: Women, Representation, and the City* (Ithaca, NY: Cornell University Press, 1995), 181–206; Susan David Bernstein, "Reading Room Geographies of Late-Victorian London: The British Museum, Bloomsbury, and the People's Palace, Mile End," in *19: Interdisciplinary Studies in the Long Nineteenth Century* 13 (2011), doi: https://www.19.bbk.ac.uk/articles/10.16995/ntn.632.

72 Amy Levy, "Middle-Class Jewish Women of To-Day," *Jewish Chronicle*, September 17, 1886, 7. Scholarship on Levy includes Naomi Hetherington and Nadia Valman, eds., *Amy Levy: Critical Essays* (Athens: Ohio University Press, 2010); Emma Francis, "Amy Levy: Contradictions? Feminism and Semitic Discourse," in *Women's Poetry, Late Romantic to Late Victorian: Gender and Genre, 1830–1900*, ed. Isobel Armstrong and Virginia Blain (Basingstoke, UK: Macmillan, 1999), 183–204; Meri-Jane Rochelson, "Jews, Gender, and Genre in Late-Victorian England: Amy Levy's *Reuben Sachs*," *Women's Studies* 25 (1996): 311–28; Ana Parejo Vadillo, *Women Poets and Urban Aestheticism: Passengers of Modernity* (Basingstoke, UK: Palgrave Macmillan, 2005), ch. 1; and Amy Levy, *Reuben Sachs: A Sketch*, ed. Susan David Bernstein (Peterborough, Canada: Broadview Press, 2006).

73 Levy, "Middle-Class Jewish Women," 7.

74 Amy Levy, "Jewish Women and 'Women's Rights,'" Letter to the Editor, *Jewish Chronicle*, February 28, 1879, 5.

75 Levy, "Middle-Class Jewish Women," 7.

76 Levy, *Reuben Sachs*, 209.

77 Nadia Valman, "Amy Levy and the Literary Representation of the Jewess," in *Amy Levy: Critical Essays*, ed. Naomi Hetherington and Nadia Valman (Athens: Ohio University Press, 2010), 90–109; Nadia Valman, "Barbarous and Mediaeval: Jewish Marriage in Fin de Siècle English Fiction," in *The Image of the Jew in European Liberal Culture, 1789–1914*, ed. Bryan Cheyette and Nadia Valman (London: Vallentine Mitchell, 2004), 111–29.

78 Valman, *The Jewess*, ch. 6; Summers, *Christian and Jewish Women*, 74–75.

79 Cohen, *Lady de Rothschild*, 110.

80 Lily H. Montagu, *The Faith of a Jewish Woman* (London: Allen & Unwin, 1943), 2, 10.

81 Montagu, *Faith of a Jewish Woman*, 27, 25, 24. For the context in which Liberal Judaism emerged, see Daniel R. Langton, *Claude Montefiore: His Life and Thought* (Portland, OR: Vallentine Mitchell, 2002); and Black, *Social Politics of Anglo-Jewry*, 67–70.

82 Montagu, *Faith of a Jewish Woman*, 22, 25.

83 Montagu, *Faith of a Jewish Woman*, 18.

84 Summers, *Christian and Jewish Women*, 105.

85 Summers, *Christian and Jewish Women*, 36–43.

86 Summers, *Christian and Jewish Women*, 91.

87 Summers, *Christian and Jewish Women*, 119, 125.

88 Lily H. Montagu, "Handwritten Letter, to Be Opened After Her Death," September 2, 1919, Liberal Jewish Synagogue Archives, London, in Ellen M. Umansky,

Lily Montagu: Sermons, Addresses, Letters, and Prayers (New York: Edwin Mellen, 1985), 380; "Short Paper with Outline of What I Want Done with Regard to My Work If I Pass Away," September 1, 1939, Liberal Jewish Synagogue Archives, London, in Umansky, *Lily Montagu*, 381–82. Umansky writes that Lewis "shared a home with Lily and Marian Montagu at the 'Red Lodge' from 1918 until her death in 1952" (Umansky, *Lily Montagu*, 403).

89 Lady Arbuthnot, "In Memoriam Agnes Zimmerman," *Musical Times*, January 1, 1926, p. 28.

90 Sophie Fuller, "'Devoted Attention': Looking for Lesbian Musicians in Fin-de-Siècle Britain," in *Queer Episodes in Music and Modern Identity*, ed. Sophie Fuller and Lloyd Whitesell (Urbana: University of Illinois Press, 2002), 80.

91 Kuzmack, *Woman's Cause*, 16–17, 107.

92 See Sharon Marcus, *Between Women: Friendship, Desire, and Marriage in Victorian England* (Princeton, NJ: Princeton University Press, 2007).

SEPHARDIC JEWISH WOMEN CONFRONT THE MODERN AGE

Becoming Bourgeois in the Eastern Mediterranean

DINA DANON

IN 1913 A YOUNG Graziella Benghiat delivered a lecture on feminism to an audience of Alliance israélite universelle alumni in the Ottoman city of Izmir. Herself an alumnus of the city's Alliance school for girls, Benghiat assessed the increasingly robust debates surrounding the emancipation of women and the movement advanced by suffragettes. Benghiat allowed that many of the suffragettes' claims were both "strong" and "just" and agreed that "from the point of view of intelligence, equality cannot be contested." Yet she argued that this equality must not obscure the inherent and incontrovertible differences between the sexes.

> Nature had certainly gifted men and women the same dose of intelligence, but one different in quality. Because a woman is naturally weaker, and consequently more tender, her intelligence tends towards sentiments at times incompatible with the strong nature of men, just as certain masculine sentiments are incompatible with our nature. . . . What remains, then, is for us to know how to share work and give to each one the task that best suits each of us in life. In theater do we not give each actor the role that best suits him?[1]

Benghiat's insistence that feminists remain attentive to "natural" differences in their demands provides a near pitch-perfect articulation of the bourgeois construction of gender that came to dominate the Sephardic world of the late Ottoman Mediterranean. As has been well documented, such a construction put women squarely in the domestic realm, as nineteenth-century writers and intellectuals in Western and Central Europe argued that women's "natural" tendencies for emotionality, morality, and religiosity were best served in their roles as wives and mothers.[2] Taking Benghiat and her hometown of Ottoman Izmir as a point of entry but drawing on Istanbul and Salonica as well, in this essay I reflect on the bourgeois construction of gender in the Sephardic Diaspora of the Eastern Mediterranean through the lens of a vibrant Ladino press. As I demonstrate, much like their Western European sisters, Sephardic women were encouraged to prioritize their role in the home as mother-educators and to devote time outside it to endeavors that would draw on their "natural" skills, such as charity. Yet, at the same time, embourgeoisement in the Sephardic world points to instructive divergences with other Jewish communities. For many Sephardic Jews, widespread impoverishment put full participation in the bourgeois culture disseminated by the press out of reach. For those who were able to adopt some bourgeois practices, the pronounced Westernization of the late Ottoman period put Sephardic women on the frontlines of a perceived opposition between life "*a la turka*" and life "*a la franka*."[3] Thus the prospect of becoming bourgeois ultimately entailed a complicated and often fraught balancing act for Sephardic women, demanding constant negotiation of new social and cultural ideals against economic realities.

A Portrait of the Ottoman Sephardic Community

THE OTTOMAN SEPHARDIC COMMUNITY of which Graziella Benghiat was a part dates back to the days of the Spanish expulsion, when scores of Iberian Jews chose exile over forced conversion to Catholicism. Upon arriving in the Islamic empire governed by sharia law, Jews were categorized as *dhimmi*s, or protected people, because of their monotheistic faith. Reconstituting their communities in such cities as Istanbul, Edirne, Salonica, and, later in the seventeenth century, Izmir, the Eastern Mediterranean became home to a vibrant Judeo-Spanish Diaspora, characterized by robust communities, institutions, schools, and presses. Given their knowledge of Mediterranean trade networks, a significant number of Jews saw marked economic success, particularly in the realms of international commerce and textile manufacturing. The financial apparatus of the state saw increased Jewish involvement, as Jews became active in both tax collection and tax farming. In addition, in the early modern period some Jews rose to prominence at the Ottoman court, serving as doctors, advisers, negotiators, and diplomats. Notably, Jewish women such as Esther Handali and Esperanza Malchi were involved in purveying goods such as clothing and jewelry to the imperial harem.[4]

The nineteenth century would bring about enormous political, cultural, social, and economic change across the empire. Increasing European encroachment in Ottoman affairs led the empire to adopt a sweeping series of Westernizing reforms known collectively as the Tanzimat (1839–1876), or "reorganization." Ottomans of all faiths negotiated new legal and financial systems, administrative structures, and educational institutions aimed at cultivating a shared sense of belonging and reinvigorating the empire. Dramatically reconfigured urban landscapes coupled with technological advances such as trains, telegraph, steamships, and a booming press both changed the texture of daily life within the *millets*, or ethnoreligious communities, and catalyzed an emerging public sphere that transcended them.[5] Such phenomena were particularly prevalent in port cities, where profound economic expansion resulting from the empire's incorporation into the world capitalist economy had spurred the growth of local bourgeoisies. Typically but by no means exclusively dominated by non-Muslim merchants and professionals, many among these bourgeoisies took cultural cues from the West.[6]

With the exception of some Jewish elites, on the whole Ottoman Sephardim were significantly outpaced by Greeks and Armenians in this emerging commercial bourgeoisie. Whereas Jews remained entrenched in the financial systems of the state, Greeks and Armenians were better prepared to operate in the new economy because of their robust market connections in the Balkans and the benefits conferred through ongoing negotiation of European protections. In the modern period the socioeconomic profile of many Sephardic Jews began to deteriorate, as they increasingly clustered in petty trade, crafts, and unskilled labor. Many Sephardic Jewish neighborhoods across the region were characterized by heavy impoverishment and indigence. The one exception to this general trend was the Jewish community of Salonica, which, because of its demographic majority in the city, saw marked representation in the city's growing commercial and industrial enterprises.[7]

The economic position of most Ottoman Sephardic Jews did not permit them full access to the bourgeois culture that surrounded them. Yet, as residents of eastern Mediterranean port cities they nonetheless felt its impact, observing new patterns of behavior, association, consumption, and leisure that have been treated as evidence of "middle-class hegemony" in the region.[8] Furthermore, new institutions in the Jewish community, such as the Alliance israélite universelle schooling network and a robust Ladino-language press, reinforced this hegemony for the broader Jewish public they addressed and constantly presented it with a new cultural ideal for which to strive.[9] It is here, in the sources bequeathed to us by new nineteenth-century institutions, that Sephardic women start to become more visible. Against the backdrop of the dislocations wrought by the dissolution of empire and war, archival material from most Ladino-speaking communities has either yet to be discovered or is lost to us. Even in the limited body of archival material that does exist, such as that of Ottoman Izmir, sources produced by women themselves are sorely lacking. With the emergence of an active Ladino press and the schools of the Alliance, new genres of sources help us understand if not the lived reality of Sephardic women, then at least the role attributed to them in the broader communal transformations envisioned by intellectuals, journalists, and communal oligarchs. The exceedingly small body of literature exploring modern Sephardic women either as part of a larger narrative or, even more rarely, as a main subject of interrogation has productively drawn on such sources.[10]

By the turn of the twentieth century, nearly thirty Alliance schools could be found across the major centers of Istanbul, Salonica, and Izmir and their environs. Of these, nine were specifically for girls and two were coeducational.[11] As Frances Malino demonstrates in this volume, the Alliance had a profound impact not only on the tens of thousands of students it reached across the Islamic world but also on generations of Eastern Jewish women who became a crucial part of its teaching staff. The influence of the Alliance extended far beyond the walls of its own schools, as many traditional institutions either came under its direct supervision or modified their curricula according to its example.[12] Central to the Westernizing mission of the Alliance was the role of the *mère éducatrice*, or "mother-educator," whose efforts in the home had implications not only for her own family but also for the moral "regeneration" of the Jewish community.[13]

Reinforcing this construction of gender were many editors of the region's Ladino press, who used the pages of their newspapers to promote the values of the French Jewish bourgeoisie, advertise its material accoutrements, and advocate for its "civilizing" potential. As Sarah Stein has demonstrated through the lens of Istanbul's *El Tiempo* and its instructional supplements, editors such as David Fresco offered readers an "itinerary for cultural transformation that fulfilled and expanded the central goal of the *Alliance Israélite Universelle*."[14] Like David Fresco, editors such as Aaron Joseph Hazan of Izmir's *La Buena Esperanza* and Saadi a-Levi of Salonica's *La Epoca* among many others devoted significant attention to the role of women in the broader cultural transformation they envisioned. As readers of these papers, Sephardic men and women encountered abundant discussion of philosophical matters regarding a "modern" woman's role in society, practical advice on child rearing and housekeeping, and advertisements for Western-style clothing and goods.[15]

Domestic Sphere

BOURGEOIS WOMANHOOD WAS DEFINED in large part by its connection to the domestic sphere. For Sephardic Jewish women in the Islamic world, associating women with the domestic was certainly not new. Yet as scholars have shown in other Middle Eastern contexts, in the late nineteenth century the discourse around women's management of the domestic sphere was reconfigured in alignment with both new political preoccupations and shifting boundaries between public and private.[16] For an Ottoman Sephardic woman, at stake in the management of her home was her ability to successfully negotiate the tensions between East and West that pervaded family life, which would ultimately not just contribute to the regeneration of her community but serve as its primary agent. In this sense, the domestic space becomes a telling portal for how the demands of modernity were interpreted by Sephardic Jews.

Among the most important attributes of the *mère-éducatrice* was her attentiveness to matters of hygiene, which intersected with anxieties spurred by frequent epidemics of communicable diseases such as cholera and the plague in Ottoman cities and with ideological preoccupations with the "dirtiness" of the "Orient." As Aaron Joseph Hazan of Izmir's *La Buena Esperanza* lamented in 1881, "Mothers do not see to the cleanliness of their children much," and he promised a series of "useful" articles on the topic penned by a famous European coreligionist.[17] Similarly, the handbook for parents of Alliance schoolchildren in Izmir urged mothers in particular to "see to the cleanliness of their children," reminding them that "they need to wash themselves every morning with cold water, comb their hair, and clean their clothes and shoes."[18] Perhaps to reinforce the idea that such mothering skills needed to be acquired even by Western women, in the winter of 1907 readers of *La Buena Esperanza* learned that a "mothers' school" had recently opened in Paris, where women took courses in hygiene and other topics, such as the architecture of the home.[19] As one columnist would later note in painting a portrait of "the perfect housewife" in Salonica's *La Epoca*, "The cleanliness that shines in all of the corners of the home, in all of the utensils and in all of the clothing is reflected in her conscience."[20] To attain such an impeccable standard, readers of *La Epoca* could purchase "Sunlight Soap," which was advertised over the course of many years in its pages. Useful for laundry and for a host of household needs, Sunlight Soap was touted for "making clothing as white as snow" and billed as "indispensable for families."[21]

Alongside a young woman's mastery of hygiene was the expectation that she cultivate a broad range of skills under the rubric of "domestic economy," or the application of efficiency and rationality to her household duties. A subject

An ad for Sunlight Soap in *La Epoca*, January 22, 1904. Image in the public domain.

in the curriculum of Alliance girls' schools,[22] domestic economy was among the most prized skills of a *buena nekuchera*, or "good housewife."[23] Calling a bride who has arrived in the home of her new husband "a queen in her kingdom," one contributor to Izmir's *El Comersial* argued that good housewives needed to "descend from the pedestal" afforded by their feminine qualities and master accounting. Requiring meticulous supervision of the household budget, such accounting demanded a keen financial savvy on the part of wives, who were expected to ably balance the payment of rent, taxes, insurance, and utilities while both guarding against smaller, unnecessary expenditures and saving for unforeseen circumstances. Citing the wisdom of Benjamin Franklin, *El Comersial* recommended that housewives assiduously check the bills of all their purchases and pay close attention to the weights and measures used in the marketplace. "Young woman," the article concluded, "no detail, no matter how small, should be above your notice."[24] Similarly, among the characteristics of an ideal wife sketched by a contributor to *La Epoca* was her "devotion to economy, order, and organization" and knowledge of how to "run a house."[25] Revealingly, advertisements for Sunlight Soap highlighted not only its cleansing properties but also its time-saving benefits in ensuring "triple economy: time, work, and money."[26]

Such constructions of a *buena nekuchera* could be found outside the Ladino press as well. In 1914 Nissim Kuri of Izmir's Liga de Pas i Solidaridad, a social club that aimed to foster unity in an often conflict-ridden community, delivered a lecture on the duties between members and their wives. Echoing the sentiments of both Alliance observers and Sephardic journalists, Kuri argued that the mastery of domestic economy had implications not only for individual families but also for the broader Sephardic community, as the transformation of each Jewish household at the hands of a capable woman would serve as the ultimate bulwark against the community's unconscious "physical and moral decadence": "You cannot imagine the serenity, the calm of both mind and soul, that reigns in a well-run and wisely balanced household," Kuri concluded. "The economic uplifting of an entire people depends on it."[27]

Even more important than a bourgeois woman's meticulous management of the home was the moral example she set for her children.[28] Finding echoes with the traditional image of an *eshet hayil*, or "woman of valor," Sephardic women were constantly reminded of the enormous influence they wielded. Izmir's *El Comersial* painted a full portrait of this influence in 1907.

> What is a woman's role? Is it not sublime and grandiose? Is it not women who pursue the noble and holy mission of raising the family? Is it not in their hands that the future of humanity is entrusted? Is it not with a remarkable vigilance and true heroism that women undertake such a difficult yet delicate mission? It is she who must bring up her children. It is she whose mandate is to educate noble citizens—human men in the real sense of the word. It is she who sees to inculcating in children, from the cradle, ideas of health, principles of good education, [and] the seed of virtues and noble qualities. Which role could be more important than this? Which mission is more noble than that of women?[29]

David Fresco, of Istanbul's *El Tiempo*, agreed, arguing that "a mother is the first teacher," adding that "her whole erudition is her moral influence."[30] Jacob Algrante, of Izmir's *El Novelista*, idealized the role of women as "providence in our youth, consolation in our illness and in the most critical moments of our life, and our blessing in moments of happiness," arguing that "it is she who forms our soul, who leads us to goodness. She is our moral and religious education. She supports us with her virtue and faith."[31] As a columnist in *La Epoca* cautioned, such enormous responsibility required a "constant vigilance" on the part of women in relation to themselves and to their children.[32]

Belief that a woman's primary role lay in the home shaped debates about the content of women's education. One contributor to Istanbul's *El Tiempo* argued that, although he was not against educating women "according to the modern spirit," many parents had misunderstood the needs of the day by prioritizing physical education over moral development. "I prefer a thousand times a woman devoid of all instruction but bearing a well brought-up soul to a very learned woman with a poorly brought-up soul," he argued.[33] Taking the issue up again in 1893, *El Tiempo* argued that, although women were indeed entitled to instruction, it need not be particularly sophisticated. "Women were not made to be engineers, lawyers, or science teachers," the article claimed. "She has no time to deal with astronomy or metaphysics."[34]

More suitable was an education centered around her role in the home, a point Rafael Immanuel Florentin of Salonica echoed a year later when he argued that the "education given to girls should help them understand the point of their existence" not only in their family or the wider Jewish community but also in society.[35] The marriage advice column in Salonica mentioned earlier reminded suitors that an ideal wife should "possess an adequate education (large doses being dangerous)" and be "educated so as to be able to present herself in society (no more)."[36]

Bourgeois Womanhood and Charity

THE CONSTRUCTION OF THE bourgeois woman as sensitive and tender handily facilitated the notion that she was particularly well suited to charitable endeavors. Endowed with "grandeur of heart, sensibility, sweetness, and piety," Jewish women, according to Izmir's *El Novelista*, were naturally predisposed to serve as "consolation for the poor, a refuge for the miserable, and a loving mother for the orphan. Oh, how capable are these women of alleviating the suffering and pain of the unfortunate."[37] So well suited were women for engaging in charity that it was cast as a domain where they might even be superior to men. Addressing readers frustrated by "inequality," *El Novelista* insisted that it would be "ridiculous for a woman to try to shine" as a man did. Instead, women needed to take pride in the distinct role nature had allotted them: "The only place where a woman can walk alongside a man or dispute his steps is in the domain of charity. . . . Among her attributes are love and devotion. Where is there not a wound to heal, an unfortunate to help, a tear to dry? It is upon the underprivileged that the affections filling women's hearts can be spread."[38]

Already by the 1870s the Ladino press had begun to profile women worthy of praise for their commitment to charitable causes. In 1874 *La Esperanza* (after February 1880, *La Buena Esperanza*) highlighted the efforts of Sinyoro de Leon Sidi during the Shabbat Albasha, an annual midwinter effort to provide the impoverished children of the Talmud Torah school with clothing and shoes, typically around Hanukkah. Crowning her "the mother of the poor and orphaned, the sustainer and consolation of widows and rabbis," the paper mobilized the imagery of a benevolent bourgeois woman caring for the needy.[39]

Many Sephardic women followed in Madame de Leon Sidi's path in the late Ottoman period. By the 1890s Istanbul was already home to numerous women's charities, among them the Women's Committee of Hasköy, the Society of Jewish Women of Galata, the Karidad i Relidjion Society, and the Charity Society of the Young Jewish Ladies of Ortaköy,[40] and Izmir saw the founding of women's charitable associations such as La Buena Veluntad, Nashim Sadka-niot, the God's Will Society, and the women's sections of the Bikur Holim and the Talmud Torah Societies.[41] Reflecting the prevailing connection between motherhood and charity, in 1894 Emilia Tedeski, president of La Sosiedad de benefezensia de las damas israelitas de Pera told her fellow members to think of their association as a "small child," urging them to see to its care and supervision.[42] Similarly, Madame Elias Pasha, wife of the eye doctor to the Imperial Palace, called on the young women of Hasköy to follow the example of the women of Pera and "alleviate the misery of the unhappy schoolchildren who are, for the most part, hungry and crying for a little bread."[43]

Eventually, some long-standing Jewish communal initiatives such as *albasha*, or providing clothing to the students of the Talmud Torah, came to be regarded as the exclusive province of newly formed women's charities. In 1902, for example, the new Women's Committee of Izmir's Talmud Torah school oversaw the production and distribution of clothing. "One must see the joy on the faces of these little and unfortunate children," *La Buena Esperanza* claimed, "when they are called by their brave female protectors who give them [each] a shirt, pants, handkerchief, *sisit*, and to some, shoes."[44] During an *albasha* initiative in 1907, *El Novelista* celebrated the "second mothers" whom the orphans had found in the women of the committee[45] and praised those "guardian angels" whose "social position might allow them to stay at home and remain indifferent to the outside world." "If the prisons curse our women for snatching away future prisoners," *El Novelista*'s Romano concluded, "human-ity and the heavens bless them," thus underscoring the profound connection between bourgeois femininity and philanthropy.[46]

Jewish women also participated in charitable work outside the Jewish community. Such was the case of Madame Elias Pasha, mentioned earlier. Cit-ing press coverage in *Le Moniteur Oriental*, *El Tiempo* reported that in addition to her "active and effective" work on behalf of Jewish charities, Madame Elias Pasha had recently demonstrated strong support of the Imperial Darülaceze, the first poorhouse in Istanbul and one of Sultan Abdülhamid II's most prized public initiatives.[47]

The "natural" ability of women to seek out suffering was regarded as especially well suited to serving the needs of the shame-faced poor, or those thrust into poverty due to particular circumstances. Protecting the anonymity of such cases was seen as paramount and was demonstrated by the work of the God's Will Society, a women's group that had come to the aid of numerous "fallen families" in advance of Passover.[48] Lamenting that "the stronger sex neglects this sort of charity," *El Novelista* marveled at how "a group of girls [with] tender hearts, future Jewish mothers, fulfill this need."[49]

The reshaping of Jewish philanthropy in the eastern Sephardic Diaspora also gave rise to new complexities regarding the changing role of women in the public sphere. In 1875 a benefit in Izmir featuring public speeches delivered by communal leaders and by Talmud Torah students was held over the course of two days to accommodate separate events for men and women.[50] Yet only a year later, *La Esperanza* reported that the presence of women and young ladies at a ball for a Jewish school had lent it "a more splendid form."[51] The notion that the presence of women served only to enhance such events found numerous echoes over the coming years. Reporting on an 1884 ball, *La Buena Esperanza* highlighted how "the elegant clothing, fine jewelry, and grace of the women lent a greater brilliance to this ball that left nothing to be desired,"[52] and in 1887, it proudly reported that more than seventy women and young ladies had attended the soirée for the Ozer Dalim Society.[53] So valuable was the presence of women at charity balls that in 1907 a proposal surfaced that would allow them to attend balls free of charge. In favor of such a step, one contributor commented that "all of our readers can attest to the fact that the brilliant success of any ball is due to the feminine sex," arguing that without women, such an event "could not be called a ball."[54]

As balls became increasingly commonplace, women took an active role not only in attending them but also in initiating them. In the winter of 1896 *El Tiempo* praised the women of the Sosieta de Damas for organizing a ball at Istanbul's famous Pera Palas, a luxurious Western-style hotel. Under the direction of president Emilia Tedeski, young ladies Ida Cohen, Emma de Castro, Adela Faraggi, Ida Matalon, Dorotea Gabbai, Emma Molia, and Klota Viterino orchestrated an event that attracted a "numerous" and "very exclusive crowd." The cultural cues provided by the West for bourgeois Sephardic women were reflected not only in the ball's location and in Ms. Faraggi's skilled recital of a French comedy that was "admired for [her] graceful accent"[55] but also in the very names of the organizers. For upwardly mobile women in the Sephardic world, names such as Dorotea, Adela, and Emilia could mark one's middle-class stature in a way that Zinbul, Mazaltov, and Jamila could not.

Even though Ms. Faraggi's performance at the 1896 ball was well received, at times women's participation in philanthropic theater performances provoked significant debate. By the early twentieth century, uneasiness surfaced with respect to the supposed detrimental impact of theater on women and their "virtue," given mixed attitudes toward theater in general and discomfort with the intimate contact that inevitably took place between the sexes onstage. *El Comersial* ardently took up the issue, arguing that true "progress" would not arrive until "old ideas that currently predominate regarding the theater disappear."[56] Allowing that theater had indeed "shocked social conventions," *El Comersial* still argued in favor of giving "a little more freedom to our young women," insisting that "with the instinct that guides the finer sex, they will know how to carry themselves. . . . If she is an honest girl, she will always remain an honest girl."[57] In future articles, *El Comersial* cast the ability of women to appear on the stage for charitable purposes as not only desirable but a requirement of modernity itself. Encouraging women to appear on the stage would only serve "to awaken their enthusiasm for generous and useful causes [and] encourage them to do praise-worthy acts." It criticized opponents of women on the stage for disseminating "backwards ideas from old times" and cast them as "incompatible with the needs of the current age." *El Comersial* encouraged its readers to "lift their sights to more noble, pure, and higher ideas" and to realize that "the twentieth century is a century of progress and civilization, a century in which men and women must think, reason, and act in accordance with its demands."[58] Only a couple of weeks later, the newspaper triumphantly reported on a recent ball held for the benefit of the Alliance. Celebrating how women had enthusiastically taken to the stage, the paper read this as proof that Izmir's Jews were finally acquainting themselves with the "demands of life in the present day."[59]

The advent of *baylar a la franka*, or "European-style" dancing, proved to be another arena in which new philanthropic activities sparked internal debate. Alexander Benghiat, editor of *El Meseret* and Graziella Benghiat's husband, emerged as a staunch critic of such dancing and used his newspaper to discourage the practice. In 1901 he criticized those "so-called '*frankeados*' who dance not with their sisters or wives, but with the daughters of their neighbors or with distant acquaintances."[60] Worried that *baylar a la franka* encouraged inappropriate contact between the sexes, Benghiat concluded that "European-style dancing is horrible for us Levantines" and saw in the "calm and peaceful" East a bulwark against the "scandalous scenes" of big European cities.[61]

The popularity of charity balls and theater performances also intersected with increasing concern regarding appropriate dress. Given the function of dress as a visible and public marker of class, attendance at such events demanded not only certain comportment but also dignified clothing and accoutrements. In announcing a ball for the Alliance to be attended by both Jewish and Christian business leaders, the organizing committee required that attendees arrive "in style."[62] Explaining that men would be required to wear all black and women their usual ball attire, *La Buena Esperanza* alerted its readers that anyone wearing "Turkish style clothing" would be barred from entering.[63] Respecting such a dress code would ensure that the ball "would be praised by all parties," demonstrating that Izmir's Jews took pride in their community.[64]

Notably, such demands to arrive "in style" were absent from announcements for the 1892 soirée held for the Ozer Dalim and Mahzikei Ani'im Societies. Given that this soirée was "but a party for families [and] is purely national," the organizers declared, "men and women may come dressed without going to great expense."[65] The relaxing of standards in the context of a Jewish communal event not anticipated to draw a mixed crowd further underscores the nature of dress as a public marker of class and the importance that Izmir's Jews attached to appearing middle class in the eyes of their neighbors.

Luxury and Sobriety

ALONGSIDE THE EMERGENCE OF new bourgeois practices in the home and in public was a growing emphasis on the virtues of self-restraint and sobriety. Such ideas found a particularly sharp resonance in a population already grappling with the supposed backwardness of its own Eastern culture. As Alliance administrator Gabriel Arié would remark in 1899 regarding the Jews of Izmir, the community's "taste for luxury [and] wild expenses," the "disproportion between the resources of each person and the needs he creates for himself," and its "spirit of improvidence and total absence of habits of economy" were among the main causes of its "decline."[66] A front-page article in La Epoca called "luxury and extravagant spending" the "two biggest enemies of our families," adding that the prevalence of poverty was due to a wider failure in "weigh[ing] our expenses against our situation."[67] Perhaps more convincingly, in his 1914 address to the Liga de Pas, Nissim Kuri emphasized the need for frugality, not as a defense against any Sephardic proclivity for luxury but rather to mitigate the "modern habits [and] the demands of the new life" that forced people to spend beyond their means.[68]

Women found themselves at the heart of such preoccupation with luxury in the Sephardic world, regardless of their socioeconomic position. Whether it was as "high society women," with their "riches and magnificence" who had become "Emilia and Ernestina,"[69] or girls who wished to emulate "the women of the aristocracy" but were "forced to work with their hands"[70] as domestic servants or as laborers in silk and tobacco mills, Sephardic women were measured against a standard that idealized bourgeois "simplicity" and denigrated the temptations of luxury and its associated vices.[71] This is particularly evident in the realm of dress. Already by 1829, Sultan Mahmud II had mandated the adoption of European garb and the fez among Ottoman officials, measures that were undertaken to openly and publicly mark the centrality of allegiance to the state over forms of social and religious belonging.[72] Although such reforms were directed only at men, by the late nineteenth century upper-class Ottoman women also experienced changes in their dress. The emergence of mass fashion in the empire saw the introduction of highly tailored European clothes that, in accentuating the shape of the body, stood in stark contrast to loose-fitting and layered Ottoman garb.[73] The choices that Ottoman Sephardic women were encouraged to make against this backdrop of expanding options for dress reflect the careful and deliberate balancing of Eastern and Western cultures that was embedded in demonstrating a commitment to simplicity.

In 1883, for example, *La Buena Esperanza* lamented the slow and uneven pace with which Izmir's Jewish women were abandoning their traditional garb. Although they had begun to adopt some Western fashions, some continued to don the *tokado*, an elaborate headdress specific to Sephardic women. *La Buena Esperanza* denigrated the practice as a "veritable scandal," claiming it negated any "progress" achieved through wearing Western attire. "Why bother going to dressmaker after dressmaker? Why spend so much money while wearing a *tokadiko* of a thousand wonders?" the paper wondered.[74] Yet, as Western-style ladies' hats became increasingly common as the decades wore on, the women who donned them were criticized for excessive extravagance. Their obstruction of the audience's view during theater performances became especially contentious, and as a result, charitable associations began to ask that women refrain from such accessories during benefits. In 1906 Izmir's Talmud Torah school stipulated that women patrons planning to attend the association's upcoming show "come without hats,"[75] and in 1907 Ozer Dalim followed suit.[76] Later that year, an impassioned editorial appeared in the pages of *El Comersial* on the subject, with its author remarking that ladies' hats had become "veritable gardens of Babylon." Recognizing the need to "harmonize the exigencies of fashion with the community of spectators," he offered numerous solutions, largely emanating from the great halls of Parisian venues such as the Opéra, the Opéra Comique, and the Comédie Française. In such establishments, he argued, not only had new rules been imposed regulating ladies' hats, but also the general attitude toward such elaborate headgear had changed. It had gradually become acceptable for women to wear lace or scarves instead of opulent hats, and he pointed out that the famous stage actress Sarah Bernhardt had banned such hats at her performances.[77] A year later, women were encouraged to join a leisurely excursion to Aydin as a way to abandon "their hats as high as the pyramids of Egypt, gala dresses, luxurious robes and 'fru-fru' skirts."[78] By spending the day engaged in wholesome field games and activities in the countryside, women could truly demonstrate that they were "adherents of simplicity."[79]

Yet another revealing critique of women's luxury was put forth by a young seamstress. She first lamented that the "demands of life today" had not only increased the cost of living, such that fathers could barely maintain their households, but had also made the "caprices of their daughters" nearly impossible to satisfy. The seamstress sarcastically described how she worked tirelessly "to increase the profits of the department stores of Frank Street" and expressed shame at occupying herself "only with exterior adornments." The seamstress also criticized the demands that her clients made on her own patterns of dress as well. "Obligated as I am to be in frequent contact with my aristocratic clients, forced to accompany many of them in buying clothes, I must be as well-dressed as they are, with artfulness, taste [and] refinement; otherwise, my clients would undoubtedly abandon me." If women were to only "give the best example of simplicity," the seamstress continued, others would quickly follow their example and begin dressing "according to [their] position." The seamstress concluded by exhorting the newspaper to continue its commitment to "the movement begun in support of the suppression of luxury," adding that it could lead to "important reforms."[80]

Critique

THE BROAD PURCHASE OF bourgeois constructions of gender in the Eastern Sephardic diaspora does not mean they were uncontested. Quite the reverse. Some began to question the implications of "civilization" and its displacement of "tradition." Again, women's dress emerged as a point of contention in this debate. For example, the European corset attracted the ire of some observers for the havoc it wrought on a woman's body and internal organs. In 1893 *El Tiempo* published an article printed in the physical outline of both a corseted and uncorseted figure. Condemning the corset for putting intense pressure on a woman's heart and lungs, the article posited that the "imprudent" women who chose to wear it "brought a series of misfortunes upon themselves" while trying to lend themselves a "beautiful figure." Criticizing this figure instead as "horrifying," the article contrasted the "disfigurement" caused by corsets to a woman's natural shape.[81]

In 1901 Alexander Benghiat attacked the *décolleté* chosen by many women attending balls, with its shorter sleeves and open display of one's neck, upper chest, and back.[82] Surprised that such a style had become popular, Benghiat wondered how "an educated and intelligent woman who calls herself honest, could go in such revealing clothing to a ball with the idea of pleasing men." Placing the blame squarely on the influence of the West, Benghiat remarked that "civilization has required us to dress ourselves, but too much civilization is causing women to get rid of some of their clothes." Benghiat continued,

טאלייה קון קורטילימו

חיסטה חיב לה
סורמה דילה עטייה
די אונה ונחיר כונדי לה
קון און חפדיעחדו קורטי-
ליטו חיס חטחדו . לחם קיקטי-
חם דיבפורנגחחדחם פיר כיד חם-
רימחדחם שיזגחן כונדי לום סינגונו-
נים חסטה קי חיליים דילייין
חינפילימום . חיל קורחסין חיל
טמנגיין חים חפדיעחדו
חי נו סימחדי חזיל כוק
סונקסייניק . חיל
חינחחדו דיצייני
אונה נחחה
חינירטה ,
חיל חיכטו-
נחגו נחחחוהחדו
נו סומחדי דיזרחר
חי חין חונה ונסקליטה טו-
דום לום חורגחנום חינטירי-
טורים כון חפדיעחדוס , חים
חבכי קי חונה נוזיר טחנספורטנדי כי
סרטחי חונה כידיחח די דיכדיחחם , נח
קחימי קי קין חיכטו חילייה טייני חונה
חינונוה סורטה. נייגנרדחם קי חין לי-
סילדחל, חיכטה סורדה חיב חובו-
רחה חי סחליקי און נונו
(מחיינונכה) חיסטרופייחדי.

מאלייה אנג'ה

חיסטה חיב לה
טחלייה נחטורא די
אונה ונחיר לה קחל
נו סולי מונקה דיקפור-
נחחלה פור חון קודכיליטו .
חיל חינטיורידיחור חיב חונה וונה
די סחלוד . חיודיספחרטי די קום
גרחחייחם, חילייה טייני טחונבין חו-
נה ליקיחה . סום פולמונים כון ליצי-
רום חי ריכפירחן קין דיסיקולטחל.
סומחדי חי סוליזה, רובוסטה חי
כחכה . טולדחם לחם פונקסייניק
סחיילולחייקהם כון ריגולחרים .
לה סירקולחסייון די לה כחנ-
גרי כי חני קון חיל ונחם
גרחחנדי מורדין . חילייה נו
חיס סחלחידה חי נו טייני לה
ריכפילחחסייון קורטחחדה. חים חון
קומחדפו לייני די צידה. אח ! קי
לחם ונחידים קינוביחן לום דחכייים
קי חיספוט קורטליטום חוין, חילייחם
חוצלירין דישחחדו לה דחנין נחטורה
חזיל סו קחונדני חי מונקה פרילה-
רילחן די סיר קונטרה חילייה.

"I do not believe that they are obligated by any 'fashion' to come half naked to a ball," and he concluded that "more important than fashion is good sense."[83]

Criticism of "civilization" extended beyond its reordering of patterns of dress. While "civilization" had exported the image of the bourgeois housewife, with its discourse of emancipation, so too did it invite consideration of women seeking opportunities outside the home. *El Tiempo* makes its suspicion apparent in the 1896 piece "The Twentieth Century Woman." The article narrates the plight of a sympathetic young man who desperately needs a button sewed onto his jacket. Yet the women in his household are otherwise occupied, with his wife studying psychology, his maid reading lectures delivered at the Sorbonne, his cook conducting scientific experiments in the kitchen, and his nanny writing poetry. Against the backdrop of a house that, though "well-furnished and graceful," was "dirty and dusty" and in "disarray," the wife scolds her husband, "I have told you more than once that twentieth-century women cannot worry about such vanities."[84] The reader is left convinced not of the benefits of "civilization" but of its costs. Similarly, an editorialist for Izmir's *El Novelista*, Joseph Romano, argued that allowing women to do the same work as men would "lower women to a level beneath that which civilization had lifted them to." He continued, "Why do we always try to copy the French, the English, and others? We, and we Jews especially, need to protect the traditional purity of our homes, the exemplary virtue of our communities," further adding that "we do not want corruption or demoralization among us."[85]

Conclusion

IT IS ONLY IN recent years that Sephardic Jewry in the modern age has begun to receive the scholarly treatment that it deserves. All the more so for Eastern Sephardic women, who have received little sustained attention. Yet their experiences invite us to rethink paradigms that have typically governed the study of Jewish women. First, the bourgeois construction of gender in the Ladino-speaking Diaspora is divergent from other case studies in the way it was predicated on a deracination from local culture. Refracted as it was through the larger prism of Westernization, becoming bourgeois often demanded a delicate negotiation of two cultures that were cast in oppositional terms. A good *mère éducatrice* spoke not Ladino but French, abandoned her elaborate *tokados* for hats, and discarded Sephardic "superstitions" in favor of rational practices informed by science. By contrast, Western European Jewish women typically saw a harmonious relationship between their Jewishness and the cultural idiom of the surrounding middle class. As Marion Kaplan has argued in the case of Germany, Jewish women there saw no contradiction between *deutschtum* and *judentum*.[86]

In addition, tracking constructions of gender in the Sephardic world also invites further reflection on the role of women in the larger study of Jews in the modern age. Like German and French Jewish women, Sephardic women were encouraged to adopt bourgeois ideals and practices. Yet unlike their Central European sisters, Sephardic women were envisioned as agents of profound social and cultural transformation, which points in turn to notable similarities with the Yiddish-speaking women of Eastern Europe. Yet this parallel is limited as well, given that the deepening politicization and secularization experienced by many Ashkenazic Jewish women was absent in the Sephardic world.

Although some points of convergence do exist between Sephardic and Ashkenazic Jewries of various diasporas, ultimately perhaps the model that holds the most interpretive potential is the one that has only started being written—that of Ottoman women, both Muslim and non-Muslim.[87] Across the empire, women of various faiths and ethnicities undoubtedly encountered similar pressures as they navigated an imbalanced power dynamic between East and West. Scholars have shown, for example, how "feminism" became a potent term in debates about Westernization,[88] as well as how shifting norms governing Muslim women's behavior intersected with questions of morality, religious tradition, and authenticity.[89] Some have recovered the expanded participation of Ottoman women in a shared and multiethnic public sphere,[90] whereas others have called attention to the ways the "women's question" was refracted through the various and sometimes competing visions of empire and nationality across different ethnoreligious groups.[91] Even as such research is being pursued, recovering the experience of Sephardic women certainly helps to promote, in the words of Paula Hyman, a "healthy skepticism about master narratives."[92]

Notes

I thank Stanford University Press for permission to republish in this chapter some material from chapter 3 of my book *The Jews of Ottoman Izmir: A Modern History* (Stanford, CA: Stanford University Press, 2020).

1 "A Sephardi Suffragette? A Jewish Woman of Izmir Lectures on Feminism," trans. Alma Rachel Heckman, in *Sephardi Lives: A Documentary History, 1700–1950*, ed. Julia Phillips Cohen and Sarah Abrevaya Stein (Stanford, CA: Stanford University Press, 2014), 231–35.

2 See, for example, Karin Hausen, "Family and Role-Division: The Polarisation of Sexual Stereotypes in the Nineteenth Century—An Aspect of the Dissociation

of Work and Family," in *The German Family: Essays on the Social History of the Family in Nineteenth and Twentieth Century Germany*, ed. Richard Evans and W. R. Lee (London: Croom Helm, 1981), 51–83; Leonore Davidoff and Catherine Hall, *Family Fortunes: Men and Women of the English Middle Class, 1780–1850* (London: Hutchinson, 1987), 149–92.

3   Alan Duben and Cem Behar, *Istanbul Households: Marriage, Family, and Fertility, 1880–1940* (Cambridge, UK: Cambridge University Press, 1991), 203–4.

4   For more on the social and economic position of Ottoman Jewry in the early modern period, see Esther Benbassa and Aron Rodrigue, *Sephardi Jewry: A History of the Judeo-Spanish Community, 14th to 20th Centuries* (Berkeley: University of California Press, 2000), 36–44.

5   For more on the public sphere in the Ottoman context, see Bedross der Matossian, "Formation of Public Sphere(s) in the Aftermath of the 1908 Revolution Among Armenians, Arabs, and Jews," in *"L'ivresse de la liberté": La Révolution de 1908 dans l'Empire Ottoman*, ed. François Georgeon (Paris: Peeters, 2012), 189–219.

6   Reşat Kasaba, Çağlar Keyder, and Faruk Tabak, "Eastern Mediterranean Port Cities and Their Bourgeoisies: Merchants, Political Projects, and Nation-States," *Review* 10, no. 1 (1986): 122, 124.

7   For more on the socioeconomic profile of Salonican Jewry, see Paul Dumont, "La structure sociale de la communauté juive de Salonique à la fin du dix-neuvième siècle," *Revue Historique* 263 (1980): 351–93.

8   Cem Emrence, *Remapping the Ottoman Middle East: Modernity, Imperial Bureaucracy, and Islam* (London: I. B. Tauris, 2012), 41.

9   For a fuller exploration of the Ladino press, see Sarah Abrevaya Stein, *Making Jews Modern: The Yiddish and Ladino Press in the Russian and Ottoman Empires* (Bloomington: Indiana University Press, 2004).

10   See, for example, Stein, *Making Jews Modern*, 123–49; Gila Hadar, "Jewish Tobacco Workers in Salonika: Gender and Family in the Context of Social and Ethnic Strife," in *Women in the Ottoman Balkans: Gender, Culture, and History*, ed. Amila Butrovic and Irvin Cemil Schick (London: I. B. Tauris, 2007), 127–52; Aron Rodrigue, *Jews and Muslims: Images of Sephardi and Eastern Jewries in Modern Times* (Seattle: University of Washington Press, 2003), 80–93; and Esther Benbassa, "L'éducation feminine en Orient: L'école de filles de l'Alliance Israélite Universelle à Galata, Istanbul (1879–1912)," *Histoire, Économie et Société* 10, no. 4 (1991): 529–59.

11   See the chart in Rodrigue, *Jews and Muslims*, 15–21.

12   Aron Rodrigue, *French Jews, Turkish Jews: The Alliance Israélite Universelle and the Politics of Jewish Schooling in Turkey, 1860–1925* (Bloomington: Indiana University Press, 1990), 95.

13   See Frances Malino in this volume; Rodrigue, *French Jews, Turkish Jews*, 78–79; and Benbassa, "L'éducation feminine en Orient."

14   Stein, *Making Jews Modern*, 124.

15   Stein, *Making Jews Modern*, 126–36, 175–87.

16   Marilyn Booth, "May Her Likes Be Multiplied: 'Famous Women' Biography and Gendered Prescription in Egypt, 1892–1935," *Signs: Journal of Women in Culture and Society* 22, no. 4 (1997): 862.

17 "La salud publika," *La Buena Esperanza*, March 23, 1881.
18 *Eskolas de la Aliansa Israelit Universal en Izmir: Informasiones para las familyas* (September–October 1890), 3.
19 "Eskolas de madres en Paris," *La Buena Esperanza*, February 22, 1907.
20 "Nuestras mujeres," *La Epoca*, April 7, 1905.
21 See, for example, "Shavon de Sunlayt," *La Epoca*, January 22, 1905; February 19, 1904; and July 24, 1903.
22 *Eskolas de la Aliansa Israelit Universal en Izmir*, 10.
23 "El orden i la ermozura en la familya," *El Comersial*, October 17, 1907.
24 "El orden i la ermozura en la familya."
25 "Despozorios i kazamientos," *La Epoca*, July 3, 1903.
26 "Shavon de Sunlayt," *La Epoca*, February 19, 1904.
27 *Los doveres entre los ermanos de la Liga de Pas i Solidaridad i sus mujeres* (Izmir: Impr. Franko, ca. 1914), 17.
28 For a fuller discussion of bourgeois womanhood, see Bonnie G. Smith, *Ladies of the Leisure Class: The Bourgeoises of Northern France in the Nineteenth Century* (Princeton, NJ: Princeton University Press, 1981).
29 "Respektamos la mujer," *El Comersial*, April 25, 1907.
30 "La instruksion de la mujer," *El Tiempo*, December 30, 1895.
31 "La mujer djudia," *El Novelista*, March 28, 1907.
32 "A las madres," *La Epoca*, October 26, 1906.
33 "Eshet hayil mi yimtza?" *El Tiempo*, December 22, 1890.
34 "La edukasion de la mujer," *El Tiempo*, September 8, 1892.
35 "La mujer," *El Tiempo*, March 9, 1893.
36 "Despozorios i kazamientos."
37 "Despozorios i kazamientos."
38 "El rolo de una mujer: La Sosiedad Bikur Holim Shel Nashim," *El Novelista*, November 30, 1906.
39 "Novedades diversas," *La Esperanza*, December 17, 1874.
40 Abraham Galante, *Histoire des Juifs de Turquie*, 9 vols. (Istanbul: Editions Isis, 1985), 1: 343–46.
41 Abraham Galante, *Histoire des Juifs d'Anatolie*, vol. 1, *Les Juifs d'Izmir* (Istanbul: Imprimerie Babok, 1937), 90–91.
42 "La sosiedad de benefezensia de las damas israelitas de Pera," *El Tiempo*, March 21, 1894.
43 "Letra al redaktor," *El Tiempo*, March 26, 1896.
44 "Karidad judia," *La Buena Esperanza*, January 6, 1902.
45 "Una tokante seremonia," *El Novelista*, February 20, 1907.
46 "Nuestros uerfanikos," *El Novelista*, March 15, 1907.
47 "Madame Elias Pasha," *El Tiempo*, July 2, 1896.
48 "God's Will," *El Novelista*, March 28, 1907.
49 "God's Will."
50 "Diskorso de Los Guerfanos de Talmud Torah," *La Esperanza*, supp. 39, 1875.
51 "Novedades Lokales," *La Esperanza*, February 17, 1876.
52 "El balo," *La Buena Esperanza*, January 31, 1884.

53 "La segunda soirée Ozer Dalim," *La Buena Esperanza*, March 17, 1887.

54 "Repuesta," *El Comersial*, July 11, 1907.

55 "Balos," *El Tiempo*, March 12, 1896.

56 "El teatro i las ovras de bienfazensia," *El Comersial*, May 2, 1907.

57 "El teatro i las ovras de bienfazensia."

58 "El teatro i las ovras de bienfazensia."

59 "Un poko de todo: nuestras ijas i el teatro," *El Comersial*, May 23, 1907.

60 "Bailar a la franka," *El Meseret*, January 11, 1901.

61 "Bailar a la franka."

62 "El estrenamiento de nuestras eskolas i el balo," *La Buena Esperanza*, January 18, 1883.

63 "El estrenamiento de nuestras eskolas i el balo."

64 "El estrenamiento de nuestras eskolas i el balo."

65 "La soirée nasionala," *La Buena Esperanza*, February 25, 1892.

66 Archives of the Alliance israélite universelle, Turquie LXXVI E 911.08, Arié, December 1, 1899.

67 "Luso i ovardalik," *La Epoca*, April 19, 1905.

68 *Los doveres entre los ermanos*, 17.

69 "Eshet hayil mi yimtza."

70 "Luso i ovardalik."

71 This trend has been documented in other Ottoman groups as well. See Haris Exertzoglou, "The Cultural Uses of Consumption: Negotiating Class, Gender, and Nation in the Ottoman Urban Centers During the 19th Century," *International Journal of Middle East Studies* 35 (2003): 81–83.

72 Donald Quataert, "Clothing Laws, State, and Society in the Ottoman Empire, 1720–1829," *International Journal of Middle Eastern Studies* 29 (1997): 403–25.

73 Charlotte Jirousek, "The Transition to Mass Fashion System Dress in the Later Ottoman Empire," in *Consumption Studies and the History of the Ottoman Empire, 1550–1922*, ed. D. Quataert (Albany: State University of New York Press, 2000), 201–42.

74 "Los vestimientos de las mujeres en Izmirna," *La Buena Esperanza*, September 21, 1883.

75 "Programa," *El Novelista*, October 3, 1906.

76 "El chapeo en el teatro," *El Comersial*, May 2, 1907.

77 "El chapeo en el teatro."

78 "La Eskorsion: Las Ijas i el Lukso," *El Comersial*, May 23, 1907.

79 "La Eskorsion: Las Ijas i el Lukso."

80 "El Lukso," *El Comersial*, May 16, 1907.

81 "Taya kon korselito," *El Tiempo*, March 6, 1893.

82 "En los balos," *El Meseret*, November 22, 1901.

83 "En los balos."

84 "Variadades: La mujer en venten siglo," *El Tiempo*, August 13, 1896.

85 "Para la mujer," *El Novelista*, July 26, 1907.

86 Marion Kaplan, *The Making of the Jewish Middle Class: Women, Family, and Identity in Imperial Germany* (Oxford, UK: Oxford University Press, 1991), 10.

87 The study of Ottoman women in the modern period has only recently attracted the attention of scholars. See, for example, Duygu Köksal and Anasta-
sia Falierou, eds., *A Social History of Late Ottoman Women: New Perspectives*
(Leiden: Brill, 2013); Nazan Maksudyan, ed., *Women and the City, Women in the
City: A Gendered Perspective on Ottoman Urban History* (New York: Berghahn,
2014); and Ebru Boyar and Kate Fleet, eds., *Ottoman Women in Public Space*
(Leiden: Brill, 2016).

88 Ayfer Karakaya-Stump, "Debating Progress in a 'Serious Newspaper for Muslim
Women': The Periodical 'Kadin' of the Post-Revolutionary Salonica, 1908–1909,"
British Journal of Middle Eastern Studies 30, no. 2 (2003): 177–80.

89 Çiğdem Oğuz, "'The Homeland Will Not Be Saved Merely by Chastity': Women's
Agency, Nationalism, and Morality in the Late Ottoman Empire," *Journal of the
Ottoman and Turkish Studies Association* 6, no. 2 (2019): 96–99.

90 Hülya Yıldız, "Rethinking the Political: Ottoman Women as Feminist Subjects,"
Journal of Gender Studies 27, no. 2 (2018): 177–91.

91 Efi Kanner, "Transcultural Encounters: Discourses on Women's Rights and Feminist Interventions in the Ottoman Empire, Greece, and Turkey from the Mid-
Nineteenth Century to the Interwar Period," *Journal of Women's History* 28, no. 3
(2016): 66–92.

92 Paula Hyman, "Gender and the Shaping of Modern Jewish Identities," *Jewish Social Studies* 8, nos. 2/3 (2003): 159.

ORIENTAL, FEMINIST, ORIENTALIST

The New Jewish Woman and
the Alliance Israélite Universelle

FRANCES MALINO

IN AN EMOTIONALLY CHARGED letter written from Tripoli on June 11, 1911, Maïr Lévy pleaded with the Alliance israélite universelle (AIU) to accept his daughter Tamo at one of the three Parisian boarding schools that trained Alliance *institutrices* (primary school teachers). What else can "[my] French-speaking, African-born, Jewish daughter" do, he asked.[1] In his plaintive query, Lévy could hardly capture the "braided identity" of his daughter or of the hundreds of other young women who brought France's civilizing mission—and that of the Jews—to Jewish girls in Muslim lands.

Six young, acculturated French Jews founded the Alliance in 1860. Heeding the rabbinic saying *kol yisrael arevim zeh bazeh* (all Jews are responsible for one another) and wedded to the conviction that French civilization was both normative and universally applicable, they set themselves the task, through the establishment of a network of primary schools, of "regenerating" the Jews of North Africa and the Middle East vocationally, linguistically, morally, and spiritually.[2] The Alliance opened its first schools in Tétouan, a luminously white city nestled against the towering Rif Mountains of northern Morocco. Using satellite imagery, immersive panoramas, and three-dimensional architectural reconstructions now accessible online through Diarna ("our homes" in Judeo-Arabic), we can wander virtually through the narrow, winding streets of Tétouan's *mellah* (Jewish quarter) and its hauntingly beautiful Castilian cemetery.[3]

Rabbi Samuel Nahon, a founding member of Tétouan's local Alliance committee and subsequently its president, provided the primary impetus for establishing Tétouan's school for girls. Until his death in 1900, he also remained the school's protector, counseling its teachers and mediating their disputes with the community. Nahon's role was not unique. Other rabbis, for example, Hazan of Alexandria and Sarfati of Fez, also vociferously supported the education of Jewish women.[4] However, their advocacy was not universally welcomed. The education of boys was tolerated by conservative spirits as a "necessary evil," but "extending it to young girls was seen as a perilous innovation," the *sécrétaire générale* of the Alliance later recalled.[5]

By the eve of World War I, the Alliance boasted a vast network of 183 schools, 85 of which were for "children of the other sex."[6] After inspecting 42 of these schools (19 of them for girls and 23 for boys), the Alliance concluded that the girls' schools were superior to those for the boys.[7] The explanation lay not in the "nefarious" street life of the *mellah*, as the Spanish consul in Tétouan had suggested, but rather in the fact that girls remained in school until they completed their studies and could thus be placed in an appropriate class regardless of age. The Alliance found another reason for the superiority of its girls' schools, though: The teachers were women. As such, they were better able "to win the hearts" of their students.

The Alliance had intended its teachers to be French-born.[8] When few Jews chose to leave Europe for the villages and towns of North Africa and the Middle East, it opted instead to provide the brightest "Orientals" with a normal-school education in Paris.[9] French teaching certificates in hand, they were then to serve the Alliance for at least ten years, just as French-born teachers were required to serve their state. However, in contrast to those in the metropole and unanticipated by the Alliance, these *institutrices*, once they returned to the "Orient," were more independent and even truculent.[10]

In this chapter I focus on the pioneering generation of French-speaking North African- and Ottoman-born *institutrices*.[11] I explore how undertaking the civilizing mission of the Alliance also transformed these Jewish women into agents of French colonialism, simultaneously decentering the empire while structurally underscoring their outsider status as Orientals in Europe and as Orientalists and feminists in North Africa and the Middle East. I also suggest that many of these *institutrices* redefined the feminism they encountered in the metropole to advance their own liberation and that of the young girls they taught. Last, I conclude that the pioneering generation of *institutrices*, indebted to an emerging constellation of new women in fin de siècle France, can be seen collectively as exemplars of the "new Jewish woman."

The period I examine is from 1892 to 1934, the years of the Alliance's greatest influence. These were also the years when Alsatian-born Jacques Bigart was the central figure (*sécrétaire général*) in the functioning and success of the Alliance. Obsessively conscientious and acutely attuned to every minute detail in the lives of "his" teachers, both male and female, Bigart dutifully answered each of their letters, often also correcting their French in blue pencil. The bureaucratization of the Alliance organization after his death robbed the archives of such personal content.

The women teachers of the Alliance confided in Bigart their dreams, frustrations, and the bitter pain of their losses. Male teachers also wrote letters, of course, in keeping with the French epistolary tradition (the Alliance believed that letter writing strengthened loyalty and connectedness among teachers).[12] But the letters from the women—they exist in the thousands, held together with rusting straight pins in the archives of the Alliance—are less self-conscious than those of their male counterparts and more personal, even confessional.[13] Never intended for the public domain (copies were destroyed when the *institutrice* left her post), they reveal worlds both intimate and beyond prescriptive dictates. Without them—they survived removal by the Nazis to Frankfurt during World War II along with the contents of the Alliance library—and the personal dossiers recently returned from Moscow, this inquiry into the lives of individual *institutrices* would not have been possible.[14]

Messody Pariente, or the Making of a Feminist Orientalist *Institutrice*

MESSODY PARIENTE'S LETTERS VIVIDLY capture the trajectory of an Alliance *institutrice* as she became feminist in her professional assertiveness, Orientalist in her assumptions about her native society, and an outsider in both metropole and colony. Born in Tétouan in 1877 to an illustrious Sephardic family (its members included her uncle, Semtob Pariente, a major figure in extending the influence of the Alliance in Turkey), Pariente studied at the local Alliance school before departing for Paris to train as an Alliance teacher. In 1895 she returned to northern Morocco as an *adjointe* (assistant) in the Alliance girls' school in Tangier. Two years later, she became an *adjointe* in Tétouan to Claire Benchimol, her mentor and former teacher. Pariente refused to accept the Alliance's presumption that marriage to Amram Elmaleh (born in Tangier in 1879 and also an Alliance teacher) meant an end to her teaching career. "I assumed that in authorizing me to leave with him for Beirut, you intended to give me a post there as well," she explained in her letter to Paris. "If there is no vacancy, I dare hope, Monsieur le Président, that on my return you will procure me one."[15] Three years later (1906), Pariente became the founding director of the Alliance girl's school in Mazagan (El-Jedida).

In Mazagan Pariente demonstrated the traits that would mark the rest of her life: indomitable strength, keen intelligence, and remarkable courage, all of which her pride and sense of self reinforced. For example, shortly after her arrival in Mazagan, local unrest necessitated that she depart for Tangier. Upon her return, she found the Alliance reluctant to send her an assistant. "You express fear for the security of a young girl who would come all alone to Morocco. She would not be alone in Mazagan. She would be with me, staying with me if it is necessary. If the situation becomes so aggravated as to present serious dangers, we shall not remain and my assistant will leave with us. This lack of tranquility could last for years. Is it because of this that you are gong to suspend our work in Morocco?"[16] Unwilling to compromise her work in Morocco (like many *institutrices* Pariente chaffed at the metropole's ignorance of conditions on the ground), she successfully arranged for two French Catholic sisters from Tangier to join her.

Pariente's confident assertion of independence stood in sharp contrast to her assessment of her African-born coreligionists. In 1909 the Alliance sent her to Fez to reopen the girls' school (it had been closed for two years). Her letters to Paris barely hid, indeed many did not, her dismay at the "retrograde ideas and strange customs" she encountered—a reaction not uncommon among northern Moroccan Sephardic Jews when interacting with their Arabic-speaking coreligionists: "Your schools in Fez," she wrote shortly after arriving, "are too important and the work that we undertake in a milieu as backward as this too interesting for you not to furnish us the means to work actively and fully for the regeneration of this population."[17] While in Fez, Pariente battled child marriage by charging parents higher fees if they enrolled only their sons in school.[18] She developed a warm working relationship with the local rabbis and a successful and demanding Hebrew program for her students. With the *tricoteuses* (knitting machines) she imported—without permission from the Alliance—she established a successful cottage industry among the women of the *mellah*. In April 1912, after the establishment of the French Protectorate and with thousands of rebelling Moroccan soldiers pillaging the *mellah*, Pariente and her husband guided the Jews of Fez to the safety of the sultan's palace. Transforming a local synagogue into a hospital and aided by a Russian Jewish female doctor, they tended to the sick and wounded.

The *école menagerie* (domestic training school) that Pariente subsequently established in Rabat was placed under the auspices of the French Protectorate rather than the Alliance. Before long she accused the French authorities—rightly believing they cared little for indigenous Jews—of modifying her programs, reducing her personnel, augmenting her work, and paying her less than her non-Jewish peers. She lost the position in 1922 after a serious illness required her to take a leave of absence.

Pariente refused to be silenced. Empowered by notions of republican justice, she brought a formal complaint against the recently appointed and increasingly conservative director of public instruction.[19] In it she demanded the 32,000 francs owed her for the remainder of her contract. After a judgment in her favor and bursting with pride at her defiance and success, Pariente wrote the Alliance, "For once justice has proven itself just. I received everything I requested except for the indemnity that was fixed at one year of my salary [Pariente had requested two and a half years]. Mr. Hardy had to pay me 12,000 francs and all the legal expenses. One never anticipated that this little *institutrice* Madame Elmaleh was going to file a complaint against the Directeur de l'Instruction Publique, des Beaux-Arts et des Antiquités. But one sees everything these days . . . *n'est ce pas!*"[20]

Pariente retired to Casablanca in 1924. As a social and political activist, she worked with deaf and blind children, obtained better pension benefits for Alliance retirees, and organized a local chapter of Oeuvre de Sécours aux Enfants. She also home-tutored her nephew Edmond Amran El Maleh (he would become one of Morocco's most beloved writers), when asthma prevented him from attending school.[21] In 1958 Pariente left Casablanca to join her children in Paris. Her last letter to Morocco was dated 1962. Her unwavering commitment to the language and ideals of the republic notwithstanding, she was not at home in France. "You have no idea," she confided to Rabbi Tajouri, Délégué de l'AIU au Maroc, "how much I live in thought and heart for everything that concerns Morocco."[22]

Exile in Paris? A Setting for Education, Outsiderdom, Orientalism, and Feminism

AS THE ODYSSEY OF Pariente suggests, she came to embody many of the ideals, values, and prejudices of the wider French colonial establishment. And yet she was also never fully French. Indeed, from their initial arrival in Paris for their teacher training, Pariente and her pioneering generation of Alliance teachers were made aware that their status was that of outsiders, notwithstanding the fact that the education they were to receive was designed for them to play a role in the French civilizing mission.

Until 1922, when it opened its own normal school for girls in Versailles, the Alliance trained its future *institutrices* at two private schools for girls, the *pensions* (boarding schools) of Madame Isaac (her father was the noted historian Léon Kahn) and Madame Weill-Kahn, and at a vocational and normal school for girls, the École Bischoffsheim, established in 1872 by Louis Bischoffsheim and his wife. Although located in different *quartiers* of the city, the schools often took the students on outings together, visiting Paris museums and gardens and attending synagogue services. The chief rabbi's eloquence, one Bischoffsheim student happily recalled, "elevated their spirit, and comforted their soul."[23]

Although the young girls who attended the *pensions* and Bischoffsheim were all Jewish, there was greater diversity among them in socioeconomic background, nationality, and religious tradition than among the boys studying at the École normale israélite orientale. Prayers at Madame Isaac's, for example, followed German and Portuguese pronunciation, reflecting the Ashkenazic and Sephardic background of the student body.[24] By 1906, however, as French Jewish girls increasingly enrolled in the public schools of France, more than half (44) of those studying at Madame Isaac's were subsidized by the Alliance.[25]

The directors of the three schools regularly informed Bigart of the progress of "his" students as well as their suitability for the profession of Alliance *institutrice*.[26] At times, however, and much to his chagrin, they also challenged Bigart. For example, Maurice Bloch, who had succeeded his father at the École Bischoffsheim, argued for more preparatory time for the *orientales*. He complained that they had two years less time than their Parisian classmates and yet they were expected to take the same written and oral exams at the Hôtel de Ville. "Is it diplomas you wish, or pedagogues?" he asked sarcastically. "Young girls matured by reading and study, or parrots?"[27]

Preparation time notwithstanding, those selected by the Alliance to study in Paris had much in common with their French-born counterparts studying in the normal schools of France.[28] They shared a curriculum that included learning about contagious diseases, proper ventilation, and vaccinations. *Normaliennes* also resided in their schools (often referred to as lay convents), where the indoctrination process was "rigorous" and "familial."[29] Moreover, modern city life and quite often the French language itself could be as foreign to them as to the young girls from North Africa and the Middle East. "I told myself that all this was finished, that I had turned a new page," one French-born *institutrice* recalled. "I was going to know a different world. The little peasant I had once been would be no more."[30]

What set all Alliance-subsidized students apart, however, regardless of place of origin, was that once they arrived in Paris, they were collectively labeled *orientales*, a category associated in the metropole with primitiveness, exoticism, and effeminacy. As late as 1927, for example, when Bischoffsheim's *directrice* bid farewell to the last class of Alliance students, she found it necessary to contrast the "elegance" and "civilization" of the "*orientales*" in the audience with the "lack of hygiene," "gaudy rags," and "guttural cries" of those who had come to Paris a half-century earlier.[31] Although Mesdames Isaac and Weill-Kahn refrained from publicly disparaging their students from the Orient, at these *pensions* as well the *orientales* stood apart. For example, on weekends and during long summer holidays when their European classmates returned to their homes, they remained at school. They remained there as well during World War I, albeit garnering praise for "bravery," "military discipline in the face of bombardments," "patriotism," and their "French hearts."[32]

The Jewish education they had received as young girls also set the Alliance students apart from their European-born classmates, most notably after the secularization of the French public school system in 1882.[33] For example, all sixty-nine girls who took the Alliance exam in 1912 for admission to one of the three normal schools could already read and write Hebrew (these students came from cities across the Mediterranean, including Aleppo, Adrianople, Beirut, Brousse, Cairo, Cavalla, Constantinople, Damascus, Haifa, Jerusalem, Larache, Monastir, Rhodes, Safed, Salonica, Smyrna, Tangier, Tétouan, Tiberias, Tripoli, and Tunis). Some even listed Hebrew as their favorite class.[34] Moreover, once in Paris they would continue their Jewish education. Indeed, they were tested regularly in both Hebrew and Jewish history. "I was truly surprised at the success of the Hebrew teaching," one examiner wrote in 1905. "Many of the students from the boys' school are inferior to some of these girls."[35]

Of course, not all Alliance-subsidized students encountered the same political climate. For example, the Revolution of 1789 loomed large, especially in the press, for Claire Benchimol (a student in Paris from 1885 to 1889) and her younger sister, Alégrina. But for Alégrina, fifteen years Claire's junior, revile of the Revolution's achievements, including its emancipation of the Jews, often took the place of celebration. Witnessing a nation and its Jews rent asunder, even as Alfred Dreyfus received a presidential pardon, marked Alégrina for the rest of her life. Whether directing schools in Tripoli, Mogador, or Casablanca, she never failed to note the virulence of anti-Semitism or the need for solidarity among Jews. That the anti-Semitism she experienced was often introduced and propagated by Europeans was a paradox she also rarely failed to note.

What these young girls felt about their *orientale* designation is difficult to ascertain (one can only imagine their reactions to the pavilions featured at the Paris Expositions Universelles showcasing "exotic" human and material cultures). A heated dispute between two teachers (each used initials that were not her own) that erupted in 1901 on the pages of the Alliance's *Revue des écoles* suggests that their responses were both emotionally charged and varied. Mademoiselle B, an experienced *directrice*, had suggested establishing a separate normal school exclusively for Alliance girls comparable to the École normale israélite orientale for boys. Its mandate would be to ensure that in the future teachers returned to the Orient not only with teaching degrees but also with training more appropriate for their profession. Mademoiselle R.S., a newly graduated *institutrice*, rejected her colleague's "reproaches" as well as her "remedies." She acknowledged that a young assistant might not fully understand the complexities of her profession when she first arrived at her post. But this was only natural, she argued, and hardly a reason to deny young girls from the Orient exposure to European classmates, especially when one observed the nefarious effects on the boys who had no such exposure. "It is in contact with these spiritual and playful children, which the little Parisians often are, that we acquire ease, character, the spirit of doing the right thing, and vivacity. In class, emulation stirs us; we wish, as they, to demonstrate some cleverness, a quick retort."[36] Mademoiselle B. had the final word. Girls are always more at ease than boys at this age, she explained; it had nothing to do with their classmates. Moreover, because candidates were carefully selected through exams and recommendations, the so-called benefits of contact with Parisians belonged to a "truth of yesterday" or merely reflected a "simple prejudice" of today.

Simple prejudice or not, for those in the metropole, the *institutrices* retained the designation *orientales*, although their return to North Africa and the Middle East certainly attenuated its significance. On the other hand, the feminism that these *orientales* appropriated while abroad ensured that they became outsiders in their homelands as well.

Transposing Familial Feminism to the Orient

IN 1900 HASSIBA BENCHIMOL (her ancestors are immortalized in a Delacroix painting) left Tangier for Fez to establish an Alliance school for girls.[37] Her first impressions are notable for their passion and fury—and for her self-identification as a feminist. "From the moment of her birth, a woman in Fez feels the weight of her inferiority. While cries of joy and endless celebration welcome the birth of a son, for a young girl, whose only sin is to have been born, there are only cries of mourning. I must confess that as a woman and a feminist, these practices revolt me."[38]

The Benchimols and their generation of *institutrices* experienced Paris during the early years of *féminisme*, a term broadly used and distinguished at the time by the expressions "familial" (often referred to as equality-in-difference feminism) and "individualist." Individualist feminists repudiated all concepts of women's special nature, espousing instead equality of opportunity for all individuals, regardless of sex, familial considerations, or national concerns.[39] The Alliance supported "familial" feminism, as did many French republicans with whom it had close ties (e.g., the *directeur de l'enseignement primaire* taught pedagogy at its normal school and provided the Alliance leadership with government regulations). Indeed, familial feminism had informed Adolphe Crémieux's call a half-century earlier to educate the Jewish girls of the Orient. They were to become, he explained in 1865, the type of mother that the new generation required.[40] That familial feminism continued to inform the Alliance's mission can be seen in the 1910 address of the president of the Association des anciennes élèves of Salonica: "Our Association must create the ideal woman of tomorrow, a noble and intelligent woman, educated and sweet, the woman a young man dreams will become his lifetime companion."[41]

Familial feminism also appeared in articles that the Alliance reproduced in its *Bulletin des écoles* (a separate journal that appeared monthly between 1910 and 1914).[42] "Let us not appear to advocate changing women into men," one such article warned. "We are no longer at a time when one asks himself if a woman has a soul or if the soul of a woman differs from that of a man. What is incontestable is that neither their destination nor their nature is the same."[43] Another concluded: "The fundamental rule of female education must be equality in difference or difference in equality."[44] The Alliance's decision to reproduce these articles or excerpts from them—at times even adding its own critical commentary and placing them in a special section titled "Questions Féminines"—suggests that it struggled with their themes. Were women the same or different from men, and, if the latter, how could one ensure their equality in the area of education and at the same time preserve their essential differences?[45]

Committed to the view that women's lives should be improved (the Alliance believed, as did many Europeans, that gender relations were an indicator of a society's level of civilization), the Alliance failed to anticipate just how radical even familial feminism might become when transplanted to the Orient. For example, in France mainstream feminists, eschewing confrontation and conflict, subscribed to the role of preserving political and social stability. Indeed, as Linda Clark has demonstrated, most children were led to expect adult lives "comparable to those of their parents."[46] On the other hand, in the Orient equality-in-difference feminism had a more destabilizing effect, for it presumed radical changes not only within the household but also beyond. "Our task," Hassiba Benchimol's cousin Messody Coriat proclaimed when establishing a school in Marrakesh in 1902, "is to make of our young girls women different from their mothers . . . who will no longer be at the mercy of their husbands' whims."[47]

The Alliance also failed to anticipate how the feminism embraced by its female teachers might shape their responses to directives from Paris. For example, in the fall of 1893 Claire Benchimol reported to Paris her fears that the situation in Tétouan would lead to a recurrence of the events of 1860 (the Spanish-Moroccan War), when Berber tribes of the Rif mountainous region had pillaged and burned the Jewish quarter. Once again these Riffians were attacking, but this time, in contrast to 1860, the Spanish were on the defensive. Benchimol wrote that there was talk of war and that wealthy families were preparing to leave the country, fearful that the Arabs would again take vengeance on the Jews. "We the employees of the school, although we are the most courageous of the quarter, are alarmed by the situation. . . . What refuge will we have? Where will we be able to go? And how can we afford to leave?"[48] From his more comfortable position in the 9th arrondissement of Paris, Bigart sought to calm Benchimol's fears, explaining that this was not 1860 and that the European consuls would protect the *mellah*. But he also complained that he would like to see more courage from the *directrice* of the school. Benchimol's response barely hid her anger. She challenged Bigart's presumption of female weakness—"I am braver," she explained, "than many of the men"—and his ignorance of the political realities on the ground, arguing that another European power should replace Spain as the protector of the Jews. In so doing, however, she also gave voice to the delicacy of her own position as both a foreign presence entitled to European protection and a spokesperson for the fears and memories of her fellow Tétouannais.[49]

Historians have argued that feminists in both France and Britain collaborated in strengthening the empire. British feminists, for example, "worked consistently to identify themselves with the national interest and their cause with the future prosperity of the nation-state."[50] The Alliance's espousal of feminism was certainly linked to its political self-representation in imperial France. That of its *institutrices*, on the other hand, was not. On the contrary, even if France loomed large in their endeavor, most *institutrices* sought in feminism personal liberation irrespective of national concerns.

The Oriental New Woman?
The Impact of the Parisian Sartorial Revolution

ASSERTIONS OF AUTONOMY AND agency, despite retribution from Paris and isolation and exile from the communities the *institutrices* served, were often indebted to yet another cultural shift in the metropole: the emerging constellation of new women. Much to the chagrin of those who feared the masculinization of French culture, these new women publicly pursued a career and explicitly challenged, in print and in dress, the prevailing ideals of femininity. Some new women were feminists; others were not. Among them could be found Margarite Durand, founder of the newspaper *La Fronde*; the writers Séverine (Caroline Rémy de Guebhard) and Gyp (Sibylle Riquetti de Mirabeau, whose works, despite their anti-Semitism, could be found on the shelves of the Alliance school library in Tripoli); and the great Jewish actress Sarah Bernhardt. As Mary Louise Roberts has shown, this *femme nouvelle* was often linked in the French cultural imagination with the Jew. Both were seen as cosmopolitan or non-French, posing a "menace" in their fluid identity and thus responsible for fin de siècle decadence.[51]

Attendance at the theater, daily strolls in the Bois de Bologne, and the increasing accessibility of journals and newspapers brought the *orientales* into almost daily contact with the new woman. Even after they returned to the Orient, the magazines they subscribed to, paid for by the Alliance, and the catalogs they received from such Parisian department stores as Le Bon Marché (which mailed 260,000 catalogs internationally in 1894) kept them informed of the radical transformations in French female fashion that reflected and contributed to changing attitudes toward female identity.[52] Whether in Tétouan or Tehran, Alliance *institutrices* were participants in Paris's evolving sartorial scene, as corsets, bustles, and plumes gave way to the masculinized *costume tailleur*.

In the ateliers they established alongside the Alliance schools, the *institutrices* (and the couturiers they hired from Europe) carefully replicated the liberating belle époque styles. "Since the Italian occupation," the *directrice* of the school in Tripoli informed the Alliance on May 5, 1912, "the situation of our young girls is even better. Their work, entirely European, is even more appreciated and thus more remunerative. Some Italian families already living here are surprised to find works of such a marvelous delicacy among *indigènes* they considered savages."[53] Although the teacher in Tripoli sought to attract European or Europeanized customers to her atelier, she made it quite clear that she also introduced the new styles with an eye to remaking the self-image of her students and facilitating their new roles as breadwinners and modern wives.

That a woman would marry and devote herself to husband and family remained the ideal of both the Alliance and French educators. By the time the Alliance issued its *Instructions generals pour les professeurs* in 1903, however, it had also recognized the need to establish apprenticeship programs for the poor.[54] Because girls could not safely apprentice *en ville*, they were placed in ateliers attached to their schools and supervised by the *institutrices*. Claire Benchimol faced numerous problems following the establishment of her dressmaking atelier—it was among the first—including finding and retaining couturiers, competition from other ateliers in the city, and conflict with wealthy members of the Jewish community who complained both that their daughters were not admitted to the atelier and that, because of the atelier, they could no longer find domestic servants. At one point, Bigart even suggested to Benchimol that she might wish to close her dressmaking atelier and use the funds to teach a less crowded trade. "But which?" he asked.[55]

Much to Bigart's delight (he underlined the report with "important" next to it), Tétouan's *atelier de couture* eventually succeeded, furnishing "excellent workers easily placed and earning a daily salary of 2 to 4 pesetas."[56] But the skills and professions appropriate and competitive for young Jewish girls in North Africa, Asia Minor, and the Middle East remained difficult to ascertain. (For example, in contrast to many other cities, Baghdad's workshops easily flourished, with the number of female Jewish apprentices in 1913 surpassing 100.)[57] Understandably, Paris often turned for advice to those on the ground. This dependence on the wisdom and experience of the *directrices*, albeit rarely acknowledged, only reinforced an autonomy never intended by the Alliance.

The sartorial revolution introduced by the *institutrices* left some Europeans—for example, Elkan Nathan Adler, son of the chief rabbi of the British Empire—nostalgic for the traditional dress of the Orient. "I sighed for the artistic draperies which our émigrés had brought over to Tangiers from Castile," he mused after observing a "smart-looking" Paris frock, in primary colors, being made for a Tétouanais Jewish bride.[58] Many years later, on visiting Fez (he made his first trip to Morocco when he was 71), Bigart also fell prey to the nostalgia for the Orient's rich sartorial past. Young girls from the Alliance school, dressed in the carefully preserved gold- and silver-embroidered outfits of their grandmothers, had welcomed him. "This spectacle of past centuries and vanished souls," he wrote, "offered me a feast for the eyes I shall find nowhere else."[59]

Adler and Bigart may have yearned for the eroticized fashions of a Delacroix painting, but the *institutrice* whose Tétouan workshop Adler visited had a profoundly different image in mind: "We have created such a change in the manner of dress," she proudly announced, "that one thinks himself in Europe."[60] If adopting Western dress signified for Jewish males in nineteenth-century Europe profound changes in their lives ("Clothes alone," the Lithuanian *maskil* Mordechai Aaron Günzburg argued, "constitute the wall that divides Jew and Christian and makes them think the other a different species of man"),[61] it was no less a significant marker for Jewish girls living in Muslim lands. Adler visited the Tétouan workshop in 1897. Three years later, at that same atelier, a rebellious student absconded with the dressmaking model (she did not want to pay the tariff for clothes made at the atelier). Because the *grand rabbin* (chief rabbi), whose support the *directrice* could have counted on in her punishment of the student, lay gravely ill, the student's father and uncle were able to exploit the incident to mobilize Tétouan's disaffected community members, many of whom, including themselves, had recently migrated from the south, spoke Judeo-Arabic, and were viewed with disdain and distrust by the Sephardim of the north. Within months the Alliance notified the *directrice* and her husband of their transfer to Tripoli. The *directrice*'s response barely hid her fury. She wrote that, by ignoring her many accomplishments in Tétouan, the Alliance had made of her "an abstraction."[62]

Unexpected Empowerment:
The *Institutrices* Appropriate the *Mission Civilisatrice*

IN HER ANGRY RESPONSE to the Alliance, Tétouan's *directrice* also exposed, intentionally or perhaps not, the paradox of equality-in-difference feminism: Grounded in a republican universalism that excluded women, it coded the "abstract individual" as masculine.[63] A similar paradox could be found in France's *mission civilisatrice* (civilizing mission). It also expressed universalist aspirations yet simultaneously divided the world into "civilization" and "barbarism," thus invoking a "discourse of difference" between French subjects and those who were colonized.[64] The Alliance incorporated this paradox into its initial 1860 *appel* (call) and into Crémieux's 1865 impassioned call to educate the women of the Orient: "Israélites of the Orient and Africa, what have you made of your daily companion, your equal before God? In what subservience do you leave her? What support do you find for the trials of life in this subaltern creature?"[65]

The *mission civilisatrice* permeated the printed instructions and *circulaires* that the Alliance regularly sent to all its teachers. Their task, they were told, was to combat "the bad habits" diffused among "Oriental" populations: "egoism, pride, exaggeration of personal feeling, platitudes, blind respect for force or fortune, and the violence of petty passions."[66] The Alliance also honed the republic's pedagogical mandate to be more appropriate for young girls living in the Orient. They should not, for example, be "encumbered" by the official programs in France concerning the learning of the French language. As for the teaching of history, there was no need for young girls to learn facts; an oral discussion of principles and causes—in short, a moral education—was sufficient.

Despite their origins, few teachers escaped viewing their charges through the Orientalist lens of the Alliance. Frustration, exhaustion, and lack of success would find some even referring to their students as *petites sauvages* (little savages). It is true, the Salonican-born *directrice* wrote from Rhodes in 1905, "that our little girls have defects, but my intention is not to depict them as ugly as the devil. . . . Although sentiment is erased in them as quickly as it is born, I hope to succeed in awakening their sensitivity and educating their heart."[67]

Writing also in 1905 from Tangier, Hassiba Benchimol could not resist comparing her Moroccan students to their more "civilized" counterparts in Tunis. More tellingly, especially given the imperfections of her own French accent—younger family members recall her saying "mon fils le chien" (my son the dog) when referring to her son Lucien—she disparaged the language of her Moroccan coreligionists in contrast to the one she had so proudly adopted as her own: "Tunis is a French city, grand and beautiful; Tangier in contrast appears ugly, even mean. I no longer have the pleasure of hearing French spoken around me, the language I love more than my mother tongue [the Judeo-Spanish spoken in the north of Morocco]. Here one vegetates, is bored, and can't help noticing the inferiority of those around us, both in their ideas and their knowledge."[68]

It is hardly surprising that eradicating Oriental habits in their students—whether manifested in their language, clothing, or moral character—was a goal shared by most of the *institutrices*. The Alliance had set the same goal for them during their four-year stay in Paris. And the Alliance succeeded: *Institutrices* returned to the "Orient" Europeanized in language and dress as well as education.

Not surprisingly, undertaking the *mission civilisatrice* was empowering for the *institutrices*. It gave them status and authority both locally and in communications with the metropole. For example, on July 28, 1912, the *directrice* of the school in Tripoli, reporting to Paris on the Italian occupation and the anti-Semitism that had emerged in its wake, explained why she believed the Jewish community might be transformed "for the better."

> For the first time notables turn their eyes to their unhappy brothers and defend them when the occasion presents itself. These occasions are sadly more frequent, as is always the case on the eve of a conquest. While anti-Semitism may be inevitable, the effect seems to have some advantages for our brothers. The Italianized notables understand that there still exists an abyss between themselves and the conquerors, and

from this deception is born quite naturally a new, solid, serious, and sacred connection between themselves and their previously ignored coreligionists. We have followed this shift with pleasure and already foresee the day when Jewish solidarity in Tripoli will form an important *faisceau* [beam] impervious to attack.[69]

Paradoxically, undertaking the *mission civilisatrice* also inspired the *institutrices* to defy the Alliance, whether by teaching historical facts rather than moral lessons to young girls, importing sewing machines without permission (because the machines took hours to learn, the Alliance wanted girls to learn to sew by hand), or exposing the racial and sexual prejudices of the metropole. Defiance even extended to the teachers' intimate lives. Although required to seek formal approval from the Alliance to marry, they often merely presented Paris with a fait accompli.[70] One *institutrice*, when announcing her decision to wed, merely assured the Alliance that she had not acted lightly and that her husband-to-be would make her as "happy" as she, on her part, would try to make him.[71] Education may have been "a massive canon in the artillery of empire," but in the hands of the *institutrices* it also became a challenge to patriarchal and colonial authority.[72]

Despite their own Orientalism and often against the mandate of the institution they served, the teachers also used their role as educator to forge solidarities of freedom and choice among themselves and their "disinherited sisters."[73] In so doing, they resembled those "imperial feminists" who, while "hewing closely" to Orientalist stereotypes, nevertheless challenged the assumptions justifying the *mission civilisatrice* and its "misogynistic underpinnings."[74] Among these feminists as well, however, Alliance *institutrices* remained structurally apart. "Colonized women, Jews, and foreigners in France could only mimic Frenchness," the radical feminist and ardent supporter of female suffrage Hubertine Auclert proclaimed. "They could become almost French, but not quite."[75]

Conclusion

THE PIONEERING GENERATION OF Alliance *institutrices*, "agents" of the empire, albeit never considered French, had an enduring impact on the young girls of the Orient, especially in the areas of literacy, eradication of child marriage, familiarity with Jewish tradition and history, and the acquisition of skills required to earn a living and maintain a modern home. Diplomats as well as educators, they also negotiated successfully with colonial authorities, with warring factions within the communities they served, and with an international organization that all too often was divorced from the reality on the ground (in this they had much in common with the pioneering generation of French Catholic women missionaries).[76] Moreover, the voluntary associations that they founded, such as the Sociétés des Dames (which in Tétouan provided a complete trousseau and food for new mothers) and the Sociétés scolaires and Associations des anciens élèves, provided public spaces in which former students could express both solidarity and activism. Last, had it not been for their network of family and friends, the Alliance's mission, certainly in relation to the young girls of the Orient, would have failed.

The *institutrices* may have also left footprints beyond their own religious community. One Moroccan Muslim woman explained long after most Jews had emigrated that everything new pertaining to women was due to the Jewish girls who opened the breaches, thus letting women believe change was possible.[77] Albeit hyperbolic, this assertion suggests an even broader legacy of the Alliance and its *institutrices*. That legacy, however, would lay dormant during a protectorate that rejected academic instruction for indigenous Muslim girls. "Overzealous French *maîtresses* [mistresses]," Georges Hardy and Louis-Hubert Lyautey have argued, might "infect their Muslim students with emancipatory ideas."[78]

Neither in their profession nor in their political and social activities do the Alliance *institutrices* resemble the constellation of new women (journalists, actresses, and writers) that emerged in belle époque France. Yet, in the cast of their character, impact of person, and fluidity of identity, Messody Pariente and her generation of Alliance teachers—Oriental, feminist, and Orientalist—were no less unconventional and unsettling in their world than the new woman of the metropole.

Notes

I thank Indiana University Press for granting me permission to modify and republish my essay from *Colonialism and the Jews*, ed. Ethan B. Katz, Lisa Moses Leff, and Maud S. Mandel, published in 2017.

1   Archives of the Alliance israélite universelle (AIU), Paris, Lybie IV.E.22, June 11, 1911.

2   The Alliance also included in its mandate sophisticated lobbying and tireless diplomacy on behalf of all their coreligionists. For a comprehensive overview of the Alliance published in commemoration of its 150th anniversary, see André Kaspi, ed., *Histoire de l'Alliance Universelle de 1860 à nos jours* (Paris: Armand Colin, 2010).

3 Diarna: The Geo-Museum of North African and Middle Eastern Jewish Life has pioneered the synthesis of digital-mapping technology and multimedia documentation. The museum was launched in 2008 as the flagship initiative of Digital Heritage Mapping, a nonprofit organization co-founded by Frances Malino. Diarna's mission is to digitally preserve the Jewish history of the Middle East and North Africa (and beyond) through dedicated research, extensive documentation, and the collection of oral histories. Diarna's work is achieved through a multinational and interfaith collaboration among students, scholars, artists, and tour guides. See Diarna.org.

4 Archives of the AIU, Egypt I.B.7 and Fez II.C.8.04f.

5 Jacques Bigart, Archives of the AIU, Moscou M 05.19, n.d. but ca. 1915.

6 For a complete list of the Alliance's schools for girls, see Georges Weill, *Émancipation et progress: L'Alliance israélite universelle et les droits de l'homme* (Paris: Nadir, 2000), 183–99.

7 *Bulletin de l'Alliance* (1908): 27.

8 Since the Revolution primary school teachers in France have been trained at departmental *écoles normales*. Although from the beginning the Alliance trained all the boys at the Ecole normale israélite orientale, it did not establish a normal school for girls until 1922. Following the Alliance's usage, the term *Oriental* refers to those Jews living in North Africa, the Middle East and the Ottoman Empire.

9 The selection process was both lengthy and rigorous. All had attended local Alliance primary schools. Their teachers recommended them to the Alliance leadership, testifying to their abilities in Hebrew and Jewish history, French history, geography, arithmetic, science, and calligraphy. Their health, intelligence, aptitude, commitment to teaching, character, and morality were scrutinized, and written permission from their parents, along with a medical certificate and their essay exams, were sent to the Alliance's central committee. See Frances Malino, "'Adieu à ma maison': Sephardi Adolescent Identities, 1932–36," *Jewish Social Studies* 15, no. 1 (2008): 131–45.

10 Frances Malino, "Institutrices in the Metropole and the Maghreb: A Comparative Perspective," *Historical Reflections* 32, no. 1 (2006): 129–43.

11 Although I refer throughout this chapter to the teachers as *institutrices*, many would be promoted to the position of *directrice* (headmistress).

12 Martha Hanna, "A Republic of Letters: The Epistolary Tradition in France During World War I," *American Historical Review* 108, no. 5 (2003): 1338–61.

13 These letters have recently been digitized by the Alliance israélite universelle.

14 Fearing the arrival of the Germans in 1940, the Alliance had arranged for politically sensitive documents kept in the office of the *secrétaire générale* to be sent by truck to the free zone. For more than sixty years this material, which had subsequently found its way to the Soviet archives, was presumed lost.

15 Letter dated July 10, 1902, Archives of the AIU, Maroc LXX.E.1041.

16 Letter dated September 22, 1907, Archives of the AIU, Maroc XXIX.E.475.

17 Letter dated June 16, 1909, Archives of the AIU, Maroc XV.E.246.

18 At the beginning of the nineteenth century, child marriage was prevalent among the Jews of Morocco, though not always among the same classes. In Tétouan, for

example, it existed only among the poorer members of the community, whereas in Fez child marriages remained the preserve of the wealthy. From the beginning the *institutrices* refused to admit to their schools students who were married, sadly acknowledging that they were thus denying an education to these young girls. The alternative, however, was to condone the practice.

19 Georges Hardy would subsequently play an important role in Vichy France.

20 Letter dated January 24, 1924, Archives of the AIU, Maroc XXIX.E.475.

21 Born in Safi in 1917, Elmaleh fought for Moroccan independence. In 1965 he left Morocco for Paris and did not return until 1980. He died there at the age of 93, having requested that four languages be transcribed on his tombstone: Arabic, Berber, Hebrew, and French. I learned of Elmaleh's relationship to Messody in an interview with him in January 2005.

22 Archives of the AIU, Delegation Casablanca E89.

23 Letter from Hélène Salzer, cited in A. H. Navon, *Les 70 Ans de l'Ecole Normale Israélite Orientale (1865–1935)* (Paris: Durlacher, 1935), 79.

24 Archives of the AIU, France V.E.Vb. The brochure, featuring a frontispiece depicting an imposing institutional façade with young girls playing in a carefully enclosed "natural" space, advertised the school in English and German. For a discussion of the school and an illustration of the brochure, see Rebecca Rogers, *From the Salon to the Schoolroom* (University Park: Pennsylvania State University Press, 2005). Interestingly, Rogers points out that "the Jewish character of the school only appears in German" (176).

25 Archives of the AIU, France V.E.Vb.

26 For example, the classes at Madame Isaac's were taught by professors from the *écoles* of Paris, except for the teaching of Hebrew, the Bible, and Jewish history, which was supervised by the *grand rabbins* of Paris.

27 Archives of the AIU, France VI.E.6c.

28 Malino, "Institutrices in the Metropole."

29 Anne Quartararo, *Women Teachers and Popular Education in Nineteenth-Century France* (Newark: University of Delaware Press, 1995), 20.

30 Émilie Carles, *Une soupe aux herbes sauvages* (Paris: Livre de Poche, 1981), 103.

31 Letter dated December 20, 1927, Archives of the AIU, France VI.E.6d.

32 Letter dated December 20, 1927, Archives of the AIU, France VI.E.6d.

33 After 1882 the teaching of Hebrew and Jewish history was relegated to private Jewish schools, such as the *écoles consistoriales*. If they chose to, Jewish girls in public schools could attend two classes a week (the boys were expected to attend four) in a supplementary system of religious courses, the *cours d'instruction religieuse*.

34 Archives of the AIU, Moscou 100-3-58.

35 Archives of the AIU, France V.E.5b. The place of Hebrew in the Alliance curriculum for both boys and girls declined as the Alliance became more directly identified with and indebted to France. Shortly before World War II, perhaps in response to the changing political climate in Europe, the Alliance intensified religious instruction in its normal schools in Paris and reintroduced the *brevet d'hébreu* for its teachers. However, interviews with female students who attended Alliance schools after the war and with *institutrices* who taught during this period

suggest that Hebrew in the Alliance curriculum never returned to the place it had occupied in the late nineteenth and twentieth centuries.

36 "Les adjointes de nos écoles," *La Revue des écoles de l'Alliance* (January–March 1902): 262.

37 Eugène Delacroix, *Saâda, the Wife of Abraham Benchimol, and Précidia, One of Their Daughters* (Tangier, 1832), Metropolitan Museum of Art, New York.

38 Letter dated November 25, 1900, Archives of the AIU, France XIV.F25. See also Aron Rodrigue, *Images of Sephardi and Eastern Jewries in Transition: The Teachers of the Alliance Israélite Universelle, 1860–1939* (Seattle: University of Washington Press, 1993), 82–84. For a discussion of *institutrices* in Palestine, see Sylvie Bijaoui, "Un chemin d'émancipation: L'Alliance israélite universelle et les femmes juives de Palestine, 1872–1939," *Archives Juives: Revue d'Histoire des Juifs de France* 46, no. 1 (2013):107–19.

39 Karen Offen, "Depopulation, Nationalism, and Feminism in Fin-de-Siècle France," *American Historical Review* 89, no. 3 (1984): 648–76.

40 "Announcement of the President, Vice-Presidents, Treasurer, and Secretary," *Bulletin de l'Alliance israélite universelle* (March 1, 1865): v.

41 *Association des ancienne éléves de l'Alliance israélite universelle salonique bulletin annuel, 1909–1910*, p. 8. I thank Paris Papamichos Chronakis for sharing this document with me.

42 For example, "What Differentiates the Education of Girls from That of Boys," "The Qualities of a Woman," "For Our Girls," and "Gymnastics for Young Girls."

43 *Bulletin des écoles* (1910): 66.

44 *Bulletin des écoles* (1911): 95.

45 In these questions concerning the nature and education of women, France's Jews may well have heard echoes from emancipation debates of a century earlier, for example, from Berr Isaac Berr's eloquent and impassioned 1791 *Lettre d'un citoyen*, in which, after assuring his coreligionists that with the required civil oath they renounced only their servitude, he outlined the educational, linguistic, and professional changes necessary to transform Jews into respected and worthy Frenchmen. Berr Isaac Berr, *Lettre d'un citoyen member de la ci-devant communauté des juifs de Lorraine, à ses confrères, à l'occasion du droit de citoyen actif rendu aux Juifs par le décret du 28 septembre 1791* (Nancy, 1791).

46 Linda L. Clark, *Schooling the Daughters of Marianne: Textbooks and the Socialization of Girls in Modern French Primary Schools* (Albany: State University of New York Press, 1984), 104.

47 Letter dated August 13, 1902, Archives of the AIU, France XIV.F.25.

48 Letter dated November 9, 1893, Archives of the AIU, Maroc L.XVIII.E.980.

49 Letter dated November 9, 1893, Archives of the AIU, Maroc L.XVIII.E.980.

50 Antoinette Burton, *Burdens of History: British Feminists, Indian Women, and Imperial Culture* (Chapel Hill: University of North Carolina Press, 1994), 5.

51 Mary Louis Roberts, *Disruptive Acts: The New Woman in Fin-de-Siècle France* (Chicago: University of Chicago Press, 2002), 13, 113–15.

52 Michael R. Miller, *The Bon Marché: Bourgeois Culture and the Department Store, 1869–1920* (Princeton, NJ: Princeton University Press, 1981) 35–37.

53 Archives of the AIU, Lybie III.E.20. Were the ateliers replicating the fashionable harem pants? If so, were they also engaged in eroticizing the "Orient."

54 *Instructions generals pour les professeurs* (Paris: Alliance israélite universelle, 1903), 82, 86–87.

55 Archives of the AIU, Série des Registres, RE 100, April 13, 1897.

56 Archives of the AIU, Maroc LXIX.E.1033.

57 For a detailed discussion of vocational training for Jewish girls in Ottoman Iraq, see Jonathan Sciaron, *Educational Oases in the Desert* (Albany: State University of New York Press, 2017).

58 Elkan Nathan Adler, *Jews in Many Lands* (Philadelphia: Jewish Publication Society of America, 1905), 172. Adler visited Tétouan in 1897.

59 Jacques Bigart, *A la Mémoire de Jacques Bigart, 1855–1934*, ed. Sylvain Halff (Paris: Alliance israélite universelle, 1934), 13.

60 Letter dated May 11, 1893, Archives of the AIU, Maroc L.XIV.E.980.

61 Israel Bartal, "Mordechai Aaron Günzburg: A Lithuanian Maskil Faces Modernity," in *Profiles in Diversity: Jews in a Changing Europe, 1750–1870*, ed. Frances Malino and David Jan Sorkin (Detroit: Wayne State University Press 1998), 135. *Maskil* is the term used by contemporaries and historians for individuals who were part of the Haskalah, or the Jewish European Enlightenment movement, based on the older use of *maskil* as an honorific for scholar or enlightened man.

62 Letter dated December 31, 1900, Archives of the AIU, Lybie III.E.21.

63 Joan Wallach Scott, *Only Paradoxes to Offer: French Feminists and the Rights of Man* (Cambridge, MA: Harvard University Press, 1996).

64 For a discussion of universalism and the civilizing mission, see Rachel Nuñez, "Rethinking Universalism: Olympe Audouard, Hubertine Auclert, and the Gender Politics of the Civilizing Mission," *French Politics, Culture, and Society* 30, no. 1 (2012): 24–25.

65 "Announcement of the President," vi.

66 *Instructions générales pour les professeurs*, 27–28.

67 Letter dated December 14, 1905, Archives of the AIU, France X.F.18.

68 Letter dated January 7, 1898, Archives of the AIU, Maroc L.I.E.827. Hassiba's younger relatives, more Europeanized than she, were unable to resist marking her as *orientale*. Interview by the author with Mesdames F.S. and S.H. in Paris on July 9, 2002. However, when Hassiba's daughter Marcelle, then living in Argentina, was asked by her grandson how many languages she knew (she had just addressed his mother in French), she answered, "Many but not one is useful anymore." David Beytelmann to Frances Malino, in an email dated August 20, 2015.

69 Letter dated July 29, 1912, Archives of the AIU, Lybie III.E.20.

70 The Alliance permitted its teachers to marry—as did the French state—and many did so (mostly to each other).

71 Letter dated May 22, 1894, Archives of the AIU, Maroc LXIV.E.980.

72 Bill Ashcroft, Gareth Griffiths, and Helen Tiffin, eds., *The Post-Colonial Studies Reader*, 2nd ed. (London: Routledge, 2006), 371.

73 Letter dated July 28, 1912, Archives of the AIU, Lybie III.E.20.

74 Nuñez, "Rethinking Universalism," 28–29.

75 Quoted in Nuñez, "Rethinking Universalism," 34.

76 Sarah A. Curtis, *Civilizing Habits: Women Missionaries and the Revival of French Empire* (Oxford, UK: Oxford University Press, 2010).

77 Emanuela Trevisan Semi and Hanan Sekkat Hatimi, *Mémoire et representations des juifs au Maroc: les voisins absents de Meknès* (Paris: Publisud, 2011), 77. Aomar Boum in his recent book *Memories of Absence* provides a fascinating perspective on Muslim memories of Jews. He did not include Muslim women in his interviews. Although he was not refused access to these women, Boum believed the presence of their male relatives prevented them from talking freely. Aomar Boum, *Memories of Absence: How Muslims Remember Jews in Morocco* (Stanford, CA: Stanford University Press, 2013), 5.

78 Spencer D. Segalla, *The Moroccan Soul: French Education, Colonial Ethnography, and Muslim Resistance* (Lincoln: University of Nebraska Press, 2009), 110.

GENDER AND THE EXPERIENCES OF ASHKENAZIC JEWISH WOMEN AND GIRLS IN THE UNITED STATES FROM THE MID-NINETEENTH THROUGH THE EARLY TWENTIETH CENTURY

MELISSA R. KLAPPER

IN MARCH 1890 THE NATIONALLY circulated *Jewish Messenger* published a month-long symposium on the topic of the "American Jewess." The editors contacted contributors from all over the country and asked them to comment on the status of American Jewish women. Without exception, they all agreed that girls were the most important members of the American Jewish community. Julia Richman, a New York school principal, explained, "The American Jewess must be regarded as a triangular unit, which requires development in three directions [grounded in the past, active in the present, and looking toward the future] lest the harmony of the whole be destroyed."[1] As Jews, women, and Americans, Jewish girls held the future in their hands. The symposium appeared at a pivotal moment, when the mass migration of millions of Eastern European Jews was transforming the American Jewish community. Yet as the discussion demonstrated, the experiences of Jewish women and girls were already widely understood as a critical part of the American Jewish experience.

Traditional periodization has divided American Jewish history into three rough stages: the "Sephardic" colonial and early national period, the "German" nineteenth century, and the "Eastern European" late nineteenth century through the first decades of the twentieth century. More recently, historians have questioned this periodization; for instance, Ashkenazim far outnumbered Sephardim well before the American Revolution. The alternative model of a long century of continuous Jewish migration from about the 1820s through the 1920s is more useful in approaching the history of Ashkenazic Jewish girls and women in the United States.[2] No one could deny the many differences in

American Jewry between 1820 and 1920. More Jewish women did immigrate from Central and Western Europe during the earlier part of that century, and they were less likely to come alone than their Eastern European counterparts, who primarily came later. The later they arrived, the more their experiences were shaped by the communal structures and organizations—and prejudices—their predecessors had developed. Yet the vast majority struggled with similar concerns: work, family, and the ramifications of the freedoms of American life. All Jewish immigrants to America passed through stages of adjustment and acculturation, and although not all rocketed up the socioeconomic ladder or maintained the same approach to Judaism, there were patterns in their experiences. In this essay the experiences of Ashkenazic Jewish girls and women in the United States from the middle of the nineteenth century through the first decades of the twentieth century are examined. Although the impact of gender on every aspect of their lives is highlighted, the focus is on immigration, family, education, religion, work, and activism.

Immigration, Family, and Education

A PRIMARY MARKER OF similarity for Ashkenazic Jewish women across a century of immigration is the central role that gender played in their lives. The late Paula Hyman incontrovertibly argued that the modern Jewish experience cannot be understood without deploying gender as a central category of analysis.[3] As post-Haskalah Jewish communities sought to integrate themselves into broader modernizing societies, gender provided a path toward that integration, though it looked different depending on the surrounding social and economic arrangements. Broadly speaking, in nineteenth-century Western Europe, the industrialization that led to a separation of home and workplace gave rise to a private domestic world for women that stood in stark contrast to the public world of work and politics inhabited by men. Although this model was achieved only by the middle and upper classes, it was aspirational for the working class as well and structured domestic and family relations, even for those women for whom retreat from economic participation remained impossible.

In Western European Jewish communities, religious practice was often assigned to the interior spaces of synagogue and home, leaving Jewish women largely responsible for keeping the faith in private settings. In Eastern Europe the home also remained a locus of Jewish practice, but because of the much larger weight placed on the traditional religious learning that remained the province of men, Jewish women there could not claim as much status in religious life. Even though only a small group of elite men actually devoted their lives to Torah study, those who did required economically competent wives. The public role these women played in the marketplace achieved social acceptance even among Jewish families that were not structured along the lines of learning men and working women. In both Western and Eastern Europe, then, gender roles shaped the social, religious, and economic ideals of Jewish communities, though in different ways.

When Jews immigrated to the United States, they found that adjusting to their new homes required recalibrating gender roles. Although some Western European Jews arrived with financial resources and were able to preserve a gendered domesticity, most immigrants experienced some period of economic hardship that did not allow women to absent themselves from whatever the family business turned out to be. Whether in larger Jewish communities in cities such as New York, Cincinnati, and San Francisco or in tiny communities all over the interior of the United States along trade routes and shipping lanes, women participated in the family economy throughout the 1800s. However, they also retained their central roles in a domestic Judaism and retreated from paid labor as soon as possible. In this way, gender roles for Jewish women from Central and Western Europe maintained some continuity.

Eastern European Jews had a harder time adjusting to the gender norms of their new environment. In the United States at the turn of the twentieth century, when men's worth was measured by financial success, there was little respect for traditions of male intellectual endeavor supported by female economic activity. In *Bread Givers*, Anzia Yezierska's novel of the immigrant Jewish experience, set around 1910 in New York, the landlady who collects the Smolinsky family's rent heaps scorn on the father, who studies all day while his daughters have jobs. "The dirty do-nothing! Go to work yourself! Stop singing prayers. Then you'll have money for rent," she says, colorfully expressing an attitude shared by many acculturating American Jews that men needed to make a living.[4] The mark of any immigrant family's success was when men could earn enough to support their families and women could retreat into the home. This role reversal from the traditional ideal—even though it was not part of the real-world experiences of most Jewish immigrants—led to difficulties for the Eastern European Jewish community, especially in the urban areas where most of them settled. The immediate effects of the gender reversal were not always felt by recent immigrants, who could rarely afford to keep women or children out of the workplace, but over the long term conflict over proper gender roles became a hallmark of the relationships between husbands and wives, parents and children, and new immigrants and the established Jewish community.[5]

As was the case in most places Jews have lived, Jewish family life in America generally followed the patterns of broader society. From the Civil War through the interwar period, middle-class Jewish families typically consisted of parents and children, though following migration other family members might live under the same roof as well. Whether living in large cities or small towns, Jewish families nearly always sent their children to elementary school and, increasingly, high school. In middle-class Jewish families, girls were more likely to graduate from high school, whereas their brothers sometimes left school early to join the family business. Such families often valued cultural activities, with many girls taking piano lessons and boys and girls alike learning the social dances of their day.[6]

By the late 1800s American Jews ran businesses all over the country, drew on trade networks of Jews in other places, and traveled abroad for both business and pleasure. However, the precarious nature of commercial interests left them vulnerable to the economic swings of the era. Like financial success, acceptance in broader society also did not travel in a straight line, especially because anti-Semitism intensified as more American Jewish families achieved some measure of success. Still, through good works and communal leadership Jewish women could sometimes gain entrance to polite society before their husbands and sons. For example, Hannah Greenebaum Solomon and her sister Henrietta Frank were invited to join the prestigious Chicago Woman's Club in 1876, several years before the men in their family were invited to join the Chicago Civic Club.[7] Middle-class Jewish families generally found equilibrium between social acceptance and religious practice, but those who made it into the upper echelons of economic success found it was more difficult to be accepted by an American elite that sometimes viewed them as parvenus with suspect religious beliefs. The wealthy Seligman family discovered this when they were turned away from the Saratoga Springs Grand Union Hotel in 1877.[8]

In contrast to their middle-class counterparts, working-class Jewish families' lives were structured around economic exigency. Even a fully employed adult man could not usually support a household on his wages, so other members of the family also had to earn. Married Jewish women were somewhat less likely to take jobs outside the home than other immigrant women, but they were still economically active. They took in boarders, disrupting the nuclear family, and did all kinds of home work, from cracking nuts to assembling match boxes. Young children often labored alongside their mothers, recalling a pre-industrial model of the home as a productive economic unit. Although even the poorest Jewish families sent their children to elementary school at a greater rate than any other ethnic group, many Jewish children who longed to attend high school had to work instead. Their individual aspirations were sublimated to the collective needs of their families. Many Jewish parents regretted the need to deprive their children of further education and did what they could to keep them in school, including deferring buying homes. As a result, more Jewish adolescents attended high school than any other ethnic group, but they could not always make it to graduation, and secondary education remained a luxury.[9] Hunter College in New York was heavily Jewish by the 1930s, and by then a substantial percentage of public school teachers in many major American cities were Jewish women, demonstrating the greater education available to a large number of Jewish girls, but there were still plenty of Jewish girls whose labor was needed to support their families.[10] Jewish women's memoirs seethe with resentment and pain around these issues. For example, at the age of 13 Hilda Satt followed her older sister into a Chicago knitting factory. "The few dollars I could earn," she wrote later, "meant more food, which we all needed, and more coal with which the stove insisted on being fed." She, like so many others, saw no choice but to sacrifice her individual desire for education on behalf of the needs of the family.[11]

When Jewish girls entered the workforce, they were generally expected, like their counterparts from other ethnic groups, to turn over their wages to their mothers, the household managers, who then gave them back small amounts with which they could enjoy the amusements of the city, such as ice cream cones, nickelodeons, and beach excursions. In the brave new world of American consumer culture, when Jewish girls earned raises, they sometimes stealthily kept the extra for themselves. Such deception carried its own risks, though, as Mollie, a Jewish girl from Milwaukee, found when she tried to explain how she had paid for a new feathered hat.[12] Plenty of working-class and immigrant Jewish families were warm, close, and supportive, but the constant strain of economic pressure also could adversely affect family relationships. By way of contrast, the more privatized life of middle-class families in America might mean fewer people to turn to in times of crisis, whereas working-class communities, accustomed to trouble, sometimes had a greater sense of communal responsibility for neighbors and friends.

One result of the continuous push and pull over gender roles among immigrants to America was a new interest in Jewish girls. From at least the 1860s, Jewish girls occupied a prominent space in the American Jewish imagination as both keepers of tradition and agents of acculturation. Middle-class Jewish girls, if dressed appropriately and exhibiting the requisite accomplishments, could help establish their families' place in America. Working-class Jewish girls, if contributing adequately to the household coffers and improving themselves through educational and recreational activities, could offer a bridge to social mobility. All Jewish girls had the power to secure greater acceptance and respectability and to create model Jewish homes that exemplified the possibilities of living a life at once fully American and Jewish. It is not surprising that the American Jewish press devoted so much attention to girls during the late 1800s and early 1900s. The *Jewish Messenger* published a series of articles under the heading "The Religious Education of Females" in 1867, long before its 1890 symposium on the "American Jewess," and the *American Israelite* published its own series, starting with the article "Our Girls," in 1875.[13]

On the one hand, Jewish girls could stem the tide of rapid assimilation by embodying both American and Jewish ideals of womanhood. Their future was assumed to be a profoundly traditional one as Jewish mothers. On the other hand, all the forces working against tradition in the freewheeling United States required educational innovation to ensure continuity of Jewish belief and practice. Just as was the case in Europe, commitment to tradition required significant departures from the past. To that end, girls participated in—indeed, were the primary targets of—organized Jewish religious education, from the Sabbath school that Rebecca Gratz founded in Philadelphia in 1838 through the establishment of the first American Bais Yaakov school for Orthodox girls a century later in New York. The two schools were entirely dissimilar. Gratz's weekly school initially used a Protestant catechism with the references to Jesus blacked out, and the full-day Bais Yaakov school was populated by Yiddish-speaking teachers fending off deviance from traditional religious observance. However, in offering formal religious education to Jewish girls, both participated in a consequential revolution of knowledge and responsibility for Jewish girls and women.[14]

Jewish girls themselves felt the weight of these communal expectations. In their diaries, letters, and memoirs, they wrote of their pleasure in the responsibilities placed on them but also their anxieties about achieving what could sometimes be seen as contradictory goals of modernization and keeping tradition alive. As an adolescent in 1896 Seattle, Bella Weretnikow lamented in her diary, "O! That problem of what I am going to be, how it does haunt me. The fear of choosing the wrong thing is continually present."[15] These anxieties intensified as broader ideas about women and gender shifted at the turn of the twentieth century. Girls and women had more opportunities for education and work than ever but were still tasked with preserving domesticity and traditional sexual mores. They were also still expected to marry Jewish men, something most of them did until well after World War II.[16]

For many Jewish women and girls, what mattered most was not necessarily where in Europe they came from but how long they or their families had been in the United States. The gradual process of acculturation in an American society that was itself evolving in terms of women's roles and rights affected all

Jews, regardless of their national origins. Most Jewish families in America—whether they came in 1850 or 1910, whether they came to pursue business opportunities or flee pogroms, whether they were traditionally observant or already secularized—harbored similar hopes of building a better future for themselves. Such aspirations were most likely to be achieved by their children and, in the Jewish case, often were. Although not all Jews in America rose from peddlers to department store magnates, many saw their children living more settled and comfortable lives. For girls that might mean more education, greater freedom in choice of marriage partners, more economic security and independence, and more societal acceptance.

It is important not to disregard the poverty, class tensions, family destabilization, and anti-Semitism that immigration carried in its wake. Class, not gender alone, always determined and sometimes limited Jewish girls' aspirations and achievements. Jewish men deserted their wives and families in numbers that attracted negative attention in both the Jewish and mainstream press.[17] Jewish communities across the United States found it necessary to establish institutions for children who were not only orphaned but might also come from families too impoverished to care for them.[18] As in most poor immigrant communities, Jewish women confronted domestic violence and sexual harassment in the workplace.[19] When 17-year-old Pearl Adler was raped by her factory foreman during World War I, she had no family to turn to because she had immigrated alone.[20] Immigration displaced huge numbers of Jews and brought great hardship to many. However, going to the United States generally turned out to be a good decision in the long run. The fortuitous combination of greater opportunity for both women and Jews overall had a positive impact on Ashkenazic American Jewish women.

Religious Lives

BECAUSE THE UNITED STATES was such a large and varied country, both physical and social geography affected Ashkenazic Jewish women's religious lives during the nineteenth and early twentieth centuries. Prairie pioneer Rachel Calof's life of physical hardship and religious deprivation in 1890s North Dakota bore little resemblance to National Council of Jewish Women (NCJW) founder Hannah Greenebaum Solomon's privileged life of social acceptance and affiliation with Reform Judaism at the same time in Chicago.[21] Jewish women who settled in small towns either longed for greater religious practice—such as access to kosher meat or *mikvehs*—or, sometimes, abandoned religious observance as impracticable and unnecessary.[22]

Women in urban Jewish centers faced less stark choices about what to retain or leave behind, although their decisions were also shaped by institutions and denominations in addition to free will.

Like all American Jews, women were affected by the growth of denominationalism.[23] Religious reform had been under way in the United States since the 1820s, but developments in Central and Western Europe led to the flowering of the American Reform movement from the mid-nineteenth century on. Many American Jews favored shortened liturgy, vernacular sermons, choirs, decorous services, and professional clergy. The move to raise women's status in the synagogue through mixed seating was widely adopted, though family pews hardly equaled religious egalitarianism. Few American Jews concerned themselves much about the ideological changes proposed by the leaders of the Reform movement at home or abroad, though many supported the founding of Hebrew Union College in 1875 as an important step toward producing American-trained rabbis. They pointed to sumptuously designed and decorated synagogues as symbols of the overall status of the American Jewish community. These synagogues, built from the start without separate women's sections, attracted more women to services, a trend noted with hearty approval by rabbis and the American Jewish press, though with concomitant consternation over the gradual disappearance of men from the pews. For women who no longer kept kosher or observed Shabbat in traditional ways, their synagogues as much as their homes became central. They joined ladies auxiliaries and sisterhoods, taught Sabbath school, took their children to services, organized charitable campaigns, and generally made Jewish activity part of women's expanding access to public life that characterized the turn of the century.[24]

More traditionally minded women did not necessarily object to a greater public role for themselves in Jewish life, but they looked askance at such innovations as mixed seating and choirs and asked pointed questions about the ability of ignorant, though well-intentioned ladies to offer meaningful religious education to Jewish children in weekly Sabbath schools. These were the women, many of them Eastern European immigrants, who did without meat when there was no ritual slaughterer available, insisted on observing Shabbat as a genuine day of rest, and preferred a Hebrew synagogue service even though they could not fully understand it. They were concerned about sustaining Jewish values and practices in an open American environment whose very freedom seemed inimical to tradition. Some of these women joined in what Jonathan Sarna has termed "The Jewish Awakening," a flowering of Jewish institutions and organizations at the turn of the century. The Jewish Theological Seminary, the American Jewish Historical Society, and the Jewish Publication Society, among others, sought to find a balance between tradition and modernity.[25] Even an organization such as the NCJW, founded in 1893 by a group of women mostly, though not exclusively, affiliated with Reform Judaism, started with the goal of reorienting American Jewish women's lives around religion and increasing their knowledge of Judaism.

Education seemed key to the projects of American Jews across the spectrum of religious observance and belief. Whereas for centuries Jewish education had been the preserve of the male intellectual elite, there was growing concern about religious schooling as a necessity in an American environment that rewarded acculturation and in which all religious affiliation was voluntary. Reform Jews urged their proliferating congregations to raise the standards for both teachers and students at their Sabbath schools. The Jewish Theological Seminary, first founded in 1886 to preserve historical Judaism, established the Teachers Institute in 1911, soon after reorganizing under the leadership of Solomon Schechter. Both male and female students at the Teachers Institute undertook rigorous training, often simultaneously studying with John Dewey at Columbia University, and had a huge impact on professionalizing American Jewish education. A number of these men and women helped develop Talmud Torah schools as an alternative model to Sabbath schools. Talmud Torahs met several afternoons a week and on weekends and prescribed a more intensive curriculum than had previously been available to American Jewish children. Some of the women who played a major role in developing Jewish education in America were highly educated rabbis' wives, such as Rebecca Aaronson Brickner and Tamar de Sola Pool.[26]

As the Conservative movement developed into a full-fledged denomination that especially appealed to the children of immigrants who sought middle ground between Reform and Orthodox Judaism, religious education became key to the maintenance of a balanced American Jewish identity. The most traditionally observant Jews were slower to include girls in their educational institutions, but by the 1930s Orthodox Judaism in America was strong enough to establish both coeducational and single-sex day schools that served children in immersive religious environments. With the exception of the rapidly disappearing heder, a school for Jewish boys with a traditional curriculum and often an untrained teacher, all these types of religious schools employed women as Jewish educators. Perhaps unsurprisingly, the career path of religious education and the knowledge necessary to achieve success in that career encouraged a few Jewish women to seek ordination as rabbis, though they did not succeed for decades.[27] Even though Jewish education never reached most American Jewish children, especially outside urban communities, and met with decidedly mixed results, it still provided new opportunities for Jewish girls and women to become knowledgeable about their religious heritage.[28]

Work and Activism

REGARDLESS OF THEIR RELIGIOUS practices, many women took for granted that Jewish values of community and *tzedakah* (charity or social justice) provided ample justification for activity in the public sphere. This was true even for women who otherwise abandoned Jewish affiliation. Their experiences of work offered one major arena for their efforts to improve not only their own lives but also the world around them. Gendered domestic ideals notwithstanding, Jewish women performed all kinds of work in America. They were artificial flower makers, shopkeepers, midwives, milliners, and clerks. They were nutcrackers, teachers, seamstresses, social workers, lecturers, and shopgirls. They were cigar rollers, inventors, actresses, farmers, nurses, lawyers, and doctors. They worked for themselves, for their families, in communal institutions, for small businesses, and for large companies. They worked at home, in stores, at schools, on farms, in small sweatshops, and in large factories. Although some Ashkenazic American Jewish women wanted only for their families to achieve enough economic success that their paid labor would no longer be necessary, others saw in the world of work the promise of expanded autonomy and opportunity. As new professions requiring an education, such as librarianship and social work, opened to women at the turn of the century, American-born Jewish girls flocked to them, often choosing to work in their own communities.[29] Jewish communal institutions offered girls classes in specific skills, such as shorthand and typing, that could increase their desirability on the job market even if they could not afford to attend professional schools.[30]

Garment industry work occupied many Eastern European Jewish women both before and after migration. As late as 1934, ten years after the United States virtually shut down immigration from Eastern Europe, more than 70% of the members of the International Ladies Garment Workers Union (ILGWU) were Jewish.[31] Virtually every woman in the Western world learned how to sew, and Jewish women were no exception. Whether coming from remote shtetls or cities such as Odessa and Vilna, Jewish women arrived in America knowing how to ply a needle and/or operate textile machinery. Along with Italian and other immigrant women, they became the foundation of the garment industry in New York, Chicago, and Los Angeles. In so doing, they also became the mainstay of women's labor activism in the United States.

Women's labor activism had historically been difficult to spark. Because so many women planned to stop factory work after they married or when their families gained a modicum of financial stability, they were sometimes less motivated to improve conditions for future workers or for themselves. Jewish women, however, seemed more invested in improving work conditions even when they hoped their employment would be temporary. As Alice Kessler-Harris, Annalise Orleck, Susan Glenn, and others have shown, Jewish women workers became the backbone of both the ILGWU and the Amalgamated Clothing Workers of America, despite the fierce resistance of both employers and their male co-workers.[32] They pioneered pushing not only for better shop conditions but also for union-sponsored social and cultural programming to enhance workers' lives. A slew of Jewish women, some immigrant and some American-born, became the most successful female labor organizers in the country. Rose Schneiderman, Pauline Newman, Rose Pesotta, Fannia Cohen, and others worked with both Jewish men, such as Sidney Hillman, and non-Jewish women, such as Leonora O'Reilly. Through the Women's Trade Union League (WTUL) they also allied with middle-class women who supported their cause.[33] At times the sheer number of Jewish women in the garment industry led to an explicitly Jewish solidarity among the workers, who conducted much of their union business in Yiddish, relied on the Yiddish press for support, and during the 1909 Uprising of the 20,000 followed Clara Lemlich Shevelson's lead in swearing a version of an old Jewish oath, "If I turn traitor to the cause I now pledge, may this hand wither from the arm I now raise."[34] But when tragedy struck, as in the Triangle Shirtwaist Factory Fire of 1911, Schneiderman was not afraid to rain curses down on the heads of the Jewish factory owners, reminding her audience at a memorial meeting, "I would be a traitor to those poor burned bodies if I were to come here to talk good fellowship."[35] She knew there were limits to Jewish solidarity and that Jewish workers suffering from intolerable labor conditions sometimes worked for Jewish employers.

Although not every Jewish woman worker joined a union, both proponents and opponents of organized labor took for granted Jewish workers' support, further underscoring a climate of activism that permeated most large urban Jewish communities during the early twentieth century. The preponderance of Jewish women in certain industrial sectors, whether the garment industry in New York and Chicago or the cigar industry in Florida, led to a wider shared culture among American Jewish women, especially the young, who were most likely to work in factories. They worked together on shop floors, learned together in night school classrooms, agitated together at mass meetings, and played together at dance halls and theaters. Their significant participation in labor activism, whether as workers or as allies who belonged to groups such as the WTUL, also helped American Jewish women make common cause with each other on a number of other issues.

One of the causes that crossed class lines for Jewish women was suffrage.[36] Working-class Jewish women such as Newman and Schneiderman felt that enfranchisement would enable them to demand labor reform and policies to address the needs of women whose economic contributions were vital to their families and to themselves. Along with their WTUL allies, they pointed to the progressive social reforms enacted in individual states that had been gradually giving women the vote. The Yiddish press that served many immigrant Jewish communities supported suffrage for these reasons, running frequent stories about the campaigns for women's rights in America and worldwide. Even the more conservative religious Jewish press generally supported suffrage, citing biblical examples of politically active figures such as Deborah and Esther. The greater acceptance of a public role for women in the immigrant Jewish community's ideas about gender also facilitated widespread acceptance. So did the socialism that many Eastern European immigrant Jews professed. Despite expressing some concern about the suffrage movement's priorities, the international socialist movement still considered enfranchisement a path to greater political power for the proletariat. The impact of working-class Jewish women on the suffrage movement was evident in the high percentage of Jewish men who supported the suffrage referendum in New York both in 1915, when it did not pass, and in 1917, when it did.[37] Young Jewish women such as Berta and Eva Ratner, who canvassed for the referendum and distributed suffrage literature at street meetings, celebrated the victory and, as Berta wrote to a friend, rejoiced that "we learned so much of existing conditions that were outside our interests" before.[38]

Middle- and upper-class Jewish women also played significant roles in the American suffrage movement.[39] Maud Nathan was probably the most famous Jewish suffragist not just in the United States but also in the international woman's movement, where she was recognized for her multilingualism and served as an interpreter at several International Woman Suffrage Alliance meetings. For Nathan and many other middle-class members of synagogue sisterhoods and such organizations as the NCJW and Hadassah, women had been proving their public worth for decades, engaging in every conceivable political activity short of voting.[40] They ran large organizations that provided a huge range of community services, from education to public health and beyond, and it was ludicrous that they should continue to be disenfranchised. Nathan was part of a large group of financially comfortable Jewish women who genuinely believed that working women needed the greater political power and protection the vote would afford them. Middle- and upper-class women who did not work outside the home also justified suffrage on the basis of motherhood, adopting a maternalist rhetoric with a particular appeal to Jewish women whose cultural and religious traditions placed great emphasis on the importance of mothers. This line of reasoning was adopted by the English-language press that targeted the established American Jewish community, and, like the Yiddish press, endorsed suffrage.

Anti-Semitism became a significant challenge for American Jews who supported suffrage. From at least the 1860s, when pioneering women's rights activist Ernestine Rose had felt compelled to defend Jewish interests even after largely disassociating herself from the Jewish community, anti-Semitism had regularly reared up in the women's movement.[41] The majority of several generations of American suffragists were white Protestant native-born women, and some had no compunction about exhibiting racist, xenophobic, and anti-Semitic prejudices. When renowned suffrage leader Elizabeth Cady Stanton presided over the publication of the *Woman's Bible* in 1895, she welcomed the inclusion of numerous anti-Semitic sections and disdainfully turned away a delegation of protesting Jewish women.[42] Alice Paul, head of the militant National Woman's Party, made no attempt to disguise her distaste for Jews, even though some of her most trusted lieutenants, such as Anita Pollitzer, were Jewish.[43] The international women's movement also encompassed anti-Semitism, as Maud Nathan found to her dismay at the 1920 International Woman Suffrage Alliance meeting in Geneva that was supposed to serve as a postwar space of reconciliation. Blaming "Jewish profiteers" for the Great War, it seemed, was something about which British, French, and German activist women could agree.[44]

The troubling persistence of anti-Semitism helps explain why American Jewish women supported enfranchisement but rarely rose to positions of leadership in the suffrage movement as they did in other women's movements of the early twentieth century. They also tended to support suffrage as individuals rather than through Jewish women's organizations. Still, whether or not Jewish women's organizations officially supported suffrage, Jewish women certainly did. They also lent a great deal of energy to two other major feminist movements during the late nineteenth and early twentieth centuries: birth control and peace.

Jewish women's fertility rates began to drop dramatically in all parts of Europe during the nineteenth century. The evidence suggests that they took advantage of whatever contraceptive practices were available.[45] The invention of the diaphragm, which put control of contraception into women's hands, proved a turning point. Starting in the 1870s, birth control clinics in many countries dispensed diaphragms, typically only to married women, though the burden of proof was low. Although poorer Jewish women and Jewish women from Eastern Europe continued to bear more children than their middle-class and Western European counterparts, by the time any of these groups arrived in the United States, Jewish couples had already begun to exert whatever control they could over their fertility.

In the United States the birth control movement followed these European patterns.[46] Margaret Sanger established the first American birth control clinic in 1916 in Brownsville, an immigrant Brooklyn neighborhood. The clinic flyers advertised it in English, Italian, and Yiddish, and immigrant women lined up for blocks, baby carriages in tow. Most wanted to have fewer children, not none at all. Sanger and her sister, both nurses, staffed the clinic along with Fania Mindell, a Yiddish-speaking social worker. The clinic served only a few hundred people before being shut down by police, but it galvanized a significant number of Jewish women into action.[47] For example, Rose Halpern, a mother of six, was one of the first clients and became a steadfast supporter of the birth control movement. She and other immigrant Jewish women dismissed out of hand the accusations of anti-Semitism that had been levied against Sanger. No one forced them to visit clinics or use diaphragms, and they almost universally saw these allegations as baseless propaganda.[48] Working-class Jewish women were desperate for the information and contraceptive devices they would otherwise have no access to, unlike their middle-class counterparts, who could often quietly secure contraception through their personal physicians. Opinion was divided within the American Jewish community, but the fact that Halakhah allowed for contraception under a variety of circumstances helped lead to support for a movement that provided something American Jews wanted: the means to plan their families.

In addition to being early adopters of contraception, American Jewish women also participated in the movement as activists and doctors. Middle-class American Jewish women's organizations, later dismissed by historians as staid and conservative, founded, funded, and staffed illegal birth control clinics in places as far-flung as St. Paul, Minnesota, and Louisville, Kentucky, taking radical political action and placing themselves in legal jeopardy. The clinic boards, which typically included local rabbis, encouraged middle-class Jewish women to meet their own contraceptive needs at the clinics and provided services for poorer women with less access to birth control. A number of Jewish women served as editors of *Birth Control Review* and held high-level positions in birth control movement organizations. A disproportionate number of birth control clinic doctors were Jewish women, both because they supported the movement and because anti-Semitism and discrimination against them as women limited their professional opportunities. One of the most prominent was Hannah Mayer Stone, medical director of the flagship Birth Control Clinical Research Bureau in New York, whose work triggered the federal court case that ultimately removed birth control from the legal category of obscenity in 1936. Stone, along with other Jewish women doctors, such as Nadine Kavinoky and Bessie Moses, earned an international reputation, making presentations at medical conferences based on their clinical work.

Whereas anti-Semitism played only a small role in the birth control movement, it had a bigger impact on the peace movement, which was another focus of American Jewish women's activism during the early twentieth century.[49] World peace became a popular cause after the first Hague Peace Conference of 1899. The NCJW added a Peace and Arbitration Committee in 1908, and peace became one of the primary activities of the National Federation of Temple Sisterhoods soon after its 1913 founding. Following World War I, a women's peace movement developed worldwide, with Jewish women playing a major part across the globe. The NCJW became known as one of the most significant participants in the American women's peace movement, and Jewish women also served in leadership roles in the Women's Peace Union and the War Resisters League. Women such as Fanny Brin, a national NCJW president, and Estelle Sternberger, executive director of World Peaceways, kept the cause of peace at the forefront of American Jewish communal life. Not all elements of the American Jewish community supported peace—for instance, some Jewish leftists initially applauded the Russian Revolution as the necessarily violent precursor to overthrowing capitalism, and there was considerable debate within the various denominations' rabbinic associations—but by the 1920s international peace activists noted American Jewish women's support for the cause. Gertrud Baer, international secretary of the Women's International League for Peace and Freedom, commented during a 1924 American lecture tour that "always whenever approached have the Jewish groups willingly and enthusiastically shown their sympathy."[50]

However, once Hitler came to power and immediately targeted Jews, American Jewish women in the peace movement faced a dilemma. As though conditions in Germany—and then increasingly throughout Europe—were not bad enough, Jewish women activists were also dismayed to find that few of their fellow peace workers seemed willing to acknowledge this new threat. Pacifists everywhere deplored Hitler, but they were reluctant to abandon the progress toward world peace they believed had been made during the 1920s to speak out on behalf of Jews. As conditions worsened during the 1930s, reluctance to condemn Nazi actions seemed to many Jewish women peace activists to shade into anti-Semitism, leading most of them to make the agonizing decision to leave the movement.[51] As pacifist Rebecca Hourwich Reyher put it, "I must take my side where the yellow star is. . . . When Jews were being persecuted it was certainly the obligation of anybody who was remotely connected with being a Jew, whether they were religious or not to do something about it."[52] Jewish identity ultimately trumped the maternalist politics that had led so many American Jewish women to peace work.

Given the persistent anti-Semitism in the women's movements of the early twentieth century, it is not surprising that many American Jewish women chose instead to devote their public activity to Jewish causes. They rioted over the price of kosher meat and created Jewish women's free loan associations.[53] They became involved with all the major Jewish causes of the day. As previously discussed, one of these was the labor movement, which was not officially Jewish but might as well have been, given the preponderance of Jewish women organizers, the influence of the Yiddish labor press, and the sheer number of Jewish workers in such major economic sectors as the garment industry. Another Jewish cause was Zionism.[54] Zionism was controversial in the United States. The 1885 Pittsburgh Platform of the Reform movement expressly abjured it, and many of the prayer books and liturgies printed in the United States removed references to a return to Zion. This rejection of centuries of tradition shocked some Eastern European Jewish immigrants. Many of those who had fled persecution sympathized with the idea of a homeland that would stand as a surety and beacon of safety for Jews worldwide. When the Federation of American Zionists was founded in 1897, the group included a mixture of people from the established American Jewish community and the immigrant Jewish community. One of the early members was Henrietta Szold, already a prominent communal figure. Following a trip to Palestine in 1909, Szold returned to the United States with the conviction that Jewish women had an important part to play in Zionism. The Zionist women's study circle she began in 1912 swiftly developed into Hadassah, which became the largest women's Zionist organization in the world and was for a long time one of the biggest women's organizations of any kind.[55]

Unlike the NCJW, which focused largely on domestic issues, Hadassah during its early decades concentrated its activities almost entirely in prestate Israel. Hadassah sent nurses Rachel Landy and Rose Kaplan to Palestine in 1913 and then supported a medical unit there during World War I. The organization became so identified with health care and education that when the Jewish Agency organized a kind of quasi-government under British Mandate rule, Hadassah had responsibility for both. Szold and a number of other American Zionist women either made aliyah or spent extended periods of time in Palestine to oversee these functions.[56] For many Ashkenazic American Jewish women, especially the daughters and granddaughters of immigrants who retained attachments to traditional expressions of Judaism, participating in Hadassah activities became a fundamental expression of Jewish identity. As the socioeconomic status of American Jewry rose, Hadassah sometimes was caricaturized for decorous luncheons and placid fashion shows, but the organization raised millions upon millions of dollars and kept Zionism and Israel at the forefront of American Jewish life.[57]

Some American Jewish women engaged in activism as a result of their Jewish ethnic, cultural, or religious identities, but others abandoned affiliation altogether. For either political or pragmatic reasons, many of the Jewish women attracted to radicalism adopted a secular stance instead, rejecting any of the traditions that had limited their aspirations and ideological commitments. Communism, socialism, anarchism, or a more generalized leftist politics replaced Jewishness as an identity category. The poor working conditions of most immigrants and the push to expand women's rights propelled Jewish women toward secular social justice work. Leftist political activity could take place outside the bounds of Jewish community, but even the most radical women, such as anarchist Emma Goldman, could not help but notice that even in their secular politics there was a preponderance of Jews. A commitment to social justice does seem to have provided a common denominator between Jewish activism and the involvement of Jews in avowedly secular leftist politics.[58]

Whatever their economic means, political affiliations, religious preferences, or cultural sensibilities, Ashkenazic American Jewish women consistently made space in their lives to work for the change they wanted to see in the world. During the nineteenth century, ladies auxiliaries and sewing circles fed the hungry and clothed the poor while also offering their members a Jewish space to socialize and study. Synagogue sisterhoods began with projects to beautify their congregational homes and help the elderly but then developed through the National Federation of Temple Sisterhoods, the Women's League of Conservative Judaism, and the Orthodox Union's Women's Branch into denominational powerhouses, running campaigns to help the Jewish blind, building dormitories for rabbinic students, and promoting observance of Shabbat and family purity laws. The NCJW, along with other women's clubs at the turn of the century, added social service and political engagement to its original religious and educational mission. Jewish women were major players in leftist politics, joining the socialist and communist parties with alacrity and working toward class equality. The largest Jewish groups operated on an international scale; for example, the NCJW, Hadassah, and the Women's Auxiliary of the Workmen's Circle set aside their considerable differences to join in reconstruction work among devastated European Jewish communities after World War I.[59] By the 1930s, American Jewish women of all backgrounds and affiliations could take pride in a rich legacy of activism that would continue to be part of American Jewish women's experiences.

Conclusion

IN THE YEARS SINCE the first and second editions of *Jewish Women in Historical Perspective*, American Jewish history has expanded past an older focus on men, communal leaders, and restrictive definitions of religion. This is due in no small part to the pioneering scholars who insisted that women's voices be heard, that they mattered, and that they had the power to transform any understanding of the American Jewish experience. Much more is known today about many aspects of American Jewish women's lives, but there is still more to learn about topics such as sexuality, material culture, religious education, traditional observance, secularization, and artistic expression. There is a disturbing lack of research on Sephardic Jewish women in America, a huge oversight given the tens of thousands of Ottoman Empire Jews who came to the United States during the period of mass migration and created communities in New York, Seattle, Los Angeles, and elsewhere.[60] In addition, gender history is never only about women, and an analysis from the perspective of masculinity has the potential to redefine American Jewish history yet again. American Jewish women have been and continue to be a diverse lot, encompassing a variety of religious affiliations, class statuses, national origins, cultural and ethnic heritages, racial identities, political persuasions, and geographic locations. For all their important differences, however, the centrality of gender to their experiences has been a constant across the centuries.

Notes

1 *Jewish Messenger*, March 14, 1890.
2 For a realignment of the periodization, see Hasia R. Diner, *The Jews of the United States, 1654 to 2000* (Berkeley: University of California Press, 2004). Surveys of American Jewish women's history include Joyce Antler, *The Journey Home: How Jewish Women Shaped Modern America* (New York: Schocken, 1997); Hasia R. Diner and Beryl Lieff Benderly, *Her Works Praise Her: A History of Jewish Women from Colonial Times to the Present* (New York: Basic, 2002); and Pamela S. Nadell, *America's Jewish Women: A History from Colonial Times to Today* (New York: Norton, 2019).

3 Paula E. Hyman, *Gender and Assimilation in Modern Jewish History* (Seattle: University of Washington Press, 1995).

4 Anzia Yezierska, *Bread Givers* (New York: Persea Books, 1999) (originally published in 1925).

5 Riv-Ellen Prell, *Fighting to Become American: Jews, Gender, and the Anxiety of Assimilation* (Boston: Beacon, 1999).

6 Melissa R. Klapper, *Jewish Girls Coming of Age in America, 1860–1920* (New York: New York University Press, 2005), chaps. 2 and 5.

7 Faith Rogow, *Gone to Another Meeting: The National Council of Jewish Women, 1893–1993* (Tuscaloosa: University of Alabama Press, 1993), 10.

8 Robert Michael, *A Concise History of American Antisemitism* (Lanham, MD: Rowman & Littlefield, 2005), 92.

9 Klapper, *Jewish Girls*, 96–102.

10 Ruth Jacknow Markowitz, *My Daughter, The Teacher: Jewish Teachers in the New York City Schools* (New Brunswick, NJ: Rutgers University Press, 1993).

11 Hilda Satt Polacheck, *I Came a Stranger: The Story of a Hull House Girl* (Urbana: University of Illinois Press, 1989), 55.

12 Melissa R. Klapper, *Small Strangers: The Experiences of Immigrant Children in the United States, 1880–1925* (Chicago: Ivan R. Dee, 2007), 120.

13 See "The Religious Education of Our Females" and subsequent articles in the *Jewish Messenger*, June 1867; "Our Girls" and subsequent articles in the *American Israelite*, January and February 1875; and Klapper, *Jewish Girls*, ch. 4.

14 Dianne Ashton, *Rebecca Gratz: Women and Judaism in Antebellum America* (Detroit: Wayne State University Press, 1997); Leslie M. Ginsparg, "Defining Bais Yaakov: A Historical Study of Yeshivish Orthodox Girls' High School Education in America, 1963–1984," PhD diss., New York University, 2009.

15 Bella Weretnikow diary, June 12, 1896, Bella Weretnikow Rosenbaum Papers, MS 179, American Jewish Archives.

16 Diner and Benderly, *Her Works Praise Her*, 201–2.

17 Anna R. Igra, *Wives Without Husbands: Marriage, Desertion, and Welfare in New York, 1900–1935* (Chapel Hill: University of North Carolina Press, 2006).

18 Reena Sigman Friedman, *These Are Our Children: Jewish Orphanages in the United States, 1880–1925* (Waltham, MA: Brandeis University Press, 1994).

19 Daniel Bender, "'Too Much of Distasteful Masculinity': Historicizing Sexual Harassment in the Garment Sweatshop and Factory," *Journal of Women's History* 15 (Winter 2004): 91–116.

20 Polly Adler, *A House Is Not a Home* (New York: Rinehart, 1953), 24–25.

21 Rachel Calof, *Rachel Calof's Story: Jewish Homesteader on the Northern Plains* (Bloomington: Indiana University Press, 1996); Hannah Greenebaum Solomon, *The Fabric of My Life: The Autobiography of Hannah G. Solomon* (New York: Bloch, 1946).

22 Linda Mack Schloff, *"And Prairie Dogs Weren't Kosher": Jewish Women in the Upper Midwest Since 1855* (St. Paul: Minnesota Historical Society, 1996); Jeanne Abrams, *Jewish Women Pioneering the Frontier Trail: A History in the American West* (New York: New York University Press, 2006).

23 Jonathan D. Sarna, *American Judaism: A History* (New Haven, CT: Yale University Press, 2004).

24 Karla Goldman, *Beyond the Synagogue Gallery: Finding a Place for Women in American Judaism* (Cambridge, MA: Harvard University Press, 2000).

25 Jonathan D. Sarna, *A Great Awakening: The Transformation That Shaped Twentieth Century American Judaism and Its Implications for Today* (New York: Council for Initiatives in Jewish Education, 1995).

26 Shuly Rubin Schwartz, *The Rabbi's Wife: The Rebbetzin in American Jewish Life* (New York: New York University Press, 2006).

27 Pamela S. Nadell, *Women Who Would Be Rabbis: A History of Women's Ordination, 1889–1985* (Boston: Beacon, 1998).

28 Jonathan B. Krasner, *The Benderly Boys and American Jewish Education* (Waltham, MA: Brandeis University Press, 2011).

29 Daniel J. Walkowitz, "The Making of a Feminine Professional Identity: Social Workers in the 1920s," *American Historical Review* 95 (October 1990): 1051–75.

30 Jenna Weissman Joselit, *Aspiring Women: A History of the Jewish Foundation for Education of Women* (New York: Jewish Foundation for Education of Women, 1996).

31 Daniel Katz, *All Together Different: Yiddish Socialists, Garment Workers, and the Labor Roots of Multiculturalism* (New York: New York University Press, 2011), 10.

32 Alice Kessler-Harris, "Organizing the Unorganizable: Three Jewish Women and Their Union," *Labor History* 17 (1976): 5–23; Susan A. Glenn, *Daughters of the Shtetl: Life and Labor in the Immigrant Generation* (Ithaca, NY: Cornell University Press, 1990); Annelise Orleck, *Common Sense and a Little Fire: Women and Working-Class Politics in the United States, 1900–1965* (Chapel Hill: University of North Carolina Press, 1995); Karen Pastorello, *A Power Among Them: Bessie Abramowitz Hillman and the Making of the Amalgamated Clothing Workers of America* (Urbana: University of Illinois Press, 2008).

33 Nancy Schrom Dye, *As Equals and as Sisters: Feminism, the Labor Movement, and the Women's Trade Union League of New York* (Columbia: University of Missouri Press, 1980).

34 Katz, *All Together Different*, 51.

35 Rose Schneiderman at the Memorial Meeting at the Metropolitan Opera House, in Robert D. Marcus and David Burner, eds., *America Firsthand: Readings from Reconstruction to the Present*, 5th ed. (Boston: Bedford/St. Martin's, 2001), 120–21.

36 Melissa R. Klapper, *Ballots, Babies, and Banners of Peace: American Jewish Women's Activism, 1890–1940* (New York: New York University Press, 2013).

37 Elinor Lerner, "Jewish Involvement in the New York City Suffrage Movement," *American Jewish History* 52 (June 1981): 442–61.

38 Berta Ratner, Brooklyn, to Mrs. H., November 1915, Berta Ratner Rosenbluth Papers, A/R8132, Schlesinger Library on the History of American Women, Harvard University.

39 Klapper, *Ballots*, ch. 1.

40 Rogow, *Gone to Another Meeting*.

41 Bonnie S. Anderson, *The Rabbi's Atheist Daughter: Ernestine Rose, International Feminist Pioneer* (New York: Oxford University Press, 2017), 128–31.

42 Kathi Kern, *Mrs. Stanton's Bible* (Ithaca, NY: Cornell University Press, 2001), 208.

43 Mabel Vernon and Amelia Fry, *Mabel Vernon: Speaker for Suffrage and Petitioner for Peace—An Interview* (Berkeley: Regional Oral History Office, Bancroft Library, University of California, 1976), 157.

44 Maud Nathan, *Once Upon a Time and Today* (New York: Putnam, 1933), 273–75. On anti-Semitism in the international women's movement, see Linda Kuzmack Gordon, *Woman's Cause: The Jewish Woman's Movement in England and the United States, 1881–1933* (Columbus: Ohio State University Press, 1990); and Leila J. Rupp, *Worlds of Women: The Making of an International Women's Movement* (Princeton, NJ: Princeton University Press, 1997).

45 ChaeRan Freeze, *Jewish Marriage and Divorce in Imperial Russia* (Waltham, MA: Brandeis University Press, 2001).

46 See Peter C. Engelman, *A History of the Birth Control Movement in America* (Santa Barbara, CA: Praeger, 2011). The discussion in this section is based on Klapper, *Ballots*, chaps. 2 and 4.

47 Judith Rosenbaum, "'The Call to Action': Margaret Sanger, the Brownsville Jewish Women, and Political Activism," in *Gender and Jewish History*, ed. Marion Kaplan and Deborah Dash Moore (Bloomington: University of Indiana Press, 2011), 251–66.

48 Carole R. McCann, *Birth Control Politics in the United States, 1916–1945* (Ithaca, NY: Cornell University Press, 1994).

49 The discussion in this section is based on Klapper, *Ballots*, chaps. 3 and 5.

50 WILPF–Massachusetts Branch Annual Report, 1924, Box 1, Folder 2, Women's International League for Peace and Freedom, Massachusetts Branch Records, 83-M23, Schlesinger Library on the History of American Women, Harvard University.

51 Melissa R. Klapper, "'Those By Whose Side We Have Labored': American Jewish Women and the Peace Movement Between the Wars," *Journal of American History* 97 (December 2010): 636–58.

52 Rebecca Hourwich Reyher, Amelia Fry, and Fern Ingersoll, *Rebecca Hourwich Reyher: Search and Struggle for Equality and Independence* (Berkeley: Regional Oral History Office, Bancroft Library, University of California, 1977), 190–92.

53 Paula E. Hyman, "Immigrant Women and Consumer Protest: The New York City Kosher Meat Boycott of 1902," *American Jewish History* 70 (September 1980): 91–105; Shelly Tenenbaum, "Borrowers or Lenders Be: Jewish Immigrant Women's Credit Networks," in *American Jewish Women's History: A Reader*, ed. Pamela S. Nadell (New York: New York University Press, 2003), 79–90.

54 Mark A. Raider, *The Emergence of American Zionism* (New York: New York University Press, 1998).

55 Joan Dash, *Summoned to Jerusalem: The Life of Henrietta Szold* (New York: Harper & Row, 1979).

56 Shulamit Reinharz and Mark A. Raider, eds., *American Jewish Women and the Zionist Enterprise* (Waltham, MA: Brandeis University Press, 2004).

57 Recent histories include Erica B. Simmons, *Hadassah and the Zionist Project* (Lanham, MD: Rowman & Littlefield, 2006); and Mira Katzburg-Yungman, *Hadassah: American Women Zionists and the Rebirth of Israel* (Liverpool, UK: Littman Library of Jewish Civilization, 2014).

58 Alice Kessler-Harris, "The Gender of Jews and the Politics of Women: A Reflection," in *Jews and Leftist Politics: Judaism, Israel, Antisemitism, and Gender*, ed. Jack Jacobs (New York: Cambridge University Press, 2017), 200–230.

59 Mary McCune, *"The Whole Wide World, Without Limits": International Relief, Gender Politics, and American Jewish Women, 1893–1930* (Detroit: Wayne State University Press, 2005).

60 Aviva Ben-Ur, *Sephardic Jews in America* (New York: New York University Press, 2009), is an important contribution, as is Devin E. Naar, "Turkinos Beyond the Empire, 1893–1924," *Jewish Quarterly Review* 105 (spring 2015): 174–205. For a model for future research, see Devi Mays, "'I Killed Her Because I Loved Her Too Much': Gender and Violence in the 20th Century Sephardi Diaspora," *Mashriq & Mahjar* 2 (2014): 4–28.

EMPOWERED YET WEAKENED

Jewish Women's Identity and National Awakening in Mandatory Palestine, 1920–1948

Lilach Rosenberg-Friedman

"Were someone to talk to us about an English woman, or a French, German, Russian, or Italian woman," wrote Eliezer Ben-Yehuda, the driving spirit behind the revival of the Hebrew language in Palestine in the late nineteenth century, "we would immediately understand what he was saying. . . . We would know—more or less—her virtues and vices, her greatness or mediocrity, her inclinations, what she likes and dislikes." The "Hebrew woman" was a different matter, however: "Who is she, where does she come from, what is she, to whom is she close, whom does she resemble, what qualities does she possess?" To Ben-Yehuda in that period, she was a complete enigma.[1]

To Ben-Yehuda in 1896, the Hebrew woman lacked a coherent national character, as only the first buds were beginning to appear at this point. But that character came into full flower in the following years. During the British Mandatory period in Palestine (1920–1948), women played an active role in both the ideal and real expressions of the national revival. Zionist national and social aspirations and the complex nature of the local society-in-formation proved fertile ground for the emergence of various paradigms. All women who formed part of this society shared in the process. Some actively contributed to it, forging new identities. Others remained more passive, preserving their traditional identities. Furthermore, although national revival empowered some women, it debilitated and weakened others.

In this chapter I examine the variegated female identity that emerged in the Jewish society of Mandatory Palestine, known as the Yishuv. I address the women's prototypes that stand out during the period under discussion: working women and pioneers; women in agricultural settlements; women in the defense forces; women's lives in the cities, kibbutzim (communal settlements founded on the principles of economic and political collaboration and equality), and moshavim (partially cooperative settlements); and women's organizations for social advancement. From the portraits of individual women unique characteristics arise alongside issues common to all. Whether a woman had children herself or not, motherhood and its status in the national enterprise were central to the gender discourse and thus the life of every woman. I dedicate a separate section to that topic. Throughout I focus on an analysis of gender ideologies and women's actual experiences. Female identity in the Yishuv was molded by numerous factors. Two of the most significant were the Zionist goal of establishing a Jewish state and creating a new society and immigration.

Historical Background

THE BRITISH MANDATORY PERIOD in Palestine witnessed a series of dramatic events in a brief span of time: the creation of a modern Western regime, mass waves of immigration, significant security issues, economic crises, a world war, the Holocaust and extermination of millions of Jews, and the declaration of the Jewish state only three years after the end of the war. The convergence of these factors led to the emergence of complex social phenomena. Jewish society was faced with the need to reconcile nationalist, religious, social, and cultural beliefs, navigating between tradition and modernity and conservativism and revolution. These challenges significantly influenced women's identities and roles.

At the beginning of the nineteenth century, the Jewish population of Palestine was about 8,000. As the century wore on, it began to increase in size, with most of the new arrivals immigrating for religious reasons and being supported by Jewish philanthropists. Known as the Old Yishuv, this group was patriarchal, conservative, and resistant to change.[2] It was built on waves of Jewish immigration mostly from Eastern Europe. Toward the end of the century and the 20th century's first decades, the numbers swelled with the arrival of new immigrants driven by modern nationalist and socialist ideas. With the rise of the Nazis in the 1930s, many more also arrived from Central and Western Europe. Only a minority came from Muslim countries.

In 1918 the Jewish population numbered 56,000 and the local Arab populace 600,000. On May 14, 1948, when the State of Israel was declared, the Jewish population of Palestine had risen to 650,000, constituting 30% of the population as a whole. In line with the goal of creating a Jewish state, the Yishuv established new urban and agricultural settlements, set up local and national political institutions, developed a democratic electoral system and leadership, and shaped a new cultural experience around the Hebrew language.

The Yishuv population was young and, in the early 1920s, predominantly male. As time went on, however, the gender divide became far more balanced. By the end of the 1940s, there were 300,000 women in the total Jewish population of 650,000.[3] This circumstance reflected the Zionist goal of creating a new society separate from the local populace to ensure a Jewish majority.[4] However, because both the British Mandatory authorities and the Zionist leadership favored the immigration of men over women, many women were forced to use various ruses to reach Palestine, including sham marriages to men with immigration certificates.[5]

Immigrants stamped an indelible imprint on the Jewish society that developed in Mandatory Palestine, weaving the worldviews and cultural values they brought with them from their countries of origin into the complex local reality.[6] Although many came from traditional patriarchal Jewish societies, some were also educated and already had professional careers, reflecting the processes of urbanization, emancipation, modernization, and secularization characteristic of the period.[7] Most lived within a familial framework, the men occupying most of the positions of power, acting as household and community heads and leaving the home to their wives.[8]

In addition to the difficulties associated with immigration in general—acclimatizing to a new geographical location and mastering a new language—women immigrants also faced those specific to the Jewish homeland: security issues, the economic distress of the region, and the demands attendant on the vision of building the infrastructure for an independent, sovereign Jewish entity and shaping a new kind of Jew. Gender issues formed an integral part of Zionism's national ideology in this regard. The "new Jew" was to be the antithesis of the "feminine" exilic Jew. This would be a healthy form of national life capable of changing the Jewish body and creating a new man, whose masculinity stood at the center of the Zionist discourse. The male body was "becoming a symbol of the new society and a means whereby to form the nation."[9] Although women were regarded as playing an important role, this role continued to center around motherhood—the role they had traditionally played, reinforced in the new country by the national society that harnessed it to its own needs.

Development of Gender-Historical Research in Israel

EVEN THOUGH THEY FORMED an integral part of society and contributed to it in various ways, the women of the Yishuv remained silent for decades.[10] Men were depicted as shouldering the burden of the revolution and becoming a new type of Jew, but women were primarily portrayed as remaining in their traditional place, playing the role of helpmate to their menfolk in the national and revolutionary project. Right through to the 1980s, however, Israeli historiography continued to preserve one of the founding myths of the Yishuv: the belief in progressive gender equality. This was based on formal political equality—the right to vote—granted to women both in the Zionist movement (from 1898) and the Yishuv (from 1926) and the supposed egalitarian nature of the kibbutzim. The fact that many women helped defend the Yishuv in the armed forces also reinforced it.

Although exceptional figures became well known, women were relegated to anecdotal status in the discussion of the formation of hegemonic Israeliness.[11] The second wave of feminism and emergence of the field of gender history in North America directly influenced developments in Israel. As the 1980s progressed, the first traces of women's voices became heard, revealing that gender equality in the Yishuv was more myth than fact.[12]

In the twenty-first century the national historiography that depicted the past in one-dimensional colors, focusing exclusively on the center and the social elite—leadership, the labor sector, agricultural settlements, and security— has begun to examine other strata of society. In line with this, gender history research has also begun to examine diverse female experiences. Women's voices have been difficult to trace in local history, most never having been documented. The sources at our disposal include the press, settlement bulletins, memoirs, and biographies together with oral testimonies by and about women.

Working Women and Pioneers

THE FIRST WOMEN TO appear in the Yishuv's historiography were the pioneers and workers who belonged to the labor sector. Many of those who arrived in the early twentieth century sought to take an active part in creating the national structure on a par with their male counterparts.[13] In their eyes, gender equality meant playing an equal part in the agricultural work that constituted the epitome of the Zionist revolution and the creation of a new Jew. Many of the pioneers who arrived during the Mandatory period were motivated by the same vision. "I set my objective on coming here," wrote R. in her diary in 1925, "training myself for agricultural work. I saw this as the facade of everything . . . a strong desire to participate in the creation and building up of the people's new economy."[14] In their view, gender equality could be achieved if they became like "men," taking on hard tasks, dressing in male attire, and so on.[15] Even though jobs such as plowing with bulls required physical strength, the male Yishuv was wary of the "new women" who sought to enter professions that had been male preserves; many of the men cold-shouldered their fellow farm laborers and relegated them to the kitchen, laundry, and other "female" realms.

Some women internalized the male view that playing this role was their destiny in the national enterprise, believing themselves to be contributing to it in the best way possible. Others suffered the indignities imposed on them, accepting the fact that they could not assimilate into other areas. Ada Fishman Maimon (1893–1973), an observant Jewish feminist who immigrated in 1912 and devoted her life to improving the status of women, helping to found the working women's movement, testified in both articles and books to the hard conditions under which women labored. In 1929 she wrote, "The working women sought to rebel against the idea that kitchen work was the women's domain. Although she wanted to, she couldn't move out of it, knowing that the gates to the fields were closed in her face, only the privileged few being allowed to enter them."[16]

Some women initiated projects for women to provide them with agricultural training, believing that they would then be able to integrate into the agricultural sector. For example, the agronomist Hannah Maisel (1883–1972) established the Kinneret Farm for women pioneers in 1911 for the purpose of training women for those jobs she regarded as befitting them—chicken houses, greenhouses, nurseries, and so on.[17] Although it existed for only a short period of time, dozens of women passed through its doors, impacting the status of women across the agricultural sector.[18] It also served as a model for the "working women's farms" created across the country in the 1920s and 1930s that sought to provide agricultural training to women. These unfortunately offered only a partial solution to the problem of gender equality.

Urban working women—the majority of Jewish working women in Palestine (23,701 in 1939)—who were neither interested in agriculture nor particularly driven by an egalitarian ideology, fared little better. The job market for women was extremely limited, affording them few opportunities and poor pay. Thus most looked to enter professions traditionally considered female. Here, they continued to be treated badly, working under poor conditions, earning little, and being restricted to casual work. Many were single women, as married women were dependent on their husbands because no legal agreements or arrangements existed that allowed them to pursue a career outside the home. They thus found it difficult to sustain themselves, suffering from unemployment, poor food, and health issues. Some even turned in despair to prostitution or suicide.[19] Even those who moved to agricultural settlements failed to find in them an avenue for achieving their ambitions and meeting their needs.

Women in the Agricultural Settlements

WOMEN PIONEERS WHO STROVE to participate actively in the implementation of Zionist socialist ideas looked to the kibbutzim and moshavim, the flagships of the Zionist enterprise. They hoped that the values these communities endorsed would enable them to take part in all activities and branches of labor, thus enabling them to play a direct role in shaping the formation of a new Jewish society.

The kibbutzim's egalitarian principles should theoretically have liberated women and afforded them the opportunity to achieve equality by transferring responsibility for housework tasks and child rearing to the collective. In fact, however, the kibbutzim continued to assign women to "female" jobs—the service branches and child rearing. The idea of the "natural mother," the belief that men were more productive than women, and the great need for (wo)manpower in the service sectors as the kibbutzim grew in size all worked against gender equality.[20] Yochebed Bat-Rachel (1901–1989), one of the founders of Kibbutz Ein Harod in 1921, which played a seminal role in the settlement enterprise, was a prominent activist on behalf of women's rights in the kibbutz movement and a member of the Yishuv leadership. She expressly observed how women were excluded from the power centers: "Even in kibbutz society, the male members are those who make all the decisions with regard to its running, in just the same way as in the family and patriarchal society."[21]

Ein Harod exemplified the fight for change in the status of women that affected not only the kibbutzim but also society at large. One of Bat-Rachel's colleagues, Lilia Bassewitz (1900–1990), was a leader in the working women's movement and a member of the editorial board of *Davar Hapoalot*, its literary organ, established in 1934 and edited by Rachel Katznelson Shazar. Bassewitz worked tirelessly to advance the status of women in the Yishuv and the kibbutz movement, documenting her life and struggles in her memoirs. Together with others, the two women sought to integrate women into the privileged sectors of the agricultural branch, also demanding that men assume roles traditionally assigned to women—that is, the service branches. By doing so, they believed that women who were customarily passive could become more actively involved in the public space.

Alongside documenting their personal experiences in the kibbutz bulletins, Yishuv journals, and books, Bassewitz and Bat-Rachel also edited a volume in which the female narrative played a central role.[22] The anthology *Women of the Kibbutz* (1943) includes the complex life stories of a hundred women kibbutz members. As Bassewitz observed in 1931: "Day chases after day, work, kids, economic issues . . . and the women members' lives successes and failures, struggles with internal and external problems, ups and downs, great accomplishments and disappointed dreams, the joy of creativity and despair."[23]

The efforts of the women of Ein Harod led to two prominent achievements that had repercussions beyond the kibbutz itself: (1) reservation of a third of the seats on all kibbutz committees for women in a type of affirmative action, an initiative that enabled women to take part in public activities; and (2) in the wake of the "women members' revolt" in 1936 that sought to draft women into guard and defense duty alongside their male counterparts, the allocation of two of the six permanent places on the defense committee to women and training in the use of firearms. Not only did other kibbutzim adopt these measures, but urban women also sought to take an active part in defense and guarding posts.

Although these struggles yielded some fruit, the integration of women into the public space on the kibbutzim remained partial at best; full equality was not achieved during that period. Women continued to press to enter the branches of public, productive, and privileged life that were, for the most part, reserved for men. Male authority was also manifest in the private space, which was heavily constricted. Thus, for example, the kibbutzim stripped the

Mothers and babies in Kibbutz Ein-Harod, 1920s. Photograph by Avraham Soskin. Bitmuna Collections, Ada Maimon's Album. Reproduced with permission.

institution of the family of its traditional substance, and all the children grew up together in children's houses. Although women accepted these measures—some even worked to implement them—quite a few found it a painful and difficult experience, impinging on their ingrained sense of motherhood.

Nor was gender equality achieved on the moshavim. These agricultural communities revolved around the family unit; however, the women who lived on them were able to combine motherhood with work outside the home—in the farmyards and fields. Although moshav life was particularly demanding on women, many of them felt self-fulfilled, believing themselves to be making a contribution to the national enterprise as both mothers and farmers.[24]

Although life on the agricultural settlements took a heavy personal toll on women, quite frequently belying the alleged principle of gender equality, many regarded it as a way they could actively participate in the building up of the country, even by fulfilling their traditional roles, either by choice or out of necessity.

The Place and Status of Women in the Defense Forces

AS IN THE AGRICULTURAL sector, the military had traditionally been a preeminently male domain in the Jewish homeland. As the Yishuv developed, it was faced with increasingly critical security issues. The Jewish-Arab conflict and British Mandatory policies as well as World War II and the military threat to the Yishuv demanded a large fighting force. Right from the beginning, both men and women answered the call to defend the homeland. Hashomer, the small first Hebrew defense force, established in 1909, was founded with help from numerous women. The most prominent of these were Manya Shochat (1878–1961) and Rachel Yana'it Ben-Zvi (1886–1979), both of whom also played a central role in the labor movement.[25] Ben-Zvi also later became one of the initiators of the Haganah in 1920, the largest defense force of the Yishuv and sort of a voluntary popular militia. The women of the Haganah constantly struggled to gain new and valued roles, cementing their positions step by step.

During the events of 1936, both men and women took an active part in defending their homes. The need to take advantage of all the people available increased the number of women serving in the Haganah. The combat-supporting roles they were given—liaison officers, medics, kitchen staff, clerks, and so on—were deemed suitable to their gender. On the eve of the War of Independence, 10,000 women formed a fifth of the total force of the Haganah.[26]

Women also participated in the Irgun and Lechi, two underground organizations active in the 1940s that opposed both the British and the Zionist leadership, sometimes using violent means. One of the most well known Irgun fighters was Esther Raziel-Naor (1911–2002), who served as both a medic and a key broadcaster on the underground radio. In 1942 she became the only woman to be appointed to its leading ranks. The British charged her with being a member of a terror organization, and she was incarcerated for eight months while pregnant and the mother of two small children. Raziel-Naor later served as a Member of Knesset, serving from its inception until 1974 on behalf of the opposition Herut Party.[27]

A place of honor in the myth of the fighting women of the Yishuv is reserved for those who served in the Palmach, the Haganah's elite fighting force established in 1941. Women began joining the Palmach in 1942, and by assuming combat roles, they strengthened the myth of equality: "They were with us in everything. They dressed in drab gray like us and wore the heavy helmets. They shouldered the immense burdens on their backs, carried the burning steel, and laid their heads on stones in the field at night."[28] When the true test arrived, however, gender equality again proved more myth than reality.

Almost 4,000 women volunteered in the British army during World War II, serving primarily as drivers, liaison officers, guards, and medics. In doing so, they had to overcome the disapprobation of the Yishuv leadership, which regarded service in a foreign military machine as inappropriate to the character of its women—a threat to their honor and a stain on the nation.[29]

The women who participated in the War of Independence (1947–1949), strengthened the myth of military equality, undermining gender boundaries by fighting alongside men on the frontlines. Even here, however, the traditional gender distinction remained; women served principally in the auxiliary services and supported the fighting men. Despite their combat training, women in the Palmach were withdrawn to the rear after the first battles. Some women found satisfaction in supporting the men, regarding this role as a way of contributing to the national enterprise. Others, however, wanted more equality. For example, Rachel Savorai (1926–2016) lamented the fact that women were viewed as constructed out of a different material, one that must be protected from injury or destruction. In her eyes, the right and duty to sacrifice one's life on behalf of the nation belonged to both men and women equally.[30]

The refusal to let women serve in combat roles reflected the belief that men were responsible for defending them on the home front. It was also buttressed by the fear that women might fall captive and suffer sexual assault. The Yishuv sought to prevent this from happening in part because it regarded women as a national symbol, representing and protecting the nation's honor. This may account for the fact that the ninety-six Jewish women taken as prisoners of war during the War of Independence did not become part of Israeli collective memory.[31]

Other figures, however, became national heroes. For example, Zohara Leviatov (1927–1948) was a Palmach fighter and pilot who fell in the War of Independence. She became famous after her death with the publication of her personal diaries and correspondence with her fiancé Shmuel Kaufman, killed earlier in the war. Mira Ben-Ari (1926–1948) was a member of Kibbutz Nitzanim. Serving as a wireless operator during the War of Independence, she refused to be evacuated with her small son, remaining on the front to defend the kibbutz and paying for her bravery with her life. In a note to her husband, tucked into the pocket of her son's jacket, she wrote, "No farewell is harder than that of a mother and child. But I am doing so that he will grow up in a safe place and become a free man in his own country."[32] Herein, Ben-Ari expressed the national identification that characterized so many women during this period. Because of these women, female sacrifice on behalf of the nation became a prominent part of collective Israeli memory.

With the development of gender research concerning the Yishuv, women who had become national symbols gained new recognition and features. Hannah Senesh (1921–1944) was long known for having volunteered as a special operations executive paratrooper in the British army during World War II and for being captured, tortured, and executed after being dropped into occupied Hungary.[33] However, a recent new study of her life based on fresh sources tells the story of her tortuous path to Palestine. Examining her disappointments and frustrations and attempts to redefine her national, class, and gender identity, this new study traces the way she transformed herself from a Hungarian bourgeois woman into a Hebrew socialist.[34] Previously a one-dimensional national emblem, Senesh is now understood as having shared the complex hopes, dreams, and challenges of many Yishuv women.

Other women, less well engraved on collective memory, have also been brought to life in recent years. For example, Ada Sereni (1905–1997) was responsible for the vital illegal immigration (Ha'apalah) route from Italy that brought European Jewish refugees to Mandatory Palestine after the Holocaust. A primary tool in the national struggle and one of the most prominent symbols of the national ethos in the Yishuv and later the state, this activity was organized by the Mossad Le'Aliyah Bet. Sereni sent dozens of ships to Palestine carrying thousands of refugees—a complex task that demanded great creativity and daring. Despite her achievements, she was never accorded full recognition in the collective memory. Gender played a large role in this silencing. Many men found it difficult to accept her authority. Over the years, people have claimed that Sereni's success stemmed from her "feminine charms," which "devalued" the organization's image. She was thus not held up as an example for the Yishuv, which championed masculinity.[35] Sereni's case not only illustrates the sexist nature of her society but also illuminates the way in which the national enterprise molded the new female identity by allowing women to participate in the public space. Although this demonstrated their capabilities, it delimited them at the same time.

When the State of Israel was declared in May 1948, it became the only Western country that, from the moment of its formation, conscripted women into the army. Although this ostensibly set the seal on the myth of gender equality in Israeli society, the establishment of the Israel Defense Forces (IDF) actually heightened the inequality between the sexes.[36] For years, women were assigned different roles, served less time than men, and were subservient to the primarily male hierarchy, rarely achieving the rank of commander or making their way into the top echelons. Thus, in reality, the most prominent emblem of gender equality, army service, widened the gap between the sexes.[37]

Women's Organizations for Women and Social Advancement

THE INSTITUTIONS AND PROJECTS necessary for the Yishuv's daily running depended heavily on voluntary service. The economic hardships that those who immigrated to Palestine experienced prompted women to set up voluntary auxiliary organizations in this prestate era. Various women's organizations, designed to help the poor in general and women in particular, arose in the labor and civic sectors. These reflected the sense that joint efforts with men did not meet women's specific needs.

Hadassah, the Women's Zionist Organization of America, founded in 1912 by Henrietta Szold (1860–1945), began its work in Palestine in 1918.[38] Dedicating her life to realizing the Zionist vision, Szold immigrated to Israel from the United States in 1920. Elected to the Zionist Executive, she headed the Department of Education and Health, working tirelessly in the areas of welfare in the Yishuv and playing a central role in its formation. Hadassah's two primary goals were to advance health and medical services in Palestine and to further the Zionist cause in the American Jewish community. Nurses sent to Palestine by Hadassah before World War I established a clinic in Jerusalem. They were followed by a mission of physicians and nurses in 1918 who founded clinics and hospitals across the country. The organization focused its work on underprivileged neighborhoods and sectors not considered to constitute part of the national collective—the Mizrahi and Orthodox communities, for example. Thus it sought to foster models of care for children, seeking to reshape the image of motherhood held by members of these populations.[39]

In civic circles the Federation of Mizrahi Women (1918) represented middle-class religious Zionist women, working on behalf of the welfare of the poor in this sector and its women workers. The Federation of Jewish Women formed in 1920 focused on social work, giving aid to pregnant women and young mothers. WIZO—the Women's International Zionist Organization— was established by British women Zionists to gain national recognition for Jewish women worldwide and to help create a national homeland in Palestine. It began operating in Palestine in 1920, organizing its official activities in the Yishuv within the framework of the National WIZO Federation in 1927. In 1933 it merged with the Jewish Women's Federation, devoting its efforts toward providing professional training for women, establishing and protecting women's rights, and setting up children's institutions.[40] All these women's groups worked in the areas of welfare, health care, and child care—the sphere traditionally assigned to women. They succeeded in bringing education, health, and hygiene within the purview of the National Council (Va'ad Le'umi). Together with the Assembly of Representatives and the Zionist Executive (known later as the Jewish Agency Executive), this constituted the Yishuv leadership. These areas became matters of public responsibility. The economic hardships of the Yishuv thus allowed women to gain access to the public space.

The Women Worker's Movement (1921) operated under the auspices of the Histadrut, the general workers' union. Governed by a Council of Women Workers, its members came from both urban and rural communities.[41] Like the Women Worker's Movement, which served as its role model, the Organization of Religious Working Women (1935) sought to advance women economically by offering professional training in diverse fields, educational projects, and cultural activities. Both set themselves the goal of helping women become independent or bring an income into the family, also encouraging them to participate in the public space.

The Union of Hebrew Women for Equal Rights (1919), the first women's party in Palestine, sought to improve the legal and political status of women in the Yishuv. Led by Rosa Welt-Strauss (1856–1939), one of the first female European eye doctors, who immigrated to Palestine in 1919, its primary goal was national regeneration: "We want to participate, as much as we possibly can, in rejuvenating our land," she wrote.[42] In Welt-Strauss's eyes, this meant giving women equal rights. The Union headed the struggle for the right to vote, won in 1926.[43]

Voting rights were no guarantee of equality, however. Neither the Zionist movement nor the Yishuv leadership was ready to relinquish its traditional attitude toward women. Many women were excluded from positions of leadership because gender norms dictated that they could not play a public role. Women themselves were also hesitant about participating in the political arena, believing themselves to be unsuited to this essentially masculine sphere by nature. The women's organizations nonetheless formed the springboard for the participation of some women in the Yishuv leadership.

In setting up their own associations to contribute to the national project, women's organizations helped women enter new areas and become more independent. They raised funds and mobilized themselves as forces working to improve the status of women in society, enabling them to enter new fields of employment. This self-organization also formed the basis for the development of female self-awareness and new goals for women's advancement.

From a Monolithic to a Diverse Female Image

As GENDER HISTORY RESEARCH expanded, other female experiences came under scrutiny. Women from disparate sectors and ethnogeographical backgrounds whose lifestyles, place of residence, and national, religious, social, and gender perceptions differed greatly gradually came out of the shadows. Women who struck out on their own, were abandoned, or who dealt with economic, personal-emotional, and social-normative hardships were recognized. Those who turned to prostitution and crossed the national collective boundaries by associating with non-Jews, in particular Arabs, also gained visibility.[44] Studies of single women on the margins of a family-oriented society shed further light on the Yishuv. For example, Henya Pekelman immigrated in 1920 and worked as a day laborer. In her autobiography published in 1935, she documents the difficulties she faced: unemployment, shortages, and transient existence. She became pregnant through rape, and the child died when only a month old in 1925. Not belonging to the Yishuv elite, Pekelman felt socially excluded, isolated, and persecuted, and she ended her life in 1940 by jumping to her death.[45] Her story serves as rare testimony of the lives of women in the Yishuv who, despite not forming part of its elite, constituted an intrinsic part of its fabric.

Other women also found it difficult to adjust to life in the new country. These included Holocaust survivors, who demonstrated their courage in various ways,[46] and religious pioneer women who sought to hold onto traditional values while participating in the new national project. In 1921 the first religious pioneer, Rachel Labkovsky (later Berkman), found herself in a new country, penniless, and without regular employment. Neither the various groups of young pioneers with their nonreligious lifestyle nor the religious pioneers' groups afforded her a home, the latter believing that the presence of a young unmarried woman in a group of religious men would threaten their moral image. Faced with the choice of abandoning religion or leaving the country, she eventually joined the religious workers' movement (Hapo'el Hamizrahi), paving the way for others to follow her example.[47]

In civic circles, educated women immigrants fought for employment in their areas of expertise—architecture, medicine, law, academic and artistic fields, and so on.[48] Their explicit goal was to advance the national enterprise and work on behalf of society, and their self-realization formed part of the national project. Some of the most prominent figures were women professionals who developed a specialization as they worked to help build the land and construct a new society. Charlotte (Lotte) Cohn, an architectural pioneer who immigrated from Germany in 1921, described herself as belonging to an ardent group of youth whose vision was to participate in the building of the country.[49] The female doctors who worked indefatigably to develop a modern medical system in the country did so out of a sense of mission, regarding medicine not only as a means of support but also as a national objective. As Batsheva Younis observed, "We were all young, full of energy and hope and a vibrant faith in the future of our land, ready to give all our efforts and knowledge on its behalf."[50]

Mizrahi women—a minority in the Yishuv—were doubly marginalized because of their gender and origin. Even within the historiography, their story was not regarded as unique or differing from that of either Ashkenazic women or Mizrahi men for many years.[51] Studies demonstrate the discrimination they faced in the labor market, education, and public domain. This inferior status is particularly prominent in the face of the Zionist vision of gathering in the exiles and the ethos of social and gender equality.[52] Others reveal that some Mizrahi women transformed their sense of having "an identity to be ashamed of and hidden" into one of pride and power.[53] All clearly illustrate the diverse and varied identities of Mizrahi women, shattering the myth of a monolithic bloc.

Motherhood

ALTHOUGH IT SOUGHT TO establish a new society, the Zionist leadership espoused traditional views regarding birthrates, believing a high rate to be crucial for survival. It thus placed great emphasis on the mother. The high birthrate among the Muslim population reinforced this attitude. The drop in immigration at the end of the 1930s and during World War II and the destruction of European Jewry during the Holocaust further entrenched it. Motherhood and birthrate levels thus became even more important precisely when the national struggle was at its height, requiring all the manpower—men and women alike—at its disposal.[54]

In all their diversity, the women of the Yishuv were first of all wives and mothers, tasked with the responsibility of rearing their families.[55] Alongside personal motherhood, which was regarded as a means for realizing national goals, the Yishuv promulgated the idea of national motherhood. This called for women to harness themselves to the national cause precisely because they were mothers, a move that on occasion paradoxically crossed gender boundaries.[56]

At the end of World War II, about 200 women left the Yishuv for the displaced persons camps set up across Europe. Their aim was to take care of orphaned children who had survived the Holocaust, helping to educate them and organizing their immigration to Palestine. This role derived from a gender perception that regarded all women, including the unmarried, as natural mothers. Some of the women emissaries were mothers who left their own children for an extended period to take care of the nation's children. Although reluctant to undertake this mission, they accepted the challenge, putting national needs before their own personal needs. This episode, and others like it during the Yishuv, demonstrates both the notion of national motherhood and the precedence it took over women's individual and personal choices concerning how to be a mother.[57]

Some women in the Yishuv sought to liberate themselves from the traditional views of patriarchal Jewish society by taking an active part in the building of the nation as workers.[58] At the same time, however, they were held responsible for rearing and educating the "new Jew." Their traditional role as mothers was even more crucial in the national project. The "new Jewish woman" who desired to contribute to the national enterprise while realizing her own potential as a person constituted a threat to the family; tension existed between their new national character and traditional identity.[59]

Many women found it difficult to assume maternal and national responsibilities simultaneously. Judith (whose surname is not recorded), a member of Moshav Kfar Yehoshua, wrote in 1943, "The contemporary mother cannot come to terms with the fact that she is only a homemaker and mother, a role that has lost its value. . . . She has sought and found other spiritual values."[60] Unfortunately, the Yishuv itself was not ready for this change in perception. As a prestate society, no constitutional bills existed to protect women's and mothers' rights. Without the necessary social conditions, the attempt to combine motherhood with pioneering and work was a daunting task. "The demand was more than we could bear," Judith observed.[61]

Many women were also forced to work outside the home to sustain their families. Although some welcomed this situation as symbolizing their new identity, it conflicted with motherhood. Journalist Hedva Nofech wrote in 1937, "Almost every woman today wants to be independent economically and earn what she needs for herself and her family. Due to the many difficulties in her work, no woman can dedicate herself to her family as mothers did in early generations. This has a direct effect on birthrate levels."[62]

Some women reacted by renouncing traditional motherhood, particularly in the kibbutzim. Others relinquished their aspiration of participating in the public sphere. Yet others sought to combine both roles. All paid a personal price at times. Retrospectively, however, we can see that the two aspects converged to a large extent. Perhaps more than any of their European or North American counterparts, the women of the Yishuv integrated family and national life. Whereas on many occasions they were forced to do so by national circumstances rather than a change in gender perceptions, they remain the accepted and conventional image of the new Israeli woman today. With one of the highest birthrate levels in the Western world and a high percentage of women with professional careers, the foundations of the current cultural reality were laid down during the period of the Yishuv.

Conclusion

JUST AS PARTICIPATION IN the national enterprise helped raise the status of women, it also afforded them opportunities for assuming new roles and shaping new identities. Women's use of traditional forms of activity challenged patriarchal control over the public space. For example, their involvement in the welfare and caregiving sectors paved the way for women to enter the public domain without raising male antagonism. The perception of women as mothers who educated their own children likewise opened up the educational field, enabling them to become pupils, students, teachers, and even principals. Although their service in active duty in the armed forces during the Yishuv period was due to circumstances and was temporary, it allowed them to demonstrate their capacities and reveal the horizons they could reach.

In her current research, Margalit Shilo demonstrates how, unlike in other places of the world where educated, professional women find it difficult to work in their fields because of gender perceptions, immigration to Palestine gave women an opportunity to pursue careers, find self-realization, and stamp their imprint on the public space as the new society sought to establish itself on new social and cultural values.[63] Teachers and kindergarten caregivers, social workers, architects, and doctors thus harnessed themselves to the national enterprise while using their professional skills and pursuing their professional development. For example, Shoshana Persitz (1893–1969), a Zionist activist and educator who immigrated in 1925 as a widow with four children, established the Hebrew publication *Omanut* (Art), which she began in Russia. In 1926 she was elected to the Tel Aviv municipal council and given charge of the Department of Education and Culture. Within this framework she supported innovative educational initiatives such as special education. Alongside her public education work, which she regarded as a national mission, she also engaged in personal development, becoming an elected member of the first through the third Knessets.[64]

Pediatrician Dr. Helena Kagan (1889–1978) likewise interwove her professional skills with the building of the nation. Immigrating from Russia in 1914, she worked as a doctor and in 1916 founded a day care center for working mothers, the first of its kind in the country. Later, she went on to open a children's home for orphans and abandoned infants (1924). In 1936 she established the children's department in Bikur Holim Hospital in Jerusalem, serving as its head for more than twenty years. She was also a public activist and one of the founders of WIZO.[65]

Women from countries in which they were regarded as particularly inferior benefited from immigration. For example, Yemenite women experienced great changes on their arrival. They were accustomed to lowly positions in their homeland, having no access to formal education. Married off at an early age, they were expected to devote themselves solely to raising their families. Viewed as their husband's property, they sometimes had to accept other wives and complete confinement to the women's quarters. Their migration afforded some of them a new, empowering identity. Although their encounter with Yishuv society was far from easy—the material hardships they endured were compounded by the contempt and condescension to which they were exposed— they came into contact with a different lifestyle. Serving as a vital part of the workforce, they integrated into their new environment more quickly than their menfolk. By overcoming their suffering and enduring the hardships, some of them gradually found a way to better themselves and improve their lives.[66]

Indeed, the difficult life in Mandatory Palestine exacted a heavy price from many women. Nevertheless, the sense of being part of something bigger than themselves infused their endeavors with significance and enabled them to cope with all the hardships they endured. As a society-in-formation, the Yishuv formed the cradle for an upheaval in female identity. Although most women were affected by this circumstance, their stories are individual and varied, covering a range of sectors, groups, and communities and influenced by a wide array of national, social, religious, and revolutionary forces, all operating in tandem. Nor can a single continuum be discerned running from a low to a high point; ebbs and flows occurred, each of which was affected by different factors. Some of these were dependent on the women themselves, others on historical conditions.

After the achievements gained in the 1920s and 1930s, during which women began taking part in the public national endeavor, the pressing national challenges of the late 1940s diverted their attention away from themselves and their status as women, mobilizing them to the national cause. For many women, the declaration of the State of Israel in May 1948 meant a reversion to their traditional status and the relinquishing of the roles they had been allowed to play in bringing it into existence. At the same time, however, it also enabled the struggle for women's rights to continue, now within a sovereign entity and the framework of new gender perceptions.

Notes

1   Eliezer Ben-Yehuda, "Yehudiyat Eretz Israel," *HaZvi* 12, no. 23 (March 6, 1896): 3 (Hebrew). Translations are my own.

2   Margalit Shilo, *Princess or Prisoner? Jewish Women in Jerusalem, 1840–1914* (Waltham, MA: Brandeis University Press, 2005).

3   Gur Alroey, "Women in the Yishuv: Demographic Aspects," in *One Law for Men and Women: Women, Rights, and Law During the British Mandate*, ed. Eyal Katvan, Margalit Shilo, and Ruth Halperin-Kaddari (Ramat-Gan: Bar-Ilan University Press, 2011), 91, 96–97 (Hebrew).

4   Lilach Rosenberg-Friedman, *Birthrate Politics in Zion: Judaism, Zionism, and Modernity in Mandate Palestine (1920–1948)* (Bloomington: Indiana University Press, 2017).

5   Aviva Halamish, "Discrimination Against Women in Immigration to Pre-State Palestine: Facts, Causes, Consequences," *Proceedings of the Twelfth World Congress of Jewish Studies* 5 (2001): 49–57 (Hebrew); Deborah S. Bernstein, "Between the Private and the Public: Fictitious Marriage During the British Mandate," *Israel* 18–19 (2011): 5–29 (Hebrew).

6   Pnina Morag Talmon and Yael Atzmon, eds., *Immigrant Women in Israel* (Jerusalem: Bialik Institute, 2013), 10 (Hebrew).

7   Sydney Stahl Weinberg, *The World of Our Mothers: The Lives of Jewish Immigrant Women* (Chapel Hill: University of North Carolina Press, 1988), 3–40; and Chae Ran Freeze's chapter in this volume.

8   Deborah S. Bernstein, "Daughters of the Nation: Between the Public and Private Spheres in Pre-State Israel," in *Jewish Women in Historical Perspective*, ed. Judith R. Baskin (Detroit: Wayne State University Press, 1998), 291–92.

9   David Biale, *Eros and the Jews: From Biblical Israel to Contemporary America* (Tel Aviv: Am Oved, 1994), 231–32 (Hebrew).

10 For the development of gender history research, see Margalit Shilo, "Women, Gender, and the History of the Yishuv: Achievements and Further Goals," *Cathedra* 150 (2014): 121–54 (Hebrew).

11 Yaffah Berlovitz, "In Search of a Profile of the 'Eretz-Israeli' Woman in Women's Literature of the 'Yishuv' Period," in *The Israeli Woman: Roots, Reality, and Images*, ed. Tova Cohen (Ramat-Gan: Bar-Ilan University Press, 2000), 91–93 (Hebrew).

12 Dafna Izraeli, "The Zionist Women's Movement in Palestine, 1911–1927: A Sociological Analysis," *Signs* 7, no. 1 (1981): 87–114.

13 Deborah S. Bernstein, *The Struggle for Equality: Women Workers in the Palestine Yishuv* (Tel Aviv: Hakibbutz Hameuchad, 1987) (Hebrew).

14 Quoted in Bernstein, *Struggle for Equality*, 157.

15 Margalit Shilo and Gideon Katz, *Gender in Israel: New Studies on Gender in the Yishuv and State*, ed. Margalit Shilo and Gideon Katz (Beersheba: Ben-Gurion Research Institute for the Study of Israel and Zionism, 2011), 1–2 (Hebrew).

16 Esther Carmel-Hakim, *Hannah Maisel's Lifelong Mission: Agricultural Training for Women* (Jerusalem: Yad-Tabenkin, 2007), 19 (Hebrew). See also Batsheva Margalit-Stern, *The Revolutionary: Ada Fishman Maimon—A Biography* (Jerusalem: Yad Ben-Zvi/Ben-Gurion Research Institute for the Study of Israel and Zionism, 2018) (Hebrew).

17 Margalit Shilo, "The Women's Agricultural Training Farm at Kinneret, 1911–1917: A Solution to the Problem of the Working Woman in the Second Aliyah," *Cathedra* 14 (1981): 112 (Hebrew).

18 Carmel-Hakim, *Hannah Maisel*.

19 Batsheva Margalit-Stern, "'A Queen Without a Kingdom': Jewish Women Workers in the Labor Force in Mandatory Palestine," in *Economy and Society in Mandatory Palestine, 1918–1948*, ed. Avi Bareli and Nahum Karlinsky (Beersheba: Ben-Gurion Research Institute, Ben-Gurion University of the Negev Press, 2003): 113–51 (Hebrew).

20 Sylvie Fogiel-Bijaoui and Rachel Sharabi, eds., *Dynamics of Gender Borders: Women in Israel's Cooperative Settlements* (Berlin: de Gruyter; and Jerusalem: Magnes, 2017).

21 Yochebed Bat-Rachel, *The Path I Followed: Chapters from My Life and Labors* (Efal: Yad Tabenkin, 1981), 94 (Hebrew).

22 Tami Kaminsky, *Their Way: The Women of Ein Harod, 1921–1948* (Sde-Boker: Ben-Gurion Research Institute for the Study of Israel and Zionism; and Efal: Yad-Tabenkin, 2019) (Hebrew).

23 Lilia Bassewitz, "Kibbutz Society," *Mibifnim* 52 (November 23, 1931): 653 (Hebrew).

24 Fogiel-Bijaoui and Sharabi, *Dynamics of Gender Borders*.

25 Smadar Sinai, *Women and Gender in Hashomer* (Efal: Yad Tabenkin/Hakibbutz Hameuchad, 2013) (Hebrew).

26 Dganit Boni-Davidi, "Women and Gender in the Haganah, 1920–1948," in *Security and Political Challenges Put to the Test: Israel in the Arab and International Arenas*, ed. Michael Laskier and Ronen Yitzhak (Ramat-Gan: Bar-Ilan University Press, 2012), 101–34 (Hebrew).

27 Naama Teitelbaum-Kari, "Female Leadership from the Ranks of the Opposition: The Profile of Esther Raziel-Naor, Irgun Commander and Opposition Leader," PhD diss., Bar-Ilan University, 2019 (Hebrew).

28 Gilad Zerubabel, "A Young Girl in Battle," in *Sefer Hapalmach: Elite Fighting Force of the Haganah*, 2 vols., ed. Gilad Zerubabel (Tel Aviv: Hakibbutz Hameuchad, 1955–1957), 2: 781–82 (Hebrew).

29 Anat Granit-Hacohen, *Hebrew Women Join the Forces: Jewish Women from Palestine in the British Forces During the Second World War* (Portland, OR: Vallentine Mitchell, 2017).

30 Yonit Efron, "Sisters, Fighters, and Mothers: The Ethos and Reality of the 1948 Generation," *Iyunim Bitkumat Israel* 10 (2000): 365–66 (Hebrew).

31 Lilach Rosenberg-Friedman, "Captivity and Gender: The Experience of Female Prisoners of War During Israel's War of Independence," *Nashim: A Journal of Jewish Women's Studies and Gender Issues* 33 (fall 2018): 64–89, https://doi.org/10.2979/nashim.33.1.04.

32 https://www.ynetnews.com/articles/0,7340,L-5232952,00.html.

33 Judy Baumel-Schwartz, *Perfect Heroes: The World War II Parachutists from Palestine and the Israeli Heroic Ethic* (Madison: University of Wisconsin Press, 2010).

34 Ruti Glick, *Captive in a New Land: The Story of the Immigrant Hanna Szenes* (Haifa: Pardes, 2013) (Hebrew).

35 Lilach Rosenberg-Friedman, "National Mission, Feminine Identity, and Female Leadership in a Mythical Masculine Organization: The Story of Ada Sireni, the Head of the Mossad Le'Aliya in Italy in the 1940s," *Women's Studies* 43, no. 5 (2014): 589–618.

36 Lilach Rosenberg-Friedman, *Revolutionaries Despite Themselves: Women and Gender in Religious Zionism in the Yishuv Period* (Jerusalem: Yad Ben-Zvi, 2005), 241–48 (Hebrew).

37 Orna Sasson-Levy, *Identities in Uniform: Masculinities and Femininities in the Israeli Military* (Jerusalem: Magnes, 2006) (Hebrew).

38 Shifra Shvartz and Zipora Shehory-Rubin, *Hadassah: For the Health of the People* (Monterey, CA: Samuel Wachtman's Sons, 2012).

39 Dafna Hirsch, "The Medicalization of Motherhood: Ethnic Relation and the Education of Jewish Mizrahi Mothers in Mandate Palestine," in *Gender in Israel: New Studies on Gender in the Yishuv and State*, ed. Margalit Shilo and Gideon Katz (Beersheba: Ben-Gurion Research Institute for the Study of Israel and Zionism, 2011), 112, 137–38 (Hebrew).

40 Hanna Herzog, "The Fringes of the Margin: Women's Organizations in the Civic Sector of the Yishuv," in *Pioneers and Homemakers: Jewish Women in Pre-State Israel*, ed. Deborah Bernstein (Albany: State University of New York Press, 1992), 283–304.

41 Batsheva Margalit-Stern, *Redemption in Bondage: The Women Workers' Movement in Eretz Israel, 1920–1939* (Jerusalem: Yad Ben-Zvi/Schechter Institute, 2006) (Hebrew).

42 Rosa Welt-Strauss, "Jewish Women's Campaign for Equal Rights," letter to the editor, *Haaretz*, September 29, 1919 (Hebrew).

43 Margalit Shilo, *Girls of Liberty: The Struggle for Suffrage in Mandatory Palestine* (Boston: Brandeis University Press, 2016).

44 Deborah S. Bernstein, *Women on the Margins: Gender and Nationalism in Mandate Tel Aviv* (Jerusalem: Yad Ben-Zvi, 2008) (Hebrew).

45 Talia Pfefferman, "Women's Silence in 'The Life of a Worker in Her Homeland' (1935) by Henya Pekelman," in *Gender in Israel: New Studies on Gender in the Yishuv and State*, ed. Margalit Shilo and Gideon Katz (Beersheba: Ben-Gurion Research Institute for the Study of Israel and Zionism, 2011), 23–49 (Hebrew).

46 Sharon Geva, *To the Unknown Sister: Holocaust Heroines in Israeli Society* (Tel Aviv: Hakibbutz Hameuchad, 2010) (Hebrew).

47 Shabtai Daniel, ed., *Rachel Berkman: Her Life, Appreciations, Recollections* (Tel Aviv: Mo'etset ha-Po'alot, 1939), 10, 66 (Hebrew); Rosenberg-Friedman, *Revolutionaries*, 7–11.

48 Zipora Shehory-Rubin and Shifra Shvartz, *Alexandra Belkind: The Story of a Pioneering Jewish Woman Doctor* (Zichron Ya'akov: Itai Bahur, 2012) (Hebrew); Margalit Shilo, *Women Build a Nation: Professional Women in the Land of Israel, 1918–1948* (Jerusalem: Carmel, 2020) (Hebrew); Ruth Markus, "Artists: Yishuv and Israel, 1920–1970," in *Jewish Women: A Comprehensive Historical Encyclopedia*, ed. E. Hayman and Dalia Ofer (Jerusalem: Shalvi, 2006) (Hebrew).

49 Sigal Davidi, "The Women Architects of Mandate Palestine and the Creation of Social Modernism," PhD diss., Tel Aviv University, 2014 (Hebrew).

50 Batsheva Younis, "Recollections from the Earliest Days," *Harufu'a* 12, no. 1 (1936): 39 (Hebrew).

51 Pnina Motzafi-Haller, "Scholarship, Identity, and Power," *Signs* 26, no. 3 (2001): 710.

52 Shlomit Lir, *To My Sister: Mizrahi Feminist Politics* (Tel Aviv: Babel, 2007) (Hebrew); Henriette Dahan Kalev, "Oriental Women: Identity and Herstory," in *Jewish Women in the Yishuv and Zionism: A Gender Perspective*, ed. Margalit Shilo, Ruth Kark, and Galit Hasan-Rokem (Jerusalem: Yad Ben-Zvi, 2002), 49, 60 (Hebrew).

53 Pnina Motzafi-Haller, "New Challenges in the Historiographic and Sociological Research of Oriental Jewish Women," in *Woman in the East, Woman from the East: The Story of the Oriental Jewish Woman*, ed. Tova Cohen and Shaul Regev (Ramat-Gan: Bar-Ilan University Press, 2005), 17 (Hebrew).

54 Rosenberg-Friedman, *Birthrate Politics in Zion*.

55 Tammy Razi, "'The Family Is Worthy of Being Rebuilt': Perceptions of the Jewish Family in Mandate Palestine, 1918–1948," in *One Law for Men and Women: Women, Rights, and Law During the British Mandate*, ed. Eyal Katvan, Margalit Shilo, and Ruth Halperin-Kaddari (Ramat-Gan: Bar-Ilan University Press, 2011), 21–56 (Hebrew); Lilach Rosenberg-Friedman, "The National Character of the

Yishuv and Its Limitations: The Committee on the Birthrate Problems of the Va'ad Leumi as a Case Study," *Cathedra* 167 (2018): 1–38 (Hebrew).

56 Lilach Rosenberg-Friedman, "Nationalism, Gender, and Feminine Identity: The Case of Post–World War II Zionist Female Emissaries," *European Journal for Jewish Studies* 8, no. 2 (2014): 194–216.

57 Rosenberg-Friedman, "Nationalism."

58 Deborah Bernstein, "Between Woman, Man, and the Homemaker: Women and Family Among Jewish Urban Workers During the Yishuv," in *Israeli Society: A Critical Perspective*, ed. Uri Ram (Tel Aviv: Breirot, 1993), 88 (Hebrew).

59 Billie Melman, "From the Periphery to the Center of History: Gender and National Identity in the Yishuv, 1890–1920," *Zion* 52 (1997): 253 (Hebrew); Bernstein, "Daughters of the Nation."

60 Judith, "[Response] to Ben-Gurion's Three Comments," *Hapoel Hatza'ir* 47 (August 12, 1943): 25 (Hebrew).

61 Judith, "[Response] to Ben-Gurion," 25.

62 Hedva Nofech, "What People Think About the Question of the Modern Woman in Palestine," *Tesha Ba'erev* 7, no. 22.4 (1937): n.p. (Hebrew).

63 Margalit Shilo, "Professional Women in the Yishuv in Mandatory Palestine: Shaping a New Society and a New Jewish Woman," *Nashim: A Journal of Jewish Women's Studies and Gender Issues* 34 (spring 2019): 33–52.

64 Judith Harari, *An Israeli Woman and Mother* (Tel Aviv: Masada, 1958), 400 (Hebrew).

65 Zipora Shehory-Rubin, "Dr. Helena Kagan: The Doctor Who Became a Legend," *Cathedra* 118 (2006): 89–114 (Hebrew).

66 Margalit Shilo, "The Absorption Narrative as the Narrative of Female Empowerment: Saida Binat the Yemenite," in *A New Spirit in the Palace of Torah*, ed. Ronit Irshai and Dov Schwartz (Ramat-Gan: Bar-Ilan University Press, 2018), 275–300 (Hebrew); Rachel Sharabi, "Confrontation and Compromise: How Yemenite Women Immigrants Dealt with the Social Framework," in *Woman in the East, Woman from the East: The Story of the Oriental Jewish Woman*, ed. Tova Cohen and Shaul Regev (Ramat-Gan: Bar-Ilan University Press, 2005), 224 (Hebrew).

GIRLS COMING-OF-AGE DURING THE HOLOCAUST

Gender, Class, and the Struggle for Survival in Eastern Europe

NATALIA ALEKSIUN

I decided not to wear plaits any longer and copying Walt Disney's Snow White *wore my long hair loose with a ribbon fastened around my head. Apparently because of this change, somebody told me I was a pretty girl, somebody else addressed me as "Miss." All this and nature itself brought home to me that I was no longer a child.*[1]

IN HER 1986 MEMOIR, *Winter in the Morning*, Janina Bauman remembers fondly the last days of the fateful summer in 1939. With her well-off and close-knit family, she celebrated her thirteenth birthday in a spa before returning to Warsaw on the eve of the German attack against Poland. She felt that her childhood ended then, but it was living in the Warsaw ghetto and in hiding on the so-called Aryan side (outside the ghetto) that molded her experience of adolescence. Conversely, her daily life in the ghetto and on the Aryan side was shaped by her own self-perception as belonging to a particular class and age group. Bauman's sense of self vacillated while she attended underground classes in the Warsaw ghetto, met up with friends, enjoyed the attention of young men, and when she found herself on the run after escaping to the Aryan side. Her self-perception shifted according to external indicators, internal feelings, and bodily changes. Indeed, *Winter in the Morning* opens a window onto the experience of coming-of-age in Eastern Europe during the Holocaust. This chapter is grounded in Bauman's recollections and other diaries and memoirs of young women who reflected on their experiences as children becoming teenagers. In considering the gap between her experiences and her later adult perspective, Bauman insisted that she "made an effort to be faithful not only to the facts but also to my own thoughts and feelings at the time."[2] This effort tested the limits of memory, self-representation, and staying true to her young self. As Bauman declared, "Mine was the small, limited world of a teenage girl living in fear, in seclusion, in ignorance of very many important facts and occurrences. That is why my account is not and does not pretend to be a historical document."[3] But diaries and memoirs are historical documents that can shed light on personal experiences, even if they require careful reading and keen awareness of the influence of the loss of family members, social taboos, and self-censorship among other constraints.[4]

A growing number of scholars are examining the experience of Jewish women in the Holocaust.[5] In her review essay on women and gender in the Holocaust, Marion Kaplan summarizes the interpretative gains: "Without women's memories we missed not only familial and domestic aspects of the Holocaust but also gendered public behaviors and humiliations and gendered

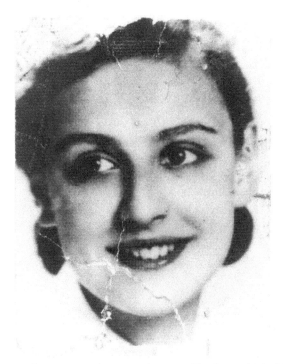

Janina Bauman in the Warsaw ghetto, early 1942. The Second World War Experience Centre, LEEWW.2000.431. Reproduced with permission.

persecutions in ghettos and camps."[6] Posing new questions of old sources, women's personal accounts, allows for a more nuanced discussion of women's sexuality, sexual violence, and survival strategies of individuals and families.[7] Likewise, scholars pay close attention to the plight of Jewish children.[8] However, Jewish female adolescence, defined here as roughly ages 10–18, has hardly been studied as a separate category. There is good reason for this, as notions of age seem blurred in the sources themselves. Different agencies exercised the power to define and redefine Jewish coming-of-age in Eastern Europe during the Holocaust. Still, I argue for the centrality of age as a key factor that, together with gender and class, shaped the experience of Jewish adolescents in the ghettos and living in hiding and the camps.

Two crucial issues shaped the experience of coming-of-age during the Holocaust: economic status and family relations, in particular those between teenage daughters and their parents. The longer families stayed together, the longer parents could act in parental capacities, even if internal family dynamics underwent transformation. Moreover, relative wealth determined the degree of continuity in retaining childhood roles. The age of puberty and its intersection with Nazi policies and individual trajectories during the Holocaust influenced experiences as well. Did a 13-year-old girl indeed cease to be a child, as Bauman boldly declared? Or did she rather indicate an awareness about changes in her body that became amplified as she continued to grow up during the war? And to what extent did the experiences of female Jewish teenagers differ from their male counterparts of a similar class? Bauman's sense of her childhood ending resembles patterns in the Jewish religious tradition. According to Halakhah (Jewish law), the age of adulthood for boys begins at 13 and for girls at 12, when they are required to perform religious commandments as adults. What role did religious definitions play—if any, for girls—and how did the Nazi way of categorizing children affect the process of coming-of-age? Nazi policy set the age for forced labor at 12, lumping young adolescents together with adults. Moreover, in the General Government in Nazi-occupied Poland, the German administration ordered every Jew over the age of 10 to display a white armband with a blue Star of David, thus setting an external mark that identified a child who was no longer to be treated as such.[9]

Jewish teenagers endured the same stages of the German anti-Jewish policy in Eastern Europe as other Jews, including dispossession, resettlement, ghettoization, exploitation, deportations, incarceration, and annihilation. The ways in which young people negotiated these shifts provide further insight into these processes and allow a glimpse into what the experience of genocide meant for young women in particular, what it signified to them as witnesses and victims.

Childhood Before the War

IN THEIR DIARIES AND memoirs middle-class Jewish women who came of age in Eastern Europe set the stage for their experiences during the Holocaust by portraying their loving, close-knit families before the war.

> I was growing up in a happy family. My father was a doctor and surgeon, dealing with people's kidneys and bladders. My mother's father, Grandad Aleksander, was a doctor too, his fame well established in Warsaw before I was born. . . . There were lots of uncles, aunts and cousins on both sides of the family, most of them doctors, others lawyers, engineers or such like.[10]

For Bauman, time spent in Konstancin, near Warsaw, in a splendid country villa built by her grandfather epitomized her prewar childhood, graced by supportive family, material security, and blissful encounters with nature. She noted, "I remember those years as a bright, warm time of sensual and emotional exploration, vivid imagination, a growing love for anything of beauty around me; as a time when I read my first books and made my first friendships."[11]

Halina Nelken also reminisced about her happy childhood in an affluent middle-class family in Kraków. Born in 1923, she grew up surrounded by a loving family who encouraged her interest in reading and art. She fondly remembered her parents' home, filled with oriental rugs and tapestries, Viennese furniture, and paintings of distinguished Polish painters, where she listened to her favorite fairy tales and Polish poetry and looked at albums.[12] Fifteen years old when the war broke out, Mary Berg lived in Łódź, where her father ran an art gallery and her mother worked as a fashion designer and where she attended a prestigious private Jewish gymnasium.[13] In October 1939 Berg reflected on the dramatic change: "I can hardly believe that only six weeks ago my family and I were at the lovely health resort of Ciechocinek, enjoying a carefree vacation with thousands of other visitors. I had no idea then what was in store for us."[14] Having experienced the beginning of the German occupation in Łódź, her family decided to flee to Warsaw. Those who managed to escape the Nazis only to experience the harsh reality of Soviet occupation in eastern Poland from 1939 until 1941 also recorded glimpses of family devotion and support. Writing in 1943 while she was in hiding on the Aryan side, 12-year-old Janina Hescheles chronicled her life in the Lwów ghetto and in Janowska camp. She recalled the delightful time she spent with her adoring parents, after her father Henryk had been released from Soviet arrest.[15]

Even though more middle-class authors survived, most Polish Jews were struggling or poor. Indeed, in juxtaposing childhood before the war and childhood loss during the Holocaust, for most, memories of large and loving families transcend class. Halina Birenbaum (Hala Grynsztejn), who was 10 years old in 1939, lived in Warsaw with her parents and two older brothers. Her father owned a small business, but her mother had to take on sewing to supplement the family's budget. Birenbaum underscored that she enjoyed a particularly close relationship with her resourceful mother, which sustained her in the early months of the war. After their apartment burned in the siege of Warsaw and they moved to a crowded place, Birenbaum wrote, "The few rescued things were kept in a box; my mother arranged for us to sleep on the floor on mattresses saved from the fire."[16] Riwka Lipszyc, who was born in Łódź in 1929 and died in Auschwitz, focused on the importance of extended family in her diary written in the ghetto. After Lipszyc lost her father in the summer of 1941 and then her mother a year later, she and her three siblings were adopted by their aunt and uncle. But in September 1942, the two youngest were deported to the death camp.[17] When their aunt died in the summer of 1943, Lipszyc and her sister were cared for by their cousin, who was 20 at the time.[18] In January 1944, after she had already lost her parents and two younger siblings, Lipszyc drew strength from the memories of her Orthodox childhood before the war: "I've noticed that I'm looking for inspiration . . . in memories. [. . .] Oh, God! I feel blessed to have been born in a family like ours, not in any other . . . After all I was lucky."[19] Even as she was missing her dead parents, she was able to find some comfort remembering her childhood with them.[20]

Still, a few testimonies preserve family disappointments over lack of family closeness. Growing up in the small town of Šamorín (Somorja) in western Slovakia, Ellie Friedmann dreamed of becoming a famous writer and yearned for her emotionally distant mother's acceptance and embrace.[21] When the town came under Hungarian occupation in 1938, her father's business was confiscated and she had to leave school. For many, however, writing about family conflicts and tensions with parents and siblings who had perished proved too difficult. Instead, they focused on their happy prewar childhoods as a coping mechanism during the war and as a way of living on after catastrophe.

Continued Education

Bauman's family did not experience drastic pauperization and an immediate decline in lifestyle in the first months of the occupation and even after the establishment of the ghetto in October 1940.[22] Owing to their parents' strong prewar financial position, Bauman, Nelken, Berg, and Hescheles were able to continue their education in underground courses. Not only were these courses costly, but also students often dropped out because they worked to support their families.[23] In Warsaw, Bauman and Berg together with their younger sisters attended gymnasium classes. During the first months in the Warsaw ghetto, Bauman, her sister, and their mother moved in with relatives. The adults divided the chores among themselves. But the children—Janina and Sophie—were "expected to continue our studies instead. This we did. There were many good teachers trapped in the ghetto, and plenty of children wanting to learn. I found a few of my old friends now living close to me, we got in touch with some teachers from a good prewar grammar school for boys called 'Spójnia' (Bond), and within a couple of days we began our third year of secondary education."[24]

Berg also attended gymnasium; most of the teachers and many classmates from her former school also had escaped from Łódź to Warsaw in the first months of the occupation. The class met at her parents' apartment because her mother's American citizenship was thought to afford a degree of security.[25] Berg marveled that the students worked hard with a sense of "strange earnestness" and that all passed demanding high school exams organized in the underground.[26] These girls were aware of their privileged position, being able to study rather than forced to work to keep their families afloat.

Despite her less privileged background, Birenbaum too continued her education, encouraged by her older brother, although she does not indicate how her family was able to pay her private tutor, who later starved to death in the Warsaw ghetto.[27] She remarked that "studying and reading in those terrible times took me into another world, a world free of Nazis, ghettos, and murder."[28] For Berg, Birenbaum, and other teenage girls from families who could afford private tutors and could join study groups, education emerges as a central theme. Teenagers who retained access to books and education in the ghettos enjoyed their childhoods longer. Lipszyc, whose means in the Łódź ghetto, sealed off in May 1940, were limited, especially after the death of her parents, still attended classes disguised as vocational training in workshops where she worked. These created a crucial sense of continuity with her prewar education.[29] Lipszyc's relationship with her mentor—Fajga Zelicka, who had attended the Bais Yaakov's Seminary for Teachers in Kraków and who supported Lipszyc's education on behalf of the Juvenile Protection Committee—further strengthened that connection.[30] Following the German occupation of Lwów in the summer of 1941, Hescheles attended underground classes because "Mommy wanted me to study. For this reason, I went three times a week to classes. There were a handful of us. . . . We met every two weeks at someone else's flat. We were taught by Miss Wasserman."[31] But all educational efforts, regardless of the prewar status of Jewish families, ceased after the German roundups and deportations began.

Family Relations and Communal Suffering

HOLOCAUST ACCOUNTS OF ADOLESCENT girls of all classes repeatedly describe the ongoing loss of family members. The girls report the fates of relatives who died early on of natural causes, although often triggered by instances of abuse or physical violence. Bauman's grandfather Maks suffered a stroke after he was assaulted by Germans who picked him up in his apartment. Bauman concluded, "So I lost my beloved grandfather, too, and had just one grandma left, the one I had never particularly liked. But as she was the only one, my feelings for her grew stronger and our relationship became closer than before."[32] Still, middle-class families were more likely to maintain a semblance of prewar life, isolating children from the horror around them. Although families suffered displacement and forced separation from the first days of the occupation, the surviving family networks continued to occupy a central place in the lives of young Jewish girls. It is through experience of family connection that they describe and explain their feelings, frustrations, fears, and hopes. Much of their early accounts focus on the fates of not only parents but also uncles, aunts, grandparents, and cousins. As members of their nuclear families perished, the existence of extended family networks become all the more important.

Even the relatively privileged girls were not oblivious to what was happening around them. Sometime in the winter of 1941, Bauman's mother received funds from a devoted Catholic companion, referred to as Aunt Maria, who sold objects on behalf of the family. And Bauman's mother took her daughters out for lunch at a restaurant in the Warsaw ghetto. Although she noticed "horrifying" prices, Bauman was delighted.

> If it hadn't been for Sophie and me, Mother would have got up and left, but she didn't want to disappoint us, so we stayed and ordered the least expensive items from the menu: chicken broth with noodles, cholent—[. . .] followed by milky pudding with cherry syrup. It was a true feast, the best meal we had had for ages. Though so far we had never starved in the ghetto, our daily meals at home were far less substantial and tasty. Sighing, Mother paid the bill, and filled with goodness we left the restaurant.[33]

At that point Bauman found herself among the privileged teenagers who were sheltered from the experience of hunger; she did not worry about earning a living or supporting her mother and younger sister. But she did not engage in self-deception. She noted the beggars, the starving, and the dead on the streets of the Warsaw ghetto.[34] At Berg's home members of the Łódź group gathered in the wake of the establishment of the Warsaw ghetto in November 1940: "We sat in a stupor and did not know what to undertake. Now all our efforts are useless. Who cares for the theater these days? Everyone is brooding over one thing and one thing only: the ghetto."[35] These relatively well-off teenage girls wrote about their sense of helplessness in changing the fate of the masses starving around them in the ghettos. But at the same time, Bauman, Nelken, and Berg accepted their privilege as a way of life, as they had done before the war.

Non-Jewish friends on the other side of the ghetto wall could also protect Jewish families from starvation. Such was the rather exceptional situation of Halina Birenbaum's family. Although not wealthy before the war, the Grynsztejns did not initially experience starvation in the Warsaw ghetto, thanks to assistance from her father's non-Jewish friends from work.[36] She observed beggars and starving children, including her own friends; unable to help them, she herself was provided with barely enough food by her parents.[37]

The pressure of living in a ghetto crept into the daily lives of all families, even when they did not immediately starve and even though in families of relative privilege shifts seemed subtler and not permanent. As the situation in the ghettos in German-occupied Poland deteriorated, many accounts testify to the changing roles of teenage daughters of all classes. Birenbaum notes that she "slowly stopped believing in my mother's assurances."[38] Even formerly middle-class daughters took on responsibility for their parents, trying to protect them from emotional anguish. Some became providers for their families. Bauman could afford not to worry about making a living in the Warsaw ghetto, but she tried to serve as a guardian of emotional well-being for her mother. Thus she decided not to tell her about the unexpected return of her friend's father in April 1941. She anticipated the pain her mother would experience, as her own father had disappeared in Soviet captivity.[39]

Harsh conditions in Eastern European ghettos accelerated emancipation of teenage children, meaning that young girls acquired agency they might not have had before. Forced to mature faster, they worked and sometimes did not fully obey their parents or follow the prewar norms of their social class, a process particularly fraught for girls who might have previously been subject to more rigid control. At the same time, this accelerated need to become an adult meant that parents treated their children as adults. Bauman remembered her own mother involving her in the intimate details of her life: "For a long time, she just kept stroking my hair. Then she started taking to me softly and frankly, as if I were not her daughter but her closest friend."[40] Again, being treated as more mature worked in different ways for females and males and with mothers and fathers.

Bauman vacillated between longing for the experience of safety provided by parents and the urge to protect her mother and younger sister. She fantasized that her absent father would have been able to protect them: "If only Father was here," she wrote in her diary in the fall of 1942. "We would be so much safer with him and so much better off. He would certainly know exactly what to do and how to cope with the worst. I know mother thinks the same."[41] When the Warsaw ghetto was transformed into a forced labor camp in the aftermath of the Great Liquidation Action in the summer of 1942 and more than 260,000 Jewish men, women, and children were deported to the extermination center in Treblinka and murdered, Bauman reported to work in cleaning emptied Jewish flats to spare her mother from the ordeal.[42]

Nazi persecution led to straining relations among relatives. As close-knit families broke up and grandparents, parents, and siblings perished, fear and hunger triggered conflicts and tensions, further adding to the sense of crisis and forcing teenagers to become adults. For Rywka Lipszyc the gradual loss of her family members contributed to her prematurely taking on adult roles. She felt bitter about the inequalities in dividing food provisions and food thefts. Lipszyc longed for the safety of childhood but at the same time also for the control of being an adult. In December 1943 she wrote with pride that her teacher admired her ability to assess her situation with the acumen of someone older than her age.[43] She also measured herself against her younger sister, who as a child had less control over her actions and was unable to resist the temptation of accepting things offered by their cousins: "I have decided, as I mentioned before, not to use what is exclusively theirs. Cipka can't overcome it, she's just a kid, but I succeeded and it pleases me."[44] Teenage girls measured their accelerated emancipation not only with regard to their parents but also by comparing themselves to their peer groups.

Peers, Friendship, and Love in the Ghetto

PEER GROUPS, OFTEN MIXED gender, served as a parallel network of reference and support. Among these, youth groups and underground activities constituted a particular category of peer group experiences key to the everyday life of teenage Jewish women. In Warsaw Berg described how her group of middle-class young Jewish refugees from Łódź organized a club to raise relief funds.

Berg took pride in the success of the show that her "Lodz Artistic Group" performed in September 1940 at the Joint Distribution Committee office.[45] In many ghettos, young women engaged in underground activities and fulfilled a particularly dangerous but crucial role as couriers.[46]

Friendship provided teenage girls with a source of emotional support and conversations about the future but, not surprisingly also with competition and petty jealousies. Some friendships continued from before the war, creating a link to lives lived in peaceful times. Other friendships were forced by the new circumstances. In the summer of 1941 Bauman juggled two close friends she had known from before the Nazi occupation. With one, Hanka, she discussed books, and with the other, Zula, she talked about boys and love, because "Hanka would dismiss the subject, blushing terribly."[47] It was a striking expression of the clinging to normalcy that scholars discuss in relation to Jewish children.[48] Teenage girls dreamed about love, experienced sexual attraction, developed crushes, and fell in love. And they lived through the entire range of emotions associated with these experiences. Relationships began more quickly and were felt intensely as young people, not knowing if they would survive, wanted to experience life to the fullest. In August 1941, working in an agricultural group sponsored by the Jewish Council (Judenrat), Bauman reflected on her envy of the romantic feelings one of her friends developed for their instructor, declaring, "It's Romeo I'm longing for."[49] On the eve of the Great Deportation with her own newfound love, Roman, she strode the streets of the ghetto vainly seeking privacy: "There is nowhere to go, there is no way to be alone. The streets moan and yell with a thousand voices, they reek of rotten fish and dying bodies. Wherever we turn, whatever we look at, all is ugliness. So we run away and hide from it all in the flat. Here at least we are safe from sounds and smells. Not from other people, though."[50] In a desperate search for intimacy, Roman proposed that they spend a night together in a secret hotel in the ghetto, although he had just enough money for one night there. But on the following morning, the Germans began deportations from the ghetto, and Bauman saw Roman again only after the liberation.[51]

Coming-of-age also meant some adolescent girls experienced strong feelings and attraction toward other women. On April 13, 1942, Melania Weissenberg, at 12 years old, noted intense feelings she developed for her friend in the ghetto of Dąbrowa Tarnowska.

If only you [Sabina Goldman] knew, Bineczka, how much I love you. . . . Oh, if only you knew. But you do not and you shall never know. Because you will not believe that such a love can exist. It is called lesbian love; that is, of a woman for another woman. I love you with all my naive, still entirely pure, tiny heart. And I am suffering.[52]

Later in hiding, Melania mourned Sabina's death during the liquidation of the ghetto.[53] In the Łódź ghetto, a peer group played an important role in the life of Rywka Lipszyc. She looked up to her educator Surcia (Sara Zelwer), who was a role model and a source of emotional support. For her, this relationship emerged as the strongest of her bonds.[54] At the same time, she seemed quite ambivalent—or simply uncomfortable or unsure—about interactions with boys, possibly because the model of Orthodox upbringing restricted social-izing in mixed-gender groups. Raised in a different cultural milieu, Bauman continued to seek attachments with young men.[55]

Longing for Nature, Fashion, Celebration, and Entertainment

Despite the omnipresent feeling of doom, or maybe because of it, young people were often oriented toward the future. Whether as younger girls play-ing hide and seek or slightly older ones dancing with young men, teenagers longed for freedom. Jewish teenage girls dreamed of beauty and nature. After working for a day outdoors for the Association to Promote Agriculture, pre-paring the grounds of the Holy Spirit Hospital for planting vegetables with a group of young boys and girls, Bauman marveled, "Eight long hours of hard physical work under the blue sky. Can't imagine anything better."[56] On March 21, 1942, Weissenberg, living in Dąbrowa Tarnowska, envisioned the upcoming spring wearing "a golden dress woven of rays of sun" and with "a wreath of primrose, its first harbingers."[57] Affectionately, if naively, she called on the spring for help: "Do not forget, remember and look everywhere! Wher-ever you looked, it became brighter and sadness disappeared. You ran away already. . . . Left for other houses, to other people and didn't look everywhere. You forgot to look into our dark, poor unfortunate Jewish souls."[58]

Birthdays reminded adolescent girls in the ghettos, in hiding, and in the camps about happier times spent with their families. At the same time, they brought to the surface a sense of profound injustice: reminders of the struggle to survive while so young, the beginning of adult life with its promise still unfulfilled. These realizations led to a sense of doom, anger, regret, and resolve to endure. Hiding in the midst of the Great Liquidation Action in the Warsaw ghetto, Bauman noted:

> The day dragged on endlessly. It was terribly hot and stuffy in the little room, deadly quiet all around. We kept straining our ears, reliving the events of the past day and night. I was trying to make out what day

it was, what date. Great-Aunt Bella, who had been keeping a diary, helped me, it was Tuesday 18 August, which meant it was my birthday, probably my last. I was sixteen.[59]

Acting according to one's age could help these young women cope, and the preoccupations of ordinary teenagers, such as one's looks, did not disappear when they entered the ghetto. When teenage girls had access to books, reading works not meant for their young age inspired their imaginations. For Bauman this occurred after the Great Liquidation Action with *The Magic Mountain*, a masterpiece of Thomas Mann.[60] Earlier, in the Warsaw ghetto, Bauman enjoyed listening to music and attending concerts.[61] She felt guilty for participating in entertainment against the background of persecution and poverty, but she still clung to these moments of forgetting about the tragic reality around her. Torn between vanity and self-awareness, Bauman scolded herself for manipulating her mother into letting her wear her mother's dress. She grew breasts and Bauman's mother insisted she wear the only dress that still fit.

> I've always hated it, ever since I got it two years ago. But I couldn't make Mother change her mind by just saying I didn't like the dress. So I told her that if I walked the streets all bright red, I might easily be spotted by that crazy German who comes to the ghetto every day on his break just to shoot dead a few Jews in the crowd. This argument did the job instantly—Mother stopped nagging and gave me one of her own dresses, the lovely grey one made of linen.[62]

Taking care of one's looks was also a survival strategy. When Birenbaum ate bread, potatoes, and grits, she was able to gain weight and it "proved advantageous to me later on, for I looked a great deal more serious and was able to deceive the executioners by concealing my real age from them—according to the Nazi law, death was the lot of children."[63] A certain look gave the adolescent girls confidence and played a role in selections during German deportations from the ghettos, when some young able-bodied Jews were allowed to stay in the ghettos or were sent to work camps rather than exterminated immediately.

Deportations and Separations

DURING THE SPRING AND summer of 1942, with the wave of deportations from the ghettos in Nazi-occupied Poland, adolescent girls experienced the breakdown of their families. Some still had one or both parents to rely on.

Birenbaum's symbiotic relationship with her mother continued, but it also shifted as she matured quickly: "Even in the ghetto, before the deportation campaigns started, I was not a good little girl. But suddenly this all changed, I began seeing everything differently, and my mother became for me the supreme, most perfect of models to imitate, which was a great joy in itself."[64] Her mother embraced the necessity for partnership: she "now spoke to me as though I were a grown-up, a friend."[65]

Birenbaum remembered in the early days of the Great Liquidation Action that her mother continued to be a beacon of strength for the whole family: "She alone could control herself, comfort the rest of us and devise new ways of saving our lives."[66] After capture Birenbaum was able to control her panic because of her mother's strength.[67] She describes her mother's courage at the Umschlagplatz in almost surreal terms: "She spoke serenely, just as though we were sitting in the tranquility of our own home."[68] It was her mother's perseverance and initiative that allowed Birenbaum and her older brother to escape death and return to the ghetto: "It was not easy. I was scared. I was scared of everything: the Nazis, the everlasting 'campaigns,' the continuous shooting that accompanied them. But what I dreaded most of all was losing my mother; I shuddered at the mere thought. I could not imagine life without her."[69]

Birenbaum was not yet 14 at the time, but her mother repeatedly told her, "Remember, you must always, everywhere, say you are nearly eighteen."[70] Indeed, Birenbaum no longer saw herself as a child. She noted the differences between herself and the children who hid with her in the Toebbens factory, a German textile company in the Warsaw ghetto, where Jewish slave laborers selected during the summer 1942 roundups worked: "We had to admire the way in which little children behaved, so patiently and sensibly, like grown-up people, as they suffered with us in the factory."[71] Yet teenage girls had to make heartbreaking decisions whether to stay with their parents or seek survival on their own. Their youth was an advantage during selections. Moreover, their bodies could be brokered to men, especially Jewish policemen, who had positions of relative power, possibly of life and death, in the ghetto structure. Presenting themselves as young women rather than children also kept them alive longer in the camps.[72]

Hiding

LEAVING THE GHETTO TO hide on the Aryan side proved critical for many adolescent girls, punctuating their experience of growing up during the Holocaust. Bauman, her sister Sophie, and their mother escaped from the Warsaw ghetto on

January 25, 1943: "At dusk we put on all the clothes we had and filled the pockets with our small belongings, in my case my diary and Roman's photographs."[73] Bauman hid with her mother and younger sister throughout most of the time until liberation. She noted the change that occurred in their family dynamic from the Great Liquidation Action of 1942 on. As her mother collapsed, Bauman took over, as she put it, as "a real head of the family." Bauman explained, "Without her brother, Mother felt insecure and helpless. Now it was I who had to take care of our day-to-day life, of settling down, finding food, even cooking. I also had to tell Mother and Sophie what to do and make all kinds of decisions for them. They gratefully accepted my leadership."[74] And she felt the burden of responsibility: "In those dark days of temporary stability, I had no close friend, nobody of my own age to talk to."[75] When evacuated from Warsaw after the defeat of the Polish uprising in the summer of 1944, however, it would be their mother who took the risk of seeking the intervention of a German officer in order not to be separated from her daughters.[76] Bauman concludes, "Though full grown, I still had a great deal to learn from my mother, and had never become as warm-hearted, forbearing and inwardly strong as she was."[77]

For many others, this was a moment of separation from their families, seeing their parents for the last time. These decisions were made collectively, by the parents, or by the young girls themselves. In September 1942 Weissenberg moved from Dąbrowa Tarnowska to a small village where a local farmer, Wiktor Wójcik, and his sister agreed to shelter her, if briefly, along with her older cousin Helena. Melania's mother, her stepfather, and her brother were unable to join them and all perished. Shortly after the liquidation of the ghetto, Melania wrote about her feelings of impending destruction of the entire Jewish community: "An enormous, black cloud is hanging over us and it surely shall descend on us. Why would you try to convince yourself that it shall not do so, that enough has already happened and that nothing else will? Why, Dąbrowa is no different, no better town than any other."[78] For Weissenberg, in hiding on the Wójciks' small farm, the constant company of her cousin was a source of tension but also emotional refuge. The two were inseparable during the whole time they were in hiding, and their conversation became their only source of distraction.[79] The context of hiding with or without other family members proved an essential setting for how adolescent girls learned about being grown-up women.

Sexuality, Sexual Barter, Exploitation, and Sexual Abuse

LIVING IN HIDING, ON the run from the Nazis and their collaborators, adolescent Jewish girls still worried about their femininity being erased. On the eve of the

Warsaw Ghetto Uprising in the spring of 1943, Bauman found herself enjoying a sense of her own attractiveness.[80] Yet experiencing attraction could be random, as those in hiding and passing as non-Jews were limited in their social interactions. Bauman flirted with the lover of her landlady, causing a painful friction as the man proposed to marry her despite their age difference to facilitate her rescue.[81]

Hiding on the Aryan side, however, rendered young Jewish women extremely vulnerable to sexual exploitation and assault. Indeed, when trying to survive in hiding or pass as a non-Jew, Jewish teenage girls had to negotiate the advances of people who helped them, knowing or not knowing about their Jewishness. Performing her assumed non-Jewish identity meant that Bauman constantly faced advances from men: landlords and blackmailers. On the run, she was propositioned by a German who worked as an armed train guard, searching for smuggled goods, partisans, and Jews. He forced her to sit next to him and offered to take her to a night club. On another occasion she was nearly raped by an extortionist who came to demand a ransom from Jews hiding on a partly destroyed floor above a German company.[82]

In December 1943 Weissenberg, who was only 13 years old, noted in her diary that she learned about sex from her cousin. She was interested in stories her cousin shared with her when they were forced to spend most of their time alone and cramped underground: "We talk a lot about having sex and Kitten shows me exactly how it is done. I convinced her to provoke Ciuruniu [Wójcik, the man hiding them] to let him know that she was also willing, despite the cold. She listened to me and she approached him and it happened."[83] Wójcik had sex with the older cousin first, but by the summer of 1944, sexual barter also involved Melania. In June 1944, Weissenberg noted: "Sex in broad daylight, behind the door on June 1. Also, on the next day. But it was no fun because it was only that."[84] Plagued by loneliness, boredom, and physical discomfort, Weissenberg derived from these encounters a sense of emotional connection and limited agency. Shortly before the arrival of the Red Army, Weissenberg considered a strategy that spelled the utter end of her childhood: "I convinced Kitten to tell that Rascal [Wójcik] that I was pregnant, so that he would per-haps take pity on me and stop being so cruel."[85] Sex with Wójcik served as a strategy to prolong their stay at his farm and improve the conditions of hiding and became part and parcel of his keeping them alive.

Camps

FOR JEWISH TEENAGE GIRLS deportation from the ghettos and arrival in the camps shattered whatever was left of the innocence of their childhoods.

Nelken registered this clearly: "Concentration Camp Kraków-Płaszów was a tremendous shock. We went straight to the sauna, and we waited in the nude, first for the clothes to come from delousing, then to be registered."[86] Upon their arrival in concentration camps, teenage girls underwent selection. Their physical appearance played a crucial role and adolescent girls who looked older could pass as able-bodied adults. Indeed, Birenbaum concluded that in Majdanek her physical appearance proved life-saving: "Fortunately . . . I was physically robust and plump enough not to be taken for a child, and the many 'selections,' during which weak, pale and thin women were sent to the gas chambers, passed me by."[87] In the first moments Birenbaum was still consoled by her mother, but after her death this role was soon to be taken up by Hela, her sister-in-law.[88] Nelken remembered: "Bewildered and ice-cold, I wrapped myself in our down quilt from home. At least I was next to my mother."[89] In the initial days at camp Płaszów, Nelken's mother took care of her daughter's clothing and hygiene, helping in the difficult physical and psychological adjustments. Therefore Nelken saw her mother as her protector during the traumatic introduction to camp reality: "My brave mother kept our whole family together with her fortitude, her common sense, and her profound wisdom about life. She would not accept that the present was not worth caring about because everything was only temporary, provisional."[90] Nelken's mother continued to care for her daughter and provide her with emotional support after they were sent together to Auschwitz in October 1944.[91] But their relationship at the camp became increasingly symbiotic and reciprocal. Time and again, Halina risked her life to rescue her mother.[92]

Among the fortunate ones who entered with their mothers and survived, Viennese-born Ruth Kluger was admitted to the women's camp in Auschwitz-Birkenau with her mother, with whom she also enjoyed a symbiotic relationship. She was only 13.[93] Sarah Cushman concludes, "Unlike the younger children, young teenagers who looked fit for work usually passed the initial camp selections. If accompanied by a parent, they could count on his or her attention and care. For mothers, arriving at a camp with young teenagers often translated into an uneven struggle to save any children."[94]

But only some entered camps with mothers, older sisters, or aunts. Most mourned for their lost family members, especially parents, while experiencing an environment of unremitting violence, extreme deprivation, and physical annihilation. Mutual aid was not just a form of resistance but a basic survival strategy. Teenage girls who had lost their relatives bonded together, creating surrogate family-like networks of support.[95] Arguably, many women imprisoned in camps bonded in this way, caring for one another and increasing individual chances of staying alive. "Camp sisters" were a source of material and psychological strength in place of parents and biological siblings.[96] Scholarship on supportive relationships in the camps suggests that survival could be a function of having a relative or creating family-like relationships. For example, Sybil Milton points to "membership in a supportive group" as one of the crucial factors determining chances for survival in concentration camps and considered "bonding and networks" as "women's specific forms of survival."[97] In her collection *Mothers, Sisters, Resisters*, Brana Gurewitsch includes accounts of powerful bonds among biological sisters and other women who, upon their arrival, decided to share food and supported one another.[98] And Nechama Tec concludes that "no matter what part of Europe they came from, no matter what camps they were transferred to and when, women formed cooperative groups."[99] Many included adolescent girls.

Conclusions

THIS ESSAY IS A foray into the experiences of female Jewish children and adolescents during the Holocaust in Eastern Europe, and I have argued that age was an important intersectional factor in the context of ghettos, hiding, and camps. Diaries and memoirs written by young women reflect their insights into their place in their families and communities, passion for life, self-scrutiny, and emergent understanding of womanhood. Most diaries and memoirs analyzed here are rooted in the middle-class status of Jewish families before the war and their trajectory of striving to retain a certain lifestyle in the first months of the occupation. The presence or absence of parents, and in particular of mothers, was a second crucial aspect of coming-of-age for teenage girls during World War II. At what point and under what circumstances did mothers, fathers, and older siblings disappear, and when did female Jewish youth begin to fend for itself? How did teens understand entering into adulthood in the extreme situation of the Nazi occupation? For those who stayed with family members and/or were older at the beginning of the war, the process may have been easier, because they could recall their parents. But younger children with no real memory of "normal" family life had only the reality of life in the ghetto, hiding, and the camps. The psychological challenge of living in closed ghettos affected family relations in myriad ways. Teenage girls negotiated new daily challenges. Those who were still protected from hunger and forced labor by the prewar status of their relatives experienced fear, separation, and loss, just like everyone else in the ghettos. Adolescent Jewish girls were forced to adopt an adult's point of view and become agents of their own survival. The process was freighted with ambivalence, longing for childhood tranquility, and a degree of autonomy in the face of impossible external conditions. By looking at the experience of young girls as expressed in diaries and memoirs, we gain access to previously neglected and often taboo histories of sexuality, emotions, family solidarity, and crisis.

Notes

I thank Halina Birenbaum, Winson W. Chu, Atina Grossmann, Anna Hájková, Marion Kaplan, Katarzyna Person, Helene J. Sinnreich, Joanna Sliwa, Zofia Trębacz, and Raphael Utz for their feedback.

1 Janina Bauman, *Winter in the Morning: A Young Girl's Life in the Warsaw Ghetto and Beyond, 1939–1945* (New York: Free Press, 1986), 15.

2 Bauman, *Winter in the Morning*, ix.

3 Bauman, *Winter in the Morning*, ix.

4 Diaries and memoirs describing coming-of-age pose a methodological challenge of focusing on the individual, on the familial, and on emotions and family relations rather than on sweeping accounts of life in the ghettos or camps. See Ewa Wiatr, "Wstęp," in *Dziennik z getta łódzkiego*, by Rywka Lipszyc (Kraków: Austeria, 2017), xvii.

5 See Dalia Ofer and Lenore J. Weitzman, eds., *Women in the Holocaust* (New Haven, CT: Yale University Press, 1998); Marcia Sachs Littell, ed., *Women in the Holocaust: Responses, Insights, and Perspectives (Selected Papers from the Annual Scholars' Conference on the Holocaust and the Churches, 1900–2000)* (Merion Station, PA: Merion Westfield Press, 2001); Martyna Grądzka-Rejak, *Kobieta żydowska w okupowanym Krakowie (1939–1945)* (Kraków: Wydawnictwo 'Wysoki Zamek', 2016); and Zoë Waxman, *Women in the Holocaust: A Feminist History* (Oxford, UK: Oxford University Press, 2017).

6 Marion Kaplan, "Did Gender Matter During the Holocaust?" *Jewish Social Studies* 24, no. 2 (2019): 39.

7 See Marion Kaplan, *Between Dignity and Despair: Jewish Life in Nazi Germany* (Oxford, UK: Oxford University Press, 1998); Helene Sinnreich, "And It Was Something We Didn't Talk About: The Rape of Jewish Women During the Holocaust," *Holocaust Studies* 14, no. 2 (2008): 1–22; Anna Hájková, "Sexual Barter in Times of Genocide: Negotiating the Sexual Economy of the Theresienstadt Ghetto," *Signs* 38, no. 3 (2013): 503–33; and Natalia Aleksiun, "Gender and Daily Lives of Jews in Hiding in Eastern Galicia," *Nashim* 27 (fall 2014): 38–61.

8 See Debórah Dwork, *Children with a Star: Jewish Youth in Nazi Europe* (New Haven, CT: Yale University Press, 1991); Danielle Bailly, ed., *The Hidden Children of France, 1940–1945: Stories of Survival* (Albany: Excelsior Editions/State University of New York Press, 2010); Emunah Nachmany-Gafny, *Dividing Hearts: The Removal of Jewish Children from Gentile Families in Poland in the Immediate Post-Holocaust Years* (Jerusalem: Yad Vashem, 2009); and Joanna Sliwa, "The Place of Jewish Children in the Nazi Scheme of Genocide," paper presented at

the Workshop on Children and Mass Violence, Clark University, October 19–20, 2017. I thank Dr. Sliwa for sharing the typescript of her presentation.

9 "Identifying Marks for Jews in the Government-General, November 23, 1939," in *Documents on the Holocaust: Selected Sources on the Destruction of the Jews of Germany and Austria, Poland, and the Soviet Union*, ed. Yitzhak Arad, Israel Gutman, and Abraham Margaliot (Lincoln: University of Nebraska Press; and Jerusalem: Yad Vashem, 1999), 178. See also "Bekanntmachung der Stadhauptmanns. Betr: Die Erfassung der arbeitszwangspflichtigen Juden," April 4, 1940, United States Holocaust Memorial Museum, ITS 1277.0035.0021, 0022; and "XLVII. Obwieszczenie Starosty Miejskiego dot.: ujęcia w ewidencję żydów obowiązanych do pracy przymusowej. 4.III.1940. Schmid," Archiwum Narodowe w Kraków (State Archives, National Archives in Kraków), SMKr reels J13923–J13926, cz. I, J13923, p. 185. In other territories under German occupation or aligned with the Third Reich, there was no age restriction for yellow stars; see "Provisional Directives by Lohse, Reichskommissar for Ostland, Concerning the Treatment of Jews, August 13 1941," in *Documents on the Holocaust: Selected Sources on the Destruction of the Jews of Germany and Austria, Poland, and the Soviet Union*, ed. Yitzhak Arad, Israel Gutman, and Abraham Margaliot (Lincoln: University of Nebraska Press; and Jerusalem: Yad Vashem, 1999), 378–83.

10 Bauman, *Winter in the Morning*, 1–2. See the testimony recorded in Warsaw in August 1957 of Alina Lewinson, Janina's mother, and her focus on the family network: Archiwum ŻIH (Archives of the Jewish History Institute in Warsaw), 301/6816.

11 Bauman, *Winter in the Morning*, 3. See also 6.

12 Halina Nelken, *And Yet I Am Here*, trans. Halina Nelken and Alicia Nitecki (Amherst: University of Massachusetts Press, 1999), 3.

13 Susan Pentlin, "Introduction," in *The Diary of Mary Berg: Growing up in the Warsaw Ghetto . . .* , ed. S. L. Shneiderman (Oxford, UK: Oneworld, 2006), xxi–xxiii.

14 S. L. Shneiderman, ed., *The Diary of Mary Berg: Growing up in the Warsaw Ghetto . . .* (Oxford, UK: Oneworld, 2006), 1, entry dated October 10, 1939.

15 Janina Hescheles, *Oczyma dwunastoletniej dziewczyny* (Warsaw: Żydowski Instytut Historyczny, 2015), 41–42.

16 Halina Birenbaum, *Hope Is the Last to Die: A Coming of Age Under Nazi Terror* (Armonk, NY: M. E. Sharpe: 1996), 3, 5.

17 Wiatr, "Wstęp," xiv.

18 See Wiatr, "Wstęp," xiv.

19 Rywka Lipszyc, *The Diary of Rywka Lipszyc, Found in Auschwitz by the Red Army in 1945 and First Published in San Francisco in 2014*, ed. Alexandra Zapruder (San Francisco: Jewish Family and Children's Services, 2014), 62, note taken on January 20, 1944.

20 See, for example, Lipszyc's note about missing the dead, 31 October, 1943, in Lipszyc, *Diary*, 44. A note on January 19, 1944, is particularly moving: "I looked into my mama's eye's (in the photo). Oh. God! How much they express and how much Tamarcia resembles her! Oh, I'll never tell you this, mommy! You've left me forever! I feel horrible, I'm suffocating! God, let me take the place of my mother.

Let me suffer for my siblings! Oh, God! It's so hard! . . . And I'm always alone!" (Lipszyc, *Diary*, 61–62).

21 Livia Bitton-Jackson, *I Have Lived a Thousand Years: Growing Up in the Holocaust* (New York: Simon & Schuster Books for Young Readers, 1997), 13–14.

22 Bauman, *Winter in the Morning*, 51.

23 See Cyla Rozenblum's account dated September 1, 1941, preserved in the Oneg Shabbat Archive, where she mentions engaging in smuggling to support her widowed mother. Cyla Rozenblym, "Jakie zmiany zaszły u mnie podczas wojny," in *Archiwum Ringelbluma: Konspiracyjne Archiwum Getta Warszawy*, vol. 2, *Dzieci-tajne nauczanie w getcie warszawskim*, ed. Ruta Sakowska (Warsaw: ŻIH, 1997), 15.

24 Bauman, *Winter in the Morning*, 39.

25 In July 1940 Berg reported in her diary, "We study all the regular subjects and have even organized a chemistry and physics laboratory using glasses and pots from our kitchen instead of test tubes and retorts. Special attention is paid to the study of foreign languages, chiefly English and Hebrew. Our discussions of Polish literature have a peculiarly passionate character" (Shneiderman, *Diary of Mary Berg*, 22, entry dated July 12, 1940). Eventually, American citizenship allowed the family to be included in the transfer from the Warsaw ghetto, leave Warsaw, and travel to New York.

26 Shneiderman, *Diary of Mary Berg*, 23, entry dated July 12, 1940.

27 Birenbaum, *Hope Is the Last to Die*, 12.

28 Birenbaum, *Hope Is the Last to Die*, 13.

29 On November 8, 1943, she mentions practicing sawing and studying Hebrew; see Lipszyc, *Diary*, 45.

30 See, for example, her note from February 10, 1944: Lipszyc, *Diary*, 74. The Juvenile Protection Committee (Komitet Opieki nad Młodocianymi) placed orphans with foster families and provided them material support.

31 Hescheles, *Oczyma dwunastoletniej dziewczyny*, 48. As the situation deteriorated after the establishment of the ghetto in November 1941 and violence became rampant with forced transfers of population, Hescheles continued to study with her last friend, Alma Zelermajer, 49.

32 Bauman, *Winter in the Morning*, 33.

33 Bauman, *Winter in the Morning*, 52.

34 Bauman, *Winter in the Morning*, 41–42, 48.

35 Shneiderman, *Diary of Mary Berg*, 29, entry dated November 22, 1940.

36 Birenbaum, *Hope Is the Last to Die*, 7.

37 Birenbaum, *Hope Is the Last to Die*, 78–79.

38 Birenbaum, *Hope Is the Last to Die*, 78.

39 Bauman, *Winter in the Morning*, 43.

40 Bauman, *Winter in the Morning*, 44.

41 Bauman, *Winter in the Morning*, 85, entry dated November 2, 1942.

42 Bauman, *Winter in the Morning*, 88.

43 Lipszyc, *Diary*, 53.

44 Lipszyc, *Diary*, 55.

45 Shneiderman, *Diary of Mary Berg*, 26–27, entry dated September 11, 1940.
46 See Lenore J. Weitzman, "Women of Courage: The Kashariyot (Couriers) in the Jewish Resistance During the Holocaust," in *Lessons and Legacies*, vol. 6, *New Currents in Holocaust Research*, ed. Jeffry M. Diefendorf (Evanston, IL: Northwestern University Press, 2004), 112–52. Among couriers, there was Chavka Folman-Raban, born in Kielce in 1924. See Chavka Folman-Raban, *Lo nifradeti me-hem* (Lohamei ha-Getaot: Beit Lohamei-hagetaot, 1997).
47 Bauman, *Winter in the Morning*, 49, entry dated August 3, 1941.
48 See Joanna Sliwa, "Coping with Distorted Reality: Children in the Krakow Ghetto," *Holocaust Studies* 16, nos. 1–2 (2015): 177–202.
49 Bauman, *Winter in the Morning*, 50, diary entry for August 3, 1941.
50 Bauman, *Winter in the Morning*, 63, entry dated July 22, 1942.
51 Bauman, *Winter in the Morning*, 66, entry dated July 22, 1942.
52 Molly Applebaum, *Buried Words: The Diary of Molly Applebaum* (Montreal: Azrieli Foundation, 2017), 4. For the original Polish, see Molly Applebaum, "Dziennik Melanii Weissenberg, 1942–1945," in *Szczęście posiadać dom pod ziemią . . . Losy kobiet ocalałych z Zagłady w okolicach Dąbrowy Tarnowskiej*, ed. Jan Grabowski (Warsaw: Stowarzyszenie Centrum Badań nad Zagładą Żydów, 2016). For queer desire, see Anna Hájková, "Den Holocaust queer erzählen," *Jahrbuch Sexualitäten* 3 (2018): 86–110.
53 See Applebaum, *Buried Words*, 19, entry dated February 22, 1943.
54 Lipszyc, *Diary*, 52–53, entry dated December 24, 1943. In the Polish edition, Lipszyc's emotional musings are more extensive; see 48–49.
55 Bauman, *Winter in the Morning*, 88–89.
56 Bauman, *Winter in the Morning*, 48.
57 Applebaum, *Buried Words*, 3.
58 Applebaum, *Buried Words*, 3.
59 Bauman, *Winter in the Morning*, 50.
60 Bauman, *Winter in the Morning*, 85, entry dated November 2, 1942. See also 86, entry dated November 12, 1942.
61 Bauman, *Winter in the Morning*, 50, 53–54.
62 Bauman, *Winter in the Morning*, 50–51, entry dated August 20, 1941.
63 Birenbaum, *Hope Is the Last to Die*, 7.
64 Birenbaum, *Hope Is the Last to Die*, 35.
65 Birenbaum, *Hope Is the Last to Die*, 34.
66 Birenbaum, *Hope Is the Last to Die*, 17.
67 Birenbaum, *Hope Is the Last to Die*, 24.
68 Birenbaum, *Hope Is the Last to Die*, 29.
69 See Birenbaum, *Hope Is the Last to Die*, 34.
70 Birenbaum, *Hope Is the Last to Die*, 18. In her communication with the author, Halina Birenbaum stressed that her mother repeatedly told her to give her age as 17 (note sent on March 21, 2019).
71 Birenbaum, *Hope is the Last to Die*, 19–20. She concluded, "There were no children in the real meaning of the word in the ghetto, and especially during the criminal deportation campaigns; they were all adults, they all feared for their lives

and struggled ferociously to prolong their lives, if only for an extra hour. Even the youngest among us understood and felt this."

72 Bauman, *Winter in the Morning*, 77–78, 87.

73 Bauman, *Winter in the Morning*, 96.

74 Bauman, *Winter in the Morning*, 73.

75 Bauman, *Winter in the Morning*, 84. The next inscription is on November 2, 1942.

76 Bauman, *Winter in the Morning*, 165.

77 Bauman, *Winter in the Morning*, 141.

78 Applebaum, *Buried Words*, 7, entry dated August 16, 1942.

79 On May 20, 1943, Mela wrote in her diary, "I am terribly bored. With Helcia we have no subject left. For months we are inseparable and without fresh impressions. Oh, how bored I am . . . [. . .] If only I could go outside . . . vain dreams, unattainable, beyond our reach . . ." (Applebaum, "Dziennik Melanii Weissenberg," 45). A few months earlier, on February 22, 1943, she complained about Helcia keeping secrets from her, 43.

80 Bauman, *Winter in the Morning*, 108.

81 Bauman, *Winter in the Morning*, 149, 153.

82 Bauman, *Winter in the Morning*, 125.

83 Applebaum, *Buried Words*, 22.

84 Applebaum, *Buried Words*, 27.

85 Applebaum, *Buried Words*, 36, entry dated January 14, 1945.

86 Nelken, *And Yet I Am Here*, 199.

87 Birenbaum, *Hope Is the Last to Die*, 79.

88 Birenbaum, *Hope Is the Last to Die*, 76–78.

89 Nelken, *And Yet I Am Here*, 199. See also 199–200.

90 Nelken, *And Yet I Am Here*, 200.

91 See Nelken, *And Yet I Am Here*, 218–22.

92 When her mother was selected away among "old women," Halina brought her back appealing to the SS staff. See Nelken, *And Yet I Am Here*, 225–26.

93 Ruth Kluger, *Still Alive: A Holocaust Girlhood Remembered* (New York: Feminist Press and City University of New York, 2003), 122.

94 Sarah M. Cushman, "The Women of Birkenau," PhD diss., Clark University, Worcester, Massachusetts, October 2010, 164.

95 See Birenbaum's account about friends being indispensable for her survival after the murder of her sister-in-law, in Birenbaum, *Hope Is the Last to Die*, 119–21, 123–25.

96 For camp sisters' mutual assistance, see Lucie Adalsberger, *Auschwitz: A Doctor's Story* (Boston: Northeastern University Press, 1995); Sara Tuvel Bernstein, Louise Loots Thornton, and Marlene Bernstein Samuels, *The Seamstress: A Memoir of Survival* (New York: Berkley Books, 1997); and Birenbaum, *Hope Is the Last to Die*. See also Joyce Parkey, "Camp Sisters: Women and the Holocaust," *VCU Menorah Review* 7 (summer–fall 2007), https://scholarscompass.vcu.edu/cgi/viewcontent.cgi?article=1064&context=menorah (accessed December 28, 2020).

97 Sybil Milton, "Women and the Holocaust: The Case of German and German-Jewish Women," in *When Biology Became Destiny: Women in Weimar Republic*

and Nazi Germany, ed. Renate Bridenthal, Atina Grossman, and Marion Kaplan (New York: Monthly Review Press, 1984), 311–16.

98 Brana Gurewitsch, ed., *Mothers, Sisters, Resisters: Oral Histories of Women Who Survived the Holocaust* (Tuscaloosa: University of Alabama Press, 1998), 95–218. See also Hans Ellger, "Die Frauen-Aussenlager des KZ Neuengamme: Lebensbedingungen und Überlebensstrategien," in *Genozid und Geschlecht: jüdische Frauen im nationalsozialistischen Lagersystem*, ed. Gisela Bock (New York: Campus, 2005), 169–84.

99 Nechama Tec, *Resilience and Courage: Women, Men, and the Holocaust* (New Haven, CT: Yale University Press, 2004), 119–204; Rochelle G. Seidel, *The Jewish Women of Ravensbrück Concentration Camp* (Madison: University of Wisconsin Press, 2004); Sarah Helm, *If This Is a Woman: Inside Ravensbrück, Hitler's Concentration Camp for Women* (London: Little, Brown, 2015). See also Waxman, *Women in the Holocaust*, 105.

ONE HUNDRED YEARS OF JEWISH WOMEN'S SPIRITUALITY IN THE UNITED STATES AND BEYOND

Dianne Ashton

AT THE BEGINNING OF the twenty-first century in the United States, spirituality is a widely used concept referring to a sense of wonder, awe, connection to the Divine, and personal renewal that can be experienced in a variety of settings by individuals or groups, both in formal religious contexts and outside them. Vehicles for expressing and communicating personal spirituality have multiplied for both women and men over the last century with new communication technologies. Among them are *diaries* (produced on paper or websites), *classes* (in homes, in communal buildings, outdoors, or in virtual space), *songs* (with music and/or lyrics written on paper, typed on laptops, sung into phones or performed, popularized on YouTube and social media), and *recitations* (including prayers with food preparation or at table). Spirituality is also *embodied* through activities with religious meaning (such as dancing, attending a *mikveh*, participating in congregational religious services, wrapping tefillin, donning a *tallit* or religiously mandated clothing). Spirituality can also be embodied literally by eating religiously prescribed or inspired foods and by using ritual objects and creating special settings in which religious activities will occur, whether in homes, synagogues, or meeting rooms. Spirituality also can be *voiced* by individuals or by leaders of organizations whose activities express religious commitments.

We owe this enlarged understanding of spirituality to several decades of scholarship on women and gender that has documented and analyzed women's religious experiences to a far greater degree than had been done in past centuries, to new institutions serving women, to revolutions in technology, and to the increasing diversity of religions in families and communities. Needing to communicate with others across those diversities, individuals often describe their personal religious experiences as "spiritual" and contrast those with the standardized group practices that they feel make up "religion." Judaism has long insisted that it promotes spiritual communities that emerge through family observances, group prayer, and study. Historically, Judaism's guidelines required men's spirituality to be shaped by synagogue attendance and Torah study, but they provided little formal guidance for women's spiritual development. Our recent understandings of spirituality provide the tools for revealing Jewish women's spirituality in many different settings, both private and public.

Judaism's many spiritual expressions provide many women with opportunities for creating fulfilling religious lives. Some of these opportunities include religious duties resting on centuries of Jewish practice. More recently, Jewish women also have undertaken formal religious leadership roles previously unavailable to them. In the United States and Canada, Reform, Reconstructionist, Renewal, and Conservative Jewish congregations commonly hire formally trained religious leaders who are women, both as rabbis and as cantors. Among Orthodox Jews, women who have obtained training in Talmud and in the *siddur* lead women's prayer groups, teach in religious schools, and provide leadership for Jewish communities in the United States, England, Germany, and Israel.[1] Although much of the impetus for egalitarian or women's formal prayer groups emerged first among American Jews, we also find them among Israeli Jews and elsewhere. Among Lubavitcher Hasidim, married couples serve as missionaries who generate Jewish communities among women and men worldwide by focusing on worship and religious observance, and wives are key to the couples' success.

The widespread influence of the twentieth century's women's movement affected religions' treatment of women and energized women's engagement in religion. Three sorts of women's spiritual expressions stand out as significant over the last hundred years, either because they have engaged significant numbers of women or because they mark new ways that women have been able to demonstrate their religious creativity. These are religious activities created and promoted by women's organizations; religious activities performed by Jewish women in their homes and kitchens, including the new ritual of the women's seder; and religious music created, performed, and taught by women in congregations and cantorial schools.

Spirituality in Organizations

JEWISH WOMEN FROM A broad spectrum of religious observance organized, led, and funded their own organizations to promote Judaism. These organizations offered women routes to advancing religious goals even when women were barred from the rabbinate. In the early twentieth century many Jewish groups relied on women's financial support, acknowledged in the Sisterhood Dormitory (opened 1923) at Hebrew Union College (the seminary for Reform Judaism) in Cincinnati. By then, American Jewish women also had established a tradition of public religious roles that included teaching in Sunday schools and publishing inspirational poetry and essays in the Jewish press. Yet, when American Reform rabbis hotly debated the ordination of women in 1922, they praised the entry of women into many secular professions and even allowed some women into rabbinic colleges, but they withheld ordination itself as being "contrary to all Jewish tradition and . . . religious teaching."[2]

Women's organizations therefore provided vehicles for religious activities that engaged many individuals. The National Federation of Temple Sisterhoods (NFTS), begun in 1913, was the first national Jewish organization linking synagogue sisterhoods; women in Conservative congregational sisterhoods gathered under their own national umbrella five years later. These national organizations maintained committees that promoted particular goals, as did the NFTS's National Committee on Religion. As Barbara Goodman, of Louisville, Kentucky, reminded the national membership in 1923 when she became that committee's chairwoman, "The NFTS is primarily a religious organization." She urged members to capitalize on the "opportunities for religious observance that each holiday represents" as well as the "religion of every day."[3] That committee also created special posters with religious sayings and imagery for each holiday in the Jewish calendar for members to purchase for display at their own local committee meetings. Lest a committee get too bogged down in the practical details of their work, these posters lent a religious tone to their environment and reminded them of their goal of promoting Judaism.[4]

A different NFTS committee devoted itself to supporting the religious schools associated with Reform congregations. Holiday celebrations created new pedagogical opportunities in those schools and also enhanced the holiday experience for students, teachers, and the women who supported them. Hanukkah was particularly ripe for development by women's groups because its simple rite does not require a rabbi and occurs at home and because Hanukkah's timing near Christmas elicited concern that Jewish children should experience a Jewish religious event in December. For example, speaking to the national membership from her home in Buffalo, New York (also in 1923), Mrs. Henry Nathan (as the NFTS records called her) advised that "there is no holiday on our Jewish calendar which gives the Committee on Religious Schools more scope for work than does . . . Chanukah." The NFTS also used their activities in religious schools to promote regular domestic observances.

Earlier, Nathan told the national membership to "cooperate with your rabbi and teachers by bringing this beautiful religious spirit of the Feast of Lights into your home. It is there that the impressions are made upon our young people. . . . Make it a happy week for your children and burn Chanukah lights with them throughout the eight days."[5] Similar involvement by NFTS women enriched the religious experience of other holidays that occurred during the school year.

Indeed, Hanukkah became a particular vehicle for women's participation in special religious activities in the synagogue. The Reform movement had urged members to create special Hanukkah activities for children in their religious schools since 1868, when the movement's leaders, Cincinnati rabbis Isaac M. Wise and Max Lillienthal, promoted the effort in their national newspapers. Women played an important role in the success of those events, whether as Sunday school teachers who helped to design and implement the event, as fundraisers, or as committee members overseeing the project. Synagogue-based Hanukkah festivals became an American tradition for Reform congregations. In 1926 the NFTS created Hanukkah greeting cards to promote the holiday among adults in addition to distributing candles and tin menorahs to children in its religious schools. In these ways, women promoted this sometimes neglected holiday among both adults and children.[6]

Hanukkah gave women room to be creative and take leadership roles for several reasons. The holiday's brief rite encouraged creative elaboration; its domestic site brought it into women's traditional domain; and, in Reform congregations, its new, school-focused religious assemblies depended on women's support. Thus Hanukkah brought hundreds of Reform women into organized religious activities and encouraged them to think about their own religious experiences and values. More traditionally religious Jewish women in the United States soon joined them.

Five years after the NFTS united Reform sisterhoods, the Women's League for Conservative Judaism (WLCJ) gathered 100 women associated with more traditional congregations under its umbrella. Begun by Mathilda Schechter (1857–1924), the creative and influential wife of the chancellor of the Jewish Theological Seminary, Solomon Schechter, the WLCJ brought women together to "perpetuate traditional Judaism in their homes, synagogues and communities," something they viewed as "a task for American Jewish women."[7] "We stand for everything Jewish and American," Schechter explained. The increasing numbers of more traditional Jewish congregations reflected the dramatic growth in the American Jewish population, which rose from 250,000 in 1880 to 3.6 million by 1924. But, as American society became more fearful of immigrants after the Bolshevik Revolution and World War I, new laws restricted Jewish immigration and "America First!" became the call of the day. Public schools became vehicles for Americanizing the children of immigrants, and American culture pressured immigrants to adapt quickly. Schechter's group aimed to "guide young women through the painful process of acculturation and Americanization while preserving their Jewishness" and disseminated their message through the publication of educational materials written in English, for use in study circles and at home.[8]

Spurred on by a felt need to quickly adapt Jewish life to American conditions, the WLCJ, like the NFTS, entered a period of creativity in the 1920s. In 1927 Deborah Marcus Melamed (1892–1954), an officer of the WLCJ, a professional educator who supervised the foreign language program in Elizabeth, New Jersey, public schools, and a faculty member at Gratz College (an institution of Jewish learning in Philadelphia), published her influential work, *The Three Pillars: Thought, Worship, Practice*. Ultimately going through nine editions, this work aimed to "instill in other women the love [Melamed] felt for Jewish tradition."[9] Like Schechter, Melamed had married a rabbi and used the role of *rebbetzin* to establish her own influence among Jews, especially among Jewish women.[10] By 1930 the exchange of programming ideas and materials among Conservative women had evolved into a full-scale Program Department; their monthly periodical, *Outlook Magazine*, which further promoted the committee's work, began publication in 1930.[11]

Melamed believed that "synagogue schools ought to be given over completely to the Sisterhoods, for these women would work with the rabbi to strengthen the school and ensure that it complemented the work of the home."[12] Women who had taken the message of *The Three Pillars* to heart could undertake running of synagogue schools in the manner Melamed hoped. The book aimed to do much more than instruct its readers in the opportunities Judaism offered women for religious activities. She hoped to inspire them to experience Judaism as a fulfilling religious life. And, because much of her audience felt both societal pressures to conform and personal hopes for success in their own Americanizing, Melamed began her book with a brief discussion of the way American and Jewish values and symbols supported and enriched each other. Covering topics such as life-cycle events, customs, dietary laws, formal prayer and prayer books, and holidays, Melamed offered her own thoughts on each element of Jewish practice. For example, in her hands, Hanukkah, although ranked as a minor festival in the Jewish calendar, became a commemoration of a pivotal event in Western history. "Civilization today would have been totally different had Judea been defeated," she explained, for it would have been unlikely that Jesus or Mohammed would have felt any of Judaism's influence. Thus the Maccabean victory was a signal event with worldwide significance.[13] The custom of increasing the light of the Hanukkah menorah each evening, she explained, symbolized the "steady march of truth, growth of the light of Israel's law of love and justice, the ultimate victory of all forces of light over darkness."[14]

In the decades following publication of Melamed's book, American society expanded its notions of freedom, as the civil rights movement challenged the country to live up to its ideals and, soon after, the women's liberation movement echoed that call. Forty-six years after Melamed's book first appeared, the WLCJ leadership considered those ideals and their implications for its members in the WLCJ's monthly magazine. Reflecting the changed expectations for women's lives generated by the women's movement's second wave, the fall 1973 issue's message considered Hanukkah's meaning for Jewish women, debated those challenges, and came up with a different message from Melamed's. The WLCJ president wrote that, because women were "emerging from the home and achieving new freedoms," Hanukkah, the feast of dedication, gave women direction. "True freedom is the right to choose how we will spend our time," she explained to readers. "We choose to use our time as volunteers to work for strengthening of the Jewish family . . . better Jewish education for our children . . . and adults . . . [and] . . . to make the world a better place."[15]

Jewish women played leading roles in the twentieth-century women's liberation movement, and in 1972 Reform Judaism answered feminism's challenge with the ordination of Sally Priesand, the first American Jewish woman rabbi. Since its early days in the nineteenth century, one of Reform's first efforts to liberalize Judaism entailed making the formal prayer service more attractive to worshipers, and that attention to keeping formal prayer meaningful to its growing membership remained a key value. The social changes prompted by the women's liberation movement convinced Reform's leaders to ordain women. Women rabbis ordained in Reform seminaries wrote sermons that taught an inclusive understanding of Judaism and its traditions.[16]

But the effort to revitalize Jewish women's spirituality by linking consciousness raising and religious experience energized women well beyond the boundaries of the Reform movement. With new attention to the holiday of Rosh Chodesh, which celebrated the new moon, Jewish feminist spirituality blossomed. Meeting in synagogues or in private homes, women adapted these celebrations to local interests. Moreover, by focusing on women, these monthly festivals highlighted the vivid contrast between a rite that made women's experience central and the more standard erasure of women in most Jewish liturgy and ritual at that time, which spurred additional reforms.[17]

By the end of the twentieth century, the Women of Reform Judaism (WRJ; formerly the NFTS) was a worldwide organization welcoming any woman who shared its liberal approach to Judaism. The WRJ collaborated with the Israeli group the Women of the Wall (women who pray at the Western Wall, the Kotel, regularly and with a Torah scroll) to produce a prayer book for Rosh Chodesh, written in both Hebrew and English. The Women of the Wall also produced a "pluralist, multi-denominational prayer book made by and for women."[18] The WRJ website explains that the Rosh Chodesh celebration was promoted in midrashic literature (ancient commentary on parts of the Hebrew Bible) as an occasion that "lifts women out of the observer realm and elevates us to initiators, full participants, leaders, and creators. We value these opportunities to define our religious identity and to embellish in our own words, amongst ourselves, both the mundane and sacred aspects of our lives." The page is capped by a quote from the Babylonian Talmud (the primary source of rabbinic law and theology): "Whoever blesses the new moon in its time welcomes in the presence of the Shechina [the divine]" (*b. Sanhedrin* 42a).

The WRJ promotes Rosh Chodesh and other religious practices, especially those associated with holidays, by making inspirational readings and guidance on celebrations available to members through its website and publications. Religious practices historically associated with women's responsibilities, such as challah making, assembling the correct ritual objects for home use, and bringing young children into holiday celebrations, are also featured. National awards are granted to local WRJ groups that are particularly creative in establishing successful holiday programming in their communities. Descriptions of those successful programs earn a place on the WRJ website and create a virtual community of active, liberal Jewish women that supplements local face-to-face communal events.

The women's liberation movement also influenced Jews who were more religiously observant than those in the Reform movement, and the WLCJ strives to bring women and their views and voices into Conservative worship. Woman-focused study guides, such as those examining the biblical books named for women (Ruth and Esther), are available for sale through its website along with booklets about studying prayer, developing spirituality, and understanding mitzvot. One example of their work is the annual Women's League Shabbat, during which women run the communal religious service in their local synagogues. Women can now regularly obtain resources for creating a women's Shabbat service on the WLCJ website. For example, the *d'var Torah* (bible lesson) for the Women's Shabbat Torah reading in March 2017 was for *parashat shemot* (the Torah portion in Exodus called Names) and the *d'var Torah* on the WLCJ website points out the list of women who are named in Exodus for their heroism. Many observers have noted that biblical women "can be active and influential," whereas the few women mentioned in the

Talmud are "far less so." Thus modern Jewish women usually turn to biblical sources to create meaningful worship experiences that draw on authoritative Jewish sources.[19]

The 2017 Women's Shabbat *d'var Torah* discusses the midwives Shifra and Puah, who refused to kill the Hebrew male babies, along with Yocheved and Miriam, who were Moses's mother and sister, and Pharaoh's daughter, who rescued him from the Nile. The author of this *d'var* concluded with a challenge to contemporary women to be inspired by those models to protect their Jewish heritage and people.[20] These biblical women are mentioned at each Passover seder, and by using those familiar names, grounded in a contemporary message in a familiar and authoritative text, the author rooted her woman-focused Torah lesson in authoritative sources.

Similarly, the Jewish Orthodox Feminist Alliance (JOFA) provides a variety of resources for research and worship through its website. Founded in 1997, the organization aims to "expand the spiritual, ritual, intellectual, and political opportunities for women within the framework of halakha."[21] Today, the JOFA counts chapters in England, Western Europe, Latin America, and Israel. Among the Chabad Lubavitch, who aim for the highest possible levels of religious observance, in the last several decades women have been urged to feel a "direct connection" to the organization "rather than being contingent on their husbands' and fathers' affiliation."[22] Menahem Mendel Schneerson, the seventh Lubavitch rebbe, founded the Lubavitch Women's Organization in 1952 and underscored the significance of the wife-husband partnership of *sheluhim* (missionaries), expanding the opportunities for women in advancing the organization's goals. As religion scholar Ada Rapoport-Albert explains, he was convinced that humanity is on the brink of the messianic age and taught that redemption would be "the revelation of God's most concealed essence," an idea that implies a reversal of power relations among people to evince new spiritual insight and strength.[23]

In the early decades of the twenty-first century, these organizations continue their work and depend increasingly on organizational websites to generate and document conversations among Jewish women that express their understandings of ways to promote their own Jewish spirituality.

Spirituality through Domestic Ritual

THE MOST TIME-HONORED SPIRITUAL practices that are expected of Jewish women have been those integral to domestic life. More than simply an attitude of piety, this spirituality requires specific recitations and acts associated with particular objects on particular occasions. Like many rituals, these aim to connect the person performing the rite with the divine, thereby bringing the household into a holy realm. Women across the broad spectrum of Jewish practice, from Reform to ultra-Orthodox, knew of or practiced at least some of these rites.

Religion scholar and Orthodox Jew Tamar Frankiel writes, "In ritual . . . a concrete, usually tangible reality . . . is taken up and consciously transformed in a dramatic context." For example, she explains that "lighting Shabbat candles . . . is not like other candle lighting." Moreover, rituals "break . . . down the hypnotic force of everyday consciousness and allow . . . some deeper consciousness to break through."[24] Frankiel points out that "to the person inside the ritual, whose consciousness is being changed in the very same acts that create the drama, the reality is unquestionable."[25] She advocates a feminine, not feminist, Jewish spirituality and points out various occasions when the feminine is featured in Judaism. Key among those occasions is Shabbat, which is spoken of and experienced as a queen, or a spirit bride who "enters the home and the synagogue on Friday night."[26]

Women are particularly adept at spiritual matters, according to Frankiel. "Women can lose or loosen their ego boundaries to be open to processes that come from other levels of consciousness, other levels of reality. . . . We are in a privileged position in opening the channels of the world to the divine flow." Those openings can often occur during religious rites, including special rites that women perform. In that process, "Women are spiritual midwives in rebirthing the world."[27] This powerful spiritual experience does not occur by itself; it requires the performance of rites with *kavannah*—intention. Moreover, women can easily connect their own sense of femininity to the consciousness required for *kavannah* during Judaism's many time-based rituals, such as those that occur on Shabbat and holidays.

That kind of femininity-linked *kavannah* might be most easily developed during Rosh Chodesh celebrations. Celebrated one or two days each month by Orthodox Jews, since ancient times Rosh Chodesh has been an occasion to hear a teaching of Torah. Women often treat it as a "kind of half holiday: we do not refrain from all work but usually avoid hard labor."[28] Because the synagogue worship service and grace after meals also recognize Rosh Chodesh, men also acknowledge it. But it is mostly considered an occasion special to women.

In the home, ritual objects that are displayed serve as reminders of ritual acts, sacred time, prayers, and beliefs. Immigrants often carried with them the Sabbath candlesticks, Havdalah spice boxes, and Hanukkah menorahs required for performing those rites.[29] Women who earned reputations for rigor in their performance of domestic rites gained reputations for spirituality, which they could convey to others. Blessings of children by such mothers and grandmothers were valued and sometimes photographed.[30] In the twentieth century, guidebooks by and for Orthodox women looked to the nineteenth century's ideal of "true womanhood" that had shaped women's gender ideal in that earlier era. Like pious-toned nineteenth-century American and British women's literature and advice manuals, twentieth-century Orthodox guidebooks urged women to liken their effort in creating Jewish homes to "service at the altar" that "consecrated" their homes to Judaism. The Women's Branch of the Union of Orthodox Jewish Congregations hoped to create "highly motivated observant American Jewish women" and, during the interwar years, published books such as *Symbols and Ceremonies of the Jewish Home* and made good use of *The Jewish Home Beautiful*, published by Conservative women.[31]

By placing objects associated with ritual acts where they are visible, even when not in use, women can redefine a domestic space as a religious one. Just as the placement of furniture signals a room's use, these objects signal an ongoing religious life that will be enacted on numerous occasions in the household. By calling attention to religious practice, even when it is not being performed, these objects create a religious setting for personal life. As an individual shifts from one setting to another, one's self-perspective shifts. Religion scholar Kerry Mitchell explains, "What may have seemed very important a few hours earlier loses its significance" while "other things take on far more importance." Moreover, it can bring "a sense of individual embeddedness within an all-encompassing global whole."[32] When outdoors, one relates to the secular, national, or natural world, but inside, ritual objects signal the divine or the Jewish past (which can have biblical content) or the worldwide network of Jewish families using similar objects at similar times. The particular objects that change the environment also can shape the content of those experiences. Objects associated with Jewish religious practices suggest Jewish religious experiences and encourage individuals to experience their own lives in relation to them. This kind of change in personal meaning has often been called a spiritual experience.[33] Moreover, rabbis across denominations commonly urge Jews to select the most beautiful ritual items they can afford, because the aesthetic experience of the sublime is often also a spiritual experience.[34]

Women across denominational lines have displayed attention to domestic ritual objects. The NFTS/WRJ, WLCJ, and Women's Branch of the Union of Orthodox Jewish Congregations in America regularly remind their members to obtain, use, and display ritual objects. In the 1920s, when the NFTS promoted home religious observances among its members through its national committees, local chapters, and mailings to members, it also urged them to purchase the requisite domestic ritual objects for their home use. The WLCJ acted similarly. By arranging to sell these objects themselves, women's organizations could raise funds to support their projects, such as funding the local religious schools.

By the 1960s, when large suburban synagogues that included classrooms and social space became the norm in the United States, women's groups typically ran small shops located in the building. Through them, congregants could purchase requisite ritual objects, such as candle sticks and menorahs along with their appropriate candles, seder plates, spice boxes, mezuzot, Hebrew-inscribed wine glasses, and matzo and challah covers as well as greeting cards, art objects, jewelry, and other gifts with Jewish content for bar mitzvah and bat mitzvah celebrants or brides and grooms. These objects served both to create a Jewish setting that encouraged family members to experience their own Jewish beliefs and identity and to remind women to perform their associated rites.[35] Shoppers could also find appropriate cookbooks displayed on the shelves of synagogue gift shops. Throughout the twentieth century, Jewish women's groups compiled their own cookbooks and sold them to raise funds. More recently, these goods are also available on websites, along with instructions for crafting items at home, such as head coverings and decorative pillows with appropriate phrases and blessings.[36]

Foods can also be considered ritual objects. In 1893 Philadelphian Mary M. Cohen defended what others disparaged as "kitchen Judaism" and argued that special foods created a "bond in sanctity" between Jewish religion and family life.[37] Her remarks rested on a long Jewish tradition linking food and divinity. The bible contains several tales of miraculous foods, most notably the "manna from heaven" described in Exodus (6:18). But there is also the prophet Elijah's miraculous filling of the widow of Zarapeth's jugs of flour and oil (1 Kings 17:12–16), Elisha's miraculous expansion of twenty loaves of bread to feed one hundred men (2 Kings 4:42–44), and other such events. One scholar of Jewish mysticism explains that the medieval mystical text, the Zohar, suggests that "when the kabbalists sat down to dine they would . . . invoke divine overflow from above and prompt its downward flow upon the individual's table, the bread upon it, and ultimately into the diner's belly."[38]

Dietary laws (kashrut) structured Jewish recipes used by cooks around the world as individuals adapted its rules to local ingredients and cuisines. In 2017 one Judaica website alone offered eighty-three kosher cookbooks for sale.[39] The WLCJ website encourages its members—and anyone else who visits the site—to purchase prayer pamphlets for the extensive table blessings that customarily occur at the close of a meal whenever ten or more people have eaten together.[40] Not surprisingly, then, historian Hasia Diner has concluded that "food in the Judaic tradition stood at the very center of the sacred zone."[41]

Friday (Sabbath) evening meals provide weekly occasions for women to sanctify their homes with a candle blessing that they alone perform and that brings the Sabbath into the home. It is an occasion for displaying domestic prowess in the service of embodied spirituality: arranging and setting the dining table to signify the special and Jewish nature of the occasion and serving a dinner prepared according to Jewish custom. In contrast, the annual preparations for Passover require a marathon of cleaning, cooking, setting and arranging the table and home, inviting guests, and the timed serving of special foods. By the 1970s, when feminism emerged in its second major wave to influence American culture, women's complaints about laboring though a holiday celebrating freedom generated a new ritual custom, the Women's Seder. In 1975 Esther Broner, Naomi Freedman, and Naomi Nimrod organized a feminist seder that foregrounded the theme of liberation that has always been central to the Passover festival.[42] They returned to the biblical Exodus account to highlight key women in the events that Passover celebrates. Whereas the traditional Passover Haggadah erases most of the human effort in the Exodus, including that of Moses, to focus praise and thanks upon God, 1970s feminists sought a retelling of the Haggadah that would feature women's roles. Their efforts highlighted women's effort in the Exodus from Egypt. Tamar Frankiel points out that "women are quite prominent in midrashic stories about Pesach. Tradition tells us that God performed the redemption from Egypt because of the merit of the Jewish women."[43]

Feminist seders draw from both biblical and rabbinic texts, and at those events the midwives who refused to obey Pharaoh's order to kill newborn Jewish males are praised as the first heroes of the Exodus. Miriam, however, is given the most prominent role, and this feature of feminist seders draws on rabbinic sources along with biblical accounts. Rabbinic scholar Tamar Meir concludes that "Miriam is portrayed as an integral member of the Moses-Aaron-Miriam leadership triumvirate." A midrashic interpretation of the cupbearer's dream (Gen. 40), understands the three as the "three branches of the vine from which the people of Israel emerged and blossomed." As sister of Moses and Aaron, Miriam figures prominently in the biblical account and is called a prophet (Ex. 15:20). Another midrashic account claims that "the Israelite camps set out only with Miriam in their lead" (*Sifrei* on Deut. 24:9). Thus Jewish women creating women's seders, whether or not they are feminists, have ample support from both biblical and rabbinic literature for focusing attention on Miriam. At women's seders a new ritual item is placed on the table: a cup of water called Miriam's cup, a reminder of her role in the Exodus story and her "association with the well that accompanied the Israelites on their wanderings in the wilderness and provided them with drinking water." Tamar Meir explains, "The well, according to the rabbis, was one of the things created on the eve of the Sabbath at twilight (*m. Avot* 5:6); they depict it as a wondrous well that flowed from itself (*t. Sukkah* 3:11)."[44] Several compilations of feminist Haggadot emerged in the ensuing years. In the 1990s a student group at Yale University called Jewish Women at Yale began holding regular women's seders. Within a few years, the students produced a *Women's Seder Sourcebook* especially for this event. Conferences and conversations on the topic over several years culminated in a collection of readings for a women's seder published by Jewish Lights Press in 2003.

Typically, women's seders are communal events held before Passover begins to avoid the food restrictions that come with the holiday itself and conflicts with family events that women often want to attend. Although they generally follow the order of a typical Passover seder, there are additional ritual objects on the table that indicate the nature of this occasion. An orange signifies welcoming people previously considered outsiders to the Jewish community. Such former outsiders may include gays or lesbians, but at women's seders—and at more traditional seders where they are being incorporated—oranges also signify bringing women into central roles in religious life.[45]

However, Miriam's cup holds special significance for including women. The special place of Miriam in Jewish women's spirituality was already clear in the writings of nineteenth-century British author and theologian Grace Aguilar.[46] Moreover, because the ritual items, including foods, on the seder table signify key elements in Judaism's founding event and God's power in its occurrence, Miriam's cup conveys the notion that women were central to Judaism, both at its founding and in current practice.

Sometimes traditional elements are easy to adapt. Among the simplest are the Four Questions that are asked early in the order of readings at the Passover seder and that set up the rest of the evening as an answer that explain the seder's meaning. The *Women's Seder Sourcebook* provides the following set of four questions that offer the event's rationale. In answering the question, "Why is this night different from all other seder nights?" it replies, first, that "at all other seders we hear the stories of our forefathers but the voices of our foremothers are silent. Tonight they will be heard." It continues, "At all other seders, the heroic deeds of our sisters, Miriam, Yocheved, Shifra, and Puah are kept hidden. Tonight we will celebrate their courage. At all other seders we denounce the Pharaoh of the past. Tonight we will also examine the pharaohs of our own day. At all other seders we rejoice only in our liberation as a people. Tonight we also celebrate our empowerment as Jewish women."[47]

Although the rewriting of the Four Questions might suggest a political rather than a spiritual focus of the women's seder, the traditional Haggadah itself is also a mixture of political and spiritual recitations. Like the traditional Haggadah, its songs provide spiritual expression in women's seders too. Hymns collectively called the Hallel are normally sung at the Passover seder, but the *Women's Seder Sourcebook* explains that the psalms of the Hallel are ascribed to David and that the Talmud "teaches us that when a psalm begins with the words L'David mizmor, it signifies that the *Shekhinah* rested upon David and inspired him to utter it. The *Shekhinah* is the mystical term for the most close-dwelling God and carries the feminine attributes of the divine." It then offers readers an original "Song of Praise" to the *Shekhinah* written by Geela Rayzel Raphael.[48] Using images such as "womb of love," and asserting that the "fountain of life flows from you," this brief hymn praises the "holy mother" who "heals the wounds of a heavy heart." Thus women's seders reflect the interests and abilities of the women who create them. Ideas and resources have been shared by women in many locales around the United States and in Europe and Israel. In the United States, Conservative, Reconstructionist, and Reform congregations often hold these events in synagogue buildings to accommodate larger crowds.

Spirituality through Singing

JEWISH WOMEN HAVE HELD a complex relationship to religious singing, despite the fact that singing is among the oldest religious activities in Judaism, evidenced by the 150 hymns that make up the biblical book of Psalms. Instrumental music became taboo in the synagogue after the destruction of the Second Temple in 70 CE, so the singing of *nusach*, or prayer melodies, provided the sole music in Jewish prayer. Different *nusach*, developed in Jewish communities around the world, and distinctive melodies for morning, afternoon, evening, Sabbath, or holiday prayers identified each prayer event. In the process community singing became a key Jewish activity. By the turn of the twentieth century, immigration brought those song customs to the United States.[49]

Yet the rabbis who set Jewish law in the Talmud banned women's singing from public prayer, justifying it with the claim in *Berakhot* 24a that *kol be'ishah 'ervah* (the voice of a woman is nakedness). Ethnomusicologist Sarah M. Ross explains that this tradition is based on a particular interpretation of the Song of Songs 2:14: "My dove . . . show me your face, let me hear your voice; for your voice is sweet, and your face is lovely." This particular reading, Ross explains, gives the sensuality of a woman's voice a negative connotation "associated with her [sexuality], which might distract men from prayer and religious duty." Once a woman's voice, whether singing or speaking, was associated with her body, it became forbidden for men to recite a prayer or benediction while listening to it. Later, this prohibition extended to men listening to any musical performance by women.[50]

But as Jews adapted to secular culture in the twentieth century, mixed singing groups arose that did not ban women. For example, Zionist clubs commonly used group singing to enliven meetings and promote esprit de corps among their members. In 1970 Hadassah member Leah Abrams explained to her sister members in programming materials sent to various local chapters that "songs are faithful messengers. The inner history of a people is contained in its songs [and] Jewish music has always reflected the Jewish heritage, values, aspirations, pains, and joys. From King David, poet and musician, throughout the generations, in many different lands and in Israel today, our people find continuous expression in song. The wealth of our musical heritage in its variety is ours to be enjoyed, to be explored."[51] A more full-throated endorsement of music's importance to Jewish life could hardly be imagined.

Lubavitcher Jews practice a form of Hasidic Judaism, and for them, singing is a central spiritual activity. They regard their paraliturgical folk and popular melodies (called *nigunim*) as a primary form of spiritual communion with the divine. In addition to worship, singing occurs also at key gatherings and especially at the important *fabrengens*, where the rebbe speaks to his gathered community. Men and women are separated at these events because of the commitment to the *kol isha* rules. Hasidic women typically will not sing in the presence of men. Yet, in the last twenty-five years, that commitment to separation has generated women's *fabrengens* and women's conventions, where Hasidic women gather for their own inspirational meetings and where they are free to sing aloud.[52] Girls who attend Lubavitcher Bais Rivkah schools, which are restricted to female students, learn songs that inspire them to religious commitment and instruct them in the meaning of their future roles as Lubavitcher women.[53]

Yet, since the mid-twentieth century, singing has not divided the vast majority of Jews. The women's liberation movement transformed gender relations in Western culture, and in recent decades new mixed-gender prayer groups have emerged, even among Orthodox Jews. Notably, Shira Hadasha, a congregation founded in Jerusalem in 2002, brings together men and women who are committed to "halakha (Jewish law), tefillah (prayer), and feminism." Although the congregation does use a *mechitzah* (curtain or temporary wall separating men and women) during prayer, the portions of the service requiring a quorum of ten adults does not begin until ten men and ten women are present. Shira Hadasha implements an opinion by modern Orthodox rabbi Mendel Shapiro, who argued for enhancing women's roles in worship. He identified various times in Jewish history when women have publicly read Torah in communal worship and analyzed the circumstances of those events. His opinion has engendered controversy and opposition, but it provides the legal ground on which Shira Hadasha rests.[54] Since 1997, when the Jewish Orthodox Feminist Alliance was founded by Jewish American writer Blu Greenberg, some Orthodox women and men have explored ways to expand women's participation in public worship, especially the thorny issue of how to welcome their singing voices.[55]

Liberal Jewish worship followed a different path, and some American congregations made early adaptations to welcome women's voices in worship. In 1818 women won the right to sing in a synagogue choir, and only seven years later, architectural changes allowed women to pray without a screen blocking their view from the balcony.[56] Liberal forms of Judaism that arose in the nineteenth and twentieth centuries eliminated the separation of men and women that had long influenced synagogue architecture and welcomed women to participate vocally in public worship. In 1840 the Charleston, South Carolina, congregation of Beth Elohim instituted a new English-language hymnal, most of which had been written by local poet Penina Moise. A much used and beloved collection, eight of its hymns entered later prayer collections used by Reform Jews into the 1940s. Musical innovations in those congregations included both mixed singing and instrumental accompaniment to communal prayer, usually in the form of an organ.[57] A few decades later, Reform Judaism brought women into the formal cantorate and invested Barbara Ostfeld as its first female cantor in 1975. Over the next twenty five years, 130 women would become Reform cantors.[58]

For some, music provided the most powerful way to feel "part of an ongoing living entity," as composer and musicologist Judith Kaplan Eisenstein (1909–1996) phrased it.[59] For composer, performer, and choir leader Debbie Friedman (1951–2011), however, music was an "immediate spiritual experience."[60] Friedman's influential career began during a Memorial Day weekend Sabbath evening service at her Reform congregation in St. Paul, Minnesota. Friedman could not read music and composed her work on guitar. She performed her creations to audiences and recorded them. Her signature work, "Sing Unto God," evolved and developed throughout her career. But its earliest performance iteration was likely that evening in Minnesota. Its lyric ran, "Sing Unto God, sing a new song / O sing praises to God, give thanks to Him with a song / O sing praises unto the Lord thy God." Friedman accompanied herself on guitar, and the style reflects both the 1960s musical and cultural revolutions and the environment created in the many Jewish summer camps where Jewish life was promoted amid easygoing camaraderie. The many veterans of summer camps in the congregations where she performed provided the vanguard of an eager audience for her new style of Jewish spiritual song. Three psalms begin with the phrase "Sing unto God" (Pss. 96, 98, and 149), providing biblical and liturgical authority for her creations. But Friedman's program that night extended well beyond the single song; she restructured the entire evening's service, touching on all its required elements. Musicologist Judah Cohen points out that both Friedman's bold creativity and her representation of tradition were "valued among Reform youth leadership and important for enforcing the legitimacy of her ideas."[61] To further balance tradition and innovation, Friedman used gender-neutral terms to refer to the divine.[62] Friedman's new melody for the Mi Shebeirach (prayer for healing) has been used in hundreds of congregations, including Orthodox, although her creations found their greatest welcome in Reform and Conservative synagogues. Some Orthodox women's prayer circles also adopted her work.

Finally, new songs have been created by feminists for use during rituals of particular interest to women. The feminist songs created for Rosh Chodesh celebrations "emphasize the aspect of gathering in all-women groups" not only to sing but also to share women's stories. Other feminist songs celebrate women's fertility, as the new moon celebrations are seen as metaphors for menstruation. Feminists have also written new songs for use in immersion in a *mikveh* (ritual bath) that identify the divine as the *Shekhinah*, or as spirit of the world, rather than using the "king of the universe" language common to most traditional Jewish blessings. In Hebrew, *king* (*melech*) is a masculine noun. In addition, a movement to promote Jewish healing, largely an effort among women, produced worship services focused on healing the soul and consist largely of new chants, songs, and instrumental music. Some of these efforts rework traditional healing prayers, whereas others are entirely new. For example, Andrea Beth Damsky's song "Heal Me, Oh God" (1997) opens with repeated lines to create a chant, followed by verses asking for strength, joy, and love.

Perhaps most feminist Jewish songs are those dealing with Shabbat, the anchor of the Jewish liturgical year. New creations rework the Hebrew hymn *Eshet Chayil* (woman of valor), which is commonly recited on Friday evening, the Sabbath candle lighting prayer, the *Lecha Dodi* welcoming the Sabbath, and, as noted, alternative *d'var Torah* lessons with which to understand the week's Torah portion.[63] Feminists have also written new prayers to be recited when a woman is immersing in a *mikveh* to highlight the healing power they find in the rite. For example, in 1989 Rabbi Sue Ann Wasserman created a healing rite for Laura Levitt after Levitt's rape.[64]

In these ways and others like them, a century of Jewish women have expressed their spirituality. Their Jewish lives often combined various activities. Women who participated in women-run organizations linked to various approaches to worship also created, to varying degrees of complexity, domestic spaces that provided the settings for their own spiritual activities. Some of those same women raised their voices in song with other women who furthered woman-focused and feminist understandings of Jewish prayer. Their work to keep their own religious lives alive during the challenges and inspirations of modern life has enriched Judaism and promises to ensure it will thrive into the future.

Notes

1 See, for example, the graduates touted on the website of Yeshivat Maharat, https://www.yeshivatmaharat.org. Yeshivat Maharat (founded in 2009 in New York City) claims to be the first institution to train Orthodox women to serve as clergy.

2 "Rabbis, F. F. Correspondence . . . re admission of women to the College for the Purpose of Ordination, 1921–1922," American Jewish Archives, Miscellaneous File: J. Lauterbach and Oscar Berman, "Minority Report of the Committee on the Question of Graduating Women as Rabbis," June 20, 1921, quoted in Pamela S. Nadell, *Women Who Would Be Rabbis: A History of Women's Ordination, 1889–1985* (Boston: Beacon Press, 1998), 62.

3 1923 NTFS National Committee on Religion, Mrs. Leon Goodman, chairman, Louisville, Kentucky, NFTS/WRJ, AJA Collection no. 73, series E, box 26, folder 1.

4 See, for example, NFTS Committee on Religion, October 28, 1919, American Jewish Archives, NFTS/WRJ Collection, ms collection no. 73, box 21, folder 1; and Sarah Kussy, *Women's League Handbook and Guide* (New York: National Women's League of the United Synagogue of America, 1947), 51.

5 1923 NFTS National Committee on Religious Schools, Mrs. Henry Nathan, Buffalo national chairwoman of this committee, November 19, 1923, Letter sent with circular, American Jewish Archives, NFTS Collection.

6 Dianne Ashton, *Hanukkah in America: A History* (New York: New York University Press, 2013), 162; Mrs. Leon Goodman, NFTS Committee on Religion, November 8, 1927, American Jewish Archives, NFTS/WRJ Collection, Series E, box 26, folder 1, MS-73.

7 https://www.wlcj.org/about/history/ (accessed August 17, 2017).

8 https://www.wlcj.org/about/history/ (accessed August 17, 2017).

9 Marjorie Lehman, "Deborah Marcus Melamed," in *Jewish Women in America*, ed. Paula Hyman and Deborah Dash Moore (New York: Routledge, 1998), 909.

10 Shuly Rubin Schwartz, *The Rabbi's Wife: The Rebbetzin in American Jewish Life* (New York: New York University Press, 2006), 53–70.

11 https://www.wlcj.org/about/history/ (accessed August 17, 2017).

12 Schwartz, *Rabbi's Wife*, 68–69.

13 Deborah M. Melamed, *The Three Pillars: A Book for Jewish Women* (New York: Women's League of the United Synagogue of America, 1927), 120–23.

14 Melamed, *Three Pillars*, 123.

15 "Our President Speaks," *Outlook* 44, no. 2 (December 1973): 4, 27.

16 See, for example, Sally J. Priesand, "Looking Backward and Ahead," in *A Treasury of Favorite Sermons by Leading American Rabbis*, ed. Sidney Greenberg (New York: Jason Aronson, 1999), 195–200.

17 Sarah M. Ross, *A Season of Singing: Creating Feminist Jewish Music in the United States* (Waltham, MA: Brandeis University Press, 2016), 18; Lori Hope Lefkovitz and Rona Shapiro, "Ritualwell.Org: Loading the Virtual Canon, Or, The Politics and Aesthetics of Jewish Women's Spirituality," *Nashim* 9 (spring 2005): 101–25.

18 https://www.womenofthewall.org.il/product/original-siddur-b-women-of-the -wall (accessed April 14, 2018).

19 See, for example, Amos Oz and Fania Oz-Salzberger, *Jews and Words* (New Haven, CT: Yale University Press, 2012), 38.

20 Julia Loeb, "D'var Torah: Parashat Shemot—On Account of the Righteous Women," www.wlcj.org/programs/womens-league-shabbat/2017-womens-league -shabbat/ (accessed April 14, 2018).

21 www.jofa.org (accessed April 14, 2018).

22 Ada Rapoport-Albert, *Hasidic Studies: Essays in History and Gender* (Liverpool, UK: Littman Library of Jewish Civilization, 2018), 448.

23 Rapoport-Albert, *Hasidic Studies*, 447–50.

24 Tamar Frankiel, "Thought, Speech, Action: Rhythms of Jewish Life," in *American Spiritualities: A Reader*, ed. Catherine Albanese (Bloomington: Indiana University Press, 2001), 113–14.

25 Frankiel, "Thought, Speech, Action," 114.

26 Frankiel, "Thought, Speech, Action," 116.

27 Frankiel, "Thought, Speech, Action," 114.

28 Frankiel, "Thought, Speech, Action," 119.

29 Jenna Wiseman Joselit, "A Set Table: Jewish Domestic Culture in the New World, 1880–1950," in *Getting Comfortable in New York: The American Jewish Home, 1880–1950*, ed. Susan L. Braunstein and Jenna Wiseman Joselit (New York: Jewish Museum, 1990), 24.

30 Joselit, "A Set Table," 65.

31 Jenna Wiseman Joselit, *New York's Jewish Jews: The Orthodox Community in the Interwar Years* (Bloomington: Indiana University Press, 1990), 97–110.

32 Kerry Mitchell, *Spirituality and the State* (New York: New York University Press, 2016), 111–12.

33 Mitchell, *Spirituality and the State*, 111.

34 See, for example, Hyman E. Goldin, *The Jew and His Duties: The Essence of the Kitzur Shulchan Aruch* (New York: Hebrew Publishing, 1953), 160; and Mitchell, *Spirituality and the State*, 112.

35 Ashton, *Hanukkah in America*, 198–99.

36 https://www.wlcj.org/about/history (accessed December 1, 2017).

37 Mary M. Cohen, "The Influence of Jewish Religion in the Home," in *Papers of the Jewish Women's Congress Held at Chicago, September 4, 5, 6, and 7, 1893* (Philadelphia: Jewish Publication Society of America, 1894), 115–21; Dianne Ashton, "Crossing Boundaries: The Career of Mary M. Cohen," *American Jewish History* 38, no. 2 (1995): 153–76; Barbara Kirschenblatt-Gimblett, "Kitchen Judaism," in *Getting Comfortable in New York: The American Jewish Home, 1880–1950*, by Jenna Weissman Joselit, Barbara Kirschenblatt-Gimblett, Irving Howe, and Susan L. Braunstein (New York: Jewish Museum, 1950), 77.

38 Joel Hecker, "The Blessing in the Belly: Mystical Satiation in Medieval Kabbalah," in *Food and Judaism*, ed. Leonard J. Greenspoon, Ronald A. Simpkins, and Gerald Shapiro (Omaha, NE: Creighton University Press, 2005), 259.

39 https://www.Judaicaplace.com (accessed July 16, 2017).

40 https://www.wlcj.org/about/history (accessed July 16, 2017).

41 Hasia R. Diner, *Hungering for America: Italian, Jewish, and Irish Foodways in the Age of Migration* (Cambridge, MA: Harvard University Press, 2002), 150.

42 Susan P. Fendrick, "The Why of Women's Seders," https://ritualwell.org/ritual/why-women%E2%80%99s-seders (accessed July 7, 2017). The compilation of counterculture documents called *The Jewish 1960s: An American Sourcebook*, edited by Michael E. Staub, appeared in 2004 but included Balfour Brickner's "Notes on a Freedom Seder," originally published in *The Reconstructionist* (June 13, 1969). The Freedom Seder was conducted by Arthur Waskow in Washington, D.C., in 1969 and invited local leading antiwar activists of all religions. The seder highlighted the theme of liberation and freedom to underscore antiwar goals. See also Hasia Diner, *Lower East Side Memories: A Jewish Place in America* (Princeton, NJ: Princeton University Press, 2002), 96–98.

43 Frankiel, "Thought, Speech, Action," 120.

44 Sharon Cohen Anisfeld, Tara Mohr, and Catherine Spector, eds., *The Women's Seder Sourcebook: Rituals and Readings for Use at the Passover Seder* (Woodstock, VT: Jewish Lights Press, 2003), 67. See also Tamar Meir, "Miriam: Midrash and Aggadah," Jewish Women's Archive Encyclopedia, March 20, 2009, https://jwa.org/encyclopedia/article/miriam-midrash-and-aggadah (accessed August 2, 2017).

45 Anisfeld et al., *Women's Seder Sourcebook*, 208.

46 Dianne Ashton, "Grace Aguilar and the Matriarchal Theme in Jewish Women's Spirituality," in *Active Voices: Women in Jewish Culture*, ed. Maurie Sachs (Urbana: University of Illinois Press, 1995), 79–93.

47 Anisfeld et al., *Women's Seder Sourcebook*, 95.

48 Anisfeld et al., *Women's Seder Sourcebook*, 250.

49 Yaffa Eliach, *There Once Was a World: A 900 Year Chronicle of the Shtetl of Eishyshok* (Boston: Back Bay Press, 1998), 80.

50 Ross, *Season of Singing*, 29–31.

51 Leah Abrams, "On Jewish Music," American Jewish Historical Society, Hadassah Archives, box 12, folder R615, program materials, KIT 1970–71.

52 Ellen Koskoff, *Music in Lubavitcher Life* (Urbana: University of Illinois Press, 2001), 5, 136.

53 Koskoff, *Music in Lubavitcher Life*, 31, 236.

54 On Shira Hadasha, see Tova Hartmann, *Feminism Encounters Traditional Judaism: Resistance and Accommodation* (Waltham, MA: Brandeis University Press, 2007), 121–34.

55 Hartmann, *Feminism*.

56 "The Issue of Women Cantors: Landmarks Along the Way," *Journal of Synagogue Music* 32 (2007): 5–14; Jonathan D. Sarna, Keynote Address given at the Milken Conference on American Jewish Music, Jewish Theological Seminary, New York, November 7, 2003.

57 Gary Phillip Zola, *Isaac Harby of Charleston* (Tuscaloosa: University of Alabama Press, 1994), 112–50. Ashton, *Hanukkah in America*, 43–44.

58 Bruce Ruben, "Cantor Barbara Ostfeld: An Unassuming Pioneer," *Journal of Synagogue Music* 32 (2007): 25–29.

59 Judith Kaplan Eisenstein, "The Spiritual Power of Music," in *Four Centuries of Jewish Women's Spirituality: A Sourcebook*, rev. ed., ed. Ellen M. Umansky and Dianne Ashton (Waltham, MA: Brandeis University Press, 2009), 306.

60 Judah M. Cohen, "Sing unto God: Debbie Friedman and the Changing Sound of Jewish Liturgical Music," *Contemporary Jewry* 35 (2015): 13–34.

61 Cohen, "Sing unto God," 24–25.

62 Ross, *Season of Singing*, 40, 45–46.

63 Ross, *Season of Singing*, 141–43.

64 Laura Levitt and Sue Ann Wasserman, "Mikvah Ceremony for Laura," in *Four Centuries of Jewish Women's Spirituality: A Sourcebook*, ed. Ellen M. Umansky and Dianne Ashton (Boston: Beacon Press, 1992), 321–26.

JEWISH LESBIANS

Contemporary Activism and Its Challenges

Marla Brettschneider

I WAKE UP TO the phone ringing. It was the early 1990s, so the phone was a landline.

My mother asks, "Have you seen the paper yet today?"

I reply, "No, lemme get it."

My mom continues, "See the article on same-sex domestic partnership in New York? Ruth Berman, that's Rockie . . ."

My parents had a childhood friend, Ruthie Berman. Everyone called her Rockie. She and my mom were in a Jewish girl gang called the Emanons. In high school Rockie dated my dad for a bit. They were all poor, living in east New York, Brooklyn, which they called the "garden spot of America" in affectionate irony. Their honored but infamous alma mater, Thomas Jefferson High School, had graduated such Jewish entertainment royalty as Danny Kaye and Steve Lawrence and Eydie Gormé.

A couple of years after completing high school, my parents began dating. During the Korean War, my dad was stationed in Germany, but after his return, they married and formed my family. By this time, my parents had mostly drifted away from Rockie, who had forged a different path. Her single mom, who used a wheelchair, had raised her within Orthodoxy. After high school, Ruthie went to Brooklyn College, and later she earned other advanced degrees. Like themselves, most of the friends my parents stayed in contact with did not go on to college. In the 1950s, Ruthie married, gave birth, and began raising three children while embarking on a career as an educator. Ruthie and her husband became friendly with another couple in her building: the Kurtz family, who had two children. The Kurtzes moved to Israel in 1970. When Connie Kurtz returned to New York for a visit in 1974, she and Ruthie fell in love. They probably went through nearly every wonderful and painful experience imaginable for two white Ashkenazic women from the 1930s Jewish immigrant ghettos of Brooklyn who fell in love with each other. They divorced their husbands for each other, endured custody battles for their kids, and over time forged a new out, loud, and proud lesbian activist life.

Their story is unique. It cannot speak for the totality of Jewish lesbian life. And yet it is also emblematic of many of the milestones and struggles of Jewish lesbians over the past half-century. In the 1970s Ruthie and Connie were founding members of Congregation Beit Simchat Torah, New York City's (and the world's) largest "gay and lesbian" synagogue, where they maintained active ties. They volunteered as activists for the National Organization for Women, where they were out lesbians, confronting and challenging the general negative perception that out lesbians participating in large feminist organizations would prove a "lavender menace," undermining the successes sought by these organizations. In 2018 Connie stepped down as president of their local Democratic club as she adapted to living with cancer, the disease from which she died later that year. Ruthie is still an avid tennis player and fan and now lives in full-time retirement at their condo in Florida. Between them, Ruthie and Connie had five children, twenty grandchildren, and nearly thirty great-grandchildren scattered around the United States and Israel. Ruthie's kids have grown and formed families of their own in the United States. Connie's kids remained in Israel; her daughter is a secular Jew living on a collective near Jerusalem, and her son and his large family are Breslov Hasidim who welcomed the couple with open arms whenever they visited.

In recent years Ruthie and Connie worked with local Black Lives Matter activists on an anti-racism initiative. The couple founded branches of Parents, Friends, and Family of Lesbians and Gays (PFLAG) in New York and Florida. They were activists for many social justice issues, including gun violence, immigrant rights, police brutality, health care, dignity for senior citizens, and Israeli-Palestinian relations. They won numerous awards and honorable mentions and were the subject of the award-winning 2002 documentary *Ruthie and Connie: Every Room in the House,* which has been featured at countless film festivals along with its 2013 epilogue. Organizing their personal lives to make room for their artistic and political work and countless speaking invitations required considerable scheduling ingenuity.

Back in 1988, after living together for fourteen years, Ruthie Berman and Connie Kurtz spearheaded a lawsuit demanding domestic partnership benefits from the New York City Board of Education. The suit went on for six years. On October 30, 1993, mayor David Dinkins, the first and, as of 2020, only black mayor of New York City, confirmed domestic partner benefits for straight and gay New York City employees.

The morning of that newspaper article in 1993, I sat on my futon in my West Village studio listening to my mother with some surprise. I was a grad student at NYU. My mother hadn't really talked to me before about LGBTQ politics. But this was about Rockie. I had heard Ruthie's story from my parents when I was growing up. Eventually, fate and the perhaps predictable synergy of Jewish dyke activists in New York City brought us together. I valued my own relationship with Ruth Berman and Connie Kurtz. Although no one has seen it all, Ruthie comes and Connie came pretty close to both experiencing and making possible a lot of what Jewish lesbian life has to offer.

The extent of Ruthie and Connie's political and cultural activism is impressive but not atypical of Jewish lesbians. In the United States Jewish lesbians have been recognized activists and trailblazers since the early-twentieth-century era of Emma Lazarus, Pauline Newman, and Gertrude Stein, Alice Toklas, and their circle. In the United States the feminist second wave included many Jewish leaders who were lesbians, bi, and trans (e.g., Susan Sontag, Andrea Dworkin, Gayle Rubin, Joan Nestle, Lillian Faderman, Judith Butler, Leslie Cagan, and Annie Leibowitz).[1] In addition, Jewish dyke public figures (many of whom were or are also feminist activists), such as athlete Renée Richards, actress and comedian Sandra Bernhard, singer-songwriter Phranc, and folk singer/songwriter Alex Dobkin are influential today.

Connie Kurtz and Ruth Berman. Reproduced with permission.

Jewish lesbians in the United States began forming a network of groups in the 1970s.[2] The field of Jewish lesbian feminist scholarly work has grown and shifted since the publication of Evelyn Torton Beck's pivotal *Nice Jewish Girls* in 1982.[3] As part of the larger Jewish feminist, feminist, and lesbian feminist movements, Jewish lesbian feminists sought to create a space for articulating their unique experiences, perspectives, and modes of inquiry. Because of ongoing omissions of explicit lesbian and Jewish work, lesbian work was often excluded from general feminist and Jewish scholarship, and Jewish work was largely absent from feminist and lesbian feminist work, rendering Jewish lesbian feminism virtually invisible in all three fields. Jewish lesbian feminist work can be seen as work that is consciously Jewish, lesbian, and feminist and/or work done by Jewish lesbian feminists that has contributed to Jewish lesbian feminist activism, thinking, and communities. Jewish lesbian feminist work began in close connection with non-Jewish lesbian and feminist scholarship and activism and was highly attentive to diversity. Even with the deepening scholarly attention to intersectionality, these two factors have changed significantly since the early 1980s, in part because of historic anti-Semitism on the U.S. left.[4] Although anti-Semitism from the right has often had more of an institutional base, it has also long been difficult to be out as Jewish on the left, given internalization of international Jewish conspiracy theories.[5]

Even though Jewish lesbians have been and continue to be active, there has been little academic study on or including Jewish lesbians per se for many years. In this essay I provide an overview of the field of Jewish lesbian studies, particularly in the United States and the English-speaking world to inform the general reader and as a guide to future study. I look at the opening of the field of Jewish lesbian feminist work and then explore ways in which Jewish lesbians have been active in religious and spiritual initiatives, the arts, politics, and history, and academic and organizational life. Jewish lesbian feminism, which grew in the 1980s in part to meet a need created from a series of exclusions, has at times produced its own exclusions. In addition, despite some decades of active and interesting Jewish lesbian work, by 2020 issues of exclusion outside Jewish circles still remain, making it difficult to note Jewish lesbian contributions.

Opening the Field: Jewish Lesbian Foremothers and Foundational Initiatives

THE MAIN PERIOD OF Jewish lesbian feminism in the United States began in the late 1970s. Our exploration can begin with Adrienne Rich. Rich was eulogized as among "America's most powerful writers" and "foremost public intellectuals" in her obituary in the *Guardian*, the U.K.'s leading newspaper; she had become increasingly outspoken as a feminist in the 1970s and by the 1980s already had a following among feminists.[6] Judith Plaskow co-edited the pivotal feminist spirituality reader, *Womanspirit Rising*, in 1979 (and the follow-up, *Weaving the Visions*, in 1989) with Carol Christ.[7] Savina Teubal published *Sarah the Priestess* in 1984, and Irena Klepfisz and Melanie Kaye/Kantrowitz were known for their writing and activism in the general lesbian feminist movement.[8] With Kaye/Kantrowitz and Klepfisz's 1986 publication of *The Tribe of Dina*, the Jewish lesbian field started off consciously exploring and purposely interrupting Ashkenazic presumptions of U.S. Jewry, for example, by including memoirs of Jewish women from Argentina and China and translations of traditional women's literature from Yiddish, Hebrew, and Ladino.[9] It also began in intense conversation with non-Jewish lesbians, both white and of color, with Elly Bulkin, Barbara Smith, and Minnie Bruce Pratt's significant dialogue in *Yours in Struggle* (1984).[10] This diversity within Jewish lesbian activism and scholarship and robust exchanges between Jewish and non-Jewish lesbian feminists quickly eroded. A growing body of work by and about Jewish lesbians of color and non-Ashkenazic-centered work today still remain outside the norm, though we should be seeing more contributions over time from such scholars as Abigail Wells and Chanda Prescod-Weinstein.

In the late 1980s in the United States Tracy Moore undertook an interesting and complex project of interviewing Israeli lesbians and then engaging mainly U.S. Jewish lesbians to edit their interviews for publication in *Lesbiōt*.[11] Jewish lesbian feminists continued to explore issues together with other Jewish queers and with gay men generally.[12] They also wrote about the benefits and limitations of identifying as lesbians and/or queer, the challenges facing the first generation of lesbian rabbis, and various issues for Orthodox Jewish lesbians and those coming from ultra-Orthodox communities.[13] Melanie Kaye/Kantrowitz and Leslie Feinberg continued their multilevel work involving class-based frameworks, critical race theory, and feminist lesbian analysis.[14] Unfortunately, outside the forum that Clare Kinberg and her cohort created in *Bridges: A Journal for Jewish Feminists and Our Friends*, this sort of work became less frequent.[15] In addition, Jewish feminism and specifically Jewish lesbian feminist work was absent in general feminist and lesbian/queer feminist work, and exclusion of Jewish feminists from these circles was growing.[16]

Religion and Spirituality

NUMEROUS RELIGIOUS AND SPIRITUAL initiatives launched and led by and for Jewish lesbians have provided crucial support. Along with gay men, Jewish lesbians have not always been welcome in the congregations in which they grew up. They often faced resistance to their participation and celebrations of partnerships. Therefore, establishing spaces for community and worship was important for many. Beginning in the 1970s, Jewish lesbians were active in the formation of LGBTQ synagogues across the United States. These include Am Tikva in Boston, founded in 1976; Congregation Bet Haverim in Atlanta, which began meeting in people's homes in 1985; the Los Angeles congregations of Beth Chayim Chadashim, founded in 1972, and Congregation Kol Ami, launched in 1992; and the largest LGBTQ synagogue in the world, the already mentioned Congregation Beit Simchat Torah in New York, which began on an informal basis in 1973 and was formally established by 1975.[17] There have also been any number of LGBTQ *havurot* (less formal groups for prayer and community), such as the New Jersey Lesbian and Gay Havurah, which formed in 1991 and continues to meet regularly.

There is also an important legacy of lesbian organizing within the mainstream religious movements of U.S. Judaism. Even in the progressive Reconstructionist movement, where lesbians such as Linda Holtzman and Rebecca Alpert were pioneers, full transformation has been a long-term challenge.[18] For three years in the 1980s, Julie Greenberg from the Reconstructionist Rabbinical College and her colleagues created Ameinu for gay, lesbian, and bisexual rabbis, cantors, and rabbinic and cantorial students, most of whom were closeted and dispersed throughout the country in the Orthodox, Conservative, Reconstructionist, and Reform movements.[19] Theirs was a long and complex road that posed even more challenges than those for Jewish gay men also on the grounds of the religious texts. As opposed to same-gender male sexual behavior, same-gender female behavior is not mentioned in the Hebrew Bible. In a commentary on Leviticus edited in the second century of the common era, Israelite women are prohibited from participating in acts such as marriage between women, said to be a practice in Rome of the time. Women's same-gender sexual activity (*mesolelot*) is discussed in the Talmud, compiled in the fifth century. These two items are referenced again by philosopher Moses Maimonides in the *Mishneh Torah* of the twelfth century.[20]

In the early 1990s Dawn Rose and allies created the Incognito Club at the Jewish Theological Seminary, the Conservative movement's New York City seminary. This initiative was prompted by a devastating anti-gay and anti-lesbian witch hunt in the institution as part of the backlash to the movement's

1983 decision to ordain women.[21] Students thought to be lesbian or gay were brought into meetings with administrators to confirm or deny charges of homosexuality. As a religious institution, under U.S. law, the school could discriminate on this basis and could dismiss anyone who confirmed that they were not heterosexual. Many students left; many were traumatized. Creating the club was one compromise resulting from the shakedown.

Spiritual initiatives outside formal Jewish movements also emerged during this time period. Savina Teubal and other well-known Jewish lesbians, such as composer-singer Debbie Friedman and scholar and rabbi Drorah Setel, founded the organization Sarah's Tent: Sheltering Creative Jewish Spirituality. This organization, aimed at Jewish feminist spiritual innovation, overlapped with other Jewish feminist initiatives with high lesbian participation and leadership (including by lesbians who were not yet out). Teubal also convened two Los Angeles–based organizations: Shabbat Sheinit and the Mikvah Ladies, which experimented with creative worship services and *mikveh* rituals, respectively.[22] In 1995 Reconstructionist rabbi Sarra Levine (now Lev) and Reform rabbi Rochelle Robins launched Bat Kol, a feminist yeshiva (Jewish house of study). Miryam Kabakov and others formed the Orthodykes, an organization dedicated to supporting Orthodox lesbians.[23] And in 2010 in the United States, Eshel was founded to support Orthodox LGBTQ Jews.[24] Rabbi Benay Lappe, ordained in the Conservative movement, created and runs Svara, a queer and traditional yeshiva.[25] Numerous other Jewish lesbian-related projects abound, such as Talmud Interrupted, a group of academics in the field of rabbinics sharing their work and strategizing together about queering the discipline.[26] In addition, queer feminist Jill Hammer is cocreator and codirector of the Kohenet Hebrew Priestess Institute, which trains and celebrates leaders of Jewish earth-based, embodied, feminist, innovative ritual; the program currently hosts many queer participants and faculty.[27]

Many lesbians who grew up ultra-Orthodox or Hasidic identify with a larger trend called OTD, or Off the Derech (path), which is supported by organizations intended for this population, such as Maagal, Footsteps, and JQY (Jewish Queer Youth). Related to this population, the 2014 film *Devout* and the 2017 film *One of Us* look at struggles of lesbians and gay men seeking to find ways to stay connected with their Orthodox commitments and communities.[28]

The Arts: Impact and Creative Outlet

JEWISH LESBIANS HAVE USED film, music, and performance art as creative outlets. Jewish lesbian Lesley Gore of "You Don't Own Me" and "It's My Party" fame—née Lesley Sue Goldstein (1946–2015)—was a singer-songwriter. Lucy Renee Mathilde Schwob (a.k.a. Claude Cahun; d. 1954) in Paris, Hannah Gluckstein (Gluck; d. 1978) in England, Denise Frohman in the United States, and Sharon Gershoni in Israel all work(ed) in the fine arts. There is also a rich body of work from Jewish lesbians publishing short stories, novels, and poetry.[29]

A study of twentieth-century Jewish lesbian poets might begin with bisexual Muriel Rukeyser. A U.S. writer and activist, Rukeyser's work focused on an array of social justice issues, receiving attention both among Jews and in the United States more broadly. In the twenty-first century in the United States, her poem "To Be a Jew in the Twentieth Century" (1944), on the theme of Judaism as a gift out of the harrowing time that was World War II, was adopted by both the U.S. Reform and Reconstructionist movements for their prayer books for its profound and hopeful articulation of Judaism being "a gift."[30]

More recently, Elana Dykewomon, who first became known in larger lesbian feminist circles for her 1974 *Riverfinger Woman*, began publishing specifically Jewish work in 1997 with *Beyond the Pale*.[31] Klepfisz and Kaye/Kantrowitz continued to publish short stories and poetry.[32] Sarah Shulman published her first novel, *The Sophie Horowitz Story*, in 1984 and is still active in the field.[33] In 1989 Jewish lesbian feminist Lesléa Newman changed the landscape with her successful children's book, *Heather Has Two Mommies*, and she continues to publish significant work. *Heather Has Two Mommies* featured a girl being raised by two lesbian mothers when such a profile was not at all common.[34] In the 1990s Jewish lesbians began publishing new poetry and fiction in a fecund cluster.[35]

Jewish lesbian and queer filmmakers have produced a number of important films on Jewish lesbian and related experiences. These projects have spanned secular and religious realms as well as personal and political stories. In addition to *Devout* (2014) and *One of Us* (2017), these films include Alisa Lebow and Cynthia Madansky's *Treyf* (nonkosher), from 1998. Through chronicling the filmmakers' lives and relationship as a couple, this film was the first to critically bring a Jewish lesbian lens to mainly secular Jewish political issues, such as Jewish culture and family in the United States, homophobia, anti-Semitism, Zionism, and social justice. Gay Jewish filmmaker Sandi DuBowski's 2001 *Trembling Before G-d* looks at a series of Orthodox Jews living across the boundaries of Orthodoxy and homosexual experience and includes lesbians among those profiled. Dickson's 2002 *Ruthie and Connie: Every Room in the House* soon followed the long-term relationship of Ruth Berman and Connie Kurtz, whose story opens this essay. In 2005 *Hineini: Coming Out in a Jewish High School* shared the story of Shulamit Izen, an out lesbian student at a Boston-area Jewish high school. Izen went on to receive rabbinic ordination, and the film is still used as an educational tool by the Jewish queer organization Keshet. The first film to focus on Jewish lesbians in Israel, *Keep Not Silent* (2004), explores the lives of three Orthodox Jewish lesbians in Jerusalem who had been involved with the Orthodykes.[36]

Jewish lesbians and queers have been central to the revitalization of Yiddish culture in the United States and abroad. Attention to Yiddish culture in the *Tribe of Dina*, discussed earlier, reflects developments in various communities.[37] Adrienne Cooper, who came out later in life, was a significant leader in the 1980s revival of klezmer (a musical tradition of the Ashkenazic Jews of Eastern Europe). The founders of one of the most popular modern klezmer bands, the Klezmatics, included out queer musicians, such as the well-known violinist Alicia Svigals. The Klezmatics named their first album *Shvaygn = Toyt*, which is Yiddish for "Silence = Death," the slogan of the AIDS activist group Act Up.[38] In 1998 Eve Sicular, who had been leading the band Metropolitan Klezmer since 1994, began giving presentations from her project "The Celluloid Closet in Yiddish Film" and formed the explicitly lesbian band Isle of Klezbos.[39] Many lesbians and other queers were active in the U.S. Klezcamp and the still-operating Canadian KlezKanada. Moreover, lesbians and queers have been central to an array of Yiddish music and performance art.[40] In addition, lesbian scholars and activists Alisa Solomon and Marilyn Neimark initiated the WBAI/New York weekly radio show *Beyond the Pale*, which ran for nineteen years, until 2014. The program featured "cutting edge Jewish culture and offer[ed] local, national, and international political debate and analysis from a Jewish perspective." Over its years on the air, the program explored aspects of queer Yiddish culture and living in the Diaspora, as well as debates on Israeli and U.S. social justice issues such as racism and economic inequality.[41]

Politics and History

JEWISH LESBIANS HAVE LONG been involved in a wide array of political issues. Often engaged through their synagogues or groups beyond the Jewish community, Jewish lesbians have been particularly active in social justice arenas. A rare example of an explicitly gay and lesbian activist group that was also Jewishly self-identified was the 1990s New York City–based Jewish Activist Gays and Lesbians (JAGL, originally named JYGL, Jewish Young Gays and Lesbians). JAGL engaged in public actions regarding treatment of gays and lesbians in the Jewish community and more broadly. The group followed queer-related developments in the Conservative movement, the main Jewish religious movement at the time struggling with queer issues, such as changes in policy regarding the ordination of out gay and lesbian clergy.[42] JAGL also created the Jewish Queer Think Tank, which ran for about seven years, to provide a space for deeper critical reflection on Jewish queer issues to accompany the activist work. The group looked at issues such as same-gender partnering ceremonies, Jewish analyses of anonymous sex, and excavation of queer themes in ancient Jewish texts.

Jewish lesbians have also had a particularly distinct role in Jewish and specifically peace work and international activism aimed at ending the Israeli-Palestinian conflict. Marcia Freedman broke new ground in the 1960s and 1970s as a U.S. immigrant to Israel and an out lesbian who became a Knesset member with the Israeli civil rights movement party Ratz. Freedman is also a feminist and peace activist.[43] Many Jewish lesbians took risks as leaders in expressly Jewish organizations and in the broader movements for Israeli, Israel-Palestine, and Middle East peace.[44] They mobilized in grassroots collectives such as Women in Black[45] and in larger initiatives, including feminist groups, such as Code Pink[46] and an array of Zionist, non-Zionist, and anti-Zionist groups.[47] Many grounded their work in activist traditions of modern Jewish history.[48]

Notable Jewish lesbian writers and activists have drawn on their personal and familial connections to the Holocaust. Evi Beck and Irena Klepfisz, mentioned earlier for their founding roles in Jewish lesbian feminism, are both child survivors of the Holocaust. The stories of Jewish lesbian Holocaust survivors, such as Annette Eick, Frieda Belinfant, Gertrude Sandmann, Thea Spyer, and Felice Rahel Schragenheim, have been preserved. Moreover, there are some well-done exhibits and memorials related to Jewish lesbians and the Holocaust, and there are groups for lesbian daughters of Holocaust survivors.[49]

Jewish Academic and Organizational Life

JEWISH LESBIANS CONTINUE TO sort through paradigms and to found and participate in a range of academic and organizational projects. Although originally resistant to homogenizing tendencies in the LGBT community's transition to the label "queer"[50] and leery of the ways that patriarchal perspectives and a focus on men's experience remained dominant in communities embracing this name, over time many Jewish lesbians began to use this label. Thus, given the ways that *queer* has become the term of preference for much of the work in the field, many of its founders no longer publish much explicitly "Jewish lesbian" analysis, but they certainly still remain productive in their research. Despite little public acknowledgment of their roles, many Jewish lesbians and queers remain active as feminist scholars, rabbis (e.g., Lisa Edwards, Karen Bender, Sharon Kleinbaum, Georgette Kennebrae, Sandra Lawson, Isaama Goldstein-Stoll, and Kohenet Keshira haLev Fife), and Jewish communal figures (e.g., Ilana Kaufman, Erika Davis, Marielle Tawil, Mirushe Zyali, and Carmel Tanaka).[51] In these areas Jewish feminists continue their critical work attending to ongoing justice matters such as anti-Semitism, climate change, anti-racism, Israel-Palestine peace, sexism, transphobia, and homophobia. Given the lack of attention to lesbian contributions, it is important to note that some important works on Jewish feminism more broadly examine the role of lesbians.[52] Academic journals occasionally publish articles on Jewish lesbian feminist subjects. In general, however, Jewish lesbian works are rarely if ever currently found in most academic outlets, including feminist journals.

Jewish lesbians helped to found and continue to keep Jewish LGBTQ projects vibrant. For example, Idit Klein founded Keshet, an organization dedicated to inclusion and equality for lesbians, gays, bisexuals, and trans-gendered people in Jewish life. This was originally a local grassroots group developed to work in the Boston area. Over time, Keshet gained recognition and merged with other LGBTQ Jewish groups across the United States. It is now a national organization.[53] They are active in creating the newer Sephardic Mizrahi Q [Queer] Network.[54]

Jewish lesbians have played central roles in creating and maintaining innovative Jewish feminist spaces over the years. B'not Esh (Daughters of Fire) was created in the early 1980s. It is a group that meets annually over a long Memorial Day weekend seeking to transform Judaism and the Jewish community from a feminist perspective. It is a spirituality-focused group that explores liturgy, creative ritual innovation, Jewish texts, and politics and the arts. B'not Esh was designed to remain a relatively small group (with about thirty members at any given time) in which the members could build ties and trust over time. Members bring their expertise from their work in the wider world to the group and share their insights from engagement with this small democratic group with the Jewish and larger world.[55] Other Jewish feminist initiatives with prominent lesbian participation and leadership have included the National Council of Jewish Women, Ma'yan, Ritual Well, the Jewish Women's Archive, Women at the Wall, and the Jewish feminist magazine *Lilith*.[56]

Jewish lesbian and queer feminists are currently active in all areas of Jewish life. Jewish lesbians remain prominent in other progressive Jewish groups, such as Jews for Racial and Economic Justice; the Jewish Multi-Racial Network; the Jews of Color Convenings; the Jews of Color Initiative; the *havurah* movement; Jewish sustainability initiatives, such as Hazon at the Isabella Freedman Jewish Retreat Center; long-term Yiddish organizations, such as the Workmen's Circle; the American Jewish World Service; the American Sephardi Federation, and the Shalom Center.[57]

Matters of Exclusion

JEWISH LESBIANS CONTINUE TO face issues of exclusion in organizational and academic life as Jews, feminists, women, and lesbians. In addition, as Jewish lesbians have sought to overcome exclusions, their work has at times produced some of its own. When people speak in the name of Jewish lesbians and dykes, they often exclude or marginalize trans lesbians, and when they represent themselves or are taken as defining Jewish women's experience beyond heterosexuality, this marginalizes bi-, multi-, and pansexuals as well.[58] Some non-Ashkenazic and nonwhite Jewish lesbian feminists have published in volumes featuring the diversity of Jewish lesbian feminists.[59] Importantly, in addition to these venues, some Jewish lesbian feminists of color have also published accounts of their experiences.[60] Still, racial and other forms of diversity remain largely lacking in Jewish lesbian feminist writing, as does scholarly work on their experiences.[61] The anthologies published after *Nice Jewish Girls* and the *Tribe of Dina*, both from the 1980s, do not emphasize these aspects of diversity.[62] Because of difficulties with Jewish lesbians doing work as Jews in lesbian and feminist movements, common to the types of anti-Semitism currently found in groups on the left, no later work comes close to the deep multicommunity engagement of *Yours in Struggle: Three Feminist Perspectives of Anti-Semitism and Racism* (1984).[63]

Despite the vivacity of the field, Jewish lesbian work is rarely published in other lesbian and feminist academic journals. A search of the top twenty feminist and LGBTQ journals demonstrates this reality. Moreover, there are almost no lesbian-focused articles published in the top ten Jewish studies journals either.[64] The contemporary field of Jewish lesbian feminist studies has narrowed again, and publishing outlets are scarce.

Conclusion

JEWISH LESBIANS HAVE LIKELY existed as long as there have been Jews, from antiquity until today. I have focused on the twentieth-century and twenty-first-century West. This region saw the development of a self-identified lesbian community and of gender-based homophobia directed at people who were, or were imagined to be, lesbians. This dynamic of self-identification and targeting of women's same-gender love and affiliations spurred dynamic new forms of relationship and movements for justice. Jewish lesbians have been central to these developments both within Jewish communities and in larger social trends. A rich body of Jewish lesbian work exists in the arenas of religion and spirituality, the arts, politics and history, scholarly endeavors, and organizational and activist life. Jewish lesbians have been vital to cultural and spiritual innovation, movements for justice, and Jewish life through terrifying periods of fascism and in different moments in the life of democratic nations.

Jewish lesbian activists such as Ruth Berman and Connie Kurtz, those before them, and those who will come after them have learned to navigate these often turbulent waters. Ruthie and Connie, Brooklynites grounded in Ashkenazic Jewish immigrant communities from the 1930s, strove to make viable lives for themselves, for other women, for lesbians, for Jews, and for all those marginalized. Emerging in their teen years in a post-Holocaust U.S. Jewish community, Ruthie and Connie found and committed to each other and remained committed to helping others create beautiful and healthy lives as individuals and in the community.

Jewish lesbians such as Ruthie and Connie and their contributions exist in multiple challenging contexts of homophobia, anti-Semitism, and patriarchy, with attendant problems of racial, environmental, and economic injustice. Given these structural constraints and even with its continued areas of vibrancy, Jewish lesbian work remains undercirculated in academic and other arenas. In part, the lack of Jewish lesbian feminist work in broader feminist and lesbian contexts corresponds to a similar lack of self-identified Jewish work in progressive academic venues generally. Following Albert Memmi's important 1966 analysis of anti-Semitism and the lack of space for Jews in leftist critical paradigms, the 1980s saw Jewish lesbian feminists analyzing the absence of Jews in lesbian and feminist frameworks and the role that anti-Semitism plays in this lack.[65] Post-1990, we continue to see Jews grappling with this problem.[66] I intend this contribution to support bridging these gaps in future work.

Notes

This chapter is dedicated to the memory of Connie Kurtz (z"l), who died soon after it was written. Many thanks to Nina Katz and Patrick Baga. Much research for this article was originally prepared for the introduction to the special issue "Jewish Lesbians: New Work in the Field" of the *Journal of Lesbian Studies* 23, no. 1 (2019) and is reprinted here with permission. The Ruth Berman and Connie Kurtz Papers are housed in the Sophia Smith Collection of Women's History at Smith College and also at the Lesbian Archives in Brooklyn.

1 The second wave is a name applied to feminist movements led by mostly Western white women in the 1960s and 1970s. (The first wave refers to efforts for women's suffrage.) Today many feminists, particularly those of color, do not limit their histories of activism to these waves. See Carole R. McCann and Seung-Kyung Kim, eds., *Feminist Theory Reader: Local and Global Perspectives*, 4th ed. (New York: Taylor & Francis, 2017).

2 Faith Rogow, "Why Is This Decade Different from All Other Decades? A Look at the Rise of Jewish Lesbian Feminism," *Bridges* 1, no. 1 (1990): 67–79; and Joyce Antler, "'For God's Sake, Comb Your Hair! You Look Like a Vilde Chaye': Jewish Lesbian Feminists Explore the Politics of Identity," in *Jewish Radical Feminism: Voices from the Women's Liberation Movement*, by Joyce Antler (New York: New York University Press, 2018), 278–314.

3 Evelyn Torton Beck, *Nice Jewish Girls: A Lesbian Anthology* (Boston: Beacon Press, 1982).

4 Kimberle Crenshaw, "Demarginalizing the Intersection of Race and Sex: A Black Feminist Critique of Antidiscrimination Doctrine, Feminist Theory, and Anti-racist Politics," *University of Chicago Legal Forum* 1989, no. 1 (1989): 139–67. See also Marla Brettschneider, *The Family Flamboyant: Race Politics, Queer Families, Jewish Lives* (Albany: State University of New York Press, 2006); and Marla Brettschneider, *Jewish Feminism and Intersectionality* (Albany: State University of New York Press, 2017).

5 See Debra Schultz, *Going South: Jewish Women in the Civil Rights Movement* (New York: New York University Press, 2001); and Joyce Antler, *Jewish Radical Feminism: Voices from the Women's Liberation Movement* (New York: New York University Press, 2018).

6 Alison Flood, "Adrienne Rich, Award-Winning Poet and Essayist, Dies," *The Guardian*, March 29, 2012, https://www.theguardian.com/books/2012/mar/29/adrienne-rich-poet-essayist-dies (accessed December 10, 2020).

7 Carol P. Christ and Judith Plaskow, eds., *Womanspirit Rising: A Feminist Reader in Religion* (San Francisco: Harper Collins, 1979); and Judith Plaskow, "Blaming the Jews for the Birth of Patriarchy," in *Nice Jewish Girls: A Lesbian Anthology*, ed. Evelyn Torton Beck (Watertown, MA: Persephone Press, 1982), 250–54.

8 Savina J. Teubal, *Sarah the Priestess: The First Matriarch of Genesis* (Athens, OH: Swallow Press, 1984).

9 Irena Klepfisz and Melanie Kaye/Kantrowitz, *The Tribe of Dina: A Jewish Women's Anthology* (Boston: Beacon Press, 1986).

10 Elly Bulkin, Minnie Bruce Pratt, and Barbara Smith, *Yours in Struggle: Three Feminist Perspectives of Anti-Semitism and Racism* (New York: Long Haul Press, 1984).

11 Tracy Moore, *Lesbiōt: Israeli Lesbians Talk About Sexuality, Feminism, Judaism, and Their Lives* (London: Cassell, 1995). See also Chava Frankfort-Nachmias and Erella Shadmi, *Sappho in the Holy Land: Lesbian Existence and Dilemmas in Contemporary Israel* (Albany: State University of New York Press, 2005).

12 See, for example, Christie Balka and Andy Rose, *Twice Blessed: On Being Lesbian or Gay and Jewish* (Boston: Beacon Press, 1989); Daniel Boyarin, Daniel Itzkovitz, and Ann Pellegrini, *Queer Theory and the Jewish Question* (New York: Columbia University Press, 2003); and Gregg Drinkwater, Joshua Lesser, David Shneer, and Judith Plaskow, *Torah Queeries: Weekly Commentaries on the Hebrew Bible* (New York: New York University Press, 2009).

13 See, for example, Rebecca Alpert, *Like Bread on the Seder Plate* (New York: Columbia University Press, 1997); David Shneer and Caryn Aviv, *Queer Jews* (New York: Routledge, 2002); Rebecca Alpert, Ellen Sue Levi Elwell, and Shirley Idelson, *Lesbian Rabbis: The First Generation* (New Brunswick, NJ: Rutgers University Press, 2001); Miryam Kabakov, *Keep Your Wives Away from Them: Orthodox Women, Unorthodox Desires* (Berkeley, CA: North Atlantic Books, 2010); Leah Lax, *Uncovered: How I Left Hasidic Life and Finally Came Home—A Memoir* (Berkeley, CA: She Writes Press, 2015); and Rebecca Halff, "There Are No Queer Chassidic Jews; Or, Why Shterna Goldbloom Is Photographing Them," *Lilith*, April 18, 2018, https://www.lilith.org/blog/2018/04/there-are-no-queer-chassidic-jews-or-why-shterna-goldbloom-is-photographing-them/ (accessed December 10, 2020).

14 Melanie Kaye/Kantrowitz, *The Issue Is Power: Essays on Women, Jews, Violence, and Resistance* (San Francisco: Aunt Lute Books, 1992); Melanie Kaye/Kantrowitz, *The Colors of Jews: Racial Politics and Radical Diasporism* (Bloomington: Indiana University Press, 2007); Leslie Feinberg, *Transgender Warriors: Making History from Joan of Arc to Dennis Rodman* (Boston: Beacon Press, 1996); and Leslie Feinberg, *Trans Liberation: Beyond Pink or Blue* (Boston: Beacon Press, 1998).

15 See *Bridges: A Journal for Jewish Feminists and Our Friends*, Special Issue: Sephardi and Mizrachi Women Write About Their Lives, 7, no. 1 (1997); *Bridges*, Special Issue: Writing and Art by Jewish Women of Color, 9, no. 1 (2001); and Elly Bulkin, "Bridges: A Journal for Jewish Feminists and Our Friends," *Jewish Women's Archive*, https://jwa.org/encyclopedia/article/bridges-journal-for-jewish-feminists-and-our-friends (accessed October 20, 2017).

16 For example, *This Bridge Called My Back*, a groundbreaking work by feminists of color, included a memoir piece by the Jewish Puerto Rican lesbian Aurora Levins Morales. In 2002 a follow-up volume, *This Bridge We Call Home*, was published with a contribution from a self-identified Jewish author, Elana Dykewomon. Jewish Latina lesbian Rosa Maria Pegueros also had a piece in this volume that did not address any specifically Jewish matters of concern. However, in *Nashim* Pegueros describes the anti-Semitism she experienced when she named herself as a second Jew participating in the project in an online discussion among contributors to *This Bridge We Call Home*. According to Pegueros, in response to identifying herself as also Jewish, many contributors wrote of a Jewish takeover of the safe space for women of color they equated with a critique of Israeli actions against Palestinians. Rosa Maria Pegueros, "Radical Feminists—No Jews Need Apply," *Nashim: A Journal of Jewish Women's Studies and Gender Issues* 8 (fall 2004): 174–80; Maria Rosa Pegueros, "The Ricky Ricardo Syndrome: Looking for

Leaders, Finding Celebrities," in *This Bridge We Call Home: Radical Visions for Transformation*, ed. Gloria Anzaldúa and AnaLouise Keating (New York: Routledge, 2002), 330–38; Gloria Anzaldúa and AnaLouise Keating, *This Bridge We Call Home: Radical Visions for Transformation* (New York: Routledge, 2002); Aurora Levins Morales, ". . . And Even Fidel Can't Change That!" in *This Bridge Called My Back: Writings by Radical Women of Color*, ed. Cherríe Moraga and Gloria Anzaldúa (Albany: State University of New York Press, 2015), 48–52.

17 Moshe Shokeid, *A Gay Synagogue in New York* (New York: Columbia University Press, 1995).

18 See https://www.reconstructingjudaism.org/search/lesbian.

19 Thanks to Julie Greenberg for information on the group. See also Julie Greenberg, "My Piece of Truth," in *Lesbian Rabbis: The First Generation*, ed. Rebecca Alpert, Sue Levi Elwell, and Shirley Idelson (Piscataway, NJ: Rutgers University Press, 2001), 181–89.

20 See Rebecca Alpert's concise summation with my updates of this material in her entry on lesbianism in the Jewish Women's Archive Encyclopedia: https://jwa .org/encyclopedia/article/lesbianism (accessed December 10, 2020).

21 Dawn Robinson Rose, "Notes from the Underground," in *Lesbian Rabbis: The First Generation*, ed. Rebecca Alpert, Sue Levi Elwell, and Shirley Idelson (Piscataway, NJ: Rutgers University Press, 2001), 217–25; and Amy Stone, "Out and Ordained," *Lilith* 38, no. 2 (2011), https://www.lilith.org/articles/out-and-ordained/ (accessed December 10, 2020).

22 Thanks to Marcia Cohen Spiegel for her leadership in and information on these organizations.

23 See http://orthodykes.blogspot.com.

24 See http://www.eshelonline.org; and Lax, *Uncovered*.

25 See http://www.svara.org.

26 Thanks to Max Strassfeld for information on this. See https://irwg.umich.edu/ news/feminist-research-seminar-2016 (accessed December 10, 2020).

27 Thanks to Jill Hammer for this information; and see http://www.kohenet.com.

28 See http://www.chanigetter.com; Maagal (https://www.keshetonline.org/work/new -york/maagal-the-keshet-ny-womens-group/); the films *Devout*, dir. Diana Neille and Sana Gulzar (USA: Neshama Productions, 2014), and *One of Us*, dir. Heidi Ewing and Rachel Grady (USA: Loki Films, 2017); and, for the OTD: Off the Derech trend, http://www.offthederech.org.

29 Irene Zahava, *Speaking for Ourselves: Short Stories by Jewish Lesbians* (Freedom, CA: Crossing Press, 1990).

30 Other earlier twentieth-century Jewish lesbian poets of note include Sophia Parnok, often referred to as Russia's Sappho (Sappho was an ancient Greek poet from the isle of Lesbos who wrote of her passionate love for other women), and Vera Lachmann, a German who engaged in anti-Nazi resistance. For the more recent poetry, see Julie Enszer, *Milk and Honey: A Celebration of Jewish Lesbian Poetry* (New York: A Midsummer Night's Press, 2011).

31 Elana Dykewomon, *Riverfinger Women* (Plainfield, VT: Daughters Inc., 1974); and Elana Dykewomon, *Beyond the Pale* (Vancouver, CA: Press Gang, 1997).

32 Melanie Kaye/Kantrowitz, *My Jewish Face and Other Stories* (San Francisco: Aunt Lute Books, 1990); Irena Klepfisz, *A Few Words in the Mother Tongue: Poems Selected and New (1971–1990)* (Portland, OR: Eighth Mountain Press, 1993).

33 Sarah Schulman, *The Sophie Horowitz Story* (Tallahassee, FL: Naiad Press, 1984); and Sarah Schulman, *Israel/Palestine and the Queer International* (Durham, NC: Duke University Press, 2012).

34 Lesléa Newman and Laura Cornell, *Heather Has Two Mommies* (New York: Alyson Books, 1989). Also see http://lesleanewman.com.

35 See, for example, Ellen Galford, *The Dyke and the Dybbuk* (Seattle: Seal Press, 1993); Jyl Lynn Felman, *Hot Chicken Wings* (London: Aunt Lute Books, 1992); Jyl Lynn Felman, *Cravings: A Sensual Memoir* (Boston: Beacon Press, 1997); Jyl Lynn Felman, *Never a Dull Moment: Teaching and the Art of Performance—Feminism Takes Center Stage* (New York: Routledge, 2001); Judith Katz, *Running Fiercely Toward a High Thin Sound* (Ann Arbor, MI: Firebrand Books, 1992); Judith Katz, *The Escape Artist* (Ann Arbor, MI: Firebrand Books, 1997); Leslie Feinberg, *Stone Butch Blues: A Novel* (Ann Arbor, MI: Firebrand Books, 1993); Leslie Feinberg, *Drag King Dreams* (New York: Carroll & Graf, 2006); and T. Kira Madden, *Long Live the Tribe of Fatherless Girls* (London: Bloomsbury, 2019).

36 *Devout* (2014); *One of Us* (2017); *Treyf*, dir. Alisa Lebow and Cynthia Madansky (USA: Women Make Movies, 1998); *Trembling Before G-d*, dir. Sandi Simcha DuBowski (USA: Cinephil, 2001); *Ruthie and Connie: Every Room in the House*, dir. Deborah Dickson (USA: The Orchard, 2002); *Hineini: Coming Out in a Jewish High School*, dir. Irena Fayngold (USA: Keshet, 2005); *Keep Not Silent*, dir. Ilil Alexander (Israel: Women Make Movies, 2004); *Lifetime Guarantee: Phranc's Adventures in Plastics*, dir. Lisa Udelson (USA: Eric D'Arbeloff, 2001).

37 See Klepfisz and Kaye/Kantrowitz, *Tribe of Dina*.

38 The Klezmatics, *Shvaygn = Toyt*, 1988, CD.

39 Eve Sicular, "Outing the Archives: From the Celluloid Closet to the Isle of Klezbos," in *Queer Jews*, ed. David Shneer and Caryn Aviv (New York: Routledge, 2002), 199–214.

40 See http://klezmatics.com; klezbos.com; https://web.archive.org/web/200203300 81924/http://klezkamp.org; and http://klezkanada.org. Of special note are Jennifer Miller and other lesbians, such as Jenny Romain, who spearheaded Circus Amok (http://www.circusamok.org); performance artist Sara Felder (http://articles.latimes.com/keyword/sara-felder); musicians Natalia Zuckerman (https://nataliazukerman.com) and Jewlia Eisenberg (http://charminghostess.com); and Jill Sobule's conceptualizing of a more trans approach to Isaac Bashevas Singer's *Yentl* (https://www.jillsobule.com/yenta). See also Jon Kalish, "KlezKamp Lives on with 'Yiddish New York,'" *The Forward*, August 11, 2015, https://forward.com/culture/yiddish-culture/318864/klezkamp-lives-on-with-yiddish-new-york (accessed May 2, 2018).

41 See http://www.beyondthepale.org. Special thanks to Eve Sicular for her extensive knowledge and support with this section. Many of these people and activities had ties with Jews for Racial and Economic Justice (JFREJ) over the years. Outside the United States, Hinda Bursten is an example of a lesbian in Australia with a Yiddish

and Bund background who activated the Jewish lesbians of Melbourne (https://jwa.org). Joanna Britton is doing similar activist work in Belgium. For more on queer *yiddishkeit*, see Ingeveb.org; Jeffrey Shandler, *Adventures in Yiddishland: Postvernacular Language and Culture* (Berkeley: University of California Press, 2005); Jeffrey Shandler, "Queer Yiddishkeit: Practice and Theory," *Shofar: An Interdisciplinary Journal of Jewish Studies* 25, no. 1 (2006): 90–113; Jonathan Freedman, *Klezmer America: Jewishness, Ethnicity, Modernity* (New York: Columbia University Press, 2008); Ezra Berkley Nepon, "Zamlers, Tricksters, and Queers: Re-Mixing Histories in Yiddishland and Faerieland," in *Transformative Language Arts in Action*, ed. Ruth Farmer and Carryn Mirriam-Goldberg (Lanham, MD: Rowman & Littlefield, 2014), 79–93; Vivi Lachs, *Whitechapel Noise: Jewish Immigrant Life in Yiddish Song and Verse, London, 1884–1914* (Detroit: Wayne State University Press, 2018); Anne Pellegrini, "After Sontag: Future Notes on Camp," in *A Companion to Lesbian, Gay, Bisexual, Transgender, and Queer Studies*, ed. George E. Haggerty and Molly McGarry (Hoboken, NJ: Blackwell, 2007), 168–93; Eleanor Mallet, *Tevye's Grandchildren: Rediscovering a Jewish Identity* (Eugene, OR: Pilgrim Press, 2004); Warren Hoffman, *The Passing Game: Queering Jewish American Culture* (Syracuse, NY: Syracuse University Press, 2009); and the Mayrent Institute for Yiddish Culture, https://mayrentinstitute.wisc.edu.

42 At this point, the Reform, Reconstructionist, and Conservative movements ordain lesbian clergy and allow same-gender marriage ceremonies. Orthodox-related movements do not.

43 Marcia Freedman, *Exile in the Promised Land: A Memoir* (Ithaca, NY: Firebrand Books, 1990).

44 Rita Falbel, Irena Klepfisz, and Donna Nevel, *Jewish Women's Call for Peace: A Handbook for Jewish Women on the Israeli/Palestinian Conflict* (Ithaca, NY: Firebrand Books, 1990); Penny Rosenwasser, *Voices from a "Promised Land": Palestinian and Israeli Peace Activists Speak Their Hearts* (Willimantic, CT: Curbstone Press, 1992); Judith Butler, *Parting Ways: Jewishness and the Critique of Zionism* (New York: Columbia University Press, 2012); Schulman, *Israel/Palestine*.

45 http://womeninblack.org/vigils-arround-the-world/middle-east/israel.

46 https://www.codepink.org.

47 Examples of current groups include Americans for Peace Now, J Street, Jewish Voice for Peace, and If Not Now. Historically, see Rosenwasser, *Voices from a "Promised Land"*; and Marla Brettschneider, *Cornerstones of Peace: Jewish Identity, Politics, and Democratic Theory* (New Brunswick, NJ: Rutgers University Press, 1996).

48 An example of a Jewish political historical grounding for contemporary activist work includes Holocaust resistance efforts in the Warsaw Ghetto Uprising during the Nazi occupation of Poland. We can also find activists claiming the legacy of the internationally acclaimed twentieth-century political philosopher Hannah Arendt and her notion of the Jew as pariah, an outsider who uses their marginalized position to ally as Jews and with others in social justice work. For a discussion of the Minneapolis-based Hannah Arendt Lesbian Peace Patrol, see Sharon Jaffe, "Minneapolis: A Report on the Hannah Arendt Lesbian Peace Patrol," in

Jewish Women's Call for Peace: A Handbook for Jewish Women on the Israeli/Palestinian Conflict, ed. Rita Falbel, Irena Klepfisz, and Donna Nevel (Ithaca, NY: Firebrand Books, 1990), 59–60.

49 See Annette Eick, *Immortal Muse* (Braunton, UK: Merlin, 1984). Readers can view an interview with Frieda Belinfante at https://collections.ushmm.org/search/catalog/irn504443 and hear Belinfante's story in *But I Was a Girl: The Story of Frieda Belinfante*, dir. Toni Boumans (USA: SND Films, 1999). Claudia Schoopman, *Days of Masquerade: Life Stories of Lesbians During the Third Reich* (Cambridge, UK: Cambridge University Press, 1996), shares Sandmann's story. Thea Spyer's 40+ year relationship with Edie Windsor is portrayed in *Edie & Thea: A Very Long Engagement*, dir. Susan Muska and Gréta Olafsdóttir (USA: Bless Bless Productions, 2009). On Felice Rahel Schragenheim, see Erica Fischer, *Aimee & Jaguar: A Love Story, Berlin 1943* (New York: Harper Perennial, 2015); *Love Story: Berlin 1942*, dir. Catrine Clay (USA: Women Make Movies, 1997); and *Aimee & Jaguar*, dir. Max Färberböck (Germany: Zeitgeist Films, 2009). See also Sonja M. Hedgepeth and Rochelle G. Saidel, *Sexual Violence Against Jewish Women During the Holocaust* (Waltham, MA: Brandeis University Press, 2010); https://www.nypl.org/blog/2017/06/06/honoring-lgbt-jewish-holocaust-survivors (accessed December 10, 2020); https://www.jewishmadison.org/community-directory/jewish-lesbian-daughters-of-holocaust-survivors (accessed December 10, 2020); https://www.ushmm.org/wlc/en/article.php?ModuleId=10005478 (accessed December 10, 2020); and http://www.cityartsydney.com.au/artwork/gay-lesbian-holocaust-memorial/ (accessed December 10, 2020).

50 The term *queer* is sometimes used to refer to the array of sexual orientations and genders beyond a heterosexual and cis-gendered (a two-pole paradigm of gender) norms. It also aims to challenge assumptions of what is natural and familiar.

51 See, for example, Martha Ackelsberg, "Spirituality, Community, and Politics: B'not Esh and the Feminist Reconstruction of Judaism," *Journal of Feminist Studies in Religion* 2, no. 2 (1986): 109–20; Martha Ackelsberg, *Free Women of Spain: Anarchism and the Struggle for the Emancipation of Women* (Oakland, CA: AK Press, 1991); Martha Ackelsberg, "Toward a Multicultural Politics: A Jewish Feminist Perspective," in *The Narrow Bridge: Jewish Views on Multiculturalism*, ed. Marla Brettschneider (New Brunswick, NJ: Rutgers University Press, 1996), 89–104; Martha Ackelsberg, *Resisting Citizenship: Feminist Essays on Politics, Community, and Democracy* (New York: Routledge, 2010); Mychal Copeland and D'vorah Rose, *Struggling in Good Faith: LGBTQI Inclusion from 13 American Religious Perspectives* (Nashville: SkyLight Paths, 2016); Judith Plaskow, *Standing Again at Sinai: Judaism from a Feminist Perspective* (San Francisco: Harper San Francisco, 1991); Judith Plaskow, *The Coming of Lilith: Essays on Feminism, Judaism, and Sexual Ethics, 1872–2003* (Boston: Beacon Press, 2005); Carol Christ and Judith Plaskow, *Goddess and God in the World: Conversations in Embodied Theology* (Minneapolis: Fortress, 2016); Barbara C. Johnson and Ruby Daniel, *Ruby of Cochin: An Indian Jewish Woman Remembers* (Philadelphia: Jewish Publication Society, 1995); Naomi Seidman, *A Marriage Made in Heaven: The Sexual Politics of Hebrew and Yiddish* (Berkeley: University of California Press, 1997); Naomi

Seidman, "Reading "Queer" Ashkenaz: This Time from East to West," *TDR/The Drama Review* 55, no. 3 (2011): 50–56; Julie Greenberg, *Just Parenting: Building the World One Family at a Time* (www.juliegreenberg.net, 2014); Rebecca Macy Lesses, *Ritual Practices to Gain Power: Angels, Incantations, and Revelation in Early Jewish Mysticism* (Harrisburg, PA: Trinity Press International, 1998); Rebecca Macy Lesses, "Exe(o)rcising Power: Women as Sorceresses, Exorcists, and Demonesses in Babylonian Jewish Society of Late Antiquity," *Journal of the American Academy of Religion* 69, no. 2 (2001): 343–76; Sarra Lev, "How the *Aylonit* Got Her Sex," *AJS Review* 31, no. 2 (2007): 297–316; Sarra Lev, "They Treat Him As a Man and See Him As a Woman: The Tannaitic Understanding of the Congenital Eunuch," *Jewish Studies Quarterly* 17, no. 3 (2010): 213–43; Rachel Neis, *Vision and Visuality in Late Antique Rabbinic Culture* (Cambridge, MA: Harvard University Press, 2007); Rachel Neis, *The Sense of Sight in Rabbinic Culture: Jewish Ways of Seeing in Late Antiquity* (Cambridge, UK: Cambridge University Press, 2016); Bat Ami Bar On and Lisa Tessman, *Jewish Locations: Traversing Racialized Landscapes* (Lanham, MD: Rowman & Littlefield, 2001); and Chava Weissler, *Voices of the Matriarchs: Listening to the Prayer of Early Modern Jewish Women* (Boston: Beacon Press, 2008).

52 See, for example, Schultz, *Going South*; Dina Pinsky, *Jewish Feminists: Complex Identities and Activist Lives* (Urbana: University of Illinois Press, 2010); and, particularly, Antler, *Jewish Radical Feminism*.

53 See https://www.keshetonline.org; and Jacob Berkman, "Keshet and Jewish Mosaic to Merge," Jewish Telegraphic Agency, June 18, 2010, https://www.jta.org/2010/06/18/united-states/keshet-and-jewish-mosaic-to-merge (accessed December 10, 2020). Keshet eventually merged with another Jewish queer organization, Mosaic. Additional examples of LGBTQ Jewish organizations with lesbian leaders and active participants include the National Union of Jewish LGBT Students and Eshel. Penina Weinberg founded and continues to shepherd the Boston-based Ruach HaYam. GLOE: GLBT Outreach & Engagement at the Washington, D.C., Jewish Community Center and other local initiatives continue to develop, as exemplified by the World Congress of GLBT Jews and many other organizations in Israel and around the world, 2004–2015. See https://en.wikipedia.org/wiki/Nehirim; NUJLS at http://awiderbridge.org/nujls-national-union-of-jewish-lgbt-students; http://www.eshelonline.org; https://www.jewishboston.com/organization; http://washingtondcjcc.org/gloe; www.glbtjews.org; https://jqinternational.org/resources.

54 http://smqn.org/who-we-are.

55 See, for example, Ackelsberg, "Spirituality, Community, and Politics"; Barbara Breitman, "Social and Spiritual Reconstruction of Self Within a Feminist Jewish Community," in *Women's Spirituality, Women's Lives*, ed. Ellen Cole and Judith Ochshorn (Binghamton, NY: Harrington Park Press, 1995), 73–82; Merle Feld, "Brigadoon," in *A Spiritual Life*, ed. Merle Feld (Albany: State University of New York Press, 2007), 281–96; and Felice Yeskel, "Coming Out About Money: Cost Sharing Across Class Lines," *Bridges: A Journal for Jewish Feminists and Our Friends* 3, no. 1 (1992): 102–14. Examples of groups created by B'not Esh and

others include Achayot Or; Bat Kol on the West Coast, often referred to by the nickname Soaring Katchkes; and Oto Makom, another largely East Coast group.

56   See https://www.ncjw.org; https://www.ritualwell.org; https://jwa.org; http://www .womenofthewall.org.il; and http://lilith.org.

57   See http://jfrej.org; www.jewishmultiracialnetwork.org; http://jewishsocialjustice .org; https://havurah.org; https://hazon.org; http://circle.org; https://ajws.org; http://americansephardi.org; and https://theshalomcenter.org.

58   Sari Dworkin, "From Personal Therapy to Professional Life: Observations of a Jewish, Bisexual Lesbian Therapist and Academic," *Women and Therapy* 18, no. 2 (1996): 37–46; Hinda Seif, "A 'Most Amazing Borsht': Multiple Identities in a Jewish Bisexual Community," *Race, Gender, and Class* 6, no. 4 (1999): 88–109; Debra R. Kolodny, *Blessed Bi Spirit: Bisexual People of Faith* (New York: Continuum, 2000); Debra R. Kolodny, "Hear, I Pray You, This Dream Which I Have Dreamed," in *Blessed Bi Spirit: Bisexual People of Faith*, ed. Debra Kolodny (New York: Continuum, 2000), 103–13; Noach Dzmura, *Balancing on the Mechitza: Transgender in Jewish Community* (Berkeley, CA: North Atlantic Books, 2010); Rebecca Gorlin, "The Voice of a Wandering Jewish Bisexual," in *Bi Any Other Name: Bisexual People Speak Out*, ed. Loraine Hutchins and Lani Kaahumanu (Bronx, NY: Riverdale Avenue Books, 2015).

59   For example, the *Bridges* special issues 1997 and 2001; Rachel Wahba, "Some of Us Are Arabic," in *Nice Jewish Girls: A Lesbian Anthology*, ed. Evelyn Torton Beck (Boston: Beacon Press, 1989), 69–72; and Joslyn C. Segal, "Interracial Plus," in *Nice Jewish Girls: A Lesbian Anthology*, ed. Evelyn Torton Beck (Boston: Beacon, 1989), 61–64.

60   See, for example, Carolivia Herron, "Pastel Meetings," *Journal of Feminist Studies in Religion* 19, no. 1 (2003): 105–10; Carol Conaway, "Journey to the Promised Land: How I Became an African-American Jew Rather than a Jewish African American," *Nashim: A Journal of Jewish Women's Studies and Gender Issues* 8, no. 1 (2004): 115–28; Pegueros, "Radical Feminists"; Andrew Anthony, "'Yes, We Were Bloody Angry,'" *The Guardian*, February 15, 2006, https://www .theguardian.com/world/2006/feb/15/gender.andrewanthony (accessed May 1, 2018); Madden, *Long Live the Tribe*; and the work of Denise Frohman, https:// www.denicefrohman.com.

61   For exceptions, see Yeskel, "Coming Out About Money"; and Felice Yeskel, "Beyond the Taboo: Talking About Class," in *The Narrow Bridge: Jewish Views on Multiculturalism*, ed. Marla Brettschneider (New Brunswick, NJ: Rutgers University Press, 1996), 42–57. For work by a mixed Ashkenazic-Sephardic trans activist, see Cole Krawitz, "A Voice from Within: A Challenge for the Conservative Jewish Movement and Its Gay/Lesbian Activists," *Nashim: A Journal of Jewish Women's Studies and Gender Issues* 8, no. 1 (2004): 165–74.

62   For example, Evelyn Torton Beck, "'Nice Jewish Girls: A Lesbian Anthology' Revisited, 1982 and 2006," in *New Feminism: Worlds of Feminism, Queer, and Networking Conditions*, ed. Marina Grzinic and Rosa Reitsamer (Vienna: Löcker, 2008), 373–83.

63   Bulkin et al., *Yours in Struggle*.

64 As an example, see Danita Mushkat, "Alienated Jews: What About Outreach to Jewish Lesbians?" *Journal of Jewish Communal Service* 75, no. 4 (1999): 239–47.

65 See Albert Memmi and Judy Hyun, *The Liberation of the Jew* (New York: Viking, 1966); Letty Cottin Pogrebin, "Anti-Semitism in the Women's Movement," *Ms.*, June 1982; Evelyn Torton Beck, "The Politics of Jewish Invisibility," *National Women's Studies Association Journal* 1, no. 1 (1988): 93–102; Annette Daum, "Blaming the Jews for the Death of the Goddess," in *Nice Jewish Girls: A Lesbian Anthology*, ed. Evelyn Torton Beck (Boston: Beacon, 1989), 303–9; and Plaskow, "Blaming the Jews."

66 See, for example, Brenda Cossman and Marlee Kline, "'And If Not Now, When?': Feminism and Anti-Semitism Beyond Clara Brett Martin," *Canadian Journal of Women and the Law* 5 (1992): 298–316; Abby L. Ferber, "The Culture of Privilege: Color-Blindness, Postfeminism, and Christonormativity," *Journal of Social Issues* 68, no. 1 (2012): 63–77; Penny Rosenwasser, *Hope Into Practice: Jewish Women Choosing Justice Despite Our Fears* (PennyRosenwasser.com, 2013); Cheryl Greenberg, "'I'm Not White—I'm Jewish': The Racial Politics of American Jews," in *Race, Color, Identity: Rethinking Discourses About "Jews" in the Twenty-First Century*, ed. Efraim Sicher (New York: Berghahn, 2013), 35–55; Brettschneider, *Jewish Feminism*; and David Hirsh, *Contemporary Left Antisemitism* (London: Routledge, 2017).

CHOICES AND CHALLENGES IN AMERICAN JEWISH WOMEN'S LIVES TODAY

A Sociological Overview

SYLVIA BARACK FISHMAN

THE ROLES, EXPECTATIONS, AND experiences of girls and women—and Jewish girls and women—have varied over centuries and societies, affected by historical, economic, social, religious, and political conditions.[1] Diverse communities construct gender roles—the complex fabric of behaviors, attitudes, and expectations woven around biological sexual differences—in different ways, producing widely varying ideas of normative maleness and femaleness.[2] In addition, the lives of Jewish women have often been circumscribed by religious prejudice and the gendered expectations of the Muslim and Christian cultures among whom historical Jewish communities made their homes and by distinctive Jewish chiastic differences between male and female socioreligious roles created by their own religious societies, as various chapters in this book have detailed.

But today, in contrast, assumptions about maleness and femaleness, sexual and gender orientation, and public and private religious roles have been transformed.[3] American Jewish women have in many ways moved beyond ethnoreligious and gendered limitations, both in the larger American economic, social, and cultural spheres and in their own Jewish communities, especially among non-Orthodox Jews. Potential choices and opportunities available to women are similar in many ways to those available to men. Scholars have examined such transformations for women in religions, relationships, families, and American society[4] using gender theory, social scientific theories about marriage,[5] families and sexuality, rational choice theory, signaling[6] and economic theories,[7] and even evolutionary biology.[8] In this essay I analyze areas of greater choice and opportunity within the broad landscape of American Jewish women's lives today and also note areas of potential concern.

One of the most visible aspects of equalization is American Jewish women's extraordinarily high levels of university, graduate, and professional school achievement, analogous to those of Jewish men. High levels of secular education were an identifying social characteristic of American Jewish men and women even during the first half of the twentieth century, as Jewish women were more likely than any other ethnoreligious group of women to attend college. But Jews experienced their own gender gap nevertheless, because Jewish women were less likely than their brothers to go to university. This pattern changed during and after the 1960s and especially in recent decades, as the American Jewish educational achievement gender gap has essentially closed. The 2000–2001 National Jewish Population Survey (2000–2001 NJPS) showed that undergraduate degrees were earned by more than 70% of Jewish men and women ages 25–44. Overall, 30% of Jewish men compared with 22.5% of Jewish women under age 65 had graduate or professional degrees, but the proportion earning different types of degrees varied by age and gender, as Harriet and Moshe Hartman indicate.[9] Today, gendered differences regarding secular education between male and female Jews are minor compared with the substantial differences between American Jews and various non-Jewish cohorts. The Hartmans summarize, "The model educational attainment of American Jews is a bachelor's degree, whereas that of the rest of the white population is a high school degree." Moreover, "Nearly four times as many Jews have completed graduate or professional degrees than the broader white population," and "the proportion of Jewish women who have completed a graduate degree is more than four times that of white women as a whole."[10]

Diverse Household and Marital Status

JEWISH WOMEN'S CONTEMPORARY EDUCATIONAL and occupational achievements proceed in the context of sweeping social change, including increasing numbers of "unconventional" Jewish households—that is, households departing from the bourgeois nuclear family constellation of working father, housewife mother, and their children. The whole social conception of family has become more fluid and egalitarian.[11] American Jewish women, like other American women in their socioeconomic and educational stratum, give birth to fewer children than the generation of their mothers. Some social commentators argue that this is part of a "broader cultural shift away from a child-centric understanding of romance and marriage," as conservative American columnist Ross Douthat argues: "In 1990, 65% of Americans told Pew [a survey research foundation] that children were 'very important' to a successful marriage; in 2007, just before the current baby bust, only 41% agreed."[12]

Contemporary lifestyles of younger American Jewish men and women in many ways epitomize broader changes in American society. Perhaps the most pervasive, dramatic change in the lives of younger American Jews, like that of other well-educated liberal white Americans, is that singlehood has expanded into an extended life stage and, for some, a lifestyle choice.[13] According to the recent Pew *Portrait of Jewish Americans*, almost three-quarters (74%) of American Jewish men and 43% of American Jewish women ages 25–34 are not married.[14] The portion of Jews never married by age 34 has risen even in comparison to the 2000–2001 NJPS, when more than half of men and almost a third of women were unmarried at that age.[15] Today, Jewish men achieve a 90% ever-married rate only at age 45, and Jewish women when they are over age 50.[16] These results are striking compared with earlier periods when American Jews achieved near "universal marriage" well before age 30.

Like others in their socioeconomic cohort, Jewish "emerging adults," American Jews in their 20s, 30s, and early 40s, often delay the five social characteristics of adulthood: completion of school or training, financial independence, marriage, parenthood, and independent living arrangements.[17] Some assume that later marriage is primarily related to the fact that American Jewish women ubiquitously attain at least a college education and well over a quarter earn advanced degrees. However, the pursuit of higher education has long been one of the identifying characteristics of American Jews, but in the 1950s and 1960s it delayed marriage for only a year or two. As Stephanie Coontz recounts, in the 1950s college attendance actually enhanced marital prospects, because the four years of college served as a virtual marriage market: "For men, going to college was the way to get a good job. For women, it was the way to get a good husband." Few middle-class Jewish women then worked for numerous years after graduation; instead, they worked for a few years, married, had children, and became homemakers, partly because they "understood the likelihood of social censure if they pursued" careers.[18] Although not always recognized, aspirations for high levels of career achievement, much more than education, may contribute to delays in romantic commitments and marriage. American Jewish men and women today report that they postpone permanent commitments until after they have completed their education and certain benchmarks in their careers.[19]

Many American Jewish women and men do not begin to focus on personal goals related to romantic commitments, marriage, and family until after their educational and occupational goals are in place or at least in process.

Over the last few decades, in marked contrast to the 1950s and 1960s, college has largely ceased to be a forum where large numbers of American Jews identify enduring romantic partners. Some report an emotionally uncommitted sexual "hookup culture" instead. Even students who do not participate in casual sexual encounters often choose friendship groups rather than pairing off in romantic dyads leading to permanent commitments. Except for religiously observant students, undergraduates commonly report themselves as "not ready" to recognize potential marriage partners.[20]

Women articulate different reasons from those of men for postponing the consideration of marriage and family, according to social scientists who study rationales for delayed marriages. "Both men and women viewed education and careers as driving forces in the delay to marry," notes Daniel Parmer, but Jewish women conveyed a great "sense of urgency to complete their education" and "establish themselves in a career," whereas Jewish men discussed personal freedom and "having fun." Women often mentioned "tension between their desire to marry and have children within their biological clocks" and their desires to achieve career goals and to enjoy personal freedoms.[21] Seemingly unaware that men also have biological clocks, men mentioned women's biological clocks but not the fact that recent medical research reveals that advanced age of first-time fathers is associated with a variety of challenges in their offspring, including autism and possibly schizophrenia.[22] Some women also articulate anxiety about committing themselves too soon.

As they pursue first jobs or graduate or professional training in the years after college, both Jewish and non-Jewish young Americans are far more likely at least initially to opt for cohabitation rather than becoming engaged. Rates of cohabitation in the United States have escalated sharply over the past half-century, with "single" Jews often living together before marriage for years or instead of marriage altogether. In-marriage within the Jewish community and intermarriage (marriage between a Jew and a non-Jew) are also connected to cohabitation: On average, intermarrying Jews marry three years later than in-marrying Jews, often cohabiting in the interim. Intermarriages between Jews and non-Jews, like marriages after uncommitted cohabitation, are more likely to culminate in divorce. American Religious Identification Survey studies released in 1990 and 2001 show that marriages across ethnic and religious boundaries end in divorce more often.[23]

Not surprisingly, the changing lifestyles of American Jewish women are associated with declines in fertility, but fertility rates vary distinctively by level of religiosity in American, Israeli, and other Diaspora communities.[24] Over the past decade, fewer American Jews have had children, and fewer Jewish children have been born, compared with most of the twentieth century.

A replacement-level number of children is defined by demographers as 2.15 children per woman. To ascertain completed fertility, the Pew study looked at American Jewish women, ages 40–59, and found that in-married Jewish women had given birth to an average of 2.8 children and intermarried Jews 1.8 children and that Orthodox Jews averaged 4.1, Conservative Jews 1.8, and Reform Jews 1.7 children. The recent study of the New York Jewish population also showed the impact of religious orientation: Among the *haredim* (ultra-Orthodox) those identified as Hasidim had an average of about 6 children and the *yeshivish* (non-Hasidic ultra-Orthodox) had an average of about 5 children. Modern Orthodox Jewish New Yorkers had an average of 2.5 children per family. In New York the non-Orthodox averaged 1.5 children. Harriet Hartman suggests that the social norm of lower fertility may already have been in place in recent decades, because the 2000–2001 NJPS showed an average of 1.6–1.7 children for Jews ages 35–54.[25]

Like men's and women's narratives around love and marriage, those regarding the priority of parenting children often differ significantly by gender. Women's reproductive capacities diminish at earlier ages than those of men. According to recent figures, 3–5% of women in their 20s experience infertility, climbing to 8% between ages 30 and 34, 15% between ages 35 and 39, 32% between ages 40 and 44, and 69% between ages 45 and 49.[26] Even the most optimistic current figures show that one in five women who wait until age 40 to attempt to conceive will not succeed. Unwanted infertility, in turn, often leads to the use of medically assisted technology to enable conception at a later age.[27]

It would be a distortion to characterize women's delayed childbirth as a deliberate delay in many cases. For many Jewish women who do not have partners or husbands, the waiting for babies is involuntary. Increasing numbers of such women are turning to strategies such as freezing their eggs.[28] Some choose to give birth to children as single mothers. Significantly, and perhaps surprisingly to some, these single mothers by choice include many who are religiously and Jewishly traditional in their orientation. Their Jewish family values of parenting children make them willing to take on parenting responsibilities without the aid of a partner or spouse.[29]

Married Jewish Women with Children in Partnership Marriages

TODAY, MOST MARRIED AMERICAN Jewish women with children at home are in dual-earner families in which women/wives/mothers have high levels of educational and occupational achievement, identified in this essay as partnership marriages. Fewer American Jewish families conform to the older pattern of the American bourgeois family, in which the father is the primary or even the sole wage earner and the mother devotes herself to children, household, and good works in the community. Among married American Jews the 2000–2001 NJPS shows that about three-quarters of the age 25–64 cohort were dual-earner couples. Strikingly, even among the 75% of dual-earner Jewish couples ages 25–44, presumably the ages most likely to have younger school-age children, 58% reported that both spouses were full-time labor force participants and 36% reported full-time husbands and part-time wives. Among the 73% of dual-earner Jewish couples ages 45–64, nearly two-thirds (65%) reported both husband and wife as full-time labor force participants.[30] Moreover, most Jewish mothers work outside the home for pay, even when they have children under age 6.

Increasingly, women living in American Jewish families with children under age 18 participate in households distinguished by their homogamy, or spousal parity—that is, husbands and wives have similar levels of educational achievement and occupational prestige. As Harriet and Moshe Hartman show in *Gender and American Jews*, one of the distinguishing characteristics of American Jews in their late 30s, 40s, and 50s is educational and occupational homogamy: "Jewish wives were more likely than wives in the broader U.S. population to have the same level of education as, or a higher level than, their husbands." Moreover, in the 1990 NJPS, the Hartmans continue, "More than half the women in dual-earner couples had the same or higher occupational prestige as, or higher prestige than, their husbands."[31]

Jewish wives working in professional positions are now more numerous than husbands: 52% compared with 44%. Women are working in meaningful careers, and not merely for a paycheck. For Jews, spousal parity is much more likely to extend to income than among the general population: In nearly half of dual-earner American Jewish households, women contribute 40–59% of the family income, compared with 30% in the general population, where most men continue to earn more on average than their wives.[32] Younger American Jewish couples are more likely than the general population to fall into the category of what Steven Nook calls "marriages of equally dependent spouses"—that is, where the spouses bring in about the same amount of money.[33] This helps to define today's Jewish families, as predicted by Calvin Goldscheider in the 1980s, as an ethnic network sharing similar social class and life expectations.[34]

Remarkably, today marriage seemingly exacts no marriage penalty in terms of professional advancements for American Jewish women. That is, Jewish women who marry and have children have achievement rates equal to their unmarried and/or childless sisters. In the past, men enjoyed a marriage advantage in their career trajectories, whereas women suffered a distinct marriage penalty.[35] Moreover, in this new economic climate the superior earning power of prospective spouses is a consideration for both men and women. According to recent studies, well-educated Jewish men today seek similarly well-educated women rather than selecting primarily for youth and putative fertility. Rosalind Barnett and Caryl Rivers highlight this economic change: "The more education a woman has the more marriageable she is."[36]

In partnership marriages, gender-role expectations have shifted. Although women demonstrably still perform more household tasks than their husbands and mothers are still regarded as the individuals responsible for household and child care, fewer women feel they are bearing the full brunt of the second shift of unpaid work.[37] Both husbands and wives expect negotiations around child care and household responsibilities rather than falling back on traditional gender roles,[38] and sociologist Barbara Risman's study found that both actively parenting married fathers and single fathers demonstrate parenting skills similar to those of mothers.[39] Child care is outsourced in many families.[40] Rates of divorce are low in these unusually stable partnership marriages. Contemporary American families, especially those high on the educational, occupational, and socioeconomic ladder, are arguably undergoing "an unfinished revolution."[41]

In most homes women are also primarily responsible for what Rachel S. Bernstein calls the Jewish third shift: In addition to a parent's first shift of paid, and often demanding, employment and the second shift of child rearing and housework, there is the just as necessary third shift, which is focused mostly on Shabbat and holiday observance and on creating a spiritual environment at home.[42] However, recent studies show that for Jewish women even more than for Jewish men, this Jewish third shift seems to have a payoff that more than compensates for the time expended.[43] Social economist Carmel Chiswick suggests that weekly Shabbat observance guarantees time for children, family, and friends—humanizing opportunities often missing in contemporary lives.[44]

Gay, Lesbian, Bisexual, and Transgender Jews and Their Families

Lesbian, gay, bisexual, transgender, and queer (LGBTQ) Jews make up about 7% of American Jews, according to a recent study by Steven M. Cohen, Caryn Aviv, and Ari Kelman. The same study reported that 31% of self-reported LGBTQ Jews are married or partnered and that another 9% are raising their own children.[45] National studies of American populations have repeatedly shown that Jews are extraordinarily liberal regarding societal acceptance of homosexual individuals and families. For example, the Pew *Portrait of Jewish Americans* (2013) reported that 82% of America's Jews say homosexuality "should be accepted by society"; that percentage increases to 89% of Jews ages 18–49 and to 89% of Jewish college graduates. The Pew authors note, "Compared with Jews, the general public is far less accepting of homosexuality (57%)." In the general population, Republicans are much less accepting than Democrats, but "Jewish Republicans are more accepting of homosexuality compared with Republicans in the general population (51% vs. 39%)."[46]

In a study of LGBTQ American Jewish families, Jonathan Krasner interviewed forty-four Jewish same-sex couple families with children and found that most of his subjects "agreed that the Jewish community was hospitable to LGBTQ people." Many of Krasner's subjects emphasized creating authentic Jewish families, a process that played itself out somewhat differently with two-woman and two-man couples. In thinking about options regarding sperm donors, egg donors, and surrogate mothers, Jewish women were more likely to express concern that their children be genetically Jewish: "Jewish background was among the most oft-cited criteria by participants in the study, second only to a clean medical history." Some gay male subjects, who were themselves halakhically observant, "mentioned halakhic considerations among the factors that they considered when choosing [an egg] donor and [gestation] surrogate," but most of the American Jewish men were not so concerned with genetic or halakhic aspects of donor choice. Israeli-born subjects, however, spoke in "more tribal" terms, and rejected female donors who were Jewish by conversion or did not have Jewish mothers.[47] Jewish communal acceptance drew many of Krasner's subjects closer to Jews and Judaism and was influential in intermarried LGBTQ Jewish households as well. As Krasner summarizes, "A significant minority of non-Jewish subjects stated that their [own] religion's negative attitudes toward homosexuality made them more receptive to their Jewish partner's arguments in favor of raising their children as Jews." However, "those families who attempted to find a home within the Orthodox community generally had a more negative experience."[48]

Women and American Intermarried Jewish Families

INTERMARRIAGES AMONG YOUNGER AMERICAN Jews today are about equal for men and women:[49] Among Jews ages 25–49, 40% of men and 40% of women were married to non-Jews. (In contrast among those age 50 and older,

27% of men and 19% of women were married to non-Jews.) Conversionary marriages—that is, marriages in which a born non-Jew converts to Judaism and becomes a "Jew by choice," to use a popular phrase—have decreased over the past 30 years, although women are still somewhat more likely to convert to Judaism than men. The Pew *Portrait of Jewish Americans* found that intermarriage rates have been fairly constant since the late 1990s, as intermarriages characterize 55% of Jews marrying in the late 1990s and 58% of those who married from 2000 until 2013. "The survey also suggests that intermarriage is much more common among Jewish respondents who are themselves the children of intermarriage. Among married Jews who report that only one of their parents was Jewish, fully 83% are married to a non-Jewish spouse. By contrast, among married Jews who say both of their parents were Jewish, 37% have a non-Jewish spouse."[50]

Gender is a relevant factor in the internal dynamics of intermarried households. In an analysis of marriages with only one Jewish parent that I conducted with Daniel Parmer, we found that even though they intermarry at equal rates, American Jewish men and women do not behave similarly with regard to Jewishness when they are intermarried.[51] This is especially true of families with a Jewish father and a non-Jewish mother who identify as Reform Jews. Jewish women married to non-Jewish men are far more likely to raise Jewish children than are Jewish men married to non-Jewish women. This is true especially of Jews who identify as Reform, even though the Reform movement's "patrilineal descent" ruling in 1983 has "presumed" that children of Jewish fathers are Jewish unless they are actively being raised in another religion.[52] The studies cited here, including both statistical and qualitative research, show that Reform Jewish men who marry non-Jewish women are often deeply ambivalent about their Jewishness and might be considered the weak link in American Jewish life today. The lack of Jewish connections in families with Jewish fathers and non-Jewish mothers is apparent in life-cycle and social network aspects as well as in religious aspects of Jewishness.

Most recent studies corroborate the differences between the behaviors of intermarried Jewish men and those of intermarried Jewish women. For example, using interviews and city studies conducted since 2000, Harriet Hartman and Ira Sheskin conclude that "women who intermarry are much more likely to maintain a Jewish identity than men" and to report that they are raising their children as Jews.[53] Some scholars are now working with data from the Pew study that may indicate the weakening of these gender differences among the most recent marriages, those that took place from 2000 to 2011; this weakening, if it proves to be so, calls for further study and analysis.

The ambivalent feelings toward Judaism of American Jewish fathers who marry non-Jewish women may be one significant reason that college students who come from intermarried families are far more likely to identify themselves as Jews if they have a Jewish mother rather than a Jewish father. Linda Sax's 2002 study of America's Jewish college freshmen showed that those with Jewish mothers were more than twice as likely to identify as Jews as those with Jewish fathers: Of those freshmen with a Jewish mother and a non-Jewish father, 38% identified as Jews; of those with a Jewish father and a non-Jewish mother, 15% identified as Jews.[54]

One vivid symbol of the extraordinary differences in the ways in which intermarried men and women behave and experience Jewishness is their widely differing commitment to the ritual circumcision of a male child, the Jewish *brit milah*. Ritual circumcision is still virtually universal among in-married Jewish parents who affiliate with any wing of American Judaism, including Reform parents. (The 2000–2001 NJPS data show that only about one in five "just Jewish/ secular" in-married parents report not providing their male children with a *brit milah*.) However, among the intermarried population the picture is quite different. In intermarried families with Jewish fathers, 61% of intermarried Reform men report that their male children have not had a *brit milah*. The figures for intermarried Reform women are exactly opposite: 69% of women report that their sons have had a *brit milah*. Intermarried Jewish men's comparative lack of commitment to the *brit milah* is perhaps surprising, because popular psychological theories say that fathers want their sons to be like them.[55] However, my previous study based on in-depth interviews with 254 geographically diverse informants (2001)[56] revealed that, although intermarried American Jewish women often take on the responsibility of raising Jewish children, with or without the cooperation of their non-Jewish husbands, in contrast many Jewish fathers are not willing to battle with their non-Jewish wives over the issue of providing ritual circumcisions for their sons or Jewish education for their children.

Changing Opportunities for Women in American Judaism

IN MOST SEGMENTS OF the American Jewish community today, historical patriarchal Jewish public religious and communal structures and behaviors are no longer the norm. Manliness in traditional Jewish societies was constructed through male Jews accepting familial, communal, and religious obligations: marriage, paternity, ritual piety, public prayer, sacred text study, societal responsibilities, and, usually, some breadwinning as well. In historical Jewish societies, women were "free," that is, not obligated. Women were not expected to engage in sacred study or participate in rituals such as communal prayer with strict time schedules. Instead, women were expected to "serve as facilitators" so that men might meet their religious "'obligation' to serve as performers, which in turn reinforced the facilitator/performer dichotomy in the family, social, and political realms," as historian Moshe Rosman emphasizes.[57]

Some argue that these and other traditional Jewish legal and social mores were (and are) structured to domesticate male aggression and libido, with putative benefits for Jewish women. Partly to accomplish this goal, rabbinic texts urged marriage in early adulthood for young men and traditional Jewish societies looked on unmarried males with suspicion. For hundreds of years, Jewish culture preferred the nonviolent, scholarly, and in many ways passive (but not asexual or celibate) male,[58] as Daniel Boyarin and others assert, and male power "was redefined as the power of the mind and intellect . . . spiritual resistance," in Aviva Cantor's words. Meanwhile, "women's enabler role was to facilitate [male religious learning and spirituality] and to accept exclusion from it." In contrast to many patriarchal cultures, in Ashkenazic Jewish communities, breadwinning "was gender neutral in most periods of Jewish history."[59]

Encounters with modernity disrupted these traditional Jewish constructions of maleness and femaleness that imposed primary religious responsibilities on men. Eventually, non-Orthodox American Jews absorbed the American assumption that women are innately more spiritual and religious than men, whereas men are innately more skeptical and detached. As Rodney Stark articulates the supposedly universal assumption, "By now it is so taken for granted that women are more religious than men that every competent quantitative study of religiousness routinely includes sex as a control variable."[60] Some researchers suggest that differential socialization creates gender differences, arguing that "men are assigned [by society] roles that are more instrumental than socio-emotional and thus are less concerned with problems of morality" but that women are socialized to be more relational in their development and more inclined toward religiosity.[61] Male disinterest in religion and religious culture is neither universal nor inevitable, an important recent study shows. In 2006 D. Paul Sullins used international data to reveal that in religions other than Christianity—especially Judaism and Islam— men are often equally or more religious than women. Sullins commented, "Worldwide there is no measure of religiousness on which Jewish females score higher than Jewish males. Jewish men report significantly higher rates of synagogue attendance and belief in life after death than do Jewish women; otherwise there is no sex difference in religiousness among Jews."[62]

How Jewish Education for Women
Transformed Contemporary Jewish Life

JEWISH EDUCATION FOR GIRLS and women is the transformation that made all the other gendered religious changes possible, although the ordination of female rabbis has attracted the most public attention. Orthodox girls as a group began to receive substantive Jewish education in (all-female) classroom settings after Sarah Schnirer created the Bais Yaakov schooling system in Poland in 1917.[63] Thereafter some level of Judaic study for girls gradually became normative, but, despite a few exceptions, rigorous text study for girls and women was neither a widespread aspiration nor a societal reality. In Orthodox congregations and until the 1950s, when bat mitzvah ceremonies first began to proliferate in many Conservative congregations, fewer Jewish girls than Jewish boys acquired liturgical competence in Hebrew, because young men but not young women were expected to participate in public prayer services. Although Reform Judaism and later Conservative Judaism brought mixed seating into their sanctuaries and abandoned the language of gendered difference, women were still not active religious leaders in either type of congregation, as both laymen and laywomen typically made up a passive audience-style congregation. In addition, in Orthodoxy it was considered immodest for women to hold public Jewish communal positions.

However, by the 1960s these historical patriarchal religious assumptions among American Jews were well on the way to widespread transformation. Even in Orthodox communities it had become unthinkable even in non-coed schools that girls would not receive substantial Judaic education. Sometimes, the subjects that girls studied were considered by teachers, students, and parents to be "inferior" to the Talmudic curriculum of boys and may well have been construed to consist of a curriculum that made them "educated but ignorant," in anthropologist Tamar El Or's pungent phrase.[64] Nevertheless, today the image of girls and young women in serious study, bent over Hebrew texts, has become commonplace in the world's two largest Jewish communities, the United States and Israel. In terms of social psychology, the normalization of the visual imagery of the studying girl was important to the eventual acceptance of women's high-level rabbinic text study, historically referred to as *lamdanut*, and women's *lamdanut* made possible a whole range of socioreligious reversals.

Today there is little gender difference in types and years of Jewish education received for American Jews under age 35, according to the Sheskin Decade 2000 data set, and in their study *Gender and American Jews*, Harriet and Moshe Hartman note that in the 2000–2001 NJPS study gender differences "have almost disappeared" among Orthodox and Conservative Jews ages 18–44.[65] In the non-Orthodox world an inverted gender gap has emerged: Girls are much more likely than boys to continue with Jewish education into their teen years, after the ages at which bat and bar mitzvah would have taken place (around 13 years and a day for boys and after 12 for girls). This is significant because of the powerful association of education in the teen years with adult Jewish connections. Boys who do not participate in some form of Jewish education with peers as teenagers may grow into adults with lower levels of Jewish ethnic capital than girls who do continue with Jewish education as teenagers.[66]

Beginning in the early to mid-1970s, while Reform and Conservative women were advocating for the ordination of female rabbis, the first women's *tefillah* (prayer) groups—all-female Orthodox worship and Torah-reading services—were beginning in several American and Israeli communities. Para-rabbinic roles began to be created by liberal Orthodox schools and institutions in the following decades; for example, some Orthodox congregations hired female "community educators" or "interns" who served quasi-rabbinic roles. In Israeli Orthodoxy female legal advocates, *toanot*, received formal credentials from educational institutions such as Nishmat in Jerusalem and became active in difficult divorce cases. Israeli *yoatzot* (female ritual advisers for women concerning religious behaviors connected with Jewish family law) received similar credentials. Although they were first viewed with suspicion by some male rabbis when they began actively advising Orthodox women, *yoatzot* and *toanot* eventually garnered appreciation by many in the Orthodox rabbinate, who began to believe that female rabbinic advisers might actually increase levels of piety among Orthodox women.

The existence of these Israeli cadres of Orthodox women trained in rabbinic texts and competently performing aspects of rabbinic functions foreshadowed the creation of an American Orthodox rabbinic seminary for women: Yeshivat Maharat, which graduated its first rabbi, Rabba Sara Hurwitz, in 2009. It had gradually become obvious that women were capable of mastering rabbinic legal texts. But the use of the term *rabba* (Hebrew for female rabbi) generated vociferous controversy in the Orthodox community. As Yeshivat Maharat moved toward the ordination of three women at its inaugural graduation ceremony on June 16, 2013, the Orthodox Rabbinical Council of America reissued a statement from 2010: "We cannot accept either the ordination of women or the recognition of women as members of the Orthodox rabbinate, regardless of the title." The school's leaders, including Rabbi Avi Weiss, founder of the modern Orthodox Yeshivat Chovevei Torah as well as Yeshivat Maharat and rabbi of the Hebrew Institute of Riverdale in the Bronx, decided to call all successive graduates *maharat,* an acronym for *manhiga hilkhatit rukhanit toranit* (female leader of Jewish law, spirituality, and Torah), instead of *rabba.*[67]

New opportunities for girls and women to acquire the intellectual tools to engage in rabbinic study were created during the same time period that American Jewish women were exploring diverse new roles in Jewish religious and liturgical settings. Some American women took advantage of educational innovations being offered in Israel, such as the nondenominational Pardes Institute of Jewish Studies in Jerusalem, a coeducational program that opened its doors in 1973 to offer men and women the opportunity to engage in the study of classic Jewish texts in an open environment. Drisha, an innovative adult women's learning environment under Orthodox leadership, opened a full-time study program in 1984 and in 1992 created a credentialing program said to parallel rabbinic ordination. Unlike female students today, most Drisha students in the 1980s and 1990s did not aspire to the rabbinate but rather simply to high-level knowledge of rabbinic texts.

Meanwhile, increasing numbers of women enrolled in the Judaic studies departments and programs that were proliferating on American college campuses in the later decades of the twentieth century. These programs, together with opportunities provided in liberal rabbinic seminaries and other institutions, gave women the ability to acquire the intellectual skills to read, understand, and analyze rabbinic materials, including the Talmud, in a setting outside the traditional yeshiva world. These academic settings added new elements to the mix: all the tools of *Wissenschaft des Judentums* (the historical, critical, and analytical study of Jewish civilization, culture, and texts), including placing textual materials in their sociohistorical contexts and trying to understand how those contexts influenced the men who contributed their opinions to the corpus of rabbinic texts.[68] This academic approach interrogates the Talmud and other rabbinic literature through the lenses of history, sociology, political theory, psychology, economics, literary analysis, and, more recently, gender theory.

Jewish Sanctification of Women's Lives

ALL CIVILIZATIONS, SOCIETIES, AND religions devise rituals and ceremonies to mark passages in the lives of their citizens and adherents. Participants find these observances meaningful for many reasons, but perhaps the most important is that they legitimate not only the life-cycle event itself but also the individual whom it affects. Although Jewish societies created meaningful ceremonies to sanctify life-cycle events of Jewish males—the *brit milah* (ritual circumcision) and naming ceremony, the celebratory bar mitzvah for coming-of-age and the assumption of religious obligations, the wedding *kiddushin* in which the bridegroom signs the document and utters the words that acquire a wife, the mournful chanting of the Kaddish prayer with which generations of Jewish males have mourned departed loved ones surrounded by a minyan (prayer quorum) community—Jewish girls and women found many of life's most profoundly moving events unmarked by formal communal and ceremonial responses.

However, over the past few decades, these lacunae have been addressed. Jewish ceremonies and naming celebrations for newborn girls, prayers to sacralize the childbearing process, and bat mitzvah services and celebrations are now ubiquitous in American Jewish communities across denominational lines, and meaningful roles for brides in their own Jewish weddings have become the norm for many American Jews. American Jewish women bereaved of loved ones—and the men among whom they worship—now assume women's public recitation of the Kaddish in the vast majority of American synagogue services. It should be noted that this is not true in Jewish communities worldwide. American Jews, male and female, frequently assume a level of Jewish religious involvement for women that is not shared among some Jewish communities in other countries.

American non-Orthodox Jewish worship environments look different from their historical predecessors. Many girls and women participate in spaces previously reserved for males, such as Torah services and sacred study halls, often wearing symbolic ritual clothing long associated with men at prayer. It is now customary in American Conservative, Reform, and other liberal wings of United States Judaism—and not unheard of in open Orthodox congregations—for women to don *kippot* (skullcaps, yarmulkes) and prayer shawls (*tallitot*) at prayer services. Recently, a modern Orthodox day school made headlines when it gave female students permission to wear tefillin (phylacteries) at morning prayers.[69]

The Challenge of the Inverse Jewish Gender Gap

As I HAVE DETAILED in this essay, American Jewish women today enjoy profoundly broader choices in every dimension of their American and Jewish lives than women in historical societies. Jewish women have played a proactive role in expanding their own secular and Jewish opportunities. To me, their achievements are unequivocally worthy of celebration.

But American Jewish women's successes over the past few decades have been accompanied by an ironic—and utterly unintended—challenge. In traditional patriarchal Jewish communities, men have been the "signifying Jews." As women have increased both leadership and grassroots participation in American Jewish religious, scholarly, and communal life, men have conversely become less involved.

This de facto feminization of almost every aspect of non-Orthodox American Jewish life is not caused by women's greater participation, but it is real and it is measurable: Girls and women greatly outnumber male counterparts as worshippers and in Jewish educational settings. Male estrangement emerges early, in boys' precipitous departure from Jewish education during their teen years, whereas girls more frequently continue after their bat mitzvah. Jewish men less often attend synagogues, join Jewish organizations, or participate in adult Jewish learning or Jewish cultural activities. They are less likely to perform Jewish rituals and ceremonies. Jewish women have increasingly assumed prominent public religious and communal roles while men's pursuit of these roles has declined.[70]

This gender imbalance is also evident in attitudes, attachments, and personal life choices. As Harriet and Moshe Hartman quantify American Jewish "significant gender differences" (from the 2000–2001 NJPS), "women express stronger religious beliefs than men, stronger (tribalistic) attachment to Jewish people than men, and a greater tendency than men to express 'being Jewish' as being active in the current Jewish community and practices." That male/female divide is especially pronounced among Reform Jews.[71] Jewish male ambivalence often includes negative feelings about other Jews—especially Jewish women.[72] In contrast, American Jewish women are more engaged than American Jewish men in the peoplehood aspects of Jewishness: visiting Israel, seeing Israel as important, having mostly Jewish friends, wanting to marry a Jewish husband and to raise Jewish children.[73]

This feminization of Judaism can be regarded partly as a form of assimilation into American norms. Whatever the complex causes, contemporary American Jewish gender imbalance has a problematic effect on the lives of individual women and on the American Jewish community as a whole. Research and honest conversations are needed to create programmatic responses that will honor egalitarian advances while seeking to re-engage the entire gendered spectrum of American Jewry in meaningful connections to Jews and Jewishness. American Jewish women will no doubt play an important role in this critical process.

Notes

1 Joan Wallach Scott, *Gender and the Politics of History* (New York: Columbia University Press, 1988).

2 Aspects of this essay are explored in Sylvia Barack Fishman, "Gender in American Jewish Life," *American Jewish Year Book 2014: The Annual Record of the North American Jewish Communities*, ed. Arnold Dashefsky and Ira Sheskin (Cham, Switzerland: Springer International, 2015); and Sylvia Barack Fishman, "Introduction: Paradoxes of a Social Revolution," in *Love, Marriage, and Jewish Families: Paradoxes of a Social Revolution*, ed. Sylvia Barack Fishman (Waltham, MA: Brandeis University Press, 2015), 1–30.

3 Paul R. Amato and Alan Booth, *A Generation at Risk: Growing Up in an Era of Family Upheaval* (Cambridge, MA: Harvard University Press, 1997).

4 Kristi Williams, "Has the Future of Marriage Arrived? A Contemporary Examination of Gender, Marriage, and Psychological Well-Being," *Journal of Health and Social Behavior* 44 (2003): 470–87.

5 Gary S. Becker, "A Theory of Marriage: Part I," *Journal of Political Economy* 81, no. 4 (1973): 813–46; Gary S. Becker, "A Theory of Marriage: Part II," *Journal of Political Economy* 82 (1974): S11–S26.

6 Michael Spence, *Market Signaling: Informational Transfer in Hiring and Related Screening Processes* (Cambridge, MA: Harvard University Press, 1974).

7 Shoshana Grossbard-Schechtman, *Marriage and the Economy: Theory and Evidence from Advanced Industrial Societies* (New York: Cambridge University Press, 2003).

8 Two intriguing recent works are Mark Pagel, *Wired for Culture: Origins of the Human Social Mind* (New York: Norton, 2012); and Steven Pinker, *The Blank Slate: The Modern Denial of Human Nature* (New York: Penguin, 2002).

9 Harriet Hartman and Moshe Hartman, *Gender and American Jews: Patterns in Work, Education, and Family in Contemporary Life* (Waltham, MA: Brandeis University Press, 2009), 14–19.

10 Hartman and Hartman, *Gender and American Jews*, 19.

11 Natalie Angier, "Families," *New York Times*, November 26, 2013.

12 Ross Douthat, "More Babies, Please," *New York Times*, December 1, 2012, p. 11.

13 Eric Klinenberg, *Going Solo: The Extraordinary Rise and Surprising Appeal of Living Alone* (New York: Penguin, 2012).

14 Luis Lugo, Alan Cooperman, and Gregory Smith et al., *A Portrait of Jewish Americans: Findings from a Pew Research Center Survey of U.S. Jews* (Washington, DC: Pew Research Center, October 1, 2013), cited in Daniel Parmer, "What's Love Got to Do With It? Marriage and Non-Marriage Among Younger American Jews," in *Love, Marriage, and Jewish Families: Paradoxes of a Social Revolution*, ed. Sylvia Barack Fishman (Waltham, MA: Brandeis University Press, 2015), 33–54, Table 2.

15 The 2000–2001 National Jewish Population Survey was conducted by the United Jewish Communities, Lawrence Kotler-Berkowitz, and others; 5,148 respondents were interviewed. See www.jewishdatabank.org for more information and to download the data.

16 Hartman and Hartman, *Gender and American Jews*, 29.

17 Robin Marantz Henig, "What Is It About Twenty-Somethings?" *New York Times Magazine*, August 10, 2010.

18 Stephanie Coontz, *A Strange Stirring: The Feminine Mystique and American Women at the Dawn of the 1960s* (New York: Basic Books, 2011), 108.

19 Parmer, "What's Love Got to Do With It."

20 Hartman and Harman, *Gender and American Jews*, 154.

21 Parmer, "What's Love Got to Do With It," 48.

22 Judith Shulevitz, "We Are Having Children Later than Ever. We Have No Idea What We're Getting Into," *New Republic*, December 20, 2012, p. 9.

23 Barry A. Kosmin, Egon Mayer, and Ariela Keysar, *American Religious Identification Survey*, 2001, https://www.gc.cuny.edu/CUNY_GC/media/CUNY-Graduate -Center/PDF/ARIS/ARIS-PDF-version.pdf?ext=.pdf (accessed January 3, 2021).

24 Sergio Della Pergola, "View from a Different Planet: Fertility Attitudes, Performances, and Policies Among Jewish Israelis," in *Love, Marriage, and Jewish Families: Paradoxes of a Social Revolution*, ed. Sylvia Barack Fishman (Waltham, MA: Brandeis University Press, 2015), figure 3.

25 Harriet Hartman, "The Intersection of Gender and Religion in the Demography of Today's American Jewish Families," paper presented at the Brandeis University Seminar on Creating and Maintaining Jewish Families, March 2007.

26 Sara Rosenthal, *The Fertility Sourcebook* (New York: McGraw-Hill Professional, 2002).

27 Miriam Zoll, "Generation I.V.F. Making a Baby in the Lab: 10 Things I Wish Someone Had Told Me," *Lilith* 38, no. 3 (2013): 22–25.

28 Elissa Gootman, "So Eager for Grandchildren, They're Paying the Egg-Freezing Clinic," *New York Times*, May 13, 2012.

29 Jason Deparle and Sabrina Tavernise, "Unwed Mothers Now a Majority Before Age of 30: New Threshold in U.S.—Most Rapid Growth Has Been Among White Women in 20s," *New York Times*, February 18, 2012.

30 Hartman and Hartman, *Gender and American Jews*, 94–95.

31 Hartman and Hartman, *Gender and American Jews*, 92–93.

32 Hartman and Hartman, *Gender and American Jews*, 107.

33 Steven L. Nock, "The Marriages of Equally Dependent Spouses," *Journal of Family Issues* 22 (2001): 245–63.

34 Calvin Goldscheider, *Jewish Continuity and Change: Emerging Patterns in America* (Bloomington: Indiana University Press, 1986), 117.

35 Hartman and Hartman, *Gender and American Jews*, 107.

36 Rosalind Barnett and Caryl Rivers, *Same Difference: How Gender Myths Are Hurting Our Relationships, Our Children, and Our Jobs* (New York: Basic Books, 2004), 79.

37 Arlie Russel Hochschild, *The Second Shift: Working Parents and the Revolution at Home* (New York: Viking, 1989).

38 Kathleen Gerson, *The Unfinished Revolution: Coming of Age in a New Era of Gender, Work, and Family* (Oxford, UK: Oxford University Press, 2010).

39 Barbara J. Risman and Danette Johnson-Sumerford, "Doing It Fairly: A Study of Postgender Marriages," *Journal of Marriage and the Family* 60 (1998): 23–40.

40 Arlie Russel Hochschild, *The Outsourced Self: Intimate Life in Market Times* (New York: Metropolitan Books/ Henry Holt, 2012).

41 Gerson, *Unfinished Revolution*.

42 Rachel S. Bernstein and Sylvia Barack Fishman, "Judaism as the Third Shift: Jewish Families Negotiating Work, Family, and Religious Lives," in *Love, Marriage, and Jewish Families: Paradoxes of a Social Revolution*, ed. Sylvia Barack Fishman (Waltham, MA: Brandeis University Press, 2015), 196–220.

43 Mark Trencher, "The Nishma Research Profile of Modern Orthodox Jews" (West Hartford, CT: Nishma Research, 2017), https://www.jewishvirtuallibrary.org/jsource/images/orthodoxsurvey2017.pdf (accessed January 3, 2021).

44 Carmel Chiswick, oral comments at the World Congress of Jewish Studies, 2017.

45 Steven M. Cohen, Caryn Aviv, and Ari Y. Kelman, "Gay, Jewish, or Both? Sexual Orientation and Jewish Engagement," *Journal of Jewish Communal Service* 84 (June 2009): 154–66.

46 Lugo et. al., *Portrait of Jewish Americans*, 101. See also Marla Brettschneider's chapter in this volume.

47 Jonathan Krasner, "'We All Still Have to Potty Train': Same Sex Couple Families and the American Jewish Community," in *Love, Marriage, and Jewish Families Today: Paradoxes of a Social Revolution*, ed. Sylvia Barack Fishman (Waltham, MA: Brandeis University Press, 2015), 73–107.

48 Krasner, "We All Still Have to Potty Train," 76.

49 This section of the chapter draws on data from Sylvia Barack Fishman and Daniel Parmer, *Matrilineal Ascent/Patrilineal Descent: The Growing Gender Imbalance in Contemporary Jewish Life* (Waltham, MA: Cohen Center for Modern Jewish Studies, 2008); and Sylvia Barack Fishman, "Fathers of the Faith? Three Decades of Patrilineal Descent," Jewish People Policy Institute (JPPI) Annual Assessment 2012–13 (Jerusalem: JPPI Annual Assessment, 2012).

50 Lugo et al., *Portrait of Jewish Americans*, 37.

51 Hartman and Hartman, *Gender and American Jews*, *121–52*; and Fishman and Parmer, *Matrilineal Descent*, 36–40.

52 See Fishman, "Fathers of the Faith"; and Fishman and Parmer, *Matrilineal Descent*.

53 Harriet Hartman and Ira Sheskin, "The Facts About Intermarriage," *Journal of Jewish Identities* 8, no. 1 (January 2015): 149–78. Hartman and Sheskin used two data sets to provide quantitative data more recent than 2000–2001 National Jewish Population Survey. The first set includes data from fifty-six communities on intermarriage rates and variables that may be related to explaining variations in intermarriage rates by community. The second set is the Decade 2000 data set, which combines the results of twenty-two local Jewish community studies conducted by Sheskin as the principal investigator between 2000 and 2010. It includes the results of 19,800 20-minute interviews and is a random sample of 547,000 Jewish households in the 22 communities.

54 Linda J. Sax, *America's Jewish College Freshmen: Current Characteristics and Recent Trends Among Students Entering College* (Los Angeles: University of California Higher Education Research Institute, Hillel Foundation for Jewish Campus Life, 2002), 227.

55 Fishman and Parmer, *Matrilineal Descent*, 56.

56 Sylvia Barack Fishman, *Double or Nothing? Jewish Families and Mixed Marriage* (Waltham, MA: Brandeis University Press, 2004), 10.

57 Moshe Rosman, *How Jewish Is Jewish History?* (Oxford, UK: Littman Library of Jewish Civilization, 2007), 150.

58 Daniel Boyarin, *Unheroic Conduct: The Rise of Heterosexuality and the Invention of the Jewish Man* (Berkeley: University of California Press, 1997).

59 Aviva Cantor, *Jewish Women, Jewish Men: The Legacy of Patriarchy in Jewish Life* (New York: Harper, 1994), 5.

60 Rodney Stark, "Physiology and Faith: Addressing the 'Universal' Gender Differences in Religious Commitment," *Journal for the Scientific Study of Religion* 41, no. 3 (2002): 496.

61 Cited in Hart Nelson and R. M. Potvin, "Gender and Regional Differences in the Religiosity of Protestant Adolescents," *Review of Religious Research* 22, no. 3 (1981): 268–85.

62 D. Paul Sullins, "Gender and Religion: Deconstructing Universality, Constructing Complexity," *American Journal of Sociology* 112, no. 3 (2006): 844.

63 Shoshana Pantel Zolty, *And All Your Children Shall Be Learned: Women and the Study of Torah in Jewish Law and History* (Northvale, NJ: Jason Aronson, 1997), 263–309.

64 Tamar El Or, *Educated but Ignorant: Ultraorthodox Jewish Women and Their World* (Boulder, CO: Lynne Rienner, 1994).

65 Hartman and Hartman, *Gender and American Jews*, 146.

66 Sylvia Barack Fishman, "Generating Jewish Connections: Conversations with Jewish Teenagers, Their Parents, and Jewish Educators and Thinkers," in *Family Matters: Jewish Education in an Age of Choice*, ed. Jack Wertheimer (Waltham, MA: Brandeis University Press, 2007), 181–210. Statistical information in this chapter is drawn from the 2000–2001 National Jewish Population Survey, analyzed in Benjamin Phillips and Sylvia Barack Fishman, "Ethnic Capital and Intermarriage: A Case Study of American Jews," *Sociology of Religion* 67, no. 4 (2006): 487–505.

67 Batya Ungar-Sargon, "Orthodox Yeshiva to Ordain Three Women. Just Don't Call Them 'Rabbi,'" in *Tablet* June 10, 2013, https://www.tabletmag.com/jewish-life-and-religion/134369/orthodox-women-ordained (accessed January 12, 2021).

68 See Michael A. Meyer, ed., *German-Jewish History in Modern Times*, vol. 2, *Acculturation, 1780–1871* (New York: Columbia University Press, 1997), 336–41.

69 Amy Sara Clark, "Ramaz Would Permit Girls to Wear Tefillin," *New York Jewish Week*, January 22, 2014, http://www.thejewishweek.com/news/new-york-news/ramaz-would-permit-girls-wear-tefillin-0 (accessed January 12, 2021).

70 Hartman and Hartman, *Gender and American Jews*, 133–38.

71 Hartman and Hartman, *Gender and American Jews*, 138.

72 Fishman, *Double or Nothing*, 17–33.

73 Fishman and Parmer, *Matrilineal Descent*, 43–46, 67.

JUDITH R. BASKIN
SELECTED BIBLIOGRAPHY

Books and Edited Collections

Editor. *The Cambridge Dictionary of Judaism and Jewish Culture*. Cambridge, UK: Cambridge University Press, 2011.

Co-editor with Kenneth Seeskin. *The Cambridge Guide to Jewish History, Religion, and Culture*. Cambridge, UK: Cambridge University Press, 2010.

Co-editor with Shelly Tenenbaum. *Gender and Jewish Studies: A Curriculum Guide*. New York: Biblio Press, 1994.

Editor. *Jewish Women in Historical Perspective*. Detroit: Wayne State University Press, 1991; 2nd ed., 1998.

Midrashic Women: Formations of the Feminine in Rabbinic Literature. Hanover, NH: University Press of New England; and Waltham, MA: Brandeis University Press, 2002.

Pharaoh's Counsellors: Job, Jethro, and Balaam in Rabbinic and Patristic Tradition. Brown Judaic Studies 47. Chico, CA: Scholars Press, 1983.

Editor. *Women of the Word: Jewish Women and Jewish Writing*. Detroit: Wayne State University Press, 1994.

Other Editorial Projects

Associate editor for new and revised entries in areas of women and gender, *Encyclopedia Judaica*, 2nd ed. New York: Macmillan Reference USA; and Jerusalem: Keter, 2006.

Postbiblical Consulting Editor. *The Torah: A Women's Commentary*. New York: Union for Reform Judaism Press, 2008.

Articles and Book Chapters

"Adding Women and Gender to the Second Edition of the *Encyclopedia Judaica*." *Journal of Modern Jewish Studies* 5, no. 3 (2006): 343–48.

"Approaches to the Representations of Women in Rabbinic Literature: Review Essay." *Nashim: A Journal of Jewish Women's Studies and Gender Issues* 9 (spring 2005): 191–203.

"Bolsters to Their Husbands: Women as Wives in Rabbinic Literature." *European Judaism* 37, no. 2 (2004): 88–102.

"The Changing Role of the Woman." In *Modern Judaism: An Oxford Guide*, ed. Nicholas de Lange and Miri Freud-Kandel, 389–400. Oxford, UK: Oxford University Press, 2004.

"Constructions of Women in Rabbinic Midrash." In *Encyclopedia of Midrash: Biblical Interpretation in Formative Judaism*, ed. Jacob Neusner and Alan J. Avery-Peck, 979–97. Leiden: Brill, 2004.

"Dolce of Worms: The Lives and Deaths of an Exemplary Medieval Jewish Woman and Her Daughters." In *Judaism in Practice: From the Middle Ages Through the Early Modern Period*, ed. Lawrence Fine, 429–37. Princeton, NJ: Princeton University Press, 2001.

"Educating Jewish Girls in Medieval Muslim and Christian Settings." In *Making a Difference: Essays in Honor of Tamara Cohn Eskenazi*, ed. David Clines, Kent Richards, and Jacob L. Wright, 19–37. Sheffield, UK: Sheffield Phoenix Press, 2012.

"The Education of Jewish Girls in the Middle Ages in Muslim and Christian Milieus." *Pe'amim: Studies in Oriental Jewry* 82 (2000): 1–17 (Hebrew).

"Erotic Subversion: Undermining Female Agency in *b. Megillah* 10b–17a." In *A Feminist Commentary on the Babylonian Talmud: Introduction and Studies*, ed. Tal Ilan, Tamara Or, Dorothea M. Salzer et al., 228–44. Heidelberg: Mohr Siebeck, 2007.

"Female Alterity and Divine Compassion: Reading the Talmud from the Perspective of Gender." In *Why Read the Talmud in the Twenty-First Century?* ed. Paul Socken, 25–40. Lanham, MD: Rowman & Littlefield, 2009.

"Female Martyrdom." In *Shalvi/Hyman Encyclopedia of Jewish Women*. www.jwa .org/encyclopedia (forthcoming in 2021).

"Four Approaches to Women and the Jewish Experience: An Introduction." In *Women and Judaism: New Insights and Scholarship*, ed. Frederick E. Greenspahn, 1–22. New York: New York University Press, 2009.

"From Separation to Displacement: The Problem of Women in *Sefer Hasidim*." *Association for Jewish Studies Review* 19, no. 1 (1994): 1–18.

"Geschlecterverhältnisse und rituelles Tauchbad im mittelalterlichen Aschkenas." In *Der Differenz auf der Spur: Frauen und Gender in Aschkenas*, ed. Christiane E. Müller and Andrea Schatz, 51–68. Berlin: Metropol, 2004.

"Images of Women in *Sefer Hasidim*." In *Mysticism, Magic and Kabbalah in Ashkenazi Judaism*, ed. Karl Erich Grözinger and Joseph Dan, 93–105. Berlin: Walter de Gruyter, 1995.

"Independent Jewish Women in Medieval Egypt: Enterprise and Ambiguity." In *From Catalonia to the Caribbean: The Sephardic Orbit from Medieval to Modern Times—Essays in Honor of Jane S. Gerber*, ed. Federica Francesconi, Stanley Mirvis, and Brian Smollett, 83–99. Leiden: E. J. Brill, 2018.

"Integrating Gender Analysis into Jewish Studies Teaching." In *Academic Approaches to Teaching Jewish Studies*, ed. Zev Garber, 173–92. Lanham, MD: University Press of America, 2000.

"Integrating Gender Studies into Jewish Studies." *Shofar: An Interdisciplinary Journal of Jewish Studies* 9, no. 4 (1991): 1–6.

"Introduction." In *Burning Lights*, by Bella Chagall, i–x. New York: Biblio Press, 1996.

"Jewish Private Life: Gender, Marriage, and the Lives of Women." In *Cambridge Guide to Jewish History, Religion, and Culture*, ed. Judith R. Baskin and Kenneth Seeskin, 357–80. Cambridge, UK: Cambridge University Press, 2010.

"Jewish Studies in North American Colleges and Universities: Yesterday, Today, and Tomorrow." *Shofar: An Interdisciplinary Journal of Jewish Studies* 32, no. 4 (2014): 9–26.

"Jewish Traditions About Women and Gender Roles: From Rabbinic Teachings to Medieval Practice." In *The Oxford Handbook of Women and Gender in Medieval Europe*, ed. Judith Bennett and Ruth Mazo Karras, 35–51. Oxford, UK: Oxford University Press, 2013.

"Jewish Women in Ashkenaz: Renegotiating Jewish Gender Roles in Northern Europe." In *Late Medieval Jewish Identities: Iberia and Beyond*, ed. Carmen Caballero Navas and Esperanza Alfonso, 79–90. Basingstoke, UK: Palgrave Macmillan, 2010.

"Jewish Women in the Middle Ages." In *Jewish Women in Historical Perspective*, 2nd ed., ed. Judith R. Baskin, 94–113. Detroit: Wayne State University Press, 1998.

"Jewish Women's Piety and the Impact of Printing in Early Modern Europe." In *Culture and Change: Attending to Early Modern Women*, ed. Margaret Mikesell and Adele Seeff, 221–40. Newark: University of Delaware Press, 2003.

"Job in Rabbinic Interpretation." In *The Voice from the Whirlwind: Interpretations of the Book of Job*, ed. W. Clark Gilpin and Leo G. Perdue, 101–10, 240–43. Nashville: Abingdon Press, 1992.

With Katja Stuerzenhofeker. "The Joy of Wisdom: An Interview with Judith R. Baskin." *Melilah: Manchester Journal of Jewish Studies* 13 (2019): 5–19.

"Male Piety, Female Bodies: Men, Women, and Ritual Immersion in Medieval Ashkenaz." *Journal of Jewish Law* 17 (2007): 11–30.

"Marriage and Mobility in Two Medieval Jewish Societies." *Jewish History* 22, nos. 1–2 (2008): 223–43.

Co-authored with Michael Riegler. "'May the Writer Be Strong': Medieval Hebrew Manuscripts Copied by and for Women." *Nashim: A Journal of Jewish Women's Studies and Gender Issues* 16, no. 2 (2008): 9–28.

"Medieval Jewish Models of Marriage." In *The Medieval Marriage Scene: Prudence, Passion, Policy*, ed. Sherry Roush and Christelle L. Baskins, 1–22. Tempe: Arizona Center for Medieval and Renaissance Studies, 2005.

"Medieval Jewish Women." In *Women in Medieval Western European Culture*, ed. Linda Mitchell, 65–80. New York: Garland, 1999.

"Medieval Jewish Women in Muslim and Christian Milieus." In *Jewish Women's History from Antiquity to the Present*, ed. Federica Francesconi and Rebecca Lynn Winer, 75–95. Detroit: Wayne State University Press, 2021.

"Piety and Female Aspiration in the Memoirs of Bella Rosenfeld Chagall and Pauline Epstein Wengeroff." *Nashim: A Journal of Jewish Women's Studies and Gender Issues* 7 (spring 2004): 65–96.

"Prophetinnen in *b. Megilla* 14a–15a." In *Die Bibel und die Frauen: Vorrabbinisches Judentum*, Band 4.1, ed. Tal Ilan, Lorena Miralles Maciá, and Ronit Nikolsky, 204–20. Stuttgart: W. Kohlhammer, 2020.

"Prostitution: Not a Job for a Nice Jewish Girl." In *The Passionate Torah: Sex and Judaism*, ed. Danya Ruttenberg, 29–35. New York: New York University Press, 2009.

"Pulcellina of Blois." In *Shalvi/Hyman Encyclopedia of Jewish Women*. www.jwa .org/encyclopedia (forthcoming in 2021).

"Rabbinic Forensics: Distinguishing Egg White from Semen in *b. Gittin* 57a." In *Sources and Interpretation in Ancient Judaism: Studies for Tal Ilan at Sixty*, ed. Meron M. Piotrkowski, Geoffrey Herman, and Saskia Dönitz, 252–67. Leiden: Brill, 2018.

"Rabbinic Judaism and the Creation of Woman." *Shofar* 13, no. 4 (1995): 68–73; reprinted in *Judaism Since Gender*, ed. Miriam Peskowitz and Laura Levitt, 125–30 (London: Routledge, 1997).

"Rabbinic-Patristic Exegetical Contacts: Some New Perspectives." *Religious Studies Review* 24 (1998): 171–73.

"Rabbinic-Patristic Exegetical Contacts in Late Antiquity: A Bibliographical Reappraisal." In *Approaches to Ancient Judaism 5: Studies in Judaism and Its Greco-Roman Context*, ed. William Scott Green, 53–80. Missoula, MT: Scholars Press, 1985.

"Rabbinic Reflections on the Barren Wife." *Harvard Theological Review* 82 (1989): 1–14.

"The Rabbinic Transformations of Rahab the Harlot." *Notre Dame English Journal: A Journal of Religion in Literature* 11 (1979): 141–57.

"Repräsentationen biblischer Frauen in den Schriften der Chasside Aschkenas." In *Die Bibel und die Frauen: Das jüdische Mittelalter*, Band 4.2, ed. Carol Bakhos and Gerhard Langer, 151–67. Stuttgart: W. Koklhammer, 2020.

"The Separation of Women in Rabbinic Judaism." In *Women, Religion, and Social Change*, ed. Yvonne Yazbeck Haddad and Ellison Banks Findly, 3–18. Albany: State University of New York Press, 1985.

"'She Extinguished the Light of the World': Justifications for Women's Disabilities in *Abot de-Rabbi Nathan B.*" In *Current Trends in the Study of Midrash*, ed. Carol Bakhos, 277–97. Leiden: Brill, 2005.

"Some Parallels in the Education of Medieval Jewish and Christian Women." *Jewish History* 5 (1991): 41–51.

"The *Taqqanah* of the *Moredet* in the Middle Ages." In *Accounting for the Commandments in Medieval Judaism: Studies in Law, Philosophy, Pietism, and Kabbalah*, ed. Jeremy P. Brown and Marc Herman, 45–57. Leiden: Brill, 2021.

"Under Gentile Eyes: My Jewish Childhood in Hamilton, Ontario." In *No Better Home? Jews, Canada, and the Sense of Belonging*, ed. David Koffman, 201–16. Toronto: University of Toronto Press, 2020.

"Woman as Other in Rabbinic Literature." In *Judaism in Late Antiquity*, pt. 3, vol. 2, *Where We Stand: Issues and Debates in Ancient Judaism*, ed. Jacob Neusner and Alan J. Avery-Peck, 177–96. Leiden: Brill, 1999.

"Women and Gender in Jacob Neusner's Writings." In *A Legacy of Learning: Essays in Honor of Jacob Neusner*, ed. Alan J. Avery-Peck, 33–47. Leiden: Brill, 2014.

"Women and Gender Relations." *Oxford Bibliographies in Jewish Studies*, ed. David Biale. Oxford Bibliographies Online, 2019.

"Women and Judaism." In *The Encyclopedia of Judaism*, ed. Jacob Neusner, Alan J. Avery-Peck, and William Scott Green, 3: 1478–1502. Leiden: Brill; and London: Continuum, 2000.

"Women and Post-Biblical Commentary." In *The Torah: A Women's Commentary*, ed. Tamara Cohn Eskenazi and Andrea L. Weiss, xlix–lv. New York: Union for Reform Judaism Press, 2008.

"Women and Ritual Immersion in Medieval Ashkenaz: The Sexual Politics of Piety." In *Judaism in Practice: From the Middle Ages Through the Early Modern Period*, ed. Lawrence Fine, 131–42. Princeton, NJ: Princeton University Press, 2001.

"Women and Sexual Ambivalence in *Sefer Hasidim*." *Jewish Quarterly Review* 96, no. 1 (2006): 1–8.

"Women at Odds: Biblical Paradigms." In *Feminist Nightmares: Women at Odds*, ed. Jennifer Fleischner and Susan Weisser, 209–24. New York: New York University Press, 1994.

"Women, Gender, and Judaism." In *The Bloomsbury Companion to Jewish Studies*, ed. Dean Phillip Bell, 229–50. London: Bloomsbury Press, 2013.

"Women in Contemporary Judaism." In *The Blackwell Companion to Judaism*, ed. Jacob Neusner and Alan J. Avery-Peck, 393–414. Hoboken, NJ: Blackwell, 2001.

"Women in Contemporary Judaism: Selected Readings." In *The Blackwell Reader in Judaism*, ed. Jacob Neusner and Alan J. Avery-Peck, 316–32. Hoboken, NJ: Blackwell, 2001.

"Women in Rabbinic Judaism: Focal Points and Turning Points." In *From Moses to Muhammed: An Interpretation—Turning Points and Focal Points*, ed. Jacob Neusner, Alan J. Avery-Peck, and William Scott Green, 303–44. Leiden: Brill, 2005.

"Women of the Word: An Introduction." In *Women of the Word: Jewish Women and Jewish Writing*, ed. Judith R. Baskin, 17–34. Detroit: Wayne State University Press, 1994.

"Women Saints in Judaism: Dolce of Worms." In *Women Saints in World Religions*, ed. Arvind Sharma, 39–69. Albany: State University of New York Press, 2000.

"Women's and Gender Studies: Historiographical Trends." In *Routledge Companion to Jewish History and Historiography*, ed. Dean Phillip Bell, 486–500. London: Routledge, 2018.

ACKNOWLEDGMENTS

A VOLUME OF THIS complexity and length could not have appeared without the support of many. The editors wish to thank all the contributors and Judith R. Baskin for her guidance throughout the project. We also thank the two anonymous peer reviewers of the collection, Sarah Abrevaya Stein, Lisa Unger Baskin, Elissa Bemporad, Ruth Berman, Hannah Bourne, Mimi Braverman, Francesca Bregoli, Justine Carré-Miller, Glenn Dynner, Pratima Gopalakrishnan, Kristin Harpster, Catherine Kerrison, Seth Koven, Marjorie Lehman, Annie Martin, Michelle Moravec, Muriel McClendon, Tirzah Meacham, Emily Nowak, Diana Riddle, David Shneer z"l, Jutta Seibert, Anna Sfard, Kristina Stonehill, Susan Storch, Carrie Downes Teefey, Paola Ugolini, Kim Webb, Kathy Wildfong, Stephanie Williams, Sarah Wipperman, and Julian Yates. This work was supported by an Individual Development Award from the United University Profession at the State University of New York, Albany, and by a grant from Villanova University's Subvention of Publication Program. Finally, Rebecca Lynn Winer wishes to thank the College of Liberal Arts and Sciences at Villanova University for a research semester in spring 2019 to devote time to co-writing her contributions and to co-editing this volume.

CONTRIBUTORS

Rachel Adelman is currently Associate Professor of Hebrew Bible in the rabbinic program at Hebrew College in Boston. Her first book, *The Return of the Repressed: Pirqe deRabbi Eliezer and the Pseudepigrapha* (Brill, 2009), was based on her doctoral dissertation; her second major book, *The Female Ruse: Women's Deception and Divine Sanction in the Hebrew Bible* (Sheffield-Phoenix Press, 2015), resulted from her work as a research associate in the Women's Studies in Religion Program at Harvard Divinity School. She is currently working on a third monograph, *Daughters in Danger in the Hebrew Bible* (forthcoming, Sheffield).

Natalia Aleksiun is Professor of Modern Jewish History at Touro College, Graduate School of Jewish Studies, New York. She has published the monograph *Where to? The Zionist Movement in Poland, 1944–1950* (2004) and numerous articles in *Yad Vashem Studies, Polish Review, Dapim, East European Jewish Affairs, Studies in Contemporary Jewry, Polin, Gal Ed, East European Societies and Politics, Nashim*, and *German History*. She coedited the twentieth volume of *Polin*, devoted to the memory of the Holocaust, and the twenty-ninth volume on writing Jewish history in Eastern Europe. Her new book is *Conscious History: Polish Jewish Historians Before the Holocaust* (The Littman Library of Jewish Civilization, 2021). She is co-editor in chief of *East European Jewish Affairs*. She is currently working on two new books: about the so-called cadaver affair in medical departments in east-central Europe in the interwar period and on daily lives of Jews in hiding in Galicia during the Holocaust.

Dianne Ashton is Professor of Religious Studies at Rowan University and the former editor of *American Jewish History*. She was the founding director of Rowan's American Studies program and a founder of its Jewish Studies Program. Her books include *Hanukkah in America: A History (New York University Press, 2013), Rebecca Gratz: Women and Judaism in Antebellum America (Wayne State University Press, 1997), Jewish Life in Pennsylvania (Pennsylvania History Association, 1998)*, and *Four Centuries of Jewish Women's Spirituality* (Brandeis University Press, 1992; revised 2005). Her articles have appeared in more than thirty scholarly venues, and her research has been funded by the National Endowment for the Humanities, the Hadassah-Brandeis Institute, the American Jewish Archives, and the Gilder Lehrman Institute.

She sits on the Academic Advisory Councils of the American Jewish Historical Society and the Jewish Women's Archive.

Benjamin M. Baader is Associate Professor of History at the University of Manitoba, where he has been instrumental in reestablishing the Jewish studies program and has been involved in leading it. Baader teaches, writes, and lectures on European history, Jewish history, historiography, gender studies, and feminist theory. He specializes in nineteenth-century German Jewish women's and gender history, and he has also done work on American Jewish gender history and on Jewish post-Shoah identity in North America and Germany. His publications include *Gender, Judaism, and Bourgeois Culture in Germany, 1800–1870* (Indiana University Press, 2006) and *Jewish Masculinities: German Jews, Gender, and History* (Indiana University Press, 2012), which he co-edited with Paul Lerner and Sharon Gillerman. His theoretical interests have also found expression in a project about theorizing Jewishness with the toolkit of gender theory, in the course of which Chaya Halberstam, Beth Berkowitz, and he co-edited a special issue of the *Journal of Jewish Identities* (vol. 11, no. 1, 2018), titled "Gender Theory and Theorizing Jewishness."

Judith R. Baskin is Philip H. Knight Professor Emerita of Humanities at the University of Oregon. Her books include *Midrashic Women: Formations of the Feminine in Rabbinic Literature* (Brandeis University Press, 2002) and the edited collections *Jewish Women in Historical Perspective* (Wayne State University Press, 1991 and 1998) and *Women of the Word: Jewish Women and Jewish Writing* (Wayne State University Press, 1994). *The Cambridge Guide to Jewish History, Religion, and Culture* (Cambridge University Press, 2010), co-edited with Kenneth Seeskin, won a 2011 National Jewish Book Award.

Marla Brettschneider is Professor of Political Theory with a joint appointment in women's studies and political science at the University of New Hampshire. Brettschneider works on Jewish diversity politics using the critical theory tools of Jewish, feminist, queer, critical race, class-based, and de-colonial paradigms; and is the author of numerous award-winning books, including *The Family Flamboyant: Race Politics, Queer Families, Jewish Lives* (SUNY Press, 2006) and *Jewish Feminism and Intersectionality* (SUNY Press, 2016). Brettschneider has also edited and co-edited many books and special issues of academic journals, such as *Jewcy: Jewish Lesbian Feminisms for the 21st Century* (Routledge, 2021), *LGBTQ Politics: A Critical Reader* (New York University Press, 2017), and *The Narrow Bridge: Jewish Views on Multiculturalism* (Rutgers University Press, 1996) with a foreword by Cornel West.

Elisheva Carlebach is Salo Baron Professor of Jewish History, Culture, and Society and co-director of the Institute for Israel and Jewish Studies, Columbia University. She is the author of *The Pursuit of Heresy* (Columbia University Press, 1994), winner of the National Jewish Book Award; *Divided Souls: Jewish Converts to Christianity* (Yale University Press, 2001); and *Palaces of Time* (Harvard University Press, 2011), awarded the Schnitzer Prize from the Association for Jewish Studies. Her most recent book is *Confronting Modernity: 1750–1880*, volume 6 of the Posen Library of Jewish Culture and Civilization (Yale University Press, 2019). She has held fellowships at the New York Public Library, the National Endowment for the Humanities, the Tikvah Center of NYU Law School, and the Katz Center for Advanced Jewish Studies, University of Pennsylvania. She served as editor-in-chief of *AJS Review* and is a past president of the American Academy for Jewish Research.

Dina Danon is Associate Professor of Judaic Studies at Binghamton University. Her research focuses on the Ladino-speaking communities of the eastern Sephardic Diaspora. She is the author of *The Jews of Ottoman Izmir: A Modern History* (Stanford University Press, 2020). She was awarded a fellowship at the Katz Center for Advanced Judaic Studies at the University of Pennsylvania in 2018–2019 for her new project "Negotiating Modernity: The Marketplace of Matchmaking, Marriage, and Divorce in the Ottoman Sephardi World."

Sylvia Barack Fishman, the author of eight books and numerous articles, writes and speaks on Jewish identity, Israel-Diaspora relations, anti-Semitism and anti-Zionism, the interplay of American and Jewish values, transformations in the American Jewish family, the impact of Jewish education, gender and sexuality in American Jewish life, and portrayals of Jews and Jewishness in fiction and film. She currently is an emerita professor of contemporary Jewish life in the Near Eastern and Judaic Studies Department at Brandeis University. Fishman was the founding co-director of the Hadassah Brandeis Institute (HBI), and she edits the HBI Series on Gender and Jewish Women. Among other honors, Fishman received the Marshall Sklare Award from the Association for the Social Scientific Study of Jewry (2014).

Federica Francesconi is Assistant Professor of History and Director of the Judaic Studies Program at the University at Albany, State University of New York. Her research and publications address the social, religious, and cultural aspects of the early modern history of Jews in Italy, focusing on the multifaceted politics and dynamics of ghetto life. She has held fellowships at the University of Oxford, the University of California, Los Angeles, and the Katz Center for Advanced Judaic Studies at the University of Pennsylvania. Francesconi recently coedited *From Catalonia to the Caribbean: The Sephardic Orbit from Medieval to Modern Times* (Brill, 2018).

She is the author of *Invisible Enlighteners: The Jewish Merchants of Modena, from the Renaissance to the Emancipation* (University of Pennsylvania Press, 2021). She is the associate editor and book review editor of the journal *Jewish History*.

ChaeRan Freeze is the Frances and Max Elkon Professor of Modern Jewish History at Brandeis University. She has focused her research on the history and culture of the Jews in Russia, Jewish family history, and women's and gender studies. Freeze's articles have appeared in a variety of academic journals and edited collections. Her first book was *Jewish Marriage and Divorce in Imperial Russia* (Brandeis University Press, 2001), which examines the impact of modernization on Jewish family practices and patterns in Imperial Russia based on newly declassified archival materials from the former Soviet Union. Her next book, *Everyday Jewish Life in Imperial Russia, 1825–1914: Select Documents* (coauthored with Jay Harris; Brandeis University Press, 2013), documents the "everyday" (*Alltags*) as a site of interaction with modernity where Jews confronted the unfamiliar and negotiated their environment in strategic and creative ways. Her most recent book, *A Woman of Distinction: The Life and Diaries of Zinaida Poliakova* (Brandeis University Press, 2019), explores how Jews successfully integrated into Russian aristocratic society.

Tal Ilan is Professor of Jewish Studies at the Freie Universität Berlin. Her chief publications include the books *Mine and Yours Are Hers: Retrieving Women's History from Rabbinic Literature* (Brill, 1997), *Integrating Women into Second Temple History* (Mohr Siebeck, 1999), *Silencing the Queen* (Mohr Siebeck, 2006), *A Lexicon of Jewish Names in Late Antiquity* (4 volumes; Mohr Siebeck, 2002–2012), and *Josephus and the Rabbis* (2 volumes; Brill, 2017). She is also the editor of the series A Feminist Commentary on the Babylonian Talmud (Mohr Siebeck) and the author of two volumes in the series: *Ta'anit* (2008) and *Hullin* (2017).

Debra Kaplan is Associate Professor at Bar Ilan University in Israel. Her work focuses on the Jewish communities in Western Europe during the early modern period. She has written about Jewish-Christian relations, women and gender, communal rituals, autobiographies, and various aspects of daily life. Her first book, *Beyond Expulsion: Jews, Christians, and Reformation Strasbourg* (Stanford University Press, 2011), explores the relationships between Jews in Alsace and Christians in Strasbourg during the Protestant Reformation. Her second book, *Patrons and Their Poor: Jewish Community and Public Charity in Early Modern Germany* (University of Pennsylvania Press, 2020), uses public charity as a window into the different populations that comprised early modern Jewish communities in Ashkenaz.

Melissa R. Klapper is Professor of History and the Director of Women's and Gender Studies at Rowan University, where she teaches American and women's history, the history of childhood and youth, and women's and gender studies. She is the author of *Jewish Girls Coming of Age in America, 1860–1920* (New York University Press, 2005), *Small Strangers: The Experiences of Immigrant Children in the United States, 1880–1925* (Ivan R. Dee, 2007), and *Ballots, Babies, and Banners of Peace: American Jewish Women's Activism, 1890–1940* (New York University Press, 2013), which won the 2013 National Jewish Book Award in Women's Studies. Her most recent book is *Ballet Class: An American History* (Oxford University Press, 2020).

Sharon Faye Koren is Associate Professor of Medieval Jewish Culture at the Hebrew Union College/Jewish Institute of Religion in New York City, where she teaches courses in medieval history, biblical commentary, Jewish philosophy, and Jewish mysticism. Her publications include *Forsaken: The Menstruant in Medieval Jewish Mysticism* (Brandeis University Press, 2011) and many articles on gender and medieval Kabbalah. She is currently completing a book on the biblical heroines in the Zohar.

Renée Levine Melammed is Professor of Jewish History at the Schechter Institute in Jerusalem. Her fields of research include the lives of conversos and Sephardic and Oriental Jewish women. Her current project deals with women's lives as reflected in the Cairo Genizah, in particular, through letters. She has published numerous articles in four languages as well as *Heretics or Daughters of Israel: The Crypto-Jewish Women of Castile* (Oxford University Press, 1999), *A Question of Identity: Iberian Conversos in Historical Perspective* (Oxford University Press, 2004), and *An Ode to Salonika: The Ladino Verses of Bouena Sarfatty* (Indiana University Press, 2013). She is also the academic editor of *Nashim*.

Frances Malino is the Sophia Moses Robison Professor of Jewish Studies and History Emerita at Wellesley College. She is author of *The Sephardic Jews of Bordeaux: Assimilation and Emancipation in Revolutionary and Napoleonic France* (University of Alabama Press, 1978; French translation, 1985) and *A Jew in the French Revolution: The Life of Zalkind Hourwitz* (Blackwell, 1996; French translation, 2000) and co-editor of *Essays in Modern Jewish History: A Tribute to Ben Halpern* (Farleigh Dickinson University Press, 1982), *The Jews in Modern France* (Brandeis University Press, 1985), *Profiles in Diversity: Jews in a Changing Europe* (Wayne State University Press, 1998), and *Voices of the Diaspora: Jewish Women Writing in the New Europe* (Northwestern University Press, 2005). Her current project is "Teaching Freedom: Jewish Sisters in Muslim Lands." In 2012 she was named Chevalier dans l'Ordre des Palmes académiques by the French Ministry of Education.

Lilach Rosenberg-Friedman is Associate Professor and the chair of the Land of Israel Studies and Archaeology Department, Bar-Ilan University, Israel. She is a historian who specializes in the history of Israel in the modern period. Her writing includes the book *Revolutionaries Despite Themselves: Women and Gender in Religious Zionism During the Yishuv Period* (Yad Ben-Zvi, 2005; in Hebrew) and various essays on women and gender in Mandatory Palestine and the State of Israel, on such topics as feminine identity and leadership, the Hebrew family, marriage and motherhood, and biographies of women in the era of national renaissance. Her most recent book is *Birthrate Politics in Zion: Judaism, Zionism, and Modernity in Mandate Palestine (1920–1948)* (Indiana University Press, 2017).

Moshe Rosman is Professor Emeritus of Jewish History at Bar Ilan University. In 1989 he pioneered the first course on the history of Jewish women to be offered in a Jewish history department in Israel. His books include *How Jewish Is Jewish History?* (The Littman Library of Jewish Civilization, 2007) and *Categorically Jewish, Distinctly Polish: Polish Jewish History Reflected and Refracted* (The Littman Library of Jewish Civilization, 2021).

Nadia Valman is Professor of Urban Literature at Queen Mary, University of London. She is the author of *The Jewess in Nineteenth-Century British Literary Culture* (Cambridge University Press, 2007) and the editor of eight books on Jewish cultural history, including *British Jewish Women Writers* (Wayne State University Press, 2014); with Laurence Roth, the *Routledge Handbook of Contemporary Jewish Cultures* (Routledge, 2014); and with Jonathan M. Hess and Maurice Samuels, *Nineteenth-Century Jewish Literature: A Reader* (Stanford University Press, 2013). She leads literature walks based on her research and recently organized a historical re-enactment of an 1889 protest march by Jewish workers in east London.

Rebecca Lynn Winer is Associate Professor of History at Villanova University. Her research focuses on women, gender, and Christian-Jewish-Muslim relations in medieval Roussillon and Catalonia, and Slavery Studies. She is the author of *Women, Wealth, and Community in Perpignan, c. 1250–1300: Christians, Jews, and Enslaved Muslims in a Medieval Mediterranean Town* (Ashgate, 2006) as well as numerous essays on Jewish women, domestic service, slavery, and notarial culture in the Middle Ages. Her work has been supported by grants and fellowships from the American Association of University Women, the American Philosophical Society, the Hadassah-Brandeis Institute, and the Herbert D. Katz Center for Advanced Judaic Studies at the University of Pennsylvania. In her current book project she analyzes the experiences of Christian and Jewish wet nurses and mothers in the medieval Crown of Aragon and beyond.

INDEX

Page references in *italics* refer to illustrative materials.

Christianity, 9–10, 128–29, 134. *See also* Catholic Church; conversion/converts to Christianity

Christians: in al-Andalus, 99; cooperation with, in Victorian Britain, 271–72, 273–74; devout, in early modern Italy, 148; in early modern family and community economies, 185; in Iberia, 103–5, 108–10; on marital patterns and sexuality, 82–83; as mystics, 141n66; in 19th-century German salon culture, 243

Christian world, medieval, 9–10, 75, 101–9

circumcision, 85, 130–31, 133–34, 179, 450, 455

cis-gender privilege, 23–25

citizenship, 243–44, 249–50

civilization, 4–5, 255, 298–300, 307, 308, 319–21

class, socioeconomic: in adolescent girls' experience of the Holocaust, 375, 377–81, 389–90; in alienation from institutional Judaism, 278–79; clothing as marker of, 295–96; in early modern central Europe, 185; in 19th-century lives and societies, 15–17; in ownership of concubines, 105–6; in rabbinic texts, 63; of Sephardic Jews, in the Eastern Mediterranean, 287; in tensions of immigration to the U.S., 335; in Victorian Britain, 16–17, 261–62. *See also* elite, Jewish; middle classes; working classes

clothing, 199, 203, 220–21, 293, 295–300, 316–19, 384, 455. *See also* fashion

clubs/club movement, 270–71, 274–75, 290–91, 381–82, 411. *See also* associationism, Jewish female; organizations, women's

cofanetto (casket), 157–58, *158*

cohabitation in the contemporary U.S., 444

Cohen, Judah, 412–13

Cohen, Mary M., 407

Cohn, Charlotte, 364

college attendance and degrees, 442, 443–44

colonialism, French, 18–19, 308, 321

Combat Organization (Socialist Revolutionary Party), 232

combat roles for women, 359–60

commandments. *See* mitzvot (commandments)

communism, 345–46. *See also* socialism

communities, Jewish: gender and domestic service in, 150–51; for LGBTQ people, 424–25; medieval, semi-autonomous, 9–10; Ottoman Sephardic, 286–88, 290–91; socioeconomic divisions of, in Victorian Britain, 261–62; synagogue attendance in bylaws of, 203; targeted by Visigoths in Iberia, 98

Compagnia delle Donne (dowering sisterhoods). *See* sisterhoods: dowering

Conat, Estellina, 176–77

concentration camps, 21–22, 381, 387–89. *See also* deportations from WWII Polish ghettos; Holocaust

concubines, enslaved, 105–6

confraternities (*hevrot*), 24–25, 155–58, 172–73

conscription of women into the military, 361

Conservative Jews/Judaism, 249–50, 337–38, 400–402, 403–4, 427–28, 444–45, 452–53. *See also* positive-historical Judaism

conversion/converts to Christianity: in Ashkenaz, 87; in contemporary intermarriage, 448–49; crypto-Judaism/crypto-Jews, 10, 108–10; in early modern Italy, 145; forced, 9–10, 97–98, 108–10, 112–13, 286; in Iberia, 97–98, 106, 107–10, 112–13; in 19th-century Germany, 241–46, 248–49; in the Russian Empire, 229, 230–31; in 17th-century Amsterdam, 11, 111–12

conversions to Judaism, 106

cookbooks, 407

Coontz, Stephanie, 443

Cooper, Adrienne, 427

Copio Sullam, Sara, 154

Coriat, Messody, 315–16

courts: civil, 172–73; Muslim, 4–5, 76–77, 78; rabbinic, 57, 83, 149, 172–73, 184, 185, 224–25

Cover, Robert, 34

creation narrative, 7–8, 54, 55–56, 125–26, 134–35. *See also* Eve

creativity, 23, 220–21, 241, 412–13, 425–27

Crenshaw, Kimberlé, 7. *See also* intersectionality

cross-dressing, 207, 223–24

crypto-Judaism/crypto-Jews (conversos). *See* conversion/converts to Christianity

culture: in al-Andalus (Iberian peninsula), 98–101; in American spirituality, 411; *Bildung* (German), 16, 247–50, 252–53, 254; clash of, in Victorian Britain, 16–17; consumer, 296–98, 333; in early modern Italy, 143, 152–53, 154–55, 157–58; of labor activism among American Jewish women, 339–40; local, in medieval social and family life, 76, 112–13; majority, influence of, 81–82; material, in early modern Italy, 157–61; of 19th-century German salons, 243; popular, in Britain, 278–79; religious, 219, 241, 249–53, 262–64, 279; secular, 152–53, 411; transnational, women's acculturation in, 1; Yiddish, LGBTQ people in, 427

Cum Nimis Absurdum (Papal bull, 1555), 145

da Fano, Menachem Azariah, 149

da Modena, Aaron Berekhiah: *Maavar Yabbok*, 153

Damsky, Andrea Beth: "Heal Me, Oh God," 413

da Pisa, Fiammetta, 155–56

d'Arpino, Anna, 159–60

daughters: gendered ideals for, 197–99; inheritance rights of, 58–59, 61, 184; and mothers during the Holocaust, 380–81, 384–86, 387–88, 389–90; of printers, in early modern central Europe, 176–77; violence against, in the Hebrew Bible, 42–44. *See also* girls

Davis, Zemon Natalie, 2–3

Deborah, story of, 39

deeds of gift, 59. *See also* inheritances

defense forces of Mandatory Palestine, 357, 358–61

de Leon, Moses, 124

denominationalism, 336, 345

dependence, economic, 203–5, 209–10, 217–18

deportations from WWII Polish ghettos, 378–79, 381, 384–85, 387–88. *See also* Holocaust

Desart, Ellen, 273–74

de Sommi Portaleone, Leone: *Le tre Sorelle*, 148–49; "Magen Nashim," 148; *Tsaoth b'Dihutha d'Kiddushin*, 148–49

devotions: kabbalistic, 111; in Reform Judaism, 249–51

Devout (2014 film), 425

diaries, 176, 373–74, 376–77, 389–90, 397

diaspora, Sephardic, 109–12, 285–301

dietary laws, 407–8. *See also* food/foodways

Din (judgment *sefirah*), 129

Dinah, story of, 35–36, 42, 43–44

Diner, Hasia, 407–8

discrimination, gendered and racial, 7, 108–10, 342–43, 364, 424–25. *See also* anti-Semitism

disengagement from Judaism, 241, 247–49, 449–50

diversity: at AIU boarding schools, 312; in American Jewish lesbian studies and activism, 422–23; in contemporary American households and marital status, 442–45; in expressions of spirituality, 397–98; of Jews in the U.S., 346

divorce: and apostasy in medieval Europe, 10, 106–8; in Ashkenaz, 81–83, 87; conversion in, 87, 106–7; documents of, 57–58, 78, 81–82, 101; in economic status in the Polish-Lithuanian Commonwealth, 205; intermarriage in, 444; in the medieval Muslim world, 78–79; in partnership marriages, 447; in rabbinic texts, 57–58, 60–61; in the Russian Empire, 217–18, 224–25 domesticity/domestic sphere: confinement to, 60, 153; in contemporary Germany, 254–55; in early modern Italy, 143, 145–46, 153–54; in the Eastern Mediterranean, 285–86, 289–92; expectations of, in the U.S., 334; industrialization in, 330; medieval expectations of, 75; in 19th-century Germany, 252–53; in rabbinic texts, 60, 62–63, 69; and spirituality, 404–10, 414; in Victorian Britain, 16–17, 262–64, 266–67. *See also* households/homes

domestic Judaism, 15–17, 19, 331

domestic partnership benefits, 420–21

donations. *See* charity; philanthropy

dowries: in Ashkenaz, 81–82; dowry funds, societies, sisterhoods, 11, 99, 112, 156–57; in early modern central Europe, 181–82; in early modern Italy, 149, 151, 153–54, 156–57, 183–84; in the medieval Muslim world, 77–78; real estate as, for widows in Poland, 204–5

Drisha (institute for Jewish education), 454

dual-earner families, contemporary, 445–47

DuBowski, Sandi: *Trembling Before G-d*, 426–27

Dykewomon, Elana: *Beyond the Pale*, 426; *Riverfinger Woman*, 426

dynasties in the Hebrew Bible, 40–42, 46

Dynner, Glenn, 6

East End of London, 268–71

École Bischoffsheim, Paris, 311–14

école managerie (domestic training school), Rabat, 310–11

economic life: in Ashkenaz, 81, 83–84, 86; in early modern central Europe, 180–85; for immigrants, in Victorian Britain, 266–68; in 19th-century Germany, 241–42; in the Polish-Lithuanian Commonwealth, 203–5, 209–10; in the Russian Empire, 226–29

economy: capitalist, in the Eastern Mediterranean, 287; in early modern central Europe, 181, 183–84; family, 181, 183–84, 208–10, 226–29, 331; household, in the Eastern Mediterranean, 289–91; and immigration to the U.S., 331; in the Polish-Lithuanian Commonwealth, 208–10; in the Russian Empire, 226–29

Eden, 36–37, 54, 55–56, 127

education: of adolescent girls during the Holocaust, 22, 377–79; AIU in, 307–8, 313; American women's activism in, 344–45; of Ashkenazi girls in the U.S., 19–20, 330–35, 337–38; in contemporary American Jewish life, 25, 442, 443–44, 452–54; curricula, 222, 288, 289–90, 312, 324–25n35, 337–38, 452–53; donations for, in Muslim Iberia, 99; in early modern central Europe, 172; in early modern Italy, 154, 160–61; in the Eastern Mediterranean, 287–88, 291–92; higher, 222–23, 228, 275, 332–33, 442, 443–44, 454; in Mandatory Palestine, 362, 365, 366; medieval, 80, 86–87; in 19th-century Germany, 243, 251; of Orthodox women and girls, 25–26, 452–53; and partnership marriages, 445–47; professionalization of, 337; in rabbinic texts, 68–69; religious, 251, 333–34, 452–53; in religious experience, 14–15; in the Russian Empire, 17–18, 222–24, 225–26; secular, 17–18, 442; socioeconomic status and family background in, 13–14; Yiddish books in, 201–2. *See also* schools

egalitarianism: in contemporary American Jewish life, 25, 442–43, 456; of God and Israel, in the Hebrew Bible, 44–45; in Hasidism, in the Russian Empire, 220; in Mandatory Palestine, 353–54, 355–56; in 19th-century German salons, 243, 245–46; in rabbinic texts, 58–59; and spirituality, 398; in the Zohar, 125–26, 135–36

Ein Harod Kibbutz, 356–57, *357*
El Comersial, 289–90, 291, 294–95, 297
Eleazar ben Judah, of Worms, 87
Eleazar ben Samuel, of Mainz, 87–88
Eliezer ben Joel Halevi, 84
elite, Jewish: in Ashkenaz, 81; as donors
   of synagogue textiles, 160; in Iberia,
   99–101, 105–6; and modernity in the
   Eastern Mediterranean, 296–98; in
   19th-century Germany, 16, 242–43;
   rabbinic, Yiddish books authored
   by, 201; in rabbinic texts, 63–64;
   relationships of, with domestic
   servants, 150–51; in the Russian
   Empire, 217–18; in the Sephardic
   diaspora, 109–10; sex segregation in
   power of, 221; sexual impropriety by,
   in the Zohar, 133–34; in the U.S., 330,
   340–41; in Victorian Britain, 261–63,
   264–65, 266, 270–75, 277–78. *See also*
   class, socioeconomic
emancipation: and embourgeoisement in
   the Eastern Mediterranean, 285, 300;
   higher education in, 222–23, 228; in
   19th-century Germany, 244–45, 246;
   in the Russian Empire, 228; of teenage
   girls during the Holocaust, 380–82; in
   Victorian Britain, 263, 266
embourgeoisement, 246–49, 251–53,
   285–301. *See also* bourgeoisie
emigration. *See* migrations
empowerment: of immigrants to
   Mandatory Palestine, 367; of the
   institutrices, 311, 319–21; women's
   seders in, 409; in the Zohar, 121, 135
Enlightenment, Jewish. *See* Haskalah
   (Jewish enlightenment) movement
Enlightenment culture, German, 241–48,
   249–50. *See also* Haskalah (Jewish
   enlightenment) movement
enslaved women, 63, 105–6
Epoca, La, 289–90, *290*, 296
equality-in-difference feminism (familial
   feminism). *See under* feminism/
   feminists
equality/inequality: in the Hebrew Bible,
   54; "inferiority" of women, 134–35; in

LGBTQ activism, 429; in Mandatory
   Palestine, 20–21, 354–55, 356–58, 359,
   362–63; myth of, 353–54, 359, 361; in
   rabbinic texts, 54, 58–59; in Victorian
   Britain, 273
eroticism, 121, 126, 131, 134–35, 225
eroticization of Jewish women, 104
Eshel, 425
Esperanza, La/Buena Esperanza, La, 293,
   295–96, 297
Esther, story of, 33–34
ethnicity: in American Jewish life, 25, 444;
   and education, in the U.S., 19–20,
   332–33; in Jewish households of early
   modern Italy, 150–51; in 19th-century
   lives and societies, 15–16; in the
   Ottoman Empire, 301; in the Polish-
   Lithuanian Commonwealth, 193, 195;
   in the Russian Empire, 232–33. *See
   also* Ashkenazim; Mizrahi women;
   Sephardim
Europe, early modern central: economic
   life and status in, 12–13, 180–85;
   readers and writers in, 169, 173–77,
   185–86; records and regulations in,
   169–73, 180–81; ritual life in, 178–80
Eve, 7–8, 54, 55–56, 134–35. *See also*
   creation narrative
everyday life: in early modern central
   Europe, 169–73, 175–76, 180–81; in
   early modern Italy, 151; in the Eastern
   Mediterranean, 287; lived experience/
   reality of, 146–61, 287–88, 351–52,
   356–58; in medieval Christian Spain,
   101–4; in the Russian Empire, 17–18,
   227; and upward mobility in 19th-
   century Germany, 246–49; in the
   WWII Polish ghetto, 373–74, 380–82
exclusion. *See* inclusion/exclusion
exemptions of women: from
   commandments, 8–9, 54–55, 67–68;
   from literacy and Torah study, 69;
   from pilgrimages, 67; from sukkot,
   67–68. *See also* inclusion/exclusion
experiences, religious, 14–15, 23, 252–53,
   397–98, 399–400, 402–3, 406. *See also*
   spirituality

exploitation, sexual, 272–73, 387. *See also* abuse: sexual; prostitution

expulsions, 9–10, 11, 80–81, 98, 109–10, 112–13

extermination camps, 21–22, 381, 388–89. *See also* concentration camps; deportations from WWII Polish ghettos; Holocaust

facilitation of male religious objectives: in historical society, 450–51; of male scholars, in Victorian Britain, 266–67; in the Polish-Lithuanian Commonwealth, 12, 198–99, 200, 209–10, 212n31; of scholars, in Mitnagdism, 221; in the Zohar, 132–33

factory work/workers, 227–30, 231–32, 267–68, 338–40

Faivilevich, Dora, 224

family: Ashkenazic, in the U.S., 330–35; background of, in agency, 13–14; in the contemporary U.S., 442–50; in experiences of adolescent girls during the Holocaust, 375, 379–81, 384–85, 389–90; German Jewish, 253–55; in Iberia, 98, 103–4; in Mandatory Palestine, 357–58; in the Polish-Lithuanian Commonwealth, 196–97, 208; in pre-WWII Poland, 376–77; in Russian imperial law, 224–26; in Victorian Britain, 268–71. *See also* households/homes

fashion, 296–98, 316–19, 384. *See also* clothing

fathers: in contemporary American Jewish families, 447, 450; in Hebrew Bible, 33; in violence against their daughters, 42. *See also* parents/parenting

Federation of American Zionists, 344

feminine, cosmic, 10, 121, 124–25, 127–28, 129–30, 405

femininity: of adolescent girls during the Holocaust, 386–87; bourgeois, and charity in the Eastern Mediterranean, 293; in the Hebrew Bible, 8–9; of the Oriental new woman, 317–18; in the

Polish-Lithuanian Commonwealth, 195, 197–99; in religious culture in 19th-century Germany, 252–53; in spirituality, 405; Victorian rhetoric of, in rescue work, 274

feminism/feminists: in academic and organizational life, 428–30; and American Jewish lesbian activism, 421–22; and American spirituality, ix–xi, 402–4, 408–10, 413; British, in imperialism, 316; in the Eastern Mediterranean, 285–86, 301; on the Fall from Eden story, 36–37; French familial, 4–5, 18–19, 314–16, 319; individualist, 314–15; and the *institutrices*, 309–11; in intersectionality, 7; in Israel, 354; in Jewish studies, ix–xi, 2–3, 240–41; LGBTQ, in the contemporary U.S., 421–22, 425, 430; of modern German Jewish women, 254–55; second-wave, 354, 402, 408–10, 421–22; in study of *salonières*, 245; 21st century, 255; in Victorian Britain, 275–76. *See also* women's movement

"Feminist Approaches to Jewish Studies" roundtable, 2–3

feminization, 12, 16, 25, 145–46, 157–59, 253, 455–56

fertility/infertility, 37–38, 195–96, 341–42, 413, 444–45, 446–47. *See also* birthrate

films on LGBTQ experiences, 426–27

financial records, early modern, 172–73

Fishman Maimon, Ada, 355

Florentin, Rafael Immanuel, 291–92

fluidity: in family definitions, 442–43; gendered, in the Zohar, 128–29, 131–32, 138n22; of identity, 5, 7, 24–26, 278–79, 316–17, 322

food/foodways, 170, 254, 381, 397, 407–8. *See also* dietary laws

foreign women, in the Hebrew Bible, 33–34, 35–36

foremothers: of Jewish lesbian studies, 422–23; in Seder, 409

Four Questions, 409–10

France, 307–22. *See also* Ashkenaz

Frances, Immanuel: "Against Women Who Pursue Religious Studies," 146

Francesca Sarah of Safed, 111

Frank, Henrietta, 332

Frankel, Zacharias, 249–50

Frankiel, Tamar, 405, 408

Franklin, Netta, 277

Freedman, Marcia, 428

Freedman, Naomi, 408

freedom: of bourgeois Sephardic women in the Eastern Mediterranean, 294–95; longing for, by adolescent girls during the Holocaust, 383; for medieval Jewish women, 76–77; of religion, in the Russian Empire, 219; in the U.S., 329–30, 334–35, 336–37, 402, 408, 444

Freeze, ChaeRan: *Polin: Jewish Women in Eastern Europe*, 5–6

Fresco, David, 288, 291

Friedman, Debbie, 425

Friedman, Debbie: "Sing Unto God," 412–13

Friedmann, Ellie, 377

friends/friendship: in German salons, 243, 245; during the Holocaust, 380, 381–83; in Victorian Britain, 270–71, 273, 276, 277–79

Frohman, Denise, 425–26

Frymer-Kensky, Tikva, 43–44

garment industry work and activism, 338–39

Geissmar, Clara, 16, 241, 246–49

gender: bourgeois construction of, 285–86, 298–301; cis-gender privilege, 23–25; in contemporary intermarried households, 449; defined, 5; double standards, 33, 104; female, in the Zohar, 124–26; gap in the contemporary U.S., 25, 442, 452–53, 455–56; and genocide, 1; of God in the Hebrew Bible, 32, 44–46; of God, in the Zohar, 124–26; in interpretive lenses, 5–6; in Judaism, 4; in 19th-century lives and societies, 15–16; in Zionism, 353. *See also* roles, gendered

genocide, 1, 21–22. *See also* Holocaust

geographic scope, 3

Germany: domestic Judaism in, 16; early modern, 171; Imperial, German Jewish women and families, 253–55; 19th-century, 239–53; postwar Jewish community in, 255; unification of, in upward mobility, 246. *See also* Ashkenaz; Europe, early modern central

Gershom ben Judah, 81–82

Gershoni, Sharon, 425–26

Gerson, Judith, 7

ghettos: in early modern Italy, 145–46, 148, 150; Warsaw, lives of adolescent girls in, 373–75, 377–90; in women's withdrawal from public life, 12

girls: in acculturation to the U.S., 333–34; adolescent, in the Holocaust, 373–75, 377–90; age of, at betrothal, 82; confirmation ceremonies for, 251; education of, 19–20, 22, 25–26, 330–35, 337–38, 377–79, 452–53; friendship for in Victorian Britain, 270–71; peers, friendship, and love in WWII ghettos, 381–83; pre-war childhood of, 376–77; schools for, 222–23, 307–8. *See also* children; daughters

Gitl of Kraków, 208

Glenn, Susan A., 2–3

Glikl Hameln (a.k.a. Glückel of Hameln, Glikl bas Yehuda, Glikl of Hamburg), x, 176, 181, 208

Gluckstein, Hannah, 425–26

God: gender of, 32, 44–46, 124–26; interventions by, in the Hebrew Bible, 33–34; in the Zohar, 121, 124–26, 128–29

godmothers, 85

God's Will Society, 293–94

Goitein, Shlomo Dov, 79

Goldman, Emma, 345

Goldschmidt, Johanna, 251

Goldsmid, Louisa, 278

Goodman, Barbara, 399

Gore, Lesley, 425–26

Great Liquidation Action of 1942, 381, 383–86. *See also* deportations from WWII Polish ghettos

Greenberg, Julie, 424

guardians, 89, 102, 103. *See also* mothers/motherhood; parents/parenting

guidebooks, Orthodox, 405–6

Guide to Factories and Plants for 1879, 227

gynecology, 127–28, 195–97. *See also* midwives/midwifery

Hadassah, 344–46, 361–62, 411

Hadassah-Brandeis Institute (HBI), 2

Haganah (Yishuv defense force and militia), 358, 359

Haggadot, feminist, 408–9, 410

Halakhah: age of adulthood in, 375; in American spirituality, 411–12; in betrothals and sexual relationships in early modern Italy, 149, 150–51; in books for women in the Polish-Lithuanian Commonwealth, 201–2; in choices of same-sex couples for child genetics, 448; and family, in the Russian Empire, 224–25; family planning in, 19–20, 342; gender in, 61, 62–63, 64–65, 70; in modernization of German religious culture, 249–50, 252–53; rabbinic legal system, 57, 59–62; wills in, 184; in women's lives in Ashkenaz, 84–87. *See also* Law

halakhic midrashim, 61, 70, 149

halitzah (release of levirate brides), 58

Hallel, 410

Halpern, Rose, 342

Hammer, Jill, 425

Ha-Nagid, Shmuel, 100

Handali, Esther, 110–11

handbooks for women, 152–53, 174–75, 200–201

Hanukkah, 23, 159, 399–402. *See also* holidays

harassment, workplace, 335

haredim (ultra-Orthodox), 444–45. *See also* Orthodox Jews/Judaism

"harlot with a big heart" trope, 36

Hartman, Harriet and Moshe, 442, 449, 456; *Gender and American Jews*, 446, 452–53

Hashomer (Hebrew defense force), 358

Hasidei Ashkenaz, 82–83

Hasidim/Hasidism, 10–11, 25–26, 135–36, 220–21, 398, 404, 411, 425, 444–45

Haskalah (Jewish enlightenment) movement, 219, 225–26, 233. *See also* Enlightenment culture, German; *maskilim*

hats/headdresses, 297–98

havurah (fellowship), Second Temple, 71

havurot (prayer and community groups) and *hevrot* (confraternities), 24–25, 155–58, 172–73, 424, 428–29

Hazan, Aaron Joseph, 288, 289

healing, Jewish spiritual, 413

health care, 267–70, 278, 344–45, 361–62. *See also* medicine/medical profession

Hebrew: bars to women learning, 17–18; in culture of Mandatory Palestine, 352–53; education in, 223–25, 313, 324n33, 324–25n35, 452; gendered literacy in, 86–87, 147, 160–61, 173–74; scholarship in, in Ashkenaz, 81; women's poetry in, 99–100

Hebrew Bible: "depatriarchalization" of the, 45–46; feminine imagery in, 133–34; feminine symbolism in, 129–31; heroines in, 37–38, 148, 403–4, 408–9; "Holiness Code," 34–35; intersectionality in, 7; life and continuity in, 35, 38, 40–41; matriarchs in, 33–34, 36–38, 40–42, 46, 126, 129–30, 148, 219; patriarchy in, 7, 8–10, 32–34, 43–44, 45–46; prophecy in, 43, 44–46; reading women and gender in, 31–46; same-sex relationships in, 424; wife-sister tales in, 33–34

Hebrew Union College, 336, 398–99

"Hebrew woman," 351–52

Heilprun, Yaakov ben Elhanan, 152–53

Henriques, Agnes, 262–63

heroines: in Ashkenaz, 9–10; biblical, 37–38, 148, 403–4, 408–9; in Mandatory Palestine military, 360

Hertz, Deborah, 244–45

Herz, Henriette, 243, *244*

Hescheles, Janina, 376, 377–79

Ḥevrat Nizharim confraternity, 155–56

hibbah (affection or sexual desire), 149

hierarchy: gendered, 32–33, 65–66, 97, 104–6, 112–13, 361; sociopolitical, 38–39, 150–51, 241–42

higher education, 222–23, 228, 275, 332–33, 442, 443–44, 454

Hillel Ba'al Shem (*Sefer Haḥeshek*), 194–97

Hineini: Coming Out in a Jewish High School (2005 film), 426–27

Hirsch, Samson Raphael, 252

Histadrut (workers' union of Mandatory Palestine), 362

historiography, national, of Israel, 354

Hokhmah (male *sefirah*), 126, 127–28

holidays: and American spirituality, 23, 399–400, 401–3, 405, 408–10, 413; in domestic space, 143; Hanukkah, 23, 159, 399–402; in ritual life of early modern Eastern Europe, 178; Rosh Chodesh, 402–3, 405, 413. *See also* celebrations

"Holiness Code," 34–35

Holocaust: adolescent girls in, 21–22, 373–75, 377–90; families in, 375, 379–81; lesbians in resistance to, 436–37n48; peers, friendship, and love in ghettos of, 381–83; scholarship on women in, 374–75; survival strategies, 22, 385–86, 389–90; women's experiences of, 21–22. *See also* Nazi Germany

homophobia, gender-based, 23–24, 430–31

Horowitz, Sara Rebecca Leah, 175, 199–200, 212n31; *Tkhine Imohos*, 13–14, 199

households/homes: *Bildung* culture in, 254; diversity of, in the contemporary U.S., 442–45; early modern conceptualization of, 13; feminization of, in early modern Italy, 157–58; parity in contemporary responsibilities in, 447; religious practice in, 330–31; in Victorian Britain, 268–71. *See also* domesticity/ domestic sphere; family

Hunter College, New York, 332–33

Hurwitz, Sara, 453–54

hygiene, 268–70, 289, 362

Hyman, Paula, 330; *Gender and Assimilation in Modern Jewish History*, 1; *Polin: Jewish Women in Eastern Europe*, 5–6

Iberia: culture and life in, 98–101; economic activities in, 97–98, 112–13; everyday lives in, 101–4; female Andalusian Sufi mystics in, 141n66; forced conversion in, 10, 107–9; gender and hierarchy in, 104–6; Sephardic diaspora, 109–12; Visigothic persecution in, 98; women and gender in, 97–113

Iberian elegies, 9–10

ibn Adret, Solomon, 105

identity: and American peace activism, 343–44; in American spirituality, 400–401; in contemporary Germany, 254–55; in contemporary intermarried households, 449–50; in early modern Italy, 145–46; fluidity of, 5, 7, 24–26, 278–79, 316–17, 322; German, in upward mobility, 247–48; Hadassah activities in, for American women, 344–45; hiding of, during the Holocaust, 387; intersectional, in the Russian Empire, 218; in intersectionalism, 7; inverted gender gap in, 456; in Mandatory Palestine, 351–52, 360, 364, 366, 367–68; in 19th-century Germany, 239–40, 247–48; religious education in, in the U.S., 337–38; in the Sephardic diaspora, 112, 300–301

ideology, 8–9, 18, 54–55, 104, 221, 266, 351–52, 356

imagery: of early modern rituals, 179–80; of female *sefirot*, 126–27; feminine, in the Zohar, 133–34; maternal, in mystical Christianity, 128–29; in songs for women's seders, 410

Imhoff, Sara, 2–3

immigrants/immigration: illegal, post-Holocaust, 360–61; in Mandatory Palestine, 352–53, 364, 367; in the U.S., 329–35; in Victorian Britain, 16–17, 261, 264–67, 268–71, 274–75. *See also* migrations

inclusion/exclusion: in the contemporary U.S., 24–25; in Hasidism, 10–11, 220–21; in kabbalistic texts, 10–11; of and by lesbians, 422, 423, 430; LGBTQ activism on, 429; in Mandatory Palestine, 362–63; in 19th-century Germany, 251; from political power, 70, 356; in rabbinic texts, 8–9, 55, 60, 61; in the Russian Empire, 17–18, 227–28, 231–32; from Torah study, 53–54, 60, 68–69; from trade, in the Middle Ages, 80–81; in Victorian Britain, 261–62

Incognito Club, Jewish Theological Seminary, 424–25

industrialization, 228–29, 239–40, 246, 330

infant mortality, 268–69, 281n34

infertility. *See* fertility/infertility

inheritances, 34, 58, 61, 76–77, 103–4, 184–85, 208

innkeeping, 205–6, 227

innovations: in American spirituality, 412–13, 425, 429; of Anglo-Jewish elite women, 278; educational, 25–26, 334, 454; of Jewish lesbians, 24–25, 430–31; in Jewish women's history, 3–6; in rabbinic texts, 56, 59; in religious life, in the U.S., 336; in Victorian health care and welfare, 269–70

Inquisition, 108–10, 145

institutrices (primary school teachers), 307–22. *See also* Alliance israélite universelle (AIU)

integration. *See* assimilation

intellectuals, 154–55, 275–76

intermarriage, 35–36, 99, 108, 243–44, 444–45, 448–50

International Ladies Garment Workers Union (ILGWU), 338–39

intersectionality, 6–8, 32, 33–34, 112–13, 217–33, 422

intimacy: and adolescent girls during the Holocaust, 382–83; household, in women's rituals, 159; of religious life in the Russian Empire, 219–20, 222–23; in theater performances, 294–95; in Victorian Britain, 273, 274–75, 277–78

Irgun (underground military), 358–59

Isaac the Blind, 124

Islamic world, 9–10, 18–19, 76–80, 285–301

Isle of Klezbos, 427

Israel: egalitarian prayer groups in, 402–3; fertility rates in, 444–45; gender-historical research in, 353–54; Jewish education in, 452, 454; Jewish lesbian film in, 426–27; lesbian Jews in, 427–28; myth of equality in, 353–54, 361; Orthodox women rabbis and para-rabbis in, 453–54; peace activism in, 428; rights of women in, 368; state of, declared, 352–53, 368; as the wife of God, 44–45; women and kings of, 40; women in the military of, 361; women's labor in national structure of, 354–55. *See also* Mandatory Palestine, Jewish society of

Israel Defense Forces (IDF), 361

Israeli-Palestinian conflict, 428

Isserles, Moses, 202

Italy, early modern: agency in, 12–13, 146–49, 150, 157–58, 160–61; apprenticeships in, 145–46, 150, 160–61; book culture and literary expression in, 151–55; fraternalism and professional activities in, 155–57; gender and domestic service in, 150–51; material culture and ritual life in, 157–61; rabbinic and secular attitudes towards women in, 146–49; women's cultural accomplishments in, 154–55

Marian cult, 134
marketplaces, 64, 102, 207–8, 227
marriage: in Ashkenaz, 82–83, 87;
    to concubines, urged in Iberia,
    105–6; consent in, 148–49; in the
    contemporary U.S., 442–48; critique
    of, in Victorian Britain, 275–76; in
    early modern central Europe, 178–79,
    183–85; and economic status in the
    Polish-Lithuanian Commonwealth,
    204–5; in the Hebrew Bible, 33–36,
    44; in Iberia, 99, 100, 102–3, 105–7;
    for *institutrices*, 321; intermarriage,
    35–36, 99, 108, 243–44, 444–45,
    448–50; levirate, 34–35, 58, 105;
    for LGBTQ people, 447–48; in the
    medieval Muslim world, 77–80;
    monogamy, 105–6, 133–34; in
    19th-century Germany, 243–45;
    partnership marriages, 445–47; in the
    Polish-Lithuanian Commonwealth,
    194; in rabbinic texts, 56–58, 61–62;
    remarriage, 82–83, 87, 102–3, 204–5;
    in the Russian Empire, 224–25; in the
    Zohar, 126, 133–34
martyrdom of medieval women, 9–10, 75,
    84, 87
Marx, Eleanor, 275
masculine-feminine binary, 11–12, 31–32,
    38–39, 121, 125–26, 128–29
masculinity, 159, 195, 240, 353, 354–55,
    450–51
masculinization, 17–18, 145–46, 152–53,
    316–17
maskilim (Enlightened male authors),
    17–18, 222, 225–26, 232. *See also*
    Haskalah (Jewish enlightenment)
    movement
Mason, Charlotte, 277
matchmakers, 182
medicine/medical profession: American
    Jewish women in, 342–43; female
    doctors in Mandatory Palestine, 364,
    367; as medieval female occupation,
    79–80; midwifery, 12–13, 38, 65, 84,
    182, 196–97; in the Polish-Lithuanian
    Commonwealth, 194–97; in rabbinic

texts, 65; in the Russian Empire, 228;
    and Soʿed Ḥolim, 156–57; study of,
    in the Russian Empire, 223. *See also*
    health care
Mediterranean, Eastern: bourgeois
    construction of gender in, 285–86,
    298–301; bourgeois womanhood
    and charity in, 292–96; critiques of
    Sephardic bourgeoisie in, 298–300;
    domestic sphere in, 285–86, 289–92;
    embourgeoisement of Sephardic
    women in, 285–301; luxury and
    sobriety in, 296–98; Sephardic
    community in, 109–12, 286–88
Meir, Tama, 408–9
Melamed, Deborah Marcus: *The Three
    Pillars: Thought, Worship, Practice*,
    401–2
Melammed, Renée Levine, 76–77
memoirs, 246–49, 373–74, 376–77,
    389–90. *See also* diaries
memory, collective: military women in,
    359–61; of women, in Holocaust
    studies, 21–22
Mendelssohn, Brendel, 243–45
Mendelssohn, Henriette, 244–45
Mendelssohn, Moses, 243–44
menstruation/menstruating women
    (*niddah*), 59–60, 85–86, 92n49, 128,
    129, 174–75, 202, 413
mère-éducatrice (mother-educator), 288,
    289, 300–301
Meseret, El, 295
messianic movements, 10, 80, 109, 404
Michal, wife of David, 40–41
middle classes: in contemporary Germany,
    253–54; as conversos, in Iberia, 108–9;
    in early modern Italy, 157–59, 160–61;
    in the Eastern Mediterranean, 287,
    295–96, 300–301; in the Holocaust,
    22, 376–78, 379–82, 389–90; in
    Mandatory Palestine, 362; in 19th-
    century Germany, 16, 239–40,
    246–49; in the U.S., 19–20, 332–34,
    339, 340–43, 443; in Victorian Britain,
    16–17, 262–64, 269–73, 278. *See also*
    class, socioeconomic

Middle East: *institutrices* in, 18–19, 307–8, 312, 314–16; Sephardic diaspora in, 111, 286–88. *See also* Mediterranean, Eastern; Ottoman Empire

midrashim: halakhic, 61, 70, 149; in medieval Kabbalah, 124, 127; modern, in depatriarchalization, 46; as rabbinic literature, 53; refusal of betrothals in, 149; women's punishment for Eve's sin in, 54; women's role in, 61, 62–63; on women's rule, 70; in women's spirituality, in the U.S., 402–3, 408–9; women's subordination in, 55–56

midwives/midwifery, 12–13, 38, 65, 84, 182, 196–97. *See also* medicine/medical profession

migrations, 3, 88, 101, 255, 266–67, 271–72, 329–30, 346. *See also* diaspora, Sephardic; immigrants/immigration

Mikvah Ladies, 425

mikveh (ritual bath), 83, 102–3, 158–59, 180, 413, 425

military, Yishuv, 358–61, 366

Mindell, Fania, 342

Miriam, story of, 408–9

Mishnah, 53, 56–57, 59–63, 67, 71

Mishnaic Order of Women (*Nashim*), 59–61

misogyny, 44–45, 53–54, 134–35, 321

missionaries, 25–26, 230–31, 398

Mitchell, Kerry, 406

Mitnagdism, 221

mitzvot (commandments): and adultery in the Hebrew Bible, 33; handbooks on, 152–53, 174–75, 200–201; on marital relations, in Ashkenaz, 86–87; performance of, as a mark of adulthood, 375; in rabbinic texts, 54–55, 61, 67–68; in ritual life in early modern Italy, 157–58; *Seder mitzvot nashim*, 152–53, 174–75, 200–201; women's education in, 13–14; women's exemption from, 8–9, 54–55, 67–68; in women's religious fulfillment, 212n31; in the Zohar, 122–24, 130–33

Mizrahi women, 21, 361–62, 364, 429

Mizrahi Women, Federation of, 362

mobility, social: for bourgeois Sephardic women, 294; education in, 68–69; female collaboration in, 16–17; in 19th-century Germany, 246–49, 254; in the Sephardic diaspora, 111; in the U.S., 333–35; in Victorian Britain, 274–75, 278

Modena, Fioretta, 153–54

Modena, Marianna, 147–48

modernization/modernity: in changing opportunities in American Judaism, 451; in the Eastern Mediterranean, 285–301; Jewish women as agents of, 26; in 19th-century Germany, 239–55; for Sephardic women, 285–301; in the U.S., 334; in Victorian Britain, 267, 274–75, 279. *See also* Westernization

modesty, 85, 147, 181–82, 197–99, 220–21, 272–73, 452

Moelin, Jacob ben Moses, 84–85

mohar (marriage gift), 77–78

Molin, Jacob, 174–75

monarchies in Hebrew Bible narratives, 40–42

moneylending, 80–81, 84, 180–81, 205

Montagu, Lily, 268, 273–75, 276, 277; *Naomi's Exodus*, 276

Montefiore, Charlotte, 263

Moore, Tracy: *Lesbiōt*, 423

moral conduct books, 197–98, 200–201, 219–20

morality: in childrearing, in the Eastern Mediterranean, 291; in early modern central Europe, 172; in early modern Italy, 147; musar (ethics), 4, 198; in the Polish-Lithuanian Commonwealth, 197–98; in Reform Judaism, 249–50, 252–53; religious education in, 252; secular, in disengagement from Judaism, 248; sexual, in expectations of Jewish girls in the U.S., 334

Moriscas (forced female converts from Islam), 109

Morocco, 307–8, 309–11

Mosessohn, Miriam Markel, 223–24

moshavim in Mandatory Palestine, 356, 358

Mossad Le'Aliya Bet, 360–61

"mother of the messaiah" trope, 48n19

mothers/motherhood: and adolescent daughters during the Holocaust, 380–81, 384–86, 387–88, 389–90; in Ashkenaz, 86–87; as basis for suffrage in the U.S., 340–41; in changes in religious education, 252; in the Eastern Mediterranean, 288, 289, 292–93, 300–301; as guardians, 89, 102, 103; in the Hebrew Bible, 36–38; immigrant, in Victorian Britain, 268–69; in Jewish identity of children in intermarried households, 449–50; in Mandatory Palestine, 20–21, 353, 356, 357–58, 361–62, 364–66; in partnership marriages, 445–47; personification of God as, 45–46; in rabbinic texts, 62–63; unwed, 229, 230, 272

Muslim women, 99–100, 104, 105–6, 141n66, 301, 322

Muslim world, medieval, 75, 76–80, 83, 88, 98–101

mysticism, 111, 121, 130–34, 135–36, 141n55, 194–97

Nahan, Samuel, 307–8

Nahmanides (Moshe ben Nahman), 124

Naimark-Goldberg, Natalie, 244–45

Nashim: A Journal of Jewish Women's Studies and Gender Issues, 2

Nasi, Gracia, 109–10

Nathan, Maud, 340–41

Nathan, Mrs. Henry, 399–400

National Council, Mandatory Palestine, 362

nationalism in Mandatory Palestine, 20–21, 358, 360–61, 363, 364–65, 366

National Jewish Population Survey, 2000–2001, 442, 445–46

National Socialism (Nazism), 255

National Union of Women Workers, 277

nature: in bourgeois constructions of gender, 285–86; longing for, by

adolescent girls during the Holocaust, 383

Nazi Germany, 343–44, 375. *See also* Holocaust

NCJW (National Council of Jewish Women), 335–37, 343, 345–46

Neimark, Marilyn: *Beyond the Pale* radio show, 427

Nelken, Halina, 376, 377–78, 380, 387–88

networks, social and familial, 254, 275–76, 379–81, 388–89, 449

Neusner, Jacob, 59–61

new Jewish Woman, 307–22, 354–55, 365–66

Newman, Lesléa: *Heather Has Two Mommies*, 426

Newman, Pauline, 339, 340

NFTS (National Federation of Temple Sisterhoods), 343, 345–46, 399–401, 406–7. *See also* Women of Reform Judaism

niddah. See menstruation/menstruating women (*niddah*)

Niddah Tractate, 59–60

Nimrod, Naomi, 408

Nizirite (consecrating) vows, 36, 62–63

Nofech, Hedva, 366

North African women as *institutrices*, 4–5, 18–19, 307–22

Novelista, El, 291, 292, 293, 300

objects: gendered, in early modern Italy, 148, 157–61; ritual, in American spirituality, 397, 403, 404–7, 408–9

occultists, 79–80

occupations for women: in Ashkenaz, 84; for Ashkenazic American women, 338–39; in the contemporary U.S., 443–44, 445–47; in early modern central Europe, 182–84; in marketplaces, 64, 102, 207–8; in medieval Christian Spain, 102; in the medieval Muslim world, 79–80; in the Polish-Lithuanian Commonwealth, 205–7; in rabbinic texts, 62–66

Off the Derech (OTD), 425

One of Us (2017 film), 425

Orah Hayyim (Way of Life), 143, *144*

Poggetti, Allegra Carmi, 153–54
pogroms, 227
Poland: Hebrew education for girls in, 223–24; Holocaust in, 373–75, 377–90, 436–37n48; pre-war childhood for girls in, 376–77. *See also* Europe, early modern central
Poliakov family, 226–28
Polish-Lithuanian Commonwealth: accessible literature for women in, 200–202; Ashkenazic settlement in, 193–94; economic agency and status of women in, 203–7; feminine ideal in, 197–200; gendered stereotypes in, 194–97; powerful women in, 208–9; women in the synagogue, 202–3
politics/political participation: in Jewish lesbian film, 426–27; leftist, of Ashkenazic American Jewish women, 345–46; LGBTQ activism in, 427–28; in Mandatory Palestine, 20–21, 353–54, 362–63; in the Russian Empire, 231–32; salons in new political space, 241–42; in Victorian Britain, 278
polygamy, 105
polygyny, 81–82, 90n20
population growth, 169–70, 261, 352–53, 400–401
populism, 231
Porges, Moses, 174
Portrait of Jewish Americans (Pew), 447–49
"Portuguese Nation," 111–12
positive-historical Judaism, 16, 249–50. *See also* Conservative Jews/Judaism
Possevino, Antonio: *Bibliotheca Selecta*, 152–53
poverty: of Ashkenazic immigrants in Victorian Britain, 264, 266, 267–68; in conversion attempts, in early modern Italy, 145; dowries in preventing, 183–84; in the Eastern Mediterranean, 285–86, 287, 293, 296; and immigration to the U.S., 335; in 19th-century Germany, 239–40, 245–46; of workers in the Russian Empire, 228–29

practice, religious: in American spirituality, 401–2, 406; disengagement from, in 19th-century Germany, 241, 247–49; in Eastern European communities, 330–31; of holiday celebrations, 403; in the U.S., 336–37; in Victorian Britain, 262–63, 267; in Western European communities, 330–31; women's status in, in Ashkenaz, 84–85
Präger, Moses, 250–51
prayer: German-language, 249–51, 252–53; interruption of public, 102; prayer groups led by women, 85–86, 398; print in disseminating, 175; public, in the Polish-Lithuanian Commonwealth, 202–3; spirituality in singing, 410–11; *tkhines*, 17–18, 175, 199–202, 203, 219; in the Zohar, 122–23
prayer groups (*tefillah*), 398, 411–12, 453
pregnancy, 13, 150–51
Priesand, Sally, 402
primogeniture, 34, 38
print, early modern revolution in, 12, 88, 173–75, 176–77, 185–86
private sphere, 17–18, 169–71, 226, 289, 357–58. *See also* domesticity/domestic sphere
procreation, 33–34, 61, 134–35
professions and professional women: in early modern Europe, 12–13, 147–48, 155–56, 160, 182–83; *institutrice* as, 309, 312, 313–14; in Mandatory Palestine, 353, 354–56, 364, 366–67; for the new German Jewish woman, 254–55; in rabbinic texts, 63–66; in the Russian Empire, 17–18; in the U.S., 19–20, 25, 337, 338, 342–43; in Victorian Britain, 275–76. *See also* medicine/medical profession
property, 103–4, 145, 203–5, 208, 226
prostitution, 104–5, 229–30, 271–75, 363. *See also* exploitation, sexual
Protestants/Protestantism, 88, 171, 248, 262–64, 341
Provident Fund, 269

public life/realm: Ashkenazic American women in, 338, 340; in the contemporary U.S., 23; in early modern central Europe, 169–71, 180, 181–82; in early modern Italy, 12–13, 145–46, 155–56, 160–61; in the Eastern Mediterranean, 287, 289; in Mandatory Palestine, 356, 357–58, 360–61, 362, 366–67; 19th-century German salons as, 241–42; Sephardic women in, 294–96, 301; study houses as, 68–69; widows in, in medieval Christian Spain, 103

purity/impurity: in handbooks, 174–75; laws on, 104–5, 108; rituals of, in early modern Italy, 153, 157–59; sexual, in the Zohar, 133–34; Victorian women as guardians of, 16–17, 266–67, 271–72, 273–74. *See also* menstruation/menstruating women (*niddah*)

Qasmuna bit Isma'il al-Yehudi, 100
queens, 40–42, 66, 67–68, 70
"queer," as label, 428–29

rabbanit (rabbi's wife), 178. See also *rebbetzin*
rabbinic texts/literature: academic approach to, 454; composition of, 53; domestic sphere in, 62–63; on early modern households, 150; exemptions from commandments in, 8–9, 54–55, 67–68; origins of *Shekhinah* in, 127; patriarchal and androcentric outlook of, 8–9, 53–54; as political history, 69–71; professional sphere in, 63–66; on study houses, 68–69; systemization of dispersed biblical texts in, 54; on women in the synagogue and Temple, 67–68; women's legal position in, 56–59; women's religion in, 66–67; women's roles in, 56–62; women's study of, 452–54. *See also* Torah
Rabbis: approach to out-of-wedlock pregnancies by, 13; concerns over unmarried women in Amsterdam,

111–12; as intellectual male elite, 53–54; lesbian, 423; ordination of women as, 25–26, 254–55, 337–38, 398–99, 402, 427–28, 453–54; Orthodox, and LGBTQ couples, 25–26; "state," in the Russian Empire, 224–25; on women in society, 8

racialization in the Russian Empire, 230–31

radicalism, 222–23, 247–48, 275–76, 315–16, 342–43, 345

Rahab of Jericho, story of, 36

Rakovsky, Puah, 223–24, 231–32

rape, 35–36, 42–44, 335, 413. *See also* abuse: sexual

Raphael, Geela Rayzel: "Song of Praise," 410

Rapoport-Albert, Ada, 220

Rashkovich Mariia, 222–23

Ratner, Berta and Eva, 340

Raziel-Naor, Esther, 358–59

reality, lived. *See under* everyday life

rebbetzin, 401

rebellious women (*moredet*), 83

reciprocity, 44–45, 122–24, 147, 150, 264–66

recitations, 200–201, 203, 397, 404–5, 410, 455

reconstruction, post-WWI, 345–46

Reconstructionist movement, x, 424

Reform Jews/Judaism: American, 336, 337, 398–401, 402–3; in American spirituality, 398–401, 402–3, 412; birthrates of, in the contemporary U.S., 444–45; in contemporary intermarried households, 449, 450; feminization in formation of, 16; inverted gender gap in, 456; in modernization, in 19th-century Germany, 249–53; ordination of women in, x, 402–3; religious education for girls in, 452, 453

refugees, 11, 145, 360–61

religion: diversity of women's experiences in, 14–15; in LGBTQ activism, 424–25; spirituality contrasted with, 397–98; women's, in rabbinic texts, 66–67

Religion, National Committee on, 399

religious life/sphere/religiosity: *Bildung* culture in, 249–51; and birthrates, in the contemporary U.S., 444–45; bourgeois, in 19th-century Germany, 241, 252–53; in early modern Italy, 145–46; early modern regulations in, 169–70; in Europe, 330–31; exclusion from, 8–9, 17–18; and gender, in American Judaism, 451; medieval, 80; in the Polish-Lithuanian Commonwealth, 194, 209–10; in the Russian Empire, 219–21; in the U.S., 23, 24–25, 330–31, 335–38, 398. *See also* spirituality

Religious Schools, NFTS Committee on, 399–400

religious workers' movement, 363–64

Religious Working Women, Organization of, 362

Republic of Letters, 243

rescue work in Victorian Britain, 271–75

residency rights in the Russian Empire, 217–18

resistance: of adolescent girls in concentration camps, 388–89; in Ashkenaz, 9–10; to biblical patriarchy, 31; to conversion, in Iberia, 107–9; to French familial feminism, by *institutrices*, 4–5; Jewish women as agents of, 26; to unionization, 339

revolution, proletarian, 231–32

Reyher, Rebecca Hourwich, 343–44

Rich, Adrienne, 422–23

Richman, Julia, 329

rights of women: in Israel, 368; in Mandatory Palestine, 362–63; in rabbinic texts, 58–59, 60–61; in the Russian Empire, 226, 232; in the U.S., 334–35

rituals/ritual life: in disengagement from Judaism, 248–49; domestic, in spirituality, 404–10; in early modern central Europe, 178–80; in early modern Italy, 153, 157–61; in spirituality, 404–10; *tkhines* in, 219; in

Victorian Britain, 278; in the Zohar, 122–23. *See also* ceremonies

Robins, Rochelle, 425

roles, gendered: in the contemporary U.S., 25, 441–42, 447–48; in early modern Italy, 143, 148; in early modern Polish communities, 12; in the Eastern Mediterranean, 285–86, 291–92; in French familial feminism, 4–5; in Iberia, 97; and immigration to the U.S., 330–31, 333–35; religious, 398–99, 441–42, 456; in the Russian Empire, 17–18, 225–26; *tkhines* in transcending, 219; in Victorian Britain, 16–17, 266–67, 270; Yiddish books in preparation for, 201–2; in the Zohar, 131–33

romance, 225–26, 382–83, 442–43

Rose, Dawn, 424–25

Rosh Chodesh, 402–3, 405, 413. *See also* holidays

Ross, Sara M., 410–11

Rothschild, Constance de, 276

Rothschild, Lionel de, 263

Rothschild, Louisa de, 262–63

Rukeyser, Muriel: "To Be a Jew in the Twentieth Century," 426

Russian Empire: disability in, 217–18; economy in, 226–29; education in, 17–18, 222–24, 225–26; ethnicity in, 232–33; family law in, 224–26; gender roles in, 17–18, 225–26; marginality in, 218, 221, 222, 229–31; new directions in, 232–33; religious life in, 219–21

Russian Society for the Protection of Women in St. Petersburg, 229–30

Ruth, story of, 35, 36

Ruthie and Connie: Every Room in the House, 420

Sabbath candles, lighting of, 132–33, 219, 405, 413

Sabbetai Tzevi movement, 111

Saloman, Gotthold, 251

salon women (*salonières*), 241–46

salvation, participatory, 130–31

Sanger, Margaret, 342
sante vive (living saints), 148
Sarah and Abraham, story of, 33–34, 38, 129–30
Sara Pyke House, 271–72
Sara's Tent: Sheltering Creative Jewish Spirituality, 425
Savorai, Rachel, 359
Schechter, Mathilda, 400–401
Schneerson, Menahem Mendel, 404
Schneiderman, Rose, 339, 340
Schnirer, Sarah, 452
scholarship: lesbian and feminist, 422, 430; religious, 81, 100, 221, 239–40, 266–67, 331 (see also Torah study)
schools: for girls, 222–23, 307–8; Jewish, 249–50, 337–38, 399–400; public, 270, 313, 332–33, 400–401; Sabbath schools, 334, 336–37; synagogue, 401–2. See also education
Schwob, Lucy Renee Mathild, 425–26
Scott, Joan Wallach, 5
Second Temple period, 69–71
secularism/secularization, 18, 248–49, 301, 313, 334–35, 345
seder mitzvot nashim (order of women's precepts) genre, 152–53, 174–75, 200–201
seders, women's, 398, 408–10
Sefer ha-Bahir (Book of Brightness), 124
Sefer Haḥeshek (Hillel Ba'al Shem), 194–97
Sefer Ḥasidim, 83–84, 86–88
sefirot (divine attributes), 122–31, 123
segregation, gendered, 68, 69, 111, 159–60, 178, 202–3, 219, 221, 233
seminaries for women, 453–54
Senesh, Hannah, 360
Sepharad. See Iberia
Sephardic Mizrahi Q [Queer] Network, 429
Sephardim, 18–19, 109–12, 285–301, 310, 346
Sereni, Ada, 360–61
servants/service, domestic: children of, 150–51; dowries for, 149; in early modern central Europe, 182, 183–84; in early modern Italy, 149, 150–51;

in medieval Christian Spain, 102; sex and sexual relationships in, 13, 150–51, 183–84; vulnerability of, in the Russian Empire, 230; as witnesses for the Spanish Inquisition, 108–9
Setel, Drorah, 425
settlements, agricultural, 356–58
sex and sexual relationships: as barter for girls in the Holocaust, 387; in the contemporary U.S., 443–44; in domestic service, 13, 150–51, 183–84; in Iberia, 97, 99, 104–9; interfaith, 99, 104–6; LGBTQ, 277–78, 424, 447–48; marital, in Ashkenaz, 82–83; prostitution and rescue work in Victorian Britain, 271–75; in the Zohar, 127–28, 131–33. See also marriage; prostitution
sexism in Mandatory Palestine, 360–61
sexuality, 10–11, 33–34, 124–25, 386–87
Shabbat: in American spirituality, 403–4, 405, 413; in early modern Italy, 143, 152–53; in rabbinic texts, 62–63; in the U.S., 336–37, 345–46, 447
Shabbat Sheinit, 425
Shabbat yetziat ha-yoledet ritual, 179
Shekhinah, 10–11, 121, 122, 127–36, 410
Sheskin, Ira, 449
Shilo, Margalit, 366–67
Shira Hadasha congregation, 411–12
Shkol'nik, Mariia, 232
Shochat, Manya, 358
Shulman, Sara: The Sophie Horowitz Story, 426
Sick Room Helps Society (SRHS), 269
Sicular, Eve: "The Celluloid Closet in Yiddish Film," 427
silk production, 12–13, 160–61
singer-songwriters, LGBTQ, 426–27
singing and song in spirituality, 410–14
sisterhoods: dowering, 11, 111–12, 156–57 (see also dowries); synagogue, 345–46, 399
Slonik, Benjamin: Seder mitzvot nashim, 174–75
sobriety, 296–98
sociability, Enlightened, 241–43

valor, women of, 147–48

values, Jewish: in contemporary U.S. households, 445; in early modern Italy, 149; in Mandatory Palestine, 252, 353, 356, 363–64, 366–67; medieval, 87–88, 112–13; modesty as, in central Europe, 181–82; in spirituality, 23, 400, 401–2; in the U.S., 336–37, 338

values, middle-class, 270, 288

Varnhagen, Rahel (Levin), 243

Veit, Brendel (née Mendelssohn), 243–45

Venice, 12–13, 145, 152–53

Verbermacher, Hannah Rochel (Maid of Ludmir), 135–36, 220

vernacular Kabbalah, 135

violence: anti-Semitic, in medieval Christian Spain, 106, 107; against daughters, in the Hebrew Bible, 42–44; domestic, and immigration to the U.S., 335; in the Middle Ages, 80–81; sexual, 35–36, 42–44, 335, 413 (*see also* abuse: sexual)

visibility of women, 81, 97–98, 154–55, 185–86, 229–30, 261–62, 287–88, 363

Visigoths, persecution by, 98

Vital, Hayyim, 111

voluntary associations/volunteer work: American Jewish lesbians in, 420; in American spirituality, 402; *institutrices* establishing, 321–22; in Mandatory Palestine, 21, 361–62; in 19th-century Germany, 242; in Victorian Britain, 269–70, 271–72, 273; in WWII, 359, 360–61

von Rothschild, Louise and Clementine, 251

vsenarodnost' (supra-ethnic nationality), 232

Vygodskaia, Anna Pavlovna, 223

Wagenseil, Johann Christoph, 176

War of Independence, 359–60

War Resisters League, 343

warriors, female, in the Hebrew Bible, 38–42

Warsaw ghetto, 22, 373–75, 377–90, 436–37n48. *See also* Holocaust

weaponry, female, 38–42

websites, organizational, 403–4

Wegner, Judith, 60–61

Weimar German society, 254–55

Weiss, Avi, 453–54

Weissenberg, Melania, 382–83, 386, 387

Weissler, Chava, 219

welfare organizations, 16–17, 278, 366

Welt-Strauss, Rosa, 362

Wengeroff, Pauline, 227–28

Weretnikow, Bella, 334

Westernization, 18–19, 285–86, 287, 288, 300–301, 316–19. *See also* modernization/modernity

wet nurses, 63, 102, 183, 230. *See also* breastfeeding

widows/widowhood: in early modern central Europe, 180–82; in early modern Italy, 153–54; in the Hebrew Bible, 34–35; in Iberia, 97–98, 102–4, 105; in the Polish-Lithuanian Commonwealth, 203–5, 206, 207, 209–10; in rabbinic texts, 58, 60–61

"Will Her Love Remember" (Ibn Labrat), 99–100

wills and testaments, women's, 108, 111–12, 150, 172, 184

Wise, Isaac M., 400

Wissenschaft des Judentums (19th-century German academic association), 239–41, 454

witches/witchcraft, 65–66. *See also* magic, women as agents of

witnesses, legal, 60

wives: in contemporary partnership marriages, 445–47; of David, 40–42; desertion of, 78–79; ideal of, in the Polish-Lithuanian Commonwealth, 199–200; in rabbinic texts, 59–60

WIZO (Women's International Zionist Organization), 362

WLCJ (Women's League of Conservative Judaism), 400–402, 405–6, 407–8

Wodzinski, Marcin, 220

Women in Black, 428

Women of Reform Judaism (WRJ), 402–3, 406–7. *See also* NFTS (National Federation of Temple Sisterhoods)

Women of the Kibbutz (Bassewitz and
Bat-Rachel), 356–57
Women of the Wall, 402–3
Women's Auxiliary of the Workmen's
Circle, 345–46
Women's League of Conservative Judaism,
345–46, 403–4
Women's League Shabbat, 403–4
women's movement, 254–55, 340–41,
356, 398, 402, 403–4, 411–12. See also
feminism/feminists
Women's Peace Union, 343
"women's question," 223, 301
Women's Seder Sourcebook, 409–10
Women's Trade Union League (WTUL),
268, 339, 340
women's work. See activities, economic;
labor; professions and professional
women
Women Worker's Movement, 362
working classes: abuse of, in Russian
factories, 228–29; early modern income
opportunities for, 183–84; in rabbinic
texts, 63; in the suffrage movement,
340; in the U.S., 332–34; in Victorian
Britain, 261–62, 267–68, 269–70,
274–75. See also class, socioeconomic
working conditions, 267–68, 339, 345, 355
World War II, 358, 359, 360–61, 373–90.
See also Holocaust
worship: communal, 84–85, 276, 411–12;
public, 14–15, 202–3, 251, 252–53,
276, 411–12. See also synagogues
writers: in early modern central Europe,
169, 175–76; in early modern Italy,
154–55, 161; male, attitudes of,
toward women, 146–49; memoirs by,
246–49, 373–74, 376–77, 389–90. See
also poets/poetry
writing culture, 11–12, 161, 169, 175–76

xenophobia, 35–36, 80–81, 341

Yagel, Abraham ben Hananiah de Gallichi,
147–48
yeshivas, 223–24, 425, 453–54. See also
education; schools
Yeshivat Maharat, 25–26, 453–54
yeshivish (non-Hasidic ultra-Orthodox),
444–45
Yesod (divine phallus), 127–28,
133–34
Yezierska, Anzia: Bread Givers, 331
Yiddish: in American activism, 339, 342;
as the language of labor and relief
in Victorian Britain, 269, 272; as
language of women's books, 173–77,
180, 197–98, 219–20; LGBTQ
people in revitalization of culture,
427; literature in, 152–53, 200–201,
209–10; music hall songs in, 267–68;
Yiddish press, 339, 340–41, 344
Yishuv. See Mandatory Palestine, Jewish
society of
yoatzot (female ritual advisers), 453
Younis, Betsheva, 364
Yours in Struggle: Three Feminist
Perspectives of Anti-Semitism and
Racism, 430
youth clubs, 270–71, 381–82

Zalman, Elijah ben Solomon, 197–200
Zelicka, Fajga, 378–79
Zimmerman, Agnes, 278
Zinger, Oded, 76–77
Zionism: American clubs and groups for,
411, 428; American Jewish support
for, 344–45; gendered ideology
of, 353; LGBTQ people in, 428; in
Mandatory Palestine, 20–21, 351–52,
353, 356, 358–59, 361–63, 364–65,
366–67; and politics, in the Russian
Empire, 231–32
Zohar (Book of Splendor), 10–11, 23,
121–36

CPSIA information can be obtained
at www.ICGtesting.com
Printed in the USA
LVHW021750121021
700249LV00004B/108